Frommer's®

San Diego 2007

with
foldout
map

D0097101

A word about the Frommer's series, on the 50th anniversary of its first guidebook

It all began with a small book called "Europe on $5 a Day," published in 1957.

It was an ode to the joys of travel. It was young and naïve, full of purple prose, and overly awed by the pleasures of that continent. But in its excitement about the possibility of crossing the Atlantic to visit the Old World—an ability confined until then to a tiny percentage of Americans—it reflected a popular mood. And its first edition became an almost instant best-seller, the cornerstone of what was soon to be a series of several hundred guides dealing with more cities, islands, nations, and regions than I could possibly have imagined.

The Frommer books, now fifty years old and known as "Frommer's," are today the largest-selling series of guides in the United States; in most weeks of the year, they account for nearly one out of every four guidebooks sold. I think I know why.

We deal with travel in a serious fashion. Our guidebooks have never looked on travel as a mere recreation, but as a far more important human function, a time of learning and introspection, an essential part of a civilized life. We stress the culture, history, lifestyle, and beliefs of the destinations we cover, and urge our readers to seek out people and new ideas as the chief rewards of travel.

We have never shied from controversy. We have, from the beginning, encouraged our authors to be intensely judgmental, critical—both pro and con—in their comments, and wholly independent. Our only clients are our readers, and we have triggered the ire of countless prominent sorts, from a tourist newspaper we called "practically worthless" (it unsuccessfully sued us) to the many rip-offs we've condemned.

And because we believe that travel should be available to everyone regardless of their incomes, we have always been cost-conscious at every level of expenditure. Though we have broadened our recommendations beyond the budget category, we insist that every lodging we include be sensibly priced. We use every form of media to assist our readers, and are particularly proud of our feisty daily website, the award-winning Frommers.com.

I have high hopes for the future of Frommer's. May these guidebooks, in all the years ahead, continue to reflect the joy of travel and the freedom that travel represents. May they always pursue a cost-conscious path, so that people of all incomes can enjoy the rewards of travel. And may they create, for both the traveler and the persons among whom we travel, a community of friends, where all human beings live in harmony and peace.

Arthur Frommer

Frommer's®
San Diego

My San Diego
by Mark Hiss

HIGH-END NIGHTCLUBS. ADVENTUROUS DINING. HYPERMODERN ARCHITECTURE.
What's going on here? What happened to that sleepy Navy town, that nice little city of San Diego? What about that killer whale?

Well, folks, that sleepy burgh has woken up and it wants to party. Growth has been fast and furious—and at times awkward, as growth can be—over the last few years; San Diego now finds itself with a new skyline and a new attitude. With 70 miles of coastline and an array of theme parks and attractions (and, yes, killer whales), it's still a family-friendly destination, but the nearly nightly bacchanalia in the Gaslamp Quarter is evidence of something young, exciting, and new.

I spent 5 years as the editor of a visitor magazine here, and I was lucky enough to play tourist in my own city. During that gig, I realized that there's no easy way to sum up San Diego. Whatever you're interested in—from astronomy to zebras—is here. It's an embarrassment of riches, really—and that's not even taking into account that San Diego undeniably has the country's best weather.

The city is currently riding the crest of a wave unlike anything seen since its rootin' tootin' boomtown days in the 1880s, when real estate speculation doubled and tripled the price of land (hmm, sounds familiar) and the population swelled. But now, San Diego's latest boom goes beyond sky-high property values and the opening of new bars and restaurants. Swords are being sculpted—not beaten—into ploughshares at NTC Promenade, a former Navy base that's on track to become one of the country's most exciting performing arts facilities. And at press time, the San Diego Museum of Contemporary Art was preparing to open its third space, a sleek downtown annex at the historic Santa Fe Depot Baggage Building.

Of course, the 1880s boom was followed by an inevitable bust that cast a pall over downtown San Diego for nearly a century. So my advice to you? Come now while the party is rolling. This is not your father's San Diego. It's more like your great-great-grandfather's San Diego. Get ready to explore.

© John Connell/Index Stock

You can reach Coronado by taking the ferry across the bay, but I get a little thrill each time I drive across the **CORONADO BAY BRIDGE (left).** I roll down my windows, let the wind fly through my hair, and inhale the salty sea air as I climb high above San Diego Bay and absorb the panoramic view of the downtown and the glistening Bay; then I follow the gentle curve of the bridge and descend onto the island-like peninsula of Coronado.

San Diego boasts an amazing variety of places from which you can watch the sun set over the Pacific. I like to wander through **TORREY PINES STATE RESERVE (above),** along the reserve's coastal trails that wind through rare Torrey pine trees. In winter, I catch sight of migrating whales; year-round, I watch dolphins patrol the shores. Each time I go hiking at twilight above the sandy limestone bluffs, catching the sunset feels like a reward for taking care of my body.

Giraffes, graceful and strong, are one of the most splendid creatures to observe on earth. I'd prefer to see them in the African wild, but the **SAN DIEGO ZOO (above)** is an amazing home for animals because it creates a natural environment, enclosing its more than 4,000 creatures with moats instead of steel bars. There's so much to see at the zoo that I usually split my visit into two days.

I love to skate, but when I strap on rollerblades I have all the grace of a newborn foal. Thankfully the beach scene consists of a variety of outdoor activities, like jogging, biking, and **BEACH VOLLEYBALL (right)**. On any given sunny day, dozens of volleyball games pepper San Diego's beaches. Remember, you don't have to play to enjoy this game—half the fun is in people-watching, or applauding a smooth slide in the sand.

LA JOLLA COVE (right) La Jolla's coastal region is beautiful and inviting, and on sunny afternoons when the underwater visibility reaches 10 to 15 feet, La Jolla Cove becomes a popular spot for photographers, sun worshipers, and explorers hoping for a glimpse of sea anemones, starfish, or hermit crabs in its tide pools.

Established in 1789, **MISSION BASILICA SAN DIEGO DE ALCALA** (below) is California's oldest mission and an active Catholic Parish; mass is conducted here daily. For me, the mission is a peaceful retreat, and a feeling of hope and serenity takes hold whenever I visit.

Seaside **LA JOLLA (above)** is a jewel in San Diego's crown. It's an easy town to stroll through after a day lounging at the beach or snorkeling at La Jolla Cove. This affluent community boasts clusters of stunning homes overlooking the sea—peek upwards as you walk along the beach and you'll get a glimpse of mansions precariously perched on the edges of the cliffs.

Finding a parking space can be frustrating (and expensive), but riding the **SAN DIEGO TROLLEY (right)** is a fun way to explore the Gaslamp Quarter, visit Old Town, and to head south of the border to the town of Tijuana.

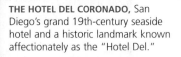

THE HOTEL DEL CORONADO, San Diego's grand 19th-century seaside hotel and a historic landmark known affectionately as the "Hotel Del."

Each Spring desert wildflowers burst into full bloom in **ANZA-BORREGO DESERT STATE PARK (above)**, home to ancient fossils, sandstone canyons, granite mountains, and over 600 types of desert plants. You can hike the park's trails (except in the summer, when temperatures rise to as high as 125°F, or 52°C) or wind around the boulders on a self-guided driving tour.

I always enjoy exploring the historic Gaslamp Quarter, full of shops, restaurants, and nightclubs. The **LOUIS BANK OF COMMERCE BUILDING (right)** was the first granite building in San Diego.

San Diego's richest concentration of museums, gardens, and performance art are within **BALBOA PARK,** the largest urban cultural park in the nation. The Botanical Building contains around 2,100 varieties of tropical and flowering plants. The adjacent reflecting pool sprouts water lilies and is home to goldfish and colorful koi. I could spend an entire day at in San Diego's favorite park (and I have) and see only a fraction of what there is to see.

San Diego's north county town of Carlsbad and neighboring Encinitas make up a noted commercial flower-growing region. The most vibrant palette of colors can be found in the acres of eye-popping blossoms that come alive between March and May at the **CARLSBAD RANCH (left)**. It is an awesome sight, like walking into a Monet painting in Southern California.

A dozen or so skyscrapers define **DOWNTOWN SAN DIEGO (above)**. No longer a desolate grid after the 9-to-5 crowd departs, this bay-facing business district is home to the Convention Center, Petco Park (the San Diego Padres' baseball stadium), and the historic Gaslamp Quarter (full of shopping, dining, and entertainment venues). And hugging downtown along the bay, the Embarcadero is a perfect waterfront strip to stroll.

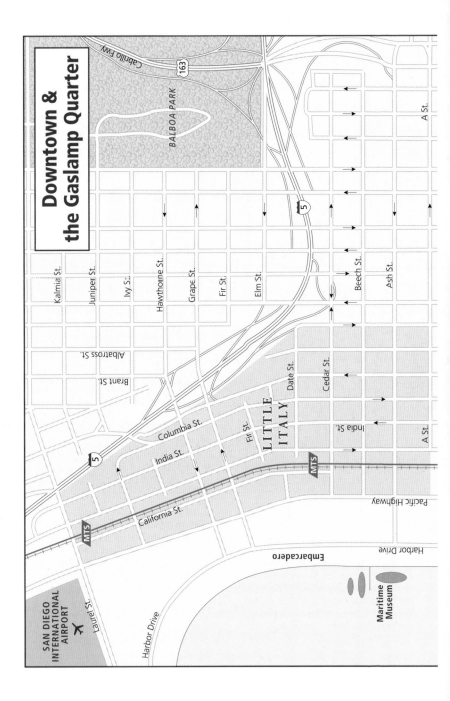

Downtown &
the Gaslamp Quarter

SAN DIEGO INTERNATIONAL AIRPORT

Cabrillo Fwy

BALBOA PARK

163

5

Kalmia St.
Juniper St.
Ivy St.
Hawthorne St.
Grape St.
Fir St.
Elm St.
Beech St.
Ash St.
A St.

Albatross St.
Brant St.

Date St.
Cedar St.
India St.
A St.

Columbia St.
India St.
Fir St.

LITTLE ITALY

MTS

California St.

5

Laurel St.

Harbor Drive

Embarcadero

Pacific Highway

Harbor Drive

Maritime Museum

MTS

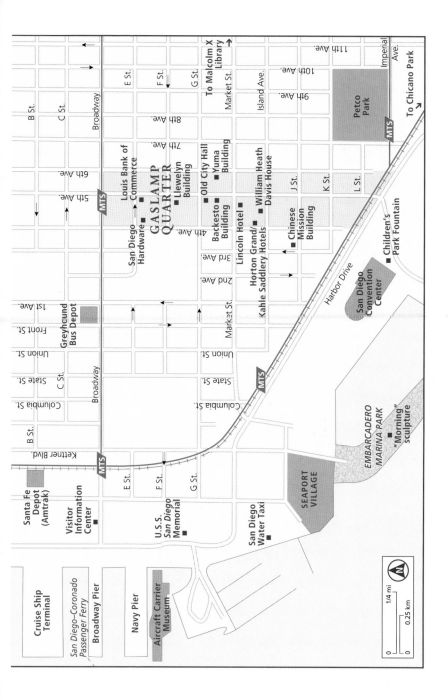

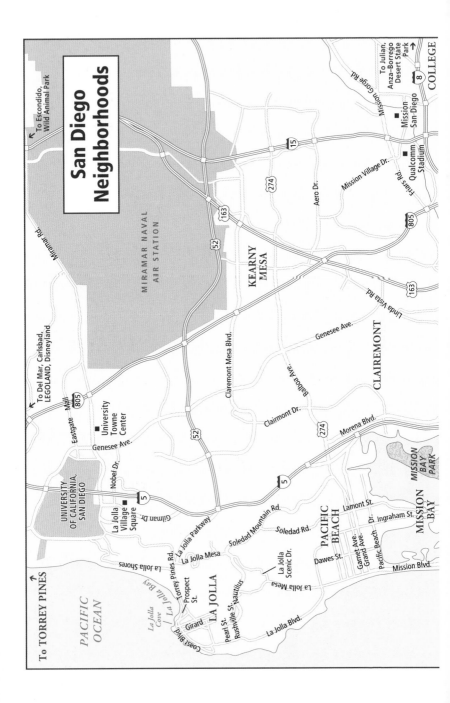

San Diego Neighborhoods

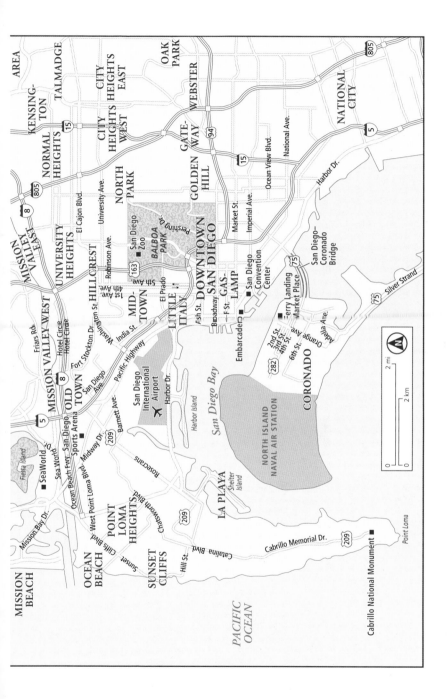

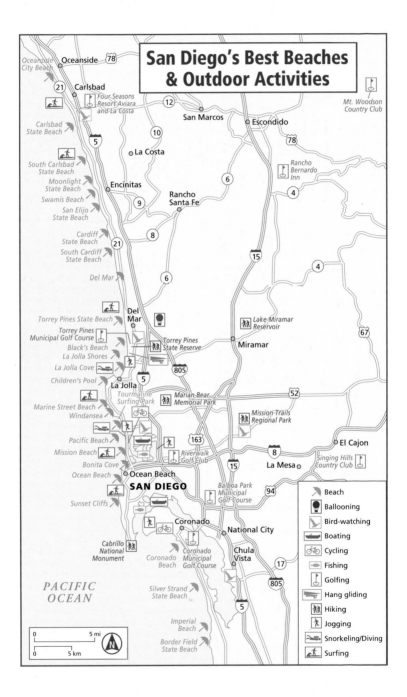

Frommer's®

San Diego

2007

by Mark Hiss

Here's what the critics say about Frommer's:

"Amazingly easy to use. Very portable, very complete."

—*Booklist*

"Detailed, accurate, and easy-to-read information for all price ranges."

—*Glamour Magazine*

"Hotel information is close to encyclopedic."

—*Des Moines Sunday Register*

"Frommer's Guides have a way of giving you a real feel for a place."

—*Knight Ridder Newspapers*

BICENTENNIAL
1807
⊛WILEY
2007
BICENTENNIAL

Wiley Publishing, Inc.

About the Author

A third-generation Southern Californian, **Mark Hiss** is a writer and photographer who has lived in San Diego for 25 years. He was the founding editor of both *Where San Diego*, the city's visitor guide, and *Performances*, the playbill magazine for the city's leading performing arts venues. He is also a recovering publicist who spent many years working for some of San Diego's top theater companies.

Published by:

Wiley Publishing, Inc.

111 River St.
Hoboken, NJ 07030-5774

ISBN-13: 978-0-470-04211-3
ISBN-10: 0-470-04211-7

Editor: Jennifer Anmuth
Production Editor: Michael Brumitt
Cartographer: Tim Lohnes
Photo Editor: Richard Fox
Production by Wiley Indianapolis Composition Services

Front cover photo: San Diego Zoo: Close-up of polar bear in water, with wood block in mouth
Back cover photo: Surfers in silhouette on beach at sunset; beach unidentified; pier in distance

For information on our other products and services or to obtain technical support, please contact our Customer Care Department within the U.S. at 800/762-2974, outside the U.S. at 317/572-3993 or fax 317/572-4002.

Wiley also publishes its books in a variety of electronic formats. Some content that appears in print may not be available in electronic formats.

Manufactured in the United States of America

5 4 3 2 1

Contents

List of Maps

An Invitation to the Reader

In researching this book, we discovered many wonderful places—hotels, restaurants, shops, and more. We're sure you'll find others. Please tell us about them, so we can share the information with your fellow travelers in upcoming editions. If you were disappointed with a recommendation, we'd love to know that, too. Please write to:

Frommer's San Diego 2007
Wiley Publishing, Inc. • 111 River St. • Hoboken, NJ 07030-5774

An Additional Note

Please be advised that travel information is subject to change at any time—and this is especially true of prices. We therefore suggest that you write or call ahead for confirmation when making your travel plans. The authors, editors, and publisher cannot be held responsible for the experiences of readers while traveling. Your safety is important to us, however, so we encourage you to stay alert and be aware of your surroundings. Keep a close eye on cameras, purses, and wallets, all favorite targets of thieves and pickpockets.

Frommer's Star Ratings, Icons & Abbreviations

Every hotel, restaurant, and attraction listing in this guide has been ranked for quality, value, service, amenities, and special features using a **star-rating system.** In country, state, and regional guides, we also rate towns and regions to help you narrow down your choices and budget your time accordingly. Hotels and restaurants are rated on a scale of zero (recommended) to three stars (exceptional). Attractions, shopping, nightlife, towns, and regions are rated according to the following scale: zero stars (recommended), one star (highly recommended), two stars (very highly recommended), and three stars (must-see).

In addition to the star-rating system, we also use **seven feature icons** that point you to the great deals, in-the-know advice, and unique experiences that separate travelers from tourists. Throughout the book, look for:

Finds	Special finds—those places only insiders know about
Fun Fact	Fun facts—details that make travelers more informed and their trips more fun
Kids	Best bets for kids and advice for the whole family
Moments	Special moments—those experiences that memories are made of
Overrated	Places or experiences not worth your time or money
Tips	Insider tips—great ways to save time and money
Value	Great values—where to get the best deals

The following **abbreviations** are used for credit cards:

AE	American Express	DISC	Discover	V	Visa
DC	Diners Club	MC	MasterCard		

Frommers.com

Now that you have the guidebook to a great trip, visit our website at **www.frommers.com** for travel information on more than 3,000 destinations. With features updated regularly, we give you instant access to the most current trip-planning information available. At Frommers.com, you'll also find the best prices on airfares, accommodations, and car rentals—and you can even book travel online through our travel booking partners. At Frommers.com, you'll also find the following:

- Online updates to our most popular guidebooks
- Vacation sweepstakes and contest giveaways
- Newsletter highlighting the hottest travel trends
- Online travel message boards with featured travel discussions

What's New in San Diego

With its upscale dining, full-throttled nightlife, world-class theater, and modern skyline, San Diego has become a big-time city. Unfortunately, you're never too big for a little city hall chicanery. San Diego has gone through an unbelievable, tragi-comic series of political embarrassments and scandals over the last several years, none bigger than the back-room financial contretemps that led the *New York Times* to label the city "Enron by the sea."

San Diego is currently (as of press time) facing the most devastating financial cri-sis in its history, thanks to a creatively maintained city pension fund that now has a deficit of more than $1.8 *billion.* An alphabet soup of agencies (FBI, IRS, SEC) is investigating, and some indict-ments have been handed out, but this is an unfolding story. Mayor Jerry Sanders says he won't raise taxes (including the hotel tax), but travelers should be on the lookout for cuts in staffing and hours at parks, beaches, libraries, and other city facilities, as well as a possible profusion of untended potholes on local streets.

In another governmental development, City Council deliberation has begun on whether or not to ban smoking from all 17 miles of San Diego beaches and 38,000-plus acres of parkland. Check for posted signs (if the city can afford to put new ones up).

For those who plan to rely on public transportation: The bus system is under-going a major countywide transforma-tion. Be aware that some, if not many, bus routes may have changed or dropped altogether after this book is published. For timely information, call the **MTS Transit Store** (📞 **619/234-1060**) or visit the website at www.sdcommute.com. To learn more, refer to chapter 4.

WHERE TO STAY Condo hotels, popular for some time in places like Las Vegas and Miami, are making splashy for-ays into the San Diego market. These pri-vately owned condos do double duty as hotel accommodations and feature lots of amenities. Ironically, the first two projects hitting town have music connections: the **Hard Rock Hotel,** at the corner of Fifth Ave. and L St. (📞 **888/230-7625;** www. hardrock.com), and **The Diegan,** 1055 Fifth Ave. (📞 **619/702-6666;** www. diegan.com), which is grafted onto the House of Blues. Both of these ventures are adding not only new rooms to the downtown scene, but also bars, restau-rants, and performance spaces. Rande Gerber's **Sky Bar** at the Hard Rock is expected to be a big draw. The Hard Rock is scheduled to open in the spring; The Diegan in the fall.

When it opens in early 2007, the **Grand Del Mar Resort & Spa,** 5200 Grand Del Mar Way (📞 **858/350-7600;** www.thegranddelmar.com), will raise the bar of luxury in the North County. This 261-room property, designed in a Mediterranean-cum-South Beach style, sits on 24 acres and cozies up to one of San Diego's top golf courses, created by Tom Fazio. The Grand Del Mar will offer the largest standard guest rooms (610 sq. ft.) in San Diego, as well as a 12-room, full-service spa.

A well-loved San Diego icon finally reopens after a long renovation. The **US Grant Hotel,** 326 Broadway (✆ **800/ 237-5029;** www.usgrant.net), was built by Ulysses S. Grant, Jr., in 1910 to honor his father; it's scheduled to welcome guests again in late 2006, following a nearly 2-year, $52 million makeover. In an interesting historical side note, the hotel is owned by the Sycuan Band of the Kumeyaay Nation, which in 1875 was granted sovereignty by President Grant. The hotel is operated as part of the Starwood Luxury Collection.

Rancho Valencia Resort, 5921 Valencia Circle (✆ **800/548-3664;** www. ranchovalencia.com), one of the area's premier romantic destination hotels, has added a spectacular new spa. The $12 million facility covers 2.5 acres and features 5 pools (including a dedicated Watsu pool), 10 treatment rooms with private patios, and state-of-the-art hydrotherapies.

WHERE TO DINE Jack's La Jolla, 7863 Girard Ave. (✆ **858/456-8111;** www.jackslajolla.com) has been at the top of everyone's list since it opened in 2006. In this three-floor, multicomponent establishment, you can sample everything from coffee and baked goods at the sidewalk cafe to oysters at the rooftop raw bar, with amazing fine dining in between.

The Gaslamp Quarter continues to propagate new restaurants (how hungry can one city be?). A few of the new standouts on the scene are **Red Pearl,** 440 J St. (✆ **619/231-1100;** www.redpearl kitchen.com); **The Palm,** 615 J St. (✆ **619/702-6500;** www.thepalm.com); and **Dussini Mediterranean Bistro,** 275 Fifth Ave. (✆ **619/233-4323;** www. dussini.com).

Red Pearl is a hip, pan-Asian affair, created by Tim and Liza Goodell, who are the masterminds behind a couple of hot restaurants in Hollywood. The Palm, part of an 80-year-old chain, is a classic, old-school steakhouse, right down to the celebrity caricatures adorning the walls. Dussini, meanwhile, is a three-level restaurant and lounge, ensconced in a historic Irving Gill–designed building; there's billiards up in the loft bar.

WHERE TO GO At press time, the **Museum of Contemporary Art San Diego** (✆ **619/234-1001;** www.mcasd. org) was working to complete its third space, a downtown wing to complement the galleries directly across the street and the flagship La Jolla location. Located on Kettner Boulevard (at C St.), the new facility extends from historic Santa Fe Depot, turning the train station's 1915 "baggage building" into a sleek museum with 10,000 square feet of exhibition space and a 130-seat lecture hall. Its opening is slated for the beginning of the year.

In Balboa Park, the **San Diego Natural History Museum** (✆ **619/232- 3821;** www.sdnhm.org) has unveiled the most elaborate exhibit in the organization's 133-year history. Three years in the making, *Fossil Mysteries* incorporates interactive technologies, artwork, and life-size reproductions of prehistoric animals, including a Megalodon shark, the largest known predator to ever inhabit the earth.

AFTER DARK San Diego's red-hot nightlife shows no signs of slowing down. On the contrary, it just keeps burning brighter. The city's latest place to see and be seen is the 22,000-square-foot dance and supper club **Stingaree,** 454 Sixth Ave. (✆ **619/544-9500;** www.sting sandiego.com). Adopting the neighborhood's tenderloin nickname from a century ago, Stingaree features pod-like dining booths, a two-story, three-paneled waterfall sculpture behind the main bar, numerous nooks and party spaces, and a rooftop patio with fire pit. It's chic and mod.

The **belo** (© **619/231-9200;** www. belosandiego.com), is San Diego's latest underground club. Literally. Below street level in the Gaslamp on E Street, between Fourth and Fifth avenues, this huge (20,000 sq. ft.), three-room space features a retro design in pop-art hues, offset by exposed brick walls. There's a restaurant too, if you can manage to sit still.

1

The Best of San Diego

Over the past 2 decades, San Diego has evolved past its old reputation as a slow-growth, conservative Navy town graced with 70 miles of fabulous sandy coastline. Of course, the military link is still present today, with a handful of large bases throughout the county. But the city—California's first and the nation's seventh largest—now hosts a diversity of neighborhoods and residents to rival Los Angeles. San Diego reflects its Spanish-Mexican heritage in every corner; you won't forget that bustling Tijuana is just across the border, less than 30 minutes away. Yet, in stark contrast to Tijuana's infamous poverty, San Diego boasts one of the nation's priciest housing markets and a biotech/tourism/telecom economy that's firing on all cylinders. A full-fledged building boom is transforming formerly seedy downtown neighborhoods and architecturally rich suburbs into upscale wonders. And the stylish young residents and shop owners they attract are, in turn, updating and enriching San Diego's dining, shopping, and entertainment options.

Amid all these changes, San Diego is still first and foremost a big outdoor playground. You can swim, snorkel, windsurf, kayak, bicycle, in-line skate, and partake of other diversions in or near the water, as well as in the mountains and desert. Top-notch civic attractions include three world-famous animal parks and Balboa Park, one of the finest urban parks in the world. Just pack a laid-back attitude along with your sandals and swimsuit, and prepare for a warm welcome to California's grown-up beach town.

1 The Most Unforgettable Travel Experiences

- **Driving over the Bridge to Coronado:** The 1st time or the 50th, there's always an adrenaline rush as you follow this engineering marvel's dramatic curves and catch a glimpse of the panoramic view to either side. Driving west, you can easily pick out the distinctive **Hotel del Coronado** (p. 93)—or as the locals say, the **Hotel Del**—in the distance before you reach the "island." See "Orientation" in chapter 4 for more about the city's neighborhoods.

- **Escaping to Torrey Pines State Reserve:** Poised on a majestic cliff overlooking the Pacific Ocean, this state park is set aside for the rarest pine tree in North America. The reserve has short trails that immerse hikers into a delicate and beautiful coastal environment. See p. 163.

- **Watching the Seals at the Children's Pool:** This tiny La Jolla cove was originally named for the toddlers who could safely frolic behind a man-made seawall. These days, seals and sea lions sunning themselves on the sand are the main attraction. The beach had been off limits to humans since 1997, but following much public debate, it was reopened to swimmers in 2005. Keep a safe distance—these are wild animals—and you'll be rewarded with a unique wildlife experience. See p. 144.

- **Taking in the City's Best Panorama:** Drive out to the tip of Point Loma on a clear day for an unsurpassed 360-degree view that takes in downtown, the harbor, military bases, Coronado, and, in the distance, Tijuana and San Diego's mountainous backcountry. See p. 153.

- **Renting Bikes, Skates, or Kayaks in Mission Bay:** Landscaped shores, calm waters, paved paths, and friendly neighbors make Mission Bay an aquatic playground like no other. Explore on land or water, depending on your energy level, and then grab a bite at the Mission. See p. 159.

- **Strolling Through the Gaslamp Quarter:** Victorian commercial buildings that fill a 16½-block area will make you think you've stepped back in time. The beautifully restored buildings, in the heart of downtown, house some of the city's most popular shops, restaurants, and nightspots. See "Walking Tour 1: The Gaslamp Quarter," on p. 187.

- **Spending a Day in Balboa Park:** Head to the San Diego Zoo and overlook the superb city park that surrounds it. The buildings that grew out of Balboa Park's 1915–16 exposition create a Spanish Golden Age fantasia, plus there are mature gardens, the acclaimed Old Globe Theatre, and 13 of San Diego's best museums. See p. 145 and 200.

- **Listening to Live Music Outdoors at Humphrey's:** An intimate, palm-fringed venue on the water at Shelter Island, Humphrey's has name acts from mid-May to October and puts those impersonal summer concert "sheds" found in other cities to shame. See "Live Entertainment," in chapter 10.

- **Floating Up, Up, and Away over North County:** Sunset hot-air balloon rides carry passengers over the golf courses and luxury homes north of the city. Do it while you can—open space for landings is fast disappearing, making ballooning an endangered species here. For details, see "North County Beach Towns: Spots to Surf & Sun," in chapter 11.

- **Wildflowers and Serenity at Anza-Borrego Desert State Park:** The largest state park in the lower 48 attracts the most visitors during the spring wildflower season, when a kaleidoscopic carpet blankets the desert. Others come year-round to hike more than 100 miles of trails. See p. 274.

- **Frolicking at La Jolla's Beaches:** It may be misspelled Spanish for "the jewel," but there is no mistaking the beauty of La Jolla's bluff-lined beaches. Each has a distinct personality: Surfers love Windansea's waves; harbor seals have adopted the Children's Pool; La Jolla Shores is popular for swimming, sunbathing, and kayaking; and the Cove is a top snorkeling and scuba diving spot, and the best place to spot the electric-orange California state fish, the garibaldi. See p. 143–144.

- **Playing a Round of Golf at Torrey Pines Golf Course** (La Jolla): Two 18-hole championship courses overlook the ocean and provide players with plenty of challenge. In February, the Buick Invitational Tournament is held here. The rest of the year, these popular municipal courses are open to everybody. See p. 180.

- **Spending a Day at San Diego Zoo, Wild Animal Park, or SeaWorld:** At the zoo, animals live in naturalistic habitats such as Monkey Trails and Forest Tails (the most elaborate enclosure it has ever created), and it's one of only four zoos in the United States where you can see giant pandas. At the Wild Animal Park, most of the 3,500 animals roam freely over an 1,800-acre spread. And Sea-World, with its water-themed rides, flashy animal shows, and detailed exhibits, is an aquatic wonderland of pirouetting dolphins and 4-ton killer whales with a fetish for drenching visitors. See p. 136.

- **Crossing the Border:** What a difference a line makes. Tijuana waits on the other side of the world's busiest border crossing. There's a raucous tourist zone, but also plentiful shopping, cultural, and culinary delights. Beyond Tijuana, check out beachside Rosarito and Ensenada. See p. 279.

2 The Best Splurge Hotels

- **Four Seasons Resort Aviara,** 7100 Four Seasons Point (© 800/332-3442 or 760/603-6800), is a AAA 5-diamond resort in Carlsbad that pulls off the hat trick of encompassing one of the best restaurants, spas, and golf courses in the county. See p. 244.
- San Diego's other AAA 5-diamond property is **The Lodge at Torrey Pines,** 11480 N. Torrey Pines Rd. (© 800/566-0087 or 858/453-4420). Not surprisingly, the Lodge also features one of the area's top restaurants and spas, and elbows up against renowned Torrey Pines Golf Course in La Jolla. See p. 89.
- If you're looking for swanky and trendy, lighten your load of cash at downtown's **W San Diego,** 421 West B St. (© 888/625-5144 or 619/231-8220). Relax on your beach-ball pillow while watching your flat-screen TV, or spend even more on a pricey cocktail at the hotel's alfresco lounge with its heated-sand floor. See p. 72.

3 The Best Moderately Priced Hotels

- You won't find a better location than the **Horton Grand Hotel,** 311 Island Ave. (© 800/542-1886 or 619/544-1886). This historic Victorian beauty has called the Gaslamp Quarter home since 1886, and some otherworldly guests have reputedly been harmlessly hanging around since then, too. See p. 73.
- In San Diego's Little Italy, **La Pensione Hotel,** 606 W. Date St. (© 800/232-4683 or 619/236-8000), feels like a small European hotel and offers tidy lodgings at bargain prices. There's an abundance of great dining in the surrounding blocks, and you'll be perfectly situated to explore the rest of town by car or trolley. See p. 74.
- Tucked away in San Diego's Mission Hills neighborhood (but only a half-mile from trendy Hillcrest), **Crone's Cobblestone Cottage B&B,** 1302 Washington Place (© 619/295-4765), is a tiny Craftsman bungalow-away-from-home. Only two rooms are available; book early. See p. 75.

4 The Most Unforgettable Dining Experiences

- When you combine a world-class chef with a romantic, seaside location in La Jolla, you're guaranteed a memorable meal. At the **Marine Room,** 2000 Spindrift Dr. (© 858/459-7222), Executive Chef Bernard

Guillas' creative, modern French cuisine provides ample evidence of how far the city's invigorated dining scene has come. Guillas uses plates like a painter uses a canvas, and his palette includes the finest local products. See p. 126.

- **Jack's La Jolla,** 7863 Girard Ave. (© **858/456-8111**), is a 3-story epicurean funhouse. It features a casual sidewalk cafe and an ocean-view, rooftop raw bar, with a swank fine-dining component sandwiched in between. Chef/owner Tony DiSalvo, a veteran of Jean-Georges in New York City, offers a cutting-edge modern American cuisine that's the toast of the town. The several bar and lounge areas stay open late, and offer live entertainment as well. See p. 126.

- **George's at the Cove/George's Ocean Terrace,** 1250 Prospect St. (© **858/454-4244**): These two longtime favorites in La Jolla share an *aah*-inspiring ocean view. The downstairs kitchen turns up the finesse factor for inventive and formal California cuisine (like Pacific swordfish in a ragout of pink grapefruit and chestnuts); the cafe offers crowd- (and wallet-) pleasing dishes (such as George's enduringly popular smoked chicken-broccoli–black-bean soup). See p. 124.

- You can't visit San Diego without **trying a fish taco.** If the city has an official food, this is probably it. Fish tacos are available everywhere, but the best places to try one are **The Fishery,** 5040 Cass St. (Pacific Beach; © **858/272-9985**), **Bay Park Fish Co.,** 4121 Ashton St. (Bay Park; © **619/276-3474**), and **Point Loma Seafoods,** 2805 Emerson St. (© **619/223-1109**). **Rubio's,** 4504 E. Mission Bay Dr. (and additional locations; © **858/272-2801**) is also worth a visit. Although it's now a chain, Rubio's original stand is where the fish taco was first popularized in the early 1980s. See p. 120.

5 The Best Things to Do for Free

- **Timken Museum of Art:** It's a small collection, and the museum's modern architecture is completely out of place in Balboa Park, but the always-free Timken (© **619/239-5548**) houses 600 years of art history. Masterpieces by Rembrandt and Rubens, as well as works by such seminal American painters as Eastman Johnson and John Singleton Copley, are among the holdings. See p. 152.

- **Organ Pavilion Concerts:** The world's largest outdoor organ is not atrophying. Its 4,518 pipes have been in nearly continuous use since 1915 at the Spreckels Organ Pavilion (© **619/702-8138**) in Balboa Park. Free concerts are presented every Sunday at 2pm. See p. 152.

- **Chicano Park Murals:** More than 40 works of art grace the support pylons of the Coronado Bridge in Barrio Logan's Chicano Park, National Avenue at Crosby Street (© **619/563-4661**). The images celebrate and honor Latino heroes and culture, and are considered the largest and most important collection of outdoor murals in the country. See p. 165.

- **Self-Realization Fellowship Temple:** This retreat in Encinitas, 215 W. K St. (© **760/753-2888**), with its distinctive lotus-shaped towers, was built by a yogi in 1937. Its cliffside meditation gardens overlook the Pacific and offer incredible vistas. Visitors are welcome free of charge. See p. 243.

2

Planning Your Trip to San Diego

This chapter contains all the practical information and logistical advice you need to make your travel arrangements a snap, from deciding when to go to finding the best airfare.

1 Visitor Information

Do your homework by contacting the **San Diego Convention & Visitor's Bureau,** 401 B St., Suite 1400, San Diego, CA 92101 (mailing address only; ℭ **619/236-1212;** www.sandiego.org). Ask for the *San Diego Vacation Planning Kit,* which includes the *Visitors Planning Guide,* featuring excellent maps and information on accommodations, activities, and attractions. The *San Diego Travel Values* insert is full of discount coupons for hotels at all price levels, restaurants, attractions, cultural and recreational activities, and tours.

You can also find information in advance of your trip online at the following websites: **www.infosandiego.com,** for general information; **www.lajollaby thesea.com,** for details on La Jolla's offerings; and **www.sandiegonorth.com,** for information on excursion areas in northern San Diego County, including Del Mar, Carlsbad, Escondido, Julian, and Anza-Borrego Desert State Park. For more helpful websites, see "The Best of San Diego Online," on p. 50.

If you're thinking of attending the theater while you're in town, contact the **San Diego Performing Arts League** (ℭ **619/ 238-0700;** www.sandiegoperforms.com) for a copy of *What's Playing?,* which contains information on upcoming shows. **San Diego Art + Sol** (ℭ **619/236-1212;** www.sandiegoartandsol.com) is a cultural marketing campaign guided by the San Diego Convention and Visitors Bureau. The website lists performances and exhibits scheduled for any specific date and you may also request a free copy of the biannual magazine, which contains a 6-month calendar of events and cultural itineraries.

2 Entry Requirements & Customs

ENTRY REQUIREMENTS
PASSPORTS

For information on how to get a passport, go to "Passports" in the "Fast Facts" section of this chapter—the websites listed provide downloadable passport applications as well as the current fees for processing passport applications. For an up-to-date, country-by-country listing of passport requirements around the world, go to the "Foreign Entry Requirement" Web page of the U.S. State Department at **http://travel.state.gov.** International visitors can obtain a visa application at the same website.

VISAS

For information on how to get a Visa, go to "Visas" in the "Fast Facts" section of this chapter.

The U.S. State Department has a **Visa Waiver Program** allowing citizens of the following countries (at press time) to enter the United States without a visa for stays of up to 90 days: Andorra, Australia, Austria, Belgium, Brunei, Denmark, Finland, France, Germany, Iceland, Ireland, Italy, Japan, Liechtenstein, Luxembourg, Monaco, the Netherlands, New Zealand, Norway, Portugal, San Marino, Singapore, Slovenia, Spain, Sweden, Switzerland, and the United Kingdom. Citizens of these nations need only a valid passport and a round-trip air or cruise ticket upon arrival. If they first enter the United States, they may also visit Mexico, Canada, Bermuda, and/or the Caribbean islands and return to the United States without a visa. Further information is available from any U.S. embassy or consulate. Canadian citizens may enter the United States without visas; they need only proof of residence.

Citizens of all other countries must have (1) a valid passport that expires at least 6 months later than the scheduled end of their visit to the United States, and (2) a tourist visa, which may be obtained without charge from any U.S. consulate.

MEDICAL REQUIREMENTS

Unless you're arriving from an area known to be suffering from an epidemic (particularly cholera or yellow fever), inoculations or vaccinations are not required for entry into the United States. If you have a medical condition that requires **syringe-administered medications,** carry a valid signed prescription from your physician—the Federal Aviation Administration (FAA) no longer allows airline passengers to pack syringes in their carry-on baggage without documented proof of medical need. If you have a disease that requires treatment with **narcotics,** you should also carry documented proof with you—smuggling narcotics aboard a plane is a serious offense that carries severe penalties in the United States.

For **HIV-positive visitors,** requirements for entering the United States are somewhat vague and change frequently. For up-to-the-minute information, contact **AIDSinfo** (© **800/448-0440** or 301/519-6616 outside the U.S.; www.aidsinfo.nih.gov) or the **Gay Men's Health Crisis** (© **212/367-1000;** www.gmhc.org).

CUSTOMS
WHAT YOU CAN BRING INTO SAN DIEGO

Every visitor older than 21 years of age may bring in, free of duty, the following: (1) 1 liter of wine or hard liquor; (2) 200 cigarettes, 100 cigars (but not from Cuba), or 3 pounds of smoking tobacco; and (3) $100 worth of gifts. These exemptions are offered to travelers who spend at least 72 hours in the United States and who have not claimed them within the preceding 6 months. It is altogether forbidden to bring into the country foodstuffs (particularly fruit, cooked meats, and canned goods) and plants (vegetables, seeds, tropical plants, and the like). Foreign tourists may carry in or out up to $10,000 in U.S. or foreign currency with no formalities; larger sums must be declared to U.S. Customs on entering or leaving, which includes filing form CM 4790. For details regarding U.S. Customs and Border Protection, consult your nearest U.S. embassy or consulate, or **U.S. Customs** (© **202/927-1770;** www.customs.ustreas.gov).

WHAT YOU CAN TAKE HOME FROM SAN DIEGO
Canadian Citizens

For a clear summary of Canadian rules, write for the booklet *I Declare,* issued by the **Canada Border Services Agency**

(© **800/461-9999** in Canada, or 204/ 983-3500; **www.cbsa-asfc.gc.ca/E/ pub/cp/rc4044**).

U.K. Citizens

For information, contact **HM Customs & Excise** at © **0845/010-9000** (from outside the U.K., 020/8929-0152), or consult their website at **www.hmce. gov.uk**.

Australian Citizens

A helpful brochure available from Australian consulates or Customs offices is *Know Before You Go.* For more information, call the **Australian Customs Service** at © **1300/363-263** or log on to **www. customs.gov.au**.

New Zealand Citizens

Most questions are answered in a free pamphlet available at New Zealand consulates and Customs offices: *New Zealand Customs Guide for Travellers, Notice no. 4.* For more information, contact **New Zealand Customs,** The Customhouse, 17–21 Whitmore St., Box 2218, Wellington (© **04/473-6099** or 0800/428-786; **www.customs.govt.nz**).

3 Money

Although costs are creeping up, San Diego is still a moderately priced destination compared to New York, Boston, or San Francisco.

ATMS

Nationwide, the easiest and best way to get cash away from home is from an ATM (automated teller machine). The **Cirrus** (© **800/424-7787;** www.mastercard.com) and **PLUS** (© **800/843-7587;** www.visa.com) networks span the country; you can find them even in remote regions. Look at the back of your bank card to see which network you're on, and then call or check online for ATM locations at your destination. Be sure you know your personal identification number (PIN) and daily withdrawal limit before you depart. *Note:* Remember that many banks impose a fee every time you use a card at another bank's ATM, and that fee can be higher for international transactions (up to $5 or more) than for domestic ones (where they're rarely more than $2). In addition, the bank from which you withdraw cash may charge its own fee. To compare banks' ATM fees within the U.S., use **www.bankrate.com**. For international withdrawal fees, ask your bank.

One of California's most popular banks is Wells Fargo, a member of the Star, PLUS, Cirrus, and Global Access systems. It has hundreds of ATMs at branches and stores (including most Vons supermarkets) throughout San Diego County. Other statewide banks include Bank of America (which accepts PLUS, Star, and Interlink cards), and First Interstate Bank (Cirrus).

CREDIT CARDS & DEBIT CARDS

These credit cards are the most widely used form of payment in the United States: **Visa** (Barclaycard in Britain), **MasterCard** (EuroCard in Europe, Access in Britain, Chargex in Canada), **American Express, Diners Club,** and **Discover.** They also provide a convenient record of all your expenses, and they generally offer relatively good exchange rates. You can withdraw cash advances from your credit cards at banks or ATMs, provided you know your PIN.

It's highly recommended that you travel with at least one major credit card. You must have one to rent a car, and hotels and airlines usually require a credit card imprint as a deposit against expenses. Visitors from outside the United States should inquire whether

What Things Cost in San Diego	US$	UK£
Taxi from the airport to downtown	15.00	8.33
Bus from the airport to downtown	2.25	1.25
Local telephone call	.50	.28
Double at the Hotel del Coronado (very expensive)	300.00	166.67
Double at the Catamaran Resort Hotel (expensive)	279.00	155.00
Double at the Sommerset Suites Hotel (moderate)	159.00	88.33
Double at La Pensione Hotel (inexpensive)	90.00	50.00
Breakfast or lunch for one at the Mission (inexpensive)	11.00	6.11
Lunch for one at Casa de Guadalajara (moderate)	14.00	7.78
Two-course dinner for one at Filippi's Pizza Grotto (inexpensive)	15.00	8.33
Two-course dinner for one at Fifth & Hawthorne (moderate)	28.00	15.56
Two-course dinner for one at Thee Bungalow (expensive)	36.00	20.00
Two-course dinner for one at Baleen (very expensive)	50.00	27.78
Pint of beer at Karl Strauss Brewery	5.95	3.31
Large coffee at Claire de Lune Coffee Lounge	2.25	1.25
All-day adult ticket aboard Old Town Trolley Tours	30.00	16.67
SeaWorld adult admission	53.00	29.44
Best seat at the Old Globe Theatre	65.00	36.11
Least-expensive seat at the San Diego Symphony	20.00	11.11

their bank assesses a 1% to 3% fee on charges incurred abroad.

ATM cards with major credit-card backing, known as **debit cards,** are now a commonly acceptable form of payment in most stores and restaurants. Debit cards draw money directly from your checking account. Some stores enable you to receive "cash back" on your debit-card purchases as well. The same is true at most U.S. post offices.

TRAVELER'S CHECKS

Traveler's checks are widely accepted in the U.S., but foreign visitors should make sure that they're denominated in U.S. dollars; foreign-currency checks are often difficult to exchange.

These days, though, traveler's checks are less essential because 24-hour ATMs are found throughout cities like San Diego, allowing you to withdraw small amounts of cash as needed. But since you will likely be charged an ATM withdrawal fee if the bank is not your own, you might be better off with traveler's checks—provided that you don't mind showing identification every time you want to cash one.

You can buy traveler's checks at most banks. Most are offered in denominations of $20, $50, $100, $500, and sometimes $1000. Generally, you'll pay a service charge ranging from 1% to 4%.

The most popular traveler's checks are offered by **American Express** (✆ 800/807-6233; ✆ 800/221-7282 for card holders—this number accepts collect calls, offers service in several foreign languages, and exempts Amex gold and platinum cardholders from the 1% fee.); **Visa** (✆ 800/732-1322; or AAA members can call ✆ 866/339-3378 or stop by a AAA office to obtain Visa checks for a $9.95 fee for checks up to $1,500); and **MasterCard** (✆ 800/223-9920).

If you do choose to carry traveler's checks, keep a record of their serial numbers separate from your checks in the event they are stolen or lost. You'll get a refund faster if you know the numbers.

4 When to Go

San Diego is blessed with a mild climate, low humidity, and good air quality. In fact, *Pleasant Weather Rankings,* published by Consumer Travel, ranked San Diego's weather number two in the world (behind Las Palmas, in the Canary Islands). It's worth keeping in mind, though, that San Diego County covers more than 4,500 square miles (11,700 sq. km) and rises in elevation from sea level to 6,500 feet (1,981m). It can be a pleasant day on the coast but blisteringly hot on the inland mesas; or conversely, it can be a foggy day at the beach but gloriously sunny just minutes away downtown.

With its coastal setting, the city of San Diego maintains a moderate climate. Although the temperature can change 20°F to 30°F between day and evening, it rarely reaches a point of extreme heat or cold; daytime highs above 100°F (38°C) are unusual, and the mercury dropping below freezing can be counted in mere hours once or twice each year. San Diego receives very little precipitation (just 10 in. of rainfall in an average year, though in 2005 that total nearly doubled); what rain does fall comes primarily between November and April, and by July, our hillsides start to look brown and parched. It's not unusual for the city to go without measurable precipitation for as long as 6 months in the summer and fall.

My favorite weather in San Diego is in the fall. The days are still warm (even hot) and the cool nights remind you that yes, even in Southern California, we have a change of seasons. February and March are also beautiful periods when the landscapes are greenest and blooming flowers at their peak, although it's still too cold for all but the heartiest to go into the ocean without a wetsuit. Beach bunnies should note that late spring and early summer tanning sessions are often compromised by a local phenomenon called **May Gray** and **June Gloom**—a layer of low-lying clouds or fog along the coast that doesn't burn off until noon (if at all) and returns before sunset. Use days like these to explore inland San Diego, where places like the Wild Animal Park are probably warm and clear.

Another more unpredictable Southern California phenomenon is **Santa Ana winds,** periods of hot, dry weather that can last for several days. These usually hit a couple times a year, typically between September and December. These desiccating winds heighten wildfire danger and can be a backcountry firefighter's worst nightmare, but Santa Anas invariably bring warm temperatures and crystal-clear skies. Occurring irregularly every 2 to 7 years, the **El Niño** weather pattern—storms created by a warming of Pacific Ocean waters—can cause unusually heavy winter rains. A 1983 El Niño storm even toppled a research platform off Mission Beach (it can now be explored by divers as part of San Diego's Wreck Alley—p. 182).

San Diego is busiest between Memorial Day and Labor Day. The kids are out

Average Monthly Temperatures (°F & °C) & Rainfall (in.)

	Jan	Feb	Mar	Apr	May	June	July	Aug	Sept	Oct	Nov	Dec
High (°F)	65	66	66	68	70	71	75	77	76	74	70	66
(°C)	18	19	19	20	21	21	24	25	25	23	21	19
Low (°F)	46	47	50	54	57	60	64	66	63	58	52	47
(°C)	8	9	10	12	14	15	17	19	17	15	10	8
Rainfall	2.1	1.4	1.6	0.8	0.2	1	0	0.1	0.2	0.3	1.1	1.4

of school and *everyone* wants to be by the seashore; if you visit in summer, expect fully booked beachfront hotels and crowded parking lots. The week of the July 4th holiday is a zoo at Mission Beach and Pacific Beach—you'll love it or hate it. But San Diego's popularity as a convention destination and its year-round weather keep the tourism business steady the rest of the year as well. The only slow season is from Thanksgiving to early February. Hotels are less full, and the beaches are peaceful and uncrowded; the big family attractions are still busy on weekends, though, with residents taking advantage of holiday breaks. A local secret: Although it's the coolest, rainiest season (relatively speaking, anyway—it rarely rains), November through February are also the sunniest months of the year.

SAN DIEGO CALENDAR OF EVENTS

You might want to plan your trip around one of these annual events in the San Diego area (including the destinations covered in chapter 11, "Side Trips from San Diego"). For even more up-to-date planning information, contact the **International Visitor Information Center** (© 619/236-1212; www.sandiego.org).

January

Nations of San Diego International Dance Festival, North Park. Founded in 1993, this festival is Southern California's largest ethnic-dance showcase, featuring more than 250 dancers and musicians representing a variety of cultures and dance companies. Performances are at the North Park Theatre.

Call © 619/220-8497 or check www. sandiegodance.org. Mid-January.

The Carlsbad Marathon & Half Marathon takes place along a scenic coastal route in San Diego's North County. For more information, call © 760/692-2900 or visit www.sd marathon.com. Mid-January.

February

Buick Invitational, Torrey Pines Golf Course, La Jolla. This PGA Tour men's tournament, an annual event since 1952, draws more than 100,000 spectators each year. It features 150 of the finest professionals in the world. For information, call © 800/888-2842 or 619/281-4653; or see www.buick invitational.com. Early to mid-February.

Wildflowers bloom in the desert between late February and the end of March at Anza-Borrego Desert State Park. The peak of blooming lasts for a few weeks and timing varies from year to year, depending on the winter rainfall (see "Anza-Borrego Desert State Park" in chapter 11). For details, call © 760/767-4684.

Mardi Gras in the Gaslamp Quarter is the largest Mardi Gras party on the West Coast. The celebration of "Fat Tuesday" features a Mardi Gras parade and an outdoor celebration in downtown's historic Gaslamp Quarter. Participating restaurants and bars offer Mardi Gras specials. This is a ticketed event for ages 21 and older. For more information, call © 619/233-5227 or visit www.gaslamp.org. February 21, 2007.

March

Kiwanis Ocean Beach Kite Festival. The late-winter skies over the Ocean Beach Recreational Center get a brilliant shot of color. Learn to make and decorate a kite of your own, participate in an all-ages flying contest, take part in all types of food and entertainment, and finish up with the grand finale: a parade down to the beach. For more information, call © **619/531-1527.** First Saturday in March.

The San Diego Latino Film Festival, Mission Valley and downtown, has grown to become one of the largest and most successful Latino film events in the country. More than 100 movies from throughout Latin America and the United States are shown, complemented by gala parties, seminars, a music series, and art exhibit. Call © **619/230-1938** or go to www.sdlatinofilm.com. Mid-March.

St. Patrick's Day Parade, Hillcrest. A tradition since 1980, the parade starts at Sixth and Juniper and ends at Sixth and Laurel. An **Irish Festival** follows in Balboa Park. For details, call © **858/268-9111** or check www.stpatsparade.org. March 17.

Flower Fields in bloom at Carlsbad Ranch. One of the most spectacular sights in North County is the yearly blossoming of a gigantic sea of bright ranunculuses during March and April, creating a striped blanket that's visible from the freeway. Visitors are welcome to view and tour the fields, which are off Interstate 5 at the Palomar Airport Road exit (see "Flower Power" in chapter 11). For more information, call © **760/431-0352.**

April

Rosarito-Ensenada 50-mile Fun Bicycle Ride, Mexico. About 10,000 participants cycle from the Rosarito Beach Hotel along the two-lane free road to Ensenada and the Finish Line Fiesta. There's another ride in September. For information, call © **858/483-8777** or visit www.rosaritoensenada.com. Mid-to late April.

San Diego Crew Classic, Crown Point Shores, Mission Bay. Since 1973, it has drawn more than 3,000 rowers from collegiate teams in the U.S. (admission $7). Call © **619/225-0300** or check out www.crewclassic.org. First weekend in April.

Del Mar National Horse Show. The first event in the Del Mar racing season takes place from late April into early May at the famous Del Mar Fairgrounds. The field at this show includes Olympic-caliber and national championship horse-and-rider teams; there are also Western fashion boutiques and artist displays and demonstrations. For more information, call © **858/792-4288** or visit www.sdfair.com.

Adams Avenue Roots Festival, Normal Heights. This is a blues, folk, Cajun, Celtic, bluegrass, and international music festival held on six stages at 35th and Adams, and free to the public. Food, beer garden, and arts-and-crafts vendors. Check it out by calling © **619/282-7329** or stopping by www.normalheights.org. Late April.

Coronado Flower Show Weekend, Spreckels Park. Organizers claim this is the largest tented flower show in the Western United States. The weekend-long event, now in its 8th decade, includes a book sale, an art show, and a lineup of classic cars. Go to www.coronadoflowershow.com for more details.

ArtWalk, Little Italy, along Kettner Boulevard and India Street. This 2-day festival, which began in 1984, is now the largest art event in the San Diego/Tijuana region, showcasing hundreds of visual and performing artists. For more information, call ☏ **619/615-1090** or visit www.artwalkinfo.com.

Day at the Docks, Harbor Drive and Scott Street, Point Loma. This sportfishing tournament and festival features food, entertainment, and free boat rides. Call ☏ **619/234-8793** or see www.sportfishing.org. Usually the last Sunday of April.

May

Fiesta Cinco de Mayo, Old Town. Uniformed troops march and guns blast to mark the 1862 triumph of Mexican soldiers over the French. The festivities include a battle re-enactment with costumed actors, mariachi music, and margaritas galore. With 200,000 attending the 3-day celebration, parking is in short supply. (*Hint:* Take the trolley and make dining reservations well in advance.) Admission is free. For further details, call ☏ **619/260-1700** or visit www.fiestacincodemayo.com. Weekend closest to May 5.

Carlsbad Spring Village Faire, Grand and State streets. This event is billed as the biggest and best arts and crafts fair in Southern California. The entire downtown area of Carlsbad is closed off to traffic. Usually mid-May. Call ☏ **760/931-8400** for more details.

June

Mainly Mozart Festival. Presenting the work of Mozart and his contemporaries, this acclaimed classical-music festival features concerts on both sides of the border. An all-star orchestra draws players from around the world. For information, call ☏ **619/239-0100;** or go online at www.mainlymozart.org. Performances throughout the month.

The Rock 'n' Roll Marathon not only offers runners a unique course through Balboa Park, downtown, and around Mission Bay, it pumps them (and spectators) up with live bands on 26 stages along the course. There is a pre-race fitness expo and post-race concert, featuring big-name talent. Call ☏ **800/311-1255** or go online to www.rnrmarathon.com. Early June.

Temecula Valley Balloon & Wine Festival. Colorful hot-air balloons dominate the sky over Lake Skinner during the 2½-day festival, which also features wine tastings, good food, jazz music, and other entertainment. General admission is $15 to $22, and slots for the early morning balloon rides ($150 per person) sell out weeks in advance (call ☏ **800/965-2122**). The lake is about 10 miles northeast of Temecula. To find out about this year's festival or purchase advance tickets, call the event organizers at ☏ **951/676-6713** or visit www.tvbwf.com. Early June.

Indian Fair, Museum of Man, Balboa Park. Native Americans from dozens of tribes across the United States gather to demonstrate tribal dances and sell arts, crafts, and ethnic food. Call ☏ **619/239-2001.** Mid-June.

Twilight in the Park Concerts, Balboa Park. These free concerts at the Spreckels Organ Pavilion, on Tuesday, Wednesday, and Thursday evenings, have been held since 1979. For information, call ☏ **619/239-0512.** The Spreckels Organ Society also holds free organ concerts on Mondays at 7:30pm in summer. Find out more at ☏ **619/702-8138** or www.sosorgan.com. Mid-June to August.

San Diego County Fair. Referred to as the Del Mar Fair by everyone locally, this is the *other* happening (besides horse racing) at the Del Mar Fairgrounds. The entire county participates in this annual fair. Livestock competitions, thrill rides, flower-and-garden shows, gem and mineral exhibits, food and crafts booths, carnival games, and home arts exhibits dominate the event. There are also grandstand concerts by name performers (some require separate admission fee). The fair lasts more than 3 weeks. For details, call © **858/793-5555** or check www.sdfair.com. Mid-June to early July.

July

World Championship Over-the-Line Tournament, Mission Bay. This popular tournament is a San Diego original. The beach softball event dates from 1953 and is renowned for boisterous, beer-soaked, anything-goes behavior—a total of 1,200 three-person teams compete, and more than 50,000 attend. It's a heap of fun for the open-minded, but a bit much for small kids. It takes place on 2 consecutive weekends, on Fiesta Island in Mission Bay, and the admission is free. For more details, call © **619/688-0817** or visit www.ombac.org. Mid-July.

San Diego Symphony Summer Pops, downtown. The symphony's summer pops series features lighter classical, jazz, opera, Broadway, and show tunes, all performed under the stars and capped by fireworks. Held most summer weekends at the Embarcadero downtown. For details, call © **619/235-0804** or visit www.sandiego symphony.com. Early July to early September.

San Diego Lesbian and Gay Pride Parade, Rally, and Festival. This parade is one of San Diego's biggest draws. It begins Friday night with a rally at the Organ Pavilion in Balboa Park, reconvenes at 11am on Saturday for the parade through Hillcrest, followed by a massive festival—held south of Sixth and Laurel in the park—that continues Sunday. For more information, call © **619/297-7683** or visit www.sdpride.org. Third or fourth weekend in July.

Thoroughbred Racing Season. The "turf meets the surf" in Del Mar during the thoroughbred racing season at the Del Mar Race Track. Post time is 2pm most days; the track is dark on Tuesdays. For this year's schedule of events, call © **858/792-4242** or 858/755-1141 or visit www.dmtc.com. Mid-July to mid-September.

U.S. Open Sandcastle Competition, Imperial Beach Pier. Here's the quintessential beach event: There's a parade and children's sandcastle contest on Saturday, followed by the main competition Sunday. Past years have seen creations of astounding complexity, but note that the castles are usually plundered right after the award ceremony. For further details, call © **619/424-6663** or visit usopensandcastle.com. Mid-July.

Comic-Con International, downtown. Upward of 60,000 people attend America's largest comic-book convention each year when it lands at the San Diego Convention Center for a weekend of auctions, dealers, autographs, and seminars focusing on graphic novels and fantasy and sci-fi movies. Past special guests include artists, stars, and filmmakers like Hugh Jackman, Matt Groening, Halle Berry, Stan Lee, Angelina Jolie, and Quentin Tarantino. For further details, call © **619/491-2475** or check www.comic-con.org. Late July.

Street Scene, Mission Valley. Lamentably, the name of this music fest has become an anachronism. Squeezed out of the Gaslamp Quarter in 2005 by redevelopment, Street Scene now takes place in the parking lot of Qualcomm Stadium. The move has provided much more space for the 2-day event, but much less character. Also lost was the fest's inclusiveness—it was once a celebration of a wide variety of musical styles; now it's focused on alt-rock and hip-hop. But if that's where your musical tastes are, Street Scene delivers one of the best concert lineups in the country. For ticket and show information, call © **888/487-4347** or visit www. street-scene.com. Late July or early August.

Acura Classic, La Costa. This week-long Women's Tennis Association event gathers the greatest female tennis players in the world at the La Costa Resort & Spa. For information, call © **760/438-5683** or log onto www. acuraclassic.com. Late July to early August.

August

La Jolla SummerFest is perhaps San Diego's most prestigious annual music event. It features a wide spectrum of classical and contemporary music, from tango to Tchaikovsky, with guest composers and musicians ranging from the likes of Chick Corea to Yo-Yo Ma. SummerFest also offers master classes, open rehearsals, and workshops. Presented by the La Jolla Music Society; call © **858/459-3728** or check the website www.ljms.org for more information. Early to mid-August.

Julian Weed & Craft Show, Julian. This is one event that's better than its name. Artwork and arrangements culled from the area's myriad woods, rocks, wildflowers, and indigenous plants (okay, weeds) are displayed and sold. The Julian Chamber of Commerce (© **760/765-1857;** www.julian ca.com) has further details. Second half of August.

Surfing Competitions. Oceanside's pier-side surfing spot attracts several competitions, including the **World Bodysurfing Championships** and the **Longboard Surf Club Competition.** The events include a trade show and gala awards presentation with music and dancers. For further details, call the Oceanside Visitors Bureau at © **800/ 350-7873** or 760/722-1534 or visit www.worldbodysurfing.org and www. oceansidelongboardsurfingclub.org. Mid- or late-August.

September

La Jolla Rough Water Swim, La Jolla Cove. The country's largest rough-water swimming competition began in 1916 and features masters, men's and women's, junior, and an amateur swim. All are 1-mile events except the junior swim and gator-man 3-mile championship. Spectators don't need tickets. For recorded information, call © **858/ 456-2100.** Downloadable entry forms are available at www.ljrws.com. Sunday after Labor Day.

Julian Fall Apple Harvest. The phenomenally popular apple harvest season runs for 2 months in early fall, and every weekend local artisans display their wares. There's also plenty of cider and apple pie, plus entertainment and brilliant fall foliage. For more information, contact the chamber of commerce at © **760/765-1857.** Mid-September to mid-November.

Rosarito-Ensenada 50-mile Fun Bicycle Ride, Mexico. Held twice yearly; see the April entry, above, for a description of this late September event.

October

Fleet Week is a bit of a misnomer. It's the nation's largest military appreciation event and it lasts the entire month. It features Navy ship tours, a college football game, an auto race of classic speedsters, an air show, and more. Call © **800/353-3893** or check out www.fleetweeksandiego.org for more information.

November

Carlsbad Fall Village Faire. Billed as the largest 1-day street fair in California, this festival features more than 850 vendors on 24 city blocks. Items for sale include ceramics, jewelry, clothing, glassware, and plants. You'll find Mexican, Italian, Japanese, Korean, and Indonesian food—along with other edible fare—at booths along the way. The epicenter is the intersection of Grand Avenue and Jefferson Street. Call © **760/931-8400** or visit www. carlsbad.org. First Sunday in November.

Fall Flower Tour and the **Poinsettia Festival Street Fair,** Encinitas. Like its close neighbor Carlsbad, Encinitas is a flower-growing center—80% of the world's poinsettia plants get their start at a single ranch here. These two events celebrate the quintessential holiday plant and other late-flowering blooms. The 1-day Street Fair takes place in late November. For the Flower Tour, make reservations by early October; the nursery tours take place in early December. For poinsettia information, call the Encinitas Visitors Center at © **800/953-6041** or 760/753-6041; for the street fair, call 760/943-1950 or see www.kennedyfaires.com.

Dr. Seuss' How the Grinch Stole Christmas!, Balboa Park. San Diego was the adopted hometown of Theodor Geisel, aka Dr. Seuss, and since 1998 the Old Globe Theatre has been transformed into Whoville each holiday season. Directed by two-time Tony Award-winner Jack O'Brien, this musical has become a family tradition, with discounted seats for kids. For

more information, call © **619/234-5623;** or check www.theoldglobe.org. Mid-November through December.

San Diego Thanksgiving Dixieland Jazz Festival. More than 20 bands from around North America and beyond perform at this annual festival, held over the long Thanksgiving weekend. Expect to hear vintage jazz sounds like ragtime, swing, and, of course, pure New Orleans Dixieland. Call © **619/297-5277** or visit www.dixielandjazzfestival.org. Late November.

December

Ocean Beach Christmas Parade and Tree Festival. Ocean Beach is San Diego's counterculture community, so this parade is a little different than your average holiday parade. It's a family affair to be sure (Santa Claus is on hand, of course), but with entries like the Off Key Choir and the Geriatric Surf Club, it's definitely quirky. Call © **619/224-4906** or see www.oceanbeachsandiego.com. First Saturday in December.

Balboa Park December Nights. San Diego's fine urban park is decked out in holiday splendor for this 2-night event. A candlelight procession, traditional caroling, and baroque music ensembles are just part of the entertainment. There are crafts displays, ethnic food, traditional hot cider, and a grand Christmas tree and Nativity scene in Spreckels Organ Pavilion. The event is free and lasts from 5 to 9pm both days; the park's museums are free during those hours. For more information, call © **619/239-0512** or visit www.balboapark.org. First Friday and Saturday in December.

College Bowl Games. San Diego is home to two college football bowl games: the **Holiday Bowl** and the **Poinsettia Bowl,** both held in late December. The Holiday Bowl pits top

Whale-Watching

The migration of the California gray whales to the warm breeding grounds off the coast of Baja California occurs every winter. Glimpse these peaceful giants of the sea from the Cabrillo National Monument or on special whale-watching cruises. Call ℭ **619/557-5450** or 619-236-1212 for more information.

teams from the Pac 10 and Big 12 Conferences, and the Poinsettia Bowl pits a team from the Mountain West Conference against an at-large opponent. The fledgling Poinsettia Bowl (ℭ **619/285-5061;** www.poinsettia bowl.net) was inaugurated in 2005; the Holiday Bowl (ℭ **619/283-5808;** www.holidaybowl.com) has been around since 1978, and features several special events, including the nation's biggest balloon parade of giant inflatable characters.

Whale-watching season traditionally takes place in the cooler months of San Diego County as more than 25,000 California gray whales make the trek from the chilly Alaskan seas to the warm-water breeding lagoons of Baja California. Cabrillo National Monument, on the panoramic Point Loma peninsula, offers a glassed-in observatory from which to spot the whales, examine whale exhibits, and listen to taped narration describing these popular mammals. Many boating excursion companies offer whale-watching tours throughout the season. For more information, visit www.sandiego.org. Mid-December to mid-March.

Mission Bay Boat Parade of Lights, from Quivira Basin in Mission Bay. Held on a Saturday, the best viewing is around Crown Point, on the east side of Vacation Island, or the west side of Fiesta Island; it concludes with the lighting of a 320-foot tower of Christmas lights at SeaWorld. Call ℭ **858/488-0501.** For more vessels dressed up like Christmas trees, the **San Diego Boat Parade of Lights** is held in San Diego Bay on two Sundays, with a route starting at Shelter Island and running past Seaport Village and the Coronado Ferry Landing Marketplace. Visit www.sdparadeoflights.org for more information. Mid-December.

5 Travel Insurance

The cost of travel insurance varies widely, depending on the cost and length of your trip, your age and health, and the type of trip you're taking, but expect to pay between 5% and 8% of the vacation itself. You can get estimates from various providers through **InsureMyTrip.com**. Enter your trip cost and dates, your age, and other information for prices from more than a dozen companies.

TRIP-CANCELLATION INSURANCE

Trip-cancellation insurance will help retrieve your money if you have to back out of a trip or depart early, or if your travel supplier goes bankrupt. Permissible reasons for trip cancellation can range from sickness to natural disasters to the State Department declaring a destination unsafe for travel.

For more information, contact one of the following recommended insurers: **Access America** (ℭ 866/807-3982; www.accessamerica.com), **Global Alert** (ℭ 800/423-3632; www.tripinsurance. com), **Travel Guard International** (ℭ 800/826-4919; www.travelguard. com), **Travel Insured International**

Travel in the Age of Bankruptcy

Airlines go bankrupt, so protect yourself by **buying your tickets with a credit card.** The Fair Credit Billing Act guarantees that you can get your money back from the credit-card company if a travel supplier goes under (and if you request the refund within 60 days of the bankruptcy). **Travel insurance** can also help, but make sure it covers against "carrier default" for your specific travel provider. And be aware that if a U.S. airline goes bust mid-trip, a 2001 federal law requires other carriers to take you to your destination (albeit on a space-available basis) for a fee of no more than $25, provided you rebook within 60 days of the cancellation.

(✆ 800/243-3174; www.travelinsured.com), and **Travelex Insurance Services** (✆ 888/457-4602; www.travelex-insurance.com).

MEDICAL INSURANCE

Although it's not required of travelers, health insurance is highly recommended. Most health insurance policies cover you if you get sick away from home—but verify that you're covered before you depart, particularly if you're insured by an HMO.

International visitors should note that unlike many European countries, the United States does not usually offer free or low-cost medical care to its citizens or visitors. Doctors and hospitals are expensive, and in most cases will require advance payment or proof of coverage before they render their services. Good policies will cover the cost of an accident, repatriation, or death. Packages, such as **Europ Assistance's Worldwide Healthcare Plan,** are sold by European automobile clubs and travel agencies at attractive rates. **Worldwide Assistance Services, Inc.** (✆ 800/777-8710; www.worldwideassistance.com) is the agent for Europ Assistance in the United States.

Though lack of health insurance may prevent you from being admitted to a hospital in nonemergencies, don't worry about being left on a street corner to die: The American way is to fix you now and bill the living daylights out of you later.

INSURANCE FOR BRITISH TRAVELERS Most big travel agents offer their own insurance and will probably try to sell you their package when you book a holiday. Think before you sign. **Britain's Consumers' Association** recommends that you insist on seeing the policy and reading the fine print before buying travel insurance. **The Association of British Insurers** (✆ 020/7600-3333; www.abi.org.uk) gives advice by phone and publishes *Holiday Insurance,* a free guide to policy provisions and prices. You might also shop around for better deals: Try **Columbus Direct** (✆ 0870/033-9988; www.columbusdirect.net).

INSURANCE FOR CANADIAN TRAVELERS Canadians should check with their provincial health plan offices or call **Health Canada** (✆ 866/225-0709; www.hc-sc.gc.ca) to find out the extent of their coverage and what documentation and receipts they must take home in case they are treated in the United States.

LOST-LUGGAGE INSURANCE

On flights within the U.S., checked baggage is covered up to $2,500 per ticketed passenger. On flights outside the U.S. (and on U.S. portions of international trips), baggage coverage is limited to approximately $9.07 per pound, up to approximately $635 per checked bag. If you plan to check items more valuable than what's covered by the standard liability, see if your homeowner's policy covers your valuables, get baggage insurance as part of your comprehensive travel-insurance package, or buy Travel Guard's "BagTrak" product.

If your luggage is lost, immediately file a lost-luggage claim at the airport, detailing the luggage contents. Most airlines require that you report delayed, damaged, or lost baggage within 4 hours of arrival. The airlines are required to deliver luggage, once found, directly to your house or destination free of charge.

6 Health & Safety

STAYING HEALTHY

We list **hospitals** and **emergency numbers** under "Fast Facts" in chapter 4, "Getting to Know San Diego" (see p. 62).

If you suffer from a chronic illness, consult your doctor before your departure. Pack **prescription medications** in your carry-on luggage, and carry them in their original containers, with pharmacy labels—otherwise they won't make it through airport security. Visitors from outside the U.S. should carry generic names of prescription drugs. For U.S. travelers, most reliable health-care plans provide coverage if you get sick away from home. Foreign visitors may have to pay all medical costs upfront and be reimbursed later. See "Medical Insurance," under "Travel Insurance," above.

Medications are readily available throughout San Diego at various chain drugstores such as Long's, Rite-Aid, and Sav-On, which sell pharmaceuticals and non-prescription products. Some branches are open 24 hours (p. 62). Local hospitals also sell prescription drugs.

Near downtown San Diego, **UCSD Medical Center-Hillcrest,** 200 W. Arbor Dr. (© **619/543-6400**), has the most convenient emergency room. In La Jolla, **UCSD Thornton Hospital,** 9300 Campus Point Dr. (© **858/657-7600**), has a good emergency room, and you'll find another in Coronado, at **Coronado Hospital,** 250 Prospect Place (© **619/435-6251**), opposite the Marriott Resort.

STAYING SAFE

Fortunately, San Diego is a relatively safe destination, by big-city standards. Of the 10 largest cities in the United States, it historically has had the lowest incidence of violent crime, per capita. Still, it never hurts to take some precautions.

Virtually all areas of the city are safe during the day. Caution is advised in Balboa Park, in areas not frequented by regular foot traffic (particularly off the walkways on the Sixth Ave. side of the park). Homeless transients are common in San Diego—especially downtown, in Hillcrest, and in the beach area. They are rarely a problem, but can be unpredictable when inebriated. Downtown areas to the east of PETCO Park are sparsely populated after dusk, and poorly lit.

Parts of the city that are usually safe on foot at night include the Gaslamp Quarter, Hillcrest, Old Town, Mission Valley, La Jolla, and Coronado.

Avoid carrying valuables with you on the street, and keep expensive cameras or electronic equipment bagged up or covered when not in use. If you're using a map, try to consult it inconspicuously—or better yet, study it before you leave your room. Hold on to your pocketbook, and place your billfold in an inside pocket. In theaters, restaurants, and other public places, keep your possessions in sight.

Always lock your room door—don't assume that once you're inside the hotel, you are automatically safe and no longer need to be aware of your surroundings. Hotels are open to the public, and security may not be able to screen everyone who enters.

DRIVING SAFETY Driving safety is important too, and carjacking is not unprecedented. Question your rental agency about personal safety and ask for a traveler-safety brochure when you pick up your car. Obtain written directions—or a map with the route clearly marked—from the agency, showing how to get to your destination. San Diego's airport area, where most car rental firms are based, is generally safe.

If you drive off a highway and end up in a dodgy-looking neighborhood, leave the area as quickly as possible. If you have an accident, even on the highway, stay in your car with the doors locked until you assess the situation or until the police arrive. If you're bumped from behind on the street or are involved in a minor accident with no injuries, and the situation appears to be suspicious, motion to the other driver to follow you. Never get out of your car in such situations. Go to the nearest police precinct, well-lit service station, or 24-hour store.

Whenever possible, always park in well-lit and well-traveled areas. Always keep your car doors locked, whether the vehicle is attended or unattended. Never leave packages or valuables in sight. If someone attempts to rob you or steal your car, don't try to resist the thief/carjacker. Report the incident to the police department immediately by calling ✆ **911.**

7 Specialized Travel Resources

TRAVELERS WITH DISABILITIES
Most disabilities shouldn't stop anyone from traveling in the United States. There are more options and resources out there than ever before, and San Diego is one of the most accessible cities in the country. Most of the city's major attractions are wheelchair friendly, including the walkways and museums of Balboa Park, the San Diego Zoo (which has bus tours to navigate the steep canyons), SeaWorld, the Wild Animal Park, and downtown's Gaslamp Quarter. Old Town and the beaches require a little more effort, but are generally accessible.

Obtain more specific information from **Accessible San Diego** (✆ 858/279-0704; www.accessandiego.org), the nation's oldest center for information for travelers with disabilities. The center has an info line that helps travelers find accessible hotels, tours, attractions, and transportation. If you call long distance and get the answering machine, leave a message, and the staff will call you back collect. Ask for the annual *Access in San Diego* pamphlet, a citywide guide with specifics on which establishments are accessible for those with visual, mobility, or hearing disabilities (cost is $5). Another organization providing info and referrals is **Access Center of San Diego** (✆ 619/293-3500; www.accesscentersd.org). *Note:* The center was severely damaged in a 2005 fire and as of press time had not resumed full operation. In the San Diego Convention & Visitors Bureau's *Dining and Accommodations* guide, a wheelchair symbol designates places that are accessible to persons with disabilities.

On buses and trolleys, riders with disabilities pay a fixed fare of $1. Because discounted fares are subsidized, *technically* you must obtain a Transit Travel ID from the **Transit Store** (✆ 619/234-1060); the ID card certifies that a rider is eligible for the discount, but most drivers use visual qualifications to establish criteria. All MTS buses and trolleys are equipped with wheelchair lifts; priority seating is available on buses and trolleys.

People with visual impairments benefit from the white reflecting ring that circles the bottom of the trolley door to increase its visibility. Airport transportation for travelers with disabilities is available in vans holding one or two wheelchairs from **Cloud 9 Shuttle** (② **800/974-8885** or 858/974-8885; www.cloud9shuttle.com).

The **Golden Access Passport** gives visually impaired persons or those with permanent disabilities (regardless of age) free lifetime entrance to all properties administered by the National Park Service, the U.S. Fish and Wildlife Service, the U.S. Forest Service, the U.S. Army Corps of Engineers, the Bureau of Land Management, and the Tennessee Valley Authority. This may include national parks, monuments, historic sites, recreation areas, and national wildlife refuges.

You may pick up a Golden Access Passport at any NPS entrance fee area by showing proof of medically determined disability and eligibility for benefits under federal law. Besides free entry, the Golden Access Passport also offers a 50% discount on federal-use fees charged for such facilities as camping, swimming, parking, boat launching, and tours. For more information, go to www.nps.gov/fees_passes.htm or call ② **888/467-2757.**

Many travel agencies offer customized tours and itineraries for travelers with disabilities. Among them are **Flying Wheels Travel** (② **507/451-5005;** www.flying wheelstravel.com); **Access-Able Travel Source** (② **303/232-2979;** www.accessable.com); and **Accessible Journeys** (② **800/846-4537** or 610/521-0339; www.disabilitytravel.com). **Avis Rent a Car** has an "Avis Access" program that offers such services as a dedicated 24-hour toll-free number (② **888/879-4273**) for customers with special travel needs; special car features, such as swivel seats, spinner knobs, and hand controls; and accessible bus service.

Organizations that offer assistance to travelers with disabilities include **Moss-Rehab** (www.mossresourcenet.org), the **American Foundation for the Blind (AFB;** ② **800/232-5463;** www.afb.org), and **SATH (Society for Accessible Travel & Hospitality;** ② **212/447-7284;** www.sath.org). **AirAmbulance Card.com** is now partnered with SATH and allows you to preselect top-notch hospitals in case of an emergency.

The community website **iCan** (www.icanonline.net/channels/travel) has destination guides and several regular columns on accessible travel. Also check out the quarterly magazine *Emerging Horizons* (www.emerginghorizons.com), and *Open World* magazine, published by SATH.

GAY & LESBIAN TRAVELERS

Despite the sometimes conservative local politics, San Diego is one of America's gay-friendliest destinations, boasting several openly gay officials, including State Sen. Christine Kehoe, City Councilwoman Toni Atkins, and the country's first openly gay District Attorney, Bonnie Dumanis. San Diego also has one of the oldest gay and lesbian theater companies, Diversionary Theatre. Gay and lesbian visitors might already know about Hillcrest, near Balboa Park, the city's most prominent "out" community. Many gay-owned restaurants, boutiques, and nightspots cater to both a gay and straight clientele, and the scene is lively most nights of the week. In the 1990s, the community's residential embrace spread west to Mission Hills, and east along Adams Avenue to Kensington.

The **Annual San Diego Lesbian and Gay Pride Parade, Rally, and Festival** are held on the third or fourth weekend in July. The parade begins at 11am on Saturday at University Avenue and Normal Street, and proceeds west on University to Sixth Avenue, ending in Balboa Park. A festival follows on Saturday.

Other events that weekend include the Pride Ball, Circuit Party Daze, and a party at the San Diego Zoo. For more information, call © **619/297-7683** or check www.sdpride.org. The **San Diego Gay Rodeo** is one of the largest rodeos on the IGRA circuit, drawing cowboys and cowgirls from across the country for bronco riding and two-stepping. It's held in late April at the rodeo grounds in the East County city of Lakeside; see www.sandiegorodeo.com for more info.

The free **San Diego Gay and Lesbian Times,** published every Thursday, is the most information-packed of several local out publications, and available at the gay and lesbian **Obelisk** bookstore, 1029 University Ave., Hillcrest (© **619/297-4171**), along with other businesses in Hillcrest and neighboring communities. And check out the **San Diego Gay & Lesbian Chamber of Commerce** online at www.gsdba.org, where you can search the 750-plus member business directory and find a variety of restaurants, cafes, hotels, and other establishments that welcome gay and lesbian clients. The **San Diego Convention and Visitors Bureau** publishes a pamphlet, *San Diego from Gay to Z,* with information on gay accommodations and events. For more information or to order the free pamphlet, go to www.sandiego.org. The CVB also has touring suggestions for gay and lesbian visitors on its cultural website: www.sandiegoartandsol.com.

The **International Gay and Lesbian Travel Association (IGLTA;** © **800/448-8550** or 954/776-2626; www.iglta.org) is the trade association for the gay and lesbian travel industry, and offers an online directory of gay- and lesbian-friendly travel businesses; go to their website and click on "Members."

Gay.com Travel (© **800/929-2268** or 415/644-8044; www.gay.com/travel or www.outandabout.com) is an excellent online successor to the popular *Out &*

About print magazine. It provides regularly updated information about gay-owned, gay-oriented, and gay-friendly lodging, dining, sightseeing, nightlife, and shopping establishments in every important destination worldwide.

The following travel guides are available at many bookstores, or you can order them from any online bookseller: *Spartacus International Gay Guide* (Bruno Gmünder Verlag; www.spartacusworld.com/gayguide) and *Odysseus: The International Gay Travel Planner* (Odysseus Enterprises Ltd.); and the *Damron* guides (www.damron.com), with separate, annual books for gay men and lesbians.

SENIOR TRAVEL

Nearly every attraction in San Diego offers a senior discount; age requirements vary, and prices are discussed in chapter 7 with each individual listing. Public transportation and movie theaters also have reduced rates. Don't be shy about asking for discounts, but always carry identification, such as a driver's license, that shows your date of birth.

Members of **AARP** (formerly known as the American Association of Retired Persons), 601 E St. NW, Washington, DC 20049 (© **888/687-2277;** www.aarp.org), get discounts on hotels, airfares, and car rentals. AARP offers members a wide range of benefits, including *AARP: The Magazine* and a monthly newsletter. Anyone over 50 can join.

The **U.S. National Park Service** offers a **Golden Age Passport** that gives seniors 62 years or older lifetime entrance to all properties administered by the National Park Service—national parks, monuments, historic sites, recreation areas, and national wildlife refuges—for a one-time processing fee of $10, which must be purchased in person at any NPS facility that charges an entrance fee. Besides free entry, a Golden Age Passport also offers a

50% discount on federal-use fees charged for such facilities as camping, swimming, parking, boat launching, and tours. For more information, go to www.nps.gov/fees_passes.htm or call (C) **888/467-2757.**

Many reliable agencies and organizations target the 50-plus market. **Elderhostel** ((C) **877/426-8056;** www.elder hostel.org) arranges study programs for those aged 55 and over. There are a variety of Elderhostel programs offered in the San Diego/Baja region, from bird-watching to cooking. Recommended publications offering travel resources and discounts for seniors include the quarterly magazine *Travel 50 & Beyond* (www.travel50andbeyond.com); *Travel Unlimited: Uncommon Adventures for the Mature Traveler* (Avalon); *101 Tips for Mature Travelers,* available from Grand Circle Travel ((C) **800/221-2610** or 617/350-7500, www.gct.com); and *Unbelievably Good Deals and Great Adventures That You Absolutely Can't Get Unless You're Over 50* (McGraw-Hill), by Joann Rattner Heilman.

FAMILY TRAVEL

With its plethora of theme parks, animal attractions, and beaches and parks, San Diego is an ideal family-vacation destination. And, of course, Disneyland is right up the road, too.

To locate accommodations, restaurants, and attractions that are particularly kid-friendly, refer to the "Kids" icon throughout this guide. Also, keep in mind some hotels offer free or discounted lodging for children who share a room with a parent or guardian—be sure to ask.

Recommended family travel websites include **Family Travel Forum** (www.familytravelforum.com), a comprehensive site that offers customized trip planning; **Family Travel Network** (www.familytravelnetwork.com), an award-winning site that offers travel features,

deals, and tips; **Travel with Your Kids** (www.travelwithyourkids.com), a comprehensive site offering sound advice for long-distance and international travel with children; and **Family Travel Files** (www.thefamilytravelfiles.com), which offers an online magazine and a directory of off-the-beaten-path tours and tour operators for families.

Frommer's *Unofficial Guide* series includes a no-nonsense look at traveling with the tribe in the Golden State in *The Unofficial Guide to California with Kids* (www.frommers.com).

MULTICULTURAL TRAVELERS

Although San Diego has a reputation as a predominantly white, middle-class, conservative-leaning metropolis, a closer look reveals a more diverse picture: 25% of the city's inhabitants are Hispanic, 13% are Asian, and 9% are African American. The **San Diego Art + Sol** website (www.san diegoartandsol.com) is an excellent place to begin researching the city's contemporary cultural attractions; it also features interesting touring itineraries.

The **San Diego Museum of Man** (p. 151) covers 4 million years of human history, with a particular focus on the native heritage of the Americas. San Diego's original residents were Native Americans, and their history is related at **Mission Trails Regional Park** and the **Junípero Serra Museum.**

With the Mexican border just 16 miles from downtown San Diego, Mexico's influence is unmistakable, and Spanish street and place names are prevalent. The **Mission Basilica San Diego de Alcalá, Junípero Serra Museum** and **Old Town** showcase Spanish-Mexican history, while contemporary culture is reflected in the murals of **Chicano Park** ((C) **619/563-4661;** www.chicano-park.org) under the San Diego-Coronado Bay Bridge. **Voz Alta** ((C) **619/230-1869;** www.vozalta. org) is a downtown gathering spot for writers, artists, and musicians with a

Chicano bent that hosts bimonthly poetry slams and other events. The **Centro Cultural de la Raza** (© **619/235-6135**; www.centroraza.com) in Balboa Park has been hobbled by internal disputes for the past several years, but still manages to present shows and exhibits. **Cinco de Mayo** (May 5) is a huge celebration in Old Town, but any day is great for shopping for Latin American handicrafts at **Bazaar del Mundo** or **Plaza del Pasado** (p. 211). Americanized Mexican food is ubiquitous, but for a taste of the real Mexico try **El Agave Tequileria** (p. 116), or head south of the border. While in Tijuana, be sure to visit the excellent **Centro Cultural Tijuana** (p. 284), which covers the history, contemporary art and culture, and performing arts of Mexico. The **Museum of Contemporary Art** (p. 162 and p. 154), with a seaside location in La Jolla and a spectacularly expanded downtown San Diego branch, often holds major shows of current Mexican artists.

Initially lured by the California gold rush in the 1850s, a small Chinese community came to live in San Diego and controlled much of the fishing industry until 1890; Chinese also helped build (and later staff) the Hotel del Coronado. Chinatown—downtown, south of Market Street—eventually merged with the rough-and-tumble Stingaree, San Diego's red-light district. The area is now largely part of the Gaslamp Quarter, but at the turn of the last century it was the hub of gambling, prostitution, and opium dens, and Chinese-raised families who ran notorious bars like the Old Tub of Blood Saloon and the Seven Buckets of Blood Saloon.

Today, an **Asian/Pacific Historic District** is beginning to materialize, concentrated between Market and J streets, and between Third and Fifth avenues. Eighteen buildings in this area have strong historical ties to the Asian/Pacific-American community. Also here is the **San Diego Chinese Historical Museum** (p. 155),

which offers walking tours of the old Chinatown the second Saturday of the month.

An African presence has been felt in small but important ways throughout San Diego history. Black slaves were part of Juan Cabrillo's expedition along the California coast in 1542, and Pío Pico, a San Diegan who became the last Mexican governor of California before it was annexed by the United States, was of African descent. The Clermont Hotel, 501 Seventh Ave., was built in 1887 and was one of the city's first black-owned businesses, a segregated hotel "for colored people" until 1956; it may be the oldest surviving historically black hotel in the nation and was designated an African-American landmark in 2001. In the mountains east of San Diego, you'll find the **Julian Gold Rush Hotel** (p. 273), built in 1897 by freed slave Albert Robinson. The **Black Historical Society of San Diego** offers tours of downtown San Diego's black history on Saturdays; call © **619/685-7215** for details or see www.blackhistoricalsociety.org. In Old Town, the ramshackle **Casa del Rey Moro African Museum** (**619/220-0022;** www.ambers.com) provides a scholarly look at black history, with a special emphasis on how it has played out in San Diego and California. The **World Beat Center** (**619/230-1190;** www.world beatcenter.org) in Balboa Park produces reggae and African music concerts, has a variety of classes, and even runs its own radio station.

Black Travel Online (www.blacktravel online.com) posts news on upcoming events and includes links to articles and travel-booking sites. **Soul of America** (www.soulofamerica.com) is a comprehensive website, with travel tips, event and family-reunion postings, and sections on historically black beach resorts and active vacations. The section on San Diego is fairly detailed and has a calendar of events.

STUDENT TRAVEL

A valid student ID will often qualify students for discounts on airfare, accommodations, entry to museums, cultural events, movies, and more. If you're planning to travel outside the U.S., you'd be wise to arm yourself with an **International Student Identity Card (ISIC),** which offers substantial savings on rail passes, plane tickets, and entrance fees. It also provides you with basic health and life insurance and a 24-hour help line. The card is available from **STA Travel** (② **800/781-4040** in North America; www.sta.com or www.statravel.com), the biggest student travel agency in the world. If you're no longer a student but are still under 26, you can get an **International Youth Travel Card (IYTC)** from the same people, which entitles you to some discounts (but not on museum admissions). **Travel CUTS** (② **800/667-2887** or 416/614-2887; www.travelcuts. com) offers similar services for both Canadians and U.S. residents. Irish students may prefer to turn to **USIT** (② **01/602-1600;** www.usitnow.ie), an Ireland-based specialist in student, youth, and independent travel.

SINGLE TRAVELERS

On package vacations, single travelers are often hit with a "single supplement" to the base price. To avoid it, you can agree to room with other single travelers or find a compatible roommate before you go with one of the many roommate-locator agencies.

TravelChums (② **212/787-2621;** www.travelchums.com) is an Internet-only travel-companion matching service with elements of an online personals-type site, hosted by the respected New York–based Shaw Guides travel service.

For more information, check out Eleanor Berman's latest edition of *Traveling Solo: Advice and Ideas for More Than 250 Great Vacations* (Globe Pequot), a guide with advice on traveling alone, either solo or as part of a group tour.

TRAVELING WITH PETS

Many of us wouldn't dream of going on vacation without our pets. And these days, more and more lodgings and restaurants are going the pet-friendly route. In chapter 5, I've noted which hotels accept pets; the **Loews Coronado Bay Resort** (p. 93), in particular, goes out of its way to welcome pets. Many San Diegans congregate with their canine friends at **Dog Beach,** at the north end of Ocean Beach, where dogs can swim, play, and socialize. After your pooch is thoroughly coated in seawater and sand, take him to the do-it-yourself **Dog Beach Dog Wash,** 2 blocks away at 4933 Voltaire St. (② **619/523-1700**). **Nate's Point** in Balboa Park is another favored place to let your pooch run loose. It's on the west end of the park, on the south side of Cabrillo Bridge.

Good resources include **www.pets welcome.com**, which dispenses medical tips, names of animal-friendly lodgings and campgrounds, and lists of kennels and veterinarians; **www.pettravel.com**; and **www.travelpets.com**. Also check out *The Portable Petswelcome.com: The Complete Guide to Traveling with Your Pet* (Howell Book House), which features the best selection of pet travel information anywhere. Another resource is *Pets-R-Permitted Hotel, Motel & Kennel Directory: The Travel Resource for Pet Owners Who Travel* (Annenberg Communications).

If you plan to fly with your pet, a list of requirements for transporting live animals is available at **http://airconsumer. ost.dot.gov**. You may be able to carry your pet on board a plane if it's small enough to put inside a carrier that can slip under the seat. Pets usually count as one piece of carry-on luggage. The ASPCA discourages travelers from checking pets as luggage at any time, as storage conditions on planes are loosely monitored, and fatal accidents are not unprecedented. Your other option is to ship your pet with a professional carrier, which can be expensive. Ask your veterinarian whether you should sedate your pet on a plane ride or give it anti-nausea medication. Never give your pet sedatives used by humans.

8 Planning Your Trip Online

SURFING FOR AIRFARE

The most popular online travel agencies are **Travelocity** (www.travelocity.com or www.travelocity.co.uk), **Expedia** (www.expedia.com, www.expedia.co.uk, or www.expedia.ca), and **Orbitz** (www.orbitz.com).

In addition, most airlines now offer online-only fares that even their phone agents know nothing about. For the websites of airlines that fly to and from your destination, go to "Getting There," p. 30.

Other helpful websites for booking airline tickets online include

- www.biddingfortravel.com
- www.cheapflights.com
- www.hotwire.com
- www.kayak.com
- www.lastminutetravel.com
- www.opodo.co.uk
- www.priceline.com
- www.sidestep.com
- www.site59.com
- www.smartertravel.com

SURFING FOR HOTELS

In addition to **Travelocity, Expedia, Orbitz, Priceline,** and **Hotwire** (see above), the following websites will help you with booking hotel rooms online:

- www.hotels.com
- www.quickbook.com
- www.travelaxe.net
- www.travelweb.com
- www.tripadvisor.com

It's a good idea to **get a confirmation number** and **make a printout** of any online booking transaction.

SURFING FOR RENTAL CARS

For booking rental cars online, the best deals are usually found at rental-car

---

Frommers.com: The Complete Travel Resource

For an excellent travel-planning resource, we highly recommend **Frommers. com** (www.frommers.com), voted Best Travel Site by *PC Magazine*. We're a little biased, of course, but we guarantee that you'll find the travel tips, reviews, monthly vacation giveaways, bookstore, and online-booking capabilities thoroughly indispensable. Among the special features are our popular **Destinations** section, where you'll get expert travel tips, hotel and dining recommendations, and advice on the sights to see for more than 3,500 destinations around the globe; the **Frommers.com Newsletter,** with the latest deals, travel trends, and money-saving secrets; our **Community** area featuring **Message Boards,** where Frommer's readers post queries and share advice (sometimes even our authors show up to answer questions); and our **Photo Center.** When your research is finished, the **Online Reservations System** (www.frommers.com/book_a_trip) takes you to Frommer's preferred online partners for booking your vacation at affordable prices.

company websites, although all the major online travel agencies also offer rental-car reservations services. Priceline and Hotwire work well for rental cars, too; the only "mystery" is which major rental company you get, and for most travelers, the difference between Hertz, Avis, and Budget is negligible.

9 The 21st-Century Traveler

INTERNET ACCESS AWAY FROM HOME
WITHOUT YOUR OWN COMPUTER

To find cybercafes in your destination, check **www.cybercaptive.com** and **www.cybercafe.com**. If you're already out and about, San Diego neighborhoods like Hillcrest, North Park, and the beach areas are good spots to find coffee and computers.

Aside from formal cybercafes, most **youth hostels** and **public libraries** offer Internet access. Avoid **hotel business centers** unless you're willing to pay exorbitant rates.

Most major airports now have **Internet kiosks** scattered throughout their gates. These give you basic Web access for a per-minute fee that's usually higher than cybercafe prices.

WITH YOUR OWN COMPUTER

More and more hotels, cafes, and retailers are signing on as Wi-Fi (wireless fidelity) "hotspots." Mac owners have their own networking technology, Apple AirPort. **T-Mobile Hotspot** (www.t-mobile.com/hotspot) serves up wireless connections at more than 1,000 Starbucks coffee shops nationwide. **Boingo** (www.boingo.com) and **Wayport** (www.wayport.com) have set up networks in airports and high-class hotel lobbies. iPass providers (see below) also give you access to a few hundred wireless hotel-lobby setups. To locate other hotspots that provide **free wireless networks** in cities around the world, go to **www.personaltelco.net/index.cgi/WirelessCommunities**.

For dial-up access, most business-class hotels in the U.S. offer dataports for laptop modems, and a few thousand hotels in the U.S. and Europe now offer free high-speed Internet access. In addition, major Internet Service Providers (ISPs) have **local access numbers** around the world, allowing you to go online by placing a local call. The **iPass** network also has dial-up numbers around the world. You'll have to sign up with an iPass provider, who will then tell you how to set up your computer for your destination(s). For a list of iPass providers, go to www.ipass.com and click on "Individuals Buy Now." One solid provider is **i2roam** (www.i2roam.com; © **866/811-6209** or 920/235-0475).

Wherever you go, bring a **connection kit** of the right power and phone adapters, a spare phone cord, and a spare Ethernet network cable—or find out whether your hotel supplies them to guests.

For information on electrical currency conversions, see "Electricity," in the "Fast Facts" section of chapter 4.

CELLPHONE USE IN THE U.S.

Just because your cellphone works at home doesn't mean it'll work everywhere in the U.S. (thanks to our nation's fragmented cellphone system). It's a good bet that your phone will work in major cities,

---

San Diego Travel Blogs
Check out **www.sandiegoblog.com** or **www.sandiegobloggers.com**.

Online Traveler's Toolbox

Veteran travelers usually carry some essential items to make their trips easier. Following is a selection of handy online tools to bookmark and use.

- **Airplane Food** (www.airlinemeals.net)
- **Airplane Seating** (www.seatguru.com and www.airlinequality.com)
- **Maps** (www.mapquest.com)
- **San Diego Events and Entertainment** (www.sdreader.com)
- **San Diego Local News and Restaurant Reviews** (www.signonsandiego.com)
- **Time and Date** (www.timeanddate.com)
- **Universal Currency Converter** (www.xe.com/ucc)
- **Visa ATM Locator** (www.visa.com), **MasterCard ATM Locator** (www.mastercard.com)
- **Weather** (www.intellicast.com and www.weather.com)

but take a look at your wireless company's coverage map on its website before heading out; T-Mobile, Sprint, and Nextel are particularly weak in rural areas. If you need to stay in touch at a destination where you know your phone won't work, **rent** a phone that does from **InTouch USA** (② 800/872-7626; www.intouchglobal.com) or a rental car location, but beware that you'll pay $1 a minute or more for airtime.

If you're venturing deep into national parks, you may want to consider renting a **satellite phone** (satphone). It's different from a cellphone in that it connects to satellites rather than ground-based towers. Unfortunately, you'll pay at least $2 per minute to use the phone, and it works only where you can see the horizon (i.e., usually not indoors). In North America, you can rent Iridium satellite phones from **RoadPost** (www.roadpost.com;

② **888/290-1606** or 905/272-5665). InTouch USA (see above) offers a wider range of satphones but at higher rates.

If you're not from the U.S., you'll be appalled at the poor reach of our **GSM (Global System for Mobiles) wireless network,** which is used by much of the rest of the world. Your phone will probably work in most major U.S. cities; it definitely won't work in many rural areas. (To see where GSM phones work in the U.S., check out www.t-mobile.com/coverage/national_popup.asp.) In addition, you may or may not be able to send SMS (text messaging) home. In a worst-case scenario, you can always rent a phone; in San Diego, **Four Points Communications,** 3956 First Ave., Hillcrest (② **800/237-3266** or 619/234-6182; www.fourpointscom.com) and **BearCom,** 4506 Federal Blvd. (② **619/263-2159;** www.bearcom.com) deliver to hotels within the metro area.

10 Getting There

BY PLANE

Flights arrive at San Diego International Airport/Lindbergh Field (airport code: SAN), named after aviation hero Charles Lindbergh. It's close to downtown San Diego and is served by most national and regional air carriers as well as AeroMéxico. Although no airline uses San Diego

Tips Prepare to Be Fingerprinted

As of January 2004, many international visitors traveling on visas to the United States will be photographed and fingerprinted at Customs in a new program created by the Department of Homeland Security called **US-VISIT**. Non-U.S. citizens arriving at airports and on cruise ships must undergo an instant background check as part of the government's efforts to deter terrorism by verifying the identity of incoming and outgoing visitors. Exempt from the extra scrutiny are visitors entering by land or those who don't require a visa for short-term visits (mostly in Europe; see p. 9). For more information, go to the Homeland Security website at **www.dhs.gov/dhspublic**.

as a hub for connections, Southwest Airlines controls one-third of the airlift into the city.

Major airlines flying into San Diego include **AeroMéxico** (© 800/237-6639; www.aeromexico.com), **Air Canada** (© 888/247-2262; www.aircanada.com), **Alaska Airlines** (© 800/252-7522; www.alaskaair.com), **Aloha Airlines** (© 800/367-5250; www.alohaairlines.com), **America West** (© 800/235-9292; www.americawest.com), **American Airlines** (© 800/433-7300; www.aa.com), **Continental Airlines** (© 800/525-0280; www.continental.com), **Delta Airlines** (© 800/221-1212; www.delta.com), **Frontier Airlines** (© 800/432-1359; www.frontierairlines.com), **Hawaiian Airlines** (© 800/367-5320; www.hawaiianair.com), **JetBlue** (© 800/538-2583; www.jetblue.com), **Northwest Airlines** (© 800/225-2525; www.nwa.com), **Southwest Airlines** (© 800/435-9792; www.southwest.com), **United Airlines** (© 800/864-8331; www.ual.com), and **US Airways** (© 800/428-4322; www.usairways.com). The Commuter Terminal, a half-mile from the main terminals, is used by regional carriers **American Eagle** and **United Express** (for flight info, contact the parent carriers listed above).

If you are staying at a hotel in Carlsbad, Encinitas, or Rancho Santa Fe, the McClellan-Palomar Airport in Carlsbad

(CLD) may be a more convenient point of entry. The airport is 42 miles north of downtown San Diego and is served by **America West Express** from Phoenix and **United Express** from Los Angeles.

IMMIGRATION & CUSTOMS CLEARANCE   Foreign visitors arriving by air, no matter what the port of entry, should cultivate patience and resignation before setting foot on U.S. soil. Clearing immigration control can take as long as 2 hours. This is especially true in the aftermath of the September 11, 2001, terrorist attacks; U.S. airports considerably beefed up security clearances. People traveling by air from Canada, Bermuda, and certain Caribbean countries can sometimes clear Customs and Immigration at the point of departure, which is much faster.

FLYING FOR LESS: TIPS FOR GETTING THE BEST AIRFARE

- Book your ticket **long in advance** or **at the last minute,** or **fly midweek** or **at less-trafficked hours** and you may pay a fraction of the full fare. If your schedule is flexible, say so.
- Search **the Internet** for cheap fares (see "Planning Your Trip Online," above).
- Keep an eye on local newspapers for **promotional specials** or **fare wars,** when airlines lower prices on their most popular routes.

- Try to book a ticket **in its country of origin.** For foreign travelers on multi-leg trips, book in the country of the first leg; for example, book New York–Chicago–Montreal–New York in the United States.
- **Consolidators,** also known as bucket shops, are great sources for international tickets, although they usually can't beat Internet fares within North America. Start by looking in Sunday newspaper travel sections, but *beware:* Bucket shop tickets are usually nonrefundable or rigged with stiff cancellation penalties, often as high as 50% to 75% of the ticket price, and some put you on charter airlines, which may leave at inconvenient times and experience delays. Several reliable consolidators are worldwide and available online. **STA Travel** has been the world's lead consolidator for students since purchasing Council Travel, but their fares are competitive for travelers of all ages. **Flights.com** (✆ 800/872-8800; www.flights.com) has excellent fares worldwide, particularly to Europe. They also have "local" websites in 12 countries. **FlyCheap** (✆ 800/359-2432; www.1800flycheap.com) has especially good fares to sunny destinations. **Air Tickets Direct** (✆ 800/778-3447; www.airtickets direct.com) is based in Montreal and leverages the currently weak Canadian dollar for low fares; they also book trips to places that U.S. travel agents won't touch, such as Cuba.
- Join **frequent-flier clubs.** To play the frequent-flier game to your best advantage, consult Randy Petersen's **Inside Flyer** (www.insideflyer.com). Petersen and friends review all the programs in detail and post regular updates on changes in policies and trends.

LONG-HAUL FLIGHTS: HOW TO STAY COMFORTABLE

- Find more details about U.S. airlines at **www.seatguru.com**. For international airlines, the research firm Skytrax has posted a list of average seat pitches at **www.airlinequality.com**.
- Emergency exit seats and bulkhead seats typically have the most legroom. Emergency exit seats are usually left unassigned until the day of a flight, (to ensure that someone able-bodied fills the seats); it's worth getting to the ticket counter early to snag one of these spots for a long flight. Many passengers find that bulkhead seating (the row facing the wall at the front of the cabin) offers more legroom, but keep in mind that bulkheads are where airlines often put baby bassinets, so you may be sitting next to an infant.
- To have two seats for yourself in a three-seat row, try for an aisle seat in a center section toward the back of coach. If you're traveling with a companion, book an aisle and a window seat. Middle seats are usually booked last, so chances are good you'll end up with three seats to yourselves. And in the event that a third passenger is assigned the middle seat, he or she will probably be more than happy to trade for a window or an aisle.
- Ask about entertainment options. Many airlines offer seatback video systems where you get to choose your movies or play video games—but only on some of their planes. (Boeing 777s are your best bet.)
- To sleep, avoid the last row of any section or the row in front of an emergency exit, as these seats are the least likely to recline. Avoid seats near highly trafficked toilet areas. Avoid seats in the back of many jets—these can be narrower than those in the rest

of coach. You also may want to reserve a window seat so you can rest your head and avoid being bumped in the aisle.

- Get up, walk around, and stretch every 60 to 90 minutes to keep your blood flowing. This helps avoid **deep vein thrombosis.**
- Drink water before, during, and after your flight to combat the lack of humidity in airplane cabins. Avoid alcohol, which will dehydrate you.
- If you're flying with kids, bring toys, books, pacifiers, and chewing gum to help them relieve ear pressure buildup during ascent and descent.

GETTING THERE BY CAR

If you're planning a road trip, being a member of the **American Automobile Association (AAA)** offers helpful perks. Members who carry their cards with them not only receive free roadside assistance, but also have access to a wealth of free travel information (detailed maps and guidebooks). Also, many hotels and attractions throughout California offer discounts to AAA members—always inquire. Call (**800/922-8228** or your local branch for membership information.

Visitors driving to San Diego from Los Angeles and points north do so via coastal route I-5. From points northeast, take I-15 and link up with Highway 163 South as you enter Miramar (use I-8 West for the beaches). From the east, use I-8 into the city, connecting to Highway 163 South for Hillcrest and downtown. Entering the downtown area, Highway 163 turns into 10th Avenue. Try to avoid arriving during weekday rush hours,

between 7 and 9am and 4 and 6pm. If you are heading to Coronado, take the San Diego–Coronado Bay Bridge from I-5. Maximum speed in the San Diego area is 65mph, and many areas are limited to 55mph.

San Diego is 130 miles (2–3 hours) from **Los Angeles;** 149 miles from **Palm Springs,** a 2½-hour trip; 532 miles, or 8 to 9 hours, from **San Francisco.**

GETTING THERE BY TRAIN

Trains from all points in the United States and Canada will take you to Los Angeles, where you'll need to change trains for the 2-hour, 45-minute journey to San Diego. You'll arrive at San Diego's Santa Fe Station, downtown at Broadway and Kettner Boulevard. A few hotels are found within walking distance. The San Diego Trolley station is across the street. For price and schedule information, call **Amtrak** ((**800/872-7245;** www.amtrak.com). Trains depart about 11 times per day, and one-way fare runs $32 (round-trip is $64).

GETTING THERE BY BUS

Greyhound buses serve San Diego from downtown Los Angeles, Phoenix, Las Vegas, and other southwestern cities, arriving at the downtown terminal, at 120 W. Broadway ((**800/231-2222** or 619/239-3266; www.greyhound.com). Several hotels, Horton Plaza, and the Gaslamp Quarter are within walking distance, as is the San Diego Trolley line. Buses from Los Angeles are as frequent as every 30 minutes, take about 2½ hours for the journey, and round-trip fare is $27 (one-way is $16).

11 Packages for the Independent Traveler

Package tours are simply a way to buy the airfare, accommodations, and other elements of your trip (such as car rentals, airport transfers, and sometimes even

activities) at the same time and often at discounted prices.

One good source of package deals is the airlines themselves. Most major airlines offer air/land packages, including **American Airlines Vacations** (© 800/321-2121; www.aavacations.com), **Delta Vacations** (© 800/221-6666; www.delta vacations.com), **Continental Airlines Vacations** (© 800/301-3800; www.co vacations.com), and **United Vacations** (© 888/854-3899; www.unitedvacations. com). The **San Diego Convention and Visitors Bureau** (© 800/350-6205; www.sandiego.org) has its own booking engine for packages incorporating air, hotel, and activities, and the **Walt Disney Travel Company** (© 714/520-5002;

www.disney.com) is the largest tour operator featuring San Diego. Several big **online travel agencies**—Expedia, Travelocity, Orbitz, Site59, and Lastminute. com—do a brisk business in packages as well.

Travel packages are also listed in the travel section of your local Sunday newspaper. Or check ads in the national travel magazines such as *Arthur Frommer's Budget Travel Magazine, Travel + Leisure, National Geographic Traveler,* and *Condé Nast Traveler.*

12 Escorted General-Interest Tours

Escorted tours are structured group tours, with a group leader. The price usually includes everything from airfare to hotels, meals, tours, admission costs, and local transportation.

Despite the fact that escorted tours require big deposits and predetermine hotels, restaurants, and itineraries, many people derive security and peace of mind from the structure they offer. Escorted tours—whether they're navigated by bus, motor coach, train, or boat—let travelers sit back and enjoy the trip without having to drive or worry about details. They take you to the maximum number of sights in the minimum amount of time with the least amount of hassle. They're particularly convenient for people with limited

mobility and they can be a great way to make new friends.

On the downside, you'll have little opportunity for serendipitous interactions with locals. The tours can be jam-packed with activities, leaving little room for individual sightseeing, whim, or adventure—plus they often focus on the heavily touristed sites, so you miss out on many a lesser-known gem.

Companies that specialize in escorted trips to San Diego include **Collette Tours** (© **800/340-5158;** www.collette vacations.com), **Globus** (© **866/755-8581;** www.globusjourneys.com), and **Tauck World Discovery** (© **800/788-7885;** www.tauck.com).

13 Getting Around San Diego

BY CAR
Unless you plan to spend the bulk of your vacation in a city where walking is the best way to get around (read: New York City or New Orleans), the most cost-effective way to travel is by car.

If you're visiting from abroad and plan to rent a car in the United States, you probably won't need the services of an additional automobile organization. If

you're planning to buy or borrow a car, automobile-association membership is recommended. **AAA,** the **American Automobile Association** (© **800/222-4357;** http://travel.aaa.com), is the country's largest auto club and supplies its members with maps, insurance, and, most important, emergency road service. *Note:* Foreign driver's licenses are usually recognized in the U.S., but you should get an international one if your home license is not in English.

BY TRAIN

International visitors can buy a USA Rail Pass, good for 15 or 30 days of unlimited travel on Amtrak (℗ 800/USA-RAIL; www.amtrak.com). The pass is available through many overseas travel agents. See Amtrak's website for the cost of travel within the western, eastern, or northwestern United States. With a foreign passport, you can also buy passes direct from some Amtrak locations, including San Francisco, Los Angeles, Chicago, New York, Miami, Boston, and Washington, D.C. Reservations are generally required and should be made as early as possible. Regional rail passes are also available.

BY BUS

Bus travel is often the most economical form of public transit for short hops between U.S. cities, but it can also be slow and uncomfortable—certainly not an option for everyone (particularly when Amtrak, which is far more luxurious, offers similar rates). **Greyhound/ Trailways** (℗ 800/231-2222; www. greyhound.com) is the sole nationwide bus line. International visitors can obtain information about the **International Ameripass** by phone through the Greyhound International Office at the Port Authority Bus Terminal in New York City (℗ 212/971-0492). The pass can be obtained from foreign travel agents or through Greyhound's website (order at least 21 days before your departure to the U.S.) and costs less than the domestic version. You can get more info on the pass at the website, or by calling ℗ 402/ 330-8552.

14 Recommended Books

While New York and San Francisco may be better known for their cosmopolitan literary icons, San Diego is no slouch when it comes to colorful characters, bigger-than-life biographies, hard-core history, and famous fiction.

Philip Marlowe, Raymond Chandler's classic detective, spent most of his time in the literary Los Angeles of the 1940s. But the last Marlowe mystery, *Playback* (Vintage Books, 1988), includes a beautiful woman who hides out in "Esmeralda" (actually La Jolla), a coastal town north of downtown San Diego, where Chandler spent his last 13 years of life.

Another hard-boiled type, cop-turned-novelist Joseph Wambaugh, has called San Diego home for more than 15 years. In the early 1970s, his novels *The New Centurions* and *The Onion Field* profoundly altered the way law enforcement was portrayed and perceived in this country. Three of Wambaugh's later works—*Floaters* (Bantam, 1997), *Lines and Shadows* (Bantam, 1995), and *Finnegan's Week* (Bantam, 1994)—are set in San Diego.

The 1980 film starring Christopher Reeve and Jane Seymour may have moved the story from the Hotel del Coronado to a turn-of-the-20th-century hotel in Mackinac Island, Michigan, but *Somewhere in Time* (St. Martin's Press, 1999), penned by master thriller novelist Richard Matheson—also known for *A Stir of Echoes* (Tor Books, 1999) and *What Dreams May Come* (Tor Books, 1998)—is one of the most famous stories set in San Diego to date. Originally published in 1975 under the title *Bid Time Return* (Buccaneer Books, 1995), this science fiction–slanted romantic fantasy works not only as a love story, but as a vivid travelogue of Southern California and Coronado.

Coronado also figures largely in L. Frank Baum's *Oz* books, including *The Wizard of Oz* (Tor Books, 1995). The author, who lived in Coronado, based his description of the Emerald City on it. Another San Diego local, Theodor Geisel (aka Dr. Seuss), wrote many of his much-loved children's books while living in La Jolla (*The Sneetches,* in fact, is a poke at snobby La Jollans).

The Pump House Gang (Bantam Doubleday Dell, 1999), a psychedelic collection of 1960s essays by Tom Wolfe, is named for the often-crazy coterie of expert surfers that hung out at La Jolla's Windansea beach; the eponymous short story vividly captures a sense of place and of an entire generation.

Max Miller, a reporter for the *San Diego Sun* during the Depression, wrote the runaway 1932 best seller *I Cover the Waterfront* (Barricade Books, 2003). Miller was the archetypal hard-drinking beat reporter of the time, but his book sketched wonderful tales of the city's seedy waterfront, fishermen, brothels, and sailors.

Thomas S. Hines's gorgeous coffee-table book, *Irving Gill and the Architecture of Reform: A Study in Modernist Architectural Culture* (Monacelli, 2000), features photographs and text showcasing the artist's early-20th-century modern style. Architectural buffs will enjoy Gill's designs; while lesser known than those of his contemporaries—like Wright, Frey, Neutra, and Schindler—they are local landmarks. Much of Gill's work is in La Jolla. The city's distinctive style is also highlighted in the useful guidebook *San Diego Architecture* by Dirk Sutro (San Diego Architectural Foundation, 2002).

Mission San Luis Rey in northern San Diego County inspired the setting for Helen Hunt Jackson's 1884 novel, *Ramona: A Story* (Signet, 2002). A love story that holds up even with today's jaded audiences, Jackson's tale incorporates a changing California (the fading Spanish order, the decline of Native American tribes, the arrival of white settlers) into its enduring drama. The Estudillo House in Old Town is sometimes called "Ramona's House" because it so closely resembles the vivid description in the book.

The brother-and-sister team of E. W. and Ellen Browning were responsible for the establishment of the Scripps Institute of Oceanography, early funding of the San Diego Zoo, creating Torrey Pines State Park, and leaving a permanent imprint on the community of La Jolla. In *Edward Willis and Ellen Browning Scripps: An Unmatched Pair* (Image Books, 1990), Charles Preece offers the best biography of these two pillars of San Diego's philanthropic Scripps family.

The dark history of class and power in the city is provided in *Under the Perfect Sun: The San Diego Tourists Never See* (New Press, 2003), by Mike Davis (author of *City of Quartz*), Kelly Mayhew, and Jim Miller. From the shady transactions of John D. Spreckels to the Ponzi schemes of C. Arnholt Smith in the '70s, the team dissects the city's militarized economy, its Republican movers and shakers, and its embrace of racial segregation. It's an anti-tourism guidebook out to deflate the city's fun-in-the-sun mythology. Miller is also editor of *Sunshine/Noir* (City Works Press, 2005), a collection of new poetry, fiction and nonfiction, all focused on the San Diego/Tijuana region.

For something a bit frothier, local restaurateur Ingrid Croce has assembled *The San Diego Restaurant Cookbook* (Avalanche, 2005). Featuring more than 300 recipes from dozens of the city's best eateries, the cookbook is a salute to San Diego's burgeoning foodie scene.

FAST FACTS: San Diego

Embassies & Consulates All embassies are in the nation's capital, Washington, D.C. Some consulates are in major U.S. cities, and most nations have a mission to the United Nations in New York City. If your country isn't listed below, call for directory information in Washington, D.C. (© **202/555-1212**) or log on to **www.embassy.org/embassies**.

The embassy of **Australia** is at 1601 Massachusetts Ave. NW, Washington, DC 20036 (© **202/797-3000**; www.austemb.org). There are consulates in New York, Honolulu, Houston, Los Angeles, and San Francisco.

The embassy of **Canada** is at 501 Pennsylvania Ave. NW, Washington, DC 20001 (© **202/682-1740**; www.canadianembassy.org). Other Canadian consulates are in Buffalo (New York), Detroit, Los Angeles, New York, and Seattle.

The embassy of **Ireland** is at 2234 Massachusetts Ave. NW, Washington, DC 20008 (© **202/462-3939**; www.irelandemb.org). Irish consulates are in Boston, Chicago, New York, San Francisco, and other cities. See the website for a complete listing.

The embassy of **New Zealand** is at 37 Observatory Circle NW, Washington, DC 20008 (© **202/328-4800**; www.nzemb.org). New Zealand consulates are in Los Angeles, Salt Lake City, San Francisco, and Seattle.

The embassy of the **United Kingdom** is at 3100 Massachusetts Ave. NW, Washington, DC 20008 (© **202/588-7800**; www.britainusa.com). Other British consulates are in Atlanta, Boston, Chicago, Cleveland, Houston, Los Angeles, New York, San Francisco, and Seattle.

Holidays Banks, government offices, post offices, and many stores, restaurants, and museums are closed on the following legal national holidays: January 1 (New Year's Day), the third Monday in January (Martin Luther King, Jr., Day), the third Monday in February (Presidents' Day), the last Monday in May (Memorial Day), July 4 (Independence Day), the first Monday in September (Labor Day), the second Monday in October (Columbus Day), November 11 (Veterans Day/Armistice Day), the fourth Thursday in November (Thanksgiving Day), and December 25 (Christmas). The Tuesday after the first Monday in November is Election Day, a federal government holiday in presidential-election years (held every 4 years, and next in 2008).

For more information on holidays see "Calendar of Events," earlier in this chapter.

Legal Aid If you are "pulled over" for a minor infraction (such as speeding), never attempt to pay the fine directly to a police officer; this could be construed as attempted bribery, a much more serious crime. Pay fines by mail, or directly into the hands of the clerk of the court. If accused of a more serious offense, say and do nothing before consulting a lawyer. Here the burden is on the state to prove a person's guilt beyond a reasonable doubt, and everyone has the right to remain silent, whether he or she is suspected of a crime or actually arrested. Once arrested, a person can make one telephone call to a party of his or her choice. International visitors should call your embassy or consulate.

Mail At press time, domestic postage rates were 24¢ for a postcard and 39¢ for a letter. For international mail, a first-class letter of up to 1 ounce costs 84¢ (63¢ to Canada and Mexico); a first-class postcard costs 75¢ (55¢ to Canada and Mexico); and a preprinted postal aerogramme costs 75¢. For more information go to **www.usps.com** and click on "Calculate Postage."

If you aren't sure what your address will be in the United States, mail can be sent to you, in your name, c/o General Delivery at the main post office of the city or region where you expect to be. (Call ℂ **800/275-8777** for information on the nearest post office.) The addressee must pick up mail in person and must produce proof of identity (driver's license, passport, etc.). Most post offices will hold your mail for up to 1 month and are open Monday to Friday from 8am to 6pm, and Saturday from 9am to 3pm.

Always include zip codes when mailing items in the U.S. If you don't know your zip code, visit www.usps.com/zip4.

Passports **For Residents of Australia:** You can pick up an application from your local post office or any branch of Passports Australia, but you must schedule an interview at the passport office to present your application materials. Call the **Australian Passport Information Service** at ℂ **131-232,** or visit the government website at www.passports.gov.au.

For Residents of Canada: Passport applications are available at travel agencies throughout Canada or from the central **Passport Office,** Department of Foreign Affairs and International Trade, Ottawa, ON K1A 0G3 (ℂ **800/567-6868;** www.ppt.gc.ca). *Note:* Canadian children who travel must have their own passport. However, if you hold a valid Canadian passport issued before December 11, 2001, that bears the name of your child, the passport remains valid for you and your child until it expires.

For Residents of Ireland: You can apply for a 10-year passport at the **Passport Office,** Setanta Centre, Molesworth Street, Dublin 2 (ℂ **01/671-1633;** www.irlgov.ie/iveagh). Those under age 18 and over 65 must apply for a 3-year passport. You can also apply at 1A South Mall, Cork (ℂ **021/272-525**) or at most main post offices.

For Residents of New Zealand: You can pick up a passport application at any New Zealand Passports Office or download it from their website. Contact the **Passports Office** at ℂ **0800/225-050** in New Zealand or 04/474-8100 or log on to www.passports.govt.nz.

For Residents of the United Kingdom: To pick up an application for a standard 10-year passport (5-yr. passport for children under 16), visit your nearest passport office, major post office, or travel agency or contact the **United Kingdom Passport Service** at ℂ **0870/521-0410** or search its website at www.ukpa.gov.uk.

Telephone & Fax Generally, hotel surcharges on long-distance and local calls are astronomical, so you're better off using your **cellphone** or a **public pay telephone.** Many convenience groceries and packaging services sell **prepaid calling cards** in denominations up to $50; for international visitors these can be the least expensive way to call home. Many public phones at airports now accept American Express, MasterCard, and Visa credit cards. **Local calls** made from public pay phones in most locales cost either 35¢ or 50¢. Pay phones do not accept pennies, and few will take anything larger than a quarter.

Most long-distance and international calls can be dialed directly from any phone. **For calls within the United States and to Canada,** dial 1 followed by the area code and the seven-digit number. **For other international calls,** dial 011 followed by the country code, city code, and the number you are calling.

Calls to area codes **800, 888, 877,** and **866** are toll-free. However, calls to area codes **700** and **900** (chat lines, bulletin boards, "dating" services, and so on) can be very expensive—usually a charge of 95¢ to $3 or more per minute, and they sometimes have minimum charges that can run as high as $15 or more.

For **reversed-charge or collect calls,** and for person-to-person calls, dial the number 0 and then the area code and number; an operator will come on the line, and you should specify whether you are calling collect, person-to-person, or both. If your operator-assisted call is international, ask for the overseas operator.

For **local directory assistance** ("information"), dial 411; for long-distance information, dial 1 and then the appropriate area code and 555-1212.

Most hotels have **fax machines** available for guest use (be sure to ask about the charge to use it). Many hotel rooms are even wired for guests' fax machines. A less expensive way to send and receive faxes may be at stores such as **The UPS Store** (formerly Mail Boxes Etc.).

Time The continental United States is divided into **four time zones:** Eastern Standard Time (EST), Central Standard Time (CST), Mountain Standard Time (MST), and Pacific Standard Time (PST). Alaska and Hawaii have their own zones. For example, when it's 9am in San Diego (PST), it's 7am in Honolulu (HST), 10am in Denver (MST), 11am in Chicago (CST), noon in New York City (EST), 5pm in London (GMT), and 2am the next day in Sydney.

Daylight saving time takes effect at 2am the first Sunday in April until 2am the last Sunday in October, except in Arizona, Hawaii, the U.S. Virgin Islands, and Puerto Rico. Daylight savings moves the clock 1 hour ahead of standard time. (A new law will extend daylight saving in 2007; clocks will change the second Sunday in March and the first Sunday in November.)

Tipping Tips are a very important part of certain workers' income, and gratuities are the standard way of showing appreciation for services provided. (Tipping is certainly not compulsory if the service is poor.) In hotels, tip **bellhops** at least $1 per bag ($2–$3 if you have a lot of luggage) and tip the **chamber staff** $1 to $2 per day (more if you've left a disaster area to clean up). Tip the **doorman** or **concierge** only if he or she has provided you with some specific service (for example, calling a cab for you or obtaining difficult-to-get theater tickets). Tip the **valet-parking attendant** $1 every time you get your car.

In restaurants, bars, and nightclubs, tip **service staff** 15% to 20% of the check, tip **bartenders** 10% to 15%, tip **checkroom attendants** $1 per garment, and tip **valet-parking attendants** $1 per vehicle.

As for other service personnel, tip **cab drivers** 15% of the fare; tip **skycaps** at airports at least $1 per bag ($2–$3 if you have a lot of luggage); and tip **hairdressers** and **barbers** 15% to 20%.

Visas For information about U.S. Visas, go to **http://travel.state.gov** and click on "Visas," or go to one of the following websites.

Australian citizens can obtain up-to-date visa information from the **U.S. Embassy Canberra,** Moonah Place, Yarralumla, ACT 2600 (© **02/6214-5600**) or by checking the U.S. Diplomatic Mission's website at **http://usembassy-australia. state.gov/consular**.

British subjects can obtain up-to-date visa information by calling the **U.S. Embassy Visa Information Line** (© **0891/200-290**) or by visiting the "Visas to the U.S." section of the American Embassy London's website at **www.us embassy.org.uk**.

Irish citizens can obtain up-to-date visa information through the **Embassy of the USA Dublin,** 42 Elgin Rd., Dublin 4, Ireland (© **353/1-668-8777**), or check the "Consular Services" section of the website at **http://dublin.usembassy.gov**.

Citizens of **New Zealand** can obtain up-to-date visa information by contacting the **U.S. Embassy New Zealand,** 29 Fitzherbert Terrace, Thorndon, Wellington (© **644/472-2068**), or get the information directly from the "For New Zealanders" section of the website at **http://usembassy.org.nz**.

3

Suggested San Diego Itineraries

by Caroline Sieg

If 1 to 3 days is all you have in San Diego, maximize your time with our ready-made itinerary. Rent a car and hit the beach—at sunset or under the almost-always shining sun. Stroll the vibrant Gaslamp Quarter, cruise across the San Diego–Coronado Bay Bridge, head up to La Jolla for upscale shopping and dining, or explore dramatic Torrey Pines State Reserve. Whatever you do, dress in layers and bring a sweatshirt— Southern California mornings are often cool and foggy (especially near the ocean), and it gets chilly after sundown.

1 The Best of San Diego in 1 Day

To get an overview of San Diego in just 1 day, you'll have to dart around town a bit. Begin with a taste of its Hispanic heritage, embrace San Diego's dazzling beaches, and end the day in the spirited downtown Gaslamp Quarter.

❶ Old Town

Old Town State Historic Park is the most-visited state park in California (and it's free). This is San Diego's original downtown, and history comes to colorful life here, especially at **Plaza del Pasado,** a once-dilapidated 1930s motel converted into shopping and dining arcades, replete with mariachi players strumming the sounds of Mexico around an inner courtyard. See p. 156.

❷ Hillcrest

Hillcrest, San Diego's equivalent of LA's West Hollywood or NYC's West Village, is an urban, pedestrian-friendly neighborhood. Its tolerant attitude fosters a large gay community and a hip, eclectic vibe.

Pop into trendy boutiques, second-hand clothing stores, and an array of restaurants and cafes. Check out the '40s-era Art Deco neighborhood sign dangling above University Avenue (at 5th Ave.).

➌ BREAKING BREAD

Bread & Cie, 350 University Ave. (© 619/683-9322), is perfect for a quick shot of java and a fresh scone or muffin, and its lunch fare features hearty Mediterranean sandwiches served on delectable homemade bread, such as rosemary and cheese baguette or olive focaccia. Relax at one of the bistro tables or take your bite to go and picnic at your next stop, Balboa Park. See the next page.

❹ Balboa Park

Balboa Park, the nation's largest urban cultural park, contains clusters of diverse museums and theaters, as well as San Diegans lolling about in the grass on any given pristine 70°F sunny day (read: pretty much every day). Wander past the Spanish Golden Age–style buildings lining El Prado (a pedestrian mall), ponder the Botanical Building's sublime lily pond, or explore the meandering park trails. See p. 145.

❺ The San Diego–Coronado Bay Bridge

Drive across the 2-mile-long, curved San Diego–Coronado Bay Bridge with the salty wind whistling in your ears. If you've rented a convertible, put the top down *now.* In a word: Invigorating. See p. 164.

❻ Hotel del Coronado & Coronado Beach

Nicknamed by locals as the "Hotel Del," this Victorian landmark, with its spiky red turrets and gingerbread trim, is a San Diego gem. Waltz through the elegant lobby (perhaps you'll meet the resident ghost, Kate Morgan), wander across the sprawling white decks facing the Pacific, and take a leisurely walk along Coronado Beach. The beach and the deck are fabulous spots to watch a sunset. See p. 164 and 142.

❼ The Gaslamp Quarter

Finish the day in the historic Gaslamp Quarter, which always promises a lively late-afternoon and evening street scene. Pick from dozens of restaurants (many housed within restored Victorian commercial buildings), and stick around for live music or dancing after dinner—if you have the energy. See p. 104, 187, and 226.

2 The Best of San Diego in 2 Days

Your second full-day tour starts with a famous San Diego theme park, but you'll need to choose which one: SeaWorld or the San Diego Zoo. You could spend the entire day at one of those places, but if you need a change of scenery halfway through the afternoon, spend a few active hours at the public aquatic park, Mission Bay, or on the Mission Beach boardwalk. If you have no desire to exercise, chill out on the beach and embrace a lazy afternoon under the sun.

❶ A Theme Park: SeaWorld or San Diego Zoo

You'll get a dose of animals at both places, but do yourself a favor and choose *either* SeaWorld *or* the San Diego Zoo; don't try to do both in 1 day. Get there when the gates open to maximize your touring time, and spend a little more than half of the day exploring. Plan to leave by early afternoon for a late lunch.

At **SeaWorld,** Shamu may be the star, but there's a whole lot more to see and do here. You'll find Journey to Atlantis (a rollercoaster), Shipwreck Rapids (a splashy river ride), lovable penguins at the Penguin Encounter, *R. L. Stine's Haunted Lighthouse* (a "4-D" interactive movie experience), and animal shows featuring dolphins, sea lions, otters, house pets, and, of course, a certain killer whale. See p. 138.

More than 4,000 creatures reside at the world-renowned **San Diego Zoo,** known not only for its giant pandas, gorillas, and tigers housed in naturalistic environments, but also for its successful animal preservation efforts. The Children's Zoo petting area is perfect for little ones (and any adult who loves animals). See p. 136.

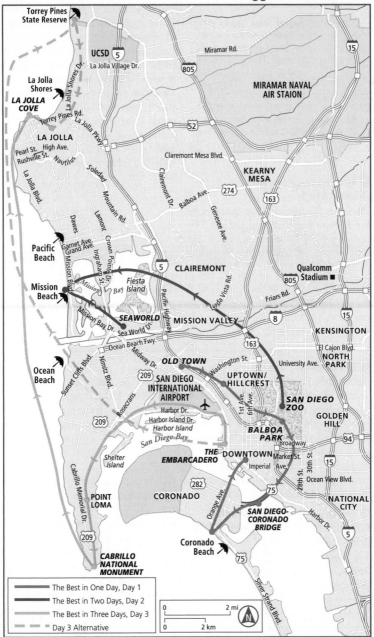

Torrey Pines State Reserve

UCSD
La Jolla Village Dr.

Miramar Rd.

MIRAMAR NAVAL AIR STAION

La Jolla Shores

LA JOLLA COVE

La Jolla Shores Dr.

Torrey Pines Rd.

La Jolla Pkwy.

LA JOLLA

Pearl St. High Ave.
Rushville St.
Nautilus

La Jolla Blvd

Soledad

Mountain Rd.

Claremont Mesa Blvd.

KEARNY MESA

Claremont Dr.

Balboa Ave.

Genesee Ave.

CLAIREMONT

Qualcomm Stadium

Friars Rd.

Pacific Beach

Garnet Ave.
Grand Ave.

Lamont

Crown Point Dr.

Ingraham St.

Mission Blvd

Dawes

Mission Beach

Fiesta Island

Mission Bay

SEAWORLD

Sea World Dr.

Pacific Highway

MISSION VALLEY

Linda Vista Rd.

KENSINGTON

Ocean Beach Fwy.

Mission Bay Dr.

Midway Dr.

OLD TOWN

Washington St.

El Cajon Blvd.
University Ave.

NORTH PARK

Ocean Beach

Sunset Cliffs Blvd.

Nimitz Blvd.

Rosecrans

SAN DIEGO INTERNATIONAL AIRPORT

UPTOWN/ HILLCREST

1st Ave.
6th Ave.

SAN DIEGO ZOO

GOLDEN HILL

Harbor Dr.
Harbor Island Dr.
Harbor Island

BALBOA PARK

San Diego Bay

Shelter Island

THE EMBARCADERO

DOWNTOWN

Broadway

Market St.

Imperial Ave.

28th St.
30th St.

Ocean View Blvd.

NATIONAL CITY

POINT LOMA

Cabrillo Memorial Dr.

CORONADO

Orange Ave.

SAN DIEGO-CORONADO BRIDGE

Coronado Beach

Harbor Dr.

CABRILLO NATIONAL MONUMENT

Silver Strand Blvd.

The Best in One Day, Day 1
The Best in Two Days, Day 2
The Best in Three Days, Day 3
Day 3 Alternative

0   2 mi
0   2 km

N

2️ A POST–THEME PARK BREAK
If you're coming from SeaWorld and you don't mind a little irony, try the fresh-off-the-boat seafood at **2A❝ The Fishery,** 5040 Cass St. (📞 858/272-9985)—a casual Pacific Beach fish market. See p. 122. If you spent the morning at the San Diego Zoo, pick up a gourmet taco at colorful **2B❝ Mamá Testa,** 1417 A University Ave. (📞 619/298-8226), a local favorite. See p. 120.

---

③ Mission Bay Park & Mission Beach
Outfitters like **Mission Bay Sportcenter** and **Mission Beach Club** (p. 182 and 176)

rent recreational gear (bikes, in-line skates, kayaks, catamarans), allowing you to wind your way around Mission Bay Park, an aquatic playground with bayside paths hopping with locals exercising alfresco. You can also have fun on two wheels on the Mission Beach boardwalk, which hugs the wide swath of sandy beach. If exercise is the last thing on your mind, grab a blanket, plop down on the sand, catch some rays, and ponder the volleyball players' sun-tanned muscles. See p. 143.

3 The Best of San Diego in 3 Days

After you've followed the previous two itineraries, spend your third day strolling the Embarcadero, taking in the ocean views from Point Loma or Torrey Pines, and exploring another spectacular beach and a bevy of outdoor dining venues in La Jolla. If you love theme parks or you have young children in tow, consider visiting the one you didn't choose on Day 2.

---

❶ The Embarcadero
Explore the Embarcadero, downtown San Diego's waterfront. You'll find harbor tours, a ferry to Coronado, and historic vessels like the aircraft carrier the USS *Midway* and the *Star of India,* the world's oldest active ship. Both are now floating museums. There are also plenty of restaurants and shops at Seaport Village, a maritime-themed retail area (p. 209).

❷ The Great Outdoors: Cabrillo National Monument or Torrey Pines State Reserve
You don't have to go far to find stunning natural environments in San Diego. The two best and closest are Cabrillo National Monument and Torrey Pines State Reserve. Hours can easily melt away at either of these magical spots, so it's best to visit just one.

You'll find **Cabrillo National Monument** at the end of Point Loma, a slice of

land jutting out into the Pacific just southeast of Coronado and downtown San Diego. This 144-acre park features a statue of Juan Rodríguez Cabrillo, the Portuguese explorer who landed in San Diego in 1542; a restored 1855 lighthouse; museum installations and a bookstore; bayside trails; tide pools; and a 422-foot-high lookout. This is an excellent vantage point to see migrating Pacific gray whales in winter; year-round, you'll enjoy awesome views of San Diego's harbor and skyline, and the rocky Pacific coastline. When skies are clear, you can also see Mexico in the distance. See p. 153.

Just north of La Jolla, **Torrey Pines State Reserve** is one of San Diego's most treasured spots. The 1,000-acre reserve is home to the distinctively gnarled tree that gives the place its name (and which is found only here and on an island off the coast). Trails range from flat and easy to steep and narrow, but all provide utterly breathtaking views of the ocean, lagoon, canyons, sandstone formations, and the famed Torrey Pines Golf Course. Take a hike or just head down to the beach. See p. 163.

---

③ FISH TACOS & DESSERTS

Stop for a snack or lunch at the harborside **③A Point Loma Seafoods**, 2805 Emerson St. (✆ 619/223-1109), a fish market (with a few outdoor picnic tables) offering sandwiches, sushi, salads, and tasty fish tacos. See p. 134. In La Jolla, sweet and savory options are available at **③B Michele Coulon Dessertier**, 7556 D Fay Ave. (✆ 858/56-5098). If you need something more substantial than sugar, the menu at this small, family-operated restaurant goes way beyond amazing desserts. Try the onion soup, Belgian endive salad, or quiche along with your flourless chocolate Cognac cake.

④ La Jolla

End your day in La Jolla, San Diego's swanky neighbor to the north. This town is upscale, expensive, and filled with stunning homes (and many mansions). Take one look at the pristine coastline and you'll instantly understand the area's allure. The main shopping and dining venues are clustered along or near Prospect Street, but La Jolla's most spectacular spot is the bluff above La Jolla Cove. Stroll along Coast Boulevard for the most scenic views. With its calm, crystal clear water, the Cove is also great for swimming. In the tide pools at its small, sandy beach, you can glimpse marine life such as starfish, sea anemones, and sea urchins. See p. 160.

4

Getting to Know
San Diego

Tucked into the sunny and parched southwest corner of the United States, San Diego is situated in one of the country's most naturally beautiful metropolitan settings. Learning the lay of the land is neither confusing nor daunting, but it helps to understand a few geographical features. Two major characteristics give San Diego its topographical personality: a superb and varied coastline; and a series of mesas bisected by inland finger canyons, inhabited by many coyotes, skunks, and raccoons.

San Diego's downtown—16 miles north of the Mexico border—sits at the edge of a large natural harbor, the San Diego Bay. The harbor is almost enclosed by two fingers of land: flat Coronado "Island" on one side, and peninsular Point Loma on the other. Both of these areas hold important military bases, bordered by classic neighborhoods dating to the 1890s and 1920s, respectively. Coronado isn't really an island—a ribbon of sand called the Silver Strand connects it to Imperial Beach, just north of the border.

Heading north from Point Loma is Mission Bay, a lagoon that was carved out of a tidal estuary in the 1940s and is now a watersports playground. A series of communities are found along the beach-lined coast: Ocean Beach, Mission Beach, Pacific Beach, La Jolla, and, just outside San Diego's city limits, Del Mar. To the south of downtown, you'll find National City, which is distinguished by shipyards on its bay side, then Chula Vista, and San Ysidro, which ends abruptly at the border (and where the huge city of Tijuana begins, equally abruptly). In the last decade, there's been intense housing development in the area from Chula Vista south.

That sums up the coast. Inland areas are perhaps best defined by Mission Valley, a mile-wide canyon that runs east-west, 2 miles north of downtown. Half a century ago, the valley held little beyond a few dairy farms, California's first mission, and the San Diego River (which is more like a creek for about 51 weeks a year). Then Interstate 8 was built through the valley, followed by a shopping center, a sports stadium, another shopping center, and lots of condos; today, Mission Valley is perhaps the most congested part of the city (and one of the least charming). In spite of this, residents all use the valley, and many live along its perimeter: On the southern rim are desirable older neighborhoods like Mission Hills, Hillcrest, Normal Heights, and Kensington; to the north are Linda Vista and Kearny Mesa—bedroom communities that emerged in the 1950s—and Miramar Naval Air Station. Just outside and to the north of the city limits is Rancho Bernardo, a quiet, clubby suburb.

The city of San Diego possesses one other vital (if man-made) ingredient: Balboa Park. Nestled in a 1,400-acre square between downtown and Mission Valley, the park contains the San Diego Zoo, many of its best museums, theaters (including the Tony Award-winning Old Globe), wonderful gardens, recreational facilities, and splendid architecture.

1 Orientation

ARRIVING

BY PLANE

We have a love-hate relationship with **San Diego International Airport** (© 619/ 231-2100; www.san.org), also known as Lindbergh Field. The facility is just 2 miles northwest of downtown, and the landing approach is right at the edge of the central business district. Pilots thread a passage between high-rise buildings and Balboa Park on their final descent to the runway—you'll get a great view on either side of the plane. The best part: We usually count the time from touchdown to gate-park in seconds, not minutes, and departures are rarely delayed for weather problems.

San Diego isn't a connecting hub for domestic airlines, and most international travel arrives via Los Angeles or points east, but Lindbergh Field is the nation's busiest single-runway commercial airport (yes, all 600 daily arrivals and departures use just one strip of asphalt). Its dainty size makes it easy for travelers to navigate, but city officials are well aware of the critical need to enlarge or move the airport if they hope to keep the city's economic engine humming. Plans have ranged from a floating airport-at-sea (no kidding) to setting it in the Anza-Borrego Desert to conscripting Miramar Naval Air Station. Hard decisions will have to be made (and fairly soon), because whether the airport is expanded at its current location or re-created elsewhere, it will have a drastic impact on its neighbors.

Planes land at Terminal 1 or 2, though most flights to and from Southern California airports use the Commuter Terminal, a half-mile away; the Airport Flyer ("red bus") provides free service from the main airport to the Commuter Terminal, or there's a footpath. General **information desks** with visitor materials, maps, and other services are near the baggage claim areas of both Terminal 1 and 2. You can exchange foreign currency at **Travelex America** (© 619/295-1501; www.travelexusa.com) in Terminal 1 across from the United Airlines ticket counter, or in Terminal 2 on the second level (*inside* the security area, near the gates). **Hotel reservation** and **car-rental courtesy phones** are in the baggage-claim areas of Terminal 1 and 2.

GETTING INTO TOWN FROM THE AIRPORT

BY BUS   The **Metropolitan Transit System** (MTS; © 619/233-3004; www.sd commute.com) operates the San Diego Transit Flyer—bus route no. 992—providing service between the airport and downtown San Diego, running along Broadway. Bus stops are at each of Lindbergh Field's three terminals. The one-way fare is $2.25, and exact change is required. Request a transfer if you're connecting to another bus or the San Diego Trolley route downtown. The ride takes about 15 minutes and buses come at 10- to 15-minute intervals.

At the **Transit Store,** 102 Broadway, at First Avenue (© 619/234-1060), you can get information about greater San Diego's mass transit system (bus, rail, and ferry) and pick up free brochures, route maps, and timetables. The store is open Monday to Friday, 9am to 5pm. *Note:* At press time, San Diego's bus routes are being significantly altered, making a trip or a call to the Transit Store all the more important if you plan on relying on MTS service.

Tips   Need a Lift into Town?

Remember to ask your hotel whether it has an **airport shuttle** from Lindbergh Field. Hotels often offer this service—usually free, sometimes for a nominal charge—and some also provide complimentary shuttles from the hotel to popular shopping and dining areas. Make sure the hotel knows when you're arriving, and get precise directions on where it'll pick you up.

BY TAXI   Taxis line up outside both terminals, and the trip to a downtown location, usually a 10-minute ride, is about $10 (plus tip); budget $20 to $25 for Coronado or Mission Beach, and about $30 to $35 for La Jolla.

BY SHUTTLE   Several airport shuttles run regularly from the airport to points around the city; you'll see designated pick-up areas outside each terminal. The shuttles are a good deal for single travelers; two or more people traveling together might as well take a taxi. The fare is about $8 per person to downtown hotels; Mission Valley and Mission Beach hotels are $10 to $12; La Jolla and Coronado hotels are around $15 to $19. Rates to a residence are about double the above rates for the first person. One company that serves all of San Diego County is **Cloud 9 Shuttle** (© 800/974-8885; www.cloud9shuttle.com).

BY CAR   If you're driving to downtown from the airport, take Harbor Drive south to Broadway, the main east-west thoroughfare, and turn left. To reach Hillcrest or Balboa Park, exit the airport toward I-5, and follow the signs for Laurel Street. To reach Mission Bay, take I-5 north to I-8 west. To reach La Jolla, take I-5 north to the La Jolla Parkway exit, bearing left onto Torrey Pines Road. For complete information on rental cars in San Diego, see "Getting Around," later in this chapter.

GETTING INTO TOWN FROM PLACES OTHER THAN THE AIRPORT

BY BUS   Greyhound buses from Los Angeles, Phoenix, Las Vegas, and other points in the southwest United States arrive at the station in downtown San Diego at 120 W. Broadway. Local buses stop in front and the San Diego Trolley line is nearby.

BY TRAIN   San Diego's Santa Fe Station is at the west end of Broadway, between Front Street and First Avenue, within a half-mile of most downtown hotels and the Embarcadero. Taxis line up outside the main door, the trolley station is across the street, and a dozen local bus routes stop on Broadway or Pacific Coast Highway, 1 block away.

BY CAR   Three main interstates lead into San Diego. **I-5** is the primary route from San Francisco, central California, and Los Angeles; it runs straight through downtown to the Tijuana border crossing. **I-8** cuts across California from points east like Phoenix, terminating just west of I-5 at Mission Bay. **I-15** leads from the deserts to the north through inland San Diego; as you enter Miramar, take **Highway 163** south to reach the central parts of the city.

VISITOR INFORMATION

There are staffed information booths at the airport and the train station, plus the following.

In downtown San Diego, the Convention & Visitors Bureau's **International Visitor Information Center** (© 619/236-1212; www.sandiego.org) is on the

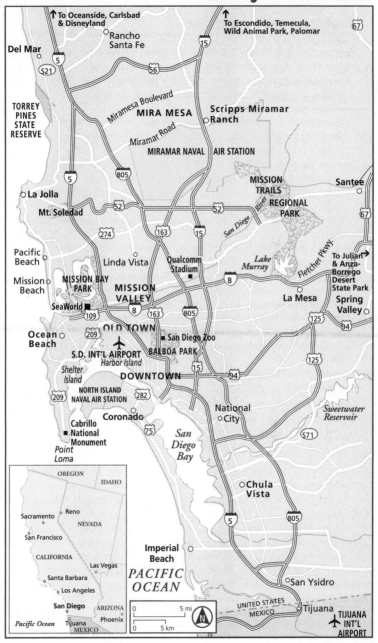

↑ To Oceanside, Carlsbad & Disneyland

Rancho Santa Fe

Del Mar

↑ To Escondido, Temecula, Wild Animal Park, Palomar

67

5

S21

56

15

TORREY PINES STATE RESERVE

Miramesa Boulevard

MIRA MESA

Scripps Miramar Ranch

Miramar Road

MIRAMAR NAVAL AIR STATION

5

805

La Jolla

MISSION TRAILS

Santee

52

52

REGIONAL PARK

67

Mt. Soledad

San Diego River

274

163

15

Pacific Beach

Linda Vista

Qualcomm Stadium

Lake Murray

To Julian & Anza-Borrego Desert State Park

Fletcher Pkwy.

Mission Beach

MISSION BAY PARK

MISSION VALLEY

8

La Mesa

Spring Valley

SeaWorld ■

109

8

163

805

125

94

Ocean Beach

209

OLD TOWN

■ San Diego Zoo

125

S.D. INT'L AIRPORT

Harbor Island

BALBOA PARK

Shelter Island

DOWNTOWN

15

94

Sweetwater Reservoir

NORTH ISLAND NAVAL AIR STATION

209

282

National City

Cabrillo ■ National Monument

Coronado

75

S71

Point Loma

San Diego Bay

Chula Vista

805

Imperial Beach

5

PACIFIC OCEAN

San Ysidro

UNITED STATES
MEXICO

Tijuana

TIJUANA INT'L AIRPORT

OREGON

IDAHO

Sacramento
Reno

NEVADA

San Francisco

CALIFORNIA

Las Vegas

Santa Barbara

Los Angeles

ARIZONA

San Diego

Phoenix

Pacific Ocean

Tijuana
MEXICO

0   5 mi

0   5 km

N

The Best of San Diego Online

You can find lots of information on San Diego on the Internet; here are a few of my favorite planning and general information sites.

- **www.sandiego.org** is maintained by the San Diego Convention & Visitors Bureau and includes up-to-date weather data, a calendar of events, and a hotel booking engine.

- **www.sandiegoartandsol.com** is the link for cultural tourism. You'll find a list of art shows and music events, plus intriguing touring itineraries that delve into the city's culture.

- **www.sandiego-online.com**, the *San Diego* magazine website, offers abbreviated stories as well as dining and events listings.

- **www.sdreader.com**, the site of the free weekly *San Diego Reader,* is a great source for club and show listings, plus edgy topical journalism. It has printable dining and other coupons you can really use, plus opinionated arts, eats, and entertainment critiques.

- **www.signonsandiego.com** is where Citysearch teams up with the *San Diego Union-Tribune,* catering as much to locals as to visitors. It offers plenty of helpful links, plus reviews of restaurants, music, movies, performing arts, museums, outdoor recreation, beaches, and sports.

- **www.sdgodowntown.com** is SignOnSanDiego's Gaslamp Quarter site, offering information on downtown events, restaurants, nightlife, and shopping.

- **www.digitalcity.com/sandiego** is a lifestyle guide targeted at locals, and therefore yields occasional off-the-beaten-tourist-path recommendations. You'll find everything from personal ads to constantly changing restaurant spotlights and daily top picks.

- **www.wheresd.com** provides information on arts, culture, special events, shopping, and dining for San Diego, Orange County, and Los Angeles. You can also make hotel reservations through the site.

Embarcadero at 1040 1/3 W. Broadway, at Harbor Drive. Daily summer hours are from 9am to 5pm; for the remainder of the year, hours are Thursday through Tuesday from 9am to 4pm. Convis offers great info and deals on its website, but you can also get your hands on the glossy *Official Visitors Planning Guide* from the Information Center. The guide includes information on member accommodations, dining, activities, attractions, tours, and transportation. At press time, it was unclear whether hard copies of the *San Diego Travel Values* pamphlet, full of discount coupons for hotels, restaurants, and attractions, would still be published. All those *Travel Values* discounts (and many more) are now available at www.sandiego.org. Convis also operates a walk-up–only facility at the **La Jolla Visitor Center,** 7966 Herschel Ave., near the corner of Prospect Street. This office is open daily in summer, from 10am to 7pm (until 6pm Sun); from September to May the center is open daily but with more limited hours.

If you're driving into town, the **Mission Bay Visitor Information Center,** 2688 E. Mission Bay Dr. (© **866/746-8440** or 619/276-8200; www.infosandiego.com), is between Mission Bay and I-5, at the Clairemont Drive exit. This private facility books hotels and sells discounted admission tickets to a variety of attractions—discounts work out to about $2 to $3 off per adult for the big-ticket items such as SeaWorld. There's plenty of parking; stop in between 9am and dusk.

The **Coronado Visitors Center,** 1100 Orange Ave. (© **619/437-8788;** www. coronadovisitors.com), dispenses maps, newsletters, and information-packed brochures. Inside the Coronado Museum, they're open Monday through Friday from 9am to 5pm, Saturday from 10am to 5pm, and Sunday from 11am to 4pm.

San Diego has two major print publications: The daily *San Diego Union-Tribune* and the alternative (and free) *San Diego Weekly Reader.* The *U-T* has woefully thin international and national coverage—mostly wire-service pick-ups—but does a decent job covering local news, and has an archly conservative editorial board. It's weekly entertainment supplement, "Night & Day," which comes out on Thursdays, has been dumbed-down to attract a new demographic but will still give you the nuts and bolts of what's going on in town that week. For a more complete list of happenings, check the *Reader,* which also comes out on Thursdays, and can be found all over the city at bookstores, cafes, liquor stores, and other outlets; a condensed version called *The Weekly* is found in hotels and tourist areas. Except for a couple of segments, the full version of the *Reader* is a bore—it's all about the listings. Check the free *San Diego CityBeat* for a truly alternative take on San Diego. It's distributed throughout the city on Wednesdays.

CITY LAYOUT
Main Arteries & Streets

It's not hard to find your way around downtown San Diego. Most streets run one way, in a grid pattern. First through Twelfth (aka Park Blvd.) avenues run north and south—odd-number avenues are northbound, even numbers run south; A through K streets alternate running east and west. Broadway (the equivalent of D St.) runs both directions, as do Market Street and Harbor Drive. North of A Street, the east–west streets bear the names of trees, in alphabetical order: Ash, Beech, Cedar, Date, and so on. Harbor Drive runs past the airport and along the waterfront, which is known as the Embarcadero. Ash Street and Broadway are the downtown arteries that connect with Harbor Drive.

The Coronado Bay Bridge leading to Coronado is accessible from I-5 south of downtown, and I-5 north leads to Old Town, Mission Bay, La Jolla, and North County coastal areas. Balboa Park (home of the San Diego Zoo), Hillcrest, and Uptown areas lie north of downtown San Diego. The park and zoo are easily reached by way of Park Boulevard (which would otherwise be Twelfth Ave.), and which leads to the parking lots. Fifth Avenue leads to Hillcrest. Highway 163, which heads north from Eleventh Avenue, leads into Mission Valley.

CORONADO   The main streets are Orange Avenue, where most of the hotels and restaurants are clustered, and Ocean Drive, which follows Coronado Beach.

DOWNTOWN   The major thoroughfares are Broadway (a major bus artery), Fourth and Fifth avenues (which run south and north, respectively), C Street (the trolley line), and Harbor Drive, which curls along the waterfront and passes the Maritime Museum, Seaport Village, the Convention Center, and PETCO Park.

HILLCREST   The main streets are University Avenue and Washington Street (both two-way, running east and west), and Fourth and Fifth avenues (both one-way, running south and north, respectively).

LA JOLLA The main avenues are Prospect and Girard, which are perpendicular to each other. The main routes in and out of La Jolla are La Jolla Boulevard (running south to Mission Beach) and Torrey Pines Road (leading to I-5).

MISSION VALLEY I-8 runs east-west along the valley's southern perimeter; Highway 163, I-805, and I-15 run north-south through the valley. Hotel Circle is an elongated loop road that parallels either side of I-8 to the west of Highway 163; Friar's Road is the major artery on the north side of the valley.

PACIFIC BEACH Mission Boulevard is the main drag, parallel to and 1 block in from the beach, and perpendicular to it are Grand and Garnet avenues. East and West Mission Bay drives encircle most of the bay and Ingraham Street cuts through the middle of it.

STREET MAPS

The **International Visitor Information Center,** 1040 1/3 W. Broadway, along the downtown Embarcadero (✆ **619/236-1212**), provides an illustrated pocket map. Also available are maps of the 59-mile scenic drive around San Diego, the Gaslamp Quarter, Tijuana, San Diego's public transportation, and a "Campgrounds and Recreation" map for the county.

The **Automobile Club of Southern California** has 10 San Diego offices (✆ **619/ 233-1000**). It distributes great maps, which are free to AAA members and to members of many international auto clubs, and sells auto insurance for those driving within Mexico.

Car-rental outfits usually offer maps of the city that show the freeways and major streets, and hotels often provide complimentary maps of the downtown area. You can buy maps of the city and vicinity at the retail stores listed under "Travel Accessories," in chapter 9 (p. 219). The **Transit Store,** 102 Broadway, at First Avenue (✆ **619/ 234-1060**), is a storehouse of bus and trolley maps, with a friendly staff on duty to answer specific questions.

If you're moving to San Diego or plan an extended stay, I recommend the *Thomas Guides,* available at bookstores, drugstores, and large supermarkets for $27 (or contact ✆ **800/899-6277;** www.thomas.com). This all-encompassing book of maps deciphers San Diego County street by street and includes a CD-ROM version.

THE NEIGHBORHOODS IN BRIEF

In this guidebook, San Diego is divided into six main areas, where most visitors spend the bulk of their visit.

Downtown After decades of intense development and restoration, downtown San Diego has emerged as a vibrant neighborhood with attractions that last long after banking hours. The city center is now a magnet for travelers, conventioneers, and locals. The business, shopping, dining, and entertainment heart of the city, the downtown area encompasses Horton Plaza, the Gaslamp Quarter, the Embarcadero (waterfront), the Convention Center, and Little Italy, sprawling over eight individual "neighborhoods." The **Gaslamp Quarter** is the center of a massive redevelopment kicked off in the mid-1980s with the opening of the Horton Plaza shopping complex; now, it's a cluster of renovated historic buildings housing some of the city's best restaurants and clubs. Immediately southeast of the Gaslamp is **PETCO Park,** home of the San Diego Padres, which opened in 2004. Also undergoing a renaissance is **Little Italy,** a small neighborhood along India Street between Cedar and Hawthorn at the northern edge of downtown, and a great place to find a variety of restaurants (especially Italian) and one-of-a-kind stores.

Hillcrest & Uptown   Part of Hillcrest's charm is the number of people out walking, shopping, and just hanging out. As the city's first self-contained suburb in the 1920s, it was also the desirable address for bankers and bureaucrats to erect their mansions. Now, it's the heart of San Diego's gay and lesbian community, but still manages to charm everyone with an eclectic blend of shops and cafes. Despite the cachet of being close to **Balboa Park** (home of the **San Diego Zoo** and numerous **museums**), the area fell into neglect in the 1960s. However, by the late 1970s, legions of preservation-minded residents began restoring Hillcrest's charms. Centrally located and brimming with popular restaurants and avant-garde boutiques, Hillcrest also offers less expensive and more personalized accommodations than any other area in the city. Other old Uptown neighborhoods of interest are **Mission Hills** to the west of Hillcrest, and **University Heights, Normal Heights, North Park,** and **Kensington** to the east.

Old Town & Mission Valley   These two busy areas wrap around the neighborhood of Mission Hills. On one end are the Old Town State Historic Park (where California "began") and several museums that recall the turn of the 20th century and the city's beginnings. Old Town is said to attract more visitors than any other sight in San Diego—it's where you can steep yourself in history while eating and shopping to your stomach and heart's content. Not far from Old Town lies the vast suburban sprawl of Mission Valley, a tribute to the automobile and to a more modern style of prosperity. Its main street, aptly named Hotel Circle, is lined with a string of moderately priced hotels as an alternative to the ritzier neighborhoods. In recent years, condo developments have made the valley a residential area.

Mission Bay & the Beaches   *Casual* is the word of the day here. Come here when you want to wiggle your toes in the sand, feel the sun warm your skin, exert yourself in physical activities, and cool off in the blue ocean waters. Mission Bay is a watery playground perfect for water-skiing, sailing, kayaking, and windsurfing. The adjacent communities of **Ocean Beach, Mission Beach,** and **Pacific Beach** are known for their wide stretches of sand, active nightlife, and informal dining. If you've come for the SoCal beach lifestyle, this is where you'll find it. The boardwalk, which runs from South Mission Beach to Pacific Beach, is a popular place for in-line skating, bike riding, people-watching, and sunsets.

La Jolla   Mediterranean in design and ambience, La Jolla is the Southern California Riviera. This seaside community of about 25,000 is home to an inordinate number of wealthy folks who could probably live anywhere. They chose La Jolla for good reason—it's surrounded by the beach, the **University of California, San Diego (UCSD),** outstanding restaurants, both pricey and traditional shops, and some of the world's best medical facilities. The heart of La Jolla is referred to as the **Village,** roughly delineated by **Pearl Street** to the south, **Prospect Street** to the north, **Torrey Pines Road** to the east, and the rugged coast to the west. This is a picturesque

Off the Beaten Path: Golden Hill and Beyond

You don't think the swank Gaslamp Quarter will be the last San Diego neighborhood to be rediscovered and gentrified, do you? If you like to explore, check out another old neighborhood that's attracting attention.

When the downtown area we now call the Gaslamp Quarter was enjoying its turn-of-the-20th-century heyday as the city's commercial center, the most convenient suburb was Golden Hill. Directly east of downtown, Golden Hill had the added advantage of being next to Balboa Park—it wraps around the southeast corner of the park. Back then, homes here enjoyed a sweeping view south to the bay, but development slowly blocked many of these views. For a drive-by look at some oldies but goodies, head east from downtown along Broadway, where finely preserved Victorians now serve as legal and medical offices, or cruise down 28th Street along the park, or any other side street that catches your eye.

Some of the neighborhood's best Victorians and bungalows show the caring touch of deep-pocketed architecture buffs, though plenty have fallen victim to the wrecking ball. Sandwiched between a natural arroyo (now the pathway of the I-94 freeway) and vast Balboa Park, Golden Hill is an area where in the still of the night you're likely to see coyotes, opossums, and even red foxes trotting down quiet streets.

South Park, a neighborhood that blends into Golden Hill (most San Diegans—except for those who live there—couldn't tell you where one begins and the other ends), has been steadily carving an identity of its own. Hipster bars and engaging restaurants have cropped up and created a buzz. Places like the **Whistle Stop Bar** (2236 Fern St., ✆ **619/284-6784**); **M-Theory Music** (3004 Juniper St.; ✆ **619/269-2963**), an independent record store that hosts in-store music appearances and also has its own recording label; and **South Park Bar and Grill** (1946 Fern St., ✆ **619/696-0096**) are leading the way.

South Park is definitely adding to the overall vibe of Golden Hill, which has such locally popular hangouts as **The Big Kitchen** (3003 Grape St.; **619/234-5789**), where a pre-fame Whoopi Goldberg once waitressed; **Krakatoa** coffeehouse (1128 25th St., ✆ **619/230-0272**) and its next-door neighbor, the retro **Turf Supper Club** (p. 230), where you cook your own steaks; and **Influx Cafe** (1948 Broadway, ✆ **619/255-9470**), with its minimalist-chic decor and home-baked goods.

And adjacent to South Park, a half-mile north of Broadway, is the sweet little enclave known as the Burlingame Historical District. The lovingly tended neighborhood—which features pink sidewalks—is made up of Spanish stucco and Craftsman-era bungalows, and is a treat to walk through. It's between 30th and 32nd streets, north of Kalmia Street.

neighborhood, which makes it perfect for simply strolling about. It's uncertain whether "La Jolla" (pronounced la-HOY-ya) is misspelled Spanish for "the jewel" or a native people's word for "cave," but once you see it, you'll no doubt go with the first definition.

Coronado You may be tempted to think of Coronado as an island, but it's actually on a bulbous peninsula connected to the mainland by a narrow sand spit, the **Silver Strand.** It's a quaint, self-contained island community inhabited by generations of old-line families living on quiet, tree-lined streets. The northern portion of the peninsula is home to the **U.S. Naval Air Station,** in use since World War I. The southern sector has a history as an elite playground for snowbirds and has a charming suburban community. Shops line the main street, Orange Avenue, and you'll find several ritzy resorts, including the landmark **Hotel del Coronado,** referred to locally as the "Hotel Del." Coronado has a lovely duned beach (one of the area's finest), plenty of restaurants, and a "downtown" reminiscent of a small Midwestern town; it's also home to more retired admirals than any other community in the country.

2 Getting Around

San Diego has many walkable neighborhoods, from the historic downtown area, to Hillcrest and nearby Balboa Park and Mission Hills, to the Embarcadero, to Mission Bay Park. You get there by car, bus, or trolley, and your feet do the rest. For inspiration, turn to chapter 8, "City Strolls."

BY CAR

We complain of increasing traffic, but San Diego is still easy to navigate by car. Most downtown streets run one-way, in a grid pattern. However, outside downtown, canyons and bays often make streets indirect. Finding a parking space can be tricky in the Gaslamp Quarter, Old Town, Mission Beach, and La Jolla, but parking lots are often centrally located. Rush hour on the freeways is generally concentrated from 7 to 9am and 4:30 to 6pm. Be aware that San Diego's gas prices are often among the highest in the country. Also note that, generally speaking, we're not the best drivers in the rain—vehicles careening out of control during the first couple of winter dousings keep the Highway Patrol and local news channels very busy.

Note on driving to Mexico: If you plan to drive to Mexico, be sure to check with your insurance company at home to verify exactly the limits of your policy. Mexican car insurance is available from various agencies (visible to drivers heading into Mexico) on the U.S. side of the border. Whether your insurance covers areas south of the border or not, Mexican car insurance may be preferable due to different liability standards.

CAR RENTALS

I'd love to tell you that public transportation is a good way to get around, as in New York City or San Francisco, but the distances between attractions and indirect bus routings usually make it inefficient. Those staying for a short time downtown will find plenty to see and do within easy reach (including Balboa Park and Old Town), but otherwise, if you don't drive to San Diego with your own car, you'll want to rent one. You *can* reach virtually all sights of interest using public transportation, but having your own wheels is a big advantage.

All the major car-rental firms have an office at the airport and several have them in larger hotels. Some of the national companies include **Alamo** (© 800/462-5266; www.alamo.com), **Avis** (© 800/230-4898; www.avis.com), **Budget** (© 800/527-0700; www.budget.com), **Dollar** (© 800/800-3665; www.dollar.com), **Enterprise**

> **Tips**   **Curb Appeal**
>
> Street parking rules are color-coordinated throughout the city. A **red curb** means no stopping at any time. **Blue curbs** are used to denote parking for people with disabilities—the fine for parking in these spaces without a distinguishing placard or a disabled license plate is $340 (out-of-state disabled plates are okay). A **white-painted curb** signifies a passenger loading zone; the time limit is 3 minutes, or 10 minutes in front of a hotel. A **yellow curb** is a commercial loading zone—which means that between 6am and 6pm Monday through Saturday, trucks and commercial vehicles are allowed 20 minutes to load or unload goods, *and* passenger vehicles can unload passengers for 3 minutes (from 6pm–6am and all day Sunday, anyone can park in a yellow curb zone, though some yellow zones are in effect 24 hours—be sure to check any nearby signage). A **green curb** designates short-term parking only—usually 15 or 30 minutes (as posted). Unpainted curbs are subject to parking rules on signs or meters.

(© 800/736-8222; www.enterprise.com), **Hertz** (© 800/654-3131; www.hertz.com), **National** (© 800/227-7368; www.nationalcar.com), and **Thrifty** (© 800/847-4389; www.thrifty.com). *Note for Mexico-bound car renters:* Some companies, including Avis, will allow their cars into Mexico as far as Ensenada, but other rental outfits won't allow you to drive south of the border.

Demystifying Renter's Insurance

Before you drive off in a rental car, be sure you're insured. Hasty assumptions about your personal auto insurance or a rental agency's additional coverage could end up costing you tens of thousands of dollars, even if you're involved in an accident that was clearly the fault of another driver.

If you already hold a **private auto insurance** policy, you're most likely covered in the United States for loss of or damage to a rental car and liability in case of injury to any other party involved in an accident. Be sure to find out whether you're covered in the area you're visiting, whether your policy extends to everyone who will be driving the car, how much liability is covered in case an outside party is injured in an accident, and whether the type of vehicle you are renting is included under your contract. (Rental trucks, SUVs, and luxury vehicles or sports cars may not be covered.)

Most **major credit cards** (especially gold and platinum cards) provide some degree of coverage as well, provided they're used to pay for the rental. Terms vary widely, however, so be sure to call your credit card company directly before you rent.

If you're **uninsured,** your credit card will probably provide primary coverage as long as you decline the rental agency's insurance and as long as you rent with that card. This means that the credit card will cover damage or theft of a rental car for the full cost of the vehicle. (In a few states, however, theft is not covered; ask specifically about state law where you will be renting and driving.) If you already have insurance, your credit card will provide secondary coverage, which basically covers your deductible.

Note: Though they may cover damage to your rental car, *credit cards will not cover liability,* or the cost of injury to an outside party, damage to an outside party's vehicle, or both. If you do not hold an insurance policy, you may seriously want to

---

---

consider purchasing additional liability insurance from your rental company, even if you decline collision coverage. Be sure to check the terms, however. Some rental agencies cover liability only if the renter is not at fault; even then, the rental company's obligation varies from state to state.

The basic insurance coverage offered by most car-rental companies, known as the **Loss/Damage Waiver (LDW)** or **Collision Damage Waiver (CDW)**, can cost as much as $20 a day. It usually covers the full value of the vehicle with no deductible if an outside party causes an accident or other damage to the rental car. Liability coverage varies according to the company policy and state law, but the minimum is usually at least $15,000. If you are at fault in an accident, you will be covered for the full replacement value of the car, but not for liability. Some states allow you to buy additional liability coverage for such cases. Most rental companies will require a police report to process any claims you file, but your private insurer will not be notified of the accident.

Saving Money on a Rental Car

Car-rental rates vary even more dramatically than airline fares. Prices depend on the size of the car, where and when you pick it up and drop it off, the length of the rental period, where and how far you drive it, whether you buy insurance, and a host of other factors. A few key questions could save you hundreds of dollars:

- Are weekend rates lower than weekday rates? Ask if the rate is the same for pickup Friday morning, for instance, as it is for Thursday night.
- Does the agency assess a drop-off charge if you don't return the car to the same location where you picked it up?
- Are special promotional rates available? If you see an advertised price in your local newspaper, be sure to ask for that specific rate; otherwise, you may be charged the standard cost.
- Are discounts available for members of AARP, AAA, frequent-flyer programs, or trade unions?
- How much tax will be added to the rental bill? Local tax? State use tax?
- How much does the rental company charge to refill your gas tank if you return with the tank less than full? Though most rental companies claim these prices are competitive, fuel is almost always cheaper in town.

PARKING

Metered parking spaces are found in downtown, Hillcrest, and the beach communities, but demand outpaces supply. Posted signs indicate operating hours—generally Monday through Saturday from 8am to 6pm. Be prepared with several dollars in quarters—some meters take no other coin, and 25¢ usually buys only 12 minutes, even on a 2-hour meter. Most unmetered areas have signs restricting street parking to 1 or 2 hours; count on vigilant chalking and ticketing during the regulated hours. Three-hour meters line Harbor Drive opposite the ticket offices for harbor tours; even on weekends, you have to feed them. If you can't find a metered space, there are plenty of hourly lots downtown. Parking in Mission Valley is usually within large parking structures and free, though congested on weekends and particularly leading up to Christmas.

Downtown parking structures on 6th Avenue (at Market and at K sts.) have helped ease parking woes, but it's still a challenge. Of special concern are game nights—and days—at PETCO Park (Apr–Sept). Unless you're staying downtown or want to attend the game, it's best to avoid the baseball traffic and head elsewhere for dining or nightlife.

DRIVING RULES

San Diegans are relatively respectful drivers, although admittedly we often speed and sometimes we lose patience with those who don't know their way around. We also have a tough time driving in the rain—watch for spinouts and hydroplaning vehicles when traveling in our rare wet weather.

There are a few rules you should be aware of. California has a seat-belt law for both drivers and passengers, so buckle up before you venture out. You may turn right at a red light after stopping unless a sign says otherwise. Likewise, you can turn left on a red light from a one-way street onto another one-way street after coming to a full stop. Keep in mind, when driving in San Diego, that pedestrians have the right of way at all times, not just in crosswalks, so stop for pedestrians who have stepped off the curb. Penalties in California for drunk driving are among the toughest in the country. Speed limits on freeways, particularly Highway 8 through Mission Valley, are aggressively enforced after dark, partly as a pretext for nabbing drivers who might have imbibed. Also beware of main beach arteries (Grand, Garnet, and Mission). Traffic enforcement can be strict.

BY PUBLIC TRANSPORTATION
BY BUS

Important Note: At press time, San Diego's bus system was beginning a countywide overhaul. In the most major reworking of the city's transportation system in 25 years, nearly the entire Metropolitan Transit System will be affected. Routes will be changed or even eliminated; outlying areas are expected to become better served, while downtown will probably see reduced service. If you plan on relying on MTS buses while traveling in San Diego this year, you'll be well served by a visit or call to the downtown MTS **Transit Store,** 102 Broadway at First Avenue (© **619/234-1060**).

The Transit Store dispenses passes, tokens, timetables, maps, brochures, and lost-and-found information. It issues ID cards for seniors 60 and older, and for travelers with disabilities, all of whom pay $1 per ride. Request a copy of the useful brochure *San Diego Fun Places,* which details the city's most popular tourist attractions and the buses that will take you to them. The office is open Monday through Friday from 9am to 5pm.

San Diego has had an adequate bus system that will get you to where you're going— eventually. Most drivers are friendly and helpful; on local routes, bus stops are marked by rectangular blue signs every other block or so, farther apart on express routes. Most **bus fares** are $2.25. Buses accept dollar bills and change, but drivers can't give change. Transfers must be used within 90 minutes, and you can return to where you started (meaning a quick round-trip might cost just the one-way fare). If transferring from the trolley, your validated ticket serves as a transfer onto the bus, valid for up to 2 hours from validation.

For assistance with route information from a living, breathing entity, call © **619/ 233-3004.** You can also view timetables, maps, and fares online—and learn how the public transit system accommodates travelers with disabilities—at **www.sdcommute.com**. There is also a downloadable version of *San Diego Fun Places.* If you know your route and just need schedule information—or automated answers to FAQs—call **Info Express** (© **619/685-4900**) from any touch-tone phone, 24 hours a day.

At press time, some of the most popular tourist attractions served by bus and rail routes are

- Balboa Park west entrance: Route 1, 3, and 25
- Balboa Park east entrances and San Diego Zoo: Route 7, 7A, and 7B
- SeaWorld: Route 9 and 27
- Cabrillo National Monument: Route 26
- Seaport Village: Route 7, 7A, 7B, and San Diego Trolley Orange Line
- Qualcomm Stadium: Route 13 and San Diego Trolley Blue and Green lines
- Tijuana: San Diego Trolley Blue Line
- San Diego International Airport: Route 992
- Wild Animal Park: Route 386 (Mon–Sat only)
- Convention Center and PETCO Park: San Diego Trolley Orange Line
- Coronado: Route 901
- Gaslamp Quarter and Horton Plaza: most downtown bus routes and San Diego Trolley Blue and Orange Lines
- Old Town: Route 5, 6, 9, 26, 28, 34, 35, 44, 908, San Diego Trolley Blue and Green lines, and the Coaster

The Coronado Shuttle, bus Route 904, runs between the Marriott Coronado Island Resort and the Old Ferry Landing, and then continues along Orange Avenue to the Hotel del Coronado, Glorietta Bay, Loews, and back again. It costs $1 per person. Route 901 goes all the way to Coronado from San Diego and costs $2.25 for adults.

When planning your route, note that schedules vary and most buses do not run all night. Some stop at 6pm, while other lines continue to 9pm, midnight, or 2am—ask your bus driver for more specific information. On Saturdays, some routes run all night.

BY TROLLEY

Although the system is too limited for most San Diegans to use for work commutes, the San Diego Trolley is great for visitors, particularly if you're staying downtown or plan to visit Tijuana. There are three routes. The **Blue Line** is the one that is the handiest for most visitors: It travels from the Mexican border north through downtown and Old Town, with some trolleys continuing into Mission Valley. The **Orange Line** runs from downtown east through Lemon Grove and El Cajon. The new **Green Line** runs from Old Town through Mission Valley to Qualcomm Stadium, San Diego State University, and on to Santee. The trip to the border crossing takes 40 minutes from downtown; from downtown to Old Town takes 10 to 15 minutes. For a route map, see the inside front cover of this guide.

Trolleys operate on a self-service fare-collection system; riders buy tickets from machines in stations before boarding. The machines list fares for each destination (ranging from $1.25 for anywhere within downtown, to $3 for the longest trips) and dispense change. Tickets are valid for 2 hours from the time of purchase, in any direction. Fare inspectors board trains at random to check tickets. A round-trip ticket is double the price, but is valid all day between the origination and destination points.

The lines run every 15 minutes during the day and every 30 minutes at night; during peak weekday rush hours the Blue Line runs every 10 minutes. There is also expanded service to accommodate events at PETCO Park and Qualcomm Stadium. Trolleys stop at each station for only 30 seconds. To open the door for boarding, push the lighted green button; to open the door to exit the trolley, push the lighted white button.

For recorded transit information, call ✆ **619/685-4900.** To speak with a customer service representative, call ✆ **619/233-3004** (TTY/TDD 619/234-5005) daily from 5:30am to 8:30pm. For wheelchair lift info, call ✆ **619/595-4960.** The trolley generally operates daily from 5am to about midnight; the Blue Line provides limited but additional service between Old Town and San Ysidro throughout the night from Saturday evening to Sunday morning; check the website at www.sdcommute.com for details.

The privately owned **Old Town Trolley Tours** (p. 172) is an excellent way to get around much of the city during a short visit. It's essentially a narrated sightseeing tour, but you can disembark at various points and join up later with the next passing group.

BY TRAIN

San Diego's express rail commuter service, the **Coaster,** travels between the downtown Santa Fe Depot station and the Oceanside Transit Center, with stops at Old Town, Sorrento Valley, Solana Beach, Encinitas, and Carlsbad. Fares range from $3.75 to $5.25 each way, depending on how far you go, and can be paid by credit card at vending machines at each station. Eligible seniors and riders with disabilities pay $1.75 to $2.50. The scenic trip between downtown San Diego and Oceanside takes 1 hour. Trains run Monday through Friday about once an hour, with four trains in each direction on Saturday; call ✆ **800/262-7837** or 619/233-3004 for the current schedule, or log on to **www.sdcommute.com**.

Amtrak (© 800/872-7245; www.amtrak.com) trains run between San Diego and downtown Los Angeles, about 11 times daily each way. Trains to Los Angeles depart from the Santa Fe Depot and stop in Solana Beach, Oceanside, San Juan Capistrano, Santa Ana, and Anaheim (Disneyland). Two trains per day also stop in San Clemente. The travel time from San Diego to Los Angeles is about 2 hours and 45 minutes (for comparison, driving time can be as little as 2 hr., or as much as 4 hr. during rush hour). A one-way ticket to Los Angeles is $32, or $45 for a reserved seat in business class. A one-way ticket to Solana Beach is $10, to Oceanside $14, to San Juan Capistrano $17, and to Anaheim $23.

BY TAXI

Half a dozen taxi companies serve the area. Rates are based on mileage and can add up quickly in sprawling San Diego—a trip from downtown to La Jolla will cost about $30 to $35. Other than in the Gaslamp Quarter after dark, taxis don't cruise the streets as they do in other cities, so you have to call ahead for quick pickup. If you're at a hotel or restaurant, the front-desk attendant or concierge will call one for you. Among the local companies are **Orange Cab** (© 619/291-3333), **San Diego Cab** (© 619/226-TAXI), and **Yellow Cab** (© 619/234-6161). The **Coronado Cab Company** (© 935/435-6211) serves Coronado. In La Jolla, use **La Jolla Cab** (© 858/453-4222).

BY WATER

BY FERRY   There's regularly scheduled ferry service between San Diego and Coronado (© 619/234-4111 for information). Ferries leave from the Broadway Pier (1050 N. Harbor Dr., at the intersection of Broadway) Sunday through Thursday on the hour from 9am to 9pm, and Friday and Saturday until 10pm. They return from the Ferry Landing in Coronado to the Broadway Pier Sunday through Thursday every hour on the half-hour from 9:30am to 9:30pm and Friday and Saturday until 10:30pm. The ride takes 15 minutes. The fare is $3 each way (50¢ extra if you bring your bike). Buy tickets at the Harbor Excursion kiosk on Broadway Pier or at the Ferry Landing in Coronado.

BY WATER TAXI   Water taxis (© 619/235-8294) will pick you up from any dock around San Diego Bay, and operate Monday through Friday from 2 to 10pm, on weekends and in summer from 11am to 11pm. If you're staying in a downtown hotel, this is a great way to get to Coronado. Boats are sometimes available at the spur of the moment, but reservations are advised. Fares are $6 per person to most locations.

BY BICYCLE

San Diego is ideal for exploration by bicycle, and many roads have designated bike lanes. Bikes are available for rent in most areas; see "Outdoor Activities" in chapter 7 for suggestions.

The San Diego Ridelink publishes a comprehensive map of the county detailing bike *paths* (for exclusive use by bicyclists), bike *lanes* (alongside motor vehicle ways), and bike *routes* (shared ways designated only by bike-symbol signs). The **San Diego Region Bike Map** is available at visitor centers; to receive a copy in advance, call © 800/266-6883.

It's possible to take your two-wheeler on the city's **public transportation.** For buses, let the driver know you want to stow your bike on the front of the bus, then board, and pay the regular fare. The trolley also lets you bring your bike on the trolley for free. Bikers can board at any entrance *except* the first set of doors behind the driver; the bike-storage area is at the back of each car. The cars carry two bikes except during weekday rush hours, when the limit is one bike per car. For more information, call the **Transit Information Line** (© 619/233-3004). Bikes are also permitted on the ferry connecting San Diego and Coronado, which has 15 miles of dedicated bike paths.

FAST FACTS: San Diego

Area Codes San Diego's main area code is **619,** used primarily by downtown, uptown, Mission Valley, Point Loma, Coronado, La Mesa, El Cajon, and Chula Vista. The area code **858** is used for northern and coastal areas, including Mission Beach, Pacific Beach, La Jolla, Del Mar, Rancho Santa Fe, and Rancho Bernardo. Use **760** to reach the remainder of San Diego County, including Encinitas, Carlsbad, Oceanside, Escondido, Ramona, Julian, and Anza-Borrego.

Babysitters **Marion's Childcare** (© 888/891-5029) has bonded babysitters available to come to your hotel room; rates start at $16 per hour with a 3-hour minimum. **Panda Services** (© 858/292-5503) is also available.

Business Hours Banks are open weekdays from 9am to 4pm or later, and sometimes Saturday morning. Stores in shopping malls tend to stay open until about 9pm weekdays and until 6pm weekends, and are open on secondary holidays.

Camera Repair Simple repairs and photographic supplies are available at **George's Camera & Video** in North Park at 3827 30th St. (© 619/297-3544), **Bob Davis' Camera Shop** in La Jolla at 7720 Fay Ave. (© 858/459-7355), **Nelson Photo Supply** in Little Italy at 1909 India St., at Fir Street (© 619/234-6621), and **Point Loma Camera Store,** 1310 Rosecrans St. (© 619/224-2719).

Currency The most common U.S. bills are the $1 (a "buck"), $5, $10, and $20 denominations. There are also $2 bills (seldom encountered), $50 bills, and $100 bills (the last two are usually not welcome as payment for small purchases). Coins come in seven denominations: 1¢ (1 cent, or a penny); 5¢ (5 cents, or a nickel); 10¢ (10 cents, or a dime); 25¢ (25 cents, or a quarter); 50¢ (50 cents, or a half dollar); the gold-colored Sacagawea coin, worth $1; and the rare silver dollar.

Dentists For dental referrals, contact the **San Diego County Dental Society** at © 800/201-0244, or call © 800/DENTIST.

Doctors **Hotel Docs** (© 800/468-3537) is a 24-hour network of physicians, dentists, and chiropractors. They accept credit cards, and their services are covered by most insurance policies. In a life-threatening situation, dial © 911.

Drugstores Long's, Rite-Aid, and Sav-On sell pharmaceuticals and nonprescription products. Look in the phone book to find the one nearest you. If you need a pharmacy after normal business hours, the following branches are open 24 hours: **Sav-On Drugs,** 8831 Villa La Jolla Dr., La Jolla (© 858/457-4390), and 313 E. Washington St., Hillcrest (© 619/291-7170); and **Rite-Aid,** 535 Robinson Ave., Hillcrest (© 619/291-3703). Local hospitals also sell prescription drugs.

Electricity Like Canada, the United States uses 110–120 volts AC (60 cycles), compared to 220–240 volts AC (50 cycles) in most of Europe, Australia, and New Zealand. Downward converters that change 220–240 volts to 110–120 volts are difficult to find in the United States, so bring one with you.

Emergencies Call © **911** for fire, police, and ambulance. The main police station is at 1401 Broadway, at 14th Street (© **619/531-2000,** or TTY/TDD 619/531-2065).

If you encounter serious problems, contact the San Diego chapter of **Traveler's Aid International** at © **619/295-8393,** or log on to www.travelersaid.org to help direct you to a local branch. This nationwide, nonprofit, social-service organization geared to helping travelers in difficult straits offers services that might include reuniting families separated while traveling, providing food and/or shelter to people stranded without cash, or even emotional counseling. If you're in trouble, seek them out.

Eyeglass Repair **Optometric Expressions,** 55 Horton Plaza (© **619/544-9000**), is at street level near the Westin Hotel, downtown. They can fill eyeglass prescriptions, repair glasses, and replace contact lenses. The major shopping centers in Mission Valley also have eyeglass stores that can fill prescriptions and handle most repairs.

Gasoline (Petrol) Petrol is known as gasoline (or simply "gas") in the United States, and petrol stations are known as both gas stations and service stations. Gasoline costs about half as much here as it does in Europe (about $3.50 per gal. at press time), and taxes are already included in the printed price. One U.S. gallon equals 3.8 liters or .85 imperial gallons. Most gas stations accept credit cards.

Hospitals Near downtown San Diego, **UCSD Medical Center-Hillcrest,** 200 W. Arbor Dr. (© **619/543-6400**), has the most convenient emergency room. In La Jolla, **UCSD Thornton Hospital,** 9300 Campus Point Dr. (© **858/657-7600**), has a good emergency room, and you'll find another in Coronado, at **Coronado Hospital,** 250 Prospect Place, opposite the Marriott Resort (© **619/435-6251**).

Hot Lines HIV Hot Line © **619/236-2352;** Alcoholics Anonymous © **619/265-8762;** Debtors Anonymous © **619/525-3065;** Mental Health referral and Suicide Crisis Line © **800/479-3339;** Traveler's Aid Society © **619/295-8393.**

Internet Access See "The 21st-Century Traveler," on p. 29.

Liquor Laws The legal age for purchase and consumption of alcoholic beverages in California is 21; proof of age is required and often requested at bars, nightclubs, and restaurants, so it's always a good idea to bring ID when you go out. Beer, wine, and hard liquor are sold daily from 6am to 2am and are available in grocery stores.

Do not carry open containers of alcohol in your car or any public area that isn't zoned for alcohol consumption—the police can fine you on the spot. Beer in a can, *not* a bottle, is allowed at San Diego beaches—check signs at beach entrances for exact rules. Nothing will ruin your trip faster than getting a citation for DUI ("driving under the influence"), so don't even think about driving while intoxicated.

Newspapers & Magazines The *San Diego Union-Tribune* is published daily, and its entertainment section, "Night & Day," is in the Thursday edition. The free *San Diego Weekly Reader* is published Thursdays and is available at many shops, restaurants, theaters, and public hot spots; it's the best source for up-to-the-week club and show listings (a visitor-friendly version called *The Weekly* is available in tourist areas). The free alternative weekly *San Diego CityBeat* is distributed on Wednesdays. It also has listings and can get you up to speed on local issues and local music. *San Diego* magazine has covered all aspects of the city since 1948, but is reportedly widening its focus for a more national appeal. It will undoubtedly still be plumped with social news and dining listings (and innumerable ads for tummy tucks and face-lifts). *San Diego Home-Garden Lifestyles* magazine highlights interior design, and also includes articles about southern California gardening and the local restaurant scene. Both magazines are published monthly and sold at newsstands. The *Los Angeles Times,* the *New York Times,* and *USA Today* are widely available.

Police The downtown police station is at 1401 Broadway (© **619/531-2000**). Call © **911** in an emergency.

Post Office San Diego's main post office is at 2535 Midway Dr., just west of Old Town; it's open Monday through Friday from 8am to 5pm, and Saturdays from 8am to 4pm. Post offices are downtown, at 815 E St. and at 51 Horton Plaza, next to the Westin Hotel. There is a post office in the Mission Valley Shopping Center, next to Macy's. These branch offices are generally open Monday through Friday during regular business hours, plus Saturday morning; for specific branch information, call © **800/275-8777** or log on to **www.usps.gov**.

Restrooms Horton Plaza and Seaport Village downtown, Balboa Park, Old Town State Historic Park in Old Town, and the Ferry Landing Marketplace in Coronado all have well-marked public restrooms. In general, you won't have a problem finding one (all restaurants, including fast-food outlets, are required to have one). Restrooms are usually clean and accessible.

Smoking Smoking is prohibited in nearly all indoor public places, including theaters, hotel lobbies, and enclosed shopping malls. In 1998, California enacted legislation prohibiting smoking in all restaurants and bars, except those with outdoor seating. *Note:* At press time, City Council debate was underway regarding the banning of smoking at all city beaches and parks.

Taxes Sales tax in restaurants and shops is 7.75%. Hotel tax is 10.5%.

Time Zone San Diego, like the rest of the West Coast, is in the Pacific Standard Time zone, which is 8 hours behind Greenwich Mean Time. Daylight-saving time is observed. To check the time, call © **619/853-1212.**

Transit Information Call © **619/233-3004** (TTY/TDD 619/234-5005). If you know your bus route and just need schedule information, call © **619/685-4900.**

Useful Telephone Numbers For the latest San Diego arts and entertainment information, call © **619/238-0700;** for half-price day-of-performance tickets, call © **619/497-5000;** for a beach and surf report, call © **619/221-8824.**

Weather Call © **619/289-1212.**

Where to Stay

Where would you prefer to sleep? Over the water or right next to the sand? In Victorian surroundings or in hip, modern digs adjacent to downtown nightlife? Facing the bay or ocean or overlooking carefully landscaped gardens? San Diego offers a variety of places to stay that range from pricey high-rise hostelries to spa- and golf-blessed resorts, from inexpensive cookie-cutter motels to out-of-the-ordinary B&Bs.

This chapter explores all the options within the city proper. Lodging recommendations for Del Mar, Encinitas, and Carlsbad (all beautifully situated along the coast and within 40 min. of the city) are found in chapter 11, as are hotels for the Disneyland area, south of the border, and inland regions.

High season is vaguely defined as the summer period between Memorial Day and Labor Day—some hotels inch rates higher still in July and August. However, as San Diego has grown into a convention destination, you'll find that rates for the larger downtown hotels and a few of the Mission Valley hotels are largely determined by the ebb and flow of conventions in town—weekend and holiday rates can be good bargains. On the other hand, leisure oriented hotels along the coast and in Mission Valley are generally busier on weekends, especially in summer, so midweek deals are easier to snag. Here's an idea to maximize your discounts: Spend the weekend at a downtown high-rise and duck into a beach bungalow on Monday.

SAVING ON YOUR HOTEL ROOM

A hotel's "rack rate" is the official published rate, and those are the prices quoted here. They will help you make an apples-to-apples comparison. The truth is, though, *hardly anybody pays rack rates,* and with the exception of smaller B&Bs, you can usually pay quite a bit less than the rates shown below. Here's how the price categories are organized:

- **Very Expensive:** $275 and up
- **Expensive:** $190 to $274
- **Moderate:** $120 to $189
- **Inexpensive:** under $120

These are all high-season prices, with no discounts applied. But *always* peruse the category above your target price—you might just find the perfect match, especially if you follow the advice below.

- Ask about special rates or other discounts.
- Dial direct.
- Book online.
- Remember the law of supply and demand.
- Look into group or long-stay discounts.
- Avoid excess charges and hidden costs.

Tips **What's Your Best Rate for Tonight?**

Trying to score the lowest rate for a downtown hotel can be an amusing exercise, providing a convention hasn't sucked up the availability. As an experiment, I called all the major downtown hotels one Tuesday morning to see what their best rate on a room for that same night would be. In all instances the rate I was quoted was 25% to 40% lower than the rack rate. When I called the Grand Hyatt, I was first quoted $240—a third off the rack rate. The price fell to $220 when I mentioned my AAA membership. I said, "Thanks, I'll get back to you." The very helpful reservations agent countered, "Let me check to see if there are any packages available." Within a few seconds she found a rate of $139 that included breakfast for two, free parking (a $15 savings), and a 15% discount off dinner at the hotel. I started to end the call again, and she cut me off to say, "Oh, here's a $99 promotional rate you might want to consider . . ."

- Book an efficiency.
- Investigate reservation services such as **Quikbook** (© **800/789-9887,** includes fax-on-demand service; www.quikbook.com), **Hotel Locators** (© **800/423-7846;** www.hotellocators.com); **Accommodations Express** (© **800/950-4685;** www.accommodationsexpress.com); and **Hotel Discounts** (© **800/715-7666;** www.hoteldiscounts.com).

Note: Rates given in this chapter do not include the hotel tax, which is an additional 10.5%.

BED & BREAKFASTS

Travelers who seek bed-and-breakfast accommodations will be pleasantly surprised by the variety and affordability of San Diego B&Bs (especially compared to the rest of California). Many B&Bs are traditional, strongly reflecting the personality of an on-site innkeeper, and offering as few as two guest rooms; others accommodate more guests in a slickly professional way. Ten B&Bs are part of the close-knit **San Diego Bed & Breakfast Guild** (© **619/523-1300;** www.bandbguildsandiego.org), whose members work actively at keeping prices reasonable; many good B&Bs average $100 to $125 a night.

HOSTELS

Those in search of less expensive accommodations should check in to San Diego's collection of hostels. You should have your own sack sheet or sleeping bag (or plan to rent one), and be prepared for shared dorm-style rooms, although private rooms are also found at most. Communal kitchens are also available at most hostels. Reservations are a good idea *any* time of year, and overbooking is not uncommon.

USAHostels (© **800/438-8622** or 619/232-3100; www.usahostels.com) is in the heart of the Gaslamp Quarter at 726 Fifth Ave., in a historic building; private rooms cost $59 and dorm rooms run $23 per person. Also in the Gaslamp is **HI Downtown Hostel** (© **888/464-4872,** ext. 156, or 619/525-1533; www.sandiegohostels.com), 521 Market St. This facility has 120 beds, including 24 private rooms; no alcohol is allowed on the premises. Private rooms start at $55 and dorm rooms start at $21. Hostelling International also has a 53-bed location in **Point Loma** (© **888/464-4872,** ext. 157, or 619/223-4778), 3790 Udall St., which is about 2 miles inland from

Ocean Beach; rates run $19 per person, and private rooms that sleep two are $48. The **Ocean Beach International Hostel,** 4961 Newport Ave. (© **800/339-7263** or 619/223-7873; www.californiahostel.com), has more than 60 beds and is just 2 blocks from the beach; bunk rates are $20 per person, and they offer free pickup from the airport, train, or bus station. There's an extensive collection of DVDs for guests, and free barbecues are held Tuesday and Friday.

1 Best Hotel Bets

- **Best Historic Hotel:** The **Hotel del Coronado,** 1500 Orange Ave. (© **800/468-3533** or 619/435-6611), positively oozes history. Opened in 1888, this Victorian masterpiece had some of the first electric lights in existence, and popular myth has it that the course of history was changed when the Prince of Wales met Wallis Simpson here at a ball. Meticulous restoration has enhanced this glorious landmark, whose early days are well chronicled in displays throughout the hotel. See p. 93.
- **Best for a Romantic Getaway:** You don't need to know much about Craftsman-style architecture to appreciate the taste and keen workmanship that went into creating **The Lodge at Torrey Pines,** 11480 North Torrey Pines Rd. (© **800/566-0087** or 858/453-4420). The lodge—one of only two AAA five-diamond hotels in the county—sits next to the Torrey Pines Golf Course, San Diego's top links. You can enjoy a fireplace in your room, sunset ocean views from your balcony, and superb meals at the hotel's A.R. Valentien restaurant. See p. 89.
- **Best for Families:** The **Paradise Point Resort & Spa,** 1404 Vacation Rd. (© **800/344-2626** or 858/274-4630), is a tropical playground offering enough activities to keep family members of all ages happy. In addition to a virtual Disneyland of on-site options, the aquatic playground of Mission Bay surrounds the hotel's private peninsula. See p. 85.
- **Best Moderately Priced Hotel:** The **Horton Grand Hotel,** 311 Island Ave. (© **800/542-1886** or 619/544-1886), is a Victorian landmark full of creature comforts that belie its friendly rates. You'll also be smack-dab in the heart of the trendy Gaslamp Quarter. See p. 73.
- **Best Budget Hotel:** In San Diego's Little Italy, **La Pensione Hotel,** 606 W. Date St. (© **800/232-4683** or 619/236-8000), feels like a small European hotel and offers tidy lodgings at bargain prices. There's an abundance of great dining in the surrounding blocks, and you'll be perfectly situated to explore the rest of town by car or trolley. See p. 74.
- **Best Bed-and-Breakfast:** The picture-perfect **Heritage Park Bed & Breakfast Inn,** 2470 Heritage Park Row (© **800/995-2470** or 619/299-6832), has it all: an exquisitely maintained Victorian house, lively and gracious hosts who delight in creating a pampering and romantic ambience, and an Old Town location equally close to downtown, Hillcrest, and Mission Bay. See p. 79.
- **Best Boutique Inn:** Smartly located in the center of La Jolla, the 20-room **Hotel Parisi,** 1111 Prospect St. (© **877/472-7474** or 858/454-1511), has the composed, quiet feel of a Zen garden, with feng shui–inspired suites, modern furnishings, and subdued color schemes. See p. 88.
- **Best Place to Stay on the Beach:** Although the Hotel Del operation is truly the grande dame of West Coast seaside resorts, if you really want to be in the heart of San Diego's beach culture, no place is better than **Tower 23,** 723 Felspar St.

(© **866/869-3723**). This sleek, modernist hotel—which takes its name from a nearby lifeguard station—sits right on the Pacific Beach boardwalk. See p. 81.

- **Best Hotel for Travelers with Disabilities:** While many of San Diego's hotels make minimal concessions to wheelchair-accessibility codes, downtown's **Manchester Grand Hyatt San Diego** 1 Market Place (© **800/233-1234** or 619/232-1234), goes the distance. There are 23 rooms with roll-in showers and lowered closet racks and peepholes. Ramps are an integral part of all the public spaces, rather than an afterthought. The hotel's Braille labeling is also thorough. See below.

- **Best Hotel Pool:** At **Hotel Solamar,** 435 Sixth Ave. (© **877/230-0300** or 619/531-8740), it's not so much the pool as the bar around it that makes it special. Jbar, as it is known, has a great vibe that lasts well into the night, thanks to the fire pits and comfy lounges. The fourth-floor setting is also a nice vantage point from which to check out the Gaslamp Quarter action. See below. For a more private, guests-only experience, the genteel pool at **La Valencia,** 1132 Prospect St. (© **800/451-0772** or 858/454-0771), is oh-so-special, with its spectacular setting overlooking Scripps Park and the Pacific. See p. 88.

2 Downtown, the Gaslamp & Little Italy

San Diego's downtown is an excellent place for leisure travelers to stay. The nightlife and dining in the Gaslamp Quarter and Horton Plaza shopping are close at hand; Balboa Park, Hillcrest, Old Town, and Coronado are less than 10 minutes away by car; and beaches aren't much farther. It's also the city's public-transportation hub, and thus very convenient for car-free visitors.

Conventions are big business, and the high-rise hotels cater primarily to the meet-and-greet crowd. While they don't offer much personality for leisure travelers, it's not hard to get rooms for 30% to 50% off the rack rates when a convention isn't taking up all the availability. Although their rack rates start in the mid-$300s, chain operations are a good place to test your wheelin'-and-dealin' skills. Start with the city's biggest hotel, the 1,625-room **Manchester Grand Hyatt San Diego** ★★, 1 Market Place (© **800/233-1234** or 619/232-1234; www.hyatt.com), a two-towered behemoth with a 40th-floor cocktail lounge with fabulous views. Then there's the 223-room **Westgate Hotel** ★★★, 1055 Second Ave. (© **800/221-3802** or 619/238-1818; www.westgatehotel.com), where the lobby looks transplanted out of the Palace of Versailles and rooms are plush, spacious, and bright. The **San Diego Marriott Gaslamp Quarter** ★★ (© **888/236-2427** or 619/696-0234; www.sandiegogaslamp hotel.com) has 306 rooms but a boutique feel, and features a popular rooftop bar that overlooks the city from 22 stories up. **Hotel Solamar** ★★ (© **877/230-0300;** www.hotelsolamar.com), a 235-room, stylishly urban Kimpton Hotels property, also draws nonguests to revel in its restaurant and bar.

Condo-hotels—privately owned apartments that serve part-time duty as hotel rooms—have been popular in Miami, New York, and Las Vegas, and now they are arriving in San Diego in a high-profile way. Ironically, both major projects are affiliated with music-based ventures: House of Blues and Hard Rock Cafe. **The Diegan** (© **619/702-6666;** www.diegan.com), scheduled to open in the fall, is a 21-story tower that rises alongside of, and connects to, the House of Blues. It will have such essential amenities as a recording studio, screening room, and sky bar. The **Hard Rock**

Where to Stay in Downtown San Diego

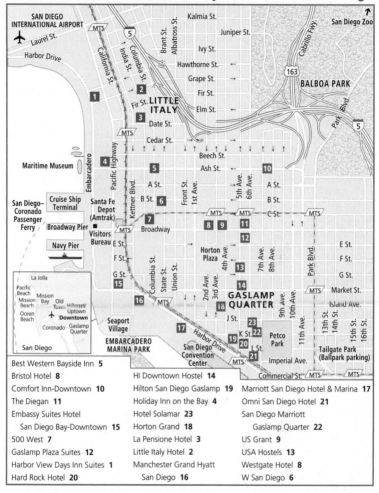

Best Western Bayside Inn **5**	HI Downtown Hostel **14**	Marriott San Diego Hotel & Marina **17**
Bristol Hotel **8**	Hilton San Diego Gaslamp **19**	Omni San Diego Hotel **21**
Comfort Inn-Downtown **10**	Holiday Inn on the Bay **4**	San Diego Marriott
The Diegan **11**	Hotel Solamar **23**	Gaslamp Quarter **22**
Embassy Suites Hotel	Horton Grand **18**	US Grant **9**
San Diego Bay-Downtown **15**	La Pensione Hotel **3**	USA Hostels **13**
500 West **7**	Little Italy Hotel **2**	Westgate Hotel **8**
Gaslamp Plaza Suites **12**	Manchester Grand Hyatt	W San Diego **6**
Harbor View Days Inn Suites **1**	San Diego **16**	
Hard Rock Hotel **20**		

Hotel (© **888/230-7625**; www.hardrock.com) is scheduled for a spring opening, adding 12 stories to the Gaslamp Quarter skyline, along with a spa, 7,000-square-foot concert venue, retail boutiques, and a lounge and bar designed by nightlife tastemaker Rande Gerber.

For a more moderate choice, in terms of price, go with the colorful, modern **Bristol Hotel,** 1055 First Ave. (© **800/662-4477** or 619/232-6141; www.bristolhotel sandiego.com), adjacent to the Gaslamp Quarter. In the budget category, the 260-room **500 West,** 500 W. Broadway (© **619/234-5252**), offers small but comfortable rooms for $69 to $89 a night in a seven-story building dating to 1924. It offers contemporary style, history, and a good location, but bathrooms are down the hall. Cheaper still are downtown's two hostels, where double rooms start at about $55 and dorm rooms are under $25: **USA Hostels** (© **800/438-8622** or 619/232-3100; www.usahostels.com) is in the heart of the Gaslamp, at 726 Fifth Ave; **HI Downtown Hostel** (© **888/464-4872,** ext. 156, or 619/525-1531; www.sandiegohostels.org) is nearby, at 521 Market St.

VERY EXPENSIVE

Embassy Suites Hotel San Diego Bay–Downtown ★★   What might seem like an impersonal business hotel can actually work out to be a good deal for families, if you can snag a room when a big convention isn't forcing up downtown rates. This spot provides modern accommodations with lots of room for families or claustrophobes. Built in 1988, the neoclassical high-rise is topped with a distinctive neon bull's-eye that's visible from far away. Every room is a suite, with a king or two doubles in the bedroom, plus a sofa bed in the living/dining area; each has convenient features like a kitchenette and a dining table that converts into a work area. All rooms open onto a 12-story atrium filled with palm trees, koi ponds, and a bubbling fountain; each also has a city or bay view. One block from Seaport Village and 8 blocks from the Gaslamp Quarter, the Embassy Suites may be a second-tier choice of convention groups (after the pricier Grand Hyatt and Marriott), but it provides solid extras like a full breakfast and complimentary evening cocktail hour.

601 Pacific Hwy. (at N. Harbor Dr.), San Diego, CA 92101. © 800/362-2779 or 619/239-2400. Fax 619/239-1520. www.embassysuites.com. 337 suites. $279–$329 suite. Extra person $20. Rates include full breakfast and afternoon cocktail. Children under 18 stay free in parent's room. AE, DC, DISC, MC, V. Valet parking $20; indoor self-parking $16. Bus: 7. Trolley: Seaport Village. **Amenities:** 2 restaurants; indoor pool; tennis court; exercise room; Jacuzzi; concierge; car-rental desk; babysitting; laundry service; self-service laundry. *In room:* A/C, TV w/pay movies, dataport, kitchenette, fridge, coffeemaker, hair dryer, iron.

Hilton San Diego Gaslamp Quarter ★★★   At the foot of the Gaslamp Quarter and across the street from the Convention Center, this hotel is ideally situated for business travelers. Yet unlike some of its competition, the Hilton doesn't overwhelm with size, making it a great place for guests who want to be close to the action (which includes loads of restaurants, nightlife, and the ballpark within a few blocks), but not get lost in the shuffle. The hotel opened in 2001 on the site of the old Bridgeworks building—part of San Diego's original wharf a century ago; much of the brick facade was incorporated into the hotel's polished design. Standard rooms boast upmarket furniture, including an overstuffed chair and ottoman, down comforters, and pillow-top mattresses. There are suites and an executive floor, but the really snazzy picks are rooms in the intimate Enclave wing, a converted office space next to the main building that features 30 oversize guest rooms with towering ceilings, custom furnishings, Frette linens, and lavish bathrooms sporting whirlpool tubs. No two of the Enclave units have the same floor plan, but they are some of the handsomest hotel rooms downtown, resembling swinging lofts more than typical chain hotel rooms.

401 K St. (at Fourth Ave.), San Diego, CA 92101. © 800/445-8667 or 619/231-4040. Fax 619/231-6439. www. hilton.com. 282 units. $329 double; from $399 suite. Children under 12 stay free in parent's room. AE, DC, DISC, MC, V. Valet parking $21. Trolley: Gaslamp Quarter. **Amenities:** 2 restaurants; 2 bars; outdoor pool; health club and full-service spa; Jacuzzi; concierge; business center; salon; 24-hr. room service; laundry service; dry cleaning. *In room:* A/C, TV w/pay movies, dataport, minibar, coffeemaker, hair dryer, iron.

Marriott San Diego Hotel & Marina ★★   In the prosperous late 1980s, well before San Diego's Convention Center was even a blueprint, this stylish mirrored tower arose. By the time a second tower took shape, adding more rooms and multiple banquet- and ballrooms, the Marriott *was* a convention center. Today it merely stands next door, garnering a large share of convention attendees. They're drawn to the scenic 446-slip marina, lush grounds, waterfall pool, and breathtaking bay-and-beyond views. The Marriott competes with the newer Grand Hyatt next door, so guests benefit from constantly improved facilities and decor. Leisure travelers can also take advantage of greatly reduced weekend rates and enjoy a free-form tropical pool area (at the edge of downtown, no less). Note that all rooms in the north tower have a small balcony, but only the suites in the south tower do. Because the Marriott tends to focus on public features and business services, guest quarters are well maintained but plain, and standard rooms are on the small side. Hallway noise can sometimes be disturbing.

333 W. Harbor Dr. (at Front St.), San Diego, CA 92101-7700. ✆ **800/228-9290** or 619/234-1500. Fax 619/234-8678. www.marriott.com. 1,408 units. $295–$429 double; from $750 suite. Children under 18 stay free in parent's room. AE, DC, DISC, MC, V. Valet parking $24; self-parking $18. Bus: 4. Trolley: Convention Center. Pets accepted. **Amenities:** 3 restaurants; bar; 2 lagoon-like outdoor pools; 6 night-lit tennis courts; fitness center; 2 Jacuzzis; sauna; boat rental; bike rental; game room; concierge; tour desk; car-rental desk; business center with secretarial services; salon; 24-hr. room service; coin-op laundry and laundry service; dry cleaning. *In room:* A/C, TV w/pay movies, dataport, minibar, coffeemaker, hair dryer, iron, safe.

Omni San Diego Hotel ★★   This downtown property is noteworthy for the fourth-floor "skybridge" that connects it with PETCO Park—it's the only hotel in the United States that's directly linked to a major-league facility. Twelve rooms even have (limited) views of the field. There's also a signature suite decked out in baseball collector's items (trimmed in the Padres' navy and orange color scheme), and the hotel's common areas are decorated with baseball memorabilia, such as Babe Ruth's 1932 contract with the Yankees and Joe DiMaggio's cleats from his 1941 streak. Packages that include tickets to a Padres game are available—so if you want to be in the heart of the baseball action, this is it. The rest of the year, this $124-million, 32-story highrise competes for the business crowd, luring conventioneers with more than 27,000 square feet of meeting space and an up-to-the-minute business center. Street-level function space is fronted by a surprisingly adventurous art gallery that focuses on the work of California artists. Rooms feature work desks, dual-line telephones, and 330-count Egyptian cotton sheets. A sixth-floor rooftop terrace has a double-sided fireplace, an outdoor swimming pool, and a Jacuzzi.

675 L St. (at Sixth Ave.), San Diego, CA 92101. ✆ **800/843-6664** or 619/231-6664. Fax 619/231-8060. www.omni hotels.com. 511 units. $329 double; from $500 suite. Children under 12 stay free in parent's room. Packages available. AE, DC, DISC, MC, V. Valet parking $24. Trolley: Gaslamp Quarter. Pets under 50 lbs. accepted with $50 nonrefundable fee. **Amenities:** 2 restaurants; 2 bars; outdoor pool; fitness center; Jacuzzi; concierge; business center; 24-hr. room service; laundry service; dry cleaning. *In room:* A/C, TV w/DVD player, dataport, minibar, coffeemaker, hair dryer, iron, safe, treadmill (upon request).

US Grant Hotel   At press time, this historic hotel was slated to reopen in late 2006 as part of Starwood Hotels & Resorts Worldwide's prestigious Luxury Collection after undergoing a huge ($52 million is the current estimate) renovation. The comprehensive restoration includes overhauling guest rooms, food and beverage facilities, lobby areas, and meeting space with a focus on returning the property to an ambience and atmosphere in keeping with its 1910 origins.

326 Broadway (at 4th Ave.), San Diego, CA 92101. ✆ **619/232-3121.** www.usgrant.net. 285 units. Call for rates. Trolley: Gaslamp Quarter. **Amenities:** Restaurant; bar; health club; Jacuzzi; concierge; room service; laundry service; dry cleaning. *In room:* A/C, TV w/pay movies, dataport, coffeemaker, hair dryer.

W San Diego ★★   The W took the city by storm when it opened in 2003, delivering swanky nightlife beyond the Gaslamp Quarter. The place is still packed on weekends, with lines out the door to get into the hotel bars. Fortunately, rooms are bright and cheery—like mod beach cabanas beamed into downtown, replete with a sexy shower. *Nouveau nautique* is the theme, with elegant aqua and sand tones accenting the whites, a window seat (great idea) for gazing down on this languid corner of downtown, and a beach-ball-shaped pillow, a blunt reminder this hotel is supposed to be fun. The WoW suite on the 19th floor is a 1,250-square-foot luxury accommodation with a host of state-of-the-art features and killer skyline views. The restaurant **Rice** stumbled out of the gate initially, but it has gotten back on track with an adventurous and playful menu of contemporary global cuisine. The adjoining bar, **Magnet,** has a sassy martini menu; while the airy lobby bar, **Living Room,** has turntables and board games (good luck concentrating on your chess match). **Beach,** on the third floor, is where the developers let it rip: The open-air bar has a sand floor (heated at night), a fire pit, and cabanas. Drinks are served in plastic, allowing you to safely roam the terrace barefoot. The cacophony dies down by Sunday when Los Angelinos depart, and for a few days, the W is a proper business hotel—albeit one with a (tiny) pool, a 24-hour open-air gym, and a bank of 18 video screens glowing with an idealized landscape of bubbles floating heavenward.

421 W. B St. (at State St.), San Diego, CA 92101. © **888/625-5144** or 619/231-8220. Fax 619/231-5779. www. whotels.com/sandiego. 259 units. $329–$469 double; $700–$3,000 suite. AE, DC, DISC, MC, V. Valet parking $23. Bus: All Broadway routes. Trolley: American Plaza or Civic Center. **Amenities:** Restaurant; 3 lounges; 24-hr. concierge; 24-hr. room service; laundry/dry-cleaning service. *In room:* A/C, TV w/VCR and DVD, CD player, dataport, minibar, coffeemaker, hair dryer, iron, safe.

EXPENSIVE

Holiday Inn on the Bay ★★ *Kids*   This better-than-average Holiday Inn is reliable and nearly always offers great deals. The three-building high-rise complex is on the Embarcadero across from the harbor and the Maritime Museum. This scenic spot is only 1½ miles from the airport (you can watch planes landing and taking off) and 2 blocks from the train station and trolley. Rooms, while basic and identical, always seem to sport clean new furnishings and plenty of thoughtful comforts. The only choice you have to make is whether you want marvelous bay views or a look at San Diego's still-evolving skyline. In either case, request the highest floor possible.

1355 N. Harbor Dr. (at Ash St.), San Diego, CA 92101-3385. © **800/465-4329** or 619/232-3861. Fax 619/232-4924. www.holiday-inn.com/san-onthebay. 600 units. $171 double; from $299 suite. Children under 18 stay free in parent's room. AE, DC, MC, V. Self-parking $18; valet $22. Bus: All Pacific Hwy. routes. Trolley: American Plaza. Pets accepted with $25 nonrefundable fee and $100 deposit. **Amenities:** 4 restaurants; lounge; outdoor heated pool; exercise room; concierge; business center; room service (6–11am and 5–11pm); babysitting; laundry service; self-service laundry. *In room:* A/C, TV w/pay movies, dataport, coffeemaker, hair dryer, iron.

MODERATE

Best Western Bayside Inn   This high-rise representative of reliable Best Western, offers quiet lodgings, even though this corner of downtown has been a hotbed of redevelopment. The area has been reshaped into an urban neighborhood saturated with upscale condos, but there's far less of the Gaslamp Quarter's hubbub here. Although calling it "bayview" would be more accurate than "bayside," rooms in the 14-story hotel reveal nice city and harbor views. Rooms and bathrooms are basic chain-hotel issue, but they are well maintained and have balconies overlooking the bay or down-town (ask for the higher floors). The accommodating staff makes this a mecca for budget-minded business travelers, and this Best Western is also close to downtown's tourist sites. It's an easy walk to the Embarcadero, a bit farther to Horton Plaza, and just 3 blocks to the train station.

555 W. Ash St. (at Columbia St.), San Diego, CA 92101. ℂ **800/341-1818** or 619/233-7500. Fax 619/239-8060. www.baysideinn.com. 122 units. $189 double. Extra person $10. Children under 12 stay free in parent's room. Rates include continental breakfast. AE, DC, DISC, MC, V. Parking $7–$15. Bus: 5 or 16. Trolley: Little Italy. **Amenities:** Restaurant (breakfast daily, dinner Mon–Fri only; no lunch); outdoor pool; Jacuzzi; laundry service; dry cleaning; air-port shuttle. *In room:* A/C, TV w/pay movies, dataport, fridge, microwave, coffeemaker, hair dryer, iron.

Horton Grand ℛ *(Finds*   A cross between an elegant hotel and a charming inn, the Horton Grand combines two hotels that date from 1886: the Horton Grand (once an infamous red-light establishment) and the Brooklyn Hotel (which for a time was the Kayle Saddlery Shop). Both were saved from demolition, moved to this spot, and con-nected by an airy atrium lobby filled with white wicker. The facade, with its graceful bay windows, is original. Each room is utterly unique, containing vintage furnishings and gas fireplaces—bathrooms are lush with reproduction floor tiles, fine brass fix-tures, and genteel appointments. Rooms overlook either the city or the fig tree–filled courtyard; they're divided between the clubby and darker "saddlery" side and the pas-tel-toned and Victorian "brothel" side. The suites (really just large studio-style rooms) are in a newer wing; choosing one means sacrificing historic character for a sitting area/sofa bed and minibar with microwave. With all the individuality, there's a room that's right for you, so query your reservationist on the different features (if you're lonely, request room 309, where the resident ghost, Roger, likes to hang out). The Palace Bar serves afternoon tea Saturdays from 2:30 to 5pm.

311 Island Ave. (at Fourth Ave.), San Diego, CA 92101. ℂ **800/542-1886** or 619/544-1886. Fax 619/239-3823. www.hortongrand.com. 132 units. $169–$199 double; from $269 suite. Extra person $20. Children under 18 stay free in parent's room. AE, DC, MC, V. Valet parking $20. Bus: 1, 4, 5, 16, or 25. Trolley: Convention Center. **Amenities:** Restaurant (breakfast Fri–Sat, dinner, and Sun brunch only); bar; business center. *In room:* A/C, TV, dataport, hair dryer.

INEXPENSIVE

Inexpensive motels line Pacific Highway between the airport and downtown. The **Harbor View Days Inn Suites,** 1919 Pacific Hwy. at Grape Street (ℂ **800/325-2525** or 619/232-1077), is within walking distance of the Embarcadero, the Maritime Museum, and the Harbor Excursion. Rates start around $90. Also see "Hostels," ear-lier on p. 66.

Comfort Inn–Downtown   In the northern corner of downtown, this place is good for business travelers without expense accounts and vacationers who just need reliable, safe accommodations. This humble chain motel must be surprised to find itself in a quickly gentrifying part of town: The landmark El Cortez Hotel across the street has been transformed into upscale condos and shops, and new residential construction is winding down on the surrounding blocks. The Comfort Inn is smartly designed so rooms open onto exterior walkways surrounding the drive-in entry courtyard, lending an insular feel in this once-dicey corner of town. There are few frills here, but coffee is always brewing in the lobby. The hotel operates a free shuttle to the airport and the train and bus stations. *Note:* The hilltop location gives thighs a workout on the walk to and from the Gaslamp Quarter, but third-floor rooms offer the best chance of a view.

719 Ash St. (at Seventh Ave.), San Diego, CA 92101. ℂ **800/404-6835** or 619/232-2525. Fax 619/687-3024. www.comfortinnsandiego.com. 67 units. $139–$174 double. Extra person $15. Children under 18 stay free in parent's room. Rates include continental breakfast. AE, DISC, MC, V. Free parking. Bus: 1, 3, 25, or 992. **Amenities:** Plunge pool; Jacuzzi; laundry service. *In room:* A/C, TV, dataport, coffeemaker, iron.

Gaslamp Plaza Suites 𝕮𝕮 ⟨*Value*⟩   You can't get closer to the center of the vibrant Gaslamp Quarter than this beautifully restored late Victorian. At 11 stories, it was San Diego's first skyscraper, built in 1913. Crafted (at great expense) of Australian gumwood, marble, brass, and exquisite etched glass, the splendid building originally housed San Diego Trust & Savings. Various other businesses (jewelers, lawyers, doctors, photographers) set up shop here until 1988, when the elegant structure was placed on the National Register of Historic Places and reopened as a boutique hotel. You'll be surprised at the timeless elegance, from the wide corridors to guest rooms furnished with European flair. Each bears the name of a writer (Emerson, Swift, Zola, Shelley, Fitzgerald, and so on). Most rooms are spacious and offer luxuries rare in this price range, like pillow-top mattresses and premium toiletries; microwaves and dinnerware; and impressive luxury bathrooms. Beware of the cheapest rooms on the back side—they are uncomfortably small (although they do have regular-size bathrooms) and have no view. The higher floors boast splendid city and bay views, as do the rooftop patio and breakfast room. Despite the welcome addition of noise-muffling windows, don't be surprised to hear a hum from the street below, especially when the Quarter gets rockin' on the weekends.

520 E St. (corner of Fifth Ave.), San Diego, CA 92101. ℂ **800/874-8770** or 619/232-9500. Fax 619/238-9945. www.gaslampplaza.com. 64 units. $109–$159 double; from $199 suite. Rates include continental breakfast. AE, DC, DISC, MC, V. Valet parking $20. Bus: 1, 3, or 25. Trolley: Fifth Ave. **Amenities:** Limited room service (lunch and dinner). *In room:* A/C, TV/VCR, dataport, fridge, microwave, coffeemaker, hair dryer, iron, safe.

La Pensione Hotel 𝕮 ⟨*Value*⟩   This place has a lot going for it: modern amenities, remarkable value, a convenient location in Little Italy within walking distance of the central business district, a friendly staff, and free parking (a premium for small hotels in San Diego). The four-story Pensione is built around a courtyard and feels like a small European hotel. The decor throughout is modern and streamlined, with plenty of sleek black and metallic surfaces, crisp white walls, and modern wood furnishings. Guest rooms, while not overly large, make the most of their space and leave you with room to move around. Each room offers a ceiling fan and minifridge; some have a small balcony. None have air-conditioning, which could be a concern on a hot day—you can open your window, but note that street cafes stay busy till midnight on weekends. If you're sensitive to noise, request a room away from the street, though this means no bay or city view. La Pensione is within walking distance of eateries (two restaurants are directly downstairs), nightspots, and a trolley station.

606 W. Date St. (at India St.), San Diego, CA 92101. ℂ **800/232-4683** or 619/236-8000. Fax 619/236-8088. www.lapensionehotel.com. 80 units. $90 double. AE, DC, DISC, MC, V. Limited free underground parking. Bus: 5 or 16. Trolley: Little Italy. **Amenities:** Self-service laundry. *In room:* TV, dataport, fridge.

Little Italy Hotel   This renovated 1910 property is a boutique bed-and-breakfast right in the heart of San Diego's Italian cultural village, just steps from quaint bakeries, delightful eateries, and hip boutiques, and a few blocks from the historic Gaslamp Quarter and Balboa Park. While preserving the building's historic architecture, they have added the latest in guest comforts, including a secluded courtyard pool (a rare treat in Little Italy) and European-style continental breakfast each morning. Wide hallways lead into a variety of unique rooms featuring luxury touches like bay views,

Jacuzzi tubs, oversize closets, wood floors, and spacious baths with plush bathrobes. Upgraded conveniences include free HBO, wireless Internet access, and free local calls.

505 W. Grape St. (at India St.), San Diego, CA 92101. **C** **800/518-9930** or 619/230-1600. Fax 619/230-0322. www.littleitalyhotel.com. 23 units. From $79 double; from $149 suite. Rates include continental breakfast. AE, DC, MC, V. *In room:* A/C, TV, safe.

3 Hillcrest & Uptown

Although they're no longer a secret, the gentrified historic neighborhoods north of downtown are still something of a bargain. They're convenient to Balboa Park and offer easy access to the rest of town. Filled with casual and upscale restaurants, eclectic shops, and percolating nightlife, the area is also easy to navigate. All of the following accommodations cater to the mainstream market and attract a gay and lesbian clientele as well.

A note on driving directions: You can reach all of these accommodations from I-5.

VERY EXPENSIVE

Britt Scripps Inn ✦✦✦   One of San Diego's most glorious Victorian houses was lovingly restored in 2005 into what is now known as the Britt Scripps Inn. Built around 1887, the property was occupied for more than 45 years by one of San Diego's most prominent families: the Scripps. To this day the name is attached locally to everything from hospitals to newspapers. The home and surrounding grounds have been converted into a 9-room "estate hotel"—part B&B, part luxury hotel. Offering first-class amenities like 1,000-thread-count sheets, flat-screen TVs (most hidden in antique armoires), free Wi-Fi, and heated towel racks, this gracious lady lays on the personal charm as well, with gourmet breakfasts including homemade pastries and breads, late-afternoon wine and cheese, and a vintage Steinway piano in the music alcove. Staff is always on site, but usually out of sight. The Britt Scripps Inn has a list of striking architectural elements—seven gables, a dramatic turret, wraparound porch, twisting oak staircase—but one feature stands out above the rest: a two-story, three-paneled stained-glass window. Be sure to catch sunset through it. And it's all just a block away from Balboa Park.

406 Maple St. (at Fourth Ave.), San Diego, CA 92103. **C** **888/881-1991** or 619/230-1991. Fax 619/230-1188. www.brittscripps.com. 9 units. $385–$525 double. Rates include full breakfast and afternoon wine and hors d'oeuvres. AE, DC, MC, V. Bus: 3, 25, 990; 15 and 115 (selected trips). Take the Laurel St. exit off I-5, make a left on Laurel, a left on Fifth Ave., and a left on Maple St. *In room:* A/C, TV w/DVD, CD player, MP3, Wi-Fi, 2-line phone, coffeemaker, hair dryer, iron, safe.

MODERATE

Crone's Cobblestone Cottage Bed & Breakfast ✦ *Finds*   After just 1 night at this magnificently restored Craftsman bungalow, you'll feel like an honored guest rather than a paying customer. Artist and bookmaker Joan Crone lives in the architectural award-winning addition to her 1913 home, which is a designated historical landmark. Guests have the run of the entire house, including a book-filled, wood-paneled den and antique-filled living room. Both cozy guest rooms have antique beds, goose-down pillows and comforters, and eclectic bedside reading. They share a full bathroom; the Eaton Room also has a private half bathroom. You can rent the entire house (two bedrooms plus the den), to sleep five or six, for $285. Crone lends a calm and

Craftsman aesthetic to the surroundings, aided by a pair of cats, who peer in from their side of the house. Mission Hills, the neighborhood a half-mile west of Hillcrest, is one of San Diego's treasures, and lots of other historic homes can be explored along quiet streets.

1302 Washington Place (4 blocks west of Goldfinch St. at Ingalls St.), San Diego, CA 92103. ℭ **619/295-4765.** www.cobblestonebandb.com. 2 units. $125 double. Rates include continental breakfast. 2-night minimum stay. No credit cards (checks accepted). Bus: 3. From I-5, take the Washington St. exit east uphill. Make a U-turn at Goldfinch, and then keep right at the Y intersection onto Washington Place. *In room:* No phone.

Sommerset Suites Hotel ☆
This five-story all-suite hotel on a busy street was originally built as apartment housing for interns at the hospital nearby. Renovated in 1999, it retains a residential ambience and unexpected amenities such as huge closets, medicine cabinets, and fully equipped kitchens in all rooms (even dishwashers). Poolside barbecue facilities encourage warm-weather mingling. The hotel has a personal, welcoming feel, from the friendly staff to the snacks, soda, beer, and wine served each afternoon and the welcome basket with cookies and microwave popcorn. Rooms are oversize and comfortably furnished, and each has a private balcony. Be prepared for noise from the busy thoroughfare below leaking in, though. Just across the street, you'll find several blocks' worth of restaurants and shops, plus a multiplex cinema. Guest services include a van to the airport, SeaWorld, the zoo, Horton Plaza, and Old Town ($8 per trip).

606 Washington St. (at Fifth Ave.), San Diego, CA 92103. ℭ **800/962-9665** or 619/692-5200. Fax 619/692-5299. www.sommersetsuites.com. 80 units. $159–$179 double. Children under 12 stay free in parent's room. Rates include upgraded continental breakfast and afternoon refreshments. AE, DC, DISC, MC, V. Free covered parking. Bus: 1, 3, 7, 11, or 25. Take the Washington St. exit off I-5. **Amenities:** Outdoor pool; Jacuzzi; coin-op laundry. *In room:* A/C, TV, dataport, kitchen, coffeemaker, hair dryer, iron.

INEXPENSIVE

Balboa Park Inn ☆
Insiders looking for unusual accommodations head straight for this small pink inn at the northern edge of Balboa Park. It's a cluster of four Spanish colonial-style former apartment buildings in a mostly residential neighborhood a half-mile east of Hillcrest's heart. The hotel is popular with gay travelers drawn to Hillcrest's restaurants and clubs, which crop up within several blocks of the property. All the rooms and standard suites are tastefully decorated; the specialty suites, however, are over-the-top. There's the "Tara Suite," as in *Gone with the Wind;* the "Nouveau Ritz," which employs every Art Deco cliché, including mirrors and Hollywood lighting; and the "Greystoke" suite, a jumble of jungle, safari, and tropical themes with a completely mirrored bathroom and Jacuzzi tub. Seven of the rooms have Jacuzzi tubs, and most have kitchens—all have a private entrance, though the front desk operates 24 hours. From here, you're close enough to walk to the San Diego Zoo and other Balboa Park attractions.

3402 Park Blvd. (at Upas St.), San Diego, CA 92103. ℭ **800/938-8181** or 619/298-0823. Fax 619/294-8070. www.balboaparkinn.com. 26 units. $99 double; $139–$219 suites. Extra person $10. Children under 12 stay free in parent's room. Rates include continental breakfast. AE, DC, DISC, MC, V. Parking available on street. Bus: 7. From I-5, take Washington St. east, follow signs to University Ave. E., and turn right at Park Blvd. *In room:* TV, fridge, microwave, coffeemaker.

The Cottage
Built in 1913, this B&B at the end of a residential cul-de-sac is surrounded by a garden and features a private hideaway—"the cottage"—tucked behind a homestead-style house. There's an herb garden in front, birdbaths, and a walkway

0 | 1/2 mi
0 | 1/2 km

La Jolla

Pacific Beach
Mission Bay
Old Town
Hillcrest/Uptown
Ocean Beach
Downtown
Coronado
Gaslamp Quarter

San Diego

1 Washington St.

3

Goldfinch St.
Falcon St.

2

Robinson Ave.

University Ave.
Essex St.

10th Ave.
Vermont St.
Normal St.

Pennsylvania Ave.

Brookes Ave.

Brookes Ave.
Myrtle Ave.

Park Blvd.
Georgia St.
Florida Dr.
Alabama St.
Mississippi St.
Texas St.

5

Walnut Ave.
Upas St.

Upas St.

Thorn St.

Spruce St. **4**

163

Redwood St.

Richmond St.

Quince St.

Palm St.

Cabrillo Fwy.

San Diego Zoo

Nutmeg St. **6**

Maple St.

5

Laurel St.

Laurel St.
Kalmia St.

Albatross St.
Front St.
1st Ave.

3rd Ave.
4th Ave.
5th Ave.
6th Ave.

El Prado

BALBOA PARK

7 Juniper St.

Ivy St.

Reynard Wy.
Curlew Dr.

Cabrillo Fwy.

Park Blvd.

U.S. Naval Hospital

Florida Dr.

Balboa Park Inn **5**
Britt Scripps Inn **6**
The Cottage **2**
Crone's Cobblestone Cottage **1**

Keating House **7**
Park Manor Suites **4**
Sommerset Suites Hotel **3**

lined with climbing roses. The cottage has a bedroom with a king-size bed, a living room with a wood-burning stove and a queen-size sofa bed, and a charming kitchen with a coffeemaker. The guestroom in the main house features a king-size bed. Both accommodations are filled with fresh flowers and antiques put to clever uses, and each has a private entrance. Owner Carol Emerick (who used to run an antiques store—and it shows!) serves a scrumptious breakfast, complete with the morning paper. Guests are welcome to use the dining room and parlor in the main house, where they sometimes light a fire and rev up the 19th-century player piano. The Cottage is 5 blocks from the cafes of Mission Hills and Hillcrest, and a short drive from Balboa Park. Book early for this find.

3829 Albatross St. (off Robinson Ave.), San Diego, CA 92103. ☎ **619/299-1564.** Fax 619/299-6213. www.sandiegobandb.com/cottage.htm. 2 units. $75–$85 double; $99–$125 cottage. Extra person in cottage $10. 2-night minimum stay. Rates include continental breakfast. AE, DISC, MC, V. Bus: 3 or 11. Take Washington St. exit off I-5, exit at University Ave.; right on First Ave., right on Robinson Ave. *In room:* TV, fridge, hair dryer.

Keating House ★★ *Finds* This grand 1880s Bankers Hill mansion, between downtown and Hillcrest and 4 blocks from Balboa Park, has been meticulously restored by two energetic innkeepers with a solid background in architectural preservation. Doug Scott and Ben Baltic not only know old houses, but they're also neighborhood devotees filled with historical knowledge. Authentic period design is celebrated throughout, even in the overflowing gardens that bloom on four sides of this local landmark. The house contains a comfortable hodgepodge of antique furnishings and appointments; three additional rooms are in the restored carriage house opening onto an exotic garden patio. The downstairs entry, parlor, and dining room all have cozy fireplaces; bathrooms—all private—are gorgeously restored with updated period fixtures. Breakfast is served in a sunny, friendly setting; special dietary needs are cheerfully considered. In contrast to many B&Bs in Victorian-era homes, this one eschews dollhouse frills for a classy, sophisticated approach. The inn draws guests ranging from Europeans to business travelers avoiding the cookie-cutter ambience of chain hotels.

2331 Second Ave. (between Juniper and Kalmia sts.), San Diego, CA 92101. (✆ **800/995-8644** or 619/239-8585. Fax 619/239-5774. www.keatinghouse.com. 9 units. $115–$165 double. Rates include full breakfast. AE, DISC, MC, V. Bus: 1, 3, 11, or 25. From the airport, take Harbor Dr. toward downtown; turn left on Laurel St., and then right on Second Ave. *In room:* Hair dryer, no phone.

Park Manor Suites 🐾 *Value*   This eight-story property was built as a full-service luxury hotel in 1926 on a prime corner overlooking Balboa Park. One of the original investors was the family of child actor Jackie Coogan. The Hollywood connection continued; the hotel became a popular stopping-off point for celebrities headed for Mexican vacations in the 1920s and 1930s. Although dated, guest rooms are huge and very comfortable, featuring full kitchens, dining rooms, living rooms, and bedrooms with a separate dressing area. A few have glassed-in terraces; request one when you book. The overall feeling is that of a prewar East Coast apartment building, complete with steam heat and lavish moldings. Park Manor Suites does have its weaknesses, particularly bathrooms that have mostly original fixtures and could use some renovation. But prices are quite reasonable for Hillcrest; there's an old-world restaurant on the ground floor, laundry service is also available, and a simple continental breakfast buffet is served in the penthouse banquet room (the view is spectacular). On Friday evenings, the penthouse bar becomes the launching pad for the gay party scene, drawing big crowds—the lone elevator gets a real workout that night.

525 Spruce St. (between Fifth and Sixth aves.), San Diego, CA 92103. (✆ **800/874-2649** or 619/291-0999. Fax 619/291-8844. www.parkmanorsuites.com. 74 units. $99–$139 studio; $169–$199 1-bedroom suite; $199–$239 2-bedroom suite. Extra person $15. Children under 12 stay free in parent's room. Rates include continental breakfast. AE, DC, DISC, MC, V. Free parking. Bus: 1, 3, or 25. Take Washington St. exit off I-5, right on Fourth Ave., left on Spruce. **Amenities:** Restaurant/bar; access to nearby health club ($5); laundry service; dry cleaning; self-service laundry. *In room:* TV, dataport, kitchen, coffeemaker, hair dryer, iron.

4 Old Town & Mission Valley

Old Town is a popular area for families because of its proximity to Old Town State Historic Park and other attractions that are within walking distance—SeaWorld and the San Diego Zoo are within a 10-minute drive. Around the corner is Mission Valley, where you'll find the city's largest collection of hotels offering rooms under $100 a night. Mission Valley lacks much homegrown personality—this is the spot for chain restaurants and shopping malls, not gardens or water views. But it caters to convention groups, families visiting the University of San Diego or San Diego State University, and leisure travelers drawn by the lower prices and competitive facilities. *A note on driving directions:* All Old Town and Mission Valley hotels are reached from either I-5 or I-8.

Where to Stay in Old Town & Mission Valley

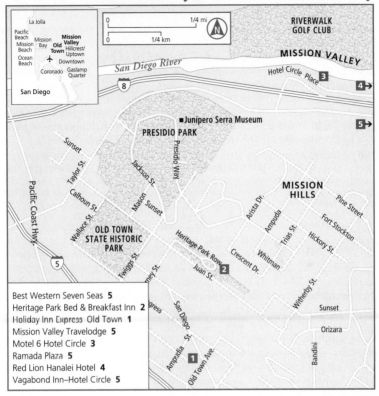

Best Western Seven Seas **5**
Heritage Park Bed & Breakfast Inn **2**
Holiday Inn Express Old Town **1**
Mission Valley Travelodge **5**
Motel 6 Hotel Circle **3**
Ramada Plaza **5**
Red Lion Hanalei Hotel **4**
Vagabond Inn–Hotel Circle **5**

MODERATE

Heritage Park Bed & Breakfast Inn ⋆⋆ This exquisite 1889 Queen Anne mansion is set in a Victorian park—an artfully arranged cobblestone cul-de-sac lined with historic buildings saved from the wrecking ball and assembled here, in Old Town, as a tourist attraction. Most of the Inn's rooms are in the main house, with a handful of equally appealing choices in an adjacent 1887 Italianate companion. Owner Nancy Helsper is an amiable and energetic innkeeper with an eye for every necessary detail; she's always eager to share tales of these homes' fascinating history and how they crossed paths with Nancy and her husband, Charles. A stay here is about surrendering to the pampering of afternoon tea, candlelight breakfast, and a number of romantic extras (champagne and chocolates, dear?) available for special celebrations. Like the gracious parlors and porches, each room is outfitted with meticulous period antiques and luxurious fabrics; the small staff provides turndown service and virtually anything else you might require. Although the fireplaces are all ornamental, some rooms have whirlpool baths. In the evenings, vintage films are shown on DVD with popcorn in the Victorian parlor.

2470 Heritage Park Row, San Diego, CA 92110. ⓒ **800/995-2470** or 619/299-6832. Fax 619/299-9465. www.
heritageparkinn.com. 12 units. $125–$280 double. Extra person $20. Rates include full breakfast and afternoon tea.
AE, DC, DISC, MC, V. Free parking. Bus: 5. Trolley: Old Town. Take I-5 to Old Town Ave., turn left onto San Diego Ave.,
and then turn right onto Harney St. *In room:* A/C, hair dryer, iron.

Holiday Inn Express–Old Town ⌘   Just a couple of easy walking blocks from the heart of Old Town, this Holiday Inn has a Spanish colonial exterior that suits the neighborhood's theme. Inside you'll find better-than-they-have-to-be contemporary furnishings and surprising small touches that make this hotel an affordable option favored by business travelers and families alike. There's nothing spectacular about the adjacent streets, so the hotel is smartly oriented toward the inside; request a room whose patio or balcony opens onto the pleasant courtyard. Rooms are thoughtfully and practically appointed, with extras like microwaves and writing tables. The lobby, surrounded by French doors, features a large fireplace, several sitting areas, and a TV. The hotel entrance, on Jefferson Street, is hard to find but worth the search.

3900 Old Town Ave., San Diego, CA 92110. © **800/465-4329** or 619/299-7400. Fax 619/299-1619. www. hiexpress.com/ex-oldtown. 125 units. $159–$169 double; from $189 suite. Extra person $10. Children under 18 stay free in parent's room. Rates include continental breakfast. AE, DC, DISC, MC, V. Parking $11. Bus: 5. Take I-5 to Old Town Ave. exit. **Amenities:** Outdoor pool; Jacuzzi; laundry service; dry cleaning. *In room:* A/C, TV, dataport, fridge, microwave, coffeemaker, iron.

Red Lion Hanalei Hotel ⌘   This Mission Valley hotel has a Polynesian theme and comfort-conscious sophistication that sets it apart from the rest of the pack. Most rooms are split between two eight-story towers, set back from the freeway and cleverly positioned so that the balconies open onto the tropically landscaped pool courtyard or the attractive links of a golf club. A few more rooms are found in the Presidio Building, which is a little too close to the freeway. The heated outdoor pool is large enough for any luau, as is the oversize Jacuzzi beside it. The hotel boasts an unmistakable 1960s vibe and Hawaiian ambience; the restaurant and bar have over-the-top kitschy decor, with waterfalls, outrigger canoes, and more. But guest rooms are outfitted with contemporary furnishings and conveniences; the sixth through eighth floors have a microwave and fridge. Services include a free shuttle to Old Town and the Fashion Valley Shopping Center, plus meeting facilities; golf packages are available.

2270 Hotel Circle N., San Diego, CA 92108. © **800/733-5466** or 619/297-1101. Fax 619/297-6049. www.hanalei hotel.com. 416 units. $159–$169 double; $275–$375 suite. AE, DISC, MC, V. Parking $8. Bus: 6. From I-8, take Hotel Circle exit, follow signs for Hotel Circle N. Pets accepted with $50 deposit. **Amenities:** 2 restaurants; bar; outdoor pool; nearby golf course; fitness center; spa/massage facility; Jacuzzi; game room; activities desk; business center; salon; limited room service (6am–10pm); laundry service; dry cleaning; coin-op laundry. *In room:* A/C, TV w/pay movies, dataport, coffeemaker, hair dryer, iron.

INEXPENSIVE

Room rates at properties on Hotel Circle are significantly cheaper than those in many other parts of the city. You'll find a cluster of inexpensive chain hotels and motels, including **Best Western Seven Seas** (© **800/421-6662** or 619/291-1300), **Mission Valley Travelodge** (© **800/255-3050** or 619/297-2271), **Ramada Plaza** (© **800/ 532-4241** or 619/291-6500), and **Vagabond Inn-Hotel Circle** (© **800/522-1555** or 619/297-1691).

Motel 6 Hotel Circle   Yes, it's a Motel 6, so you know the drill: No mint on the pillow and you have to trundle down to the front desk to retrieve a cup of coffee in the morning. On the other hand, these budget hotels—now part of the mammoth Accor chain, one of the world's largest hotel companies—know how to provide a consistent product at dependably inexpensive rates, and this one is very central to San Diego's sightseeing. The modern, four-story motel sits at the western end of Hotel Circle. Rooms are sparingly but adequately outfitted, with standard motel furnishings; bathrooms are perfunctory. Stay away from the loud freeway side—rooms in the four-story structure in back overlook a scenic 18-hole golf course and river. The hotel doesn't have a restaurant, but a fair steakhouse is across the street.

2424 Hotel Circle N., San Diego, CA 92108. ℂ **800/466-8356** or 619/296-1612. Fax 619/543-9305. www.motel6.com. 204 units. $69–$84 double. Extra person $3. Children under 18 stay free in parent's room. AE, DC, DISC, MC, V. Free parking. Bus: 6. From I-8, take Taylor St. exit. **Amenities:** Outdoor pool; coin-op laundry. *In room:* A/C, TV.

5 Mission Bay & the Beaches

If the beach and aquatic activities are front-and-center in your San Diego agenda, this part of town may be just the ticket. Although the beach communities don't offer much in the way of cultural or upscale attractions, downtown and Balboa Park are only a 15-minute drive away. Some hotels are right on Mission Bay, San Diego's water playground; they're usually good choices for families. Ocean Beach is more neighborhood-oriented and easygoing, while Mission Beach and Pacific Beach provide a taste of the transient beach-bum lifestyle—they can be a bit raucous at times, especially in summer, and dining options are focused on chain eateries. If you're looking for a more refined landing, head to La Jolla or Coronado.

Accommodations here tend to book up solid on summer weekends and even some weekdays (rates shown are for summer). But discounts can be found, especially for those who try walk-up bookings on the afternoon of arrival—admittedly, a risky proposition on a Friday or Saturday in July and August. *A note on driving directions:* All directions are provided from I-5.

VERY EXPENSIVE

Tower 23 ⭐⭐   Named for a nearby lifeguard station, Tower 23 is a modernist beach resort that opened in 2005. Sitting on the Pacific Beach (aka P.B.) boardwalk, the hotel's sky-high people-watching quotient is matched by first-class contemporary amenities, including wireless Internet access right on the beach, wall-mounted high-definition TVs, in-room Xbox systems, and Egyptian-cotton linens. The hotel's Tower Bar and Jordan restaurant, which serves contemporary steak and seafood and has an eight-seat sushi bar, have become the sophisticated heart of the P.B. scene. Jordan did not get off to a good start, especially in the service department (a common San Diego complaint), but you can always endure long waits while enjoying a cocktail and the hypnotic, 75-foot-long "wave wall" and its morphing color scheme. Featuring clean lines and glass-box architecture, the three-story Tower 23 has 44 rooms, all with private balconies (though not all with ocean views), and a guest-only second-story deck with fire pit. Seaside digs for the 21st century.

723 Felspar St., San Diego, CA 92109. ℂ **866/869-3723**. Fax 858/274-2333. www.t23hotel.com. 44 units. $319–$399 double; $499–$739 suite. Children 17 and under stay free in parent's room. AE, DC, DISC, MC, V. Valet parking $15. Bus: 27, 30, or 34. Take I-5 to Grand/Garnet exit, left on Grand Ave., right on Mission Blvd., left on Felspar St. Pets accepted with a $250 cleaning charge for dogs 25 pounds and under. **Amenities:** Restaurant; bar; private deck; Wi-Fi; 24-hour room service; laundry; valet. *In room:* A/C, TV w/DVD, CD player, Xbox, on-demand video, hair dryer, iron, safe, massage and spa services by request, Jacuzzi tubs (suites only), 2-line phone, hypoallergenic bedding (on request), daily newspaper.

EXPENSIVE

Best Western Blue Sea Lodge   The three-story Blue Sea Lodge is a reliable choice in a prime location which keeps up with the other properties in the Best Western chain. And, despite the rates listed, this can be a bargain. There are many ways to get a discount—including just asking. Aesthetically, the original rooms are a snore, but nevertheless boast a balcony or patio and a handful of necessary comforts. Rooms with full ocean views overlook the sand and have more privacy than those on the street, but the Pacific Beach boardwalk has never been known for quiet or solitude. If an ocean view is not important, save a few bucks and check into one of the units in an expansion building that opened in 2003; the decor is brighter, more enticing. The lobby offers a cafe for guests in the morning, and its heated pool and Jacuzzi are steps from the beach.

707 Pacific Beach Dr., San Diego, CA 92109-5094. ✆ **800/258-3732** or 858/488-4700. Fax 858/488-7276. www. bestwestern-bluesea.com. 128 units. $225–$275 double; from $359 suite. Children under 18 stay free in parent's room. AE, DC, DISC, MC, V. Underground and outdoor parking $6. Bus: 27 or 34. Take I-5 to Grand/Garnet exit, follow Grand Ave. to Mission Blvd. and turn left; then turn right onto Pacific Beach Dr. **Amenities:** Outdoor pool; Jacuzzi; coin-op laundry. *In room:* A/C, TV w/pay movies, dataport, microwave, coffeemaker, hair dryer, iron, safe.

Catamaran Resort Hotel ⭐⭐ (Kids)

Right on Mission Bay, the Catamaran has its own beach, complete with watersports facilities. Built in the 1950s, the hotel has been fully renovated to modern standards without losing its trademark Polynesian theme; the atrium lobby holds a 15-foot waterfall and full-size dugout canoe, koi-filled lagoons meander through the property, and the pool is surrounded by a real bamboo fence, rather than a fake metal one. Numerous varieties of bamboo and palms sprout in the lush gardens, tropical birds chirp away, and torches blaze after dark. Guest rooms—in a 13-story building or one of the six two-story buildings—have subdued South Pacific decor, and each has a balcony or patio. High floors of tower rooms have commanding views, and studios and suites have kitchenettes. A 9,300-square-foot spa was added in 2005, featuring a menu of South Pacific and Asian-inspired treatments. It's a heated-stone's throw away from the bay's jogging-and-biking path, and runners with tots in tow can rent jogging strollers at the hotel. The Catamaran is also within a few blocks of Pacific Beach's restaurant-and-nightlife scene. A Mississippi-style stern-wheeler, the *Bahia Belle*, cruises the bay Friday and Saturday evenings (nightly in summer) and is free to hotel guests.

3999 Mission Blvd. (4 blocks south of Grand Ave.), San Diego, CA 92109. ✆ **800/422-8386** or 858/488-1081. Fax 858/488-1387. www.catamaranresort.com. 315 units. $275–$399 double; from $319 suite. Children under 12 stay free in parent's room. AE, DC, DISC, MC, V. Valet parking $11; self-parking $9. Bus: 27 or 34. Take Grand/Garnet exit off I-5 and go west on Grand Ave., and then south on Mission Blvd. **Amenities:** Restaurant; 2 bars; outdoor pool; fitness room; full-service spa; Jacuzzi; watersports equipment rental; bike rental; children's programs; concierge; limited room service (5am–11pm); in-room massage; laundry service; dry cleaning. *In room:* A/C, TV w/pay movies, dataport, fridge in most units, coffeemaker, hair dryer, iron.

Crystal Pier Hotel ⭐⭐ (Finds) (Kids)

If historic charm is higher on your wish list than hotel-style service, head to this utterly unique cluster of cottages sitting literally over the surf on the vintage Crystal Pier at Pacific Beach. This place is like a self-contained hideaway—you'll get a separate living room and bedroom, fully equipped kitchen, and private patio with breathtaking ocean views—all within the whitewashed walls of sweet, blue-shuttered cottages that date from 1936 but have been carefully renovated. Each of the Cape Cod–style cottages has a deck—the more expensive units farthest out have more privacy. Six units are not actually on the pier, but still offer sunset-facing sea views; these accommodations are cheaper. The sound of waves is soothing, yet the boardwalk action is only a few steps (and worlds) away, and the pier is a great place for watching sunsets and surfers. Guests drive right out and park beside their cottages, a real boon on crowded weekends. But this operation is strictly BYOBT (bring your own beach towels), and the office is open only from 8am to 8pm. These accommodations

Where to Stay in Mission Bay & the Beaches

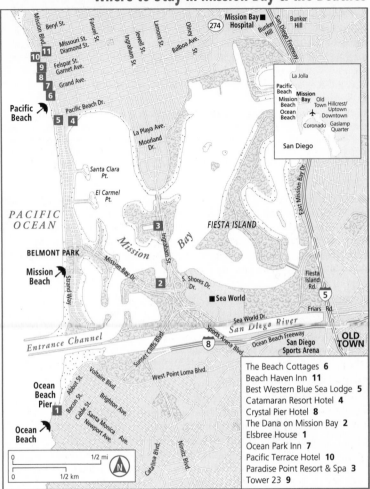

The Beach Cottages **6**
Beach Haven Inn **11**
Best Western Blue Sea Lodge **5**
Catamaran Resort Hotel **4**
Crystal Pier Hotel **8**
The Dana on Mission Bay **2**
Elsbree House **1**
Ocean Park Inn **7**
Pacific Terrace Hotel **10**
Paradise Point Resort & Spa **3**
Tower 23 **9**

book up fast, especially with long-term repeat guests; reserve for summer and holiday weekends several months in advance.

4500 Ocean Blvd. (at Garnet Ave.), San Diego, CA 92109. ☎ **800/748-5894** or 858/483-6983. Fax 858/483-6811. www.crystalpier.com. 29 units. $195–$320 double; $270–$400 for larger units sleeping 4 or 6. 3-night minimum in summer. DISC, MC, V. Free parking. Bus: 27, 30, or 34. Take I-5 to Grand/Garnet exit; follow Garnet to the pier. **Amenities:** Beach equipment rental. *In room:* TV, kitchen.

The Dana on Mission Bay ⚘   The Dana completed a $20-million renovation and expansion in 2004, which added 74 contemporary rooms in a three-story arc wrapping around an infinity pool. These rooms are a fair upgrade from the sleepy old Dana, and the old rooms, in two-story buildings, were spruced up at the same time. Some overlook bobbing sailboats in the recreational marina; others face onto the original kidney-shaped pool whose surrounding Tiki torch-lit gardens offer shuffleboard and Ping-Pong. You'll pay a little extra for bay and marina views; if the view doesn't matter, save your money—every one of the old rooms is the same size, with plain but well-maintained furnishings. The new rooms are bigger and feature water views and reclaimed redwood beam ceilings. Beaches and SeaWorld are a 15-minute walk away (there's also a complimentary shuttle). Meals and room service (including poolside food and cocktail ministrations) are available through the new restaurants, Firefly Bar & Grill and Blue Pearl.

1710 W. Mission Bay Dr., San Diego, CA 92109. ℂ **800/345-9995** or 619/222-6440. Fax 619/222-5916. www. thedana.net. 270 units. $219–$289 double (sleeps up to 4); from $339 suites. AE, DC, DISC, MC, V. Free parking. Bus: 27 or 34. Follow I-8 west to Mission Bay Dr. exit; take W. Mission Bay Dr. **Amenities:** 2 restaurants; outdoor heated pool; fitness room; Jacuzzi; watersports equipment/rentals; bike rental; limited room service (7am–8:30pm); laundry service; dry cleaning; coin-op laundry. *In room:* A/C, TV, dataport, fridge, coffeemaker, hair dryer, iron.

Ocean Park Inn ⍟   This oceanfront motor hotel offers simple, attractive, spacious rooms with contemporary furnishings. Although the inn has a smidgen of sophistication uncommon in this casual, surfer-populated area, you won't find much solitude with the boisterous scene outside. But you can't beat the sand access (directly on the beach) and the view (ditto). Rates vary according to view, but most rooms have at least a partial ocean view; all have a private balcony or patio. Units in front are most desirable, but it can get noisy directly above the boardwalk; try for the second or third floor, or pick one of the three junior suites, which have huge bathrooms and pool views.

710 Grand Ave., San Diego, CA 92109. ℂ **800/231-7735** or 858/483-5858. Fax 858/274-0823. www.ocean parkinn.com. 73 units. $199–$249 double; $239–$269 suite. Rates include continental breakfast. AE, DC, DISC, MC, V. Free indoor parking. Bus: 34 or 34A/B. Take Grand/Garnet exit off I-5; follow Grand Ave. to ocean. **Amenities:** Outdoor pool; Jacuzzi; laundry service; dry cleaning. *In room:* A/C, TV, dataport, fridge, microwave, coffeemaker, hair dryer, iron, safe.

Pacific Terrace Hotel ⍟   This modern hotel on the boardwalk swaggers with a heavy-handed South Seas–meets–Spanish Colonial ambience. Rattan fans circulate in the lobby and hint at the sunny Indonesian-inspired decor in guest rooms, which are named after Caribbean islands. Hands-on owners kicked up the luxury factor (and prices) following a renovation, resulting in a more upscale atmosphere than most of the casual beach pads nearby are able to muster, and the staff is friendly and accommodating. It's at the north end of the Pacific Beach boardwalk; the surfer contingent tends to stay a few blocks south. Large, comfortable guest rooms each come with balconies or terraces and fancy wall safes; bathrooms, designed with warm-toned marble and natural woods, have a separate sink/vanity area. About half the rooms have kitchenettes, and top-floor rooms in this three-story hotel enjoy particularly nice views—you'll find yourself mesmerized by the rhythmic waves and determined surfers below. Management keeps cookies, coffee, and iced tea at the ready throughout the day; the lushly landscaped pool and hot tub overlook a relatively quiet stretch of beach. Four nearby restaurants allow meals to be billed to the hotel, but there's no restaurant on the premises.

610 Diamond St., San Diego, CA 92109. ℂ **800/344-3370** or 858/581-3500. Fax 858/274-3341. www.pacificterrace. com. 73 units. $309–$415 double; from $485 suite. Rates include continental breakfast. AE, DC, DISC, MC, V. Parking $8; limited free parking in off-street lot. Bus: 30 or 34. Take I-5 to Grand/Garnet and follow Grand or Garnet west to Mission Blvd., turn right (north), and then left (west) onto Diamond. **Amenities:** Pool; access to nearby health club ($5); Jacuzzi; bike rental nearby; activities desk; limited room service (11am–10:30pm); in-room massage; laundry service; dry cleaning; coin-op laundry. *In room:* A/C, TV w/pay movies, dataport, minibar, coffeemaker, hair dryer, iron.

Paradise Point Resort & Spa *(Kids)*   Smack-dab in the middle of Mission Bay, this hotel complex is almost as much a theme park as its closest neighbor, SeaWorld (a 3-min. drive). Single-story accommodations are spread across 44 tropically land-scaped acres of duck-filled lagoons, lush gardens, and swim-friendly beaches; all have private lanais and plenty of thoughtful conveniences. Standard "lanai" rooms range considerably in price, based solely on view. The resort was updated to keep its low-tech 1960s charm but to lose tacky holdovers—rooms now have a refreshingly color-ful beach cottage decor. And despite daunting high-season rack rates, you can usually get a deal here. There's an upscale waterfront restaurant, Baleen (fine dining in a con-temporary, fun space), and a stunning Indonesian-inspired spa that offers cool seren-ity and aroma-tinged Asian treatments—this spa is a vacation in itself.

1404 Vacation Rd. (off Ingraham St.), San Diego, CA 92109. © 800/344-2626 or 858/274-4630. Fax 858/581-5924. www.paradisepoint.com. 457 units. $279–$455 double; from $479 suite. Extra person $20. Children 17 and under stay free in parent's room. AE, DC, DISC, MC, V. Parking $10. Bus: 9. Follow I-8 west to Mission Bay Dr. exit; take Ingra-ham St. north to Vacation Rd. **Amenities:** 3 restaurants; bar; pool bar; 6 outdoor pools; 18-hole putting course; 5 ten-nis courts; fitness center; full-service spa; Jacuzzi; bike rental; limited room service (6am–midnight); laundry service; dry cleaning. *In room:* A/C, TV w/pay movies, dataport, fridge, coffeemaker, hair dryer, iron.

MODERATE

Elsbree House *(Finds)*   Katie and Phil Elsbree turned this modern Cape Cod–style building into an immaculate, exceedingly comfortable B&B, half a block from the water's edge in Ocean Beach. One condo unit with a private entrance rents for a 4-day minimum (breakfast not included); the Elsbrees occupy another. Each of the six guest rooms has a patio or balcony. Guests share the cozy living room (with a fireplace and TV), breakfast room, and kitchen. Although other buildings on this tightly packed street block the ocean view, sounds of the surf and fresh sea breezes waft into open windows, and a charming garden—complete with trickling fountain—runs the length of the house. This Ocean Beach neighborhood is eclectic, occupied by ocean-loving couples, dedicated surf bums, and the occasional contingent of punk skater kids who congregate near the pier. Its strengths are proximity to the beach, a casual-but-pleasing selection of eateries that attract mostly locals, and San Diego's best antiquing (along Newport Ave.).

5054 Narragansett Ave., San Diego, CA 92107. © 800/607-4133 or 619/226-4133. www.bbinob.com. 7 units. $150–$250 double; $1,800 per week 3-bedroom condo (lower rates if only 1 or 2 rooms used). Rates include conti-nental breakfast. MC, V. Bus: 23 or 35. From airport, take Harbor Dr. west to Nimitz Blvd. to Lowell St., which becomes Narragansett Ave. *In room:* Hair dryer, iron, no phone.

INEXPENSIVE

The Beach Cottages   This family-owned operation has been around since 1948 and offers a variety of guest quarters, most of them geared to the long-term visitor. It's the 17 cute, little detached cottages just steps from the sand that give it real appeal, though some of them lack a view (of anything); each has a patio with tables and chairs. Adjoining apartments are perfectly adequate, especially for budget-minded families who want to log major hours on the beach—all cottages and apartments sleep four or more and have full kitchens. There are also standard motel rooms that are worn but cheap (most of these sleep two). The property is within walking distance of shops and restaurants—look both ways for speeding cyclists before crossing the boardwalk—and enjoy shared barbecue grills, shuffleboard courts, and table tennis. The cottages them-selves aren't pristine, but they have a rustic charm that makes them popular with young honeymooners and those nostalgic for the golden age of laid-back California beach culture. Reserve the beachfront cottages well in advance.

4255 Ocean Blvd. (1 block south of Grand Ave.), San Diego, CA 92109-3995. ✆ **858/483-7440.** Fax 858/273-9365. www.beachcottages.com. 61 units, 17 cottages. $75–$125 double; from $210 cottages and apts. for 4 to 6. Monthly rates available mid-Sept to Mar. AE, DC, DISC, MC, V. Free parking. Bus: 27, 30, or 34. Take I-5 to Grand/Garnet exit, go west on Grand Ave. and left on Mission Blvd. **Amenities:** Self-service laundry. *In room:* TV, fridge, microwave, coffeemaker.

Beach Haven Inn   A great spot for beach lovers who can't quite afford to be on the beach, this motel lies 1 block from the sand. Rooms face an inner courtyard, where guests enjoy a secluded ambience for relaxing by the small pool. On the street side it looks kind of marginal, but once on the property you'll find all quarters well maintained and sporting clean, up-to-date furnishings; nearly all units have eat-in kitchens. The friendly staff provides free coffee in the lobby and rents VCRs and movies.

4740 Mission Blvd. (at Missouri St.), San Diego, CA 92109. ✆ **800/831-6323** or 858/272-3812. Fax 858/272-3532. www.beachhaveninn.com. 23 units. $69–$205 double; 2-night minimum on weekends. Extra person $5. Children under 12 stay free in parent's room. Rates include continental breakfast. AE, DC, DISC, MC, V. Free parking. Bus: 30 or 34. Take I-5 to Grand/Garnet exit, follow Grand Ave. to Mission Blvd. and turn right. **Amenities:** Outdoor pool; Jacuzzi. *In room:* A/C, TV, kitchenette in most units.

6 La Jolla

The name "La Jolla" is often translated from Spanish as "the jewel," a fitting comparison for this section of the city with a beautiful coastline, as well as a compact downtown village that makes for delightful strolling. You'll have a hard time finding bargain accommodations in this upscale, conservative community. But remember, most hotels—even those in the "Very Expensive" category—have occupancy-driven rates (you can score surprising discounts during the off season).

If a modern business hotel is more your style, chain hotels farther afield include the **Hyatt Regency** 𝓖𝓖, 3777 La Jolla Village Dr. (✆ **800/233-1234** or 858/552-1234). It's a glam, business-oriented place with several good restaurants next door. The **Marriott Residence Inn** 𝓖, 8901 Gilman Dr. (✆ **800/331-3131** or 858/587-1770), is a good choice for those who want a fully equipped kitchen and more space. Both are near the University of California, San Diego.

A note on driving directions: From **I-5 north,** use the La Jolla Parkway exit or from **I-5 south** take the La Jolla Village Drive West exit, both of which merge with Torrey Pines Road.

VERY EXPENSIVE

Estancia La Jolla Hotel and Spa 𝓖𝓖𝓖   Opened in 2004, this California rancho-style property was built on the remains of a horse farm and was named one of the world's hottest new hotels in 2005 by *Condé Nast Traveler.* Estancia also made the magazine's Gold List 2006. The 9.5-acre spread has some pretty cool neighbors: the Louis I. Kahn–designed Salk Institute, UC San Diego, the Torrey Pines Gliderport, and Blacks Beach. You won't see any of those things from this self-contained retreat, but the romance created by the hacienda flavor and the meticulously maintained gardens with their native flora and bubbling fountains is diversion enough. Guest rooms face a central courtyard, and many rooms have balconies or patios. All rooms are tastefully appointed with comfy furnishings that would be at home in an upscale residence. With its old *Californio* exterior, outdoor fireplace, and live Spanish guitar music, the

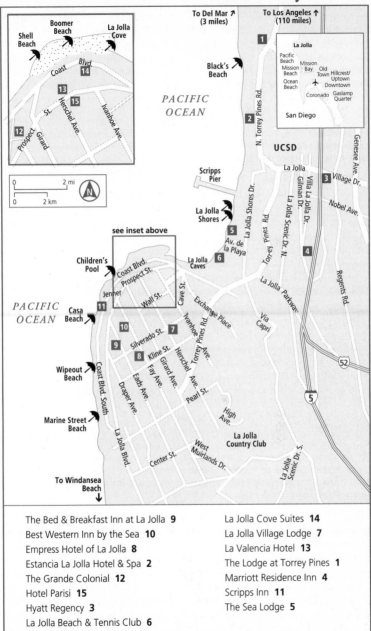

The Bed & Breakfast Inn at La Jolla **9**
Best Western Inn by the Sea **10**
Empress Hotel of La Jolla **8**
Estancia La Jolla Hotel & Spa **2**
The Grande Colonial **12**
Hotel Parisi **15**
Hyatt Regency **3**
La Jolla Beach & Tennis Club **6**

La Jolla Cove Suites **14**
La Jolla Village Lodge **7**
La Valencia Hotel **13**
The Lodge at Torrey Pines **1**
Marriott Residence Inn **4**
Scripps Inn **11**
The Sea Lodge **5**

Mustangs & Burros lounge and bar is a great place to chill out. There's also an award-winning restaurant on the premises. The full-service spa offers organic-based signature treatments like the red rose hydrating treatment and the garden vegetable wrap, while the high-tech meeting facilities offer more than 21,000 square feet of space, including a main conference room that looks ready to host the United Nations.

9700 N. Torrey Pines Rd., La Jolla, CA 92037. (℃) 877/437-8262 or 858/550-1000. Fax 858/550-1001 www.estancialajolla.com. 210 units. $249–$299 double; $399 suite. Bed-and-breakfast packages available for an additional $20. AE, DC, DISC, MC, V. Valet parking $20; self-parking $16. Bus: 101. From I-5 take the Genesee Ave. exit westbound, go left on N. Torrey Pines Rd. **Amenities:** Restaurant; bar; pool; fitness center; full-service spa; Jacuzzi; yoga and personal training; business center; 24-hour room service; secretarial support; babysitting service; free area transportation (5-mile radius); car rental; laundry service; dry cleaning. *In room:* A/C, TV w/pay movies, Wi-Fi, 2-line phone, minibar, coffeemaker, hair dryer, iron, safe, daily newspaper.

Hotel Parisi ★★★ *Finds*   Nestled among clothing boutiques and across the street from the vaunted pink lady, La Valencia, the sleek boutique Hotel Parisi caters to the traveler seeking inner peace for both entertainment and relaxation. The intimate hotel is on the second floor overlooking one of La Jolla's main intersections (street-facing rooms are well insulated from the modest din). Parisi's nurturing, wellness-inspired intimacy first becomes evident in the lobby, where elements of earth, wind, fire, water, and metal blend according to feng shui principles. The Italy-meets-Zen composition is carried into the 20 rooms, where custom furnishings are modern yet comfy. Parisi calls the spacious rooms "suites" (some are more like junior suites) and each has an ergonomic desk, dimmable lighting, goose-down superluxe bedding, and creamy, calming neutral decor—10-foot ceilings and original art throughout allow your eyes to wander. Each darkly cool marble bathroom boasts a shower (some with dual shower heads), separate tub with contoured backrest, and smoothly sculpted fixtures. Less expensive rooms are smaller with little or no view. Though primped and elegant, Parisi is not stuffy, and yet the personal service stops at nothing—there's a menu of 24-hour in-room holistic health services (from individual yoga to Thai massage, psychotherapy, and obscure Asian treatments). If the W Hotel is too swinging, but chic design by the seashore is your style, the Parisi may be just right.

1111 Prospect St. (at Herschel Ave.), La Jolla, CA 92037. (℃) 877/472-7474 or 858/454-1511. Fax 858/454-1531. www.hotelparisi.com. 28 units. $295–$425 double; from $475 suite. Rates include continental breakfast. AE, DC, DISC, MC, V. Free covered parking. Bus: 30 or 34. Take Torrey Pines Rd. to Prospect Place and turn right; Prospect Place becomes Prospect St., turn left on Herschel Ave. **Amenities:** Restaurant; 24-hr. in-room spa treatments; limited room service (11:30am–2:30pm and 5:30–10pm); laundry service; dry cleaning. *In room:* A/C, TV/VCR, dataport, minibar w/complimentary beverages, coffeemaker, hair dryer, iron, safe.

La Valencia Hotel ★★★   Within its bougainvillea-draped walls and wrought-iron garden gates, this bastion of gentility does a fine job of resurrecting elegance from the golden age, when celebrities like Greta Garbo and Charlie Chaplin vacationed here. The blufftop hotel, which looks much like a Mediterranean villa, has been the center-piece of La Jolla since opening in 1926, and a $10-million renovation in 2000 refined some of the details and added 15 villas and an enlarged pool, without breaking with its historical glamour. Brides still pose in front of the lobby's picture window (against a backdrop of the Cove and Pacific Ocean), well-coiffed ladies lunch in the dappled shade of the garden patio, and neighborhood cronies quaff libations in the clubby Whaling Bar (La Jolla's version of the power lunch). The latter was once a western Algonquin for literary inebriates as well as a watering hole for Hollywood royalty, who performed at the Playhouse at the urging of La Jolla resident Gregory Peck. One chooses La Valencia for its history and unbeatably scenic location, but you won't be disappointed by the old-world standards of service and style. Most rooms are quite comfortable, each boasting lavish appointments, and all-marble bathrooms with signature toiletries. Because rates vary wildly according to view (from sweeping to *nada*), my advice is to get a cheaper room and enjoy the scene from one of the many lounges, serene garden terraces, or the amazing pool, which fronts the Pacific and nearby Scripps Park. Room decor, layouts, and size (starting at a snug 246 sq. ft.) are all over the map, too—take a few extra minutes with the reservationist to get the right match for you. If you've got the bucks, spring for one of the newer villas featuring fireplaces and butler service. The hotel's 12-table Sky Room is one of the city's most exclusive dining rooms.

1132 Prospect St. (at Herschel Ave.), La Jolla, CA 92037. © **800/451-0772** or 858/454-0771. Fax 858/456-3921. www.lavalencia.com. 117 units. $275–$575 double; from $775 suites and villas. 2-night minimum summer weekends. AE, DC, DISC, MC, V. Valet parking $15. Bus: 30 or 34. Take Torrey Pines Rd. to Prospect Place and turn right. Prospect Place becomes Prospect St. **Amenities:** 3 restaurants; bar; outdoor pool; exercise room with spa treatments; Jacuzzi; sauna; concierge; secretarial services; 24-hr. room service; babysitting; laundry service; dry cleaning. *In room:* A/C, TV/VCR, dataport, minibar, coffeemaker, hair dryer, iron, safe.

The Lodge at Torrey Pines ★★★   Ten minutes north of La Jolla proper, this triumphant trompe l'oeil creation at the edge of the Torrey Pines Golf Course is the fantasy of local hotelier Bill Evans (of the Catamaran), who took his appreciation for Craftsman-style homes and amplified it into a 175-room upscale hotel. The Lodge brims with clinker-brick masonry, art glass windows and doors, Stickley furniture, and exquisite pottery. Most rooms fall into two main categories. The least expensive are an unstinting 520 square feet and lavished with Tiffany-style lamps, period wallpaper, framed Hiroshige prints, and lots of wood accents; views face a courtyard carefully landscaped to mimic the rare coastal environment that exists just beyond the hotel grounds. More expensive rooms overlook the golf course and the sea in the distance; most of these have balconies, fireplaces, and giant bathrooms with separate tub and shower. The 9,500-square-foot spa specializes in treatments utilizing coastal sage and other local plants, and there's an elegant pool. An excellent restaurant named after painter A. R. Valentien features superb seasonal vegetables; Valentien's wildflower watercolors line the walls, and his personal effects and medals are found in glass bookcases. The embrace of local artists and the native natural environment is inspired, and with every whim catered to by a mindful staff, The Lodge is unsurpassed as a luxury destination in San Diego.

11480 N. Torrey Pines Rd., La Jolla, CA 92037. © **800/656-0087** or 858/453-4420. Fax 858/453-7464. www.lodgetorreypines.com. 175 units. $450–$625 double; from $900 suite. Children under 18 stay free in parent's room. AE, DC, DISC, MC, V. $22 valet parking; $16 self-parking. Bus: 101. From I-5 take La Jolla Village Dr. west, bear right (north) onto N. Torrey Pines Rd. **Amenities:** 2 restaurants; outdoor pool; fitness center; Jacuzzi; spa; preferential tee times at the golf course; concierge; 24-hr. room service; laundry service; dry cleaning. *In room:* A/C, TV, dataport in many units, minibar, coffeemaker, hair dryer, safe.

EXPENSIVE

Best Western Inn by the Sea ★   Occupying an enviable location at the heart of La Jolla's charming village, this independently managed property puts guests just a short walk from the cliffs and beach. The low-rise tops out at five stories, with the upper floors enjoying ocean views (and the highest room rates). The Best Western (and the more formal Empress, a block away) offers a terrific alternative to pricier digs nearby. Rooms here are Best Western standard issue—freshly maintained, but nothing special. All rooms do have balconies, though, and refrigerators are available at no extra charge; the hotel offers plenty of welcome amenities.

7830 Fay Ave. (between Prospect and Silverado sts.), La Jolla, CA 92037. ✆ **800/526-4545** or 858/459-4461. Fax 858/456-2578. www.bestwestern.com/innbythesea. 132 units. $219–$259 double; from $469 suite. Rates include continental breakfast. AE, DC, DISC, MC, V. Parking $11. Bus: 30 or 34. Take Torrey Pines Rd. to Prospect Place and turn right. Prospect Place becomes Prospect St.; proceed to Fay Ave. and turn left. **Amenities:** Outdoor heated pool; car-rental desk; laundry service; dry cleaning; coin-op laundry. *In room:* A/C, TV w/pay movies, dataport, coffeemaker, hair dryer, iron.

Empress Hotel of La Jolla ✸

The Empress Hotel offers spacious quarters with traditional furnishings a block or two from La Jolla's main drag and the ocean. It's quieter here than at the premium cliff-top properties, and you'll sacrifice little other than direct ocean views (many rooms on the top floors afford a partial view). If you're planning to explore La Jolla on foot, the Empress is a good base, and it exudes a classiness many comparably priced chains lack, with warm service to boot. Rooms are tastefully decorated and well equipped. Bathrooms are average size but well appointed, and four "Empress" rooms have sitting areas with full-size sleeper sofas. Breakfast is set up next to a serene sun deck.

7766 Fay Ave. (at Silverado), La Jolla, CA 92037. ✆ **888/369-9900** or 858/454-3001. Fax 858/454-6387. www. empress-hotel.com. 73 units. $239–$259 double; $359 suite. Rates include continental breakfast. AE, DC, DISC, MC, V. Valet parking $8. Bus: 30 or 34. Take Torrey Pines Rd. to Girard Ave., turn right, and then left on Silverado St. **Amenities:** Restaurant; fitness room; spa; limited room service (lunch and dinner hours). *In room:* A/C, TV, dataport, fridge, coffeemaker, hair dryer, iron.

The Grande Colonial ✸✸ *Finds*

Possessed of an old-world European flair that's more London or Georgetown than seaside La Jolla, the Grande Colonial earned accolades for the complete restoration in 2001 of its polished mahogany paneling, brass fittings, and genteel library and lounge. During the original heyday of the La Jolla Playhouse, it was the temporary home for everyone from Groucho Marx to Jane Wyatt. Today, a large spray of fresh flowers is the focal point in the lounge, where guests gather in front of the fireplace for drinks—often before enjoying dinner at the hotel's Nine-Ten restaurant (p. 127). Guest rooms are quiet and elegantly appointed, with beautiful draperies and traditional furnishings. The hotel is 1 block from the ocean, but many rooms have sea views. The guest rooms have thoughtful amenities; terry robes are available on request. Relics from the early days include oversize closets and meticulously tiled bathrooms. Numerous historic photos on the walls illustrate the hotel's fascinating story, which started as a full-service apartment hotel in 1913. Among La Jolla's minihorde of deluxe properties, the Grande Colonial is often overlooked. In fact, the centrally located hotel is a sleeper that provides comparatively good value.

910 Prospect St. (between Fay and Girard), La Jolla, CA 92037. ✆ **800/826-1278** or 858/454-2181. Fax 858/ 454-5679. www.thegrandecolonial.com. 75 units. $249–$435 double; from $429 suite. Children under 12 stay free in parent's room. AE, DC, DISC, MC, V. Valet parking $14. Bus: 30 or 34. Take Torrey Pines Rd. to Prospect Place and turn right. Prospect Place becomes Prospect St. **Amenities:** Restaurant; outdoor pool; access to nearby health club; limited room service (6:30am–10:30pm); laundry service; dry cleaning. *In room:* A/C, TV w/pay movies, dataport, hair dryer, iron, safe.

La Jolla Beach & Tennis Club ✸ *Overrated*

You're supposed to pack your best tennis whites for a stint at La Jolla's private "B&T" (as it's locally known), where CEOs and MDs come for some R&R. The location is unbeatable—right on the La Jolla

Shores beach—and the physical property is attractive, in a Spanish-hacienda sort of way. However, standard guest rooms are unbelievably plain and outmoded (think late-1970s Holiday-Inn styling); most have full kitchens that are appropriate for families or longer stays. Beachfront rooms are tiny—the showers are tight enough to give broad-shouldered types claustrophobia—but they're brighter, and the wide ocean panorama at the foot of your bed is undeniably splendid (if unprivate). A variety of suites are available, ranging from one-bedroom street-side digs to deluxe two- and three-bedroom accommodations facing the ocean. The beach is popular and staff stays busy shooing away nonguests, in between primping the comfy sand chairs and umbrellas, and keeping guests stocked with fluffy towels, beverages, and snacks. Kayaks and watersports equipment can be rented; there's a sand croquet court; and you can even make arrangements for your own private beach barbecue in the evening. There's no room service, but the hotel's distinctive Marine Room restaurant (p. 126) is one of San Diego's very best, and several times a year the waves literally smash against its broad windows, inches away from diners. This historic property was founded in the 1920s, when original plans included constructing a yacht harbor; today it's known primarily for tennis and for the $45,000 it takes to become a member. You get better room value for your money at the club's sister hotel next door, the Sea Lodge (see below), but you don't stay here for the quality—B&T guests are chasing exclusive, old-money atmosphere and fawning service.

2000 Spindrift Dr., La Jolla, CA 92037. (C) **800/640-7702** or 858/454-7126. Fax 858/456-3805. www.ljbtc.com. 90 units. $219–$489 double; from $349 suite. Extra person $20. Children under 12 stay free in parent's room. AE, DC, MC, V. Free parking. Bus: 34. Take La Jolla Shores Dr., turn left on Paseo Dorado, and follow to Spindrift Dr. **Amenities:** 2 restaurants; seasonal beach snack bar; 75-ft. pool; 12 championship tennis courts; 9-hole pitch-and-putt course; fitness room; watersports equipment/rentals; massage; babysitting; laundry service; dry cleaning; coin-op laundry. *In room:* TV w/pay movies, dataport, coffeemaker, hair dryer, iron.

La Jolla Cove Suites   Tucked in beside prime ocean-view condos across from Ellen Browning Scripps Park, this family-run 1950s-era catbird seat actually sits closer to the ocean than its pricey uphill neighbor La Valencia. The to-die-for ocean view is completely unobstructed, and La Jolla Cove—one of California's prettiest swimming spots—is steps away from the hotel. The six-story property is peaceful at night, but Village dining and shopping are only a short walk away. You'll pay according to the quality of your view; about 80% of guest quarters gaze upon the ocean. On the plus side, most rooms are wonderfully spacious, each featuring a fully equipped kitchen, plus private balcony or patio. On the minus side, their functional but almost institutional furnishings have drawn complaints from *Frommer's* readers. An ocean-view rooftop deck offers lounge chairs and cafe tables; breakfast is served up there each morning, indoors or outdoors depending on the weather.

1155 Coast Blvd. (across from the Cove), La Jolla, CA 92037. (C) **888/525-6552** or 858/459-2621. Fax 858/551-3405. www.lajollacove.com. 90 units. $219–$269 double; from $324 suite. Extra person $15. Children under 12 stay free in parent's room. Rates include continental breakfast. Pets accepted with $15 nightly fee. AE, DC, DISC, MC, V. Parking $8. Bus: 30 or 34. Take Torrey Pines Rd. to Prospect Place and turn right. When the road forks, veer right (downhill) onto Coast Blvd. **Amenities:** Outdoor (nonview) pool; Jacuzzi; car-rental desk; coin-op laundry. *In room:* TV, kitchen, safe.

Scripps Inn ★★ *Finds*   This meticulously maintained inn is tucked away behind the Museum of Contemporary Art, and you'll be rewarded with seclusion even though the attractions of La Jolla are just a short walk away. Only a small, grassy park comes between the inn and the beach, cliffs, and tide pools; the view from the second-story deck can hypnotize guests, who gaze out to sea indefinitely. Rates vary depending on ocean view (all have one, but some are better than others); rooms have a pleasant pale cream/sand palette, and are furnished in "early American comfortable," with new bathroom fixtures and appointments. All rooms have sofa beds; two have wood-burning fireplaces, and four have kitchenettes. The inn supplies beach towels, firewood, and French pastries each morning. Repeat guests keep their favorite rooms for up to a month each year, so book ahead for the best choice.

555 Coast Blvd. S. (at Cuvier), La Jolla, CA 92037. © **858/454-3391.** Fax 858/456-0389. www.scrippsinn.com. 14 units. $225–$255 double; from $295 suite. Extra person $10. Children under 5 stay free in parent's room. Rates include continental breakfast. AE, DC, DISC, MC, V. Free parking. Bus: 30 or 34. Take Torrey Pines Rd., turn right on Prospect Place; past the museum, turn right onto Cuvier. *In room:* TV, fridge, coffeemaker, hair dryer, iron, safe.

The Sea Lodge ★ *Kids*   This three-story 1960s hotel in a mainly residential enclave is under the same management as the La Jolla Beach & Tennis Club next door. It has an identical on-the-sand location, minus the country club ambience—there are no reciprocal privileges. About half the rooms have some view of the ocean, and the rest look out on the pool or a tiled courtyard. The rooms are pretty basic, with perfunctory, outdated furnishings, priced by view and size. Bathrooms feature separate dressing areas with large closets; balconies or patios are standard, and some rooms have fully equipped kitchenettes. From the Sea Lodge's beach you can gaze toward the top of the cliffs, where La Jolla's village hums with activity (and relentless traffic). Like the "B&T," the Sea Lodge is popular with families but also attracts business travelers looking to balance meetings with time on the beach or the tennis court.

8110 Camino del Oro (at Avenida de la Playa), La Jolla, CA 92037. © **800/237-5211** or 858/459-8271. Fax 858/456-9346. www.ljbtc.com. 128 units. $249–$559 double; $739 suite. Extra person $20. Children under 12 stay free in parent's room. AE, DC, DISC, MC, V. Underground parking $10. Bus: 34. Take La Jolla Shores Dr., turn left onto Avenida de la Playa, turn right on Camino del Oro. **Amenities:** Restaurant; 2 pools (including a wading pool for kids); 2 tennis courts; fitness room; Jacuzzi; babysitting; laundry service; dry cleaning. *In room:* A/C, TV, dataport, fridge, coffeemaker, hair dryer, iron.

MODERATE

The Bed & Breakfast Inn at La Jolla ★★ *Finds*   A 1913 Cubist house designed by San Diego's first important architect, Irving Gill—and occupied in the 1920s by John Philip Sousa and his family—is the setting for this cultured and elegant B&B. Reconfigured as lodging, the house has lost none of its charm, and its appropriately unfrilly period furnishings add to the sense of history. The inn also features lovely enclosed gardens and a cozy library and sitting room. Sherry and fresh-cut flowers await in every room, some of which feature a fireplace or ocean view. Each room has a private bathroom, most of which are on the compact size. The furnishings are tasteful and cottage-style, with plenty of historic photos of La Jolla. Gourmet breakfast is served wherever you desire—dining room, patio, sun deck, or in your room. Picnic baskets (extra charge) are available with a day's notice. The gardens surrounding the inn were originally planned by Kate Sessions, who went on to create much of the landscaping for Balboa Park.

7753 Draper Ave. (near Prospect), La Jolla, CA 92037. © **800/582-2466** or 858/456-2066. Fax 858/456-1510. www.innlajolla.com. 15 units. $179–$359 double; $399 suite. 2-night minimum on weekends. Rates include full breakfast and afternoon wine and cheese. AE, DISC, MC, V. Bus: 30 or 34. Take Torrey Pines Rd. to Prospect Place and turn right. Prospect Place becomes Prospect St.; proceed to Draper Ave. and turn left. *In room:* A/C, hair dryer, iron.

INEXPENSIVE

Wealthy, image-conscious La Jolla is really *not* the best place for deep bargains, but if you're determined to stay here as cheaply as possible, you won't do better than the **La Jolla Village Lodge,** 1141 Silverado St., at Herschel Avenue (*©* **877/551-2001** or 858/551-2001; www.lajollavillagelodge.com). This 30-room motel is standard Americana, arranged around a small parking lot with cinder-block construction and small, basic rooms. Rates vary wildly by season and day of the week—a room that costs $80 midweek in February almost doubles in price for a summer weekend. Plan your stay accordingly.

7 Coronado

The "island" (really a peninsula) of Coronado is a great escape—with quiet, architecturally rich streets, a small-town, Navy-oriented atmosphere, and laid-back vacationing on one of the state's most beautiful and welcoming beaches. Coronado's resorts are especially popular with Southern California and Arizona families for weekend escapes. Although downtown San Diego is just a 10-minute drive or 20-minute ferry ride away, you may feel a bit isolated in Coronado, so it isn't your best choice if you're planning to spend lots of time in more central parts of the city. The 438-room **Loews Coronado Bay Resort** 🏖🏖, 4000 Coronado Bay Rd. (*©* **800/235-6397** or 619/424-4000; www.loewshotels.com), is San Diego's most removed hotel, 6 miles down the Silver Strand. It works for those who want to get away from it all in a self-contained resort; it's good for convention groups as well.

A note on driving directions: To reach the places listed here, take I-5 to the Coronado Bridge, and then follow individual directions.

VERY EXPENSIVE

Hotel del Coronado 🏖🏖🏖   Opened in 1888 and designated a National Historic Landmark in 1977, the "Hotel Del," as it's affectionately known, is the last of California's stately old seaside hotels. This monument to Victorian grandeur boasts tall cupolas, red turrets, and gingerbread trim, all spread out over 31 acres. Even if you don't stay at the Hotel Del, be sure to stroll through its sumptuous, wood-paneled lobby or along the pristine, wide beach. Rooms—almost no two alike—run the gamut from compact to extravagant, and all are packed with antique charm; most have custom-made furnishings. The least expensive rooms are snug and have views of a roof or parking lot. The best are junior suites with large windows and balconies fronting one of the state's finest white-sand beaches, but note that even here, bathrooms are modest in size. Almost half the hotel's rooms are in the seven-story contemporary tower and offer more living space, but none of the historical ambience; personally, I can't imagine staying here in anything but the Victorian structure, but you pay a premium for the privilege (especially for an ocean view), and 2-night minimums often apply. The Del's Prince of Wales fine dining emporium has been dethroned in favor of **1500 Ocean,** a new restaurant scheduled to open at press time—it's slated to offer a California seafood menu. There are plenty of other alternatives on-site as well: **Casual Sheerwater,** also serving California cuisine, offers outdoor, ocean-view seating (and fireplaces to keep the evening chill away); there are cocktails, sushi, and entertainment in the **Babcock & Story Bar;** afternoon tea is served Sundays in the **Palm Court;** and

Fun Fact   **A Century of Intrigue: Scenes from the Hotel del Coronado**

San Diego's romantic Hotel del Coronado is an unmistakable landmark, filled with enchanting and colorful memories.

When it opened in 1888, it was among the first buildings with Thomas Edison's new invention, electric light. Its own electrical power plant supplied the entire city of Coronado until 1922. Author L. Frank Baum, a frequent guest, designed the Crown Room's frumpy crown-shaped chandeliers. Baum wrote several of the books in his beloved *Wizard of Oz* series in Coronado, and some believe he modeled the Emerald City's geometric spires after the Del's conical turrets.

The hotel has played host to royalty and celebrities as well. The first visiting monarch was Kalakaua, Hawaii's last king, who spent Christmas here in 1890. But the best-known royal guest was Edward, Prince of Wales (later King Edward VIII, and then Duke of Windsor). He came to the hotel in April 1920, the first British royal to visit California. Of the many lavish social affairs held during his stay, at least two were attended by Wallis Simpson (then Navy wife Wallis Warfield) 15 years before her official introduction to the prince in London. Though some like to speculate that their love affair, which culminated in his abdication of the throne, might have begun right here, it's very unlikely it did.

In 1927, San Diego's beloved son, Charles Lindbergh, was honored here following his historic 33½-hour solo flight across the Atlantic. Hollywood stars including Mary Pickford, Greta Garbo, Charlie Chaplin, and Esther Williams have flocked to the Del. Henry James wrote in 1905 of "the charming sweetness and comfort of this spot." The hotel has also hosted 10 U.S. presidents. Perhaps most famously, director Billy Wilder filmed *Some Like It Hot* at the hotel; longtime staffers remember stars Marilyn Monroe, Tony Curtis, and Jack Lemmon romping on the beach. *The Stunt Man,* starring Peter O'Toole, was also filmed here, in 1980. And some guests have never left: The ghost of Kate Morgan, whose body was found in 1892 where the tennis courts are today, supposedly still roams the halls—room 3327 has a reputation for being haunted. Visitors and guests intrigued by the Hotel Del's past can stroll through the lower-level History Gallery, a mini-museum of hotel memorabilia.

Sunday brunch in the amazing **Crown Room** is a San Diego tradition. In 2001, the Del completed a painstaking $55-million, 3-year restoration that returned this priceless grande dame to its turn-of-the-20th-century splendor. That was just the beginning, though. In 2005, the guest rooms were given a $10 million sprucing, kicking off a 15-year master plan that will include the creation of a state-of-the-art spa with 22 treatment rooms (slated to open in the summer of '06) and the Beach Village, featuring 78 privately held one-, two-, and three-bedroom oceanfront cottages and villas.

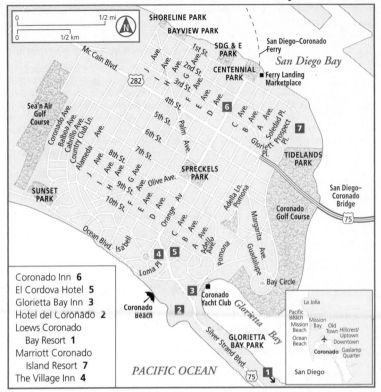

Coronado Inn **6**
El Cordova Hotel **5**
Glorietta Bay Inn **3**
Hotel del Coronado **2**
Loews Coronado
   Bay Resort **1**
Marriott Coronado
   Island Resort **7**
The Village Inn **4**

1500 Orange Ave., Coronado, CA 92118. ℂ 800/468-3533 or 619/435-6611. Fax 619/522-8238. www.hoteldel. com. 688 rooms. $305–$580 double; from $780 suites. Extra person $25. Children under 18 stay free in parent's room. Minimum stay requirements apply most weekends. AE, DC, DISC, MC, V. Valet parking $21; self-parking $16. Bus: 901 or 902. From Coronado Bridge, turn left onto Orange Ave. **Amenities:** 5 restaurants; 4 bars; 2 outdoor pools; 3 tennis courts; health club; spa; 2 Jacuzzis; bike rental; children's activities; concierge; shopping arcade; 24-hr. room service; babysitting; laundry service; dry cleaning. *In room:* A/C, TV w/pay movies, dataport, minibar, hair dryer, iron, safe.

EXPENSIVE

Marriott Coronado Island Resort 👁👁   Once expected to give competitor Loews a run for its money in the leisure market, this Marriott seems content with the substantial group business it gets from the convention center across the bay. Elegance and luxury here are understated. Although the physical property is generic, with impersonal architecture, the staff goes out of its way to provide upbeat attention: Guests just seem to get whatever they need, be it a lift downtown (by water taxi from the private dock), a tee time at the neighboring golf course, or a prime appointment at the spa. Despite its mostly business clientele, the hotel offers many enticements for the leisure traveler: a prime waterfront setting offering a sweeping view of the San Diego skyline; a location within a mile of Coronado shopping and dining, and walking distance from the ferry landing; lushly planted grounds filled with preening exotic birds; and a wealth of sporting and recreational activities. Guest rooms are generously sized and attractively furnished and decorated—in colorful French country style, and all feature balconies or patios. The superbly designed bathrooms hold an array of fine toiletries. In terms of room size and amenities, your dollar goes a lot further here than at the Hotel Del.

2000 Second St. (at Glorietta Blvd.), Coronado, CA 92118. © **800/228-9290** or 619/435-3000. Fax 619/435-3032. www.marriotthotels.com/sanci. 300 units. $315–$399 double; from $449 suites and villas. Children under 12 stay free in parent's room. AE, DC, MC, V. Valet parking $20; self-parking $15. Bus: 901 or 902. Ferry: From Broadway Pier. From Coronado Bridge, turn right onto Glorietta Blvd., take 1st right to hotel. **Amenities:** 2 restaurants; bar; 3 outdoor pools; 6 night-lit tennis courts; fitness center; spa; 2 Jacuzzis; watersports equipment/rentals; bike rental; concierge; courtesy shuttle to Horton Plaza; water taxi to convention center ($5); business center; salon; 24-hr. room service; babysitting; laundry service; dry cleaning. In room: A/C, TV w/pay movies, dataport, minibar, coffeemaker, hair dryer, iron, safe.

MODERATE

Coronado Inn ✦ Centrally located and terrifically priced, this renovated 1940s courtyard motel has such a friendly ambience, it's like staying with old friends. Iced tea, lemonade, and fresh fruit are even provided in the lobby each afternoon. It's still a motel, though—albeit with tropical floral decor—so rooms are pretty basic. The six rooms with bathtubs also have small kitchens; microwaves are available for the rest, along with hair dryers and irons (just ask up front). Rooms close to the street are noisiest, so ask for one toward the back. The Coronado shuttle stops a block away; it serves the shopping areas and Hotel Del.

266 Orange Ave. (corner of 3rd St.), Coronado, CA 92118. © **800/598-6624** or 619/435-4121. www. coronadoinn.com. 30 units (most with shower only). $135–$195 double (sleeps up to 4). Rates include continental breakfast. AE, DISC, MC, V. Free parking. Bus: 901 or 902. From Coronado Bridge, stay on 3rd St. Pets accepted with $10 nightly fee. **Amenities:** Outdoor pool; coin-op laundry. In room: A/C, TV, fridge.

El Cordova Hotel ✦ This Spanish hacienda across the street from the Hotel del Coronado began life as a private mansion in 1902. By the 1930s, it had become a hotel; the original building was augmented by a series of attachments housing retail shops along the ground-floor arcade. Shaped like a baseball diamond and surrounding a courtyard with meandering tiled pathways, flowering shrubs, a swimming pool, and patio seating for Miguel's Cocina Mexican restaurant, El Cordova hums pleasantly with activity. Each room is a little different from the next—some sport a Mexican colonial ambience, while others evoke a comfy beach cottage. All feature ceiling fans and brightly tiled bathrooms, but lack the frills that would command exorbitant rates. El Cordova has a particularly inviting aura, and its prime location makes it a popular option; reserving several months in advance is advised for summer months. Facilities include a barbecue area with picnic table.

1351 Orange Ave. (at Adella Ave.), Coronado, CA 92118. © **800/229-2032** or 619/435-4131. Fax 619/435-0632. www.elcordovahotel.com. 40 units. $155–$189 double; from $269 suite. Children under 12 stay free in parent's room. Weekly/monthly rates available in winter. AE, DC, DISC, MC, V. Parking in neighboring structure $6/day. Bus: 901 or 902. From Coronado Bridge, turn left onto Orange Ave. **Amenities:** Restaurant; outdoor pool; shopping arcade; coin-op laundry. In room: A/C, TV.

Glorietta Bay Inn ✦✦ Right across the street from, and somewhat in the (figurative) shadow of, the Hotel Del, this pretty white hotel consists of the charmingly historic John D. Spreckels mansion (1908) and several younger, motel-style buildings. Only 11 rooms are in the mansion, which boasts original fixtures, a grand staircase, and old-fashioned wicker furniture; the guest rooms are also decked out in antiques, and have a romantic and nostalgic ambience. Rooms and suites in the 1950s annexes are much less expensive but were upgraded from motel-plain to better match the main house's classy ambience (though lacking the mansion's superluxe featherbeds); some have kitchenettes and marina views. The least expensive units are small and have parking-lot views. Wherever your room is, you'll enjoy the inn's trademark personalized service, including extra-helpful staffers who remember your name and happily offer dining and sightseeing recommendations or arrange tee times. Special attention is also paid to repeat guests and families with toddlers. In addition to offering bikes and boat rentals on Glorietta Bay across the street, the hotel is within easy walking distance of the beach, golf, tennis, watersports, shopping, and dining. Rooms in the mansion are booked early, but are worth the extra effort and expense.

1630 Glorietta Blvd. (near Orange Ave.), Coronado, CA 92118. ⓒ **800/283-9383** or 619/435-3101. Fax 619/435-6182. www.gloriettabayinn.com. 100 units. Double $170–$220 annex; from $275 mansion. Extra person $10. Children under 18 stay free in parent's room. Minimum stays in summer. Rates include continental breakfast and afternoon refreshment. AE, DC, DISC, MC, V. Self-parking $10. Bus: 901 or 902. From Coronado Bridge, turn left on Orange Ave. After 2 miles, turn left onto Glorietta Blvd.; the inn is across the street from the Hotel del Coronado. **Amenities:** Outdoor pool; Jacuzzi; in-room massage; babysitting; laundry service; dry cleaning; coin-op laundry. *In room:* A/C, TV w/pay movies, dataport, fridge, coffeemaker, hair dryer, safe.

INEXPENSIVE

The Village Inn _Value_ Its location—a block or two from Coronado's main sights, including the Hotel Del, the beach, shopping, and cafes—is this inn's most appealing feature. Historic charm runs a close second; a plaque outside identifies the three-story brick-and-stucco hotel as the once-chic Blue Lantern Inn, built in 1928. The charming vintage lobby sets the mood in this European-style hostelry; each simple but well-maintained room holds antique dressers and armoires, plus lovely Battenberg lace bedcovers and shams. Front rooms enjoy the best view, and coffee and tea are available all day in the kitchen where breakfast is served. The appealing inn's only Achilles' heel is tiny, tiny bathrooms, so cramped that you almost have to stand on the toilet to use the small-scale sinks (though surprisingly, some bathrooms have been updated with Jacuzzi tubs).

1017 Park Place (at Orange Ave.), Coronado, CA 92118. ⓒ **619/435-9318.** www.coronadovillageinn.com. 15 units. $85–$95 double. Rates include continental breakfast. AE, MC, V. Parking available on street. Bus: 901 or 902. From Coronado Bridge, turn left onto Orange Ave., and then right on Park Place.

8 Near the Airport

San Diego's airport has the unusual distinction of being virtually in the downtown area. Although immediate neighbors grouse about the noise and decreased property values, this is good news for travelers: The accommodations reviewed in the downtown, Hillcrest, and Old Town/Mission Valley sections are only 5 to 15 minutes from the airport.

For those who wish to stay even closer, there are two good airport hotels—these bayside properties won't remind you of the dives found near most airports. The 1,045-room **Sheraton San Diego Hotel & Marina,** 1380 Harbor Island Dr. (ⓒ **800/325-3535** or 619/291-2900; www.starwoodhotels.com), offers rooms from $249. At the 208-room **Hilton San Diego Airport/Harbor Island,** 1960 Harbor Island Dr. (ⓒ **800/445-8667** or 619/291-6700; www.hilton.com), rooms start at $269. Both hotels offer a marina view, a pool, and a 10-minute drive to downtown San Diego—as always, hefty discounts are usually available.

6

Where to Dine

San Diego's dining scene, once a culinary backwater, has come into its own during the past decade. The spark for this new spirit of experimentation and style has been an explosion in the transplant population and cultural diversification. But other factors are at play. A bustling economy helps, motivating folks to step out and exercise their palates. These new foodies have learned to respect the seasonality of vegetables, and chefs revel in the bounteous agriculture of San Diego County by focusing on produce when flavors are at their peak at specialized North County growers like Chino Farm and Be Wise Ranch.

Top young cooks are increasingly lured by San Diego's agreeable lifestyle and the chance to make a fast impression in the region's dining scene. I've met more than one chef seduced by the idea that you can surf in the ocean each morning, and then in the afternoon hand-select fresh produce at the farm where it was grown to serve guests that night. And although we import chefs from around the world, we've also started exporting them—Marine Room wizard Bernard Guillas represents America at illustrious events like the Masters of Food and Wine, and nearly 20 locals, including Michael Stebner of **Region** (p. 113), Amiko Gubbins of **Parallel 33** (p. 112), and Riko Bartolome of **Asia-Vous** (p. 252), have cooked at the prestigious James Beard House in New York.

As you can imagine, San Diego offers terrific seafood: Whether at unembellished market-style restaurants that let the fresh catch take center stage or at upscale restaurants that feature extravagant presentations, the ocean's bounty is everywhere. California cuisine and Italian fare still dominate the scene, but eclectic fusion food has carved out a substantial niche here as well. Of course, San Diego still has plenty of clubby steak-and-potatoes stalwarts, and we're loaded with the chain restaurants you'll probably recognize from home.

But number one on most every visitor's list of priorities is Mexican food—a logical choice given the city's history and location. You'll find lots of highly Americanized, fairly satisfying interpretations of Mexican fare (that is, combo plates heaped with melted cheddar cheese) along with a few hidden gems, like **El Agave** (p. 116) and Escondido's **Hacienda de Vega** (p. 253), which serve true south-of-the-border cuisine. And don't miss our humble fish taco, perhaps the city's favorite fast food.

San Diego's multicultural fabric ensures that ethnic foods are a good option when you want something more exotic than Mexican or Italian fare. While Chinese restaurants have long had a place at the table, Asian cuisine today also includes Japanese, Thai, Vietnamese, and Cambodian restaurants. A drive through the heart of Kearny Mesa reveals a panoply of Asian eateries at all prices, along with vast grocery stores brimming with quirky delicacies. But also note that many intrepid "mainstream" chefs fuse Asian ingredients and preparations with more familiar Mediterranean or French menus.

In this chapter, restaurants in San Diego proper are indexed by location and price category. However, note that some of San Diego's best dining venues lie 30 to 40 minutes to the north, in the communities of Rancho Santa Fe, Del Mar, and Carlsbad. These are found in chapter 11, as are dining options for the Disneyland area and south of the border.

In keeping with our beach culture, even in the more pricey places, dress tends to be casual. Some notable exceptions are downtown, La Jolla's more expensive restaurants, and the hotels on Coronado, where jeans are a no-no and gentlemen may feel more comfortable in a sports coat.

For diners on a budget, the more expensive San Diego restaurants are usually accommodating if you want to order a few appetizers instead of a main course, and many offer reasonably priced lunch menus. Worthwhile discount coupons are found in the *San Diego Weekly Reader,* available free on Thursdays (and known as *The Weekly* in an edited version distributed at local hotels). And quite a few restaurants, like **Chez Loma** (p. 132) and **Café Pacifica** (p. 116), offer "early bird" specials—discounted dining for those who don't mind being seated by 6pm or so.

Restaurants are categorized by price, which includes the average cost of one entree, an appetizer (if the entree does not come with a side dish or appetizer), one *nonalcoholic* drink, tax, and tip. **Very Expensive** means a meal averages $50 per person and up; **Expensive** means it costs $30 to $50; **Moderate** means it's $15 to $30; and **Inexpensive** means it's less than $15.

A note on parking: Unless a listing specifies otherwise, drivers can expect to park within 2 or 3 blocks of the restaurants listed here. If you can't find a free or metered space on the street, you can seek out a garage or lot; most Gaslamp Quarter and La Jolla venues offer valet parking.

1 Best Bets for Dining

- **Best Spot for a Business Lunch: Dobson's Bar & Restaurant,** 956 Broadway Circle, downtown San Diego (© 619/231-6771), has been mixing business and pleasure for more than 20 years. You'll literally rub shoulders (thanks to the restaurant's cozy set-up) with power brokers and politicos from both sides of the border. See p. 104.
- **Best View:** Many restaurants overlook the ocean, but only from **Brockton Villa,** 1235 Coast Blvd., La Jolla (© 858/454-7393), can you see sublime La Jolla Cove. Diners with a window seat will feel as if they're looking out on a gigantic picture postcard. See p. 128.
- **Best Value:** The word "huge" barely begins to describe the portions at **Filippi's Pizza Grotto,** 1747 India St. (© 619/232-5095), where a salad for one is enough for three, and an order of lasagna must weigh a pound. There's a kids' menu, and Filippi's has locations all over, including Pacific Beach, Mission Valley, and Escondido. See p. 110.

- **Best Seafood:** At **Star of the Sea,** 1360 N. Harbor Dr. (© **619/232-7408**), you'll find the city's best package of fresh seafood, exquisite preparations, graceful service, and memorable views from the edge of San Diego Bay. See p. 106.
- **Best Contemporary American Cuisine:** Young Turk Tony DiSalvo has set the San Diego dining scene on fire with his three-floor, multitasking dining complex, **Jack's La Jolla,** 7863 Girard Ave. (© **858/456-8111**). DiSalvo, a veteran of Jean-Georges in New York City, quickly established Jack's at the top of the San Diego food chain with a sophisticated menu that incorporates plenty of local products. See p. 126.
- **Best Mexican Cuisine:** Rather than the "combination plate" fare that's common on this side of the border, **El Agave Tequileria,** 2304 San Diego Ave., Old Town (© **619/220-0692**), offers a memorable combination of freshly prepared recipes from Veracruz, Chiapas, Puebla, and Mexico City—along with an impressive selection of boutique and artisan tequilas and mezcals. See p. 116.
- **Best Pizza:** For gourmet pizza from a wood-fired oven, head for **Sammy's California Woodfired Pizza,** a local institution with several locations, including 770 Fourth Ave., in the Gaslamp Quarter (© **619/230-8888**). For the traditional Sicilian variety, line up for **Filippi's Pizza Grotto** (see "Best Value," above).
- **Best Desserts:** You'll forget your diet at **Extraordinary Desserts,** 2929 Fifth Ave., Hillcrest (© **619/294-2132**) and 1430 Union St., Little Italy, (© **619/294-7001**). Heck, it's so good you might forget your name. Proprietor Karen Krasne has a *Certificat de Patisserie* from Le Cordon Bleu in Paris and makes everything fresh on the premises daily. See p. 113.
- **Best Late-Night Dining:** Open later than just about anyplace else downtown, **Café Lulu,** 419 F St. (© **619/238-0114**), serves eclectic sandwiches and inventive espresso drinks until 1am during the week, 3am on weekends. See p. 110.
- **Best Fast Food:** A fish taco may sound strange to the uninitiated, but once you taste one, you'll know why locals line up for them. They're served at eateries throughout the city, but try one from the original location of **Rubio's,** 4504 E. Mission Bay Dr. (© **619/272-2801**). Now a burgeoning chain, Rubio's popularized fish tacos here nearly 25 years ago. See "Baja Fish Tacos" on p. 120.
- **Best People Watching:** The food is nothing to write home about, but **The Green Flash,** 701 Thomas Ave. (© **858/270-7715**), is the place to take in the Pacific Beach scene, the good, the bad, and the ugly. Skaters, surfers, joggers, bikers, suntanners, dog-walkers, spring breakers—you name 'em, they're all here. The boardwalk is just inches from the tables, and the view changes every few seconds. See p. 122.
- **Best Picnic Fare:** Pack a superb sandwich from the **Bread & Cie.,** 350 University Ave., Hillcrest (© **619/683-9322**), where the hearty breads are the toast of the city; see p. 114. Or head to one of several locations of **Whole Foods,** where the deli houses a smashing selection of delicious hot and cold items, a great cheese collection, and a crisp salad bar; you'll find one outpost in Hillcrest at 711 University Ave. (© **619/294-2800**), and another in La Jolla at 8825 Villa La Jolla Dr. (© **858/642-6700**).

2 Restaurants by Cuisine

AMERICAN

Bay Beach Cafe (Coronado, $$, p. 132)

Bertrand at Mister A's ✦✦✦ (Hillcrest/ Uptown, $$$$, p. 111)

The Brigantine (Coronado, $$$, p. 131)

Clayton's Coffee Shop (Coronado, $, p. 133)

Corvette Diner (Hillcrest/Uptown, $, p. 115)

Crest Cafe (Hillcrest/Uptown, $, p. 115)

Dakota Grill & Spirits ✦ (Downtown, $$, p. 108)

Fat City Steakhouse (Little Italy, $$, p. 109)

The Green Flash (Pacific Beach, $$, p. 122

Hash House a Go Go ✦ (Hillcrest/ Uptown, $$, p. 111)

Hodad's (Ocean Beach, $, p. 120)

Jack's Grille ✦✦ (La Jolla, $$, p. 129)

Jack's La Jolla ✦✦✦ (La Jolla, $$$$, p. 126)

Karl Strauss Brewery & Grill (Downtown, La Jolla, $$, p. 109)

Kensington Grill ✦✦ (Kensington, $$$, p. 135)

Lou & Mickey's ✦ (Downtown, $$$, p. 108

Rainwater's on Kettner ✦✦ (Downtown, $$$$, p. 105)

Rhinoceros Cafe & Grille ✦ (Coronado, $$, p. 132)

Rocky's Crown Pub (Pacific Beach, $, p. 120)

South Beach Bar & Grill (Ocean Beach, $, p. 120)

BREAKFAST

Brockton Villa ✦ (La Jolla, $$, p. 128)

Cafe 222 ✦ (Downtown, $$, p. 104)

Clayton's Coffee Shop (Coronado, $, p. 133)

The Cottage ✦ (La Jolla, $, p. 131)

Crest Cafe (Hillcrest/Uptown, $, p. 115)

Hash House a Go Go (Hillcrest/ Uptown, $$, p. 111)

Kono's Surf Club Café (Pacific Beach, $, p. 120)

The Mission ✦ (Mission Beach, North Park, Downtown, $, p. 123)

Villa Nueva Bakery Café ✦ (Coronado, $, p. 133)

CALIFORNIAN

Azzura Point ✦✦ (Coronado, $$$$, p. 131)

Baleen ✦✦ (Mission Bay, $$$$, p. 120)

Brockton Villa ✦ (La Jolla, $$, p. 128)

Cafe Pacifica ✦✦ (Old Town, $$$, p. 116)

California Cuisine ✦✦ (Hillcrest/ Uptown, $$$, p. 112)

Chive ✦✦✦ (Downtown, $$$, p. 107)

Confidential ✦ (Downtown, $$$, p. 104)

Dobson's Bar and Restaurant ✦ (Downtown, $$, p. 104)

Fresh ✦✦ (La Jolla, $$$, p. 127)

George's at the Cove ✦✦✦ (La Jolla, $$$$, p. 124)

Hawthorn's ✦ (Hillcrest/Uptown, $$, p. 113)

Indigo Grill ✦✦ (Little Italy, $$$, p. 107)

The Marine Room ✦✦✦ (La Jolla, $$$$, p. 126)

Napa Valley Grille ✦ (Downtown, $$, p. 109)

Nick's at the Beach (Ocean Beach, $$, p. 123)

Nine-Ten ✦✦ (La Jolla, $$$$, p. 127)

Ocean Terrace Bistro and Pacific View Bar ✦✦ (La Jolla, $$, p. 129)

Key to Abbreviations: $$$$ = Very Expensive; $$$ = Expensive; $$ = Moderate; $ = Inexpensive

Region ✶✶ (Hillcrest/Uptown, $$$, p. 113)

Stingaree ✶ (Downtown, $$$, p. 104)

CHINESE

China Max ✶ (Kearny Mesa, $$, p. 134)

Jasmine ✶✶ (Kearny Mesa, $$, p. 134)

Red Pearl Kitchen (Downtown, $$$, p. 104)

Spicy City ✶ (Kearny Mesa, $$, p. 134)

COFFEE & TEA

Café Lulu (Downtown, $, p. 110)

Living Room Coffeehouse (Old Town, $, p. 118)

Mrs. Burton's Tea Parlor (Old Town, $$, p. 115)

DESSERTS

Extraordinary Desserts ✶✶✶ (Hillcrest/Uptown, Little Italy, $$, p. 113)

Michele Coulon Dessertier ✶✶ (La Jolla, $$, p. 124)

FRENCH

3rd Corner ✶✶ (Ocean Beach, $$, p. 120)

Cafe Cerise ✶✶ (Downtown, $$, p. 104)

Cafe Chloe ✶✶ (Downtown, $$, p. 108)

Chez Loma ✶ (Coronado, $$$, p. 132)

El Bizcocho ✶✶✶ (Rancho Bernardo, $$$$, p. 135)

Laurel ✶✶ (Hillcrest/Uptown, $$$, p. 110)

Le Fontainebleau ✶✶✶ (Downtown, $$$$, p. 104)

The Marine Room ✶✶✶ (La Jolla, $$$$, p. 126)

Modus (Hillcrest/Uptown, $$, p. 110)

Sky Room ✶✶ (La Jolla, $$$$, p. 124)

Tapenade ✶✶✶ (La Jolla, $$$, p. 124)

Thee Bungalow ✶✶ (Ocean Beach, $$$, p. 121)

Top of the Cove ✶✶ (La Jolla, $$$$, p. 124)

INTERNATIONAL

Bandar ✶ (Downtown, $$, p. 104)

Café Sevilla ✶ (Downtown, $$, p. 104)

Cantina Panaderia ✶ (Pacific Beach, $$, p. 118)

Costa Brava (Pacific Beach, $$, p. 118)

Isola (Pacific Beach, $$, p. 118)

Parallel 33 ✶✶ (Hillcrest/Uptown, $$$, p. 112)

ITALIAN

Buon Appetito ✶ (Little Italy, $$, p. 104)

Caffè Bella Italia ✶✶ (Pacific Beach, $$, p. 121)

Filippi's Pizza Grotto (Downtown, Pacific Beach, and other locations, $, p. 110)

Piatti ✶ (La Jolla, $$, p. 129)

Pizza Nova (Hillcrest, Point Loma, $$, p. 114)

Po Pazzo ✶ (Little Italy, $$$, p. 104)

Sammy's California Woodfired Pizza (Downtown, Mission Valley, La Jolla, and other locations, $$, p. 114)

Sogno DiVino ✶ (Little Italy, $, p. 104)

Trattoria Acqua ✶✶ (La Jolla, $$$, p. 128)

LATIN AMERICAN

Berta's Latin American Restaurant ✶ (Old Town, $$, p. 116)

LIGHT FARE

Bread & Cie. ✶✶ (Hillcrest/Uptown, $, p. 114)

Café Lulu (Downtown, $, p. 110)

The Cottage ✶ (La Jolla, $, p. 131)

Living Room Coffeehouse
(Old Town, $, p. 118)
The Mission ✫ (Mission Beach,
North Park, downtown, $, p. 123)
Villa Nueva Bakery Café ✫
(Coronado, $, p. 132)

MEDITERRANEAN

Bertrand at Mister A's ✫✫✫
(Hillcrest/Uptown, $$$$, p. 110)
Bread & Cie. ✫✫ (Hillcrest/Uptown,
$, p. 114)
Laurel ✫✫ (Hillcrest/Uptown, $$$,
p. 110)
Napa Valley Grille ✫ (Downtown, $$,
p. 109)
Piatti ✫ (La Jolla, $$, p. 129)
Sally's ✫✫ (Downtown, $$$, p. 104)
Trattoria Acqua ✫✫ (La Jolla, $$$,
p. 128)

MEXICAN

Candelas ✫✫ (Downtown, $$$,
p. 106)
Casa Guadalajara (Old Town, $$,
p. 117)
El Agave Tequileria ✫✫ (Old Town,
$$$, p. 116)
El Zarape ✫ (Hillcrest/Uptown, $,
p. 120)
Gringo's ✫ (Pacific Beach, $$, p. 103)
Mamá Testa ✫ (Hillcrest/Uptown, $,
p. 120)
Miguel's Cocina (Coronado, $$,
p. 131)
Old Town Mexican Café (Old Town,
$, p. 118)
Ranchos Cocina ✫ (North Park, $$,
p. 135)
Rubio's Baja Grill (throughout the
city, $, p. 120)
Su Casa (La Jolla, $$, p. 124)
Wahoo's Fish Taco (La Jolla/
Mission Valley, $, p. 120)

PACIFIC RIM/ASIAN FUSION

Roppongi ✫ (La Jolla, $$$, p. 127)

SEAFOOD

Baleen ✫✫ (Mission Bay, $$$$,
p. 120)
Bay Park Fish Co. ✫ (Bay Park, $$,
p. 120)
Blue Water Seafood Market and
Grill ✫ (Mission Hills, $$, p. 120)
The Brigantine (Coronado, $$$,
p. 131)
Cafe Pacifica ✫✫ (Old Town, $$$,
p. 116)
The Fishery ✫ (Pacific Beach, $$,
p. 122)
The Fish Market/Top of the
Market ✫ (Downtown, $$, p. 109)
Fresh ✫✫ (La Jolla, $$$, p. 127)
Island Prime ✫ (Harbor Island, $$$,
p. 130)
Jordan (Pacific Beach, $$$, p. 118)
Lou & Mickey's ✫ (Downtown, $$$,
p. 108)
The Oceanaire Seafood Room ✫✫
(Downtown, $$$, p. 104)
Point Loma Seafoods ✫ (Point Loma,
$, p. 120)
Star of the Sea ✫✫✫ (Downtown,
$$$$ p. 106)

SUSHI

The Fish Market/Top of the Market
✫ (Downtown, $$, p. 109)
Harney Sushi (Old Town, $$, p. 115)
Sushi Ota ✫✫ (Pacific Beach, $$,
p. 123)
Zenbu ✫ (La Jolla, $$, p. 124)

THAI

Rama ✫ (Downtown, $$, p. 104)
Saffron Chicken ✫ (Mission Hills, $$,
p. 111)
Spice & Rice Thai Kitchen ✫
(La Jolla, $$, p. 130)

VEGETARIAN

Jyoti Bihanga (Normal Heights, $,
p. 135)
Kung Food (Hillcrest/Uptown, $,
p. 111)
Spread (North Park, $$, p. 135)

3 Downtown, Gaslamp Quarter & Little Italy

Two decades ago, downtown was the domain of a few high-priced and highfalutin Continental and American restaurants—and little else. But the area was turned on its ear when the new convention center opened. Swank spots began moving into the Gaslamp Quarter's restored Victorian buildings in the late 1980s. Although the initial trend—no doubt designed to cater to the expense-account crowd—leaned toward thick steaks and heaping plates of pasta, the overall menu has evolved toward lighter and more ethnic food. Today, the Gaslamp positively percolates with its concentration of dining options, at all price levels and showcasing a variety of cuisine.

You can grab breakfast at a quirky stalwart like **Cafe 222** ✱, 222 Island Ave. (© **619/236-9902**), have lunch with the powerbrokers at **Dobson's Bar & Restaurant** ✱, 956 Broadway Circle (© **619/231-6771**), and enjoy dinner with the party crowd at sexy supper clubs like **Stingaree** ✱, 454 Sixth Ave. (© **619/544-9500**), and **Confidential** ✱, 901 Fourth Ave. (© **619/696-8888**). International choices include Thai at **Rama** ✱, 327 Fourth Ave. (© **619/501-8424**), tapas at **Café Sevilla** ✱, 555 Fourth Ave. (© **619/233-5979**), and Persian at **Bandar** ✱, 825 Fourth Ave. (© **619/238-0101**). At press time, hot restaurateurs Tim and Liza Goodell had just opened a San Diego edition of **Red Pearl Kitchen,** 440 J St. (© **619/231-1100**), a hip Chinese/East Asian restaurant that has been a mainstay up the road in Orange County.

Downtown encompasses many more options beyond the 16½-block Gaslamp Quarter. Hotel restaurants like the palatial **Le Fontainebleau** ✱✱✱ at the Westgate Hotel, 1055 Second Ave. (© **619/557-3655**), or bayside **Sally's** ✱✱ along the Embarcadero at the Manchester Grand Hyatt, 1 Market Place (© **619/358-6740**), are attractive choices; chef Jason Seibert has also impressed with his **Cafe Cerise** ✱✱, 1125 Sixth Ave. (© **619/595-0153**).

Little Italy, still in the midst of an upscale makeover, is home to various eateries including, of course, fine Italians like **Po Pazzo** ✱, 1917 India St. (© **619/238-1917**), and **Buon Appetito** ✱, 1609 India St. (© **619/238-9880**). The owners of Buon Appetito also recently created a sister property next door, the wine bar **Sogno DiVino** ✱, 1607 India St. (© **619/531-8887**).

A word on parking: On evenings when the Padres are playing, or when a big convention fills area hotels, you'll compete for parking downtown. Fortunately, pedicabs—three-wheeled bikes that carry two passengers each—are easy to hire. But if you take a taxi or the trolley downtown on game nights, you'll find most restaurants easy to get into once the baseball crowd has made its way into the ballpark and the first pitch is thrown. Locals not going to the game tend to avoid the Gaslamp Quarter on those nights.

VERY EXPENSIVE

The Oceanaire Seafood Room ✱✱ SEAFOOD   As you sweep up the dramatic staircase of the Oceanaire, the retro-nautical decor may evoke the grand elegance of a Titanic-style luxury liner. The only iceberg ahead is of the lettuce variety, though, and this seafood eatery made it through its maiden voyage with flying colors to become a popular Gaslamp Quarter addition. A Minneapolis-based chain that opened here in 2004, Oceanaire features top local products as well as fish brought in daily from around the globe. Executive chef Brian Malarkey's preparations incorporate elements of Pacific Rim, Italian, classic French, and Asian cuisine; or you can have your

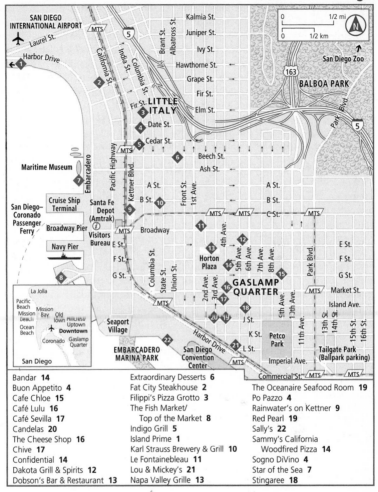

Bandar **14**
Buon Appetito **4**
Cafe Chloe **15**
Café Lulu **16**
Café Sevilla **17**
Candelas **20**
The Cheese Shop **16**
Chive **17**
Confidential **14**
Dakota Grill & Spirits **12**
Dobson's Bar & Restaurant **13**

Extraordinary Desserts **6**
Fat City Steakhouse **2**
Filippi's Pizza Grotto **3**
The Fish Market/
   Top of the Market **8**
Indigo Grill **5**
Island Prime **1**
Karl Strauss Brewery & Grill **10**
Le Fontainebleau **11**
Lou & Mickey's **21**
Napa Valley Grille **13**

The Oceanaire Seafood Room **19**
Po Pazzo **4**
Rainwater's on Kettner **9**
Red Pearl **19**
Sally's **22**
Sammy's California
   Woodfired Pizza **14**
Sogno DiVino **4**
Star of the Sea **7**
Stingaree **18**

catch-of-the-day simply grilled or broiled. There are classic starters like oysters Rockefeller, clams casino, and Maryland jumbo lump crab cakes. Entrees might include local mako shark with sweet onion confit and Roquefort blue cheese butter, or whole flash-fried striped bass in a citrus-ginger glaze. Non-fish eaters can enjoy top-quality prime beef, chicken, and pork.

400 J St. (at Fourth Ave.), Gaslamp Quarter. ℰ 619/858-2277. www.theoceanaire.com. Reservations recommended. Main courses $15–$50. AE, DISC, MC, V. Sun–Thurs 5–10pm; Fri–Sat 5–11pm. Valet parking from 6pm Sun–Thurs $10; Fri–Sat $15. Bus: 3, 5, or 16. Trolley: Convention Center.

Rainwater's on Kettner ✵✵ AMERICAN   Venerable, locally owned, and the power lunch choice of more than a few downtown business types and politicos, Rainwater's breaks no new ground in the steakhouse wars, but that's one of the reasons this spot is dependable. Lunch options include expectedly robust sandwiches and burgers, but you'll also find a good selection of entree salads. The restaurant's claim to fame is as an East Coast–style chophouse, and so the big hitters are rolled out for dinner: prime rib-eye, prime T-bone, and even a prime New York strip for two, all expertly chosen and grilled to your specifications. The dinner menu also includes rack of lamb, pork chops, a selection of seafood and pasta entrees, and I've heard the three-cheese meatloaf is a winner. But you came for the steaks, right? The spectacular wine list specializes in large-bottle formats and trophy labels (a vertical tasting of Screaming Eagle anyone?), but still finds room for eclectic picks under $50.

1202 Kettner Blvd. (at B St., next to the Santa Fe depot), downtown. © 619/233-5757. www.rainwaters.com. Reservations recommended. Main courses $10–$18 lunch, $25–$50 dinner. AE, DISC, MC, V. Mon–Fri lunch from 11:30am, dinner nightly from 4–11pm (till midnight Fri–Sat). Bus: 5. Trolley: Santa Fe Depot or American Plaza.

Star of the Sea ★★★ SEAFOOD   An Embarcadero fine-dining bastion since 1966, the former Anthony's Star of the Sea Room slumbered through the 1990s, the subject of mournful disdain by the city's emerging foodies. But a millennium makeover banished its stuffy, outmoded aura to the past, and the restaurant reopened with a new look, new attitude, and new name (to better differentiate it from the unexceptional waterfront fish houses next door, also in the Anthony's restaurant family). Gone is that dated dress code and off-putting formality, replaced by a comfortable, intimate ambience and modern decor matched to the still-glorious harbor view—the tables face the 1863 sailing ship *Star of India*. Stay tuned to the fine dining, though: executive chef Jesse Paul imbues the menu with sophisticated touches that show he's in touch with today's gourmands. The menu is seasonally composed: representative dishes include Tasmanian king salmon with wild mushrooms and hazelnuts, and perfectly seared diver scallops nuzzling a truffle risotto. There are always a few offerings for carnivores, but otherwise try the always-fresh seafood accompanied by equally stimulating vegetable creations. There's a reasonably priced wine list and a welcoming bar with its own abbreviated menu.

1360 N. Harbor Dr. (at Ash St.), Embarcadero. © 619/232-7408. www.starofthesea.com. Reservations recommended. Main courses $26–$40. AE, DC, DISC, MC, V. Daily 5:30–9:30pm (till 10pm Fri–Sat). Valet parking $8. Bus: All Harbor Dr. routes. Trolley: America Plaza.

EXPENSIVE

Candelas ★★ MEXICAN   This Gaslamp Quarter restaurant will forever alter your notion of Mexican food. If you're looking for tacos and burritos, go somewhere else. But if you're in the mood for a sophisticated, romantic fine dining experience, look no further than Candelas. Owner Alberto Mestre and executive chef Eduardo Baeza are both natives of Mexico City and they brought with them that city's culinary influences, which often blend Mexican and European elements. After all, not so long ago Spanish and French flags flew over Mexico. "I never got to try a burrito until I got to San Diego," Mestre told me. "If that's what you call Mexican food, then I'm lost." Candelas' appetizers include *estructura de aguacate* (avocado fanned and stuffed with scallops, crab, and shrimp) and *alcachofas Mestre* (artichoke hearts stuffed with ahi tuna and marinated with citrus). Look for main courses like baked lamb chops covered with mustard, basil, and garlic crust on a bed of sautéed sweet peppers, and sea bass in grape sauce. The chef's signature creation is *langosta Baeza:* fresh lobster in its shell, stuffed with mushrooms, chiles, onions, bacon, and tequila. Awesome. Candelas also has a sexy lounge next door.

416 Third Ave. (at J St.), Gaslamp Quarter. ℂ 619/702-4455. www.candelas-sd.com. Reservations recommended. Main courses $11–$15 lunch, $22–$35 dinner. AE, DC, DISC, MC, V. Mon–Fri 11am–2pm; Mon–Sun 5–11pm. Valet parking Thurs–Sat $10. Bus: 7 or 11. Trolley: Convention Center.

Chive ✹✹✹ CALIFORNIAN   This big city–style Gaslamp venue introduced San Diego to the sleek and chic dining rooms of the East Coast, and to daring kitchen inventions. The culinary adventure starts with a fashionable cocktail, of course—perhaps something like a blueberry *mojito,* Chive's twist on the Cuban classic. An ambient jazz soundtrack permeates the background while the practiced servers help decipher such unfamiliar menu ingredients as *picholine* (a tiny French olive) or *endigia* (an endive and radicchio hybrid from France). The menu changes every 6 to 8 weeks, but popular dishes found more often than not include lamb tagine served with harissa gnocchi, a roasted baby beet salad, the caramelized onion and potato pastilla, a nightly "noodle" (pasta) of the chef's whim, and salads that balance crispy greens with pungent, creamy cheeses and sweet fruit accents. But don't be surprised if you encounter curiosities like foie gras with banana bread and caramelized bananas— diners who take a chance on such eccentricities are usually richly rewarded. The always-evolving wine list offers many intriguing selections by "cork" or "stem" from all corners of the globe, like quality bottles from South Africa, Temecula, or Mexico. Chive balances its angular, wide space with cozy lighting, warm fabrics, and a pervasive sense of relaxed fun. One lament: In pursuit of elegant modernity, the cement floors and other hard surfaces amplify the noise level.

558 Fourth Ave. (at Market St.), Gaslamp Quarter. ℂ **619/232-4483.** www.chiverestaurant.com. Reservations recommended. Main courses $20–$32. AE, DC, DISC, MC, V. Daily 5–11pm. Live jazz Sat. Bus: 3, 5, 16, or 25. Trolley: Convention Center.

Indigo Grill ✹✹ CALIFORNIAN   Bracing "aboriginal" cuisine of the Pacific coast—from Mexico to Alaska—is showcased at Chef Deborah Scott's Little Italy adventure. This dance of diverse cooking ingredients and styles is as perilous as a tango, but memorable for its quantity of shrewd moves. Root veggies, game, and fruit are integral to the menu, and unusual spices are used liberally. Yes, occasionally the reach is too far, but no matter: This place is a treat for the palates of foodies yearning for something original. Start with the Oaxaca Fire, a tequila-based cocktail with a salt-and-pepper rim (lotsa kick there), and then tame the heat with the stacked beet salad with orange slices and shaved fennel. The alderwood plank salmon, served with a tangle of squid-ink pasta spotted with smoky Oaxacan cheese is a wonderful entree, or go for the blueberry-lacquered rack of lamb—all dishes are extravagantly garnished. Although the menu is primarily meat- and fish-oriented, there are always a couple of excellent vegetarian entrees and a throng of meatless appetizers (many of the starters are big enough that two will make a meal). The room is filled with native iconography, rippling water, and glass dividers that mimic sheets of ice; sharp angles, masks, and varied textures of wood, stone, metal, and leather invoke elements of the geographical territory encompassed by the menu. Scott made her name in the mid-1990s at **Kemo Sabe** (where Pacific Rim meets Southwestern), and juggles helming duties between these two, as well as her latest venture, **Island Prime,** a steak-and-seafood restaurant with killer views. If you enjoy one, it's worth checking out the others; Kemo Sabe is located at 3958 Fifth Ave., between University Avenue and Washington Street, Hillcrest (ℂ **619/220-6802**); Island Prime is on Harbor Island, near the airport, 880 Harbor Dr. (ℂ **619/298-6802**).

1536 India St. (at Cedar St.), Little Italy. © **619/234-6802.** www.cohnrestaurants.com. Reservations recommended. Main courses $9–$13 lunch, $18–$29 dinner. AE, DC, DISC, MC, V. Mon–Fri 11:30am–2:30pm; Mon–Thurs 5–9pm; Fri–Sat 5–10pm. Bus: 5 or 16. Trolley: Little Italy.

Lou & Mickey's ⑂ AMERICAN/SEAFOOD   Across the street from the Convention Center, and next to the GASLAMP sign, this old-school chophouse's best asset is a gorgeous dining room filled with exquisite hardwoods and lavish mosaic tiles, reminders of the restaurant's previous incarnation as a 1940s French bistro. The menu is more successful and varied than you might expect, ranging from bone-in steaks and prime seafood, to an oyster bar and scrumptiously good gulf shrimp served in curry-like "Manales" style. Another holdover from the old brasserie days is the popular Fruits of the Sea iced shellfish platter. For lighter eaters, there's a selection of sandwiches and pasta dishes, or you can pick a couple of items from the worthwhile appetizer list (the grilled artichokes are especially pleasing). Throw in unpretentious ambience and service that isn't predatory (like some unnamed steak houses in the Gaslamp) and you can count on a very enjoyable evening here.

224 Fifth Ave. (at Harbor Dr.), Gaslamp Quarter. © **619/237-4900.** www.louandmickeys.com. Reservations recommended. Main courses $20–$45. AE, DISC, MC, V. Sun–Thurs 5–10pm; Fri–Sat 5–11pm. Trolley: Gaslamp Quarter.

MODERATE

Cafe Chloe ⑂⑂ FRENCH   When it opened in 2004, this East Village restaurant created an immediate buzz. Had the owners struck upon some cutting-edge trend? No, it was a simple idea, really; something you'll find everywhere from Amsterdam to Zanzibar. It's a bistro. Creative, whimsical touches abound—such as a children's area, a retail space, and a patio built for two—but this is an otherwise straightforward enterprise, infused with the refined tastes and *joie de vivre* of its proprietors. So what's the fuss about? Cafe Chloe is small, it's loud when at capacity, and its tiny kitchen can get backed up. The fact is, though, while this kind of eatery can be found easily in other cities, it's a rarity here. The neighborly conviviality—combined with a short-but-sweet French-inspired menu covering breakfast, lunch, and dinner—makes for a winning dining experience, and one unique enough to create a stir in ever-morphing San Diego.

721 Ninth Ave. (at G St.), East Village. © **619/232-3242.** www.cafechloe.com. Reservations for parties of 5 or more only. Main courses $8–$13 breakfast, $9–$13 lunch, $15–$28 dinner. AE, MC, V. Mon 11am–10pm; Tues–Fri 7am–10pm; Sat 8am–10pm; Sun 9am–9pm. Bus: 7, 11, 20, 50, or 901.

Dakota Grill & Spirits ⑂ AMERICAN   This downtown business-lunch favorite is always busy and noisy; the Southwestern cowboy kitsch matches the cuisine in a beautiful room on the ground floor of San Diego's first high-rise. An open, copper-accented kitchen bustles smoothly; enjoy watching it from the second-level terrace that circles the room. Among the most popular items are the spit-wood–fired, horse-radish-crusted salmon, a chargrilled pork prime rib with apricot and mustard glaze, and the mesquite "knife and fork" baby back ribs. There's also a selection of burgers, pastas, and pizzas that can keep the dinner bill at a moderate level. When the kitchen is on, Dakota's innovation makes it a solid Gaslamp choice, and the atmosphere is the right mix of informal and smooth. There's live piano music Wednesday through Saturday evenings.

901 Fifth Ave. (at E St.), Gaslamp Quarter. © **619/234-5554.** www.cohnrestaurants.com. Reservations recommended. Main courses $9–$18 lunch, $11–$43 dinner. AE, DC, DISC, MC, V. Mon–Fri 11:30am–2:30pm; Mon–Thurs 5–10pm; Fri–Sat 5–11pm; Sun 5–9pm. Valet parking $10–$15. Bus: 3, 5, 16, or 25. Trolley: Gaslamp Quarter.

Fat City Steakhouse AMERICAN   If you need a steak but don't want to get caught up with the Gaslamp's roster of pricey chophouses and also don't want to settle for one of those chain eateries, Fat City is your place. Overlook the vaguely scary name (the owner's name is Tom Fat) and the vivid hot-pink paint job (the building is vintage Art Deco), and settle in to one of the cushy booths, beneath a canopy of Tiffany lamps. Skip the skimpy list of appetizers since the entrees come with a side of potato or rice, and specials on the blackboard include a salad for a couple bucks more. The steaks are USDA Choice, aged 21 days, and grilled-to-order over mesquite charcoal. Better yet, aim for the USDA Prime top sirloin: A hunky 12-ounce cut is just $17, and miles ahead in flavor of what you get at a Black Angus–type joint. You'll also find teriyaki salmon, chicken in a peppercorn sauce, and a couple of pasta dishes.

2137 Pacific Hwy. (at Hawthorn), Little Italy. © 619/232-9303. www.fatcitysteakhouse.com. Main courses $14–$24. Reservations accepted. AE, MC, V. Daily 5–10pm. Free parking. Bus: 34.

The Fish Market ⊀ (Value) SEAFOOD/SUSHI   The bustling Fish Market at the end of the G Street Pier on the Embarcadero is a San Diego institution. Chalkboards announce the day's catches—be it Mississippi catfish, Maine lobster, Canadian salmon, or Mexican yellowtail—which are sold by the pound or available in a number of classic, simple preparations in the casual, always-packed restaurant. Upstairs, the fancy offshoot **Top of the Market** offers sea fare with souped-up presentations (and jacked-up prices). Either way, the fish comes from the same trough, so I recommend having a cocktail in Top's plush, clubby atmosphere to enjoy the panoramic bay views, and then head downstairs for more affordable fare or treats from the sushi and oyster bars. There's another Fish Market in Del Mar at 640 Via de la Valle (© **858/ 755-2277**), and a counter outlet in Mission Valley at 2401 Fenton Pkwy. (© **619/ 280-2277**).

750 N. Harbor Dr., Embarcadero © **619/232-3474**. www.thefishmarket.com. Reservations not accepted. Main courses $10–$25 lunch, $13–$32 dinner (Top of the Market main courses $13–$35 lunch, $18–$45 dinner). AE, DC, DISC, MC, V. Daily 11am–9:30pm (till 10pm Fri–Sat). Valet parking $5. Bus: 7/7B. Trolley: Seaport Village.

Karl Strauss Brewery & Grill AMERICAN   Brewmaster Karl Strauss put San Diego on the microbrewery map with this unpretentious factory setting, now all but engulfed by the W Hotel. The smell of hops and malt wafts throughout, and the stainless-steel tanks are visible from the bar. Brews, all on tap, range from pale ale to amber lager. Five-ounce samplers are $1.75 each (or six for $8.95); if you like what you taste, 12-ounce glasses, pints, and hefty schooners stand chilled and ready. There's also nonalcoholic beer and wine by the glass. It used to be that the Cajun fries, hamburgers, German sausage (sans sauerkraut), and other greasy bar foods were secondary to the stylin' suds, but they've dressed up the lunch and dinner menu with items like mango chicken salad and filet mignon. Beer-related memorabilia and brewery tours are available. There's another location in La Jolla at 1044 Wall St. (© **858/551-2739**).

1157 Columbia St. (at B St.), downtown. © 619/234-2739. www.karlstrauss.com. Main courses $9–$25 (most entrees $11–$15). AE, MC, V. Kitchen Sun 11:30am–10pm, Mon–Thurs 11am–10pm, Fri 11am–11pm, Sat 11:30am–11pm; bar Sun–Thurs till 11pm, Fri–Sat till 1am. Bus: 5 or 16. Trolley: America Plaza.

Napa Valley Grille ⊀ CALIFORNIAN/MEDITERRANEAN   Proving that a shopping mall doesn't have to be a wasteland when it comes to dining, Napa Valley Grille is a popular, moderately upscale lunch spot for downtown workers, where entree-sized salads, sandwiches, and pasta dishes are rolled out. Come back at dinner when the atmosphere is often subdued, and you'll find a satisfying, seasonal selection of grilled items like Angus New York strip or duck breast in a pomegranate syrup, plus coriander-crusted ahi tuna or braised lamb shank with French lentils. Despite the mall bustle outside, the dining room is pleasant and appealing.

Horton Plaza Shipping Center (top floor), downtown. © 619/238-5440. www.napavalleygrille.com. Main courses $10–$16 lunch, $18–$32 dinner. AE, DC, DISC, MC, V. Mon–Thurs 11:30am–9pm; Fri–Sat 11:30am–10pm; Sun 11:30am–9:30pm. Bus: All Broadway routes. Trolley: Civic Center.

INEXPENSIVE

Café Lulu COFFEE & TEA/LIGHT FARE   Smack-dab in the heart of the Gaslamp Quarter, Café Lulu aims for a hip, bohemian mood, but if you're straight-arrow conservative, don't be put off—it's an inclusive place. Ostensibly a coffee bar, the cafe also makes a good choice for casual dining; if the stylishly dark interior is too harsh for you, watch the street action from a sidewalk table. The food is health conscious, largely prepared with organic ingredients. Soups, salads, cheese melts, and veggie lasagna are on the list; breads come from **Bread & Cie.** uptown (p. 114). Try one of the inventive coffee drinks, like cafe Bohème (mocha with almond syrup) or cafe L'amour (iced latte with a hazelnut tinge). Beer and wine are also served.

419 F St. (near Fourth Ave.), Gaslamp Quarter. © 619/238-0114. Main courses $6–$9. No credit cards. Sun–Thurs 11am–1am; Fri–Sat 11am–3am. Bus: 3, 5, 16, or 25. Trolley: Convention Center.

Filippi's Pizza Grotto (Kids) (Value) ITALIAN   For longtime locals, when we think "Little Italy," Filippi's comes to mind—it was a childhood fixture for many of us. To get to the dining area, decorated with Chianti bottles and red-checked tablecloths, you walk through a "cash and carry" Italian grocery store and deli strewn with cheeses, pastas, wines, bottles of olive oil, and salamis. You might even end up eating behind shelves of canned olives, but don't feel bad—this has been a tradition since 1950. The intoxicating smell of pizza wafts into the street; Filippi's has more than 15 varieties (including vegetarian), plus old-world spaghetti, lasagna, and other pasta. Children's portions are available, and kids will feel right at home under the sweeping mural of the Bay of Naples. On Friday and Saturday night, the lines to get in can look intimidating, but they move quickly. The original of a dozen branches throughout the county, this Filippi's has free parking. Other locations include 962 Garnet Ave. in Pacific Beach (© 858/483-6222).

1747 India St. (between Date and Fir sts.), Little Italy. © 619/232-5095. Reservations not accepted on weekends. Main courses $5–$13. AE, DC, DISC, MC, V. Sun–Mon 9am–10pm; Tues–Thurs 9am–10:30pm; Fri–Sat 9am–11:30pm. Free parking. Bus: 5. Trolley: Little Italy.

4 Hillcrest & Uptown

Hillcrest and the other gentrified uptown neighborhoods to its west and east are jam-packed with great food for any palate (and any wallet). Some are old standbys filled nightly with loyal regulars; others are trendy experiments that might be gone next year. Whether it's ethnic food, French food, health-conscious bistro fare, retro comfort food, specialty cafes and bakeries, or California cuisine, it's often mastered with the innovative panache you'd expect in the most nonconformist part of town.

Laurel ✦✦, 505 Laurel St. (© 619/239-2222), long a popular option for prtheater dining adjacent to Balboa Park, was reinvented by the owner of **Chive** (p. 107). The new menu, divided into small-plate grazing and traditional entree sections, offers French and Mediterranean cuisine with Asian influences. The west side of the park is also the site of **Modus,** 2202 Fourth Ave. (© 619/236-8516), which was set to open

Where to Dine in Hillcrest & Uptown

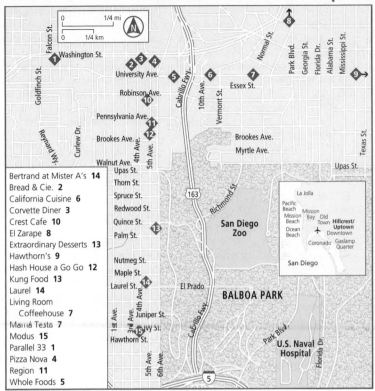

Bertrand at Mister A's **14**
Bread & Cie. **2**
California Cuisine **6**
Corvette Diner **3**
Crest Cafe **10**
El Zarape **8**
Extraordinary Desserts **13**
Hawthorn's **9**
Hash House a Go Go **12**
Kung Food **13**
Laurel **14**
Living Room
    Coffeehouse **7**
Mama Testa **7**
Modus **15**
Parallel 33 **1**
Pizza Nova **4**
Region **11**
Whole Foods **5**

at press time. Modus is the creation of Nathan Coulon, a third-generation San Diego restaurateur, whose mother runs **Michele Coulon Dessertier** (p. 124) in La Jolla. **Hash House a Go Go** ✸, 3628 Fifth Ave. (© 619/298-4646), occupies a reconverted building with an eclectic pun-filled menu of upscale comfort food. They serve three meals a day, but breakfast is the most popular choice. Whatever meal you're here for, though, you'd better be hungry, because portions are mountainous any time of day.

For many years, **Kung Food,** 2949 Fifth Ave. (© 619/298-7302), was one of San Diego's few vegetarian outposts. It closed for several years, but has reemerged at its old spot near Balboa Park. Another casual spot favored by locals is **Saffron Chicken** ✸, 3737 India St. (© 619/574-7737), serving Thai-style grilled chicken from a low-key storefront space on the west side of Mission Hills. Also note that the popular **Whole Foods** supermarket, 711 University Ave. (© 619/294-2800), has a mouthwatering deli and a robust salad bar—you can pack for a picnic or eat at the tables up front.

VERY EXPENSIVE

Bertrand at Mister A's ✸✸✸ AMERICAN/MEDITERRANEAN   Since 1965, San Diegans have come to high-rise Mister A's for proms, anniversaries, power meals, and other special occasions. Mister A's star began to wane in the '80s, though, despite its unsurpassed views of Point Loma, downtown, and Balboa Park. In 2000, it finally closed—only to reopen 4 months later, after a reported $1 million makeover under the stewardship of one of San Diego's most successful and charismatic restaurateurs, Bertrand Hug. The original Mister A's, with its dark, red-velvet interiors and cocktail waitresses in campy one-shouldered gowns, was reborn into Bertrand at Mister A's— an elegant, bright, sophisticated space, with an array of modern art. The vistas are still the best in town, although condo towers have sprouted up on the Balboa Park side of the restaurant. Seasonal menus with fresh ingredients are a highlight, and fare may include items such as sautéed boneless frog legs in Riesling sauce, Maine lobster strudel, and paella. Hug is also the proprietor of romantic **Mille Fleurs** (p. 250) in the wealthy North County neighborhood of Rancho Santa Fe.

2550 Fifth Ave. (at Laurel St.), Hillcrest. © 619/239-1377. www.bertrandatmisteras.com. Reservations recommended. Main courses $15–$20 lunch, $20–$45 dinner. AE, DC, MC, V. Mon–Fri 11:30am–2:30pm; Mon–Fri 5:30–9:30pm; Sat–Sun 5–9:30pm. Valet parking $6. Bus: 1, 3, or 25.

EXPENSIVE

California Cuisine ✦✦ CALIFORNIAN   This long-popular restaurant encountered a rocky patch when its identity as a place for light, cutting-edge food was in jeopardy. But the kitchen got an overhaul and the menu was slimmed down to bring back the qualities that put this restaurant on the map when it originally opened in 1982. Since its trademarks—no freezers, no can openers—are now well established at many serious restaurants across town, it's not as easy to stand out from the crowd, but the menu here is once again fresh and contemporary. The spare, understated dining room and delightfully romantic patio set the stage as a smoothly professional and respectful staff proffers fine dining at fair prices to a casual crowd. Under the supervision of Chef Todd Atcheson, the menu is a seasonal, market-driven affair that changes regularly. You may find jumbo lump crab cake with red pepper coulis and mango salsa or Niman ranch pork chops in an apple compote and bourbon glacé. Whatever you order, just make sure you leave enough room for the scintillating desserts such as buckwheat-mascarpone crepes with peach-plum compote, and banana and Belgian chocolate strudel with dulce de leche ice cream, whipped up on a daily basis. Allow time to find parking, which can be scarce along this busy stretch of University Avenue.

1027 University Ave. (east of 10th St.), Hillcrest. © 619/543-0790. www.californiacuisine.cc. Reservations recommended. Main courses $18–$35 dinner. AE, DC, DISC, MC, V. Daily 5–10pm. Bus: 908.

Parallel 33 ✦✦ (Finds) INTERNATIONAL   Pop quiz: What do Morocco, Lebanon, India, China, Iran, Iraq, and San Diego all have in common? Answer: They're all intersected by the same latitude—the 33rd parallel. Bringing together the unique flavors of those far-flung locales is the inspired idea behind Parallel 33, located in the upscale neighborhood of Mission Hills. The concept would be little more than a gimmick without the magic touch of Chef/owner Amiko Gubbins, and she definitely delivers. Just sit back and savor the creativity displayed in a menu that leaps enthusiastically from fragrant Moroccan chicken *b'stilla* to oven-roasted *za'atar* chicken with basmati rice, English peas, and harissa. The ahi *poke* (raw tuna) appetizer fuses a Hawaiian mainstay with Asian pear, mango, and Japanese wasabi—it's a winner. The decor is a hodgepodge, too: a touch of Hindu here, a dash of Islam there, a little bit of Buddhism—all contemporized by cement floors and iron accents. Call it contemplative industrial. Next door is the restaurant's intimate, very chill lounge, Blue Lotus, which not only handles waiting diners (and also serves food from the same menu), but warrants a visit all on its own.

741 W. Washington St. (at Falcon), Mission Hills. ℂ **619/260-0033.** www.parallel33sd.com. Reservations recommended. Main courses $18–$27. AE, DISC, MC, V. Mon–Thurs 5:30–10pm; Fri–Sat 5:30–11pm. Bus: 3, 16, or 908.

Region ✰✰ CALIFORNIAN   This restaurant is one of the shining stars in San Diego's restaurant scene—you'll find no better expression of "California cuisine" than at Region. It's the personal project of Chef Michael Stebner (formerly of Nine-Ten) who, with sous chef Allyson Colwell, continues to celebrate locally grown produce and "slow food" (the Italian cooking movement that's the opposite of fast food). Blackboards announce which farms provided each night's vegetables; another heralds "your artisans," the cheese-makers, the bakers, and so on. The menu is short—little more than a half-dozen appetizers and maybe five entrees, allowing the kitchen to keep an eye on perfecting each dish. But preparations are not fancy; the idea is to let peak-of-the-season ingredients speak for themselves without burdening them with heavy sauces or arduous techniques. Dishes might include flawlessly grilled scallops garnished with artichokes, oregano, lemon, capers, and an old-world vegetable like cardoon; or organic chicken served with turnips, broccoli, and green garlic risotto—chicken so good you'll swear off supermarket fowl forever. The food is rarely rich and the portions aren't gluttonous, so you have no excuses for cutting out before dessert.

3671 Fifth Ave. (at Pennsylvania), Hillcrest. ℂ **619/299-6499.** www.regionrestaurant.com. Reservations recommended. Main courses $19–$25. AE, DISC, MC, V. Tues–Fri and Sun 6–10pm; Sat 5:30–10pm. Bus: 1, 3, or 25.

MODERATE

Extraordinary Desserts ✰✰✰ DESSERTS   If you're a lover of sweets—heck, even if you eat dessert only once in a while—you owe it to yourself to visit this unique cafe. Chef and proprietor Karen Krasne's talent surpasses the promise of her impressive pedigree, which includes a *Certificat de Patisserie* from Le Cordon Bleu in Paris. Dozens of divine creations are available daily, and many are garnished with edible gold or flowers. Among them: a passion fruit ricotta torte bursting with kiwis, strawberries, and bananas; a *gianduia* of chocolate cake lathered with hazelnut butter cream, chocolate mousse, and boysenberry preserves, and sprinkled with shards of praline; or the *bête noir,* which is a dark-chocolate cake layered with vanilla crème brûlée, chocolate mousse, and chocolate truffle cream. Originally educated in Hawaii, Krasne likes to incorporate island touches like macadamia nuts, fresh coconut, fruit, and pure Kona coffee, but her Parisian experience is always present. She also sells her own exclusive line of jams, chutneys, syrups, spices, and confections, both at the original location and at an architecturally striking second space in Little Italy, 1430 Union St. (ℂ **619/ 294-7001**).

2929 Fifth Ave. (between Palm and Quince sts.) ℂ **619/294-2132.** www.extraordinarydesserts.com. Desserts $2–$9. MC, V. Mon–Thurs 8:30am–11pm; Fri 8:30am–midnight; Sat 10am–midnight; Sun 10am–11pm. Street parking usually available. Bus: 1, 3, or 25.

Hawthorn's ✰ CALIFORNIAN   It was a bad-news/great-news scenario for the longtime neighborhood favorite Fifth & Hawthorn. Redevelopment claimed the corner that gave the restaurant its name, but another new project came along to provide owner David Witt a new (business) lease on life. Reborn as Hawthorn's, this California fusion–style restaurant still finds itself serving theatergoers, but now it's not the people heading to the Old Globe from the restaurant's old Balboa Park–area location, but patrons of the magnificently rehabilitated North Park Theatre, just east of Hillcrest. Hawthorn's is located within the beautiful theater facility, which was originally built in 1928 and reopened in 2005 after an $8 million renovation. At press time, the

Wood-Fired Pizza

It all started with Wolfgang Puck, that crafty Austrian chef who dazzled Hollywood diners at Spago and went on to build a dynasty of California cuisine. Today, for a whole generation of Californians, pizza means barbecued chicken, tomato-basil, or goat cheese and sun-dried tomato, and kitchens all over San Diego stoke their wood-fired ovens to keep up with the demand. Two locally based chains deserve special note, and despite being alike, each chain thrives by covering neighborhoods the other doesn't. Prices are inexpensive to moderate.

Always a favorite in San Diego polls is **Sammy's California Woodfired Pizza** at 770 Fourth Ave., at F Street, in the Gaslamp Quarter (© 619/230-8888); 1620 Camino de la Reina in Mission Valley (© 619/298-8222); 702 Pearl St., at Draper Street, La Jolla (© 858/456-5222); and 12925 El Camino Real, at Del Mar Heights Road, Del Mar (© 858/259-6600). Sammy's serves creations like duck sausage, potato garlic, or Jamaican jerk shrimp atop 10-inch rounds. It also excels at enormous salads, making it easy to share a meal and save a bundle.

A similar menu is available at **Pizza Nova,** a local minichain with a vibrant atmosphere. You'll find them at 3955 Fifth Ave., north of University Avenue in Hillcrest (© 619/296-6682); 5120 N. Harbor Dr., west of Nimitz Boulevard in Point Loma (© 619/226-0268); and 945 Loma Santa Fe Dr., near I-5 in Solana Beach (© 858/259-0666).

menu was still being worked out, but Witt promises the same fresh fish, pastas, salads, and filet mignon that earned Fifth & Hawthorn a loyal following. Business hours are a bit up in the air as of press time, too, but Witt believes he'll be serving weekday lunch, nightly dinner (pre- and post-curtain), and Saturday/Sunday brunch.

2891 University Ave. (at 29th St.), North Park. © 619/544-0940. www.northparktheatre.com. Main courses $15–$25 dinner. AE, MC, V. Paid parking across the street. Bus: 7.

INEXPENSIVE

Bread & Cie. ✯✯ LIGHT FARE/MEDITERRANEAN   Delicious aromas permeate this cavernous Hillcrest bakery, where the city's most treasured breads are baked before your eyes all day long. The traditions of European artisan bread-making and attention to the fine points of texture and crust quickly catapulted Bread & Cie. to local stardom—they now supply bread to more than 75 local restaurants. Among my favorites (available daily) are anise and fig, black olive, jalapeño, and cheese—even the relatively plain sourdough *bâtard* is tart, chewy perfection. Others are available just 1 or 2 days a week, like the garlic and goat cheese (Sun and Thurs), or the hunky walnut and scallion (Wed and Sat). Ask for a free sample or order one of the many Mediterranean-inspired sandwiches. Try tuna niçoise with walnuts and capers; mozzarella, roasted peppers, and olive tapenade on focaccia; or roast turkey with hot-pepper cheese on rosemary/olive oil bread. A specialty coffee drink, delivered in a bowl-like mug, perfectly accompanies a light breakfast of fresh scones, muffins, and homemade granola with yogurt. Seating is at bistro-style tables in full view of the busy ovens and tattooed staff. Bread & Cie.'s phone line includes the usual prerecorded directional and hours of operation prompts, as well as a children's ditty sung in Dutch and a museum curator's dissertation on postmodern neo-Gothic impressionism.

350 University Ave. (at Fourth St.), Hillcrest. © 619/683-9322. Reservations not accepted. Sandwiches and light meals $4–$9. DISC, MC, V. Mon–Fri 7am–7pm; Sat 7am–6pm; Sun 8am–6pm. Bus: 1, 3, 16, 25, or 908.

Corvette Diner *Kids* AMERICAN   Travel back in time to the rockin' 1950s at this theme diner, where the jukebox is loud, the gum-snapping waitresses slide into your booth to take your order, and the decor is neon and vintage Corvette to the highest power. Equal parts *Happy Days* hangout and Jackrabbit Slim's (as in *Pulp Fiction*), the Corvette Diner is a comfy, family-friendly time warp in the midst of Hillcrest, and the diner-esque eats ain't bad for the price either. Burgers, sandwiches, appetizer munchies, blue-plate specials, and salads share the menu with a *very* full page of fountain favorites. Beer and wine are served, and there's a large bar in the center of the cavernous dining room. The party jumps a notch at night, with a DJ providing more entertainment (on top of the already captivating atmosphere)—the decibel level is always high. A reliable favorite for preteen birthdays.

3946 Fifth Ave. (between Washington St. and University Ave.), Hillcrest. © 619/542-1001. www.cohnrestaurants. com. Reservations not accepted. Main courses $7–$12, kids' plates $6. AE, DC, DISC, MC, V. Sun–Thurs 11am–10pm; Fri–Sat 11am–11pm. Valet parking $4. Bus: 1, 3, 16, 25, or 908.

Crest Cafe AMERICAN/BREAKFAST   This long-popular Hillcrest diner is a great refuge from sleek designer food and swank settings. The cheery pink interior announces 1940s style, and the room bubbles with upbeat waiters and comfort food doled out on Fiestaware. The church-pew–like booths are comfortable enough, but the small stucco room doesn't do much to mask the near constant clang of plates. No matter: Burger-lovers will fall in love with the spicy, rich "butter burger"—a dollop of herb butter is buried in the patty before cooking (it's even better than it sounds). And the East Texas fried chicken breast crusted with hunks of jalapeño peppers is none too subtle either, but it's tasty. A variety of sandwiches and salads, the popular steamed vegetable basket, and broiled chicken dishes are healthier options. During the early evening, the joint brims with neighborhood bohemians in search of a cholesterol fix, while later the club contingent swoops in; breakfast of omelets or crème brûlée French toast is a happy eye-opener.

425 Robinson Ave. (between Fourth and Fifth Ave.), Hillcrest. © 619/295-2510. www.crestcafe.net. Reservations not accepted. Main courses $5–$14. AE, DISC, MC, V. Daily 7am–midnight. Bus: 1, 3, 25, or 908.

5 Old Town & Mission Valley

Visitors usually have at least one meal in Old Town, and although this area showcases San Diego at its most touristy, I can't argue with the appeal of dining in California's charming original settlement. Mexican food and bathtub-size margaritas are the big draws, as are mariachi music and colorful decor. For a change of pace, stop by the hip sushi joint **Harney Sushi,** 3964 Harney St. (© **619/295-3272**), or **Mrs. Burton's Tea Parlor** in Heritage Park (© **619/294-4600**). Mrs. Burton's serves afternoon tea with an assortment of sandwiches, scones, tarts, and fresh fruit for $18 ($15 for children 12 and under); reservations are requested, and it's closed on Mondays.

Old Town is also the gateway to the decidedly less historic Mission Valley. There are plenty of chain eateries, both good and bad. We don't discuss them in depth here, but know that in the very busy Fashion Valley Shopping Center complex, you'll find the

Cheesecake Factory, California Pizza Kitchen, and P.F. Chang's—expect long waits for a table at each. In or near the Mission Valley Shopping Center, you'll find an Outback Steakhouse, Hooters, and Mimi's Cafe.

EXPENSIVE

Cafe Pacifica ★★ CALIFORNIAN/SEAFOOD   You can't judge a book by its cover: Inside this cozy Old Town casita, the decor is cleanly contemporary (but still romantic) and the food is anything but Mexican. Established in 1980, Cafe Pacifica serves upscale, imaginative seafood at decent prices and produces kitchen alumni who go on to enjoy local fame. Among the temptations are crab-stuffed portobello mushrooms topped with grilled asparagus, anise-scented bouillabaisse, and daily fresh fish selections served grilled with your choice of six sauces. Signature items include Hawaiian ahi with shiitake mushrooms and ginger butter, griddled mustard catfish, and the "Pomerita," a pomegranate margarita. To avoid the crush, arrive before 6:30pm—you'll also get to take advantage of the early bird special: an entree with soup or salad for $26.

2414 San Diego Ave., Old Town. ⓒ **619/291-6666**. www.cafepacifica.com. Reservations recommended. Main courses $14–$28. AE, DC, DISC, MC, V. Mon–Sat 5–10pm; Sun 4:30–9:30pm. Valet parking $5. Bus: 5/5A. Trolley: Old Town.

El Agave Tequileria ★★ MEXICAN   Don't be misled by this restaurant's less than impressive location above a liquor store on the outskirts of Old Town. This warm, bustling eatery continues to draw local gourmands for the regional Mexican cuisine and rustic elegance that leave the touristy fajitas-and-cerveza joints of Old Town far behind. El Agave is named for the agave plant from which tequila and its smoky cousin mezcal are derived, and the restaurant boasts more than 850 boutique and artisan tequilas and mezcals—bottles of every size, shape, and jewel-like hue fill shelves and cases throughout the dining room. Needless to say, El Agave serves some of the best margaritas in town. But even teetotalers will enjoy the restaurant's authentically flavored mole sauces (from Taxco, rich with walnuts; tangy tomatillo from Oaxaca; and the more familiar dark mole flavored with chocolate and sesame), along with giant shrimp and sea bass prepared in a dozen variations, or El Agave's signature beef filet with goat cheese and dark tequila sauce. On the other hand, I could almost make a meal out of the warm watercress salad dressed with onions and bacon, folded into tortillas. Lunches are simpler affairs without the exotic sauces, and inexpensive.

2304 San Diego Ave., Old Town. ⓒ **619/220-0692**. www.elagave.com. Reservations recommended. Main courses $8–$11 lunch, $16–$32 dinner. AE, MC, V. Daily 11am–10pm. Street parking. Bus: 5. Trolley: Old Town.

MODERATE

Berta's Latin American Restaurant ★ LATIN AMERICAN   Berta's is a welcome change from the nacho-and-fajita joints that dominate Old Town dining. Housed in a charming, basic cottage tucked away on a side street, Berta's faithfully re-creates the sunny flavors of Central and South America, where slow cooking mellows the heat of chiles and other spices. Everyone starts with a basket of fresh flour tortillas and mild salsa verde, which usually vanishes before you're done contemplating such mouthwatering dishes as Guatemalan *chilemal,* a rich pork-and-vegetable casserole with chiles, tomatoes, cornmeal *masa,* cilantro, and cloves. Try the Salvadoran *pupusas* (at lunch only)—dense corn-mash turnovers with melted cheese and black beans, their texture perfectly offset with crunchy cabbage salad and one of Berta's special salsas. Or opt for a table full of Spanish-style tapas, grazing alternately on crispy empanadas (filled

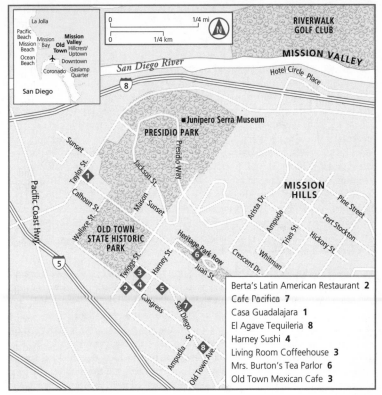

La Jolla
Pacific Beach
Mission Beach
Ocean Beach
Mission Bay
Coronado
Mission Valley
Old Town
Hillcrest/Uptown
Downtown
Gaslamp Quarter
San Diego

RIVERWALK GOLF CLUB

MISSION VALLEY

San Diego River

Hotel Circle Place

Junipero Serra Museum

PRESIDIO PARK

Presidio Way

MISSION HILLS

Sunset

Taylor St.

Jackson St.

Calhoun St.

Mason

Sunset

Arista Dr.

Ampudia

Trias St.

Hickory St.

Pine Street

Fort Stockton

Pacific Coast Hwy.

Wallace St.

OLD TOWN STATE HISTORIC PARK

Twiggs St.

Harney St.

Heritage Park Row

Juan St.

Crescent Dr.

Whitman

Congress

San Diego St.

Ampudia

Old Town Ave.

Berta's Latin American Restaurant **2**
Cafe Pacifica **7**
Casa Guadalajara **1**
El Agave Tequileria **8**
Harney Sushi **4**
Living Room Coffeehouse **3**
Mrs. Burton's Tea Parlor **6**
Old Town Mexican Cafe **3**

turnovers), strong Spanish olives, or *Pincho Moruno,* skewered lamb and onion redolent of spices and red saffron.

3928 Twiggs St. (at Congress St.), Old Town. ✆ 619/295-2343. www.bertasinoldtown.com. Main courses $7–$9 lunch, $11–$16 dinner. AE, MC, V. Tues–Sun 11am–10pm (lunch menu till 3pm). Free parking. Bus: 5/5A. Trolley: Old Town.

Casa Guadalajara *Kids* MEXICAN   Bazaar Del Mundo Shops, a warren of mostly Latin–themed gift stores, operates this Mexican restaurant situated a block away from Old Town State Historic Park. Not only is Casa Guadalajara better than what you'll find in the park, it's often less crowded than its counterparts (though waits of 30 min. or more are not unusual here Fri–Sat). Mariachi tunes played by strolling musicians enliven the room nightly, and you can also dine alfresco, in a picturesque courtyard occupied by a 200-year-old pepper tree. Birdbath-size margaritas start most meals, while dining ranges from simple south-of-the-border fare to more gourmet items like tequila lime shrimp and mango chipotle chicken—but the extensive menu features all the fajita and combo plates most people expect. Breakfast is also served on weekends. This place (like the Bazaar) is touristy, but out-of-towners looking for old California ambience and reliable Mexican food will find it here.

4105 Taylor St. (at Juan St.), Old Town. ℂ 619/295-5111. www.casaguadalajara.com. Reservations recommended. Main courses $8–$11 breakfast, $9–$16 lunch and dinner. AE, DC, DISC, MC, V. Mon–Thurs 11am–10pm; Fri 11am–11pm; Sat 8am–11pm; Sun 8am–10pm. Free parking. Bus: 5/5A. Trolley: Old Town.

INEXPENSIVE

Living Room Coffeehouse COFFEE & TEA/LIGHT FARE You may hear the whir of laptops from students, who use this spot as a sort of off-campus study hall. Grab a sidewalk table and enjoy the people-watching any time of day; indoors you'll find faux antiques, appropriately weathered for a lived-in feel. The pastries are fine, but it's the light meals—breakfast, lunch, and dinner—that make it a good choice. Breakfast includes omelets and waffles, while the rest of the fare is posted on a chalkboard menu; try the turkey lasagna, chicken Dijon, tuna melt, or one of several hearty entree salads. Plus you'll find exotic iced and hot coffee drinks, like the Emerald Isle (espresso, white chocolate, and mint). Other locations are in La Jolla at 1010 Prospect St. (ℂ **858/459-1187**); in Hillcrest at 1417 University Ave. (ℂ **619/295-7911**); in the Sports Arena area at 1018 Rosecrans (ℂ **619/222-6852**); and in the College area near San Diego State University, at 5900 El Cajon Blvd. (ℂ **619/286-8434**).

2541 San Diego Ave., Old Town. ℂ 619/325-4445. www.livingroomcafe.com. Most menu items $6–$8. AE, DISC, MC, V. Sun–Thurs 7am–10pm; Fri–Sat 7am–midnight. Bus: 5. Trolley: Old Town.

Old Town Mexican Café *(Overrated* MEXICAN This place is so popular that it's become an Old Town tourist attraction in its own right. But proceed with caution. The original structure is wonderfully funky and frayed, while the restaurant long ago expanded into additional, less appealing dining rooms and outdoor patios—and the wait for a table is often 30 minutes or longer. You can pass the time by gazing in from the sidewalk as tortillas are hand-patted the old-fashioned way, soon to be a hot-off-the-grill treat accompanying every meal, or by watching the chickens spinning around the barbecue. But the place is loud and crowded, and the food usually fails to impress. The best things here are the margaritas, served neat, in a shaker for two; the deliciously simple rotisserie chicken accompanied by tortillas, guacamole, sour cream, beans, and rice; and the cheap breakfasts, when the place is pleasantly sleepy and throng-free. Otherwise, the fried *carnitas*—reputedly a specialty—remind me of mystery meat that's been pitched into the deep-fat fryer.

2489 San Diego Ave., Old Town. ℂ 619/297-4330. www.oldtownmexcafe.com. Reservations accepted only for parties of 10 or more. Main courses $6–$9 breakfast, $9–$15 lunch and dinner. AE, DISC, MC, V. Sun–Thurs 7am–11pm; Fri–Sat 7am–midnight (bar till 1am nightly). Bus: 5. Trolley: Old Town.

6 Mission Bay & the Beaches

Restaurants at the beach exist primarily to provide an excuse for sitting and gazing at the water. Because this activity is most commonly accompanied by steady drinking, it stands to reason the food isn't often remarkable. Happily, the past few years have seen an influx of places bucking the trend, or at least raising the level of sophistication. The beautiful party people get their groove and their feed bag on in Pacific Beach at **Jordan** in the swank Tower 23 hotel, 723 Felspar (ℂ **866/869-3723**), and **Isola,** 1269 Garnet Ave. (ℂ **858/274-7014**). The creator of **The Mission** (p. 123) opened hip **Cantina Panaderia** ✸, 966 Felspar (ℂ **858/272-8400**), an Asian-Latino fusion cafe serving breakfast, lunch, and dinner, in the remnants of an old bakery; while **Costa Brava,** 1653 Garnet Ave. (ℂ **858/273-1218**), serves traditional Spanish tapas.

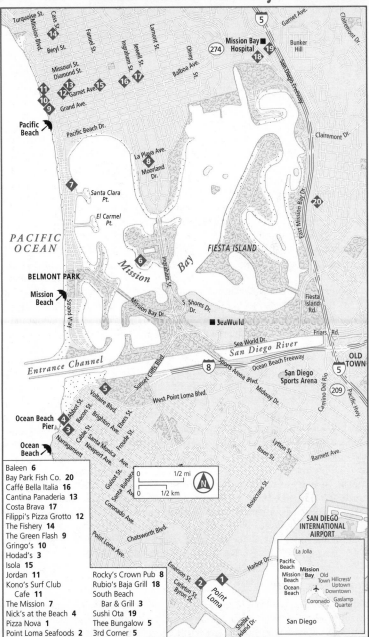

PACIFIC OCEAN

Turquoise St.
Cass St.
Mission Blvd.
Beryl St.
Fanuel St.
Missouri St.
Diamond St.
Garnet Ave.
Grand Ave.
Lamont St.
Jewell St.
Ingraham St.
Olney St.
Balboa Ave.
St.

Pacific Beach
Pacific Beach Dr.

La Playa Ave.
Moorland Dr.

Santa Clara Pt.

El Carmel Pt.

PACIFIC OCEAN

BELMONT PARK

Mission Beach
Strand Way
Mission Bay Dr.

Mission St.
Ingraham St.
Mission Bay

FIESTA ISLAND

S. Shores Dr.
Fiesta Island Rd.
Friars Rd.

SeaWorld

Sea World Dr.
San Diego River
Ocean Beach Freeway
Sports Arena Blvd.
Midway Dr.

OLD TOWN

Clairemont Dr.
Garnet Ave.
Bunker Hill

Mission Bay Hospital

East Mission Bay Dr.

San Diego Freeway

San Diego Sports Arena

Camino Del Rio
Pacific Hwy.

Voltaire Blvd.
Abbott St.
Bacon St.
Brighton Ave.
Ebers St.
Cable St.
Santa Monica Ave.
Froude St.
Newport Ave.

Ocean Beach Pier

Ocean Beach
Narragansett

Sunset Cliffs Blvd.
West Point Loma Blvd.

Entrance Channel

Guizot St.
Santa Barbara
Coronado Ave.
Point Loma Ave.
Chatsworth Blvd.

Ibsen St.
Lytton St.
Barnett Ave.

Rosecrans St.

SAN DIEGO INTERNATIONAL AIRPORT

Emerson St.
Carleton St.
Byron St.

Harbor Dr.

Shelter Island Dr.

Point Loma

La Jolla
Pacific Beach
Mission Bay
Mission Beach
Ocean Beach
Old Town
Hillcrest/Uptown
Downtown
Coronado
Gaslamp Quarter
San Diego

0   1/2 mi
0   1/2 km

N

Baleen **6**
Bay Park Fish Co. **20**
Caffé Bella Italia **16**
Cantina Panaderia **13**
Costa Brava **17**
Filippi's Pizza Grotto **12**
The Fishery **14**
The Green Flash **9**
Gringo's **10**
Hodad's **3**
Isola **15**
Jordan **7**
Kono's Surf Club Cafe **11**
The Mission **7**
Nick's at the Beach **4**
Pizza Nova **1**
Point Loma Seafoods **2**

Rocky's Crown Pub **8**
Rubio's Baja Grill **18**
South Beach Bar & Grill **3**
Sushi Ota **19**
Thee Bungalow **5**
3rd Corner **5**

Baja Fish Tacos

One of San Diego's culinary ironies is that, although the city is conscious of its Hispanic roots—not to mention within visual range of the Mexican border—it's hard to find anything other than gringo-ized combo plates in many local Mexican restaurants. But one item you'll see on many menus here is the fish taco—a native of Baja California. Consisting of batter-dipped, deep-fried filets wrapped in a corn tortilla with shredded cabbage, salsa, and a tangy sauce, fish tacos were popularized in San Diego by **Rubio's Baja Grill** (p. 100) in the early 1980s. Rubio's has since grown into a sizable chain, and it's a good option if you're on the go—the original stand is still operating at the east end of Pacific Beach, 4504 E. Mission Bay Dr., at Bunker Hill Street (© **858/272-2801**).

Fish tacos are a casual food, served in casual settings. Here are some of the best places to taste one: **Bay Park Fish Co.** ✸, 4121 Ashton St., Bay Park (© **619/276-3474**); **Blue Water Seafood Market and Grill** ✸, 3667 India St., Mission Hills (© **619/497-0914**); **The Brigantine** (p. 131); **The Fishery** ✸ (p. 122); **Mamá Testa** ✸, 1417A University Ave., Hillcrest (© **619/298-8226**); **Point Loma Seafoods** ✸, 2805 Emerson St., Point Loma (© **619/223-1109**); **South Beach Bar & Grill**, 5059 Newport Ave., Ocean Beach (© **619/226-4577**); **Wahoo's Fish Taco**, 639 Pearl St., La Jolla (© **858/459-0027**) and 2195 Station Village Way, Mission Valley (© **619/299-4550**); and **El Zarape** ✸, 4642 Park Blvd., University Heights (© **619/692-1652**).

3rd Corner ✸✸, 2265 Bacon St., Ocean Beach (© **619/223-2700**), shifted its focus from traditional seafood to become a wine shop and bistro with smashing results. The menu is focused on small plates (with a French-Mediterranean flair), but there are also a half-dozen entrees, making it an excellent option for lunch or dinner. Seating for dining is limited, but there's a full bar, lounge, and patio. You can also browse through aisles of wines—they're for sale. Best of all, 3rd Corner serves food and drinks late—until 1am (except Mon).

Start your day at the beach at **Kono's Surf Club Cafe,** 704 Garnet Ave., Pacific Beach (© **858/483-1669**), a Hawaiian-themed boardwalk breakfast shack that's cheap and delicious. A plump Kono's breakfast burrito provides enough fuel for a day of surfing or sightseeing, while a side order of savory "Kono Potatoes" is a meal in itself. And if you're looking for San Diego's best burgers, you'll find them at **Hodad's,** 5010 Newport Ave., Ocean Beach (© **619/224-4623**), and **Rocky's Crown Pub,** 3786 Ingraham, Pacific Beach (© **858/273-9140**).

VERY EXPENSIVE

Baleen ✸✸ SEAFOOD/CALIFORNIAN   This attractive waterfront eatery at the Paradise Point Resort in the middle of Mission Bay is exactly the touch of class this hotel needed when celebrity restaurateur Robbin Haas (creator of Baleen in Florida) was lured to open a venue here. With a lush bayfront view (and a dining deck that's sublime on warm evenings), it's easy to miss the design details indoors—from a

THE TRAVELOCITY GUARANTEE

...THAT SAYS EVERYTHING YOU BOOK WILL BE RIGHT, OR WE'LL WORK WITH OUR TRAVEL PARTNERS TO MAKE IT RIGHT, RIGHT AWAY.

*To drive home the point,
we're going to use the word "right" in every single sentence.*

Let's get right to it. Right to the meat! Only Travelocity guarantees everything about your booking will be right, or we'll work with our travel partners to make it right, right away. Right on!

The Guarantee covers all but one of the items pictured to the right.

Here's a picture taken smack dab right in the middle of Antigua, where the Guarantee also covers you.

For example, what if the ocean view you booked actually looks out at a downright ugly parking lot? You'd be right to call – we're there for you. And no one in their right mind would be pleased to learn the rental car place has closed and left them stranded. Call Travelocity and we'll help get you back on the right track.

Now, you may be thinking, "Yeah, right, I'm so sure." That's OK; you have the right to remain skeptical. That is until we mention help is always right around the corner. Call us right off the bat, knowing our customer service reps are there for you 24/7. Righting wrongs. Left and right.

Now if you're guessing there are some things we can't control, like the weather, well you're right. But we can help you with most things – to get all the details in righting,* visit travelocity.com/guarantee.

*Sorry, spelling things right is one of the few things not covered under the Guarantee.

I'd give my right arm for a guarantee like this, although I'm glad I don't have to.

monkey motif that includes simians hanging off chandeliers to specialized serving platters for many of Baleen's artistically arranged dishes. Start with chilled lobster in a martini glass (but avoid sticker shock by asking the price first), a warm salad of roasted mushrooms and asparagus, or fresh oysters delivered in a small cart and shucked table-side. Then savor a selection of seafood simply grilled, wood-roasted, or sautéed with hummus crust, honey wasabi glaze, or ginger sauce. Wood-roasted meats include Roquefort-crusted filet mignon and Sonoma Farms chicken with goat cheese dumplings and forest mushroom sauté. *Note:* This is a family-oriented resort, so knee-high types may be sharing the space; service is pleasantly casual.

1404 Vacation Rd. (Paradise Point Resort), Mission Bay. (✆ 858/490-6363. www.paradisepoint.com. Reservations recommended. Main courses $19–$60. AE, DC, DISC, MC, V. Sun–Thurs 5–9pm; Fri–Sat 5–10pm. Free parking. Bus: 9.

EXPENSIVE

Thee Bungalow ✿✿ FRENCH   Local foodies were shocked when they heard restaurateur Ed Moore (**3rd Corner, Nick's at the Beach,** p. 120 and 123) was sell-ing the beloved Thee Bungalow in 2006. For some 35 years this small cottage, stand-ing alone at the edge of Robb Field near the Ocean Beach channel, has been a romantic hideaway beckoning diners for consistently rewarding Continental cuisine. By far the fanciest restaurant in laid-back Ocean Beach, Thee Bungalow has endeared itself with its excellent wine list and house specialties such as crispy roast duck served with a choice of sauces (like black cherry), decadent made-to-order dessert soufflés for two (chocolate or orange liqueur), and *osso buco*–style lamb shank adorned with shal-lot–red wine purée. Thee Bungalow fans probably breathed a sigh of relief when they learned the restaurant has been taken over by the Cohn Group, which operates a string of the city's most successful restaurants, including **Kemo Sabe** and **Dakota Grill & Spirits** (p. 107 and 108). Company president David Cohn says there will be very few changes—an updated menu over time and a bit of a sprucing up, but otherwise, "99% of the people won't notice any changes." Whew.

4996 W. Point Loma Blvd. (at Bacon St.), Ocean Beach. (✆ 619/224-2884. www.cohnrestaurants.com. Reservations recommended. Main courses $19–$32, early bird specials $15–$17. AE, DC, DISC, MC, V. Mon–Thurs 5:30–9:30pm; Fri–Sat 5–10pm; Sun 5–9pm. Free parking. Bus: 35 or 923.

MODERATE

Caffè Bella Italia ✿✿ ITALIAN   If the odd-looking stucco exterior in a less-than-promising section of P.B. looks like a dry cleaner adorned with umbrellas, well, it once was a spot for all your 1-hour Martinizing needs. But in just a few short years, this charmer has found a niche in the community—despite this, many non-beach San Diegans have never heard of it. Although it's well away from the surf, it's lovely inside, and the food can knock your socks off. It's the best spot in the area for shellfish-laden pasta, wood-fired pizzas, and management that welcomes guests like family. Roman-tic lighting, sheer draperies, and warmly earthy walls create a vaguely North African ambience, assisted by the lilting Milan accents of the staff (when the din of a few dozen happy diners doesn't drown them out, that is). Every item on the menu bears the unmistakable flavor of freshness and homemade care—even the simplest curled-edge ravioli stuffed with ricotta, spinach, and pine nuts is elevated to culinary perfec-tion, while salmon is dealt with unusually firmly, endowed with olives, capers, and thick hunks of tomato in wine and garlic. You may leave wishing you could be adopted by this gracious family. As of press time, owners Stefano and Roberta Ceresoli

were working on opening a second restaurant, **Solare,** in Point Loma's Liberty Station urban-development project.

1525 Garnet Ave. (between Ingraham and Haines), Pacific Beach. (C) 858/273-1224. www.caffebellaitalia.com. Reservations suggested for dinner. Main courses $9–$14 lunch, $10–$28 dinner. AE, DC, DISC, MC, V. Tues–Sat noon–10pm; Sun 5–10pm. Free (small) parking lot. Bus: 9 or 27.

The Fishery ★ *Finds* SEAFOOD   You're pretty well guaranteed to get fresh-off-the-boat seafood at this off-the-beaten-track establishment: It's really a wholesale warehouse and retail fish market with a casual restaurant attached. The decor is clean and calm without being overly utilitarian, and the prices are fair considering the quality of the raw ingredients. Regular menu favorites include spicy mahimahi, chargrilled and topped with jalapeño butter; king salmon oscar, layered with garlic mashed potatoes and grilled asparagus, Dungeness crab and hollandaise; or—the favorite—sea bass, charbroiled with a soy-ginger marinade. You can keep it simple at lunch or dinner with bacon-wrapped scallops over a delectable salad, or the very reliable fish-and-chips, and there are always a couple of vegetarian stir-fry entrees. The menu is printed fresh daily, and a loyal crowd ventures away from the Mission/Garnet/Grand strips to enjoy this dependable neighborhood haunt.

5040 Cass St. (at Opal, ¾-mile north of Garnet), Pacific Beach. (C) 858/272-9985. No reservations, but "preferred seating" available (call ahead). Main courses $6–$21 lunch, $8–$27 dinner. AE, DC, DISC, MC, V. Daily 11am–10pm. Street parking usually available. Bus: 9.

The Green Flash AMERICAN   Known throughout Pacific Beach for its location and local clientele, the Green Flash serves adequate (and typically beachy) food at decent prices. The menu includes plenty of grilled and deep-fried seafood, straightforward steaks, and giant main-course salads. You'll also find appetizer platters of shellfish (oysters, clams, shrimp) and jalapeño "poppers" (cheese-stuffed fried peppers). The glassed-in patio is one of P.B.'s best places for people-watching, and locals congregate at sunset to catch a glimpse of the optical phenomenon for which this boardwalk hangout is named. It has something to do with the color spectrum at the moment the sun disappears below the horizon, but the scientific explanation becomes less important—and the decibel level rises—with every round of drinks.

701 Thomas Ave. (at Mission Blvd.), Pacific Beach. (C) 858/270-7715. Reservations not accepted. Main courses $4–$9 breakfast, $8–$13 lunch, $8–$35 dinner. AE, DC, DISC, MC, V. Daily 8am–10pm (bar till 2am). Bus: 27 or 34.

Gringo's ★ MEXICAN   Aiming for a more accurate reflection of south-of-the-border cooking, the awkwardly monikered Gringo's is well located at P.B.'s busiest intersection, providing visitors and locals alike with an option beyond the neighborhood's ubiquitous fast-food emporiums. This upscale space is quite agreeable to dine in, with warm woods, cool flagstone, and trendy lighting providing a modern feel, and a large patio is primed with heaters and fire pits most evenings—the venue bears little resemblance to typical Mexican restaurants (no off-key mariachis here!). Although the menu does offer a tip of the hat to dishes the average gringo will recognize (quesadillas, fajitas, burritos), flip it over and you'll see that the focus is on regional specialties from all over Mexico, the food of Oaxaca, the Yucatan, and Mexico's Pacific Coast. So, a chicken breast is stuffed with goat cheese and corn, and then lathered in a sauce of *huitlacoche* (a delicious fungus that grows on corn); a poblano chile is stuffed with picadillo and draped in a walnut cream sauce and a drizzle of pomegranate reduction. The margarita options are well worth inspection (there are more than 100 tequilas available), as is the selection of Mexican wines—drink specials run Sunday through Thursday. Sunday brunch is from 10am to 3pm.

4474 Mission Blvd. (at Garnet Ave.), Pacific Beach. ✆ 858/490-2877. www.gringoscantina.com. Reservations suggested for weekends. Main courses $6–$20 lunch, $10–$23 dinner, $7–$11 brunch. AE, DC, DISC, MC, V. Daily 11am–11pm. Bus: 27 or 34.

Nick's at the Beach CALIFORNIAN   Restaurateur Ed Moore has reshuffled the deck. He sold his longtime local favorite **Thee Bungalow** (p. 121), changed everything about **3rd Corner** (p. 120) except for the name, and then set his sights on a new challenge: reinvigorating the Ocean Beach institution formerly known as Qwiig's. It's now called Nick's at the Beach and it's got the nicest view of any restaurant in O.B., overlooking the pier—but as of press time, that's about all Moore plans to keep. He's "gutting it to the 2x4s" and pouring $2 million into the renovation. Scheduled to open in summer 2006, Nick's menu will be casual and moderately priced, leaning toward seafood with a Latin flair, and also featuring salads, sandwiches, and pastas. Moore also plans to offer a strong wine program (no surprise—his places have always been known for their wine lists) and an oyster bar. Given his track record—and that view—Nick's should be a winner. Look for it to be more sedate than his original Nick's at the Beach, which is in Pacific Beach, 809 Thomas Ave. (✆ **858/270-1730**).

5083 Santa Monica Ave. (at Abbott St.), Ocean Beach. ✆ 619/222-1101. www.nicksatthebeach.com. Reservations accepted. Main courses $7–$15 lunch, $13–$20 dinner. AE, MC, V. Daily 11am–1am. Street parking available. Bus: 35 or 923.

Sushi Ota ✿✿ SUSHI   Masterful chef-owner Yukito Ota creates San Diego's finest sushi. This sophisticated, traditional restaurant (no Asian fusion here) is a minimalist bento box with stark white walls and black furniture, softened by indirect lighting. The sushi menu is short, because discerning regulars look first to the daily specials posted behind the counter. The city's most experienced chefs, armed with nimble fingers and seriously sharp knives, turn the day's fresh catch into artful little bundles accented with mounds of wasabi and ginger. The rest of the varied menu features seafood, teriyaki-glazed meats, feather-light tempura, and a variety of small appetizers perfect to accompany a large sushi order. This restaurant is difficult to find, mainly because it's hard to believe that such outstanding dining would hide behind a laundromat and convenience store in the rear of a mini-mall that's perpendicular to the street. It's also in a nondescript part of Pacific Beach—a stone's throw from I-5—but none of that should discourage you from seeking it out.

4529 Mission Bay Dr. (at Bunker Hill), Pacific Beach. ✆ 858/270-5670. www.sushiota.com. Reservations strongly recommended on weekends. Main courses $6–$12 lunch, $9–$20 dinner, sushi $4–$12. AE, MC, V. Tues–Fri 11:30am–2pm; Tues–Thurs 5:30–10:30pm; Fri–Sun 5–10:30pm. Free parking (additional lot behind the mall). Bus: 27.

INEXPENSIVE

The Mission ✿ *Value* BREAKFAST/LIGHT FARE   Located alongside the funky surf shops, bikini boutiques, and alternative galleries of bohemian Mission Beach, the Mission is the neighborhood's central meeting place. The menu features all-day breakfasts, from traditional pancakes to nouvelle egg dishes to burritos and quesadillas—standouts include tamales and eggs with tomatillo sauce, chicken-apple sausage with eggs and a mound of rosemary potatoes, and cinnamon French toast with blackberry purée. At lunch, the menu expands for sandwiches, salads, and a few Chino-Latino items like ginger-sesame chicken tacos. Seating is casual, comfy, and conducive to lingering (tons of students, writers, and surfers hang out here), if only with a soup-bowl–size latte. Expect waits of half an hour or more on weekends. Other locations: 2801 University Ave. in North Park (© **619/220-8992**) and 1250 J St. downtown (© **619/632-7662**); they have a similar menu and hours.

3795 Mission Blvd. (at San Jose), Mission Beach. © 858/488-9060. www.themission1.signonsandiego.com. All items $5–$9. AE, MC, V. Daily 7am–3pm. Bus: 27 or 34.

7 La Jolla

As befits an upscale community with time (and money) on its hands, La Jolla has more than its fair share of good restaurants. Thankfully, they're not all expensive, and they're more ethnically diverse than you might expect in a community that still supports a haberdashery called the Ascot Shop. While many restaurants are clustered in the village, on Prospect Street and the few blocks directly east, you can also cruise down La Jolla Boulevard or up by the La Jolla Beach & Tennis Club for additional choices.

There are old-school favorites that still impress, like the 12-table, utterly romantic **Sky Room** ✹✹ at the La Valencia Hotel, 1132 Prospect St. (© **858/454-0771**), and the nearby **Top of the Cove** ✹✹, 1216 Prospect St. (© **858/454-7779**), both of which feature fabulous views and French-inspired cuisine. Chef Jean-Michel Diot doesn't have an ocean view at his French restaurant, **Tapenade** ✹✹✹, 7612 Fay Ave. (© **858/551-7500**), but once you experience his exceptional creations (which include special menus for vegetarians and children), you'll never notice. And there are even more Gallic goings-on just down the street at **Michele Coulon Dessertier** ✹✹, 7556D Fay Ave. (© **858/456-5098**). This small cafe and bakery specializes in decadent desserts, but also serves very good lunches and dinner. Lest you think it's all about the continent, though, you can find great sushi and seafood at **Zenbu** ✹, 7660 Fay Ave. (© **858/454-4540**). If you're looking for someplace as peaceful and sedate as a Zen rock garden, this probably isn't the right fit; but Zenbu offers top-quality product, as well as local fish brought in by the owner's personal fishing fleet. For traditional Mexican, head down La Jolla Boulevard to **Su Casa** (© **858/454-0369**), a family-friendly joint that serves above-average margaritas and tasty, made-at-the-table guacamole.

VERY EXPENSIVE

George's at the Cove ✹✹✹ CALIFORNIAN   You'll find host and namesake George Hauer at his restaurant's door most nights; he greets loyal regulars by name, and his confidence assures newcomers that they'll leave impressed with this beloved La Jolla institution. George's wins consistent praise for impeccable service, gorgeous views of the cove, and outstanding California cuisine. The menu, in typical San Diego fashion, presents many inventive seafood options, filtered through the myriad influences of chef Trey Foshee, selected as one of America's top 10 chefs by *Food & Wine*. Classical culinary training, Hawaiian ingenuity, and a stint at Robert Redford's Utah Sundance resort are among his many accomplishments. Foshee starts each day with a trek up to Chino Farm to select the evening's produce, which work their way into exquisite starters like the buttermilk squash soup with hazelnut cream. Mains combine divergent flavors with practiced artistry, ranging from the Niman Ranch pork tenderloin to roasted lamb loin and braised lamb shoulder with a spicy golden raisin date couscous and baby spinach. George's signature smoked chicken, broccoli,

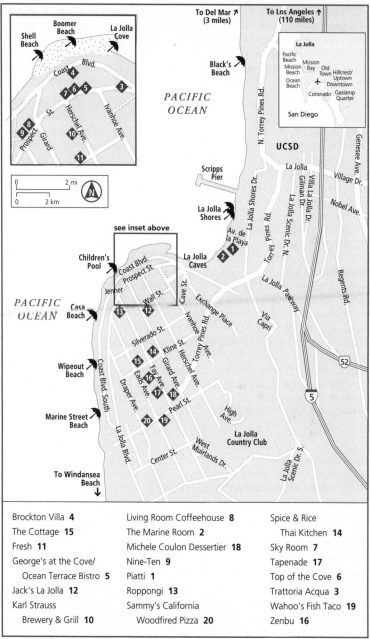

Brockton Villa **4**

The Cottage **15**

Fresh **11**

George's at the Cove/
   Ocean Terrace Bistro **5**

Jack's La Jolla **12**

Karl Strauss
   Brewery & Grill **10**

Living Room Coffeehouse **8**

The Marine Room **2**

Michele Coulon Dessertier **18**

Nine-Ten **9**

Piatti **1**

Roppongi **13**

Sammy's California
   Woodfired Pizza **20**

Spice & Rice
   Thai Kitchen **14**

Sky Room **7**

Tapenade **17**

Top of the Cove **6**

Trattoria Acqua **3**

Wahoo's Fish Taco **19**

Zenbu **16**

and black-bean soup is still a mainstay at lunch; they'll even give out the recipe for this local legend. As an alternative to dinner's pricey main courses, try the tasting menu, which offers a seasonally composed five-course sampling for $62 per person. The informal Ocean Terrace Bistro and Pacific View Bar (see review below) are upstairs.

1250 Prospect St., La Jolla. © **858/454-4244.** www.georgesatthecove.com. Reservations strongly recommended. Main courses $26–$42. AE, DC, DISC, MC, V. Sun–Thurs 5:30–10pm; Fri–Sat 5–10:30pm. Valet parking $7. Bus: 34.

Jack's La Jolla ✦✦✦ AMERICAN Is it possible to be all things to all people? Conventional wisdom says no, but conventional wisdom probably hasn't spent any time at Jack's La Jolla. It's unlike any other dining experience in San Diego: A 3-floor Epicurean funhouse that rises from sidewalk coffee stop to rooftop oyster bar, with a fine dining component and a couple of bars and lounges (with live music and DJs) thrown in for good measure. Usurping what was once a small shopping complex—there are still a few retail stores and offices that jut into the space—Jack's is built around an open-air courtyard that can take full advantage of sunny days and mild nights, but can also button up when it gets chilly. Jack's is also built around the talents and modern American cuisine of chef/owner Tony DiSalvo. Formerly executive chef at Jean-Georges in New York City, DiSalvo's arrival was preceded by high expectations, which were more than met by all. Jack's middle level features the chic Wall Street Bar, the most sedate of Jack's lounge areas, and The Dining Room at Jack's. This formal dining space is modern but warm, with the only caveat being the closer you get to the atrium, the more sound you'll hear welling up from the lower depths. Entrees here may include Muscovy duck breast with kumquat preserve, cocoa, and clove; slow-baked king salmon with artichokes and bacon; Jidori chicken in a pineapple-cardamom broth; and lamb loin with spice crumbs and sour cherries. There is also a daily seven- and nine-course tasting menu and a prix-fixe meal on Monday and Tuesday. Jack's Grille (p. 129) provides more casual, less expensive dining.

7863 Girard Ave., La Jolla. © **858/456-8111.** www.jackslajolla.com. Reservations recommended. Main courses $28–$42. AE, DC, DISC, MC, V. Sun–Thurs 5:30–10pm; Fri–Sat 5:30–10:30pm. Bars and lounges daily 5pm–1:30am. Valet parking Tues–Sat (daily in summer) 11:30am–close $7. Bus: 34.

The Marine Room ✦✦✦ (Moments) FRENCH/CALIFORNIAN For more than 6 decades, San Diego's most celebrated dining room has been this shorefront institution, perched within kissing distance of the waves that snuggle up to La Jolla Shores. But it wasn't until the 1994 arrival of Executive Chef Bernard Guillas of Brittany that the food finally lived up to its glass-fronted room with a view. A 2001 spruce-up did away with most of the dated decor, and today the Marine Room is the city's top "special occasion" destination. Guillas and Chef de Cuisine Ron Oliver work with local produce, but never hesitate to pursue unusual flavors from other corners of the globe. A favored entree includes barramundi, a delicate white fish from Australia, encrusted with chanterelle mushrooms, garnished with duck sausage and a lacy crisp of heirloom apple. Then there's the pork osso buco with morels, white asparagus, truffle oil, and plum wine sauce, or the pomegranate-macadamia–coated organic salmon with red quinoa, bok choy, Serrano ham, and a Kaffir lime-leaf infusion. The vigilant service is charmingly deferential, yet never condescending. The Marine Room ranks as one of San Diego's most expensive venues, but usually is filled to the gills on weekends; weekdays it's much easier to score a table. Ideally, schedule your reservation a half-hour or so before sunset—this will give you a chance to enjoy the scampering sandpipers and fishing pelicans while the sand takes on a honeyed aura at dusk. If you can't get in at that magic hour, experience sundown by the bar—you'll still get to enjoy the parade of illuminated rollers throughout dinner.

2000 Spindrift Dr., La Jolla. © 858/459-7222. www.marineroom.com. Reservations recommended, especially weekends. Main courses $14–$19 lunch, $28–$44 dinner; Sun brunch $42. AE, DC, DISC, MC, V. Tues–Sat 11:30am–1:30pm; Sun–Thurs 5:30–8:30pm; Fri–Sat 5:30–9pm; Sun brunch 11am–2pm. Valet parking $5. Bus: 34.

Nine-Ten ✦✦ CALIFORNIAN   This warmly stylish and understated space is the place for "market fresh" cuisine, prepared by Jason Knibb, another member of San Diego's cadre of skilled young chefs. Knibb, who was mentored by such culinary figures as Wolfgang Puck, Roy Yamaguchi, and Hans Rockenwagner, presides over a shape-shifting, seasonal menu that's best enjoyed via small-plate grazings—past offerings have included espresso and chocolate-braised boneless short ribs, Maine scallops with apple risotto, and harissa marinated shrimp. Or better yet, you can turn yourself over to the "Mercy of the Chef," a five-course tasting menu for $60, or $90 with wine pairings (your whole table has to play along, though). With star pastry chef Jack Fisher in the kitchen, be sure to leave room for desserts such as sweet goat-cheese napoleon with vanilla-poached quince, bittersweet chocolate custard with candied fennel and tangerine sorbet, or any of the house-made ice creams and sorbets. When you're looking for a classy fine-dining experience—without the old-guard attitude—this hotel eatery fits the bill very nicely.

910 Prospect St. (between Fay and Girard), La Jolla. © 858/964-5400. www.nine-ten.com. Reservations recommended. Main courses $6–$15 breakfast, $9–$14 lunch, $19–$40 dinner. AE, DC, DISC, MC, V. Daily 6:30–11am, 11:30am–2:30pm, and 6–10pm. Bus: 34.

EXPENSIVE

Fresh ✦✦ CALIFORNIAN/SEAFOOD   This fine seafood-plus restaurant was a hit right from its 2003 debut, thanks to Chef Matthew Zappoli and his pleasing, modestly adventurous menu. Zappoli, another one of San Diego's adroit young guns, offers a tapas-style menu perfect for sharing, as well as traditional entrees. Look for small plates like the ahi poke, pan-seared scallops, and shredded duck spring rolls. Entrees include a surprisingly delicate coriander-crusted mahimahi, shellfish-stuffed rainbow trout with a lemon-thyme emulsion, and "land" offerings like pepper-seared beef Delmonico in a Cabernet reduction. The desserts, also overseen by Zappoli, are well worth investigating, as is the creative lineup of martinis, available in flights of three—don't worry, they're small. The dining room itself is soothingly modern, with billowing waves of fabric across the elevated ceilings and broad windows that successfully integrate the outside dining area. Fresh is one of La Jolla's standout haunts and features live music every night, though its business has been dinged by the arrival of Jack's La Jolla down the street.

1044 Wall St. (at Hershel), La Jolla. © 858/551-7575. www.freshseafoodrestaurant.com. Reservations strongly recommended. Main courses $9–$17 lunch, $18–$31 dinner. AE, DISC, MC, V. Daily 11:30am–9:30pm (Fri–Sat till 10:30pm). Free 2-hr. validated parking. Bus: 34.

Roppongi ✦ ASIAN FUSION/PACIFIC RIM   At Roppongi, the cuisines of Japan, Thailand, China, Vietnam, Korea, and India collide, sometimes gracefully, in a vibrant explosion of flavors. You might not get past the first menu page, a long list of small tapas dishes designed for sharing—each table is even preset with a tall stack of plates that quietly encourage a communal meal of successive appetizers. It takes an adventuresome palate to hip-hop from Thai satay to Chinese pot stickers to a Mongolian duck quesadilla and then back to Indonesian spicy shrimp without missing a beat, but when you order right, it works (note that a number of the dishes are sweet, so ask your waiter for a good balance). Highlights include the Polynesian crab stack, and the seared scallops on potato pancakes floating in a silky puddle of Thai basil hollandaise. Options increase exponentially when you start considering the sushi bar menu. There are also traditionally sized main courses featuring seafood, meat, and game, all colorfully prepared; and at lunch there's a selection of bento boxes, including a vegetarian option. If your sweet tooth hasn't been sated, indulge in dessert—the caramelized Tahitian banana, framed by dollops of ice cream and topped with crispy almond brittle, is scrumptious. Day or night, the best seating is on the outdoor patio, anchored by a leaping fire pit and accented with ponds and torches.

875 Prospect St. (at Fay Ave.), La Jolla. ⓒ 858/551-5252. www.roppongiusa.com. Reservations recommended. Main courses $11–$15 lunch, $9–$18 tapas, $18–$32 dinner. AE, DC, DISC, MC, V. Sun–Thurs 11:30am–9:30pm; Fri–Sat 11:30am–10:30pm. Valet parking $7; garage parking available for dinner. Bus: 34.

Trattoria Acqua 😊😊 ITALIAN/MEDITERRANEAN Nestled on tiled terraces close enough to catch ocean breezes, this northern Italian spot has a relaxed ambience with rustic walls and outdoor seating shaded by flowering vines, vaguely evoking a romantic Tuscan villa. A mixed crowd of suits, couples, and families gather to enjoy expertly prepared seasonal dishes; every table starts with bread served with an indescribably pungent Mediterranean spread. Acqua's pastas (all available as appetizers or main courses) are luscious—rich, heady flavor combinations like orecchiette with spicy shrimp, ham, broccoli, white beans, and wine, or lobster ravioli with tomato-and-chive beurre blanc. Other specialties include *osso buco alla pugliese* (veal shank braised with tomatoes, olives, capers, and garlic and served over pappardelle pasta), *quaglie a beccafico* (roasted Sonoma quails with Italian bacon, spinach, raisins, and pine nuts), and *brazino al limone* (roasted sea bass with Algerian spice, preserved lemons, and a roasted-vegetable beurre blanc). Saturday and Sunday brunch features stuffed crêpes, frittatas, and calzones (including a seasonal fruit and mascarpone number).

1298 Prospect St. (on Coast Walk), La Jolla. ⓒ 858/454-0709. www.trattoriaacqua.com. Reservations recommended. Main courses $10–$12 brunch, $9–$20 lunch, $12–$34 dinner. AE, DC, MC, V. Daily 11:30am–2:30pm; Sun–Thurs 5–9:30pm; Fri–Sat 5–10:30pm. Validated self-parking. Bus: 34.

MODERATE

Brockton Villa 😊 BREAKFAST/CALIFORNIAN In a restored 1894 beach bungalow, this charming cafe named for an early resident's hometown (Brockton, Massachusetts) is imbued with the spirit of artistic souls drawn to a breathtaking perch overlooking La Jolla Cove. Rescued by the trailblazing Pannikin Coffee Company, the restaurant is now independently run by a Pannikin alum. The biggest buzz is at breakfast, when you can enjoy inventive dishes such as soufflélike "Coast Toast" (the house take on French toast) and Greek "steamers" (eggs scrambled with an espresso steamer, and then mixed with feta cheese, tomato, and basil). Breakfasts are served till noon weekdays (till 3pm weekends) and the dozens of coffee drinks include one "Keith Richards"—four shots of espresso topped with Mexican hot chocolate. Lunch highlights include homemade soups and salads, plus sandwiches like turkey meatloaf on toasted sourdough bread with spicy tomato-mint chutney. The somewhat less successful supper menu includes Moroccan halibut with a spicy tomato relish, plus pastas, stews, and grilled meats. But, not to put too fine a point on it, any time you can actually enjoy the sea view, Brockton's food tastes good. Steep stairs from the street limit wheelchair access.

1235 Coast Blvd. (across from La Jolla Cove), La Jolla. ℭ 858/454-7393. www.brocktonvilla.com. Reservations recommended for weekend brunch. Main courses $6–$10 breakfast, $8–$13 lunch, $18–$26 dinner. AE, DISC, MC, V. Mon 8am–3pm; Tues–Sun 8am–9pm.

Jack's Grille ✿✿ AMERICAN   This is the more casual side of the hot, 3-level dining emporium that has been the toast of the city since (and even before) it opened in early 2006. Situated on the bottom level, the Grille is anchored in the center of the atrium by a long, glass-top table that reveals an industrial trough of water just beneath it, flowing toward a flaming, sculptural rubble. For lunch or dinner, this is a stylish but relatively inexpensive place to taste the work of talented chef Tony DiSalvo, as opposed to the fine-dining component upstairs, perhaps La Jolla's priciest restaurant. Look for creations like roasted beet and candied walnut salad with Gruyère emulsion, black truffle and Fontina thin-crust pizza, and Prince Edward Island mussel-chorizo soup. The Grille also serves in the adjacent Jack's Wine Bar Lounge, the laid-back Sidewalk Cafe along Girard Avenue, the Beach (which offers great people-watching opportunities from its second-floor perch), the refined Wall Street Bar, and the rooftop Ocean View Room & Oyster Bar, where you'll find fresh shellfish, a wood-burning fireplace, and turntablists.

7863 Girard Ave., La Jolla. ℭ 858/456-8111. www.jackslajolla.com. Main courses $9–$14. AE, DC, DISC, MC, V. Daily 11:30–1:30am. Sidewalk Cafe daily 8:30am–10pm (only serving Bread & Cie. baked goods before 11:30am). Valet parking Tues–Sat (daily in summer) 11:30am–close $7. Bus: 34.

Ocean Terrace Bistro and Pacific View Bar ✿✿ *Value* CALIFORNIAN   The legendary main dining room at George's at the Cove (see above) has won numerous awards for its haute cuisine. But George's also accommodates those seeking good food and a spectacular setting with a more reasonable price tag: The upstairs Ocean Terrace Bistro and Pacific View Bar prepare their creations in the same kitchen as the high-priced fare. The two areas offer indoor and spectacular outdoor seating overlooking La Jolla Cove. For dinner, you can choose from several seafood or pasta dishes, or have something out of the ordinary, such as the Niman Ranch pork chop grilled with ancho chilies and pineapple salsa or Thai-inspired fish stew in a coconut-milk broth. The smoked chicken, broccoli, and black-bean soup is a lunchtime favorite.

1250 Prospect St., La Jolla. ℭ 858/454-4244. www.georgesatthecove.com. Reservations recommended. Main courses $9–$13 lunch, $13–$21 dinner. AE, DC, DISC, MC, V. Daily 11am–10pm (Fri–Sat till 10:30pm). Valet parking $6. Bus: 34.

Piatti ✿ ITALIAN/MEDITERRANEAN   La Jolla's version of the reliable neighborhood hangout is this pasta-centric trattoria, a couple blocks inland from La Jolla Shores. Come here on busy Friday or Saturday evenings—well, any night, really—and you're likely to be surrounded by a crew of regulars that pop in weekly and know the staff by name. You won't feel left out, however, and the food is well priced. The lemon herb-roasted chicken and *bistecca* (rib-eye) are fantastic, but it's the pastas that parade out to most tables. Try orecchiette bathed in gorgonzola, grilled chicken, and sun-dried tomatoes, or pappardelle "fantasia"—shrimp-crowned ribbons of saffron pasta, primed with garlic, tomato, and white wine; and those who are concerned with carbo-loading can substitute spinach for pasta. The outdoor patio, beneath the romantic sprawl of an enormous ficus tree, is always ideal thanks to the cozy heaters.

2182 Avenida de la Playa, La Jolla. ℭ 858/454-1589. www.piatti.com. Reservations recommended. Main courses $10–$26; Sat–Sun brunch $7–$12. AE, DC, MC, V. Mon–Thurs 11:30am–10pm; Fri 11:30am–11pm; Sat 11am–11pm; Sun 11am–10pm. Street parking usually available. Bus: 34.

Moments **Appetizing Views**

Incredible ocean vistas, a glittering skyline, and sailboats fluttering by off-shore—it's the classic backdrop for a memorable meal. So where can you find the best views?

Downtown, the **Fish Market** and its pricier cousin **Top of the Market** (p. 109) overlook San Diego Bay, and the management even provides binoculars for getting a good look at aircraft carriers and other vessels. Not far is **Star of the Sea** (p. 106), where an intimate room faces the elegant tall ship *Star of India.* The downtown area's latest visual overachiever is **Island Prime,** 880 Harbor Island Dr. (© **619/298-6802**), a creative steak-and-seafood spot near the airport. Across the harbor in Coronado, the **Bay Beach Cafe** (p. 132), **Il Fornaio,** 1333 First St. (© **619/437-4911**), and **Peohe's,** 1201 First St. (© **619/437-4474**), offer gorgeous views of the San Diego skyline, and the tony **Azzura Point** (p. 131), at Loews Coronado Bay Resort, provides a unique north-facing look across the bay.

In Ocean Beach, **Nick's at the Beach** (p. 123) sits on a second-floor perch across the street from the sand, while in Pacific Beach, the **Green Flash** (p. 122) is just 5 feet from the sand (although the year-round parade of bodies may prove a distraction from the ocean). In La Jolla, the **Sky Room** (p. 124), **George's at the Cove** (p. 124), and **Top of the Cove** (p. 124) are near the water and offer sweeping, elevated views, but **Brockton Villa** (p. 128) actually offers the La Jolla Cove outlook as advertised on every postcard stand in town. Somewhat inland, but 11 stories up, is **Elario's Bistro & Sky Lounge,** 7955 La Jolla Shores Dr. (© **858/551-3620**).

My two favorite vistas to feast on give you a choice of city or sea view. **Bertrand at Mister A's** (p. 111) sits on the 12th floor at Fifth and Laurel and the panorama here encompasses Balboa Park (as well as the living rooms of some ritzy condo towers) to the east, downtown to the south, and the San Diego Harbor to the west, and it's punctuated every few minutes by aircraft on their final approach. If you want to get up close and personal with the oceanic scene, head to **The Marine Room** (p. 126). The restaurant's windows utilize SeaWorld technology to withstand the seasonal tides that crash into the glass, and special high-tide brunches are served several times each winter to take maximum advantage of Mother Nature's show. But the beachside setting is incredible any time of year.

Spice & Rice Thai Kitchen ✦ THAI   The lunch crowd at this attractive Thai restaurant consists of shoppers and curious tourists, while dinner is quieter; all the local businesses have shut down. The food is excellent, with polished presentations and expert renditions of classics like pad Thai, satay, curry, and glazed duck. The starters often sound as good as the entrees: Consider making a grazing meal of house specialties like "gold bags" (minced pork, vegetables, glass noodles, and herbs wrapped in crispy rice paper and served with earthy plum sauce) or prawns with yellow curry lobster sauce; crispy calamari is flavored with tamarind and chili sauces.

The romantically lit covered front patio has a secluded garden feel, and inside tables also have indirect lighting. Despite the passage of time, this all-around satisfier remains something of an insider's secret.

7734 Girard Ave., La Jolla. © 858/456-0466. www.spiceandrice.com. Reservations recommended. Main courses $8–$16. AE, DISC, MC, V. Mon–Fri 11am–3pm and 5–10pm (Fri till 11pm); Sat 11:30am–3:30pm and 5–11pm; Sun 5–10pm. Bus: 34.

INEXPENSIVE

The Cottage ⑂ BREAKFAST/LIGHT FARE   La Jolla's best—and friendliest—breakfast is served at this turn-of-the-20th-century bungalow on a sunny village corner. The cottage is light and airy, but most diners opt for tables outside, where a charming white picket fence encloses the trellis-shaded brick patio. Omelets and egg dishes feature Mediterranean, Cal-Latino, and classic American touches; homemade granola is a favorite as well (it's served here, but also sold in packages to take away). The Cottage bakes its own muffins, rolls, and coffee cakes. While breakfast dishes are served all day, toward lunchtime the kitchen begins turning out freshly made, healthful soups, light meals, and sandwiches. Summer dinners (never heavy, always tasty) are a delight, particularly when you're seated before dark on a balmy seaside night. If you like what you taste, The Cottage has a cookbook available that includes many of its most popular recipes.

7702 Fay Ave. (at Kline St.), La Jolla. © 858/454-8409. www.cottagelajolla.com. Reservations accepted for dinner only. Main courses $7–$10 breakfast, $7–$12 lunch, $10–$18 dinner. AE, DISC, MC, V. Daily 7:30am–3pm; dinner (June–Aug only) Tues–Sat 5–9:30pm. Bus: 34.

8 Coronado

Rather like the conservative, old-school Navy aura that pervades the entire "island," Coronado's dining options are reliable and sometimes quite good, but the restaurants aren't exactly breaking new culinary ground.

A couple exceptions are the resort dining rooms, which seem to be waging a little rivalry over who can attract the most prestigious, multiple-award-winning executive chef. If you're in the mood for a special-occasion meal that'll knock your socks off, consider **Azzura Point** ⑂⑂ (© 619/424-4000), in Loews Coronado Bay Resort (p. 93). With its plushly upholstered, gilded, and view-endowed setting, this stylish dining room wins continual raves from deep-pocketed San Diego foodies willing to cross the bay for inventive and artistic California-Mediterranean creations. At press time, the Hotel del Coronado (p. 93) was preparing to unveil its new signature restaurant, tentatively called **1500 Ocean** (© 619/522-8496). Dethroning **Prince of Wales,** the hotel's former fine dining option, 1500 Ocean will serve a California coastal cuisine, and feature a wine list that's heavily Californian. The menu will also include Baja California vintages and recipes, and the historic Hotel Del's beachfront setting is, of course, can't-miss.

If you seek ethnic or funky food, head back across the bridge. Mexican fare (gringostyle, but well practiced) is served on the island at popular **Miguel's Cocina,** inside El Cordova Hotel (© 619/437-4237).

EXPENSIVE

The Brigantine AMERICAN/SEAFOOD   The Brigantine is best known for its oyster-bar happy hour (3–6pm and 10–11pm Mon–Thurs; 3–6pm and 10–11:30pm

Fri; 10–11:30pm Sat; 4:30pm–close on Sun). Beer, margaritas, and food are heavily discounted, and you can expect standing room only. Early bird "sundowner" specials include a seafood, steak, or chicken entree served with soup or salad, a side of veggies, and bread for $17 (5–6:30pm Mon–Thurs; 4:30–6:30pm Sun). The food is good, not great, but the congenial atmosphere is a certifiable draw. Inside, the decor is upscale and resolutely nautical; outside, there's a pleasant patio with heaters to take the chill off the night air. At lunch, you can get everything from crab cakes or fish and chips to fresh fish or pasta. There are several other Brig locations, including Point Loma (the original), 2725 Shelter Island Dr. (© **619/224-2871**), and Del Mar, 3263 Camino del Mar (© **858/481-1166**).

1333 Orange Ave., Coronado. © 619/435-4166. www.brigantine.com. Reservations recommended on weekends. Main courses $8–$17 lunch, $16–$45 dinner. AE, DC, MC, V. Mon–Sat 11:30am–2:30pm; Mon–Thurs 5–10pm; Fri–Sat 5–10:30pm; Sun 4:30–9:30pm. Small parking lot. Bus: 901, 902, or 904.

Chez Loma ⑆ FRENCH   This intimate Victorian cottage filled with antiques and subdued candlelight makes for romantic dining. The house dates from 1889, the French-Continental restaurant from 1975. Tables are scattered throughout the house and on the enclosed garden terrace; an upstairs wine salon, reminiscent of a Victorian parlor, is a cozy spot for coffee or conversation. Among the entrees are salmon with smoked-tomato vinaigrette, and roast duckling with lingonberry, port, and burnt-orange sauce; main courses are served with soup or salad, rice or potatoes, and fresh vegetables. Follow dinner with a silky crème caramel or Kahlúa crème brûlée. California wines and American microbrews are available, in addition to a full bar, and early birds enjoy specially priced meals: $25 for a three-course meal before 6pm. The restaurant's only downfall—predictability—is also its main strength.

1132 Loma (off Orange Ave.), Coronado. © 619/435-0661. www.chezloma.com. Reservations recommended. Main courses $21–$34. AE, DC, DISC, MC, V. Daily 5–10pm. Bus: 901, 902, or 904.

MODERATE

Bay Beach Cafe AMERICAN   This gathering place isn't on a real beach, but it enjoys a prime perch on San Diego Bay. Seated indoors (which can be loud) or on a glassed-in patio, diners gaze at the city skyline, which is dramatic by day and breathtaking at night. The cafe is popular at happy hour, when the setting sun glimmers on downtown's mirrored high-rises. The ferry docks at a wooden pier a few steps away, discharging passengers into the complex of gift shops and restaurants with a New England fishing-village theme. Alas, the food takes a back seat to the view, but the lunchtime menu of burgers, sandwiches, salads, and appetizers is modestly priced and satisfying; dinner entrees—steaks, seafood, and pastas—aren't quite good enough for the price.

1201 First St. (Ferry Landing Marketplace), Coronado. © 619/435-4900. www.baybeachcafe.com. Reservations recommended for dinner on weekends. Main courses $7–$10 breakfast, $9–$12 lunch, $12–$33 dinner. AE, DISC, MC, V. Mon–Fri 11am–8:30pm; Sat–Sun 8–11am. Free parking. Bus: 901, 903, or 904.

Rhinoceros Cafe & Grille ⑆ AMERICAN   With its quirky name and something-for-everyone menu, this light, bright bistro is a welcome addition to the Coronado dining scene. It's more casual than it looks from the street and offers large portions, though the kitchen can be a little heavy-handed with sauces and spices. At lunch, every other patron seems to be enjoying the popular penne à la vodka in creamy tomato sauce; favorite dinner specials are Italian cioppino, Southwestern-style meatloaf, and salmon poached and crusted with herb sauce. Plenty of crispy fresh salads

Where to Dine in Coronado

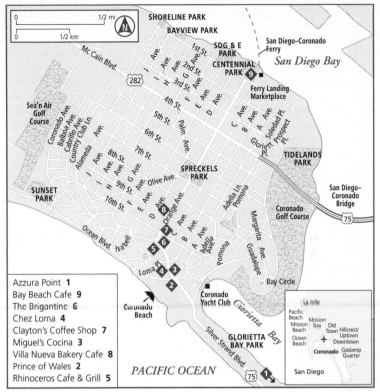

balance out the menu. For drinks, choose from the fair wine list or try Rhino Chaser's American Ale.

1166 Orange Ave., Coronado. ☎ 619/435-2121. www.rhinocafe.com. Main courses $11–$25. AE, DC, DISC, MC, V. Daily 11am–2:30pm; Sun–Thurs 5–9pm; Fri–Sat 5–10pm. Street parking usually available. Bus: 901, 902, or 904.

INEXPENSIVE

Clayton's Coffee Shop AMERICAN/BREAKFAST   The Hotel Del isn't the only relic of a bygone era in Coronado—just wait until you see this humble neighborhood favorite. Clayton's has occupied this corner spot seemingly forever, at least since a time when *everyone's* menus were full of plain American good eatin' in the $4 to $5 range. Now their horseshoe counter, chrome barstools, and well-worn pleather-lined booths are "retro," but the burgers, fries, and turkey noodle soup are timeless and quite good—plus you can still play three oldies for a quarter on the table-side jukebox. Behind the restaurant, Clayton's Mexican takeout kitchen does a brisk business in homemade tamales.

959 Orange Ave., Coronado. ☎ 619/435-5425. All menu items under $8. No credit cards. Mon–Sat 6am–8pm; Sun 6am–2pm. Bus: 901, 902, or 904.

Villa Nueva Bakery Café ★ (Value) BREAKFAST/LIGHT FARE   This wonderful little cafe is the best of its kind on the island. In addition to fresh-roasted coffee and

Picnic Fare

San Diego's benign climate lends itself to dining alfresco. An excellent spot to pick up sandwiches is **The Cheese Shop,** a gourmet deli with locations downtown at 627 4th Ave. ((*©* **619/232-2303**) and in La Jolla Shores at 2165 Avenida de la Playa (*©* **858/459-3921**). Other places to buy picnic fare include **Girard Gourmet,** 7837 Girard Ave., La Jolla (*©* **858/454-3321**); **Bread on Market** (*©* **619/795-2730**), an excellent bakery and small cafe with a menu of overstuffed sandwiches; and **Old Town Liquor and Deli,** 2304 San Diego Ave. (*©* **619/291-4888**).

Another spot that's very popular is **Point Loma Seafoods,** on the water's edge in front of the Municipal Sportfishing Pier, at 2805 Emerson near Scott Street, south of Rosecrans and west of Harbor Drive (*©* **619/223-1109**). There's a fish market here, and you can pick up seafood sandwiches, fresh sushi, and salads to go. If you decide to make your own sandwiches, the best bread in the county comes from **Bread & Cie.,** 350 University Ave., Hillcrest (*©* **619/683-9322**). **Villa Nueva Bakery Café,** 956 Orange Ave., Coronado (*©* **619/435-4191**), is a close runner-up.

espresso drinks, it serves omelets, bagels and lox, and other breakfast treats (until 2pm), deli sandwiches on the delicious house bread, and a daily fresh soup. It's the kind of spot where half the customers are greeted by name. Locals rave about the "Yacht Club" sandwich, a croissant filled with yellowfin tuna, and the breakfast croissant, topped with scrambled ham and eggs and cheddar cheese. Those fat, gooey cinnamon buns are every bit as good as they look.

956 Orange Ave., Coronado. *©* **619/435-4191**. Main courses $5–$8. AE, DISC, MC, V. Daily 6:30am–6pm. Bus: 901, 902, or 904.

9 Off the (Tourist) Beaten Path

Don't limit your dining experience in San Diego to the main tourist zones outlined above. Five minutes north of Mission Valley is the mostly business neighborhood of Kearny Mesa, home to San Diego's best Asian venues. One to try is **Jasmine** ⭐⭐, 4609 Convoy St. (*©* **858/268-0888**), which, at lunch, showcases wonderful Hong Kong–style dumplings that are wheeled around the room on carts; dinners are more elaborate— seafood dishes and the Peking duck served two ways are good choices. Nearby is **China Max** ⭐, 4698 Convoy St. (*©* **858/650-3333**), which occupies a nondescript building near the junction of the 805 and 163 freeways; the room is spare, but the kitchen exhibits finesse with southern Chinese delicacies and always has excellent (sometimes pricey) live fish specials. Another place easy to miss, thanks to its strip-mall hideout, is **Spicy City** ⭐, 4690 Convoy St. (*©* **858/278-1818**). This is Szechuan food, the real deal. Insiders claim it's best to order off the Chinese–language menu, as some dishes are left off the English menu, plus there are no descriptions of the food. And with dishes like Husband, Wife, and Piece of Lung, you're going to want to know exactly what you're getting, so brush up on your Mandarin.

Just east of Hillcrest (south and parallel to Mission Valley) is Adams Avenue, one of the city's streets of character, with antiques shops and bistros en route to Kensington. Here you'll find the **Kensington Grill** ✸✸, 4055 Adams Ave., next to the Ken Cinema (© **619/281-4014**), owned by the same crew in charge of the Gaslamp's hip Chive and featuring contemporary American cuisine in a chic setting that draws lots of neighborhood types. In nearby Normal Heights, **Jyoti Bihanga,** 3351 Adams Ave. (© **619/282-4116**), caters to followers of Sri Chinmoy and delivers a vegetarian menu of Indian-influenced salads, wraps, and curries; the "neatloaf," made with grains and tofu, is a winner. All items are priced around $10.

South of Adams Avenue, University Avenue runs through North Park. This working-class neighborhood is in the process of a major facelift, which includes the reopening of the resurrected North Park Theatre, a performing arts venue originally built in 1928. Next door to the theater is **Spread,** 2879 University Ave. (© **619/543-0406**), where the "nouveau comfort food" menu is vegetarian/vegan, relying on a daily influx of seasonal, organic products. Excellent, health-conscious Mexican food (yes, it does exist) is found at **Ranchos Cocina** ✸, 3910 30th St. (© **619/5741288**), just off University Avenue. This popular eatery will even prepare you something vegan—try asking for *that* in Old Town.

Out in the far-flung 'burb of Rancho Bernardo awaits one of San Diego's most memorable dining experiences. **El Bizcocho** ✸✸✸ is the fine-dining restaurant at the golf and tennis resort Rancho Bernardo Inn, 17550 Bernardo Oaks Dr. (© **858/675-8550**). El Biz is one of the last of San Diego's formal, gourmet experiences, and even though the name is Spanish and the decor Mexican colonial, the food is classic French with a California twist. With more than 1,600 selections, the wine list is one of the most extensive in California.

7

What to See & Do

You won't run out of things to see and do in San Diego especially if outdoor activities are high on the agenda. The San Diego Zoo, SeaWorld, and the Wild Animal Park are the city's three top attractions, but Balboa Park's museums, downtown's Gaslamp Quarter, the beaches, shopping in Old Town, and a performance at one of our prized live theaters or a Padres game at downtown PETCO Park are all attractions worth visiting. See chapter 3 for itineraries and advice on how to organize your time.

1 The Three Major Animal Parks

If you're looking for wild times, San Diego supplies them. The world-famous **San Diego Zoo** is home to more than 800 animal species, many of them rare and exotic. A sister attraction, the **Wild Animal Park,** offers another 3,500 creatures representing 429 species in an au naturel setting. And Shamu and his friends form a veritable chorus line at **SeaWorld San Diego**—waving their flippers, waddling across an ersatz Antarctica, and blowing killer-whale kisses—in more than a dozen shows a day.

San Diego's "Big Three" family attractions are joined by **LEGOLAND California,** which is about 30 miles away in the seaside community of Carlsbad. You'll find full information on visiting the park on p. 241.

San Diego Zoo ★★★ *Kids*   More than 4,000 creatures reside at this celebrated, influential zoo, started in 1916 and run by the Zoological Society of San Diego. In the early days, the zoo's founder, Dr. Harry Wegeforth, traveled around the world and bartered native Southwestern animals such as rattlesnakes and sea lions for more exotic species. The zoo is also an accredited botanical garden, lavished with more than 700,000 plants; "Dr. Harry" brought home plants from every location where he acquired animals, ensuring what would become the zoo's naturalistic and mature environment.

The zoo is one of only four in the United States with giant pandas, and many other rare species live here, including Buerger's tree kangaroos of New Guinea, long-billed kiwis from New Zealand, wild Przewalski's horses from Mongolia, lowland gorillas from Africa, and giant tortoises from the Galapagos. The Zoological Society is involved with animal preservation efforts around the world and has engineered many "firsts" in breeding. The zoo was also a forerunner in creating barless, moated enclosures that allow animals to roam in sophisticated environments resembling their natural ones.

The newest habitat, **Monkey Trails and Forest Tales** is the largest, most elaborate in the zoo's history, recreating a wooded forest full of endangered species such as the mandrill monkey, clouded leopard, and pygmy hippopotamus. An elevated trail through the treetops allows for close observation of the primate, bird, and plant life

What to See & Do in San Diego

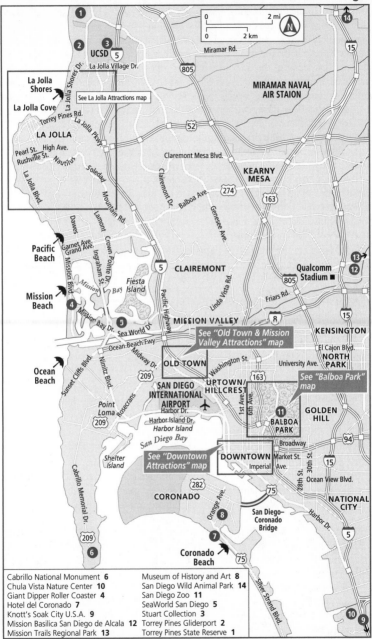

0		2 mi
0		2 km

Miramar Rd.

MIRAMAR NAVAL AIR STAION

UCSD **5**

La Jolla Village Dr.

La Jolla Shores

See La Jolla Attractions map

La Jolla Cove

Torrey Pines Rd.

La Jolla Pkwy.

LA JOLLA

Pearl St. High Ave.
Rushville St. Nautilus

Soledad

Claremont Mesa Blvd.

KEARNY MESA

La Jolla Blvd.

Mountain Rd.

Claremont Dr.

Balboa Ave.

Genesee Ave.

Pacific Beach

Garnet Ave.
Grand Ave.

Dawes

Lamont

Crown Point Dr.

Ingraham St.

CLAIREMONT

Linda Vista Rd.

Qualcomm Stadium ■

Mission Beach

Mission Blvd.

Mission Bay

Fiesta Island

Pacific Highway

Friars Rd.

Mission Bay Dr.

Sea World Dr.

MISSION VALLEY

KENSINGTON

El Cajon Blvd.

Ocean Beach

Sunset Cliffs Blvd.

Nimitz Blvd.

Ocean Beach Fwy.

Midway Dr.

OLD TOWN

Washington St.

University Ave.

NORTH PARK

See "Old Town & Mission Valley Attractions" map

UPTOWN/ HILLCREST

1st Ave.
6th Ave.

See "Balboa Park" map

Point Loma

Rosecrans

SAN DIEGO INTERNATIONAL AIRPORT

Harbor Dr.

Harbor Island Dr.
Harbor Island

BALBOA PARK

GOLDEN HILL

San Diego Bay

Shelter Island

See "Downtown Attractions" map

Broadway

DOWNTOWN Market St.

Imperial Ave.

28th St.
30th St.

Ocean View Blvd.

Cabrillo Memorial Dr.

CORONADO

282

Orange Ave.

San Diego–Coronado Bridge

75

NATIONAL CITY

Harbor Dr.

209

Coronado Beach

75

Silver Strand Blvd.

Cabrillo National Monument **6**	Museum of History and Art **8**
Chula Vista Nature Center **10**	San Diego Wild Animal Park **14**
Giant Dipper Roller Coaster **4**	San Diego Zoo **11**
Hotel del Coronado **7**	SeaWorld San Diego **5**
Knott's Soak City U.S.A. **9**	Stuart Collection **3**
Mission Basilica San Diego de Alcala **12**	Torrey Pines Gliderport **2**
Mission Trails Regional Park **13**	Torrey Pines State Reserve **1**

that thrives in the forest canopy. **Absolutely Apes** showcases orangutans and siamangs of Indonesia, while next door is **Gorilla Tropics,** where two troops of Western low-land gorillas roam an 8,000-square-foot habitat. Despite the hype, I find the **Giant Panda Research Center** *not* worth the hassle when a long line is in place (lines are shortest first thing in the morning or toward the end of the day). More noteworthy are **Ituri Forest,** which simulates a central African rainforest with forest buffalos, otters, okapis, and hippos, which are viewed underwater from a glassed-in enclosure, and the **Polar Bear Plunge,** where you'll find a 2¼-acre summer tundra habitat pop-ulated by Siberian reindeer, yellow-throated martens, and diving ducks, as well as polar bears. The **Children's Zoo** features a nursery with baby animals and a petting area where kids can cuddle up to sheep, goats, and the like. There's also a **sea lion show** at the 3,000-seat amphitheater (easy to skip if you're headed to SeaWorld).

If a lot of walking—some of it on steep hills—isn't your passion, a 40-minute **Guided Bus Tour** provides a narrated overview and covers about 75% of the facility. It costs $10 for adults, $5.50 for children 3 to 11; it's included in the so-called "Best Value" admission package. Since you get only brief glimpses of the enclosures, and animals won't always be visible, you'll want to revisit some areas. Included in the bus ticket is access to the unnarrated **Express Bus,** which allows you to get on and off at one of five different stops along the same route. You can also get an aerial perspective from the **Skyfari,** which costs $3 per person each way, though you won't see many creatures. Ideally, take the complete bus tour first thing in the morning, when the ani-mals are more active (waits for the bus tour can top an hour by midday). After the bus tour, take the Skyfari to the far side of the park and wend your way back on foot or by Express Bus to revisit animals you missed.

In addition to several fast-food options, the restaurant **Albert's** is a beautiful oasis at the lip of a canyon and a lovely place to take a break.

2920 Zoo Dr., Balboa Park. ℭ **619/234-3153** (recorded info), or 619/231-1515. www.sandiegozoo.org. Admission $22 adults, $15 children 3–11, free for military in uniform; "Best Value" package (admission, guided bus tour, round-trip Skyfari aerial tram) $32 adults, $29 seniors, $20 children. AE, DISC, MC, V. Sept to mid-June daily 9am–4pm (grounds close at 5 or 6pm); mid-June to Aug daily 9am–8pm (grounds close at 9pm). Bus: 7 or 7A/B. Interstate 5 south to Pershing Dr., follow signs.

SeaWorld San Diego 🎯🎯 *Kids*

One of California's most heavily marketed attrac-tions, SeaWorld is a big draw for a number of visitors coming to San Diego. The aquatic theme park celebrated its 40th year of operation in 2004. With each passing year the educational pretext increasingly takes a back seat to slick shows and rides, but the park—owned by the Anheuser-Busch Corporation—is perhaps still the country's premiere showplace for marine life, made politically correct with a nominally inform-ative atmosphere. At its heart, SeaWorld is a shoreside family entertainment center where the performers are dolphins, otters, sea lions, orcas, and seals. The 20-minute shows run several times each throughout the day, with visitors rotating through the various open-air amphitheaters and aquarium features.

Several successive 4-ton black-and-white killer whales have functioned as the park's mascot, and **Believe** 🎯🎯🎯, starring Shamu, is SeaWorld's most popular show. Per-formed in a 5,500-seat stadium, the stage is a 7-million-gallon pool lined with Plexi-glas walls that magnify the huge performers. But think twice before you sit in the seats down front—a high point of the act is multiple drenchings of the first 12 or so rows of spectators. Most days, the venue fills before the two or three performances even start, so arrive early to get the seat you want. The slapstick **Clyde and Seamore in**

Value Now *That's* a Deal!

San Diego's three main animal attractions offer combo tickets—and big savings. Here's how it works: If you plan to visit both the zoo and Wild Animal Park, a two-park ticket (the "Best Value" zoo package, plus Wild Animal Park admission) is $55 for adults, $34 for children 3 to 11 (for a $61/$38 value). You get one visit to each attraction, to be used within 5 days of purchase. Or throw in SeaWorld within the same 5 days, and the combo works out to $100 for adults, $77 children ages 3 to 9 (a $114/$81 value).

Other value options include the **San Diego Passport** ($79 for adults, $45 for children 3–11), which includes zoo admission, an Old Town Trolley city tour, Hornblower bay cruises, and more; passports are sold at the attractions themselves. **City Pass** (© **707/256-0490,** www.citypass.com) covers the zoo, SeaWorld, Disneyland Resorts, and Knott's Berry Farm in Orange County; passes are $199 for adults, and $159 for kids age 3 to 9 (a $238/$182 value), valid for 14 days. The **Go San Diego Card** (© **800/887-9103;** www.gosandiegocard.com) offers unlimited general admission to more than 35 attractions, including the zoo and LEGOLAND, as well as deals on shopping, dining, and day trips to Los Angeles, Mexico, and the local wine country. One-day packages start at $49 for adults and $39 for children (ages 3–12).

Deep, Deep Trouble (sea lions and otters), the fast-paced **Dolphin Discovery** 𝕬, and **Pets Rule!** are other performing animal routines, each in arenas seating more than 2,000. There are also shows focusing on humans: *R.L. Stine's Haunted Lighthouse,* a "4-D" movie starring a roster of multisensory effects, and in summer, **Cirque de la Mer,** which features acrobatic acts.

The collection of rides is led by **Journey to Atlantis** 𝕬, a 2004 arrival that combines a roller coaster and log flume with Atlantis mythology and a simulated earthquake. **Shipwreck Rapids** 𝕬 is a splashy adventure on raftlike inner tubes through caverns, waterfalls, and wild rivers, and **Wild Arctic** is a motion simulator helicopter trip to the frozen north. The **Skytower** and **Skyride** each cost an additional $3 to ride.

Guests disembarking Wild Arctic (or those using the ride bypass) find themselves in the midst of one of SeaWorld's real specialties: simulated marine environments. In this case, it's an **arctic research station** 𝕬, surrounded by beautiful beluga whales, walruses, and polar bears. Other animal environments worth seeing are **Manatee Rescue, Shark Encounter,** and the **Penguin Encounter.** Each of these attractions exits into a gift shop selling theme merchandise. The 2-acre hands-on area called **Shamu's Happy Harbor** is designed for kids, and features everything from a pretend pirate ship, with plenty of netted towers, to tube crawls, slides, and chances to get wet.

The **Dolphin Interaction Program** creates an opportunity for people to meet bottlenose dolphins. Although the program stops short of allowing you to swim with the dolphins, it does offer the opportunity to wade waist-deep, and plenty of time to stroke the mammals and to try giving training commands. This 1-hour program includes some classroom time before you wriggle into a wet suit and climb into the water for 20 minutes with the dolphins. It costs $150 per person (not including park admission); participants must be age 6 or older. One step further is the **Trainer for a Day** program, which is a 7-hour work shift with an animal trainer. Food preparation, feeding, a training session with a dolphin, and lunch is included; the price is $495 per person ($150 to be an observer). This program is limited to three participants daily, and the minimum age is 13. Advance reservations are required for both programs (✆ **800/257-4268,** press 7).

Although SeaWorld is best known as the home to pirouetting dolphins and fluke-flinging killer whales, the facility also plays a role in rescuing and rehabilitating beached animals found along the West Coast—including an average of 200 seals, sea lions, marine birds, and dolphins annually, almost 65% of which are rehabilitated and returned to the wild.

500 SeaWorld Dr., Mission Bay. ✆ **800/257-4268** or 619/226-3901. www.seaworld.com. Admission $53 adults, $43 children 3–9, free for children under 3. AE, DISC, MC, V. Hours vary seasonally, but always at least daily 10am–5pm; most weekends and during summer 9am–11pm. Parking $8. Bus: 9 or 27. From I-5, take SeaWorld Dr. exit; from I-8, take W. Mission Bay Dr. exit to SeaWorld Dr.

San Diego Wild Animal Park ✸✸✸ *Kids*   Thirty-four miles north of San Diego, outside of Escondido, this "zoo of the future" will transport you to the African plains and other faraway landscapes. Originally a breeding facility for the San Diego Zoo, the 1,800-acre Wild Animal Park now holds 3,500 animals representing 429 different species. What makes the park unique is that many of the animals roam freely in vast enclosures, allowing giraffes to interact with antelopes, much as they would in Africa. You'll find the largest crash of rhinos at any zoological facility in the world, an exhibit for the endangered California condor, and a mature landscape of exotic vegetation from many corners of the globe. Although the San Diego Zoo may be "world famous," it's the Wild Animal Park that many visitors celebrate as their favorite.

The central focus is the 5-mile **Wgasa Bush Line Railway,** a 60-minute monorail ride included in the price of admission. Trains leave every 10 minutes or so from the station, and lines build up by late morning, so make this your first or last attraction of the day (the animals are more active then anyway). The monorail passes through areas designated as East Africa, South Africa, Asian Plains, and the Eurasian Water-hole, through swaying grasses and along rocky outcrops.

Other exhibits bring you closer to the animals, like the three self-guided **walking tours,** which visit various habitats, including the most recent, **Lion Camp. Nairobi Village** is the commercial hub of the park, but even here, animal exhibits are interest-ing, including the **nursery area,** where irresistible young'uns can be seen frolicking, bottle-feeding, and sleeping; a **petting station;** the **lowland gorillas;** and the **African Aviary.** There are amphitheaters for a bird show and another featuring elephants, scheduled two or three times daily. Nairobi Village has souvenir stores and several spots for mediocre dining. Visitors should be prepared for sunny, often downright hot weather; it's not unusual for temperatures to be 5° to 10° warmer here than in San Diego.

If you want to get up-close-and-personal with the animals, take one of the park's **Photo Caravans,** which shuttle groups in flatbed trucks out into the open areas that are inaccessible to the general public. There are a variety of itineraries (some are sea-sonal and have varying age requirements), and each is a minimum of 2 hours long. Prices start at $90, and you'll want to make reservations ahead of your visit (✆ **619/ 718-3050**). Another unique perspective is provided by the **Balloon Safari**—a teth-ered helium balloon takes you 400 feet (121 meters) above the park, providing amaz-ing views of the grounds and the surrounding San Pasqual Valley. Rides are about 15 minutes and cost $15. The **Cheetah Run Safari** allows a limited number of guests

Moments **Things That Go Bump in the Night**

The Wild Animal Park's **Roar & Snore** and **Beastly Bedtime programs,** which are held on most Fridays and Saturdays from April to October (with extended dates in summer), let you camp out next to the animal compound and observe the nocturnal movements of rhinos, lions, and other creatures. To request information by mail or to make reservations, call ℂ **619/718-3050.**

(reservations required; ℂ **619/718-3000**) to watch the world's fastest land mammal in action, sprinting after a mechanical lure. Cost is $69 per person, excluding park admission.

15500 San Pasqual Valley Rd., Escondido. ℂ 760/747-8702. www.wildanimalpark.org. Admission $29 adults, $26 seniors 60 and over, $18 children 3–11, free for children under 3 and military in uniform. AE, DISC, MC, V. Daily 9am–4pm (grounds close at 5pm); extended hours during summer and Festival of Lights (2 weekends in Dec). Parking $8. Take I-15 to Via Rancho Pkwy.; follow signs for about 3 miles.

2 San Diego's Beaches

The promo materials from the local Convention and Visitors Bureau say it all: San Diego County is blessed with 70 miles of sandy coastline and more than 30 individual beaches. Even in winter and spring, when water temperatures drop to the high 50s, the beaches are great places to walk and jog, and surfers happily don wet suits to pursue their passion. In summer, the beaches teem with locals and visitors alike—the bikinis come out, the pecs are bared, and a spring-break atmosphere threatens to break loose. But common sense and good taste usually prevail and regardless of your taste, you can enjoy a fun day at the beach.

A word (rather, four) to the wise: **May Gray** and **June Gloom.** They're both names for a local weather pattern that can be counted on to foil sunbathing most mornings (and sometimes all day) from mid-May to mid-July. Overcast skies appear as inland deserts like Anza-Borrego heat up at the end of spring and suck the marine layer—a thick bank of fog—inland for a few miles each night. Be prepared for moist mornings and evenings (and sometimes afternoons) at the beaches this time of year. But *remember:* Just because the sun's not brightly shining, doesn't mean you're not being exposed to harmful UV rays. Some of the worst sunburns can happen during cloud cover, so always wear sunscreen during prolonged outdoor exposure. Another beach precaution worth remembering is the "stingray shuffle." At beaches where the water is calm, such as Mission Bay and La Jolla Shores, it's a good idea to shuffle your feet as you walk through the surf—it rousts any stingrays that might be in your path. They can deliver an extremely painful, but nonlethal, wound.

Exploring **tide pools**—pot-holed, rocky shores that retain ponds of water after the tide has gone out, providing homes for a plethora of sea creatures—can be a lot of fun. You can get a tide chart free or for a nominal charge from many surf and diving shops, including **Emerald City Surf & Sport,** 1118 Orange Ave. in Coronado (ℂ **619/435-6677**), and **San Diego Divers Supply,** 4004 Sports Arena Blvd., near SeaWorld (ℂ **619/224-3439**). Among my favorite places for tide-pooling are Cabrillo National Monument at the oceanside base of Point Loma, at Sunset Cliffs in Ocean Beach, and the rocky coast immediately south of the cove in La Jolla.

Here's a list of San Diego's most noteworthy beaches, each with its own personality and devotees. They're listed geographically from south to north. All California beaches are open to the public to the mean high-tide line, and you can check **www.sannet. gov/lifeguards/beaches** for descriptions and water quality. For the daily beach, tide, and surf report, call ✆ **619/221-8824.** *Note:* All beaches are good for swimming except as indicated. For a map of San Diego's beaches, see the color map at the beginning of this book.

IMPERIAL BEACH

A half-hour south of downtown San Diego by car or trolley, and only a few minutes from the Mexican border, is Imperial Beach. It's popular with surfers and local youth, who can be somewhat territorial about "their" sands in summer. The beach boasts 3 miles of surf breaks plus a guarded "swimmers only" stretch; check with lifeguards before getting wet, though, since sewage runoff from nearby Mexico can sometimes foul the water. I.B. also plays host to the annual **U.S. Open Sandcastle Competition** in late July—the best reason to come here—with world-class sand creations ranging from sea scenes to dragons to dinosaurs.

CORONADO BEACH ✿

Lovely, wide, and sparkling, this beach is conducive to strolling and lingering, especially in the late afternoon. At the north end, you can watch fighter jets in formation flying from the Naval Air Station, while just south is the pretty section fronting Ocean Boulevard and the Hotel del Coronado. Waves are gentle here, so the beach draws many Coronado families—and their dogs, which are allowed off-leash at the most northwesterly end. South of the Hotel Del, the beach becomes the beautiful, often deserted **Silver Strand.** The islands visible from here, Los Coronados, are 18 miles away and belong to Mexico.

OCEAN BEACH

The northern end of Ocean Beach Park is officially known as **Dog Beach** and is one of only a few in the county where your pooch can roam freely on the sand (and frolic with several dozen other people's pets). Surfers generally congregate around the O.B. Pier, mostly in the water but often at the snack shack on the end. Rip currents can be strong here and sometimes discourage swimmers from venturing beyond waist depth (check with the lifeguard stations). Facilities at the beach include restrooms, showers, picnic tables, volleyball courts, and plenty of metered parking lots. To reach the beach, take West Point Loma Boulevard all the way to the end.

MISSION BAY PARK

This inland, 4,600-acre aquatic playground contains 27 miles of bayfront, picnic areas, children's playgrounds, and paths for biking, in-line skating, and jogging. The bay lends itself to windsurfing, sailing, water-skiing, and fishing. There are dozens of access points; one of the most popular is off I-5 at Clairemont Drive (though this is not my favorite area for swimming because it is farthest from fresh ocean currents). Also accessed from this spot is **Fiesta Island,** where the annual **Over the Line Tournament** is held to raucous enthusiasm in July (see "When to Go," in chapter 2); a 4-mile road loops around the island.

BONITA COVE/MARINER'S POINT & MISSION POINT

Also enclosed in Mission Bay Park (facing the bay, not the ocean), this pretty and protected cove's calm waters, grassy picnic areas, and playground equipment make it

Beach Snack Staples: Quick (& Cheap) Taco Stands

Here are a few favorites within a burrito's throw of the sand (from south to north):

Across from the Big Dipper roller coaster—step inside **Roberto's Taco Shop,** 3202 Mission Blvd., Mission Beach (© **858/488-1610**), for family-recipe Mexican favorites.

When time is of the essence, roll through the 24-hour drive-through window at **Ramiro's,** 4525 Mission Blvd., Pacific Beach (© **858/273-5227**), for tasty burritos and tacos at rock-bottom prices.

The name says it all at **Taco Surf,** 4657 Mission Blvd., Pacific Beach (© **858/272-3877**), the most "formal" of the bunch—meaning there's table service.

As you make your way toward La Jolla, join the throngs of beachgoers and lunch-breakers at tiny **Los Dos Pedros #1,** 723 Turquoise St., Pacific Beach (© **858/488-3102**); surfers from Windansea fuel their day at **Los Dos Pedros #2,** 6990 La Jolla Blvd., La Jolla (© **858/456-2692**).

perfect for families—or as a paddling destination if you've rented kayaks elsewhere in the bay. The water is cleaner for swimming than in the northeastern reaches of Mission Bay. Get to Bonita Cove from Mission Boulevard in south Mission Beach; reach Mariner's Point via Mariner's Way, off West Mission Bay Drive.

MISSION BEACH
While Mission Bay Park is a body of saltwater surrounded by land and bridges, Mission Beach is actually a beach on the Pacific Ocean, anchored by the **Giant Dipper** roller coaster. Always popular, the sands and wide cement "boardwalk" sizzle with activity and great people-watching in summer; at the southern end there's always a volleyball game in play. The long beach and path extend from the jetty north to Belmont Park and Pacific Beach Drive. Parking is often tough, with your best bets being the public lots at Belmont Park or at the south end of West Mission Bay Drive. This busy street is the centerline of a 2-block-wide isthmus that leads a mile north to . . .

PACIFIC BEACH
There's always action here, particularly along **Ocean Front Walk,** a paved promenade featuring a human parade akin to that at L.A.'s Venice Beach boardwalk. It runs along Ocean Boulevard (just west of Mission Blvd.) to the pier. Surfing is popular year-round here, in marked sections, and the beach is well staffed with lifeguards. You're on your own to find street parking. Pacific Beach is also the home of **Tourmaline Surfing Park,** a half-mile north of the pier, where the sport's old guard gathers to surf waters where swimmers are prohibited; reach it via Tourmaline Street, off Mission Boulevard.

WINDANSEA BEACH
The fabled locale of Tom Wolfe's *Pump House Gang,* Windansea is legendary to this day among California's surf elite and remains one of San Diego's prettiest strands. Reached by way of Bonair Street (at Neptune Place), Windansea has no facilities, and

street parking is first-come, first-served. Not ideal for swimming, so come to surf, watch surfers, or soak in the camaraderie and party atmosphere.

CHILDREN'S POOL ⚲

Think clothing-optional Black's Beach is the city's most controversial sun-sea-sand situation? Think again—the Children's Pool is currently home to the biggest man-vs.-beast struggle since *Moby Dick*. A seawall protects this pocket of sand, originally intended as a calm swimming bay for children, but since 1994, when a rock outcrop off the shore was designated as a protected mammal reserve, the beach has been cordoned off for the resident **harbor seal** population. On an average day you'll spot dozens lolling in the sun. Some humans did not take kindly to their beach banishment, and the fight was on. After much heated debate (and even acts of civil disobedience), swimming was reinstated—to the displeasure of many. So while it is possible to now swim at the Children's Pool, keep in mind those are federally protected *wild* animals, and it is illegal to approach them or harass them in any way. Volunteers keep watch to make sure bathers don't interfere with the colony, and their speed dials are at the ready—scofflaws will get arrested. The beach is at Coast Boulevard and Jenner Street; there's limited free street parking.

LA JOLLA COVE ⚲⚲

The protected, calm waters—celebrated as the clearest along the coast—attract snorkelers and scuba divers, along with a fair share of families. The stunning setting offers a small sandy beach, as well as, on the cliffs above, the **Ellen Browning Scripps Park.** The cove's "look but don't touch" policy protects the colorful garibaldi, California's state fish, plus other marine life, including abalone, octopus, and lobster. The unique Underwater Park stretches from here to the northern end of Torrey Pines State Reserve and incorporates kelp forests, artificial reefs, two deep submarine canyons, and tidal pools. The cove is terrific for swimming, cramped for sunbathing, and accessible from Coast Boulevard; parking nearby is scarce.

LA JOLLA SHORES

The wide, flat mile of sand at La Jolla Shores is popular with joggers, swimmers, kayakers, novice scuba divers, and beginning body- and board-surfers, as well as families. It looks like a picture postcard, with fine sand under blue skies, kissed by gentle waves. Weekend crowds can be enormous, though, quickly claiming fire rings and occupying both the sand and the metered parking spaces in the lot. There are restrooms, showers, and picnic areas here, as well, the grassy, palm-lined Kellogg Park across the street.

BLACK'S BEACH ⚲

The area's unofficial (and illegal) nude beach, 2-mile-long Black's lies between La Jolla Shores and Torrey Pines State Beach, at the base of steep, 300-foot-high cliffs. The beach is out of the way and not easy to reach, but it draws scores with its secluded beauty and good swimming conditions—the graceful spectacle of paragliders launching from the cliffs above adds to the show. To get here, take North Torrey Pines Road, watch for signs for the Gliderport (where you can park), and clamber down the makeshift path, staying alert to avoid veering off to one of several false trails. To bypass the cliff descent, you can walk to Black's from beaches north (Torrey Pines) or south (La Jolla Shores). *Note:* There's no permanent lifeguard station, though lifeguards are usually present from spring break to October, and no restroom facilities. The beach's notoriety came about when, from 1974 to 1977, swimsuits *were* optional—the only such beach in the U.S. to be so designated at the time. Rich neighbors on the cliffs above complained enough to the city about their property being denigrated that the clothing-optional status was reversed. But today, citations for nude sunbathing are rarely issued.

TORREY PINES BEACH ⤞

The north end of Black's Beach, at the foot of Torrey Pines State Park is this fabulous, underused strand, accessed by a pay parking lot at the entrance to the park. In fact, combining a visit to the park with a day at the beach is my concept of the quintessential San Diego outdoor experience. It's rarely crowded, though you need to be aware of high tide (when most of the sand gets a bath). In almost any weather, it's a great beach for walking. *Note:* At this and any other bluff-side beach, never sit at the bottom of the cliffs. The hillsides are unstable and could collapse.

DEL MAR BEACH

The Del Mar Thoroughbred Club's slogan, as famously sung by DMTC founder Bing Crosby, is "where turf meets the surf." This town beach represents the "surf" portion of that phrase. It's a long stretch of sand backed by grassy cliffs and a playground area. This area is not heavily trafficked, and you can get a wonderful meal on the beach at Jake's. Del Mar is about 15 miles from downtown San Diego; see "North County Beach Towns: Spots to Surf & Sun" in chapter 11 on p. 235.

NORTHERN SAN DIEGO COUNTY BEACHES

Those inclined to venture farther north in San Diego County won't be disappointed. Pacific Coast Highway leads to inviting beaches, such as these in Encinitas: peaceful **Boneyard Beach, Swami's Beach** for surfing, and **Moonlight Beach,** popular with families and volleyball buffs. Farthest north is Oceanside, which has one of the West Coast's longest wooden piers, wide sandy beaches, and several popular surfing areas. See "North County Beach Towns: Spots to Surf & Sun" in chapter 11 on p. 235 for more information.

3 Attractions in Balboa Park

New York has Central Park; San Francisco has Golden Gate Park. San Diego's crown jewel is Balboa Park, a 1,174-acre city-owned playground and the largest urban cultural park in the nation. The park was established in 1868 in the heart of the city, bordered by downtown to the southwest and fringed by the early communities of Hillcrest and Golden Hill to the north and east. Originally called City Park, the name was eventually changed to commemorate the Spanish explorer Balboa. Tree plantings started in the late 19th century, while the initial buildings were created to host the 1915–16 Panama-California Exposition; another expo in 1935–36 brought additional developments.

The park's most distinctive features are its mature landscaping, the architectural beauty of the Spanish Golden Age buildings lining El Prado (the park's east-west thoroughfare), and the outstanding and diverse museums contained within it. You'll also find eight different gardens, walkways, 4½ miles of hiking trails in Florida Canyon, an ornate pavilion with the world's largest outdoor organ, an IMAX domed theater, the acclaimed **Old Globe Theatre** (p. 168), and the **San Diego Zoo** (p. 136).

Value Balboa Park Money-Savers

Most Balboa Park attractions are open free of charge one Tuesday each month; there's a rotating schedule so two or more participate each Tuesday (see "Free of Charge & Full of Fun," later in this chapter). If you plan to visit more than three of the park's museums, buy the **Passport to Balboa Park,** a $30 coupon booklet that allows entrance to 13 major museums (the rest are always free) and is valid for 1 week. If you plan to spend a day at the zoo and return for the museums another day, buy the **Best of Balboa Park Combo,** which provides one ticket to the zoo, and 3 days' admission to the 13 museums, for $55. The passports can be purchased at any participating museum or the visitor center.

The park is divided into three distinct sections, separated by Highway 163 and Florida Canyon. The narrow western wing of the park is largely grassy open areas that parallel Sixth Avenue; there are no museums in this section, but it's a good place for picnics, strolling, sunning, and dog walking. The eastern section is also devoid of cultural attractions, but has the **Balboa Park Municipal Golf Course** (p. 178). The central portion of the park, between Highway 163 and Florida Drive, contains the zoo and all of the museums.

If you really want to visit the zoo and a few of the park's museums, don't try to tackle them both the same day. Allow at least 5 hours to tour the zoo; the amount of time you spend in the 13 major museums will vary depending on your personal interests. I've also mapped out a **walking tour** that takes in most of the park's highlights (p. 200). There are informal restaurants serving sandwiches and snacks throughout the park. For breakfast, **Tobey's 19th Hole** at the municipal golf course is a find (p. 178); try lunch at the Japanese Friendship Garden's **Tea Pavilion** or in the **San Diego Museum of Art's sculpture garden** (p. 202). The **Prado Restaurant** (p. 206) is also a San Diego favorite for lunch or dinner.

There are two primary **road entrances** into the heart of the park. The most distinctive is from Sixth Avenue and Laurel Street: Laurel turns into El Prado as it traverses the beautiful **Cabrillo Bridge** across Highway 163. You can also enter via Presidents Way from Park Boulevard. Major **parking areas** are at Inspiration Point just east of Park Boulevard at Presidents Way, in front of the zoo, and along Presidents Way between the Aerospace Museum and Spreckels Organ Pavilion. Other lots, though more centrally located, are small and in high demand, especially on weekends.

Public **bus routes** 7, 7A, and 7B run along Park Boulevard; for the west side of the park, routes 1, 3, and 25 run along Fourth/Fifth avenues (except for the Marston House, all museums are closer to Park Blvd.). Free **tram** transportation within the park runs daily from 8:30am to 6pm, with extended hours in summer months. The red trolley trams originate at the Inspiration Point parking lot to circuit the park, arriving every 8 to 10 minutes and stopping at designated pickup areas. Stop by the **Balboa Park Visitors Center,** in the House of Hospitality (© **619/239-0512;** www.balboapark.org) to learn about free walking and museum **tours,** or to pick up a brochure about the **gardens** of the park.

Botanical Building and Lily Pond ✦ *Moments*   This serene park within the park is one of my favorite hideouts. Ferns, orchids, impatiens, begonias, and other plants—about 2,100 tropical and flowering varieties, plus rotating exhibits—are sheltered

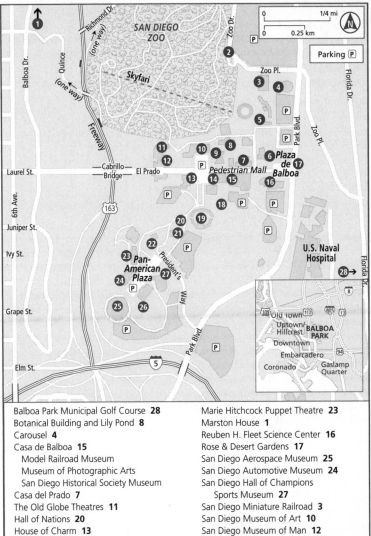

Parking P

SAN DIEGO ZOO

Skyfari

Cabrillo Bridge

El Prado

Pedestrian Mall

Plaza de Balboa

U.S. Naval Hospital

Pan-American Plaza

President's Way

Old Town
Uptown/Hillcrest
BALBOA PARK
Downtown
Embarcadero
Coronado
Gaslamp Quarter

beneath a domed lath house. The graceful 250-foot-long building, part of the 1915 Panama-California Exposition, is one of the world's largest wood lath structures, and emerged from a complete renovation in 2002. Kids love the "touch and smell" garden and the smelly bog of carnivorous plants. The lily pond out front attracts sun worshipers, painters, and street entertainers.

El Prado. ℂ 619/235-1100. Free admission. Fri–Wed 10am–4pm; closed Thurs and major holidays. Bus: 7 or 7A/B.

House of Pacific Relations International Cottages   This cluster of 17 charming one- and two-room cottages disseminates information about the culture, traditions, and history of 30 countries. Light refreshments are served, and outdoor lawn programs are presented by one of the nations every Sunday, 2 to 3pm, March through October. The adjacent **United Nations Building** houses an international gift shop where you can buy jewelry, toys and books, and UNICEF greeting cards (ℂ **619/ 233-5044**); it's open daily from 10am to 4:30pm.

Adjacent to Pan American Plaza. ℂ 619/234-0739. Free admission (donations welcome). Sun noon–4pm; 4th Tues of each month 11am–3pm. Bus: 7 or 7A/B.

Japanese Friendship Garden _Finds_   Of the 11½ acres designated for the garden, only 2 acres have been developed. Yet to come are herb and tea gardens, a cherry tree grove, a lily pond, and an amphitheater. What is here, though, is beautifully serene and is referred to as San-Kei-En, or "three-scene garden." It represents ties to San Diego's sister city of Yokohama, which has a similarly named garden. From the main gate, a crooked path (to confound evil spirits, who move only in a straight line) threads its way to the information center in a Zen-style house; here you can view the most ancient kind of garden, the _sekitei,_ made only of sand and stone (a self-guided tour is available). Teas, sushi, noodles, and more, are served on a Japanese-style deck to the left of the entrance; imported gifts are also for sale. Japanese holidays are celebrated here, and the public is invited.

2125 Park Blvd., adjacent to the Organ Pavilion. ℂ 619/232-2721. www.niwa.org. Admission $3 adults, $2.50 seniors, $2 students and military, free for children 6 and under. Free 3rd Tues of each month. Tues–Sun 10am–4pm (also on Mon 10am–4pm in summer). Bus: 7 or 7A/B.

Marston House _♠_   Noted San Diego architect Irving Gill designed this craftsman house in 1905 for George Marston, a local businessman and philanthropist. Listed on the National Register of Historic Places and now managed by the San Diego Historical Society, the house is a classic example of prairie-style architecture, reminiscent of the work of Frank Lloyd Wright. Some of its interesting features are wide hallways, brick fireplaces, and redwood paneling. Opened to the public in 1991, it is now fully furnished with Roycroft, Stickley, and Limbert pieces, as well as art pottery. Tours take about 45 minutes.

3525 Seventh Ave. (northwest corner of Balboa Park at Balboa Dr. and Upas St.). ℂ 619/298-3142. Guided tour $5 adults, $4 seniors and students, $2 children 6–17, free for children 5 and under. Fri–Sun 10am–4pm (last tour at 3:15pm). Bus: 1, 3, or 25.

Mingei International Museum _♠♠_   This captivating museum (pronounced "_min_-gay," meaning "art of the people" in Japanese), offers changing exhibitions generally describable as folk art. The rotating exhibits—usually four at a time—feature artists from countries across the globe; displays include textiles, costumes, jewelry, toys, pottery, paintings, and sculpture. The permanent collection includes whimsical contemporary sculptures by the late French artist Niki de Saint Phalle, who made San

Diego her home in 1993. Martha Longenecker, a potter and professor emeritus of art at San Diego State University, opened the museum in 1978. It is one of only a few major museums in the United States devoted to folk crafts on a worldwide scale, and well worth a look. Allow half an hour to an hour to view the exhibits; there's also a wonderful gift store that is worth a visit on its own. An Escondido branch has additional exhibits (p. 251).

1439 El Prado, in the House of Charm. © 619/239-0003. www.mingei.org. Admission $6 adults, $3 children 6–17 and students with ID, free for children under 6. Free 3rd Tues of each month. Tues–Sun 10am–4pm. Bus: 7 or 7A/B.

Museum of Photographic Arts ★★   If names like Ansel Adams and Edward
Weston stimulate your fingers to do the shutterbug, then don't miss a taste of the 7,000-plus collection of images housed by this museum—one of few in the United States devoted exclusively to the photographic arts (which, at MoPA, encompasses cinema, video, and digital photography). A 1999 expansion allowed the museum to display even more of the permanent collection, while leaving room for provocative traveling exhibits that change every few months. Photos by Alfred Stieglitz, Margaret Bourke-White, Imogen Cunningham, Paul Strand, and Manuel Alvarez Bravo are all in the permanent collection, and the plush cinema illuminates classic films on an ongoing basis. Allow 30 to 60 minutes to see the collection.

1649 El Prado. © 619/238-7559. www.mopa.org. Admission $6 adults, $4 seniors, students and military, free for children under 12 with adult. Free 2nd Tues of each month. Daily 10am–5pm (Thurs until 9pm). Bus: 7 or 7A/B.

Reuben H. Fleet Science Center ★ (Kids)   A must-see for kids of any age is this tantalizing collection of interactive exhibits and rides designed to provoke the imagination and teach scientific principles. The Virtual Zone includes **Comet Impact,** a motion simulator ride that rockets you into the heart of a comet, and other virtual-reality attractions with a scientific bent. The Fleet also houses a 76-foot-high IMAX Dome Theater that shows films so realistic that ocean footage can actually give you motion sickness. And in 2001, the Fleet unveiled a spiffy new planetarium simulator powered by computer graphics. Planetarium shows are the first Wednesday of each month ($7 adults, $6 kids age 3–12, $6 seniors).

1875 El Prado. © 619/238-1233. www.rhfleet.org. Fleet Experience admission includes an IMAX film and exhibit galleries: $12 adults, $10 seniors, $9 children 3–12 (exhibit gallery can be purchased individually). Free 1st Tues of each month (exhibit galleries only). Hours vary but always daily 9:30am–5pm; later closing times possible. Bus: 7 or 7A/B.

San Diego Aerospace Museum ★★ (Kids)   The other big kid-pleaser of the museums (along with the Reuben H. Fleet Science Center, above), this popular facility provides an overview of the nation's air-and-space history, from the days of hot-air balloons to the space age, with plenty of biplanes and military fighters in between. It emphasizes local aviation history, particularly the construction here of the *Spirit of St. Louis.* Highlights include the Apollo 9 Command Module and motion simulator rides that allow you to take a space walk or take off from the deck of a pitching aircraft carrier in a jet fighter. The museum is housed in a stunning cylindrical hall built by the Ford Motor Company in 1935 (for the park's 2nd international expo), and has an imaginative gift shop with items like old-fashioned leather flight hoods and new-fashioned freeze-dried astronaut ice cream. Allow at least an hour for your visit.

2001 Pan American Plaza. © 619/234-8291. www.aerospacemuseum.org. Admission $9 adults, $7 seniors, $4 juniors 6–17, free for active military with ID and children under 6. Free 4th Tues of each month. Sept–May daily 10am–4:30pm; June–Aug daily 10am–5:30pm. Bus: 7 or 7A/B.

Tips **Balboa Park Guided Tours**

In addition to the walking tour we map out in chapter 8, guided tours of the park cater to a wide variety of interests. The visitor center conducts free rotating tours on Saturdays at 10am that highlight either the palm trees and vegetation or park history; they meet at the visitor center. The park rangers lead free 1-hour tours focusing on the park's history, architecture, and botanical resources Tuesday and Sunday at 1pm, also meeting in front of the visitor center. The author of *Discover Balboa Park* conducts free walking tours of the park on Fridays at 1pm, meeting at the visitor center; call © **619/239-0512** for more information.

The Committee of 100 (© **619/223-6566**), an organization dedicated to preserving the park's Spanish colonial architecture, offers a free exploration of the Prado's structures on the first Wednesday of the month at 9:30am, starting from the visitor center. The Old Globe Theatre Tour visits the three performance venues and backstage areas on Saturdays and Sundays at 10:30am; the tour costs $5 for adults, $3 for seniors and students (© **619/ 231-1941**, ext. 2142). Plant Day at the San Diego Zoo is held the third Friday of each month and features self-guided and guided horticultural tours and functions; the orchid house is open to the public 10am to 2pm on this day, as well as the first Sunday of March, June, September, and December, for Orchid Odyssey (zoo admission required; call © **619/231-1515** for more details).

San Diego Automotive Museum *Rids* Even if you don't know a distributor from a dipstick, you're bound to ooh-and-aah over the classic, antique, and exotic cars here. Every one is so pristine you'd swear it just rolled off the line, from an 1886 Benz to a 1931 Rolls-Royce Phaeton to the 1981 DeLorean. Most of the time, temporary shows take over the facility, so check ahead to see if it's one you're interested in. Some days you can take a peek at the ongoing restoration program, and the museum sponsors many outdoor car rallies and other events. Allow 30 to 45 minutes for your visit.

2080 Pan American Plaza. © 619/231-2886. www.sdautomuseum.org. Admission $7 adults, $6 seniors and active military, $3 children 6–15, free for children under 6. Free 4th Tues of each month. Daily 10am–5pm (last admission 4:30pm). Bus: 7 or 7A/B.

San Diego Hall of Champions Sports Museum From Padres great Tony Gywnn to skateboard icon Tony Hawk, from legendary surfer Skip Frye to Hall of Fame quarterback Dan Fouts, this slick museum celebrates San Diego's best-ever athletes and the sports they played. More than 25 exhibits surround a centerpiece statue, the *Discus Thrower,* including memorabilia from the around the world of sport (the biggies and the niche ones), rotating art shows, and interactive stations where you can try out your play-by-play skills. One particularly interesting exhibit is devoted to athletes with disabilities. You can see it all in under an hour.

2131 Pan American Plaza. © 619/234-2544. www.sdhoc.com. Admission $6 adults, $4 seniors 65 and older and military, $3 children 6–17, free for children under 6. Free 4th Tues of each month. Daily 10am–4:30pm. Bus: 7 or 7A/B.

San Diego Historical Society Museum   A good place to start if you are a new-comer to San Diego, this museum offers permanent and changing exhibits on topics related to the history of the region. Past shows have examined such subjects as San Diego's role as a Hollywood film location to the city's architectural heritage. Many of the museum's photographs depict Balboa Park and the growth of the city. Plan to spend about 30 to 45 minutes here. Books about San Diego's history are available in the gift shop, and the research library downstairs is open Thursday through Saturday.

1649 El Prado, in Casa del Balboa. © 619/232-6203. www.sandiegohistory.org. Admission $5 adults, $4 students, seniors and military with ID, $2 children 6–17, free for children 5 and under. Free 2nd Tues of each month. Daily 10am–5pm. Bus: 7 or 7A/B.

San Diego Miniature Railroad and Carousel *Kids*   Just east of the zoo entrance, these antiquated enticements never fail to delight the preteen set. The open-air rail-road takes a 3-minute journey through a grove of eucalyptus trees, while the charm-ing carousel is one of the last in the world to still offer a ring grab (free ride if you seize the brass one). The carousel, built in 1910, is a classic, with hand-carved wood frogs, horses, and pigs.

Zoo Dr., next to San Diego Zoo entrance. Railroad © 619/231-1515, ext. 4219; carousel © 619/460-9000. www.balboapark.org. Admission $1.75, free for children under 1. Daily in summer 11am–6:30pm; 11am–4:30pm weekends and holidays only Sept–May. Bus: 7 or 7A/B.

San Diego Model Railroad Museum *Kids*   Okay, so it's not exactly high cul-ture, but this museum is cool and pleasing, and worth your time, especially if you have kids in tow. Six permanent, scale-model railroads depict Southern California's trans-portation history and terrain with an astounding attention to miniature details—the exhibits occupy a 27,000-square-foot space. Children will enjoy the hands-on Lionel trains, and train buffs of all ages will appreciate the interactive multimedia displays. Allow a half-hour to an hour for your visit.

1649 El Prado (Casa de Balboa), under the Museum of Photographic Arts. © 619/696-0199. www.sdmrm.com. Admission $5 adults, $4 seniors, $3 student, $2.50 military; free for children under 15. Free 1st Tues of each month. Tues–Fri 11am–4pm; Sat–Sun 11am–5pm. Bus: 7 or 7A/B.

San Diego Museum of Art *Kids*   This museum is known in the art world for its col-lection of Spanish baroque painting and possibly the largest horde of Asian Indian paintings outside India. The American collection includes works by Georgia O'Keeffe and Thomas Eakins. Only a small percentage of the 12,000-piece permanent collec-tion is on display at any given time, in favor of varied, often prestigious touring shows. In 2007, the work of Henri de Toulouse-Lautrec is scheduled to be the summer block-buster show. This internationally touring exhibition is being organized by SDMA and the Musée Toulouse-Lautrec in France.

1450 El Prado. © 619/232-7931. www.sdmart.org. Admission $10 adults, $8 seniors and military, $7 college stu-dents, $4 children 6–17, free for children under 6. Admission to traveling exhibits varies. Free 3rd Tues of each month. Tues–Sun 10am–6pm (Thurs until 9pm). Bus: 7 or 7A/B.

San Diego Museum of Man *Kids*   Under the iconic, rococo, tiled **California building and bell tower** just inside the park entrance at the Cabrillo Bridge, this museum is devoted to anthropology, with an emphasis on the peoples of North and South America. Favorite exhibits include life-size replicas of a dozen varieties of *Homo sapiens,* from Cro-Magnon and Neanderthal to Peking Man, and a small room featur-ing Egyptian mummies and artifacts. Don't overlook the annex across the street, which houses more exhibits, or the lady making fresh tortillas and quesadillas Wednesday through Sunday. The museum's annual Indian Fair, held in June, features American Indians from the Southwest demonstrating tribal dances and selling food, arts, and crafts. Allow at least an hour for your visit.

1350 El Prado. ℰ **619/239-2001.** www.museumofman.org. Admission $6 adults, $5 seniors, $3 children 6–17, free for children under 6. Free 3rd Tues of the month. Daily 10am–4:30pm. Bus: 1, 3, 7, 7A/B, or 25.

San Diego Natural History Museum   This museum focuses on the flora, fauna, and mineralogy of Southern and Baja California. Kids marvel at the animals they find here, including live snakes, tarantulas, and turtles. As a binational museum, research is done on both sides of the border and most exhibits are bilingual. You can see them all in about an hour. There's a 300-seat, large-format movie theater, and two films are included in the price of admission. In 2006, the museum opened the largest, most detailed exhibit in its history, *Fossil Mysteries.* The interactive installation also includes life-size models of prehistoric animals, including the Megalodon shark, the largest predator the world has ever known. Call or check the museum's website for a current schedule of special visiting exhibits.

1788 El Prado. ℰ **619/232-3821.** www.sdnhm.org. Admission $9 adults, $6 seniors, college students, and active-duty military, $5 children 3–17, free for children under 3. Free 1st Tues of each month. Daily 10am–5pm. Bus: 7 or 7A/B.

SDAI Museum of the Living Artist   Around since 1941, the San Diego Art Institute now has a museum to house exhibits of new artworks by local artists. The 10,000-square-foot municipal gallery rotates juried shows in and out every 4 to 6 weeks, ensuring a variety of mediums and styles. It's a good place to see what the local art community is up to. Plan to spend about half an hour here.

1439 El Prado. ℰ **619/236-0011.** www.sandiego-art.org. Admission $3 adults, $2 seniors, students, and military, free to children 12 and under. Free 3rd Tues of the month. Tues–Sat 10am–4pm; Sun noon–4pm. Bus: 7 or 7A/B.

Spreckels Organ Pavilion   Given to San Diego citizens in 1914 by brothers John D. and Adolph Spreckels, the ornate, curved pavilion houses a magnificent organ with 4,518 individual pipes. They range in length from the size of a pencil to more than 32 feet. With only brief interruptions, the organ has been in continuous use, and today visitors can enjoy free hour-long concerts on Sundays at 2pm, given by civic organist Carol Williams. There's seating for 2,400 but little shade, so bring an umbrella on warm days.

South of El Prado. ℰ **619/702-8138.** www.sosorgan.com. Free 1-hr. organ concerts Sun 2pm year-round; free organ concerts late June–Aug Mon 7:30pm (see website for a schedule); free Twilight in the Park concerts Tues–Thurs mid-June to Aug (call ℰ **619/239-0512** for schedule). Bus: 7 or 7A/B.

Timken Museum of Art ☆ *Finds*   How many art museums invite you to see great works of art, free of charge? This jewel-like repository houses the Putnam Foundation's collection of 19th-century American paintings and works by European old masters, as well as a worthy display of Russian icons. Yes, it's a small collection, but the marquee attractions include a Peter Paul Rubens, *Portrait of a Young Man in Armor;* San Diego's only Rembrandt, *St. Bartholomew;* and a masterpiece by Eastman Johnson, *The Cranberry Harvest.* You'll find a spot each for works by Bierstadt, Inness, Corot, and Brueghel (the elder). Since you can tour all of the museum in well under an hour, the Timken also makes for an easy introduction to fine art for younger travelers—pick up a copy of the free family guide, which turns a museum visit into a scavenger hunt.

Docent tours are available Tuesday through Thursday from 10am to noon, and the third Tuesday of the month from 1 to 3pm, or by appointment.

1500 El Prado. © **619/239-5548.** www.timkenmuseum.org. Free admission. Tues–Sat 10am–4:30pm; Sun 1:30–4:30pm. Closed Sept. Bus: 7 or 7A/B.

4 More Attractions

DOWNTOWN & BEYOND

In 2004, downtown San Diego completed a huge construction project, the Padres' **PETCO Park** (p. 184), which has extended the rebuilt downtown a few blocks farther east. Real estate developers in the "East Village" are stepping up to the plate in hopes of cashing in on a home run.

In the meantime, you can wander from the turn-of-the-20th-century **Gaslamp Quarter** ✿✿ to the joyful, modern architecture of the **Horton Plaza** ✿ shopping center (see "Walking Tour 1: The Gaslamp Quarter," in chapter 8). The Gaslamp consists of 16½ blocks of restored historic buildings. It gets its name from the old-fashioned street lamps that line the sidewalks. You'll find dozens of restaurants and our most vigorous nightlife scene here. At Horton Plaza, you can shop, stroll, snack or dine, enjoy free entertainment, see a movie, and people-watch—all within a unique and playful village framework (p. 208).

Seaport Village is a shopping and dining complex on the waterfront (p. 209). It was designed to look like a New England seaport community. If you find the views across the water alluring, another way to experience San Diego's waterfront is with one of several harbor tours (see "Organized Tours," later in this chapter).

Cabrillo National Monument ✿✿✿   Breathtaking views mingle with the early history of San Diego, which began when Juan Rodríguez Cabrillo arrived in 1542. His statue dominates the tip of Point Loma, 422 feet above sea level, which is also a vantage point for watching migrating Pacific gray whales en route from the Arctic Ocean to Baja California (and back again) December through March. A self-guided tour of the restored lighthouse, built in 1855, illuminates what life was like here more than a century ago (fog and low clouds made the lighthouse ineffective, so another was built close to the water in 1891). National Park Service rangers lead walks at the monument, and there are tide pools to explore at the base of the peninsula. On the other side of the point is the Bayside Trail, a 3.2-mile round-trip down to a lookout over the bay. Free 30-minute videos and slide shows on Cabrillo, tide pools, and the whales are shown on the hour daily from 10am to 4pm. Note the view from the visitor center to the left (north); the blocky structure on the water is the Navy's nuclear submarine base. The drive from downtown takes about 20 minutes.

1800 Cabrillo Memorial Dr., Point Loma. © **619/557-5450.** www.nps.gov/cabr. Admission $5 per vehicle, $3 for walk-ins. Daily 9am–5:15pm (till 6:15pm July–Aug). Bus: 26. By car, take I-8 west to Rosecrans St., right on Canon St., left on Catalina, and follow signs.

Firehouse Museum *Kids*   Appropriately housed in San Diego's oldest firehouse, the museum features shiny fire engines, including hand-drawn and horse-drawn models, a 1903 steam pumper, and memorabilia such as antique alarms, fire hats, and foundry molds for fire hydrants. There's also a small gift shop. Allow about half an hour for your visit.

1572 Columbia St. (at Cedar St.). © **619/232-3473.** www.thesdfirehousemuseum.org. Admission $3 adults, $2 seniors, military in uniform, and youths 13–17, free for children under 13. Wed–Fri 10am–2pm; Sat–Sun 10am–4pm. Bus: 5 or 16. Trolley: America Plaza.

Maritime Museum ⭐⭐ *Kids*   This flotilla of classic ships is led by the full-rigged merchant vessel *Star of India* (1863), a National Historic Landmark and the world's oldest ship that still goes to sea. The gleaming white San Francisco–Oakland steam-powered ferry *Berkeley* (1898) worked round-the-clock to carry people to safety following the 1906 San Francisco earthquake; she now pulls duty as a museum with fine ship models on display. The elegant *Medea* (1904) is one of the world's few remaining large steam yachts, and the *Pilot* (1914) was San Diego Bay's official pilot boat for 82 years. Recent additions include the HMS *Surprise,* a painstakingly accurate reproduction of an 18th-century Royal Navy Frigate, which played a supporting role to Russell Crowe in the film *Master and Commander: Far Side of the World,* and a 300-foot-long Cold War–era B-39 Soviet attack submarine. You can board and tour each vessel.

1492 N. Harbor Dr. ⓒ **619/234-9153.** www.sdmaritime.org. Admission $10 adults; $8 seniors over 62, youths 13–17, and active military with ID; $7 children 6–12; free for children under 6. Daily 9am–8pm (till 9pm in summer). Bus: 2, 4, 20, 23, or 29. Trolley: America Plaza.

Museum of Contemporary Art San Diego Downtown ⭐⭐   At a time when many cultural institutions are battening the hatches, the Museum of Contemporary Art continues to boldly press forward. As of press time, MCASD was scheduled to open its third facility, at a location directly across the street from its 1993 downtown annex (the flagship space is in La Jolla). The new complex takes over what was once historic Santa Fe Depot's "baggage building"; it will provide an additional 10,000 square feet of gallery space and include a lecture hall and room for educational programs. Across the street at America Plaza, two large and two smaller galleries present changing exhibitions of nationally and internationally distinguished contemporary artists; lectures and special events for adults and children are also offered. The first Thursday evening of every month is "TNT" (Thursday Night Thing), an engaging music and arts program that's part cocktail party, part gallery opening. Docent tours are usually given on weekends at 2pm, but this may change; call for new tour information. Plan to spend at least an hour at the two spaces.

1001 Kettner Blvd. (at Broadway). ⓒ **619/234-1001.** www.mcasd.org. Admission $10 adults, $6 seniors and military, free for anyone 25 and under, paid ticket good for admission to MCASD La Jolla within 7 days. Thurs–Tues 11am–5pm. Parking $2 with validation at America Plaza Complex. Bus: 2, 4, 7, 7A/B, 15, 20, 23, 34, or 115. Trolley: America Plaza.

San Diego Aircraft Carrier Museum   On January 10, 2004, the USS *Midway* made her final voyage into San Diego Bay. The aircraft carrier had a 47-year military history that began 1 week after the Japanese surrender of WWII in 1945. By the time the *Midway* was decommissioned in 1991, the warship had patrolled the Taiwan Straits in 1955, operated in the Tonkin Gulf, served as the flagship from which Desert Storm was conducted, and evacuated 1,800 people from volcano-threatened Subic Bay Naval Base in the Philippines—in all, more than 225,000 men served aboard the *Midway.* The carrier is now moored at the Embarcadero and has become the world's largest floating naval-aviation museum. A self-guided audio tour takes visitors to several levels of the ship, telling the story of life on board. The highlight is climbing up the superstructure to the bridge and gazing down on the 1,001-foot-long flight deck, with various aircraft poised for duty. What really brings the experience to life is how the ship has not been restored cosmetically—incomplete paint jobs litter the walls with the occasional graffiti, the austere bunkers look like the inhabitants just stepped out. Check into docent tours, many given by Midway vets, to add insight to your visit.

What to See & Do in Downtown & Beyond

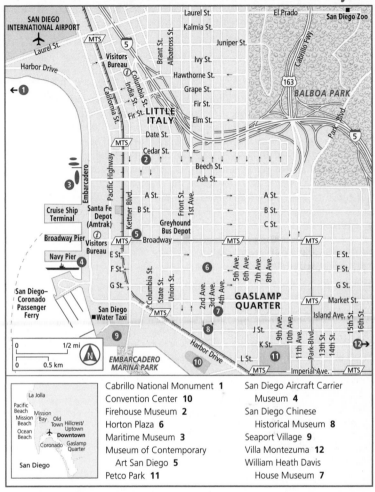

Cabrillo National Monument **1**
Convention Center **10**
Firehouse Museum **2**
Horton Plaza **6**
Maritime Museum **3**
Museum of Contemporary Art San Diego **5**
Petco Park **11**
San Diego Aircraft Carrier Museum **4**
San Diego Chinese Historical Museum **8**
Seaport Village **9**
Villa Montezuma **12**
William Heath Davis House Museum **7**

910 Harbor Dr. (at Navy Pier). © 619/544-9600. www.midway.org. Admission $15 adults; $10 seniors, students, and military; $8 children 6–17, free for children under 6 and military in uniform. Daily 10am–5pm. Limited parking on Navy Pier, $7 for 4 hours; metered parking available nearby.

San Diego Chinese Historical Museum   In the former Chinese Mission, where Chinese immigrants learned English and adapted to their new environment, this small museum contains antique Chinese lottery equipment, a series of panels documenting the gold rush, and artifacts unearthed from San Diego's old Chinatown (south of Market, between Third and Fifth aves.). There's a nice gift shop, and a pleasant garden in back with a bronze statue of Confucius. Allow about half an hour for your visit. Walking tours of the Asian Pacific Historic District start here on the second Saturday of the month; the cost is $2.

404 Third Ave. (at J St.). ℂ **619/338-9888**. www.sdchm.org. Admission $2 adults, free for children under 12. Tues–Sat 10:30am–4pm; Sun noon–4pm. Bus: 4. Trolley: Convention Center.

Villa Montezuma ☆ *Finds*   This exquisite mansion just southeast of downtown was built in 1887 for internationally acclaimed musician and author Jesse Shepard. Lush with Victoriana, it features more stained glass than most churches are blessed with; windows depict Mozart, Beethoven, Sappho, Rubens, St. Cecilia (patron saint of musicians), and other notables. The striking ceilings are of Lincrusta Walton—pressed canvas coated with linseed oil, a forerunner of linoleum, which never looked this good. Shepard lived here with his life companion, Lawrence Tonner, for only 2 years, and died in obscurity in Los Angeles in 1927. The San Diego Historical Society painstakingly restored the house, which is on the National Register of Historic Places, and furnished it with period pieces. The neighborhood is not as fashionable as the building, but it's safe to park your car in the daytime. If you love Victorian houses, don't miss this one for its quirkiness. Join the 45-minute docent-led tour, which begins every hour on the hour (the last starts at 4pm); for tours by request, call ℂ **619/232-6203**.

1925 K St. (at 20th St.). ℂ **619/239-2211**. Admission $5 adults; $4 seniors, military, and students; $2 children 6–17; free for children 5 and under. Fri–Sun 10am–4pm. Bus: 3, 3A, 5, or 16. By car, follow Market St. east, turn right on 20th St., and follow it to K St.

William Heath Davis House Museum   Shipped by boat to San Diego in 1850 from Portland, Maine, this is the oldest structure in the Gaslamp Quarter. It is a well-preserved example of a prefabricated "saltbox" family home and has remained structurally unchanged for more than 150 years. A museum on the first and second floors is open to the public, as is the small park adjacent to the house. The house is also home to the Gaslamp Quarter Historical Foundation, which sponsors walking tours of the quarter for $10 ($8 for seniors, students, and military), every Saturday at 11am. The foundation also has a small gift store here.

410 Island Ave. (at Fourth Ave.). ℂ **619/233-4692**. www.gaslampquarter.org. Admission $5; $4 seniors, military, and students. Tues–Sat 10am–6pm; Sun 9am–3pm. Bus: 1, 3, 5, 16, or 25. Trolley: Gaslamp Quarter or Convention Center.

OLD TOWN & MISSION VALLEY

The birthplace of San Diego—indeed, of California—Old Town takes you back to the Mexican California, which existed here until the mid-1800s. **Plaza del Pasado** is a 1930s-era motel that was turned into a collection of shops and restaurants selling pottery, ceramics, home decor, books, and freshly baked goodies. The complex suffers a tourist invasion daily, but for good reason. Plaza del Pasado occupies a lovely corner of Old Town State Historic Park (p. 159). It's also a popular spot for California-style Mexican meals and margaritas. "Walking Tour 3: Old Town" in chapter 8 covers Old Town's historic sights.

Mission Valley, which starts just north of Presidio Park and heads straight east, is decidedly more modern: Until I-8 was built in the 1950s, it was little more than cow pastures with a couple of dirt roads. Shopping malls, motels, a golf course, condos, car dealerships, and a massive sports stadium fill the expanse today, following the San Diego River upstream to the **Mission Basilica San Diego,** and just a few miles beyond, an outstanding park with walking trails. Few visitors make it this far, but **Mission Trails Regional Park** reveals what San Diego looked like before the Spanish arrived.

What to See & Do in Old Town & Mission Valley

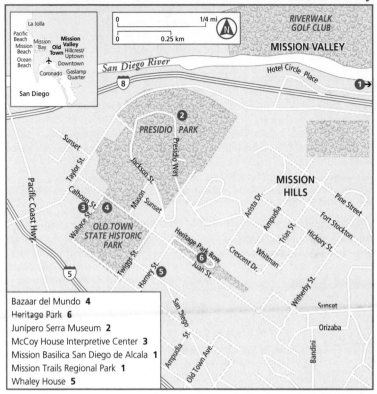

Bazaar del Mundo **4**
Heritage Park **6**
Junípero Serra Museum **2**
McCoy House Interpretive Center **3**
Mission Basilica San Diego de Alcala **1**
Mission Trails Regional Park **1**
Whaley House **5**

Heritage Park   This 7.8-acre county park, dedicated to preservation of Victorian architecture of the 1880s, contains seven original 19th-century houses moved here from other places and given new uses. Among them are a bed-and-breakfast, a doll shop, and a gift shop. The small charming synagogue at the entrance, Temple Beth Israel, was built in 1889 in Classic Revival style and relocated here in 1989. The San Diego County Parks department operates an information and reservation center out of the Sherman-Gilbert House; hours are Monday through Friday, 8am to 5pm.

2450 Heritage Park Row (corner of Juan and Harney sts.). © **877/565-3600** or 858/694-3049. www.sdparks.org. Free admission. Bus: 5, 5A, or 6. Trolley: Old Town.

Junípero Serra Museum ★   Perched on a hill above Old Town, this Spanish Mission–style structure overlooks the slopes where, in 1769, the first mission, first presidio, and first nonnative settlement on the West Coast of the United States and Canada were founded (in 1774 the Mission Basilica San Diego de Alcalá was relocated 6 miles up Mission Valley; see below). The museum's exhibits introduce visitors to the Native American, Spanish, and Mexican people who first called this place home. On display are their belongings, from cannons to cookware, a Spanish furniture collection, and one of the first paintings brought to California, which survived being damaged in an Indian attack. Follow the stairs up the tower and notice the map mural that documents the arduous journey Father Serra made to San Diego. From the

70-foot tower, visitors can compare the view with historic photos to see how this land has changed over time. Designed by William Templeton Johnson in 1929, the stately building can be seen from miles around. (And incidentally, the Spanish revival structures on the opposite side of the valley are contemporary and part of the University of San Diego.)

The settlement remained San Diego's only European village until the 1820s, when families began to move down the hill into what is now Old Town. An archaeological dig on the lower slopes is ongoing to uncover more of the items used by early settlers; the large cross overlooking the site is made of floor tile from the presidio ruins. Park rangers lead a free outdoor tour the second Sunday of every month from 1 to 2pm; **Presidio Park,** which was established around the museum, is a nice place for a picnic, and has surprisingly extensive walking trails.

2727 Presidio Dr., Presidio Park. ⓒ 619/297-3258. www.sandiegohistory.org. Admission $5 adults; $4 seniors, students, and military; $2 children 6–17; free for children under 6. Daily 10am–4:30pm. Bus: 5, 5A, or 6. Trolley: Old Town. Take I-8 to the Taylor St. exit. Turn right on Taylor, and then left on Presidio Dr.

Mission Basilica San Diego de Alcalá   Established in 1769 above Old Town, this was the first link in a chain of 21 missions founded by Spanish missionary Junípero Serra. In 1774, the mission was moved from Old Town to its present site for agricultural reasons, and to separate Native American converts from the fortress that included the original building. The mission was burned by Native Americans a year after it was built—Father Serra rebuilt the structure using 5- to 7-foot-thick adobe walls and clay tile roofs, rendering it harder to burn. In the process, he inspired a bevy of 20th-century California architects. A few bricks belonging to the original mission can be seen in Presidio Park in Old Town. Mass is said daily in this active Catholic parish. Other missions in San Diego County include Mission San Luis Rey de Francia in Oceanside, Mission San Antonia de Pala near Mount Palomar, and Mission Santa Ysabel near Julian. Known as "the King of Missions," the San Luis Rey is the largest of California's missions and one of its most beautiful (see "North County Beach Towns: Spots to Surf & Sun," in chapter 11).

10818 San Diego Mission Rd., Mission Valley. ⓒ 619/281-8449. www.missionsandiego.com. Admission $3 adults, $2 seniors and students, $1 children under 12. Free Sun and for daily Masses. Daily 9am–4:45pm; Mass daily 7am and 5:30pm. Bus: 13. Trolley: Mission San Diego. Take I-8 to Mission Gorge Rd. to Twain Ave., which turns into San Diego Mission Rd.

Mission Trails Regional Park 🎯 (Finds)   Well off the beaten track for tourists, this is one of the nation's largest urban parks, a 5,800-acre spread that includes abundant bird life, two lakes, a picturesque stretch of the San Diego River, the Old Mission Dam (probably the first irrigation project in the West), and 1,592-foot Cowles Mountain, the summit of which reveals outstanding views over much of the county. There are trails up to 4 miles in length—including a 1.5-mile interpretive trail—some of which are designated for mountain bike use, and a 46-space campground (ⓒ **619/ 668-2748**). The park came about in 1974 when the area surrounding Cowles Mountain began to experience a housing boom; city and county representatives worked with Navajo community planners to make an initial purchase of land. In 1989, the first park ranger was hired, and in 1995 the visitor center opened, cementing a place for Mission Trails in the hearts of outdoor-loving San Diegans. The 2003 fires licked at the northern edge of the park, leaving scars that are all but healed now.

1 Father Junípero Serra Trail, Mission Gorge. ⓒ **619/668-3275** or 619/668-3281. www.mtrp.org. Free admission. Daily sunrise to sundown (visitor center 9am–5pm). Take I-8 to Mission Gorge Rd.; follow for 4 miles to entrance.

Old Town State Historic Park ✻ Dedicated to recreating the early life of the city from 1821 to 1872, this is where San Diego's Mexican heritage shines brightest. The community was briefly Mexico's informal capital of the California territory; the Stars and Stripes were finally raised over Old Town in 1846. Of the park's 20 structures, 7 are original, including homes made of adobe; the rest are reconstructed. The park's headquarters is at the Robinson-Rose House, 4002 Wallace St., where you can pick up a map and peruse a model of Old Town as it looked in 1872. Among the park's attractions are La Casa de Estudillo, which depicts the living conditions of a wealthy family in 1872; and Seeley Stables, named after A. L. Seeley, who ran the stagecoach and mail service in these parts from 1867 to 1871. The stables have two floors of wagons, carriages, stagecoaches, and other memorabilia, including washboards, slot machines, and hand-worked saddles. On Wednesdays and the fourth Saturday of the month, from 10am to 1pm, costumed park volunteers reenact life in the 1800s with cooking and crafts demonstrations, a working blacksmith, and parlor singing. Free 1-hour walking tours leave daily at 11am and 2pm from the Robinson-Rose House. Note that on weekdays throughout the school year, Old Town buzzes with fourth-graders.

4002 Wallace St., Old Town. ℂ **619/220-5422.** www.parks.ca.gov. Free admission (donations welcome). Daily 10am–5pm. Bus: 5, 5A, or 6. Trolley: Old Town.

Whaley House In 1856, this striking two-story brick house (the first one in these parts) was built for Thomas Whaley and his family. Whaley was a New Yorker who arrived via San Francisco, where he had been lured by the gold rush. It's probably an urban legend that Whaley's house is designated as "one of only two authenticated haunted houses in California," yet 100,000 people visit each year to see for themselves. It is said up to four spirits haunt the structure, including the ghost of Yankee Jim Robinson, who was hanged on the site where the house now stands in 1852. Exhibits include a life mask of Abraham Lincoln, one of only six made; the spinet piano used in the movie *Gone with the Wind;* and the concert piano that accompanied Swedish soprano Jenny Lind on her final U.S. tour in 1852. The Whaley complex includes several other historic structures, including the Verna House and two false-front buildings, both dating from the 1870s. The Verna House is now an excellent little gift shop run by the Save Our Heritage Organisation, offering beautiful Arts and Crafts pottery, architecture-themed books, and crafts (and it's the place to buy your admission tickets). Behind the gift shop is a small cafe, where the outdoor dining makes for a lovely respite on a hot day.

2482 San Diego Ave. ℂ **619/297-7511.** www.whaleyhouse.org. Admission before 5pm $5 adults, $4 seniors over 60, $3 children 3–12; admission after 5pm $10 adults, $5 children 3–12. Mon–Tues 10am–5pm; Thurs and Sun 10am–9pm; Fri–Sat 10am–11pm. Bus: 5/5A. Trolley: Old Town.

MISSION BAY & THE BEACHES

Mission Bay is a man-made, 4,600-acre aquatic playground created in 1945 by dredging tidal mud flats and opening them to sea water. Today, this is a great area for walking, jogging, inline skating, biking, and boating. The boardwalk connecting Mission Beach and Pacific Beach is almost always bustling and colorful. For all of these activities, see the appropriate headings in "Outdoor Activities," later in this chapter. For **SeaWorld San Diego,** see p. 138.

The surf is always up at Belmont Park's **Wavehouse** (ℂ **858/228-9300;** www. wavehouse.com). This self-described "royal palace of youth culture" has as its center-piece Bruticus Maximus, a unique wave machine designed to create stand-up rides.

You have to get certified (about a 1-hour process) before attempting "B-Max." The Wavehouse is also the location of the historic Roaring '20s relic **The Plunge,** a 175-foot-long indoor pool (Southern California's largest). It was recently closed for repairs but reopened in March 2006.For a **spectacular view,** drive north on Mission Boulevard, past Turquoise Street, where it turns into La Jolla Mesa Drive. Proceed up the hill ¾-mile and turn around. From here you'll see the beaches and Point Loma in front of you, Mission Bay and the San Diego Bay, downtown, the Hillcrest/Uptown area, and (on a clear day) the hills of Tijuana, and to the east, San Diego's backcountry.

Giant Dipper Roller Coaster *(Kids)*   A registered national-historic landmark, the Giant Dipper dates to 1925 and is one of two surviving fixtures from the original Belmont Amusement Park (the other is The Plunge swimming pool). After sitting dormant for 15 years, this wooden roller coaster, with more than 2,600 feet of track and 13 hills, underwent extensive restoration and reopened in 1990. If you love roller coasters, do yourself a favor and take a spin on this grande dame. You must be at least 50 inches tall to ride. You can also ride on the Giant Dipper's neighbor, the **Liberty Carousel** ($2), and other carnie-style rides (unlimited ride wristband, $20).

3190 Mission Blvd., corner of W. Mission Bay Dr. © **858/488-1549.** www.giantdipper.com. Ride on the Giant Dipper $5. Daily 11am–7 or 8pm (weekend and summer hours later; closed weekdays Jan and Feb). Bus: 34 or 34A. Take I-5 to the SeaWorld exit, and follow W. Mission Bay Dr. to Belmont Park.

LA JOLLA

One of San Diego's most scenic spots—the star of postcards for more than 100 years—is **La Jolla Cove** *(★★)* and the **Ellen Browning Scripps Park** *(★★)* on the bluff above it. The walk through the park, along Coast Boulevard (start from the north at Prospect St.), offers some of California's finest coastal scenery. Swimming, sunning, picnicking, barbecuing, reading, and strolling along the oceanfront walkway are all ongoing activities, and just south is the **Children's Pool** *(★)*, a beach where dozens of harbor seals can be spotted lazing in the sun. The 6,000-acre **San Diego–La Jolla Underwater Park,** established in 1970, stretches for 10 miles from La Jolla Cove to the northern end of Torrey Pines State Reserve, and extends from the shoreline to a depth of 900 feet. The park is a boat-free zone, with undersea flora and fauna that draw scuba divers and snorkelers, many of them hoping for a glimpse of the state fish, the brilliant orange garibaldi.

Sightseeing highlights in town include **Mary Star of the Sea,** 7727 Girard (at Kline), a beautiful Roman Catholic church; and **La Valencia Hotel,** 1132 Prospect St., a fine example of Spanish colonial structure. The **La Jolla Woman's Club,** 7791 Draper Ave.; the adjacent **Museum of Contemporary Art San Diego;** the **La Jolla Recreation Center;** and **The Bishop's School** are all examples of village buildings designed by architect Irving Gill.

At La Jolla's north end, you'll find the 1,200-acre, 22,000-student **University of California, San Diego (UCSD),** which was established in 1960 and represents the county's largest single employer. The campus features the **Geisel Library** *(★★)*, a striking and distinguished contemporary structure, as well as the **Stuart Collection** of public sculpture and the **Birch Aquarium at Scripps** (see individual listings, below). One of famed architect Louis I. Kahn's masterpieces is the **Salk Institute for Biological Studies** *(★★★)*, 10010 N. Torrey Pines Rd., a research facility named for the creator of the polio vaccine (for tours, see "For Architecture Buffs," later in this chapter). Farther north is an ersatz jewel, **The Lodge at Torrey Pines** (p. 89), a modern,

What to See & Do in La Jolla

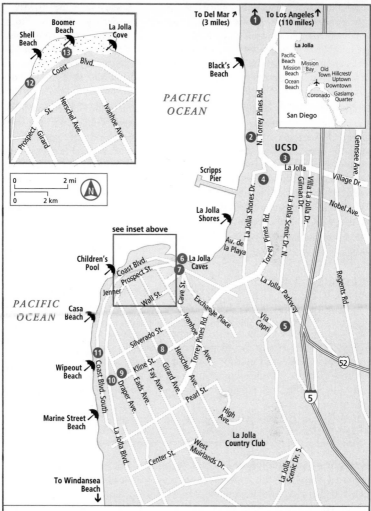

Birch Aquarium at Scripps **4**

Coast Walk **12**

Ellen Browning Scripps Park **13**

La Jolla Recreation Center **9**

La Jolla Woman's Club **10**

Mary Star of the Sea Church **8**

Mount Soledad **5**

Museum of Contemporary Art San Diego **11**

Salk Institute for Biological Studies **2**

San Diego–La Jolla Underwater Park **6**

Stuart Collection **3**

Sunny Jim Cave **7**

Torrey Pines State Reserve **1**

175-room luxury resort in the guise of an early-20th-century Craftsman-style manse; it overlooks the revered **Torrey Pines Golf Course** (p. 180).

For a fine scenic drive, follow La Jolla Boulevard to Nautilus Street and turn east to get to 800-foot-high **Mount Soledad** ⊛, which offers a 360-degree view of the area. The appropriateness of the 43-foot-tall cross on top, erected in 1954 in this public park, has been a subject of a nearly 20-year legal fight involving the ACLU (religious symbols are prohibited on public land). The debate goes on.

Birch Aquarium at Scripps ⊛⊛ *Kids*

This beautiful facility is both an aquarium and a museum, operated as the interpretive arm of the world-famous Scripps Institution of Oceanography. To make the most of the experience, be sure to pick up a visitor guide from the information booth just inside the entrance, and take time to read the text on each of the exhibits. The aquarium affords close-up views of the Pacific Northwest, the California coast, Mexico's Sea of Cortez, and the tropical seas, all presented in more than 60 marine-life tanks. The giant kelp forest is particularly impressive. Exotic highlights include the fanciful white anemones and the ethereal moon jellies, which look like elegant parachutes. The sea horse propagation program here has met with excellent results—9 different species of sea horse are on display in one of the aquarium's best exhibits. The outdoor demonstration tide pool not only shows visitors marine coastal life but also offers an amazing view of Scripps Pier, La Jolla Shores Beach, the village of La Jolla, and the ocean. The museum section has numerous interpretive exhibits on current and historic research at the Scripps Institution, which was established in 1903 and became part of the University of California system in 1912. You'll learn what fog is and why salt melts snow; discover the surprising number of supermarket products with ingredients that come from the sea (including toothpaste and ice cream); feel what an earthquake is like; and experience a variety of virtual worlds with the simulator ride Morphis. The bookstore is well stocked with textbooks, science books, educational toys, gifts, and T-shirts. Off-site adventures, such as tide-pooling, and grunion and whale watching, are also conducted year-round (call for more details).

2300 Expedition Way. ⓒ **858/534-3474.** www.aquarium.ucsd.edu. Admission $11 adults, $9 seniors, $8 college students with ID, $7.50 children 3–17, free for children under 3. Daily 9am–5pm. Docent tours for groups on request (call ahead). Free parking. Bus: 34. Take I-5 to La Jolla Village Dr. exit, go west 1 mile, and turn left at Expedition Way.

Museum of Contemporary Art San Diego La Jolla ⊛⊛⊛

Focusing on work produced since 1950, this museum is known internationally for its permanent collection and thought-provoking exhibitions. MCASD's collection of contemporary art comprises more than 3,000 works of painting, sculpture, drawings, prints, photography, video, and multimedia works. The holdings include every major art movement of the past half-century, with a strong representation by California artists. You'll see particularly noteworthy examples of minimalism, light and space work, conceptualism, installation, and site-specific art—the outside sculptures were designed specifically for this location. The museum itself is perched on a cliff overlooking the Pacific Ocean, and the views from the galleries are gorgeous. The original building on the site was the residence of the legendary Ellen Browning Scripps, designed by Irving Gill in 1916. It became an art museum in 1941, and the original Gill building facade was uncovered and restored in 1996. More than a dozen exhibitions are scheduled each year (*Transactions: Contemporary Latin American and Latino Art* is presented through Sept. 9, 2007); and MCASD also offers lectures, cutting-edge films, and special events on an ongoing basis. Guided docent tours are available daily at 2pm, with a second tour Thursdays at 5:30pm; and beginning this year, the museum offers free daily admission to anyone 25 and under. A paid ticket will get you into the beautiful new downtown space for free, if visited within 7 days. The bookstore is also a great place for contemporary gifts, and the cafe is a pleasant stop before or after your visit.

700 Prospect St. (C) 858/454-3541. www.mcasd.org. Admission $10 adults, $6 seniors and military, free for anyone 25 and under; paid ticket good for admission to MCASD Downtown within 7 days. Fri–Tues 11am–5pm; Thurs 11am–7pm. Bus: 30, 34, or 34A. Take I-5 north to La Jolla Pkwy or take I-5 south to La Jolla Village Dr. west. Take Torrey Pines Rd. to Prospect Place and turn right; Prospect Place becomes Prospect St.

Stuart Collection ☆

Consider the Stuart Collection a work in progress on a large scale. Through a 1982 agreement between the Stuart Foundation and UCSD, the still-growing collection consists of site-related sculptures by leading contemporary artists. Start by picking up a map from the information booth, and wend your way through the 1,200-acre campus to discover the 16 highly diverse artworks. Among them is Niki de Saint Phalle's *Sun God*, a jubilant 14-foot-high fiberglass bird on a 15-foot concrete base. Nicknamed "Big Bird," it's been made an unofficial mascot by the students, who use it as the centerpiece of their annual celebration, the Sun God Festival. Also in the collection are Alexis Smith's *Snake Path*, a 560-foot-long slate-tile pathway that winds up the hill from the Engineering Mall to the east terrace of the spectacular Geisel Library (breathtaking architecture that's a fabulous sculpture itself); and Terry Allen's *Trees*, three eucalyptus trees encased in lead. One tree emits songs, and another poems and stories, while the third stands silent in a grove of trees the students call "The Enchanted Forest." Allow at least 2 hours to tour the entire collection.

University of California, San Diego. (C) 858/534-2117. http://stuartcollection.ucsd.edu. Free admission. Bus: 30, 34, 41, or 101. From La Jolla, take Torrey Pines Rd. to La Jolla Village Dr., turn right, go 2 blocks to Gilman Dr. and turn left into the campus; in about 1 block the information booth will be visible on the right.

Torrey Pines State Reserve ☆☆☆ (Moments)

The rare Torrey pine tree grows in only two places in the world: Santa Rosa Island, 175 miles northwest of San Diego, and here, at the north end of La Jolla. Even if the twisted shape of these awkwardly beautiful trees doesn't lure you to this spot, the equally scarce undeveloped coastal scenery should. The city first donated 369 acres as a public park, and the 1,750-acre reserve was established in 1921, from a gift by Ellen Browning Scripps. The reserve encompasses the beach below, as well as a lagoon immediately north, but the focus is the 300-foot-high, water-carved limestone bluffs, which provide a precarious footing for the trees. In spring, the wildflower show includes bush poppies, Cleveland sage, agave, and yucca. A half-dozen trails (all under 1.5 miles in length) travel from the road to the cliff edge or down to the beach, and there's a small visitor center, built in the traditional adobe style of the Hopi Indians and featuring a lovely 12-minute video about the park. Watch for migrating gray whales in winter or dolphins who patrol these shores year-round. For a taste of what Southern California's coast looked like a couple hundred years ago, this delicate spot is one of San Diego's unique treasures. Interpretive nature walks are held weekends and holidays at 10am and 2pm. *Note:* There are no facilities for food or drinks inside the park. You can bring a picnic lunch, but you have to eat it on the beach—food and drink (other than water) are not allowed in the upper portion of the reserve.

Hwy. 101, La Jolla. (C) 858/755-2063. www.torreypine.org. Admission $6 per car, $5 seniors. Daily 8am–sunset. Bus: 101. From I-5, take Carmel Valley Rd. west; turn left at Hwy. 101.

CORONADO

It's hard to miss San Diego Bay's most noteworthy landmark: the **San Diego–Coronado Bay Bridge** ✸. Completed in 1969, this graceful five-lane bridge spans 2¼ miles and links the city and the "island" of Coronado. At 246 feet in height, the bridge was designed to be tall enough for the Navy's aircraft carriers to pass beneath, but it still looks more elegant than utilitarian, with a sweeping curve that maximizes the view. Heading to Coronado by car is a thrill because you can see Mexico and the shipyards of National City to the left, the San Diego skyline to the right, and Coronado, the naval station, and Point Loma in front of you (designated drivers have to promise to keep their eyes on the road). When the bridge opened, it put the antiquated commuter ferries out of business (though in 1986 passenger-only ferry service restarted—see "By Water" within the "Getting Around," section in chapter 4). Bus no. 901 from downtown will also take you across the bridge.

Hotel del Coronado ✸✸ Built in 1888, this turreted Victorian seaside resort remains an enduring, endearing national treasure. Whether you are lucky enough to stay, dine, or dance here, or simply to wander through to tour its grounds and photo gallery, prepare to be enchanted. See "A Century of Intrigue: Scenes from the Hotel del Coronado" on p. 94 for more details.

1500 Orange Ave., Coronado. ✆ 619/435-6611. www.hoteldel.com. Free admission. Parking $5–$6 per hour. Bus: 901. Ferry: Broadway Pier, and then ½-hr. walk, or take a bus or the Coronado trolley, or rent a bike.

Museum of History and Art This museum offers archival materials about the development of Coronado, as well as tourist information. Exhibits include photographs of the Hotel Del in its infancy, the old ferries, Tent City (a seaside campground for middle-income vacationers from 1900 to 1939), and notable residents and visitors. Other memorabilia include army uniforms, old postcards, and even recorded music. You'll also learn about the island's military aviation history during World Wars I and II. Plan to spend up to half an hour here. The museum has a gift store with Coronado-themed items, and offers guided and self-guided walking tours of the area. Guided tours ($10 for ages 12 and above) take place Wednesdays at 2pm and Fridays at 10:30am.

1100 Orange Ave. ✆ 619/435-7242. www.coronadohistory.org. Suggested donation $4 adults, $3 seniors and military, $2 youths 9–18, free to children 8 and under. Mon–Fri 9am–5pm; Sat 10am–5pm; Sun 11am–4pm. Bus: 901.

FARTHER AFIELD

Chula Vista Nature Center ✸ *Finds* *Kids* Sweetwater Marsh is one of San Diego's top bird-watching spots, and the nature center provides walking trails and a facility for experiencing the bird life (including aviaries with shore birds and raptors), as well as stingrays and small sharks in kid-level open tanks. At press time, the center was in the process of a $3 million renovation (expected to be completed in summer 2006) of its Discovery Center. When finished, it will feature **Turtle Lagoon,** San Diego's only habitat for native sea turtles. Most San Diegans are unaware we even have sea turtles, but legend has it these reptiles are the descendants of captured Baja turtles that escaped from a pen on Coronado more than 100 years ago. The parking lot is located away from the center and a shuttle bus ferries guests between the two points every 10 to 15 minutes.

1000 Gunpowder Point Dr., Chula Vista. ✆ 619/409-5900. www.chulavistanaturecenter.org. $4 adults, $2.50 seniors and students, $1 children 6–11. Tues–Sun 10am–5pm (last shuttle at 4pm). Free parking. Bus: 708. Trolley: Bayfront/E St. From I-5 south take the E St. exit.

Knott's Soak City U.S.A. *(Kids)* Themed to replicate San Diego's surfer towns around the 1950s and 1960s, this 32-acre water park is San Diego's only facility of its type. There are 22 slides of all shapes and sizes, a 500,000-gallon wave pool, a ¼-mile lazy river, and assorted snack facilities. The park is about 25 minutes south of downtown, just north of the border line.

2052 Entertainment Circle, Chula Vista. (C) 619/661-7373. www.knotts.com. Admission $27 adults, $15 seniors and children ages 3–11; reduced admission after 3pm. Mid-May to Aug daily 10am–6pm or later; weekends late Apr to mid-May and Sept. Parking $7. Take I-5 or I-805 to Main St.; turn right on Entertainment Circle.

5 Free of Charge & Full of Fun

It's easy to get charged up on vacation—$10 here, $5 there, and pretty soon your credit card balance looks like the national debt. To keep that from happening, here's a summary of free San Diego activities, most of which are described in detail earlier in this chapter. In addition, scan the lists of "Special-Interest Sightseeing," below, and "Outdoor Activities" and "Spectator Sports," later in this chapter, and the "San Diego Calendar of Events" in chapter 2. Many events listed in these sections, such as the U.S. Open Sandcastle Competition, are no-charge affairs. Also note that the walking tours outlined in chapter 8 are free to anyone.

DOWNTOWN & BEYOND

It doesn't cost a penny to stroll around the **Gaslamp Quarter,** which brims with restaurants, shops, and historic buildings, or along the Embarcadero (waterfront), and around the shops at Seaport Village or Horton Plaza. And don't forget: **Walkabout International** offers free guided walking tours (described in "Organized Tours," later in this chapter), and Centre City Redevelopment Corporation's Downtown Information Center (p. 171) gives bus tours two Saturdays a month.

If you'd rather drive around, ask for the map of the **52-mile San Diego Scenic Drive** when you're at the International Visitor Information Center.

The **murals** in **Chicano Park** ((C) 619/563-4661; www.chicano-park.org), painted on the support system of the San Diego–Coronado Bay Bridge, are a colorful road map through Mexican and Chicano history. South of downtown (exit Cesar Chavez Pkwy. from I-5), the 40-plus murals represent some of San Diego's most important pieces of public art. The **Museum of Contemporary Art San Diego**'s two downtown spaces are free to everyone 25 and under; for those who have to pay, your ticket will get you into MCA's La Jolla museum for free, if visited within 7 days.

And you can fish free of charge from any municipal pier (that is, if you bring your own pole). Fishing license is not required.

BALBOA PARK

All the **museums** in Balboa Park are open to the public without charge one Tuesday a month. Here's a list of the free days:

First Tuesday of each month: Natural History Museum, Reuben H. Fleet Science Center, Model Railroad Museum, Centro Cultural de la Raza
Second Tuesday: Museum of Photographic Arts, Historical Society Museum, Veterans Museum & Memorial Center
Third Tuesday: Museum of Art, Museum of Man, Mingei International Museum, Japanese Friendship Garden, Museum of the Living Artist
Fourth Tuesday: Aerospace Museum, Automotive Museum, Hall of Champions Sports Museum

These Balboa Park attractions are always free: The Botanical Building and Lily Pond, House of Pacific Relations International Cottages, and Timken Museum of Art. Free 1-hour Sunday afternoon organ concerts year-round, and free concerts Monday through Thursday evenings in summer are given at the **Spreckels Organ Pavilion.** There are four free **tours** of the park available, leaving from in front of the visitor center. See "Balboa Park Guided Tours" earlier on p. 150 for more information. Although it's a local best-kept secret, the **San Diego Zoo** is free to all on the first Monday of October (Founders Day), and children under 12 enter free every day during October.

OLD TOWN & MISSION VALLEY

Explore **Heritage Park, Presidio Park,** or **Old Town State Historic Park.** A 1-hour walking tour of Old Town is conducted twice daily. There's free entertainment (mariachis and folk dancers) at the **Plaza del Pasado** (p. 211) on Saturdays and Sundays, and the **Old Town Market** (San Diego Ave. and Twiggs St.), has costumed storytellers. **Mission Trails Regional Park,** which offers hiking trails and an interpretive center, is reached by following Highway 8 east to Mission Gorge Road.

MISSION BAY, PACIFIC BEACH & BEYOND

Walk along the **beach** or around the bay—it's free, fun, and holding hands at sunset is a proven aphrodisiac. Bring a picnic lunch to enjoy on the **Ocean Beach Pier** or the **Crystal Pier** in Pacific Beach.

LA JOLLA

The half-mile **Coast Walk** between the La Jolla Cove and Children's Pool is San Diego at its most beautiful—dabble in the tide pools along the way and enjoy the harbor seal colony at Seal Rock and the Children's Pool.

It's also fun to meander around the campus of the University of California, San Diego, and view the **Stuart Collection** (bring a pocketful of quarters for the hungry parking meters). The main branch of the **Museum of Contemporary Art San Diego** is always free to those 25 and under; a paid ticket will get you into the new downtown space for free (within 7 days).

Watching the hang gliders and paragliders launching from the **Gliderport** near Torrey Pines is a blast (p. 180). For the **best vista,** follow the SCENIC DRIVE signs to Mount Soledad in La Jolla and a 360-degree view of the area.

CORONADO

Drive across the toll-free San Diego-Coronado Bay Bridge and take a self-guided tour of the **Hotel del Coronado's** grounds and photo gallery. A walk on beautiful Coronado **beach** costs nothing—nor does a lookie-loo tour of the neighborhood's restored Victorian and Craftsman homes.

FARTHER AFIELD

You can self-tour the **U.S. Olympic Training Center** in Chula Vista year-round, or take a guided tour during the warmer months. This is the country's first warm-weather, year-round, multisport Olympic training complex. It's on the western shore of Lower Otay Reservoir in Chula Vista, and is one of four United States Olympic training centers. Visitors can see a 10-minute film about the Olympic movement, shop in the gift store, and then check out the highlights of the 150-acre center. Guided tours take place Tuesday through Saturday at 1:30pm. Call ✆ **619/656-6222** or go to www.usolympicteam.com for more information. To get there, take I-805 south to the Olympic Parkway exit, and then go east 7 miles until you reach a sign directing you to the Copley Visitor Center; turn right.

6 Especially for Kids

If you didn't know better, you would think that San Diego was designed by parents planning a long summer vacation. Activities abound for toddlers to teens. Dozens of public parks, 70 miles of beaches, and many museums are just part of what awaits kids and families. For current information about activities for children, pick up a free copy of the monthly *San Diego Family Magazine,* or check it out online at www.sandiego family.com; its calendar of events is geared toward family activities and kids' interests. The **International Visitor Information Center,** 1040 1/3 West Broadway at Harbor Drive (© **619/236-1212**), is also a great resource. The **Children's Museum of San Diego** (downtown on Island St.) has had trouble raising funds to complete its new space. The project has seemingly been in limbo for several years, but at latest report was scheduled to open in fall 2007; for an update see www.sdchildrensmuseum.org.

THE TOP FIVE ATTRACTIONS FOR KIDS

- **Balboa Park** (p. 145) has street entertainers and clowns that always rate high with kids. They can usually be found around El Prado on weekends. The **Natural History Museum,** the **Model Railroad Museum,** the **Aerospace Museum,** and the **Reuben H. Fleet Science Center**—with its hands-on exhibits and IMAX theater—draw kids like magnets.
- The **San Diego Zoo** (p. 136) appeals to children of all ages, and the double-decker bus tours bring all the animals into easy view of even the smallest visitors. There's a Children's Zoo within the zoo, and kids adore the performing sea lion show.
- **SeaWorld San Diego** (p. 138), on Mission Bay, entertains everyone with killer whales, pettable dolphins, and plenty of penguins—the park's penguin exhibit is home to some 350 birds, including the stars of the penguin world, Antarctica's emperor penguin. Try out the family adventure land, "Shamu's Happy Harbor," where everyone is encouraged to explore, crawl, climb, jump, and get wet in more than 20 interactive areas; or, brave a raging river in Shipwreck Rapids.
- The **San Diego Wild Animal Park** (p. 140) brings geography classes to life when kids find themselves gliding through the wilds of Africa and Asia in a monorail. For visitors age 4 and up, the Roar & Snore camping program—held April through October on weekends—is immensely popular.
- **LEGOLAND California** (p. 241), in Carlsbad, features impressive models built entirely with LEGO blocks. There are also rides, refreshments, and LEGO and DUPLO building contests. The park advertises itself as a "country just for kids"—need I say more?

OTHER TOP ATTRACTIONS

- **Birch Aquarium at Scripps** (p. 162), in La Jolla, is an aquarium that lets kids explore the realms of the deep and learn about life in the sea.
- **Seaport Village** (p. 209) has an old-fashioned carousel for kids, lots of shops and outdoor eateries that children enjoy, plus harbor views of some very impressive ships.
- **Whale-Watching Tours** (p. 173) offer a chance to get up close to 40-foot gray whales that migrate close to San Diego Bay each winter.

- **Old Town State Historic Park** (p. 159) has a one-room schoolhouse that rates high with kids. They'll also enjoy the freedom of running around the safe, park-like compound to discover their own fun.
- **San Diego Trolley** (p. 60) kids love these speedy trains that link downtown to the Mexico border crossing, to Old Town, and Mission Valley.
- **The Gliderport** will entertain kids as they watch aerial acrobats swoop through the skies. See "Hang Gliding & Paragliding," later in this chapter for details.
- **Chula Vista Nature Center** (p. 164) is a small facility near the bottom of San Diego Bay that has a walk-through aviary and tanks for getting up close with stingrays and small sharks.

THAT'S ENTERTAINMENT

The **Old Globe Theatre** (© **619/234-5623;** www.theoldglobe.org) in Balboa Park showcases *Dr. Seuss' How the Grinch Stole Christmas!* each year during the holidays—performances are scheduled mid-November through December. Tickets are priced $20 to $55 for adults, $15 to $25 for kids under 17. **San Diego Junior Theatre** (© **619/239-8355;** www.juniortheatre.com) is the oldest continuing children's theater program in the country, operating since 1948. The productions (shows like *Peter Pan* and *Little Women*) are acted and crewed by kids 8 to 18, and are staged at three different theaters: Balboa Park's Casa del Prado Theatre, the Theatre on Third in Chula Vista, and the YMCA Firehouse in La Jolla. Ticket prices are $9 to $15 for adults, $7 to $10 for seniors, and $5 to $10 children (ages 2–14). More than a dozen shows are staged each season, with performances held on Friday evenings and Saturday and Sunday afternoons, as well as some weekday matinees.

Sunday afternoon is a great time for kids in **Balboa Park.** They can visit both the outdoor Spreckels Organ Pavilion for a free concert (the mix of music isn't too high-brow for a young audience) and the House of Pacific Relations to watch folk dancing on the lawn and taste food from many nations. Or try the **Marie Hitchcock Puppet Theatre,** in Balboa Park's Palisades Building (© **619/544-9203**). Individual shows might feature marionettes, hand puppets, or ventriloquism, and the stories range from classic *Grimms' Fairy Tales* and *Aesop's Fables* to more obscure yarns. Performances are Wednesday through Friday at 10 and 11:30am and Saturday and Sunday at 11am, 1pm, and 2:30pm. The shows cost $5 for adults, $4 for seniors, and $3 for children over 2; they're free for children under 2.

7 Special-Interest Sightseeing

FOR ARCHITECTURE BUFFS

San Diego's historical architecture is most often defined by the abundance of Spanish mission structures, a style that was introduced to California by Father Junípero Serra at the **Mission Basilica San Diego.** Ostensibly, the adobe walls and tile roofs made it harder for Native Americans to burn down his churches. Spanish colonial style was revived gloriously for the 1915–16 **Panama-California Exposition** in Balboa Park by New York architect Bertram Goodhue, who oversaw a romantic fantasia abounding with Mediterranean flourishes.

But San Diego's first important architect was Irving Gill, who arrived in the city in 1893 and soon made his mark by designing buildings to integrate into the desertlike landscape. Gill's structures include numerous homes in Uptown and La Jolla; Gill's **First Church of Christ Scientist** building, 2444 Second Ave. (at Laurel) in Hillcrest, is on the National Historic Landmark list. Following the Expo, prolific local architects like William Templeton Johnson and Richard Requa integrated the Spanish/Mediterranean concept into their structures around the city, most famously the **Serra Museum** at Presidio Park, downtown's **County Administration Center,** the **Plaza del Pasado** (formerly the Casa de Pico Motel), and the **Torrey Pines Visitors Center.**

Modernism swept through the city after World War II, championed by Lloyd Ruocco, and the city's steady growth after the war allowed many inspired architects to leave their handprint on San Diego. The fast development has led to more than a few blunders along the way; the expansion of the **San Diego Convention Center,** for instance, proves most effective as a ludicrous barrier to any view of the waterfront from downtown.

Historic buildings of particular interest include houses like the Victorian **Villa Montezuma** (p. 156) and the Craftsman-style **Marston House** (p. 148). The **Gaslamp Quarter** walking tour (see chapter 8) will lead you past the area's restored Victorian commercial buildings. A stroll along the **Prado of Balboa Park** (also described in chapter 8) is a must, and turn-of-the-20th-century neighborhoods like **Bankers Hill** (just west of Balboa Park) and **Mission Hills** (west of Hillcrest) are feasts of Victorian mansions and Craftsman abodes. In **La Jolla,** you'll find the classic buildings created by Irving Gill (see "More Attractions," earlier in this chapter).

Downtown blends old and new with mixed results, though no one can deny the value of saving the **Gaslamp Quarter** from probable demolition in the 1970s. **Little Italy,** the quaint business and residential district along India Street (between Ash and Laurel sts.), is both endangered by the current building craze and also thriving amid some of the city's most progressive architecture. While you're in the central business district, take a look at the sprawling scale model of the city at the Centre City Development Corporation's Downtown Information Center, 225 Broadway (© **619/235-2222**); it gives a taste of where the city is headed.

A splendid corridor of contemporary architecture has sprouted around the University of California, San Diego, including the campus' spacecraftlike **Geisel Library,** by William Pereira. Nearby is the Louis I. Kahn–designed **Salk Institute,** and the **Neurosciences Institute,** a 1996 creation by Tod Williams-Billie Tsien. A free tour of the Salk Institute, one of Kahn's masterpieces, is held Monday, Wednesday, and Friday at noon; reservations are recommended, call © **858/453-4100,** ext. 1287.

For more information on San Diego architecture, call the local branch of the **AIA** (© **619/232-0109**). And for a self-guided tour of the city's highlights, Dirk Sutro's *San Diego Architecture* (San Diego Architectural Foundation, 2002; $25) is indispensable, with maps, addresses, and descriptions of hundreds of important structures throughout the city and county.

FOR GARDENERS

Although most years we struggle with too little rain, San Diego is a gardener's paradise, thanks in large part to the efforts and inspiration of Kate Sessions, who planted the initial trees that led to today's mature landscapes in **Balboa Park** (p. 145). While in the park, be sure to visit the **Japanese Friendship Garden,** the **Botanical Building and Lily Pond,** and the **rose and desert gardens** (across the road from Plaza de Balboa). And you'll notice that both the **San Diego Zoo** (p. 136) and **Wild Animal Park** (p. 140) are outstanding botanical gardens. Many visitors who admire the landscaping at the zoo don't realize that the plantings have been carefully developed over the years. The 100 acres were once scrub-covered hillsides with few trees. Today, towering eucalyptus and graceful palms, birds of paradise, and hibiscus are just a few of the 6,500 botanical species from all over the world that flourish here.

Garden enthusiasts will also want to stop by the 30-acre **Quail Botanical Gardens** in Encinitas (see "North County Beach Towns: Spots to Surf & Sun" in chapter 11). If you'd like to take plants home with you, visit some of the area's nurseries, starting with the charming neighborhood one started in 1910 by Kate Sessions, the **Mission Hills Nursery,** 1525 Fort Stockton Dr. (© **619/295-2808**). **Walter Andersen's Nursery,** 3642 Enterprise St. (© **619/224-8271**), is also a local favorite. See chapter 11 for information on nurseries in North County. Flower growing is big business in this area, and plant enthusiasts could spend a week just visiting the retail and wholesale purveyors of everything from pansies to palm trees.

Founded by Kate Sessions, the **San Diego Floral Association,** the oldest garden club in Southern California and based in the Casa del Prado in Balboa Park (© **619/232-5762;** www.sdfloral.org), offers day tours involving places of horticultural interest, and has events featuring speakers, classes, and exhibits.

FOR MILITARY BUFFS

San Diego's military history dates to the U.S. Navy's aviation achievements at Coronado in the 1910s. Today, one-third of the Navy's Pacific Fleet is home ported in the city's natural harbor. San Diego salutes its armed forces during **Fleet Week,** which lasts throughout the month of October and is headlined by the popular Miramar Air Show, with aerial performances by the Blue Angels. For more information, see www.fleet weeksandiego.org or www.miramarairshow.com.

The city's flagship (pardon the pun) military attraction is the USS *Midway,* making its final tour of duty as the **San Diego Aircraft Carrier Museum.** The *Midway* served from the end of World War II until the first Gulf War, and it's now docked along the Embarcadero (p. 194). The **San Diego Aerospace Museum** in Balboa Park (p. 149) celebrates the history of flight, and has a strong focus on aviation's military heroes and heroines. The park is also the location of the **Veterans Museum & Memorial Center** (© **619/239-2300;** www.veteranmuseum.org), a museum and resource center with holdings that date back to the Civil War.

Both **San Diego Harbor Excursion** and **Hornblower Cruises** tour San Diego Bay, providing an inside glimpse of naval activities (p. 171); and **Old Town Trolley Tours** offers an amphibious Sea and Land (SEAL) tour of the bay (p. 172). At **Cabrillo National Monument** in Point Loma, visitors gain an excellent view of the harbor, including the nuclear submarine base, and a small museum tells about the gun batteries established on the peninsula during World War II.

The public is also invited to the **recruit graduation** at the Marine Corps Recruit Depot, off Pacific Coast Highway (near Barnett St.), held most Fridays at 10am (© **619/524-8383**). There's a museum on the base as well (© **619/524-4426;** www. mcrdmuseumhistoricalsociety.org).

FOR WINE LOVERS

Visit **Orfila Vineyards** (© **760/738-6500;** www.orfila.com), on the way to the Wild Animal Park (p. 140) in Escondido. Italian-born winemaker Leon Santoro is a veteran of Napa Valley (Louis Martini and Stag's Leap). Besides producing excellent Chardonnay and Merlot, the winery also makes several Rhône and Italian varietals, including Sangiovese. The tasting room is open daily from 10am to 6pm, and guided tours are offered at 2pm. The property includes a parklike picnic area and a shop.

Other North County wineries include the **Bernardo Winery,** just south of Escondido (✆ **858/487-1866;** www.bernardowinery.com), which has several gift stores and dining options on site; and **Fallbrook Winery** in Fallbrook (✆ **760/728-0156;** www.fallbrookwinery.com). If you have time, the wineries along Rancho California Road in **Temecula,** just across the San Diego County line, are open for tours and tastings; for details, see "Touring Temecula's Wineries" on p. 252.

8 Organized Tours

It's almost impossible to get a handle on the diversity of San Diego in a short visit, but one way to maximize your time is to take an organized tour that introduces you to the city. Many tours are creative, not as touristy as you might fear, and allow you a great deal of versatility in planning your day.

Centre City Development Corporation's **Downtown Information Center,** 225 Broadway, Suite 160 (✆ **619/235-2222;** www.ccdc.com), offers free downtown bus tours the first and third Saturdays of the month at 10am and noon. Aimed at prospective home buyers in the downtown area, as well as curious locals trying to stay abreast of any developments, reservations are recommended for the 90-minute tour. Go inside the information center to see models of the Gaslamp Quarter and the downtown area. The office is open Monday through Saturday from 9am to 5pm.

WATER EXCURSIONS

The Gondola Company   This unique business operates from Loews Coronado Bay Resort, plying the calm waters between pleasure-boat docks in gondolas crafted according to centuries-old designs from Venice. It features all the trimmings, right down to the striped-shirt–clad gondolier with ribbons waving from his or her straw hat. Mediterranean music plays while you and up to five friends recline with snuggly blankets, and the company will even provide antipasto appetizers (or chocolate-dipped strawberries) and chilled wineglasses and ice for the beverage of your choice (BYOB). Dinner packages can also be arranged at the resort's stylish Azzura Point restaurant.

4000 Coronado Bay Rd., Coronado. ✆ 619/429-6317. www.gondolacompany.com. Mon–Fri 3pm–midnight; Sat–Sun 11am–midnight. 1-hr. cruise $70 per couple, $15 for each additional passenger (up to 6 total).

Hornblower Cruises   These 1-hour or 2-hour narrated tours lead passengers through the San Diego harbor on one of seven different yachts, ranging from a 61-passenger antique yacht to a three-deck, 800-passenger behemoth. You'll see the *Star of India,* cruise under the San Diego–Coronado Bridge, and swing by a submarine base and an aircraft carrier or two. Guests can visit the captain's wheelhouse for a photo op, and harbor seals and sea lions on buoys are a regular sighting. Whale-watching trips (mid-Dec to late Mar) are a blast, a 2-hour Sunday (and Sat in summer) champagne brunch cruise departs at 11am, and dinner/dance cruises run nightly.

1066 N. Harbor Dr. ✆ 888/467-6256 or 619/686-8715. www.hornblower.com. Harbor tours $17–$22 adults, $2 off for seniors and military, half price children 4–12. Dinner cruises start at $59; brunch cruise $45; whale-watching trips $30 (both $2 off for seniors and military, half price for children). Bus: 2. Trolley: Embarcadero.

San Diego Harbor Excursion   This company also offers daily 1- and 2-hour narrated tours of the bay, using its fleet of eight boats ranging from a 1940s passenger launch to plush, modern vessels. There are two 1-hour itineraries, each covering about 12 miles—the south bay tour includes the San Diego–Coronado Bridge and Navy shipyards, the north bay route motors past Naval Air Station North Island and Cabrillo National Monument. The 25-mile, 2-hour tour encompasses the entire bay.

Tips　San Diego by Land & Sea at the Same Time

If you can't decide between a bus tour or a bay cruise, opt for both—an amphibious tour on Old Town Trolley Tour's **Sea and Land Adventures**. The 90-minute SEAL tour departs from Seaport Village and motors along the Embarcadero until splashing into San Diego Bay. This specially built craft holds 46 passengers, and the narrated tour gives you the maritime and military history of San Diego from the right perspective. The trips are usually scheduled daily, depending on the season, with departure times varying. The cost is $30 for adults and $15 for kids 4 to 12. For information and tickets, call ✆ **619/298-8687**, or visit www.historictours.com.

In winter, whale-watching excursions feature naturalists from the Birch Aquarium, and the 2-hour Sunday brunch cruise aboard a sleek yacht is popular; dinner cruises embark nightly.

1050 N. Harbor Dr. (foot of Broadway). ✆ **800/442-7847** or 619/234-4111. www.sdhe.com. Harbor tours $17–$22 ($2 off for seniors and military, half price for children 4–12). Dinner cruises start at $58; brunch cruise $50 adults, $30 children; whale-watching trips $27–$30 adults, $21 seniors and military, $15 children. Bus: 2. Trolley: Embarcadero.

Xplore Offshore 😊😊 *(Finds)*　San Diego's best thrill ride is in plying the region's coastal waters from Coronado to Catalina. There are only two small boats in this fleet, and the one to ride is the tricked-out, 24-foot RIB (rigid-inflatable boat), similar to the crafts used by Navy SEALS. Capable of cruising at up to 45mph, the RIB is built for speed and comfort—there's lots of padding and straddle seating up front, and even a surprisingly roomy head (not bad for a 24-ft. boat). Other special features include hot water for showering after a swim and an underwater camera, for those who want to look but not get wet. Trips are unscripted; you can do what you want to do, and go wherever you want to go. Rip-roaring wave riding or serene pleasure boating, whale watching or night diving, booze cruise to bayside restaurants and concerts or camping on a remote Catalina beach—it's your call.

Pick-up points are flexible, but usually Dana Landing in Mission Bay. ✆ **858/456-1636**. www.xploreoffshore.com. 3-hour rates start at $49. Bus: 9 (for Dana Landing).

BUS TOURS

Family-owned **Contact Tours** (✆ **800/235-5393** or 619/477-8687; www.contactours. com) offers city sightseeing tours, including a "Grand Tour" that covers San Diego, Tijuana, and a 1-hour harbor cruise. It also runs trips to the San Diego Zoo, Wild Animal Park, LEGOLAND, SeaWorld, Disneyland, Universal Studios, Tijuana, Rosarito Beach, and Ensenada. Prices range from $29 for the 3½-hour City Tour to $57 for the full-day Grand Tour, which includes a visit to Tijuana (prices range $15–$27 for children 3–11). Multiple tours can be combined for discounted rates. Contact picks up passengers at most area hotels.

TROLLEY TOURS

Not to be confused with the public transit trolley, the narrated **Old Town Trolley Tours** (✆ **619/298-8687**; www.historictours.com) offers an easy way to get an overview of the city, especially if you're short on time. The open-air trolleys are also a good way to tie together visits to several of San Diego's major attractions without driving or resorting to pricey cabs. The trackless trolleys do a 30-mile circular route, and you can hop off at any one of eight stops, explore at leisure, and reboard when you please (the trolleys run every half-hour). Stops include Old Town, the Gaslamp Quarter and downtown area, Coronado, the San Diego Zoo, and Balboa Park. You can begin wherever you want, but you must purchase tickets before boarding (most stops have a ticket kiosk). The tour costs $30 for adults ($15 for kids 4–12, free for children 3 and under) for one complete loop; the route by itself takes about 2 hours. The trolleys operate daily from 9am to 4pm in winter, and from 9am to 5pm in summer.

WALKING TOURS

Walkabout International, 4639 30th St., Suite C, San Diego (*©* **619/231-7463;** www.walkabout-int.org), sponsors more than 100 free walking tours every month that are led by local volunteers, listed in a monthly newsletter and on the website. Walking tours hit all parts of the county, including the Gaslamp Quarter, La Jolla, and the beaches, and there's a hike in the mountains most Wednesdays and Saturdays.

Urban Safaris (*©* **619/944-9255;** walkingtoursofsandiego.com), provides walking tours of 10 San Diego neighborhoods, including Ocean Beach and Hillcrest. Tours depart from designated meeting places in the neighborhood where the walk will take place. All tours are $10.

Where You Want to Be Tours (*©* **619/917-6037;** www.wheretours.com) puts a lighthearted touch on its offerings, which include a walking (or biking) tour of San Diego's beach Tiki culture. Other itineraries include an Old Town power-walk, a La Jolla gallery stroll, and a downtown nightlife primer. Prices start at $20.

The **Gaslamp Quarter Historical Foundation** offers 2-hour tours of the quarter every Saturday at 11am. Tours depart from the William Heath Davis House Museum, 410 Island Ave., and cost $10 for adults and $8 for seniors, students, and military. For more information, contact the foundation directly at *©* **619/233-4692** or www.gaslampquarter.org.

Volunteers from the Canyoneer group of the **San Diego Natural History Museum** (*©* **619/255-0203;** www.sdnhm.org/canyoneers) lead free guided nature walks throughout San Diego County. The walks are held every Saturday and Sunday (except July–Aug), and usually focus on the flora and fauna of a particular area, which might be a city park or as far away as Anza-Borrego Desert. The hikes are great fun.

At the **Cabrillo National Monument** on the tip of Point Loma (p. 153), rangers often lead free walking tours. Docents at **Torrey Pines State Reserve** in La Jolla (p. 163) lead interpretive nature walks at 10am and 2pm on weekends and holidays. And guided walks are often scheduled at **Mission Trails Regional Park** (p. 158).

Also see "Balboa Park Guided Tours" (p. 150) for organized walks through Balboa Park, and "Hiking & Walking," later in this chapter, for unguided trail options.

WHALE-WATCHING

Along the California coast, whale-watching is an eagerly anticipated wintertime activity, particularly in San Diego—the Pacific gray whale passes close by Point Loma on its annual migratory trek. Local whaling in the 1870s greatly reduced their numbers, but federal protection has allowed the species to repopulate, and current estimates number about 27,000 grays in the ocean today. If you've ever been lucky enough to spot one of these gentle behemoths swimming gracefully and resolutely through the ocean, you'll understand the thrill. When they approach San Diego, the 40- to 50-foot gray whales are more than three-quarters of the way along their nearly 6,000-mile journey from Alaska to breeding lagoons in the Sea of Cortez, around the southern tip of Baja California. After mating and calving they will pass by again, calves in tow, heading back to the rich Alaskan feeding grounds. The epic journey for these cetaceans is one of the longest migrations of any mammal. From mid-December to mid-March is the best time to see the migration, and there are several ways to view their parade.

The easiest (and cheapest) is to grab a pair of binoculars and head to a good land-bound vantage point. The best is **Cabrillo National Monument,** at the tip of Point Loma, where you'll find a glassed-in observatory and educational whale exhibits, 400 feet above sea level. When the weather cooperates, you can often spot the whales as they surface for breathing—as many as eight grays per hour at peak commute (mid-Jan). Each January the rangers conduct a special "Whale Watch Weekend" featuring presentations by whale experts, children's programs, and entertainment. For more information on Cabrillo National Monument, see p. 153.

If you want to get a closer look, head out to sea on one of the excursions that locate and follow gray whales, taking care not to disturb their journey. **Classic Sailing Adventures** (© **800/659-0141** or 619/224-0800; www.classicsailingadventures.com) offers two trips per day (8:30am and 1pm); each lasts 4 hours and carries a maximum of six passengers. Sailboats are less distracting to the whales than motorized yachts, but more expensive; the cruises are $65 per person (minimum two passengers), including beverages and snacks. **Sail San Diego** (© **619/297-7426;** www.sailsandiego.com) also does whale-watching under sail, leaving weekends at 11:30am. The 4-hour trip is $85 per person and includes lunch and drinks (champagne, even). Shorter weekday motored trips ($65) are aboard a small Mexican-style fishing boat.

Companies that offer traditional, engine-driven expeditions include **Hornblower Cruises** and **San Diego Harbor Excursions** (see "Water Excursions," above). Excursions are 3 or 3½ hours, and fares run $30 for adults, with discounts for kids.

In La Jolla, the **Birch Aquarium at Scripps** celebrates gray whale season with classes, educational activities, and exhibits, and the outdoor terrace offers another vantage point for spotting the mammals from shore. Multi-day trips to San Ignacio in Baja California, where the whales mate and calve are offered in February and March, and Birch provides naturalists to accompany the whale-watching done by San Diego Harbor Excursions (see "Water Excursions," above). Call © **858/534-7336** for more information.

The **San Diego Natural History Museum** also offers multi-day, naturalist-led whale-watching trips to Baja. For a schedule and preregistration information, call © **619/255-0203** or check www.sdnhm.org/education.

9 Outdoor Activities

See section 2 of this chapter for a complete rundown of San Diego's beaches. To find the locations of the following outdoor activities, refer to the color map at the beginning of this book.

BALLOONING & SCENIC FLIGHTS

A peaceful dawn or dusk balloon ride reveals sweeping vistas of the Southern California coast, wine country, rambling estates, and golf courses. For a champagne-fueled glimpse of the county at sunrise or sunset, followed by an hors d'oeuvres party, contact **Skysurfer Balloon Company** (© **800/660-6809** or 858/481-6800; www. sandiegohotairballoons.com). The rate for a 40- to 60-minute flight is $165 per person weekdays, $175 weekends; sunrise flights leave from Temecula (70 min. north of downtown) and sunset flights are from Del Mar (25 min. from downtown). Or call **California Dreamin'** (© **800/373-3359** or 760/438-3344; www.californiadreamin. com). They charge $128 per person weekday, $148 weekend (children 5–12 always $118) for a 1-hour sunrise breakfast flight in Temecula, or $168 for sunset flights in Del Mar that last up to 1 hour ($188 on Sat); both include champagne and a personalized flight photo. California Dreamin' also offers a **biplane adventure** over Temecula's wine country starting at $248 for two people. You may also be interested in the **Temecula Balloon & Wine Festival** held in early June; call © **951/676-6713** or visit www.tvbwf.com for information.

BIRD-WATCHING

The birding scene is huge: More than 480 species have been observed in San Diego County, more than in any other county in the United States. The area is a haven along the Pacific Flyway—the migratory route along the Pacific Coast—and the diverse range of ecosystems also helps to lure a wide range of winged creatures. It's possible for birders to enjoy four distinct bird habitats in a single day.

Among the best places for bird-watching is the **Chula Vista Nature Center** at Sweetwater Marsh National Wildlife Refuge (© **619/409-5900;** www.chulavista aturecenter.org), where you may spot rare residents like the light-footed clapper rail and the western snowy plover, as well as predatory species like the American peregrine falcon and northern harrier. The nature center, which is going through an extensive renovation scheduled to be completed by summer 2006, also has aquariums for turtles, sharks and rays, aviaries featuring raptors and shorebirds, and a garden featuring native plants (p. 164). Also worth visiting along the coast is the 25-acre **Kendall-Frost Marsh** on the east side of Crown Point, in Mission Bay, which draws skimmers, shorebirds, brant, and, in winter, the large-billed savannah sparrow; and the **Torrey Pines State Reserve** (p. 163), north of La Jolla, a protected habitat for swifts, thrashers, woodpeckers, and wren tits. Inland, **Mission Trails Regional Park** (p. 158) is a 5,800-acre urban park that is visited by orange-crowned warblers, swallows, raptors, and numerous riparian species; and the **Anza-Borrego Desert State Park** (see chapter 11) makes an excellent day trip from San Diego—268 species of birds have been recorded here.

Birders coming to the area should obtain a copy of the free brochure *Birding Hot Spots of San Diego,* available at the Port Administration Building, 3165 Pacific Hwy., and at the San Diego Zoo, Wild Animal Park, San Diego Natural History Museum, and Birch Aquarium. It is also posted online at www.portofsandiego.org/sandiego_ environment/bird_brochure.asp. The **San Diego Audubon Society** is another source of birding information (© **619/682-7200;** www.sandiegoaudubon.org).

BIKING

San Diego is on the verge of becoming the nation's preeminent bicycling destination, with millions of dollars earmarked for bicycle paths throughout the city and county, including one that will parallel the rail line as far as Oceanside. But already, San Diego is cyclist friendly, and was named "one of the top 10 cities in the U.S. to bicycle" by *Bicycling* magazine. Many major thoroughfares offer bike lanes; but downtown is definitely a challenge. To obtain a detailed map by mail of San Diego County's bike lanes and routes, call **Ride Link Bicycle Information** (© 800/266-6883). You might also want to talk to the **San Diego County Bicycle Coalition** (© 858/487-6063). For information on taking your bike onto public transportation, turn to "By Bicycle," in the "Getting Around" section on p. 55 in chapter 4. Bicycle helmets are legally required for those under 18.

The paths around Mission Bay, in particular, are great for leisurely rides. The ocean-front boardwalk between Pacific Beach and Mission Beach can get very crowded, espe-cially on weekends (but that's half the fun). Coronado has a 16-mile round-trip bike trail that starts at the Ferry Landing Marketplace and follows a well-marked route around Coronado to Imperial Beach, along the Silver Strand. The road out to Point Loma (Catalina Dr.) offers moderate hills and wonderful scenery. Traveling old State Route 101 (aka the Pacific Coast Hwy.) from La Jolla north to Oceanside offers ter-rific coastal views, along with plenty of places to refuel with coffee, a snack, or a swim. The 13-mile climb up steep switchbacks to the summit of 6,140-foot Mt. Palomar is perhaps the county's most invigorating challenge, and offers its most gleeful descent.

Cycling San Diego by Nelson Copp and Jerry Schad (Sunbelt Publications) is a good resource for bicyclists and is available at most local bike shops.

RENTALS, ORGANIZED BIKE TOURS & OTHER TWO-WHEEL ADVENTURES

Downtown, call **Bike Tours San Diego,** 509 Fifth Ave. (© 619/238-2444), which offers delivery ($5) as far north as Del Mar. Rates for a city/hybrid bike start at $20 for a day, and include helmet, lock, maps, and roadside assistance. Other downtown shops include **San Diego Bike Shop,** 619 C St. (© 619/237-1245), and across the street **Pennyfarthing's Bicycle Store,** 630 C St. (© 619/233-7696); hourly rates about $5, or $25 for a 24-hour rental.

In Mission Bay, there's **Mission Beach Club,** 704 Ventura Place, off Mission Boulevard at Ocean Front Walk (© 858/488-8889), for one-speed beach cruisers; **Cheap Rentals,** 3685 and 3221 Mission Blvd. (© 858/488-9070), for mountain bikes and more; and **Hilton San Diego Resort,** 1775 E. Mission Bay Dr. (© 619/276-4010), for multispeed bikes. In La Jolla, try **California Bicycle,** 7462 La Jolla Blvd. (© 858/454-0316), for front-suspended mountain bikes. In Coronado, check out **Bikes and Beyond,** 1201 First St. at the Ferry Landing Marketplace (© 619/435-7180), for beach cruisers and mountain bikes; they also offer surrey and skate rentals. Expect to pay $7 and up per hour for bicycles, $30 for 24 hours.

Adventurous cyclists might like to participate in the **Rosarito-Ensenada 50-mile Fun Bicycle Ride,** held every April and September just across the border in Mexico. This event attracts more than 8,000 riders of all ages and abilities. It starts at the Rosarito Beach Hotel and finishes in Ensenada and rides along paved highway. For information, contact **Bicycling West, Inc.** (© 858/483-8777; www.rosarito ensenada.com).

FISHING

In the late 1940s, the waters off San Diego supplied as much as two-thirds of the nation's supply of tuna, so it's no wonder that San Diego offers exhilaration to sport-fishers. The sportfishing fleet consists of more than 75 large commercial vessels and several dozen private charter yachts, and a variety of half-, full-, and multi-day trips are available. The saltwater fishing season kicks off each spring with the traditional

Port of San Diego Day at the Docks, held the last weekend in April or at the beginning of May at Sportfishing Landing, near Shelter Island; for more information, call 𝄫 619/234-8793 or see www.sportfishing.org. Anglers of any age can fish free of charge without a license off any municipal pier in California. Public fishing piers are on Shelter Island (where there's a statue dedicated to anglers), Ocean Beach, and Imperial Beach.

Summer and fall are ideal for fishing, when the waters around Point Loma are brimming with bass, bonito, and barracuda; the Islas los Coronados, which belong to Mexico but are only about 18 miles from San Diego, are popular for yellowtail, yellowfin, and big-eyed tuna. Some outfitters will take you farther into Baja California waters on multi-day trips. Fishing charters depart from Harbor and Shelter Islands, Point Loma, the Imperial Beach pier, and Quivira Basin in Mission Bay (near the Hyatt Islandia Hotel). Participants over 16 need a California fishing license.

Rates for trips on a large boat average $37 for a half-day trip or $75 for a ¾-day trip, or you can spring $120 for a 20-hour overnight trip to the Islas los Coronados—call around and compare prices. Prices are reduced for kids, and discounts are often available for twilight sailings; charters or "limited load" rates are also available. The following outfitters offer short or extended outings with daily departures: **H & M Landing,** 2803 Emerson St. (𝄫 **619/222-1144;** www.hmlanding.com); **Lee Palm Sportfishers,** 2801 Emerson St. (𝄫 **619/224-3857;** www.redrooster3.com); **Point Loma Sportfishing,** 1403 Scott St. (𝄫 **619/223-1627;** www.pointlomasportfishing.com); and **Seaforth Sportfishing,** 1717 Quivira Rd. (𝄫 **619/224-3383;** www.seaforth landing.com). All of these shops rent tackle. Fly fishing for sea bass or halibut is also possible: **Andy Montana's,** 957 Orange Ave., Coronado (𝄫 **619/435-9992;** www.andymontanas.com), rents equipment and provides guides (starting at $150) for shoreline fishing around Coronado and San Diego Bay; classes are also offered on an ongoing basis.

For freshwater fishing, San Diego's lakes and rivers are home to bass, channel and bullhead catfish, bluegill, trout, crappie, and sunfish. Most lakes have rental facilities for boats, tackle, and bait, and they also provide picnic and (usually) camping areas. A 1-day California State Fishing License costs $12; a 1-year license is $35. For information on lake fishing, call the city's **Lakes Line** 𝄫 **619/465-3474.**

For information on fishing at **Lake Cuyamaca,** 1 hour from San Diego near Julian, see "Julian: Apple Pies & More" in chapter 11. For more information on fishing in California, contact the **California Department of Fish and Game** (𝄫 **858/467-4201;** www.dfg.ca.gov). For fishing in Mexican waters, including the area off the Coronado Islands, angling permits are required. Most charter companies will take care of the details, but if not, contact the **Mexican Department of Fisheries,** 2550 Fifth Ave., Suite 15, San Diego, CA 92103-6622 (𝄫 **619/233-4324**).

GOLF

With 90-plus courses, more than 50 of them open to the public, San Diego County offers golf enthusiasts innumerable opportunities to play their game. Courses are diverse: Some have vistas of the Pacific, others views of country hillsides or desert landscapes. For a full listing of area courses, including fees, stats, and complete scorecards, visit www.golfsd.com, or request the *Golf Guide* from the **San Diego Convention and Visitors Bureau** (𝄫 **619/236-1212;** www.sandiego.org). In addition to the well-established courses listed below, other acclaimed links include **The Grand Del**

Mar Golf Club (℃ 858/792-6200; www.thegrandgolfclub.com), **Maderas Golf Club** (℃ 858/451-8100; www.maderasgolf.com), **Barona Creek Golf Club** (℃ 619/387-7018; www.barona.com), **Steele Canyon Golf Club** (℃ 619/441-6900; www.steelecanyon.com), **The Auld Course** (℃ 619/482-4666; www.theauld course.com), and **La Costa Resort and Spa** (p. 245).

San Diego Golf Reservations (℃ 866/701-4653 or 858/964-5980; www.san diegogolfreservations.com) can arrange tee times for you at San Diego's premiere golf courses. They will consult with you on the courses you are interested in and charge a $10 per person/per tee time coordination fee. And when you just want to practice your swing, head to **Stadium Golf Center,** 2990 Murphy Canyon Rd., in Mission Valley (℃ 858/277-6667; www.stadiumgolfcenter.com). They're open daily from 7am to 10pm, with 72 artificial turf and natural grass hitting stations, plus greens and bunkers to practice your short game. A complete pro shop offers club rentals at $1 each (free for youths 17 and under); a bucket of balls costs $7 to $17. Golf instruction and clinics are also available.

Balboa Park Municipal Golf Course

Everybody has a humble municipal course like this at home, with a bare-bones 1920s clubhouse where old guys hold down lunch counter stools for hours after the game—and players take a few more mulligans than they would elsewhere. Surrounded by the beauty of Balboa Park, this 18-hole course features pure greens, fairways sprinkled with eucalyptus leaves, and distractingly nice views of the San Diego skyline. It's so convenient and affordable that it's the perfect choice for visitors who want to work some golf into their vacation rather than the other way around. The course even rents clubs. Nonresident greens fees are $36 week-days, $41 weekends; the twilight rate is $21; cart rental is $26, pull carts $5. Reservations are suggested at least a week in advance.

You don't have to be a golfer to enjoy **Tobey's 19th Hole,** the clubhouse's simple cafe, offering splendid views of Point Loma, downtown, and the park from a deck. The food is cheap and diner-esque—omelets, biscuits and gravy, corned beef hash for breakfast; chiliburgers and sandwiches for lunch—but this local hangout is a nice find for visitors.

2600 Golf Course Dr. (off Pershing Dr. or 26th St. in the southeast corner of the park), San Diego. ℃ 619/239-1660. www.sandiego.gov/golf.

Coronado Municipal Golf Course

This course is mostly for people who are vaca-tioning in Coronado and just can't bear to leave the "island." It's an 18-hole, par-72 course overlooking Glorietta Bay, and there's a coffee shop, pro shop, and driving range. It's tough to get a tee time here, so 2-day prior reservations are strongly recom-mended; call after 7am (there's a $38 nonrefundable advance registration charge). Greens fees are $25 to walk and $40 to ride for 18 holes; after 4pm, it's $13 to walk and $28 to ride. Club rental is $40 ($25 twilight rate), and pull-cart rental is $5.

2000 Visalia Row, Coronado. ℃ 619/435-3121. www.coronadogolf.com.

Four Seasons Resort Aviara Golf Club ☆☆

Uniquely landscaped to incorporate natural elements compatible with the protected Batiquitos Lagoon nearby, Aviara doesn't infringe on the wetlands bird habitat. The course is 7,007 yards from the championship tees, laid out over rolling hillsides with plenty of bunker and water challenges. Casual duffers may be frustrated here. Greens fees are $195 (including mandatory cart) during the week, and $215 Friday through Sunday; afternoon rates start at 1pm in winter, 3pm in summer. There are practice areas for putting, chipping, sand play, and driving, and the pro shop and clubhouse are fully equipped. Golf packages are available for guests of the Four Seasons.

7447 Batiquitos Dr., Carlsbad. ✆ **760/603-6900**. www.fourseasons.com. From I-5 north, take the Aviara Pkwy. exit east to Batiquitos Dr. Turn right and continue 2 miles to the clubhouse.

Mt. Woodson Golf Club ⚐

One of San Diego County's most dramatic golf courses, Mt. Woodson is a par-70, 6,180-yard course on 150 beautiful acres. The award-winning 18-hole course, which opened in 1991, meanders up and down hills, across bridges, and around granite boulders. Elevated tees provide striking views of Ramona and Mount Palomar, and on a clear day you can see for almost 100 miles. It's easy to combine a game of golf with a weekend getaway to Julian (see chapter 11). Nonresident greens fees for 18 holes (including mandatory cart) are $60 Monday through Thursday, $70 Friday, $85 Saturday, and $80 Sunday. Early bird, afternoon, and twilight rates are available, and seniors get a discount. Mt. Woodson is about 40 minutes north of San Diego.

16422 N. Woodson Dr., Ramona. ✆ **760/788-3555**. www.mtwoodson.com. Take I-15 north to Poway Rd. exit; at the end of Poway Rd., turn left (north) onto Rte. 67 and drive 3¾ miles to Archie Moore Rd.; turn left. Entrance is on the left.

Rancho Bernardo Inn ⚐

Rancho Bernardo has a mature 18-hole, 72-par championship course with different terrains, water hazards, sand traps, lakes, and waterfalls. It was recently renovated and now plays to more than 6,600 yards; there are also four sets of tees for all level of play. Stay-and-play golf packages are available. Greens fees are $90 weekdays and $115 weekends, including a cart. Twilight rates (after 1pm winter, 2pm summer) are available.

17550 Bernardo Oaks Dr., Rancho Bernardo. ✆ **858/675-8470**. www.ranchobernardoinn.com. From I-15 north, exit at Rancho Bernardo Rd. Head east to Bernardo Oaks Dr., turn left, and continue to the resort entrance.

Riverwalk Golf Club ⚐

Completely redesigned by Ted Robinson and Ted Robinson Jr., these links wander along the Mission Valley floor and are the most convenient courses for anyone staying downtown or near the beaches. Replacing the private Stardust Golf Club, the course reopened in 1998, sporting a slick, upscale new clubhouse, four lakes with waterfalls (in play on 13 of the 27 holes), open, undulating fairways, and one peculiar feature: trolley tracks. The bright red trolley speeds through now and then, but doesn't prove too distracting. Nonresident greens fees, including cart, are $95 Monday through Thursday, $105 Friday through Sunday; senior, twilight, and bargain evening rates are available.

1150 Fashion Valley Rd., Mission Valley. ✆ **619/296-4653**. www.riverwalkgc.com. Take I-8 to Hotel Circle south, and turn on Fashion Valley Rd.

Sycuan Resort & Casino

The only resort in Southern California offering 54 holes of golf (two championship courses and a 2,500-yard par-54 executive course), Sycuan takes advantage of the area's natural terrain. Mountains, natural rock outcroppings, and aged oaks and sycamores add character to individual holes. Greens fees are $45 Monday through Thursday, $50 Friday, and $64 weekends for the two par-72 courses, and $16 to $22 on the shorter course. Cart rental costs $12. Twilight rates are available and there's a golf school for women taught by women; the resort also offers a variety of good-value packages. The course was formerly known as Singing Hills.

3007 Dehesa Rd., El Cajon. ✆ **800/457-5568** or 619/442-3425. www.sycuanresort.com. Take Calif. 94 to the Willow Glen exit. Turn right and continue to the entrance.

Torrey Pines Golf Course 🏌️🏌️ These two gorgeous, municipal 18-hole championship courses are on the coast between La Jolla and Del Mar, only 20 minutes from downtown San Diego. Home of the Buick Invitational Tournament, and the setting for the 2008 U.S. Open, Torrey Pines is second only to Pebble Beach as California's top golf destination. Situated on a bluff overlooking the ocean, the north course is picturesque and has the signature hole (no. 6), but the south course is more challenging, has more sea-facing play, and benefits from a $3.5-million overhaul in 2002.

In summer, course conditions can be less than ideal due to the sheer number of people lined up to play, and "tee scalpers" aren't uncommon. Tee times are taken by computer, starting at 7pm, up to 7 days in advance and by automated telephone only—it takes only 20 to 30 minutes for all tee times for a given day to sell out. Confirmation numbers are issued, and you must have the number and photo identification with you when you check in with the starter 15 minutes ahead of time. If you're late, your time may be forfeited. Golf packages add about $70 to the cost, but give you much better odds of actually getting onto the course. Golf professionals are available for lessons, and the pro shop rents clubs. Greens fees on the south course are $115 weekdays, $135 weekends; the north course is $75 weekdays and $85 weekends. Cart rentals are $32, and twilight rates are available.

Tip: Single golfers stand a good chance of getting on the course if they just turn up and get on the waiting list for a threesome. The locals also sometimes circumvent the reservation system by spending Friday or Saturday night in a camper in the parking lot. The starter lets these diehards on before the reservations made by the computer go into effect at 7:30am.

11480 Torrey Pines Rd., La Jolla. ℂ **858/570-1234** or 858/452-3226 for the pro shop and packages. www.torreypinesgolfcourse.com or www.sandiego.gov/torreypines. From I-5, take Genesee Ave., exit west, and go left on N. Torrey Pines Rd. Bus: 101.

HANG GLIDING & PARAGLIDING

The windy cliffs at the **Torrey Pines Gliderport,** 2800 Torrey Pines Scenic Dr., La Jolla (ℂ **877/359-8326** or 858/452-9858; www.flytorrey.com), create one of the country's top spots for hang gliding and paragliding, sports that aren't for the timid, yet deliver a bigger thrill than your average roller coaster. The difference between the two nonmotorized sports? Hang gliders are suspended from a fixed wing, while paragliders hang from a parachute. In both instances, watching the pilots control these delicate crafts for hours along the brink of the precipice is awesome. A 20- to 30-minute tandem flight with a qualified instructor costs $150 for paragliding and $175 for hang gliding. Even if you don't muster the courage to try a tandem flight, sitting at the cafe here and watching the graceful acrobatics is stirring.

If you already have experience, you can rent or buy equipment from the shop at the Gliderport—note that the conditions here are considered "P3"—or take lessons from the crew of able instructors. A 3- to 5-day beginning paragliding package is $895; advanced hang-gliding lessons run $195 per day and must be scheduled ahead of time. Winds in December and January are slightest (that is, least conducive for the activities here), while March through June is best. The Gliderport is open daily from 9am to sunset.

HIKING & WALKING

San Diego's mild climate makes it a great place to walk or hike most of the year, and the options are diverse. Walking along the water is particularly rewarding. The best

beaches for walking are Coronado, Mission Beach, La Jolla Shores, and Torrey Pines, but pretty much any shore is a good choice. You can also walk around most of Mission Bay on a series of connected footpaths. If a four-legged friend is your walking companion, head for Dog Beach in Ocean Beach or Fiesta Island in Mission Bay—two of the few areas where dogs can legally go unleashed. The **Coast Walk** in La Jolla offers supreme surf-line views.

The **Sierra Club** sponsors regular hikes in the San Diego area, and nonmembers are welcome to participate. There's frequently a Wednesday mountain hike, usually in the Cuyamaca Mountains, sometimes in the Lagunas; there are evening and day hikes as well. Most are free of charge. Call the office at © **619/299-1743** weekdays from noon to 5pm, or consult the website, www.sandiego.sierraclub.org. Volunteers from the **Natural History Museum** (© **619/232-3821**) also lead nature walks throughout San Diego County.

Marian Bear Memorial Park, also known as San Clemente Canyon (© **858/581-9952** for park ranger), is a 7-mile, round-trip trail that runs directly underneath Highway 52. Most of the trail is flat, hard-packed dirt, but some areas are rocky. There are benches and places to sit and have a quiet picnic. From Highway 52 west, take the Genesee South exit; at the stoplight, make a U-turn and an immediate right into the parking lot. From Highway 52 east, exit at Genesee and make a right at the light, and then an immediate right into the parking lot.

Lake Miramar Reservoir has a 3.5-mile, paved trail with a wonderful view of the lake and mountains. Take I-15 north and exit on Mira Mesa Boulevard. Turn right on Scripps Ranch Boulevard, then left on Scripps Lake Drive, and make a left at the Lake Miramar sign. Hours are sunrise to sunset, 7 days a week; parking is free. There's also a pleasant path around **Lake Murray.** Take the Lake Murray Boulevard exit off I-8 and follow the signs.

Other places for scenic hikes listed earlier in this chapter include **Torrey Pines State Reserve** (p. 163), **Cabrillo National Monument** (p. 153), and **Mission Trails Regional Park** (p. 158). Guided walks are also offered at each of these parks.

JOGGING

An invigorating route downtown is along the wide sidewalks of the Embarcadero, stretching around the bay. A locals' favorite place to jog is the sidewalk that follows the east side of Mission Bay. Start at the Visitor Information Center and head south past the Hilton to Fiesta Island. A good spot for a short run is La Jolla Shores Beach, where there's hard-packed sand even when it isn't low tide. The beach at Coronado is also a good place for jogging, as is the shore at Pacific Beach and Mission Beach—just watch your tide chart to make sure you won't be there at high tide.

Safety note: When jogging alone, avoid secluded areas of Balboa Park, even during daylight hours.

SAILING & MOTOR YACHTS

There are more than 55,000 registered water craft docked at 26 marinas throughout San Diego County. Sailors have a choice of the calm waters of 4,600-acre **Mission Bay,** with its 26 miles of shoreline; the exciting **San Diego Bay,** one of the most beautiful natural harbors in the world; or the **Pacific Ocean,** where you can sail south to the Islas los Coronados (the trio of uninhabited islets on the Mexico side of the border). Joining a chartered sailing trip is easy.

The **Maritime Museum of San Diego** (© 619/234-9153; www.sdmaritime.org) offers half-day and 3-day sailing adventures aboard the *Californian,* the official tall ship of the state. This ship is a replica of an 1847 cutter that sailed the coast during the Gold Rush. Half-day sails depart Saturday and Sunday at 1pm from the Maritime Museum downtown and are priced $30 for adults; $21 for seniors over 62, juniors age 13 to 17, and active military; and $17 for kids 12 and under. Reservations are required for multi-day trips, which make for Catalina Island ($465) and take place in summer and fall. For sailing schedules or more information, call or check the website.

Based at Shelter Island Marina, **Classic Sailing Adventures** (© **800/659-0141** or 619/224-0800; www.classicsailingadventures.com) offers two 4-hour sailing trips daily aboard the *Soul Diversion,* a 38-foot Ericson. The afternoon cruise leaves at 1pm and a champagne sunset sail departs at 5pm. The yacht carries a maximum of six passengers (minimum two), and the $65-per-person price includes beverages and snacks.

Sail aboard the **Jada** (© **619/236-9211;** www.jadasailing.com) for sunset champagne cruises, complete with full dinner ($75 per person). Jada is a 71-foot wooden sailing yacht, built in 1938, and she's mighty yare. Dinner cruises are Wednesday through Sunday, and whale-watching sails take place in winter.

You can pretend you're racing for your country's honor with **Next Level Sailing** (© **800/644-3454;** www.nextlevelsailing.com), which offers bay sails aboard one of two 80-foot America's Cup Class racing yachts. The 2-hour excursions, either on *Stars and Stripes* or *Abracadabra,* are $99.

If you have sailing or boating experience, go for a nonchartered rental. **Seaforth Boat Rental,** 1641 Quivira Rd., Mission Bay (© **888/834-2628** or 619/223-1681; www.seaforthboatrental.com), has a wide variety of boats for bay and ocean. It rents 15- to 240-horsepower powerboats ranging from $48 to $130 an hour, 16- to 36-foot sailboats starting at $30 an hour, and ski boats and jet skis starting at $80 an hour. Half- and full-day rates are available. Canoes, kayaks, and pedal boats are also available, as well as fishing boats and equipment. Seaforth has locations downtown at the Marriott San Diego Hotel & Marina, 333 W. Harbor Dr. (© **619/239-2628**) and in Coronado at 1715 Strand Way (© **619/437-1514**).

Mission Bay Sportcenter, 1010 Santa Clara Place (© **858/488-1004;** www. missionbaysportcenter.com), rents sailboats, catamarans, sailboards, kayaks, jet skis, and motorboats. Prices range from $18 to $100 an hour, with discounts for 4-hour and full-day rentals. Private instruction is available for $30 per hour.

SCUBA DIVING & SNORKELING

San Diego's underwater scene ranges from the magnificent giant kelp forests of Point Loma to the nautical graveyard off Mission Beach called Wreck Alley. There's an aquatic Ecological Reserve off the La Jolla Cove; fishing and boating activity has been banned in the 533-acre reserve since 1929, but diving and snorkeling is welcome, and it's a reliable place to spot garibaldi, California's state fish, as well as the rare giant black sea bass. Shore diving here, or at nearby La Jolla Shores is common, and there are dive shops to help you get set up. But boat dives are the rule. Check out the Islas los Coronados, a trio of uninhabited islets off Mexico (a 90-min. boat ride from San Diego), where seals, sea lions, eels, and more cavort against a landscape of boulders (watch for swift currents), and the *Yukon,* a 366-foot Canadian destroyer that was intentionally sunk there in 2000. The ship is part of Wreck Alley, an artificial reef less than 1 mile out from Mission Beach that includes several other vessels and the remains of a research platform toppled by a storm in 1988. Water visibility in San Diego is best in the fall; in the spring, plankton blooms can reduce visibility.

The **San Diego Oceans Foundation** (✆ 619/523-1903; www.sdoceans.org) is a local nonprofit organization devoted to the stewardship of local marine waters. The website features good information about the local diving scene; www.sandiegodiving. com is another good resource. **San Diego Divers Supply,** 4004 Sports Arena Blvd. (✆ 619/224-3439; www.comedivewithus.com), will set you up with scuba and snorkeling equipment. **Ocean Enterprises** (✆ 858/565-6054; www.oceanenterprises. com), **Lois Ann Dive Charters** (✆ 800/201-4381; www.loisann.com), and **Scuba San Diego** (✆ 800/586-3483 or 619/260-1880; www.scubasandiego.com) are other good outfits.

SKATING
Gliding around San Diego, especially the Mission Bay area, on inline skates is the quintessential Southern California experience. In Pacific Beach, rent a pair of regular or inline skates from **Resort Watersports** (✆ 858/488-2582), based at the Catamaran Resort, 3981 Mission Blvd.; or **Play It Again Sports,** 1401 Garnet Ave. (✆ 858/ 490-0222). In Coronado, go to **Bikes and Beyond,** 1201 First St. at the Ferry Landing (✆ 619/435-7180). Be sure to ask for protective gear.

If you'd rather ice skate, try **Ice Town** at University Towne Center, La Jolla Village Drive at Genesee Street (✆ 858/452-9110).

SURFING
With its miles of beaches, San Diego is a popular surf destination. Some of the best spots include Windansea, La Jolla Shores, Pacific Beach, Mission Beach, Ocean Beach, and Imperial Beach. In North County, you might consider Carlsbad State Beach and Oceanside. The best waves are in late summer and early fall; surfers visiting in winter or spring will want to bring along a wetsuit. For surf reports, check out www.surfing sandiego.com or www.surfline.com.

Boards are available for rent at stands at many popular beaches. Many local surf shops also rent equipment; they include **La Jolla Surf Systems,** 2132 Avenida de la Playa, La Jolla Shores (✆ 858/456-2777), and **Emerald City–The Boarding Source,** 1118 Orange Ave., Coronado (✆ 619/435-6677).

For surfing lessons, with all equipment provided, check with **Kahuna Bob's Surf School** (✆ 800/524-8627 or 760/721-7700; www.kahunabob.com) based in Encinitas; **San Diego Surfing Academy** (✆ 800/447-7873 or 760/230-1474; www. surfsdsa.com), which offers lessons at South Carlsbad State Beach; and **Surf Diva** (✆ 858/454-8273; www.surfdiva.com), a surfing school for women and girls, based in La Jolla. The Surf Diva company has become so popular, it now does private lessons for guys on the side.

SWIMMING
Most San Diego hotels have pools, and there are plenty of other swimming options for visitors. The centrally located Mission Valley **YMCA,** 5505 Friars Rd. (✆ 619/ 298-3576; www.missionvalley.ymca.org) has varying afternoon and evening pool hours—call for details. The nonmember fee is $5 for adults ($10 for lap lanes), $1.50 for seniors and children under 12. In Balboa Park, you can swim in the **Kearns Memorial Swimming Pool,** 2229 Morley Field Dr. (✆ 619/692-4920). The fee for using the public pool is $5 for adults, $1.50 for seniors and children 15 and under;

call for seasonal hours and laps-only restrictions. In Mission Bay, you'll find the fabulous indoor pool, **The Plunge,** 3115 Oceanfront Walk (© **858/228-9300;** www.wavehouse.com), part of Belmont Park since 1925. The huge pool, recently renovated, has 10 lap lanes and a viewing area inside, plus a full gym facility. Call for hours and prices.

In La Jolla, you can swim at the **Jewish Community Center,** 4126 Executive Dr. (© **858/457-3030**). It has an ozone pool (kept clean by an ozone generator), instead of the typical chlorinated pool. It's open to the public Monday through Thursday from 6am to 7:30pm, Friday from 6am to 5pm, Saturday from 11am to 5pm, and Sunday from 8:30am to 5pm. Admission is $10.

TENNIS

There are 1,200 public and private tennis courts in San Diego. Public courts include the **La Jolla Tennis Club,** 7632 Draper, at Prospect Street (© **858/454-4434;** www.ljtc.org), which is $5 for adults and free for those 18 and under; it's open daily from dawn until the lights go off at 9pm. The **Balboa Tennis Club,** 2221 Morley Field Dr., in Balboa Park (© **619/295-9278;** www.balboatennis.com), has more than 2 dozen courts, including a stadium court. Day passes are $5 adults, $3 seniors 65 and above, $2 for 17 and under; reservations are for members only. The courts are open weekdays from 8am to 8pm, weekends from 8am to 6pm; for lessons, call © **619/ 291-5248.** The ultramodern **Barnes Tennis Center,** 4490 W. Point Loma Blvd., near Ocean Beach and SeaWorld (© **619/221-9000;** www.tennissandiego.com), has 20 lighted hard courts and 4 clay courts; they're open Monday through Friday from 8am to 9pm, Saturday and Sunday 8am to 7:30pm. Court rental is $5 to $15 per hour, drop-in classes run $18 to $25.

10 Spectator Sports

BASEBALL & SOFTBALL

The **San Diego Padres** play April through September at downtown's $474-million **PETCO Park.** Mired in litigation and revelations of influence peddling that drove a city council member from office, the 42,000-seat ballpark finally opened in 2004 to enthusiastic acclaim from San Diegans and out-of-town fans alike. A total of seven historic buildings were incorporated into the stadium, most prominently the Western Metal Supply building, a four-story brick structure dating to 1909 that now sprouts left field bleachers from one side.

The ballpark isn't the first to offer sushi alongside the usual franks and fries, but you'll find plenty of dining options, notably La Cocina, a Mexican food court with grilled ahi sandwiches and Rubio's fish tacos, and Pacific Wok, where you can munch on spring rolls and Asian salads. The local barbecue stand is run by former Padres pitcher Randy Jones. PETCO parking is limited, and costly—for a space within a couple blocks of the facility, expect to pay at least $17. Less expensive lots are found around the Santa Fe depot at Kettner Blvd. and Broadway—a 15-minute walk from the ballpark. Better yet, take the San Diego Trolley, with three stops right outside the park. For schedules, information, and tickets, call © **877/374-2784** or 619/795-5000, or visit www.padres.com.

The highlight of many San Diegans' summer is the racy softball event known as the **World Championship Over-the-Line Tournament,** held on Fiesta Island in Mission Bay on the second and third weekends of July. For more information, see the "San Diego Calendar of Events," on p. 13.

BOATING

San Diego has probably played host to the America's Cup for the last time, but several other boating events of interest are held here. Check with the **San Diego Association of Yacht Clubs** (© 619/282-5050; www.sdayc.org) for information on races and other boating to-dos. Yearly happenings include the **America's Schooner Cup,** held every March or April (© 619/223-3138), and the **Annual San Diego Crew Classic,** held on Mission Bay the first weekend in April (© 619/225-0300). The Crew Classic rowing competition draws teams from throughout the United States and Canada. The **Wooden Boat Festival** is held on Shelter Island every June over Father's Day weekend (© 619/222-9051). Approximately 90 boats participate in the festival, which features nautical displays, food, music, and crafts.

FISHING TOURNAMENTS

Enthusiasts will want to attend the **Day at the Docks** event, held at the San Diego Sportfishing Landing, at Harbor Drive and Scott Street, in Point Loma, every April. For more details, see the "San Diego Calendar of Events" on p. 13; for more information, call © 619/234-8793.

FOOTBALL

It's very possible that 2007 could be the last season San Diego's professional football team, the **Chargers,** play here. As of January 1, the franchise is free to shop around for another city. The team has tried to generate interest (and lots of city funding) for an audacious plan to create a huge urban village around a new stadium in Mission Valley. Thus far, investors and the general population aren't biting. With San Diego on the verge of bankruptcy (see "What's New in San Diego," p. 1), it's unlikely the city will commit to a sweetheart deal like that which the Padres received for their downtown stadium. For now, the **Chargers** (© 877/242-7437; www.chargers.com) play at **Qualcomm Stadium** ("The Q"), 9449 Friars Rd., Mission Valley. The season runs from August to December. The Chargers Express bus (© 619/685-4900 for information) costs $5 round-trip and picks up passengers at several locations throughout the city, beginning 2 hours before the game; the stadium is also easily reached via the San Diego Trolley.

San Diego also hosts two college bowl games, both held in December at Qualcomm Stadium. The **Holiday Bowl** (© 619/283-5808; www.holidaybowl.com) pits the Western Athletic Conference champion against a team from the Big 10; while a Mountain West Conference squad and an at-large opponent face off in the fledgling **Poinsettia Bowl** (© 619/285-5061; www.poinsettiabowl.net).

GOLF

San Diego is the site of some of the country's most important golf tournaments, including the **Buick Invitational,** which takes place in February at Torrey Pines Golf Course in La Jolla (© 800/888-2842 or 619/281-4653; www.buickinvitational.com), and the **Accenture Match Play Championship** put on by World Golf Championships and held at La Costa, also in February (© 800/918-4653; www.world golfchampionships.com). Now you know why February is celebrated as Golf Month by the Convention and Visitors Bureau. The **U.S. Open** will be held at Torrey Pines in 2008.

HORSE RACING & SHOWS

Live thoroughbred racing takes place at the **Del Mar Racetrack** (© 858/755-1141 for information and racing schedules; www.delmarracing.com) from late July to mid-September. Post time for the nine-race program is 2pm (except for Fri, when it's 4pm; 3:30pm on the final 3 Fridays); there's no racing on Tuesdays. Admission to the club-house is $8, including program; stretch run seating is $5 with program and includes infield access; and reserved seats are $5–$10. The infield area has a jungle gym where kids can play or watch exhibition shows put on by BMX riders and skateboarders. "Four O'Clock Fridays" is designed to lure a party crowd, with a 4pm post time and big-name rock bands at 7pm.

The **Del Mar National Horse Show** takes place at the Del Mar Fairgrounds from late April to early May. Olympic-caliber and national championship riders participate. For information, call © **858/792-4288** or 858/755-1161, or check www.sdfair.com.

ICE HOCKEY

The **San Diego Gulls** of the ECHL National Conference skate at the ipayOne Center at the Sports Arena from late October into March. For schedules, tickets, and information, call © **619/224-4625** or 619/224-4171, or visit www.sandiegogulls. com.

MARATHONS & TRIATHLONS

San Diego is a wonderful place to run or watch a marathon because the weather is usually mild. The **Carlsbad Marathon and Half Marathon** (© **760/692-2900**; www.sdmarathon.com) takes place in January. The course stretches mostly along the coastline, about 35 miles north of San Diego.

Drawing about 20,000 runners, the **Rock 'n' Roll Marathon** (© **800/311-1255**; www.rnrmarathon.com) is held in early June and features a route lined with rock bands, capped off by a headline act performing at a large venue.

Another popular event is the **La Jolla Half Marathon** (© **858/454-0777**; www.lajollahalfmarathon.com), held in late April. It begins at the Del Mar Fairgrounds and finishes at La Jolla Cove.

The **America's Finest City Half Marathon** (© **760/692-2900**; visit www.afchalf.com) is held in August every year. The race begins at Cabrillo National Monument, winds through downtown, and ends in Balboa Park.

The **San Diego International Triathlon** (© **858/268-1250** or check www.koz enterprises.com), held in late June, includes an international course comprised of a 1,000m swim, a 30km bike ride, and a 10km run, plus a shorter sprint course. A kids triathlon precedes the event by a week. It starts at Spanish Landing on San Diego Bay.

POLO

The public is invited to watch polo matches on Sundays from June to October at the **San Diego Polo Club,** 14555 El Camino Real, Rancho Santa Fe (© **858/481-9217**; www.sandiegopolo.com). Admission is $5.

TENNIS

San Diego plays host to several major tennis tournaments, notably the **Acura Tennis Classic,** held at the La Costa Resort and Spa in Carlsbad. The tournament is usually held between late July and early August. For information and tickets, call © **760/438-5683** or check www.acuraclassic.com.

8

City Strolls

Wandering a city's streets and parks gives you insights that are hard to come by any other way—and the exercise can't be beat, especially under the warm (but usually not unbearably hot) Southern California sun. From the history-heavy Gaslamp Quarter to thriving Balboa Park, San Diego easily lends itself to the long, leisurely stroll. The four walking tours in this chapter will give you a special sense of the city, as well as a look at some of its most unique and appealing sights and structures.

WALKING TOUR 1   THE GASLAMP QUARTER

Start:	Fourth Avenue and E Street, at Horton Plaza.
Finish:	Fourth Avenue and F Street.
Time:	Approximately 1½ hours, not including shopping and dining.
Best Times:	During the day.
Worst Times:	Evenings, when the area's popular restaurants and nightspots attract big crowds.

A National Historic District covering 16½ city blocks, the Gaslamp Quarter contains many Victorian-style commercial buildings built between the Civil War and World War I. The quarter—set off by electric versions of old gas lamps—lies between Fourth Avenue to the west, Sixth Avenue to the east, Broadway to the north, and L Street and the waterfront to the south. The blocks are not large; developer Alonzo Horton knew corner lots were desirable to buyers, so he created more of them. This tour hits some highlights of buildings along Fourth and Fifth avenues. If it whets your appetite for more, the **Gaslamp Quarter Historic Foundation,** 410 Island Ave. (© **619/233-4692;** www.gaslampquarter.org), offers walking tours every Saturday at 11am ($10, including museum admission, or $8 for seniors, students, and military). The book *San Diego's Historic Gaslamp Quarter: Then and Now,* by Susan H. Carrico and Kathleen Flanagan, makes an excellent, lightweight walking companion. It has photos, illustrations, and a map.

The tour begins at:

❶ Horton Plaza

It's a colorful conglomeration of shops, eateries, and architecture—and a tourist attraction. Ernest W. Hahn, who planned and implemented the redevelopment and revitalization of downtown San Diego, built the plaza in 1985. This core project, which covers 11½ acres and 6½ blocks in the heart of downtown, represents the successful integration of public and private funding.

The ground floor at Horton Plaza is home to the 1906 Jessop Street Clock. The timepiece has 20 dials, 12 of which tell the time in places throughout the world. Designed by Joseph Jessop, Sr., and built primarily by Claude D. Ledger, the clock stood outside Jessop's Jewelry Store on Fifth Avenue from 1927 until being moved to Horton Plaza in 1985. In 1935, when Mr. Ledger died, the clock stopped; it was restarted, but it stopped again 3 days later—the day of his funeral.

Exit Horton Plaza on the north side, street level, near Macy's. At the corner of Fourth and Broadway is:

❷ **Horton Plaza Park**

Its centerpiece is a fountain designed by well-known local architect Irving Gill and modeled after the choragic monument of Lysicrates in Athens. Dedicated October 15, 1910, it was the first successful attempt to combine colored lights with flowing water. On the fountain's base are bronze medallions of Juan Rodríguez Cabrillo, Father Junípero Serra, and Alonzo Horton, three men who were important to San Diego's development.

Walk south along Fourth Avenue, to the:

❸ **Balboa Theatre**

Constructed in 1924, the Spanish Renaissance–style building, at the southwest corner of Fourth Avenue and E Street, has a distinctive tile dome, striking tile work in the entry, and two 20-foot-high ornamental waterfalls inside. In the past, the waterfalls ran at full power during intermission; however, when turned off, they would drip and irritate the audience. In the theater's heyday, plays and vaudeville took top billing. It's currently closed, awaiting renovation.

Cross Fourth Avenue and proceed along E Street to Fifth Avenue. The tall, striking building to your left at the northeast corner of Fifth and E is the:

❹ **Watts-Robinson Building**

Built in 1913, this was one of San Diego's first skyscrapers. It once housed 70 jewelers and is now a boutique hotel (see the review for Gaslamp Plaza Suites on p. 74). Take a minute to look inside at the marble

wainscoting, tile floors, ornate ceiling, and brass ornamentation.

Return to the southwest corner of Fifth Avenue and E Street. On the opposite side of the street, at 837 Fifth Ave., is the unmistakable "grand old lady of the Gaslamp," the twin-towered baroque revival:

❺ **Louis Bank of Commerce**

You can admire the next few buildings from the west side of the street and then continue south from here. Built in 1888, this proud building was the first in San Diego made of granite. It once housed a 24-hour ice-cream parlor for which streetcars made unscheduled stops; an oyster bar frequented by Wyatt Earp; and, upstairs, the Golden Poppy Hotel, a brothel run by a fortuneteller, Madame Coara. After a fire in 1903, the original towers of the building, with eagles perched atop them, were removed.

On the west side of Fifth Avenue, at no. 840, near E Street, you'll find the:

❻ **F. W. Woolworth Building**

Built in 1910, it housed San Diego Hardware since 1922. Sadly, despite all the residential construction in the neighborhood, the hardware store has vacated. It's unknown what's going in at this point, but if it's possible, take a peek inside this huge space, with its tin ceiling, wooden floors, and storefront windows.

Across the street, at 801 Fifth Ave., stands the two-story:

❼ **Marston Building**

This Italianate Victorian-style building dates from 1881 and housed humanitarian George W. Marston's department store for 15 years. In 1885, San Diego Federal Savings' first office was here, and the Prohibition Temperance Union held its meetings here in the late 1880s. After a fire in 1903, the building was remodeled extensively.

The redbrick, Romanesque revival on the northwest corner of Fifth Avenue and F Street is the:

Walking Tour 1: The Gaslamp Quarter

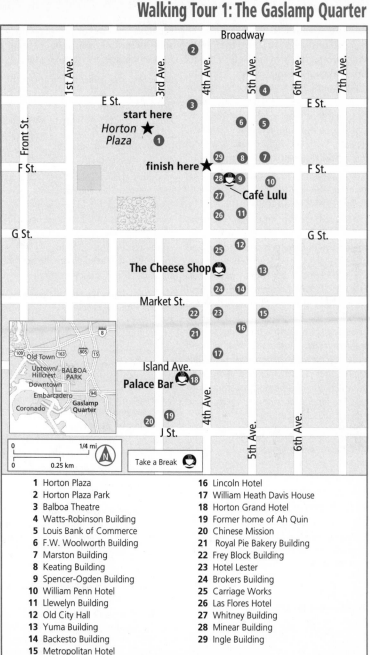

1 Horton Plaza	**16** Lincoln Hotel
2 Horton Plaza Park	**17** William Heath Davis House
3 Balboa Theatre	**18** Horton Grand Hotel
4 Watts-Robinson Building	**19** Former home of Ah Quin
5 Louis Bank of Commerce	**20** Chinese Mission
6 F.W. Woolworth Building	**21** Royal Pie Bakery Building
7 Marston Building	**22** Frey Block Building
8 Keating Building	**23** Hotel Lester
9 Spencer-Ogden Building	**24** Brokers Building
10 William Penn Hotel	**25** Carriage Works
11 Llewelyn Building	**26** Las Flores Hotel
12 Old City Hall	**27** Whitney Building
13 Yuma Building	**28** Minear Building
14 Backesto Building	**29** Ingle Building
15 Metropolitan Hotel	

⑧ Keating Building

A San Diego landmark dating from 1890, Mrs. Keating built it as a tribute to her late husband, George, whose name can still be seen in the top cornice. Originally heralded as one of the city's most prestigious office buildings, it featured conveniences such as steam heat and a wire-cage elevator. Note the architecturally distinctive rounded corner and windows.

Continuing south on Fifth Avenue, cross F Street and stand in front of the:

⑨ Spencer-Ogden Building

It's located on the southwest corner at 770 Fifth Ave. Built in 1874, it was purchased by business partners Spencer and Ogden in 1881 and has been owned by the same families ever since. *San Diego's Historic Gaslamp Quarter: Then and Now* notes that a number of druggists leased space in the building over the years, including the notorious one "who tried to make firecrackers on the second floor and ended up blowing away part of the building." Other tenants included realtors, an import business, a home-furnishing business, and dentists, one of whom called himself "Painless Parker."

Directly across the street stands the:

⑩ William Penn Hotel

Built in 1913, in the building's former life it was the elegant Oxford Hotel, and touted itself as "no rooming house but an up-to-the-minute, first-class, downtown hotel"; a double room with private bathroom and toilet cost $1.50. It reopened in 1992 as apartments—with substantially higher prices.

On the west side of the street, at 726 Fifth Ave., you'll find the:

⑪ Llewelyn Building

Built in 1887 by William Llewelyn, the family shoe store was here until 1906. Of architectural note are its arched windows, molding, and cornices. Over the years, it has been home to hotels of various names with unsavory reputations. Today the Llewelyn houses a colorful hostel.

On the southwest corner of Fifth Avenue and G Street is the:

⑫ Old City Hall

Dating from 1874, when it was a bank, this Florentine Italianate building features 16-foot ceilings, 12-foot windows framed with brick arches, antique columns, and a wrought-iron cage elevator. Notice that the windows on each floor are different. (The top two stories were added in 1887, when it became the city's public library.) The entire city government filled this building in 1900, with the police department on the first floor and the council chambers on the fourth.

Across the street in the middle of the block, at 631–633 Fifth Ave., is the:

⑬ Yuma Building

The striking edifice was built in 1882—it later expanded upward two floors to feature inviting bay windows. It was one of the first brick buildings downtown.

Continue down Fifth Avenue toward Market Street, and you'll notice the three-story:

⑭ Backesto Building

Built in 1873, this classical revival and Victorian-style building fills most of the block. Originally a one-story structure on the corner, it expanded to its present size and height over its first 15 years.

At the turn of the last century, this part of the Gaslamp was known as the Stingaree, the city's notorious red-light district. Gambling, opium dens, and wild saloons were also part of the mix.

Across Market Street, on the east side of the street, is the former:

⑮ Metropolitan Hotel

The building had bay windows when it was built in 1886. To the casual observer, it looks decidedly contemporary—until you spot the rugged 19th-century columns still visible on the street level. The Metropolitan also features arrestingly realistic *trompe l'oeil* effects painted on the facade by artists Nonni McKinnoon and Kitty Anderson. Today the Metropolitan is another of San Diego's well-located hostels.

In the middle of the block, at 536 Fifth Ave., is the small but distinctive:

🄯 Lincoln Hotel

It dates from 1913—the date cast in a grand concrete pediment two stories up. An equally grand stone lion's head once reigned atop the parapet, but tumbled to the street during an earthquake in 1986 and was quickly snatched by a passerby. The building's unusual green-and-white ceramic tile facade is thankfully intact.

Proceed to Island Avenue and turn right. The saltbox house at the corner of Fourth Avenue is the:

🄯 William Heath Davis House

Downtown's oldest surviving structure, this 157-year-old New England prefabricated lumber home was shipped to San Diego around Cape Horn in 1850. Alonzo Horton lived in the house in 1867, at its original location at the corner of Market and State (near where the *Star of India* is now docked). It was relocated to this site in 1984, completely refurbished, and the first floor and the small park next to it are open to the public. The Gaslamp Quarter Historical Foundation has its headquarters on the second floor. The house is open for guided tours Tuesday through Sunday from 11am to 3pm.

At the southwest corner of Island and Fourth avenues you'll see the bay windows of a building that's sure to steal your heart, the:

🄯 Horton Grand Hotel

Two 1886 hotels were moved here—very gently—from other sites, and then renovated and connected by an atrium; the original Horton Grand is to your left, the Brooklyn Hotel to your right. Now it's all one: the Horton Grand Hotel. The life-size papier-mâché horse (Sunshine), in the sitting area near reception, stood in front of the Brooklyn Hotel when it was a saddlery—Wyatt Earp lived here for most of his 7 years in San Diego. The reception desk is a recycled pew from a choir loft, and old post-office boxes now hold guests' keys. In the Palace Bar, look for the portrait of Ida Bailey, a local madam whose establishment, the Canary Cottage, once stood on this spot.

> ### TAKE A BREAK
> The **Cheese Shop**, 627 Fourth Ave. (📞 619/232-2303), is open for breakfast or lunch with home-made corned beef hash, fresh soups, and tasty pork sandwiches. The tables are topped with acrylic, encasing old packaging (candies, and so on) now frozen in time. After 4pm, try the **Palace Bar** (📞 619/544-1886) in the Horton Grand Hotel, another good place to relax. The bar is part of the same choir-loft pew that has been turned into the reception desk.

Around the corner from the Horton Grand, at 433 Third Ave., stands the:

🄯 Former home of Ah Quin

One of the first Chinese merchants of San Diego, Ah Quin arrived in 1879 at the age of 27 and became known as the "Mayor of Chinatown" (an area bound by Market and J sts., and Third and Fifth aves.). Ah Quin helped hundreds of Chinese immigrants find work on the railroad and owned a successful general merchandise store on Fifth Avenue. He was a respected father (of 12 children), leader, and spokesperson for the city's Chinese population. When he died in 1914—after he was hit by a motorcycle—his wealth included farmland, a mine, and other real estate.

The Ah Quin home is not open to the public, but across the street is the:

⑳ Chinese Mission

Originally located on First Avenue, this charming brick building built in 1927 was a place where Chinese immigrants (primarily men) could learn English and find employment. Religious instruction and living quarters were also provided. The building was rescued from demolition and moved to its present location, where it now contains the San Diego Chinese Historical Museum (p. 155). There's a gift shop with Chinese wares, a small Asian garden with a gate memorializing Dr. Sun Yat-sen, and a statue of Confucius. Admission is $2.

When you leave the museum, retrace your steps back to Fourth and Island and walk north; in the middle of the block on the west side you will come to the:

㉑ Royal Pie Bakery Building

Erected in 1911, this building was a bakery for most of its existence. Something else was cooking upstairs, though—the second floor housed the Anchor Hotel, which was eventually closed because of "rampant immorality."

At the southwest corner of Fourth Avenue and Market Street stands the:

㉒ Frey Block Building

Built in 1911, this was first a secondhand store, then a home for Chinese restaurants. But real fame arrived in the 1950s when it became the Crossroads, one of San Diego's most important jazz clubs. It was a venue for local and touring African-American artists.

Across the street on the southeast corner, at 401–417 Market St., is the:

㉓ Hotel Lester

This hotel dates from 1906. It housed a saloon, pool hall, and hotel of ill repute when this was a red-light district. It's still a hotel (cheap but not tawdry); while Café Bassam, a welcoming tearoom and espresso bar, and the cheerfully informal Wyatt Earp Museum operate at street level.

On the northeast corner of Fourth Avenue and Market Street, at 402 Market St., stands the:

㉔ Brokers Building

Constructed in 1889, this building has 16-foot wood-beam ceilings and cast-iron columns. Recently, it was converted to artists' lofts, with the ground floor dedicated to the downtown branch of the Hooters chain.

At the north end of this block, you will find the:

㉕ Carriage Works

Established in 1890, it once served as storage for wagons and carriages. It now houses restaurants and clubs catering to the Gaslamp Quarter's bohemian residents and those looking for energetic nightlife.

Cross G Street and walk to the middle of the block to the:

㉖ Las Flores Hotel

The gray building with blue-and-red trim at 725–733 Fourth Ave. was built in 1912, financed by Roscoe Hazard, who bought the property for an unbelievable $10 (plus an agreement to take on the seller's mortgage). With business deals like that, it's no wonder the Hazard name is still very much a part of the city. The Roscoe Hazard Bridge crosses I-805, there's a statue of Roscoe in the Mission Valley shopping center that bears his family name, and the construction company he founded is still a major player here.

Next door, at 739–745 Fourth Ave., is the:

㉗ Whitney Building

Dating from 1906, it has striking arched windows on the second floor. The inside was once used as a union meeting hall. While you're studying details, take a look at the trim on the top of the:

㉘ Minear Building

Built in 1910, it's located at the end of the block, on the southeast corner of Fourth Avenue and F Street.

Across the street is the:

㉙ Ingle Building

It dates from 1907 and now holds the Hard Rock Cafe. The mural on the F Street side of the building depicts a group of deceased rock stars (including Hendrix, Joplin, and Elvis, of course) lounging at sidewalk tables. Original stained-glass windows from the original Golden Lion Tavern (1907–32) front Fourth Avenue. Inside, the restaurant's stained-glass ceiling was taken from the Elks Club in

Stockton, California, and much of the floor is original.

WINDING DOWN
Walk to **Café Lulu,** 419 F St. (✆ 619/238-0114), near Fourth Avenue, for casual coffeehouse fare; or try **Horton Plaza,** where you can choose from many kinds of cuisine, from California to Chinese, along with good old American fast food.

WALKING TOUR 2 — THE EMBARCADERO

Start:	The Maritime Museum, at Harbor Drive and Ash Street.
Finish:	The Convention Center, at Harbor Drive and Fifth Avenue.
Time:	1½ hours, not including museum and shopping stops.
Best Times:	Weekday mornings (when it's less crowded and easier to park).
Worst Times:	Weekends, especially in the afternoon, when the Maritime Museum and Seaport Village are crowded; also when cruise ships are in port (days vary).

San Diego's colorful Embarcadero, or waterfront, cradles a bevy of seagoing vessels—frigates, ferries, yachts, cruise ships, a merchant vessel, an aircraft carrier, and even a Soviet submarine. You'll also find equally colorful Seaport Village, a shopping and dining center with a nautical theme.

Start at the:

❶ Maritime Museum

It's located at Harbor Drive at Ash Street (see the review on p. 154). Making up part of the floating museum is the magnificent *Star of India,* the world's oldest merchant ship still afloat, built in 1863 as the *Euterpe.* The ship, whose billowing sails are a familiar sight along Harbor Drive, once carried cargo to India and immigrants to New Zealand, and it braved the Arctic ice in Alaska to work in the salmon industry. Another component of the museum is the 1898 ferry *Berkeley,* built to operate between San Francisco and Oakland. In service through 1958, it carried survivors to safety 24 hours a day for 4 days after the 1906 San Francisco earthquake. You can also check out the HMS *Surprise,* which had a star turn in

the film *Master and Commander: The Far Side of the World;* a Soviet-era B-39 attack submarine; the *Californian,* a replica of a 19th-century revenue cutter; *Medea,* a 1904 steam yacht; and *Pilot,* which served as San Diego Bay's official pilot boat for 82 years.

From this vantage point, you get a fine view of the:

❷ County Administration Center

This place was built in 1936 with funds from the Works Progress Administration, and was dedicated in 1938 by President Franklin D. Roosevelt. The 23-foot-high granite sculpture in front, *Guardian of Water,* was completed by Donal Hord—San Diego's most notable sculptor—in 1939. It represents a stoic woman shouldering a water jug. The building is even more impressive from the other side because of the carefully tended gardens; it's well worth the effort and extra few minutes to walk around to Pacific Highway for a look. On weekdays, the building is open from 8am to 5pm; there are restrooms and a cafeteria inside.

> **TAKE A BREAK**
> The cafeteria on the fourth floor of the **County Administration Center** (℡ 619/515-4258) has lovely harbor views; it's open weekdays until 3:35pm and entrees are priced around $5. If you can't pass up the chance to have some seafood, return to the waterfront to **Anthony's Fishette** (℡ 619/232-5105), the simplest entity in the Anthony's clan of seafood houses, which serves fish-and-chips, shrimp, and other snacks alfresco. Next door is the **Star of the Sea** restaurant (℡ 619/232-7408), one of the city's finest seafood restaurants; it's open for dinner only.

Continue south along the Embarcadero. The large carnival-colored building on your right is the:

❸ San Diego Cruise Ship Terminal

Located on the B Street Pier, it has a large nautical clock at the entrance. Totally renovated in 1985, the flag-decorated terminal's interior is light and airy. Inside, you'll also find a snack bar and gift shop.

Farther along is the location for the:

❹ Harbor Cruises

They depart from sunup to sundown on tours of San Diego's harbor; ticket booths are right on the water. See "Organized Tours" in chapter 7 for more details.

A little farther south, near the Broadway Pier, is the:

❺ Coronado Ferry

It makes hourly trips between San Diego and Coronado. Buy tickets from the Harbor Excursion booth—you can make the round-trip in about 50 minutes. See "By Ferry" within the "Getting Around" section in chapter 4 for more information.

To your left as you look up Broadway, you'll see the two gold mission-style towers of the:

❻ Santa Fe Depot

This mosaic-draped railroad station was built in 1915, and provides one of the city's best examples of Spanish Colonial Revival style. It's only 1½ blocks away, so walk over and look inside at the vaulted ceiling, wooden benches, and walls covered in striking green-and-gold tiles. A scale model of the aircraft carrier USS *Midway* is on display inside. At the north end of the station, what was once the baggage building, is now the Museum of Contemporary Art San Diego's dynamic new space (p. 154).

Continuing south on Harbor Drive, you'll stroll through a small tree- and bench-lined park and suddenly encounter the:

❼ USS *Midway*

This aircraft carrier had a 47-year military history that started 1 week after the Japanese surrender of WWII in 1945. By the time the *Midway* was decommissioned in 1991, more than 225,000 men had served aboard. The carrier is now a naval museum, telling the story of life onboard the ship, of the wars she fought, and of the records she set (*Midway* was tasked with setting new standards throughout much of her career). For more information, see p. 154.

South of the *Midway*, at Pier 11, is the:

❽ U.S. Air Carrier Memorial

Erected in 1993, this compact black granite obelisk honors the nation's carriers and crews. It stands on the site of the old Navy fleet landing, where thousands of servicemen boarded ships over the years.

Continue along the walkway to:

❾ Tuna Harbor

This is where the commercial fishing boats congregate. San Diego's tuna fleet, with about 100 boats, was once the world's largest.

Walking Tour 2: The Embarcadero

start here

1 Maritime Museum
2 County Administration Center
3 San Diego Cruise Ship Terminal
4 Harbor cruises
5 Coronado Ferry
6 Santa Fe Depot
7 USS *Midway*
8 U.S. Air Carrier Memorial
9 Tuna Harbor
10 Seaport Village
11 Manchester Grand Hyatt
12 Marriott San Diego Hotel & Marina
13 Convention Center

Beech St.
Ash St.
A St.
B St.
C St.
Broadway
E St.
G St.
Market St.

Harbor Dr.
Pacific Highway
India St.
Kettner Blvd.

B Street Pier
Broadway Pier
Navy Pier
G Street Pier
Tuna Lane
G St.

International Visitor Information Center

PANTOJA PARK

San Diego Bay

To 11 12 13 →
finish here→

EMBARCADERO MARINA PARK

Old Town
Uptown/Hillcrest
Downtown
Embarcadero
Coronado
BALBOA PARK
Gaslamp Quarter

Information *i*
Take a Break
Trolley Line

0   2 mi
0   2 km

TAKE A BREAK
The red building on the peninsula to your right houses the **Fish Market** (© 619/232-3474), a market and casual restaurant, and its upscale counterpart, **Top of the Market** (© 619/234-4867), just upstairs. You can be assured that a meal here is fresh off the boat. Both serve lunch and dinner, and the Fish Market has a children's menu and an oyster and sushi bar. It's acceptable to drop in just for a drink and to savor the mighty view. Prices are moderate downstairs, expensive upstairs. For dessert or coffee, go inside Seaport Village to **Upstart Crow** (© 619/232-4855), a bookstore and coffeehouse, and sip cappuccino in the company of your favorite authors.

Keep walking south, where you can meander along the winding pathways of:

⑩ Seaport Village

This outdoor area contains a myriad of shops and restaurants. The carousel is pure nostalgia. Charles Looff of Coney Island carved the animals out of poplar in 1895. Kids love to spin on this classic ride. As you stroll, you will no doubt notice the official symbol of Seaport Village. The 45-foot-high detailed replica of the famous Mukilteo Lighthouse of Everett, Washington, towers above the other buildings.

From Seaport Village, continue your waterfront walk southeast to the:

⑪ Manchester Grand Hyatt, Marriott San Diego Hotel & Marina

Adjacent to Embarcadero Marina Park, which is well used by San Diegans for

strolling and jogging, these four towers contain the city's two big convention hotels. The waterfront provides a view of the San Diego–Coronado Bay Bridge. A concession at the marina office rents boats by the hour at reasonable rates and arranges diving, water-skiing, and fishing outings.

The waterfront walkway continues to the:

⑫ Convention Center

This building is another striking piece of architecture hugging the city's waterfront. When it was first completed in late 1989, its presence on the waterfront was a major factor in the revitalization of downtown San Diego. It was later enlarged to an even more imposing size, to less acclaim.

To access the Gaslamp Quarter or San Diego Trolley, you'll need to head back to Seaport Village or cut through the lobbies of the Hyatt or Marriott hotels.

WINDING DOWN
The Marriott's waterfront bar, the **Yacht Club** (© 619/230-8910), looks out onto the marina and the bay beyond. It's a choice spot for watching the harbor at dusk. You can get drinks, appetizers, and light fare here. Alternatively, the eastern tower of the Manchester Grand Hyatt has **Top of the Hyatt** (© 619/232-1234), a 40th-floor lounge with sweeping views of the city and harbor. It opens at 3pm daily and is a great spot for a sunset martini.

WALKING TOUR 3   OLD TOWN

Start:	The McCoy House, overlooking the San Diego Trolley's Old Town station.
Finish:	Heritage Park.
Time:	2 hours, not including shopping or dining.
Best Times:	Weekends (except the first one in May—Cinco de Mayo). There are daily 1-hour free tours at 11am and 2pm, so you'll either want to plan to avoid or join those.
Worst Times:	Weekdays, when numerous school groups are touring (although it's fun to watch on-site education in action). On Cinco de Mayo weekend, the first weekend in May, Old Town is a madhouse (the holiday celebrates Mexico's defeat of the French on May 5, 1862, in the Battle of Puebla).

Old Town is the Williamsburg of the West. When you visit, you go back to a time of one-room schoolhouses and village greens, when many of the people who lived, worked, and played here spoke Spanish. Even today, life moves more slowly in this part of the city, where the buildings are old or built to look that way. The stillness inside the state park is palpable, especially at night, when you can stroll along the unpaved streets and look up at the stars. You don't have to look hard or very far to see yesterday.

Begin at the McCoy House, at the northwestern end of this historic district, which preserves the essence of the small Mexican and fledgling American communities that existed here from 1821 to 1872. The core of Old Town State Historic Park is a 6-block area with no vehicular traffic and a few businesses.

The headquarters are near the intersection of Wallace and Calhoun, the location of the:

❶ McCoy House

This interpretive center and main entry-way is a historically accurate replication of the home of James McCoy, San Diego's larger-than-life lawman/legislator who lived on this site until the devastating fire of 1872. The house contains exhibits, artifacts, and visitor information.

After checking in here and getting your bearings, head to the neighboring:

❷ Robinson-Rose House

Built in 1853 as a family home, it also served as a newspaper and railroad office; now, it's the visitor center for the park. Here you'll see a large model of Old Town the way it looked prior to 1872, the year a large fire broke out (or was set). It destroyed much of the town and initiated the population exodus to New Town, now downtown San Diego. Old Town State Historic Park contains seven original buildings, including the Robinson-Rose House, and replicas of other buildings that once stood here.

From here, turn left and stroll into the colorful world of Mexican California called:

❸ Plaza del Pasado

Located at 2754 Calhoun St., this is where colorful shops and restaurants spill into a flower-filled courtyard. Costumed employees and weekend entertainment create an early California atmosphere, taking over what was once a 1930s motel (albeit one designed by acclaimed architect

Richard Requa). See p. 211 in chapter 9 for additional information.

> **TAKE A BREAK**
> This is a good opportunity to sample the Mexican food in and around Plaza del Pasado. In addition to **Casa Guadalajara** (located outside the plaza and reviewed on p. 117), there are several other restaurants in the immediate area—**Jolly Boy** (☎ 619/291-3200), **The Cosmopolitan Restaurant and Hotel** (☎ 619/209-3525), and **Casa de Reyes** (☎ 619/220-5040). All offer indoor and outdoor dining, a lively ambience, and steaming platters of enchiladas, burritos, and other familiar fare. The food, prices, and atmosphere are pretty comparable at all four; if the wait for a table is long at one, put your name on the list at another. The Cosmopolitan is in historic Casa de Bandini, completed in 1829. It was the home of Peruvian-born Juan Bandini, who became a Mexican citizen; in 1869, the building, with a second story added, became the original Cosmopolitan Hotel. The restaurants are open from 10 or 11am to 9 or 10pm (The Cosmopolitan and Casa de Reyes serve weekend breakfast), and Plaza del Pasado shops are open from 10am to 9pm, with sometimes shorter winter hours.

From Plaza del Pasado, stroll into the grassy plaza, where you'll see a:

❹ Large Rock Monument

This commemorates the first U.S. flag flown in Southern California (on July 29, 1846). In the plaza's center stands a flag-pole that resembles a ship's mast. There's a reason: The original flag hung from the mast of an abandoned ship.

Straight ahead, at the plaza's eastern edge, is:

⑤ La Casa de Estudillo

An original adobe building dating from 1827, the U-shaped house has covered walkways and an open central patio. The patio covering is made of corraza cane, the seeds for which were brought by Father Serra in 1769. The walls are 3 to 5 feet thick, holding up the heavy beams and tiles, and they work as terrific insulators against summer heat. In those days, the thicker the walls, the wealthier the family. The furnishings in the "upperclass" house are representative of the 19th century (don't overlook the beautiful four-poster beds); the original furniture came from the East Coast and from as far away as Asia. The Estudillo family, which then numbered 12, lived in the house until 1887; today family members still live in San Diego.

After you exit La Casa de Estudillo, turn left. In front of you is the reconstruction of the three-story:

⑥ Colorado House

Built in 1851, it was destroyed by fire in 1872—as were most buildings on this side of the park. Today it's the home of the Wells Fargo Historical Museum, but the original housed San Diego's first two-story hotel. The museum features an original Wells Fargo stagecoach, numerous displays of the overland-express business, and a video show. Next door to the Wells Fargo museum, and kitty-corner to La Casa de Estudillo, is the small, redbrick San Diego Court House & City Hall. (A reconstruction of the three-story Franklin House is planned to the right of the Colorado House.)

From here, continue along the pedestrian walkway 1 short block, turn right, and walk another short block to a reddish-brown building on your right. This is the one-room:

⑦ Mason Street School

An original building dating from 1865, this school was commissioned by Joshua Bean, uncle of the notorious "hanging judge" Roy Bean; Joshua Bean was also San Diego's first mayor. If you look inside, you'll notice the boards that make up the walls don't match; they were leftovers from the construction of San Diego homes. Mary Chase Walker, the first teacher, ventured here from the East when she was 38 years old. She enjoyed the larger salary but hated the fleas, mosquitoes, and truancy; after a year, she resigned to marry the president of the school board.

When you leave the schoolhouse, retrace your steps to the walkway (which is the extension of San Diego Ave.) and turn right. On your left, you'll see two buildings with brown shingle roofs. The first is the:

⑧ Pedrorena House

No. 2616 is an original Old Town house built in 1869, with stained glass over the doorway. The shop inside now sells fossils, minerals, and gems. The original owner, Miguel Pedrorena, also owned the house next door, which became the:

⑨ San Diego Union Printing Office

The newspaper was first published in 1868. This house arrived in Old Town after being prefabricated in Maine in 1851 and shipped around the Horn (it has a distinctly New England appearance). Inside you'll see the original handpress used to print the paper, which merged with the *San Diego Tribune* in 1992. The offices are now in Mission Valley, about 3 miles from here.

At the end of the pedestrian part of San Diego Avenue stands a railing; beyond it is Twiggs Street, dividing the historic park from the rest of Old Town, which is more commercial. In this part of town, you'll find shops, galleries, and restaurants.

Walking Tour 3: Old Town

1 McCoy House
2 Robinson-Rose House
3 Bazaar del Mundo
4 Large rock monument
5 La Casa de Estudillo
6 Colorado House
7 Mason Street School
8 Pedroreña House
9 San Diego Union Printing Office
10 Immaculate Conception Catholic Church
11 Whaley House
12 Heritage Park

At the corner of Twiggs Street and San Diego Avenue stands the Spanish mission–style:

⑩ Immaculate Conception Catholic Church

The cornerstone was laid in 1868, but with the movement of the community to New Town in 1872, it lost its parishioners and was not dedicated until 1919. Today the church serves about 300 families in the Old Town area. (Visitors sometimes see the little church and on a whim decide to get married here, but arrangements have to be made months in advance.)

Continue along San Diego Avenue 1 block to Harney Street. On your left is the restored:

⑪ Whaley House

The first two-story brick structure in Southern California, it was built from 1856 to 1857. The house is said to be haunted by several ghosts, including that of Yankee Jim Robinson, a convicted thief who was hanged on the site in 1852. The house is beautifully furnished with period pieces and features the life mask of Abraham Lincoln, the spinet piano used in the film *Gone with the Wind,* and the concert piano that accompanied Swedish soprano Jenny Lind on her final U.S. concert tour in 1852. The house's north room served as the county courthouse for a few years, and the courtroom looks now as it did then.

From the Whaley House, walk uphill 1½ blocks along Harney Street to a Victorian jewel called:

⑫ Heritage Park

The seven buildings in this grassy finger canyon were moved here from other parts of the city and are now used in a variety of ways. Among them are a winsome bed-and-breakfast inn (in the Queen Anne shingle-style Christian House, built in 1889), a doll shop, a teahouse, a lingerie store, and offices. Toward the bottom of the hill is the classic revival Temple Beth Israel, dating from 1889. On Sundays, local art is often exhibited in the park. If you've brought picnic supplies, enjoy them under the sheltering coral tree at the top of the park.

WINDING DOWN
At the end of your walk, wend your way back down Harney Street, and turn left at San Diego Avenue. Just ahead on the right, stop outside **Old Town Mexican Café**, 2489 San Diego Ave. (© **619/297-4330**), and watch corn and flour tortillas being hand-patted the old-fashioned way. Even if you thought you'd had your fill of Mexican food, this fresh spectacle—or the hungry looks from fellow patrons—might convince you to stop in for a refreshing margarita, *cerveza*, or fresh-squeezed lemonade along with a basket of warm tortillas and salsa.

WALKING TOUR 4 | BALBOA PARK

Start: Cabrillo Bridge, entry at Laurel Street and Sixth Avenue.

Finish: San Diego Zoo.

Time: 2½ hours, not including museum or zoo stops. If you get tired, hop on the free park tram.

Best Times: Anytime. If you want to get especially good photographs, come in the afternoon, when the sun lends a glow to the already photogenic buildings. Most museums are open until 4 or 5pm, and several are free every Tuesday.

Worst Times: More people (especially families) visit the park on weekends. But there is a festive, rather than overcrowded, spirit even then—particularly on Sunday afternoons, when you can catch a free organ concert at the outdoor Spreckels Organ Pavilion at 2pm.

Established in 1868, Balboa Park is the second oldest city park in the United States, after New York's Central Park. Much of its striking architecture was the product of the 1915–16 Panama-California Exposition and the 1935–36 California Pacific International Exposition. The structures now house a variety of museums and contribute to the overall beauty. But what makes Balboa Park truly unique is the extensive and mature botanical collection, thanks largely to Kate Sessions, a horticulturalist who devoted her life to transforming the desolate mesas and scrub-filled canyons (and other San Diego parks) into the oases they are today. Originally called "City Park," it was renamed in 1910 when Mrs. Harriet Phillips won a contest, naming it in honor of the Spanish explorer Balboa, who in 1513 was the first European to see the Pacific Ocean.

Take bus no. 1 or 3 along Fifth Avenue or bus no. 25 along Sixth Avenue to Laurel Street, which leads into Balboa Park through its most dramatic entrance, the:

❶ Cabrillo Bridge

It has striking views of downtown San Diego and straddles scenic, sycamore-lined Highway 163 (which John F. Kennedy

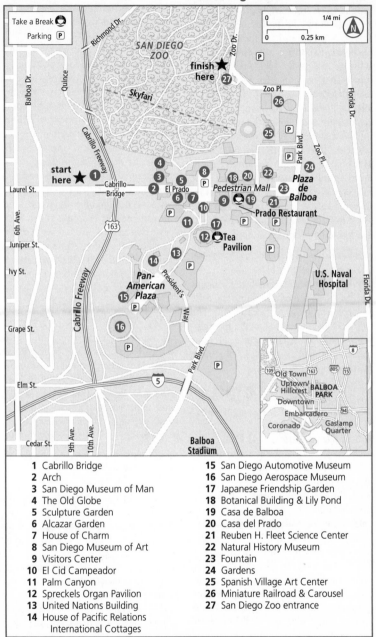

Take a Break ☕
Parking Ⓟ

San Diego Zoo

finish here ★ 27

Skyfari

start here ★ 1

Cabrillo Bridge

Laurel St.

El Prado 2

Pedestrian Mall

Prado Restaurant

Plaza de Balboa

Tea Pavilion

Pan-American Plaza

U.S. Naval Hospital

Balboa Stadium

Old Town
Uptown/Hillcrest BALBOA PARK
Downtown
Embarcadero
Coronado Gaslamp Quarter

1 Cabrillo Bridge	**15** San Diego Automotive Museum
2 Arch	**16** San Diego Aerospace Museum
3 San Diego Museum of Man	**17** Japanese Friendship Garden
4 The Old Globe	**18** Botanical Building & Lily Pond
5 Sculpture Garden	**19** Casa de Balboa
6 Alcazar Garden	**20** Casa del Prado
7 House of Charm	**21** Reuben H. Fleet Science Center
8 San Diego Museum of Art	**22** Natural History Museum
9 Visitors Center	**23** Fountain
10 El Cid Campeador	**24** Gardens
11 Palm Canyon	**25** Spanish Village Art Center
12 Spreckels Organ Pavilion	**26** Miniature Railroad & Carousel
13 United Nations Building	**27** San Diego Zoo entrance
14 House of Pacific Relations International Cottages	

proclaimed as "the most beautiful highway I've ever seen," during his 1963 visit to San Diego). Built in 1915 for the Panama-California Exposition and patterned after a bridge in Ronda, Spain, the dramatic cantilever-style bridge has seven pseudo-arches. As you cross the bridge, to your left you'll see the yellow cars of the zoo's aerial tram and, directly ahead, the distinctive California Tower of the Museum of Man. The delightful sounds of the 100-bell Symphonic Carillon can be heard every quarter-hour. Sitting atop this San Diego landmark is a weathervane shaped like the ship in which Cabrillo sailed to California in 1542. The city skyline lies to your right.

After you've crossed the bridge, go through the:

❷ Arch

The two figures represent the Atlantic and Pacific oceans and lead into the park, where you'll find a treasure of nature and culture. For now, just view the museums from the outside (you can read more about them, and all the park's museums, in chapter 7).

You have entered the park's major thoroughfare, El Prado—if you're driving a car, you'll want to find a parking space (the map on p. 201 shows all public lots) and go to the:

❸ San Diego Museum of Man

Architect Bertram Goodhue designed this structure, originally known as the California Building, in 1915—it now houses an anthropological museum. Goodhue, considered the world's foremost authority on Spanish-colonial architecture, was the master architect for the 1915–16 exposition. The exterior doubled as part of Kane's mansion in the 1941 Orson Welles classic *Citizen Kane;* historical figures carved on the facade include conquistador Juan Rodríguez Cabrillo, Spanish Kings Charles I and Phillip III, and, at the very top, Father Junípero Serra.

Just beyond and up the steps to the left is the nationally acclaimed:

❹ Old Globe Theatre

This is actually a three-theater complex that includes the Old Globe, an outdoor stage, and a small theater-in-the-round. The Old Globe was built for the 1935 exposition as a replica of Shakespeare's Globe Theatre. It was meant to be demolished after the exposition but was saved by a group of dedicated citizens. In 1978, an arsonist destroyed the theater, which was rebuilt into what you see today. It's California's oldest professional theater. If you have the opportunity to go inside, you can see the bronze bust of Shakespeare that miraculously survived the fire, battered but unbowed. The summer Shakespeare series is always popular. See p. 168 for additional information.

Beside the theater is the:

❺ Sculpture Garden of the Museum of Art

The San Diego Museum of Art Sculpture Garden features works by Joan Miró and Alexander Calder, as well as a signature piece, *Reclining Figure: Arch Leg,* by Henry Moore. *Reclining Figure* was damaged by a falling branch several years ago, but was seamlessly repaired and resumed its spot in the garden. Admission is free.

Across the street, to your right as you stroll along the Prado, is the:

❻ Alcazar Garden

It was designed in 1935 by Richard Requa and W. Allen Perry. They patterned it after the gardens surrounding the Alcazar Castle in Seville, Spain. The garden is formally laid out and trimmed with low clipped hedges; in the center walkway are two star-shaped yellow-and-blue tile fountains. The large tree at the rear is an Indian laurel fig, planted by Kate Sessions when the park was first landscaped.

Exit to your left at the opposite end of the garden, and you'll be back on El Prado. Proceed east to the corner; on your right is the:

❼ House of Charm

This is the site of the San Diego Art Institute Gallery and the Mingei International Museum of World Folk Art. The gallery is a nonprofit space that primarily exhibits works of local artists; the museum offers changing exhibitions that celebrate human creativity expressed in textiles, costumes, jewelry, toys, pottery, paintings, and sculpture.

To your left is the imposing:

❽ San Diego Museum of Art

This exquisite facade was patterned after the famous university in Salamanca, Spain. The 3 life-size figures over the scalloped entryway are the Spanish painters Bartolomé Murillo, Francisco de Zurbarán, and Diego Velázquez. The museum holds San Diego's most extensive collection of fine art, and major touring shows also swing through.

Across the street are the House of Hospitality and the park's:

❾ Visitors Center

Pick up maps, souvenirs, and discount tickets to the museums here. In the courtyard behind it, you'll find the beautiful *Woman of Tehuantepec* fountain sculpture by Donal Hord, as well as the attractive **Prado** restaurant (p. 206).

Head back toward the House of Charm, passing the statue of the mounted:

❿ El Cid Campeador

Created by Anna Hyatt Huntington and dedicated in 1930, this sculpture of the 11th-century Spanish hero was made from a mold of the original statue in the court of the Hispanic Society of America in New York. A third one is in Seville, Spain. A decidedly more modern alligator sculpture by Niki de Saint Phalle, a

French artist who made San Diego her home until her death in 2002, is found outside the entrance to the Mingei Museum—kids love climbing over the "Nikigator."

Continue to your left toward the ornamental outdoor Organ Pavilion. Before reaching the pavilion, the wooden bridge above the ravine on your right will take you into:

⓫ Palm Canyon

It's secluded, and probably should not be walked solo, but you can get a good sense of its beauty by venturing only a short distance along the path. Fifty species of palm, plus magnolia trees and a Moreton Bay fig tree, provide a tropical canopy.

From the top of Palm Canyon, continue to the ornate:

⓬ Spreckels Organ Pavilion

Donated to San Diego by brothers John D. and Adolph B. Spreckels, famed contralto Ernestine Schumann Heink sang at the December 31, 1914, dedication. A brass plaque honors her charity and patriotism. Free, lively recitals featuring the largest outdoor organ in the world (its vast structure contains 4,518 pipes) are given Sundays at 2pm, with additional concerts and events scheduled during summertime.

As you continue on, you'll see the Hall of Nations on your left, and beside it, the:

⓭ United Nations Building

This building also houses the United Nations International Gift Shop, a favorite for its diverse merchandise, much of it handmade around the world. You'll recognize the shop by the United States and United Nations flags out front. Check the bulletin board, or ask inside, for the park's calendar of events. If you need to rest, there's a pleasant spot with a few benches opposite the gift shop.

You will notice a cluster of small houses with red-tile roofs. They are the:

⑭ House of Pacific Relations International Cottages

These charming dollhouse cottages promote ethnic and cultural awareness and are open to the public on Sunday afternoons year-round. From March to October, there are lawn programs with folk dancing.

Take a quick peek into some of the cottages, and then keep heading south to see more of the park's museums; to your right, the notable:

⑮ San Diego Automotive Museum

Whether you're a gear-head into muscle cars or someone who appreciates the sculptural beauty of fine design, this museum has something for you. It features a changing roster of exhibits, as well as a permanent collection of fabulous wheels.

And the cylindrical:

⑯ San Diego Aerospace Museum

The museums in this part of the park operate in structures built for the 1935–36 Exposition. It is not necessary to walk all the way to the Aerospace Museum (located appropriately enough in the flight path of San Diego's airport), but it's one of San Diego's finest examples of Art Deco architecture. Across the parking lot on the left you'll also find the Hall of Champions Sports Museum, with another fun Niki de Saint Phalle sculpture in front.

Go back past the parking lot and the Organ Pavilion. Take a shortcut through the pavilion, exit directly opposite the stage, and follow the sidewalk to your right. Almost immediately, you'll come to the:

⑰ Japanese Friendship Garden

This 11½-acre canyon has been carefully developed to include traditional Japanese elements. At the entrance is an attractive teahouse whose deck overlooks the entire ravine, with a small meditation garden beside.

TAKE A BREAK
Now is your chance to have a bite to eat, sip a cool drink, and review the tourist literature you picked up at the Visitors Center. The **Tea Pavilion** ((C) **619/231-0048**) at the Japanese Friendship Garden serves fresh sushi, noodle soups, and Asian salads—it also carries quirky imported Japanese candies and beverages in addition to some familiar American snacks.

Return to El Prado, which is strictly a pedestrian mall to the east of the El Cid sculpture, and set your sights on the fountain at the end of the street and head toward it. Stroll down the middle of the street to get the full benefit of the lovely buildings on either side. On weekends, you'll probably pass street musicians, artists, and clowns—one of their favorite haunts is around the fountain.

The latticework building you see to the left is the:

⑱ Botanical Building & Lily Pond

An open-air conservatory, this delicate wood lath structure dates to the 1915–16 Exposition, and is filled with 2,100 permanent plants, plus seasonal displays. Particularly noteworthy is the collection of cycads and ferns. Admission is free, and the gardens are a cool retreat on a hot day. Immediately in front is the Lily Pond.

Back on El Prado, left of the Lily Pond, you'll see the:

⑲ Casa de Balboa

Inside, you'll find the Museum of Photographic Arts, the Model Railroad Museum, and the Museum of San Diego History, with engaging exhibits that interpret past events in the city and relate them to the present. Note the realistic-looking bare-breasted figures atop the Casa de Balboa. These shameless caryatids were the perfect complement to the nudist colony that temporarily sprouted in Zoro Garden—the canyon immediately east of the building—during the 1935–36 Exposition.

On the other side of El Prado, on your left, note the ornate work on the:

⑳ Casa del Prado

While it doesn't house a museum, it's one of the best—and most ornate—of the El Prado buildings, featuring baroque Spanish Golden Age ornamentation.

At the end of El Prado, on either side of the fountain, are two museums particularly popular with children; the first, on the right, is the:

㉑ Reuben H. Fleet Science Center

This science fun house has plenty of hands-on attractions, as well as a giant-screen IMAX theater. See p. 149 for a complete review of this popular attraction.

To the left is the:

㉒ Natural History Museum

Look for the sundial that's inscribed PRESENTED BY JOSEPH JESSOP; DECEMBER 1908; I STAND AMID YE SOMMERE FLOWERS TO TELL YE PASSAGE OF YE HOURES. This sundial, which is accurate to the second, was originally presented to the San Diego Public Library, and moved here in the mid-1950s when the library relocated. In 2006, the museum opened the largest exhibit in its 130-plus year history: *Fossil Mysteries*.

In the center of the Plaza de Balboa is the high-spouting:

㉓ Fountain

This seemingly ordinary installation, built in 1972, spouts 50 to 60 feet into the air. What makes it unique is a wind regulator on top of the Natural History Museum—as the wind increases, the fountain's water pressure is lowered so that the water doesn't spray over the edges. The fountain fascinates children, who giggle when it sprays them and marvel at the rainbows it creates. It's especially beautiful at night, when it's illuminated by colored lights.

From here, use the pedestrian bridge to cross the road and visit the nearly secret:

㉔ Gardens

They are tucked away on the other side of the boulevard: to your left, a Desert Garden for cacti and other plants at home in an arid landscape; to your right, the Inez Grant Parker Memorial Rose Gardens, home to 2,400 roses. The World Rose Society voted the latter as one of the top 16 rose gardens in the world—blooms peak March through May (but there are almost always some flowers visible, except in January and February when they are pruned). After you've enjoyed the flowers and plants, return to El Prado.

Just past the Natural History Museum, take a right. Behind the museum is another voluptuous Moreton Bay fig tree, planted in 1915 for the exposition; it's now more than 62 feet tall, with a canopy 100 feet in diameter.

Farther on is the sleepy:

㉕ Spanish Village Art Center

Artists are at work here daily from 11am to 4pm. They create jewelry, paintings, and sculptures in tile-roofed studios around a courtyard. There are restrooms here, too.

Exit at the back of the Spanish Village Art Center and take the paved, palm-lined sidewalk that will take you past the:

㉖ Miniature Railroad and Carousel

If members of the knee-high set are along on your tour, these treats are the perfect payoff for those on their best behavior. The tiny train makes a 3-minute loop through the eucalyptus trees, while the charming 1910 carousel offers a ride atop hand-carved wood frogs, horses, and pigs. The train and carousel are open daily in summer, weekends the rest of the year.

On the left is the entrance to the world-famous:

㉗ San Diego Zoo

You can also retrace your steps and visit some of the tempting museums you just passed, saving the zoo for another day.

Bus tip: From here, you can walk out to Park Boulevard through the zoo parking lot to the bus stop (a brown-shingled kiosk), on your right. The no. 7 bus will take you back to downtown San Diego.

WINDING DOWN

Back on El Prado (in the House of Hospitality), the **Prado Restaurant** (© 619/557-9441) has a handsome view of the park from oversize windows. Far from your average park concession, the Prado is run by the restaurant group responsible for some of San Diego's smartest eateries, and boasts a zesty menu with colorful ethnic influences—plus inventive margaritas and Latin cocktails. Lunch starts at 11:30am (Sat–Sun at 11am), and a festive (expensive) dinner menu takes over at 5pm (daily except Mon; reservations advisable). In between, a long list of tapas will satisfy any hunger pangs.

Shopping

Whether you're looking for a souvenir, a gift, or a quick replacement for an item inadvertently left at home, you'll find no shortage of stores in San Diego. This is, after all, Southern California, where looking good is a high priority and shopping in sunny outdoor malls is a way of life.

1 The Shopping Scene

Okay, so we've embraced the suburban shopping mall with vigor. Many San Diegans do the bulk of their shopping at two massive complexes in Mission Valley where every possible need is represented. Downtown has even adopted the mall concept at whimsical Horton Plaza, and historic Old Town features textiles with great flair and color from south-of-the-border lands.

Local neighborhoods, on the other hand, offer specialty shopping that meets the needs—and mirrors the personality—of that part of town. For example, modish Hillcrest is the place to go for offbeat boutiques, while conservative La Jolla offers many upscale traditional shops, especially jewelers. And don't forget that Mexico is only 20 minutes away; *tiendas* (stores) in Tijuana, Rosarito Beach, and Ensenada stock colorful crafts perfectly suited to the California lifestyle. Visitors head across the border each weekend in search of bargains and cheap margaritas.

If you want to dedicate a day to shopping but let someone else do the driving, **The Shopping Tour** offers a variety of full- and half-day tours, taking in San Diego malls, outlet malls, and destinations ranging from Palm Springs to Tijuana. Full-day tours range from $48 to $59; half-day tours are $25. For more information, call ℂ **877/ 868-7411** or go to www.theshoppingtour.com.

Shops tend to stay open late, particularly in malls like Horton Plaza and Fashion Valley, tourist destinations like Seaport Village, and areas like the Gaslamp Quarter and Hillcrest that see a lot of evening foot traffic. Places like these keep the welcome mat out until 9pm on weeknights and at least 6pm on weekends. Individual stores elsewhere generally close by 5 or 6pm.

Sales tax in San Diego is 7.75%, and savvy out-of-state shoppers have larger items shipped directly home at the point of purchase, avoiding the tax.

2 The Top Shopping Neighborhoods

DOWNTOWN, THE GASLAMP & LITTLE ITALY

Space is at a premium in the Gaslamp Quarter, and high rents have led to the influx of deep-pocketed chains and brand names, such as **Adidas,** 925 Fifth Ave. (ℂ **619/615-0287**), **Urban Outfitters,** 665 Fifth Ave. (ℂ **619/231-0102**), and **Quiksilver,** 402

Fifth Ave. (© **619/234-3125**). Fortunately, though, a few intrepid boutiques can still be found among the big retailers and the area's multitudinous eateries.

For hip and glamorous women's clothing and a great selection of jewelry, **Villa Moda,** 363 Fifth Ave. (© **619/236-9068**), is a Gaslamp standout. **Bubbles Boutique,** 226 Fifth Ave. (© **619/236-9003**), is where you'll find all manner of handmade soap products, from Mary Jane hemp and Adam & (st)Eve fig oil and brown-sugar soap bars to Almond Joy massage bars and banana shake–flavored bath "bombs."

You can spoil your little ones with some new threads from the children's store **Pout,** 701 Eighth Ave. (© **619/255-6506**), or pamper your pooch with something from **Lucky Dog Pet Boutique,** 557 Fourth Ave. (© **619/696-0364**), where you'll find supplies swank and chic: collars, snacks, soaps, bowls. **Kita Ceramics & Glassware,** 517 Fourth Ave. (© **619/231-9902**), stocks fine Japanese pottery and colorful Italian glass products. Although it can be found in many cities, **Design Within Reach,** 393 Seventh Ave. (© **619/744-9900**), is just too cool to pass by. DWR offers modern furniture and accessories from names like Knoll, Miller, and Eames.

You can continue your search for serious art, design, and home furnishings in Little Italy. The conglomeration of cool stores and galleries along Kettner Boulevard and India Street, from Laurel to Date streets, has become known as the **Art & Design District.** Throughout the year, TADD throws Friday evening open-house parties known as Kettner Nights; for information call © **619/546-5121** or go to www.taddsd.com. Among the district's highlights are **Vetro** (© **619/546-5120**) for vintage glass art, **Mixture** (© **619/239-4788**) for modern furniture and accessories, and **David Zapf Gallery** (© **619/232-5004**) and **Scott White Contemporary Art** (© **619/501-5689**), two of the city's most prominent galleries.

As the number of downtown condos multiplies, watch for shopping to diversify. Otherwise, browsing is primarily concentrated in two destination malls.

Horton Plaza ⚓   The Disneyland of shopping malls, Horton Plaza is the heart of the revitalized city center, bounded by Broadway, First and Fourth avenues, and G Street. Covering 6½ city blocks, the multilevel shopping center has more than 135 specialty shops, including art galleries, clothing and shoe stores, fun shops for kids, and a bookstore. There's a performing arts venue (the Lyceum Theatre, home to the San Diego Repertory Theatre, p. 223), a 14-screen cinema, two major department stores, and a variety of restaurants and short-order eateries. It's almost as much an attraction as SeaWorld or the San Diego Zoo, transcending its genre with a conglomeration of rambling paths, bridges, towers, piazzas, sculptures, fountains, and live greenery. Designed by the local Jerde Partnership and inspired by European shopping streets and districts like Athens's Plaka and London's Portobello Road, Horton Plaza opened in 1985 to rave reviews and provided an initial catalyst for the Gaslamp Quarter's redevelopment.

Anchor stores are Macy's and Nordstrom, while name outlets like Abercrombie & Fitch, Nine West, and Louis Vuitton are also in the mix. The top-level food court has a good variety of meal options. Parking is free with validation for the first 3 hours (4 hours at sit-down restaurants, the movie theater, and the Lyceum), $2 per 20 minutes thereafter. The parking levels are confusing, and temporarily losing your car is part of the Horton Plaza experience. The third floor of Macy's has a Visitor Information Center, open daily 10am to 6pm. 324 Horton Plaza. © **619/238-1596.** www.westfield.com/horton plaza. Bus: 2, 7, 9, 29, 34, or 35. Trolley: Civic Center.

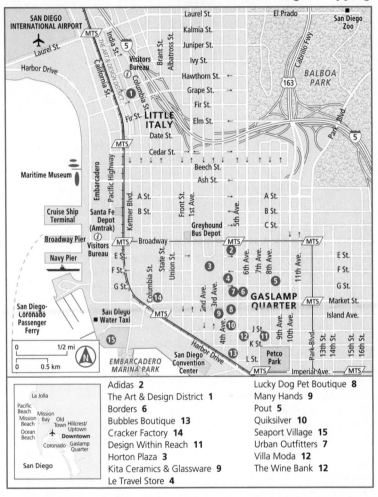

SAN DIEGO INTERNATIONAL AIRPORT

Laurel St.

Harbor Drive

THE ART & DESIGN DISTRICT

India St.
California St.
Columbia St.
Fir St.

5
Visitors Bureau

Laurel St.
Kalmia St.
Juniper St.
Ivy St.
Hawthorn St.
Grape St.
Fir St.
Elm St.
Date St.

Brant St.
Albatross St.

LITTLE ITALY

El Prado

San Diego Zoo

Cabrillo Fwy.

163

BALBOA PARK

Park Blvd.

5

Maritime Museum

Cruise Ship Terminal

Broadway Pier

Navy Pier

San Diego-Coronado Passenger Ferry

Embarcadero
Pacific Highway
Kettner Blvd.

Santa Fe Depot (Amtrak)

Visitors Bureau

Columbia St.
State St.
Union St.

Cedar St.
Beech St.
Ash St.

A St.
B St.

Front St.
1st Ave.

Greyhound Bus Depot

Broadway
E St.
F St.
G St.

2nd Ave.
3rd Ave.
4th Ave.

A St.
B St.
C St.

5th Ave.
6th Ave.
7th Ave.
8th Ave.

E St.
F St.
G St.

GASLAMP QUARTER

Market St.
Island Ave.

11th Ave.

San Diego Water Taxi

14

3
4
7 6
8
9
10
12 11
13

5
15

J St.
K St.
L St.

9th Ave.
10th Ave.

Petco Park

Park Blvd.
13th St.
14th St.
15th St.
16th St.

Harbor Drive

EMBARCADERO MARINA PARK

San Diego Convention Center

Imperial Ave.

0   1/2 mi
0   0.5 km

N

La Jolla

Pacific Beach
Mission Beach
Ocean Beach

Mission Bay

Old Town

Hillcrest/Uptown

Downtown

Coronado   Gaslamp Quarter

San Diego

Adidas **2**	Lucky Dog Pet Boutique **8**
The Art & Design District **1**	Many Hands **9**
Borders **6**	Pout **5**
Bubbles Boutique **13**	Quiksilver **10**
Cracker Factory **14**	Seaport Village **15**
Design Within Reach **11**	Urban Outfitters **7**
Horton Plaza **3**	Villa Moda **12**
Kita Ceramics & Glassware **9**	The Wine Bank **12**
Le Travel Store **4**	

Seaport Village *Kids*   Designed to resemble an ersatz Cape Cod community, this choice, 14-acre bayfront outdoor mall provides an idyllic setting that visitors love. Many of the 57 shops are of the Southern California cutesy variety, but the atmosphere is pleasant, and there are a few gems. Favorites include the **Tile Shop,** featuring hand-painted tiles from Mexico and beyond; the **San Diego City Store,** with all your local signage needs; **Island Hoppers,** for resort wear; and the **Upstart Crow** bookshop and coffeehouse, with the Crow's Nest children's bookstore inside—other stores specialize in Scandinavian items, hammocks, gifts for the left-handed, and more. There are four sit-down restaurants and a variety of sidewalk eateries, and live music is often scheduled for weekend afternoons. You get 2 hours of free parking with purchase ($3 per hour thereafter). Open daily September through May 10am to 9pm,

and daily June through August 10am to 10pm. 849 W. Harbor Dr. (at Kettner Blvd.).
℧ 619/235-4014. www.seaportvillage.com. Bus: 7. Trolley: Seaport Village.

HILLCREST & UPTOWN

Compact Hillcrest is an ideal shopping destination. As the hub of San Diego's gay and lesbian community, swank inspiration and chic housewares rule. There are plenty of establishments selling cool trinkets, used books, vintage clothing, and memorabilia, and of course, bakeries and cafes. You'll also find a panoply of modestly priced globe-hopping dining options, too.

There's no defined zone in which shops are found, so you may as well start at the neighborhood's axis, the busy intersection of University and Fifth avenues. From this corner the greatest concentration of boutiques spreads for 1 or 2 blocks in each direction, but farther east on University—between 10th Avenue and Vermont Street—you'll find another aggregation of good options, especially in the home furnishing category. **Pomegranate Home,** 1037 University Ave. (℧ **619/220-0225**), has got you covered for modern home accessories; **Co-Habitat,** 1433 University Ave. (℧ **619/688-1390**), has colorful decor and textiles from India; and **Metropolis Mall,** 1003 University Ave. (℧ **619/220-0632**), is an airy, stylish space where nearly 20 merchants feature a little of everything: furniture, clothing, fine linens, soaps and lotions, and jewelry from local designers. Next door is the fun **Ace Hardware,** 1007 University Ave. (℧ **619/291-5988**); across the street is a small shopping complex where the best bet is the little contemporary clothing store **Studio 1220,** 1220 Cleveland Ave. (℧ **619/220-7344**).

Street parking is available; most meters run 2 hours and devour quarters at a rate of one every 12 minutes, so be armed with plenty of change. You can also park in a lot—rates vary, but you'll come out ahead if you're planning to stroll for several hours.

If you're looking for postcards or provocative gifts, step into wacky **Babette Schwartz,** 421 University Ave. (℧ **619/220-7048**), a pop-culture emporium named for a local drag queen, and located under the can't-miss HILLCREST street sign. You'll find books, clothing, and accessories that follow current kitsch trends. A couple of doors away, **Cathedral,** 435 University Ave. (℧ **619/296-4046**), is dark and heady, filled with candles of all scents and shapes, plus unusual holders.

If all this walking is wearing a hole in your shoes, you can get a pair of urban-fabulous sneakers at **Mint,** 525 University Ave. (℧ **619/291-6468**). Headgear—from straw hats to knit caps to classy fedoras—fills the **Village Hat Shop,** 3821 Fourth Ave. (℧ **619/683-5533**), whose best feature may be its minimuseum of stylishly displayed vintage hats. Also on this street is **Plasticland,** 3940 Fourth Ave. (℧ **619/692-3291**), with edgy "fashion forward" clothing for women and juniors, including shoes, handbags, and accessories.

Lovers of rare and used books will want to poke around the **used bookstores** on Fifth Avenue, between University and Robinson avenues. Though their number has decreased with the advent of online shopping, you can always find something to pique your interest. This block is also home to **Shwoomp!,** 3827 Fifth Ave. (℧ **619/574-2535**), which looks like a deli but in fact provides "adventures in bathing" products like apricot-and-oat face masks, tomato-mint foot scrub, shea-butter products for dry-weather skin (all made in the on-premises kitchen), and, of course, yellow rubber duckies. A few doors down is **Wear It Again Sam,** 3823 Fifth Ave., north of Robinson (℧ **619/299-0185**). This classy step back in time sells quality vintage clothing—for both men and women—from the 1920s through the '50s.

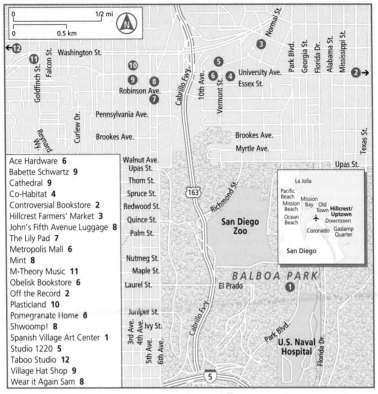

Ace Hardware **6**
Babette Schwartz **9**
Cathedral **9**
Co-Habitat **4**
Controversial Bookstore **2**
Hillcrest Farmers' Market **3**
John's Fifth Avenue Luggage **8**
The Lily Pad **7**
Metropolis Mall **6**
Mint **8**
M-Theory Music **11**
Obelisk Bookstore **6**
Off the Record **2**
Plasticland **10**
Pomegranate Home **6**
Shwoomp! **8**
Spanish Village Art Center **1**
Studio 1220 **5**
Taboo Studio **12**
Village Hat Shop **9**
Wear it Again Sam **8**

North of Hillcrest, running east from where Park Boulevard t-bones Adams Avenue, is **Adams Avenue Antique Row.** Antiques and collectible stores, vintage-clothing boutiques, and dusty used book and record stores dot the street, providing many hours of happy browsing and treasure hunting. It stretches a couple miles from Arizona Street to Normal Heights, so it's best tackled by car, but there are plenty of coffeehouses, pubs, and small restaurants to break up the excursion. For more information and an area brochure with a map, contact the **Adams Avenue Business Association** (© **619/282-7329;** www.gothere.com/adamsave).

OLD TOWN & MISSION VALLEY

Old Town Historic Park is a restoration of some of San Diego's historic sites and adobe structures, a number of which now house shops that cater to tourists. Many have a "general-store" theme and carry gourmet treats and inexpensive Mexican crafts alongside the obligatory T-shirts, baseball caps, and other San Diego–emblazoned souvenirs. **Plaza del Pasado,** 2754 Calhoun St. (© **619/297-3100;** www.plazadel pasado.com), maintains the park's old *Californio* theme and features 11 specialty shops, three restaurants, and a boutique hotel. Costumed employees, special events and activities, and strolling musicians add to the festive flavor.

Mission Valley is home to two giant malls (**Fashion Valley** and **Mission Valley**), with more than enough stores to satisfy any shopper, and free parking—both can be reached via San Diego Trolley from downtown. Book lovers will find local outposts of **Barnes & Noble,** 7610 Hazard Center Dr. (© **619/220-0175**), and **Borders,** 1072 Camino del Rio N. (© **619/295-2201**).

MISSION BAY & THE BEACHES

The beach communities offer laid-back shopping in typical California fashion, with plenty of surf shops, recreational gear, casual garb, and college-oriented music stores. If you're looking for something more distinctive than T-shirts and shorts, you'd best head east to Mission Valley.

For women in need of a new bikini, the best selection is at **Pilar's,** 3745 Mission Blvd., Pacific Beach (© **858/488-3056**), where choices range from stylish designer suits to hot trends like suits inspired by surf- and skate-wear. There's a smaller selection of one-piece suits, too. Across the street is **Liquid Foundation Surf Shop,** 3731 Mission Blvd. (© **858/488-3260**), which specializes in board shorts for guys. For affordable shoes, check out the **Skechers Footwear Outlet** at 4475 Mission Blvd. (© **800/678-5019**), at the corner of Garnet Avenue.

In Pacific Beach, **Pangea Outpost,** 909 Garnet Ave. (© **858/581-0555**), gathers 60 ethnically diverse shops under one roof; while San Diego's greatest concentration of antiques stores is found in the **Ocean Beach Antique District,** along the 4800 block of Newport Avenue, the community's main drag. Several of the stores are mall-style, featuring multiple dealers under one roof. The hundreds of individual sellers cover the gamut—everything from Asian antiquities to vintage watches to mid-20th-century collectibles. Although you won't find a horde of pricey, centuries-old European antiques, the overall quality is high enough to make it interesting for any collector. Highlights include **Newport Avenue Antiques,** 4836 Newport Ave. (© **619/224-1994**), which offers the most diversity: Its wares range from Native American crafts to Victorian furniture and delicate accessories, from Mighty Mouse collectibles to carved Asian furniture. **Ocean Beach Antique Mall,** 4847 Newport Ave. (© **619/223-6170**), has a more elegant setting and glass display cases filled with superb American art pottery and china. Names like Roseville, McCoy, and Royal Copenhagen abound, and there's a fine selection of quality majolica and Japanese tea sets. The 600-pound gorilla of the bunch is the **Newport Ave. Antique Center,** 4864 Newport Ave. (© **619/222-8686**), with 18,000 square feet of retail, and even a small espresso bar. One corner is a haven for collectors of 1940s and 1950s kitchenware (Fire King, Bauer, melamine); there's a fine selection of vintage linens and chinoiserie. This is also where you'll find Quakehold Gel, to hold your crystal in place in the event of a rumble (only in California, right?). Most of the O.B. antiques stores are open daily from 10am to 6pm, with somewhat reduced hours Sunday.

LA JOLLA

It's clear from the look of La Jolla's village that shopping is a major pastime in this upscale community. Precious gems and pearl necklaces sparkle in their cases, luxurious Persian rugs await your caress, crystal goblets prism the light—even if you're not in the market for any of it, it makes for great window shopping.

Women's clothing boutiques tend to be conservative and costly, like those lining Girard and Prospect streets (**Ann Taylor, Armani Exchange, Polo Ralph Lauren,**

La Jolla Shopping

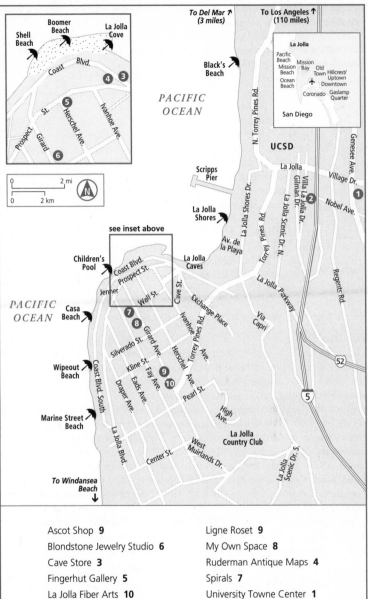

To Del Mar ↗ (3 miles)

To Los Angeles ↑ (110 miles)

Shell Beach

Boomer Beach

La Jolla Cove

Coast Blvd.

Prospect

Girard

St.

Herschel Ave.

Ivanhoe Ave.

PACIFIC OCEAN

Black's Beach

N. Torrey Pines Rd.

La Jolla
- Pacific Beach
- Mission Beach
- Ocean Beach
- Mission Bay
- Old Town
- Hillcrest/ Uptown
- Downtown
- Coronado
- Gaslamp Quarter

San Diego

UCSD

La Jolla

Villa La Jolla Dr.

Gilman Dr.

Village Dr.

Nobel Ave.

Genesee Ave.

0   2 mi
0   2 km
N

Scripps Pier

La Jolla Shores

La Jolla Shores Dr.

Torrey Pines Rd.

La Jolla Scenic Dr. N.

Regents Rd.

see inset above

Children's Pool

Coast Blvd.

Prospect St.

Jenner

Wall St.

La Jolla Caves

Av. de la Playa

La Jolla Parkway

Via Capri

PACIFIC OCEAN

Casa Beach

Cave St.

Exchange Place

Girard Ave.

Ivanhoe Ave.

Torrey Pines Ave.

Silverado St.

Kline St.

Eads Ave.

Fay Ave.

Herschel Ave.

Pearl St.

52

5

Wipeout Beach

Coast Blvd. South

Draper Ave.

Marine Street Beach

La Jolla Blvd.

Center St.

West Muirlands Dr.

High Ave.

La Jolla Country Club

La Jolla Scenic Dr. S.

To Windansea Beach ↓

Ascot Shop **9**

Blondstone Jewelry Studio **6**

Cave Store **3**

Fingerhut Gallery **5**

La Jolla Fiber Arts **10**

La Jolla Village Square **2**

Ligne Roset **9**

My Own Space **8**

Ruderman Antique Maps **4**

Spirals **7**

University Towne Center **1**

Warwick's Books **10**

Talbots, and **Sigi's Boutique**). But you'll also find less pricey venues like **Banana Republic** and **American Apparel.**

Recommended stores include **Blondstone Jewelry Studio,** 7925 Girard Ave. (© 858/456-1994), for creative, one-of-a-kind baubles; the venerable **Ascot Shop,** 7750 Girard Ave. (© 858/454-4222), for conservative men's apparel and accessories; and **La Jolla Fiber Arts,** 7644 Girard Ave. (© 858/454-6732), where hand-woven creations make the store something of an art gallery, as well as a fashion outlet. Other places worth noting are **My Own Space,** 7840 Girard Ave. (© 858/459-0099), where midcentury modernism meets Hello Kitty; **Ligne Roset,** 7726 Girard Ave. (© 858/454-3366), where minimalist furniture is on display in what was one of the last single-screen theaters in San Diego; and **Spirals,** 7906 Girard Ave. (© 858/551-8199), which has hand-painted ceramics and whimsical folk art. History buffs should not miss **Ruderman Antique Maps,** 1298 Prospect St., Suite 2C (© 858/551-8500), which sells maps, atlases, and books that date from the 15th through 19th centuries.

A unique experience awaits at the **Cave Store,** 1325 Coast Blvd., just off Prospect Street (© 858/459-0746). This clifftop shop is equal parts art gallery and antiques store, but the main attraction is the **Sunny Jim Cave,** a large and naturally occurring sea cave reached by a steep and narrow staircase through the rock (admission $4 for adults, $3 for kids 3–16, free for 2 and under). The **Crescent Café**—not much more than a coffee cart today—is a local institution that has stood on this site for decades. Black-and-white photo enlargements line the walls, depicting this quirky corner of La Jolla through the years, and making the store well worth a stop. The Coast Walk extends here along the coastline into a posh neighborhood.

CORONADO

This rather insular, conservative Navy community doesn't have a great many shopping opportunities; the best of the lot line Orange Avenue at the western end of the island. You'll find some scattered housewares and home-decor boutiques, several small women's boutiques, and the gift shops at Coronado's major resorts.

Coronado has an excellent independent bookshop, **Bay Books,** 1029 Orange Ave. (© 619/435-0070), which carries a selection in many categories, plus volumes of local historical interest, books on tape, and Mexican and European magazines. **La Provençale,** 1122 Orange Ave. (© 619/437-8881), is a little shop stocked with fabric, tablecloths, pottery, and tableware items from the French countryside; nearby **In Good Taste,** 1146 Orange Ave. (© 619/435-8356), has a small but choice selection of gourmet and food gift items—in addition to a tempting display of luscious truffles and sweets. And, if you're in pursuit of swimwear, poke your head into **Dale's Swim Shop,** 1150 Orange Ave. (© 619/435-7301), a tiny boutique jam-packed with suits to fit all bodies, including rare European makers seldom available in this country.

Ferry Landing Marketplace   Approached by ferry, the entrance is impressive— turreted red rooftops with jaunty blue flags that draw closer to you as the boat pulls in. As you stroll up the pier, you'll find yourself in the midst of about 20 souvenir and other shops filled with gifts, jewelry, and crafts. You can get a quick bite to eat or have a leisurely dinner with a view, wander along landscaped walkways, or laze on a beach or grassy bank. There's a farmers' market every Tuesday from 2:30 to 6pm. 1201 First St. (at B Ave.), Coronado. © 619/435-8895. Daily 10am–7pm or later. Bus: 901. Ferry: From Broadway Pier. Take I-5 to Coronado Bay Bridge, to B Ave., and turn right.

ELSEWHERE IN SAN DIEGO COUNTY

The **Cedros Design District** ⚓, along the 100 and 200 blocks of South Cedros Avenue in Solana Beach, is an outstanding place for designer interior decorating goods. Many of the shops are housed in a row of Quonset huts that were constructed for a company that made spy plane photographic equipment. Today, you can find more than two dozen chic shops selling furniture, original art, imported goods, home decor, antiques, and clothing, plus a couple good cafes. The strip is located just northwest of the Del Mar racetrack; reach it by taking the Via de la Valle exit off I-5 and going right on Cedros Avenue. The Coaster commuter train stops at the Solana Beach station next to the district.

Garden fanciers will find North County the best hunting grounds for bulbs, seeds, and starter cuttings. **North County nurseries** are known throughout the state for rare and hard-to-find plants—notably begonias, orchids, bromeliads, succulents, ranunculuses, and unusual herbs. For more information on the area's largest growers, **Flower Fields at Carlsbad Ranch** and **Weidners' Gardens,** turn to chapter 11.

3 Shopping A to Z

Large stores and shops in malls tend to stay open until about 9pm on weekdays, 6pm on weekends. Smaller businesses usually close at 5 or 6pm or may keep odd hours. When in doubt, call ahead.

ANTIQUES

See also the "Hillcrest & Uptown" and "Mission Bay & the Beaches" sections in "The Top Shopping Neighborhoods," earlier in this chapter.

The Cracker Factory Antiques Shopping Center   Prepare to spend some time here, exploring three floors of a dozen individually owned and operated shops filled with antiques and collectibles. It's across the street from the Manchester Grand Hyatt, a block north of Seaport Village. 448 W. Market St. (at Columbia St.). ℃ 619/233-1669. Daily 11am–5pm. Bus: 7. Trolley: Seaport Village.

ART & CRAFTS

While San Diego is not known as a powerhouse art city, you'll find more than 30 galleries in La Jolla village alone; downtown and Little Italy also offer a concentration of galleries.

Fingerhut Gallery   Fingerhut is a minichain offering fine-quality lithographs and etchings from masters like Picasso, Chagall, and Matisse. This branch, however, is notable for the "secret" art of La Jolla's own Dr. Seuss, whose whimsical-yet-provocative unpublished works explode with the same color and exuberance of illustrations from his famous books. 1205 Prospect St., La Jolla. ℃ 800/774-2278 or 858/456-9900. www.fingerhut art.com.

Four Winds Kiva Gallery   Located in the heart of Old Town, this shop has a beautiful bevy of authentic Native American crafts. Browse among pottery (including the sought-after Mata Ortiz), oil and watercolor paintings (originals and prints), and silversmith products (Zuni, Kumeyaay, Navajo, Isleta Pueblo), rugs, kachinas, and baskets. 2448 San Diego Ave., Old Town. ℃ 619/692-0466.

Many Hands   This cooperative gallery, in existence since 1972, has more than 25 members who engage in a variety of crafts, including making toys, jewelry, posters, pottery, baskets, and wearable art, much of it reasonably priced. A different artist is featured each month in Many Hands' Little Gallery. 302 Island Ave., Suite 101, Gaslamp Quarter. ℂ 619/557-8303. www.manyhandscraftgallery.com.

Spanish Village Art Center ✴   Another cooperative gallery, Spanish Village is a charming and historic collection of buildings and courtyards in Balboa Park dating to the 1935–36 California-Pacific Exposition. Today, 37 artists specialize in various mediums, including oil and watercolor painting, enamel, pottery, jewelry, metal art, origami, fused and blown glass, wood carving, and wearable art—many of the artists work on site, allowing you to see their products in the making. 1770 Village Place, Balboa Park. ℂ 619/233-9050. www.spanishvillageart.com.

Taboo Studio   This impressive shop exhibits and sells the work of jewelry designers from throughout the United States. The jewelry is made of silver, gold, platinum, and inlaid stones, in one-of-a-kind pieces, limited editions, or custom work. The gallery represents more than 65 artists. 1615½ W. Lewis St., Mission Hills. ℂ 619/692-0099. www.taboostudio.com.

BOOKS

For travel-related books, also note the shops listed under "Travel Accessories," below.

Barnes & Noble   The main San Diego branch of this book discounter sits amid one of Mission Valley's smaller malls, Hazard Center, just off Friar's Road (east of Highway 163). Besides a wide selection of paperback and hardcover titles, it offers a comprehensive periodicals rack. 7610 Hazard Center Dr., Mission Valley. ℂ 619/220-0175. Daily 10am–9pm.

Borders   This full-service book and CD store offers discounts on many titles. Borders also stocks a stylish line of greeting cards and encourages browsing; there's an adjoining coffee lounge. Of the two locations, the Mission Valley store is slightly larger. 668 Sixth Ave., Downtown; ℂ 619/702-4200. 1072 Camino del Rio N., Mission Valley; ℂ 619/295-2201. Hours for both locations: Mon–Thurs 9am–11pm; Fri–Sat 9am–midnight; Sun 10am–10pm.

Controversial Bookstore   San Diego's oldest metaphysical and spiritual bookstore started out in 1963, originally heavy on conspiracy and political tomes, as far right and far left as possible—hence the moniker. The store has evolved to embrace books on healing and alternative medicine, magic and witchcraft, astrology and UFO studies, women's issues, and spiritual pathways, plus crystals, New Age music, incense, and jewelry. 3021 University Ave., North Park. ℂ 619/296-1560. Mon–Fri 10am–7pm; Sat 10am–6pm; Sun 11am–5pm.

Obelisk Bookstore   San Diego's main gay and lesbian bookstore is where Clive Barker and Greg Louganis do their book signings. You'll find every gay magazine there is, as well as gay-themed movies for rent on DVD and video. 1029 University Ave., Hillcrest. ℂ 619/297-4171. Sun–Thurs 10am–10pm; Fri–Sat 10am–11pm.

Warwick's Books   This popular family-run bookstore is a browser's delight, with more than 40,000 titles, a large travel section, gifts, cards, and stationery. The well-read Warwick family has been in the book and stationery business since 1896. The La Jolla store was established in the mid-1930s, and the fourth generation is now involved with the store's day-to-day operation. Authors come in for readings about twice a week. 7812 Girard Ave., La Jolla. ℂ 858/454-0347. www.warwicks.com. Mon–Sat 9am–6pm; Sun 11am–5pm.

DEPARTMENT STORES

You'll find plenty of major retailers here in San Diego, in large shopping centers that provide ample opportunity to browse for gifts, mementos, or necessities.

Macy's   There are several branches of this comprehensive store, which carries clothing for women, men, and children, as well as housewares, electronics, and luggage. Macy's also has stores in the Fashion Valley (clothing only), Mission Valley Center (housewares only), University Towne Center, and North County Fair (Escondido) malls. Horton Plaza, Downtown. ℂ 619/231-4747. Mon, Wed, Thurs 10am–9pm; Fri, Tues 10am–10pm; Sat 9am–9pm; Sun 11am–7pm. Bus: 2, 7, 9, 29, 34, or 35.

Nordstrom   A San Diego favorite, Nordstrom is best known for its outstanding customer service and fine selection of shoes. It features a variety of stylish fashions and accessories for women, men, and children. Tailoring is done on the premises, and there's a full-service restaurant on the top floor. Nordstrom also has stores in the Fashion Valley, University Towne Center, and North County Fair (Escondido) malls, and there's an outlet store—Nordstrom Rack—in the Mission Valley Shopping Center. Horton Plaza, Downtown. ℂ 619/239-1700. Mon–Fri 10am–9pm; Sat 10am–8pm; Sun 11am–7pm. Bus: 2, 7, 9, 29, 34, or 35.

FARMERS' MARKETS

We love our open-air markets. Throughout the county no fewer than two dozen regularly scheduled street fests are stocked with the freshest fruits and vegetables from Southern California farms, augmented by crafts, fresh-cooked ethnic foods, flower stands, and other surprises. San Diego County produces more than $1 billion worth of fruits, flowers, and other crops each year. Avocados, known locally as "green gold," are the most profitable crop and have been grown here for more than 100 years. Citrus fruit follows close behind, and flowers are the area's third most important crop; ranunculus bulbs from here are sent all over the world, as are the famous Ecke poinsettias.

Here's a schedule of noteworthy farmers' markets in the area:

In **Hillcrest,** the market runs Sundays from 9am to 1pm at the corner of Normal Street and Lincoln Avenue, 1 block north of University Avenue. The atmosphere is festive, and exotic culinary delights reflect the eclectic neighborhood. For more information, call the **Hillcrest Association** at ℂ **619/299-3330.**

In **Ocean Beach,** a fun-filled market is held Wednesday evenings between 4 and 7pm (until 8pm in summer) in the 4900 block of Newport Avenue. In addition to fresh-cut flowers, produce, and exotic fruits and foods laid out for sampling, the market features art and entertainment. For more information, call the **Ocean Beach Business Improvement District** at ℂ **619/224-4906.**

Head to **Pacific Beach** on Saturday from 8am to noon, when Mission Boulevard between Reed Avenue and Pacific Beach Drive is transformed into a bustling marketplace.

In **Coronado,** every Tuesday afternoon the Ferry Landing hosts a produce and crafts market from 2:30 to 6pm; see p. 214 for a full review.

FLEA MARKETS

Kobey's Swap Meet *(Value* Since 1976, this gigantic open-air market positioned at the west end of the ipayOne Center Sports Arena parking lot has been a bargain-hunter's dream come true. More than 1,000 vendors fill row after row with new and used clothing, jewelry, electronics, hardware, appliances, furniture, collectibles, crafts, antiques, auto accessories, toys, and books. There's produce, too, along with food stalls and restrooms. Although Kobey's is open Friday, the weekend is when the good stuff is out—and it goes quickly, so arrive early. ipayOne Center Sports Arena, 3500 Sports Arena Blvd. © 619/226-0650. www.kobeyswap.com. Open Fri–Sun 7am–3pm. Admission Fri 50¢, Sat–Sun $1, free for children under 12. Take I-8 west to Sports Arena Blvd. turnoff, or I-5 to Rosecrans St. and turn right on Sports Arena Blvd.

MALLS

See p. 208 for details on **Horton Plaza.** Also see "Outlet Malls," below.

Fashion Valley Center   The Mission Valley corridor, running east-west about 2 miles north of downtown along I-8, contains San Diego's major shopping centers. Fashion Valley is the most attractive and most upscale, with six anchor stores: **JCPenney, Macy's, Neiman Marcus, Nordstrom, Bloomingdale's,** and **Saks Fifth Avenue** (most of which keep extended hours), plus more than 200 specialty shops and an 18-screen AMC movie theater. Other noteworthy shops include **M.A.C, Louis Vuitton, Burberry, Tiffany & Co., Max Studio, Z Gallerie, Smith & Hawken,** and **Bose.** 7007 Friars Rd. © 619/688-9113. www.simon.com. Mon–Sat 10am–9pm; Sun 11am–7pm. Bus: 6, 16, 25, 43, or 81. Hwy. 163 to Friars Rd. W.

Mission Valley Center   This old-fashioned outdoor mall predates sleek Fashion Valley and has found a niche with budget-minded stores like **Loehmann's, Nordstrom Rack,** and **Target;** you'll also find **Macy's Home & Furniture, West Elm, Sport Chalet,** and **Bed Bath & Beyond.** There's a 20-screen AMC movie theater and more than 150 other stores and places to eat. Across the streets to the north and west are separate complexes that feature Saks Fifth Avenue's **Off Fifth** (an outlet store), **Borders,** and more. 1640 Camino del Rio N. © 619/296-6375. www.westfield.com/missionvalley. Mon–Sat 10am–9pm; Sun 11am–6pm. Bus: 6, 16, 25, 43, or 81. I-8 to Mission Center Rd.

University Towne Center (UTC)   This outdoor shopping complex has a landscaped plaza and more than 180 stores, including some big ones like **Nordstrom, Sears,** and **Macy's.** It is also home to a year-round ice-skating rink, **Ice Town,** and has an outlet of Encinitas-based **Chuao Chocolatier,** a fabulous artisan chocolate shop. 4545 La Jolla Village Dr. © 858/546-8858. www.westfield.com/utc. Mon–Fri 10am–9pm; Sat 10am–7pm; Sun 11am–6pm. Bus: 50 express, 34, or 34A. I-5 to La Jolla Village Dr. and go east, or I-805 to La Jolla Village Dr. and go west.

MUSIC

In addition to dwindling mega-chains like Tower Records and the Wherehouse, you'll find a good crop of independent outlets. Probably the best place for serious collectors is **Lou's Records,** 434 Hwy. 101 in Encinitas, about 30 minutes north of downtown (© 760/753-1382; www.lousrecords.com). Here you'll find a building devoted to new and import CDs, one to used CDs and vinyl, and yet another catering to DVD and VHS fanatics. More central are **Off the Record,** 2912 University Ave., North Park (© 619/298-4755; www.otrvinyl.com), and **M-Theory Music,** which has two locations, 915 W. Washington St. in Mission Hills (© 619/220-0485), and the original location in South Park, 3004 Juniper St. (© 619/269-2963). Each has a good selection of indie releases and used CDs; M-Theory also has its own studio and hosts lots of in-store band appearances (check the website at www.mtheorymusic.com). Die-hard headbangers should make the trek to **Blue Meanie Records,** 1164 N. 2nd St. in El Cajon, 20 minutes east of downtown (© 619/442-5034), where a head-shop ambience adds to the selection of metal and punk albums, T-shirts, and posters. Last but not least is **Folk Arts Rare Records,** 2881 Adams Ave. in Normal Heights (**(C) 619/282-7833**), which is nirvana for serious jazz, folk, and blues collectors. Operated since 1967 by local legend Lou Curtiss, you'll find first-edition rarities on vinyl and 78s, most of them fairly priced. If you're not a collector or don't have a turntable, the store specializes in creating custom recordings of the vintage music on CD or cassette.

OUTLET MALLS

Carlsbad Premium Outlets   With some 90 stores, this mall includes the usual outlet favorites like **Barneys New York, Crate & Barrel, Tommy Hilfiger, Dooney & Bourke,** and **Wilsons Leather.** The mall also has several unique specialty shops, like **Thousand Mile Outdoor Wear** (**(C) 760/804-1764**), which sells outerwear manufactured from recycled products and makes the swimsuits worn by Southern California lifeguards. These outlets are located 32 miles north of downtown San Diego, close to LEGOLAND. 5600 Paseo del Norte **(C) 888/790-7467** or 760-804-9000. www.premium outlets.com. Daily 10am–8pm. I-5 north to Palomar Rd. exit; the mall is next to the freeway.

Las Americas   This outlet mall, San Diego's largest, is located in San Ysidro, immediately north of the Tijuana border crossing. Currently home to more than 115 stores, including **Neiman Marcus, Nike, Banana Republic, Guess, Liz Claiborne,** and **Ritmo Latino** (the largest Latin music store in the U.S.), it's located 16 miles south of downtown 4211 Camino de la Plaza **(C) 619/934-8400.** www.lasamericas.com. Mon–Fri 10am–9pm; Sat 10am–8pm; Sun 10am–6pm. Trolley: Border Crossing. I-5 south to Camino de la Plaza, the last U.S. exit; go right at the light.

Viejas Outlet Mall   More discount name-brand shopping is found at the Viejas Casino, east of El Cajon. Here you'll find **Big Dog, Eddie Bauer, GAP, Liz Claiborne, Nike, Perry Ellis, Polo Ralph Lauren,** and **Tommy Hilfiger**—nearly 50 stores in all. Tuesdays are Senior Citizen Days, with additional discounts at some stores. There is also daily entertainment at the Showcourt with pyrotechnics and music—and if that's not enough, there's a casino next door. Viejas is about 30 miles east of downtown. 5005 Willows Rd., Alpine **(C) 619/659-2070.** www.shopviejas.com. Mon–Sat 10am–9pm; Sun 10am–7pm. Bus: 864. I-8 east to Willows Rd. exit; turn left and follow the signs to Viejas Casino.

TOYS

The Lily Pad   This colorful shop in Hillcrest features old-fashioned toys that let creativity soar. Anker stone building blocks and puzzles (made in Germany since the 1880s), marionettes and hand puppets, wooden castles, and paintable teepees are available. Baby clothes, furniture, books, and musical instruments, too. The Lily Pad also schedules performances, lectures, and workshops. 3746 6th Ave. **(C) 619/220-8555.** www.thelilypadsd.com. Mon–Thurs 10am–5pm; Fri–Sat 10am–7pm; Sun 11am–5pm.

TRAVEL ACCESSORIES

Along with the stores listed below, try **Eddie Bauer** at Fashion Valley (**(C) 619/688-6544**) or University Towne Center (**(C) 858/552-9224**) for travel gear.

John's Fifth Avenue Luggage   This San Diego institution carries just about everything you can imagine in the way of luggage, travel accessories, business cases, pens, and gifts. The on-premises luggage-repair center is an authorized airline repair facility. There is also a store in the Fashion Valley mall, with extended hours. 3833 Fourth Ave., Hillcrest ℂ **619/298-0993**. Mon–Fri 9am–5:30pm; Sat 9am–4pm.

Le Travel Store   In business since 1976, Le Travel Store has a good selection of soft-sided luggage (particularly the Eagle Creek brand), travel books, language tapes, maps, and lots of travel accessories, plus an STA outlet. The extended hours and central location make this spot extra handy. 745 Fourth Ave. (between F and G sts.). ℂ **619/544-0005**. www.letravelstore.com. Mon–Sat 10am–7pm; Sun noon–6pm. Bus: 2, 7, 9, 29, 34, or 35. Trolley: Gaslamp.

The Map Centre   This shop in Kearny Mesa has the whole world covered—in maps, that is. From topographical maps and nautical charts to GPS global positioning toys, the Map Centre makes for terrific browsing. Local needs are a particular focus, with San Diego, California, and Baja maps galore. 7576 Clairemont Mesa Blvd. (west of Convoy St.). ℂ **619/291-3830**. www.mapworld.com. Mon–Fri 10am–5:30pm; Sat 10am–5pm.

Traveler's Depot   Around since 1985, this shop offers an extensive selection of travel books and maps, plus a great array of travel gear and accessories, with discounts on backpacks and luggage. The well-traveled owners, Ward and Lisl Hampton, are happy to give advice about restaurants in a given city while pointing you to the right shelf for an appropriate book or map. 1655 Garnet Ave., Pacific Beach. ℂ **858/483-1421**. www.travelersdepot. com. Mon–Fri 10am–6pm; Sat 10am–5pm; Sun noon–5pm, with later hours in summer.

WINE

San Diego has several unique places where you can combine wine shopping with dining. You'll feel like you've really accomplished something when you finally find **Wine-Sellar & Brasserie** in its odd business park setting, 9550 Waples St. in Sorrento Mesa (ℂ **888/774-9463** or 858/450-9557; www.winesellar.com). It started out as a wine storage facility, hence the strange locale, but not only has it grown into one of the area's best wine stores, there's an excellent French–inspired restaurant upstairs. Pick a bottle and head on up (reservations definitely recommended). Ocean Beach's **3rd Corner,** 2265 Bacon St. (ℂ **619/223-2700;** www.the3rdcorner.com), is more centrally located and has an informal, casual air. You can browse for a bottle to go with the mostly small-plate offerings. It serves late and has become popular with local bar and restaurant workers.

The Wine Bank   San Diego's best wine shop is actually one of the finest on the West Coast, featuring a great selection from around the world, but without the steep prices common at some shops. You'll find rare wines from France, Italy, and Spain, and bottles from virtually every winery in California, plus ample choices around $10. The small trove of Mexican wines is worth checking out. 363 Fifth Ave., Downtown. ℂ **619/234-7487**. www.sdwinebank.com. Mon–Sat 9am–7pm; Sun 11am–4pm.

San Diego After Dark

Historically, San Diego's cultural scene has lounged in the shadows of Los Angeles and San Francisco, content to take a back seat to the beach, the zoo, and our meteorologically inspired state of affairs. But the dot-com influence brought new blood and money into the city, and arts organizations felt the impact. The biggest winner was the San Diego Symphony, which in 2002, received the largest single donation to a symphony anywhere, ($120 million). More recently, individual donors have lavished big bucks on other arts groups: the Old Globe Theatre received a $20 million gift, while the Museum of Contemporary Art San Diego was bestowed with a $3 million donation. But don't think "after dark" in this city is limited to highfalutin affairs for the Lexus crowd—rock and pop concerts, swank martini bars, and nightclubs crank up the volume on a nearly nightly basis.

FINDING OUT WHAT'S ON

For a rundown of the week's performances, gallery openings, and other events, check the listings in the free, weekly alternative publications, *San Diego CityBeat* (www.sd citybeat.com), published on Wednesday, and *San Diego Weekly Reader* (www.sdreader. com), which comes out on Thursday (also distributed in hotels and tourist areas under the name *The Weekly*). The *San Diego Union-Tribune*'s entertainment section, "Night and Day," also appears on Thursday (www.uniontrib.com). For what's happening at the gay clubs, get the weekly *San Diego Gay & Lesbian Times*.

The local convention and visitors bureau's *Art + Sol* campaign provides a calendar of events covering the performing and visual arts, and more; see www.sandiegoartand-sol.com. The San Diego Performing Arts League produces *What's Playing?*, a performing arts guide, every 2 months. You can pick one up at the ARTS TIX booth or write to 110 W. B St., Suite 1414, San Diego, CA 92101 (© **619/238-0700;** www.sandiego performs.com).

Thankfully, San Diego's orgy of development has included more than high-rise condos and high-end supper clubs. The **NTC Promenade** in Point Loma (© **619/226-1491;** www.ntcpromenade.org) consists of 26 historic buildings on 28 acres. It's the remnants of a huge Navy base transformed into a flagship hub of creative activity and includes office, studio, and performance space for more than a dozen arts groups. The **North Park Theatre,** 2891 University Ave. (© **619/231-5714;** www.northpark theatre.com), is a 1928 vaudeville and movie house resurrected to its original glory. It's now the home base for Lyric Opera San Diego and plays host to numerous other groups throughout the year. The **La Jolla Playhouse** (p. 223) has gotten in on the act as well, completing its three-theater complex, complete with a restaurant for pre- and post-theater dining and entertainment.

GETTING TICKETS

Half-price tickets to theater, music, and dance events are available at the **ARTS TIX** booth in Horton Plaza Park, at Broadway and Third Avenue. Pull into the Horton Plaza garage (where you can validate your parking) or, if there's room, just pause at the curb. The kiosk is open Tuesday through Thursday at 11am, Friday through Sunday at 10am. The booth stays open till 6pm daily except Sunday, when it closes at 5pm. Half-price tickets are available only for same-day shows except for Monday performances, which are sold on Sunday. For a daily listing of offerings, call © **619/497-5000** or check www.sandiegoperforms.com; the website also sells half-price tickets for some shows. There is also an ARTS TIX North, at the San Diego North Convention & Visitors Bureau in Escondido, 360 N. Escondido Blvd. (© **800/848-3336** or 760/745-4741). Hours are Monday through Friday, 8:30am to 5pm.

Full-price advance tickets are also available; the Horton Plaza kiosk doubles as a Ticketmaster outlet, selling seats to concerts throughout California. As always, although Ticketmaster sells seats for a majority of local events, you'll avoid bruising "convenience" fees by purchasing directly from the venue's box office.

1 The Performing Arts

THEATER

These listings focus on the best known of San Diego's many talented theater companies. Don't hesitate to try a less prominent venue if the show appeals to you. Smaller companies doing notable work include **Cygnet Theatre** (© 619/337-1525; www.cygnet theatre.com), **Sledgehammer Theatre** (© 619/544-1484; www.sledgehammer.org), **North Coast Repertory Theatre** (© 858/481-1055; www.northcoastrep.org), and **Moxie Theatre** (© 760/634-3965; www.moxietheatre.com). This may also be the year the city's groundbreaking **Sushi Performance and Visual Art** (© 619/235-8466; www.sushiart.org) returns to a permanent home. Keep in mind, too, that the **California Center for the Performing Arts** in Escondido has its own productions (see "North County Inland: From Rancho Santa Fe to Palomar Mountain," in chapter 11). For shows oriented toward kids, see "That's Entertainment," in chapter 7.

Diversionary Theatre   Founded in 1985 and focusing on plays with gay and lesbian themes, Diversionary's past hits have included *M Butterfly, Love! Valour! Compassion!*, and *Psycho Beach Party*. The 104-seat theater is in the charming neighborhood of University Heights, 2 blocks north of El Cajon Boulevard. The box office is open Wednesday through Saturday from noon to 8pm (when shows are playing). It's a parking-challenged area, so a good idea is to come early and have dinner at one of the neighborhood eateries. 4545 Park Blvd. © **619/220-0097.** www.diversionary.org. Tickets $23–$27, $9 student rush 1 hour prior to curtain. Bus: 1, 11, 15, or 115.

The Old Globe Theatre 𝄢𝄢   This Tony Award–winning complex of three performance venues is inside Balboa Park, behind the Museum of Man. Though best known for the 581-seat Old Globe—fashioned after Shakespeare's—it also includes the 225-seat Cassius Carter Centre Stage and the 612-seat open-air Lowell Davies Festival Theatre. More than a dozen plays are scheduled here year-round, from world premieres (and subsequent Broadway hits) like *The Full Monty* and *Into the Woods* to the excellent summer Shakespeare festival when the theater goes into true repertory style, alternating performances each night. *Dr. Seuss' How the Grinch Stole Christmas!* has been a popular family draw during the holidays since 1997. Leading actors regularly grace the stage—past performers include John Lithgow, John Goodman, Hal Holbrook, and Ellen Burstyn. Backstage tours are offered Saturday and Sunday at 10:30am and cost $5 for adults, $3 for students, seniors, and military. The box office is open Monday (and other nonperformance days) noon to 6pm, and Tuesday through Sunday noon to 8pm. Balboa Park. © 619/234-5623. www.theoldglobe.org. Tickets $19–$65. Senior, student, and military discounts available. Free parking in the park's public lots. Bus: 1, 3, 7, or 25.

La Jolla Playhouse 🎭🎭 The Playhouse boasts a Hollywood pedigree (it was founded in 1947 by Gregory Peck, Dorothy McGuire, and Mel Ferrer) and a 1993 Tony Award for outstanding regional theater. With the recent completion of a third theater and the addition of an on-site restaurant at its UCSD location, the Playhouse plans to run productions, staged readings, and educational programs year-round. The Playhouse is known for its contemporary takes on classics and commitment to *commedia dell'arte* style, as well as producing Broadway-bound blockbusters. Past world-premiere hits include Billy Crystal's *700 Sundays, Jersey Boys, Thoroughly Modern Millie,* The Who's *Tommy,* and *Big River.* For each show, one Saturday matinee is a "pay what you can" performance, and every night, unsold tickets are $15 each ($20 for musicals) in a "public rush" sale 10 minutes before curtain. Box office hours are Monday noon to 6pm, Tuesday through Saturday noon to 8pm, and Sunday noon to 7pm when shows are in performance, or Monday through Saturday noon to 6pm when there are no shows running. 2910 La Jolla Village Dr. (at Torrey Pines Rd.). © 858/550-1010. www.lajollaplayhouse.com. Tickets $28–$72. Parking $2, free on weekends. Bus: 30, 34, or 34A.

Lamb's Players Theatre One of the few professional companies in the country with a true resident ensemble, the theater celebrated its 35th anniversary last year. Lamb's features five shows annually in a 350-seat theater in Coronado's historic Spreckels Building (where no seat is more than seven rows from the stage), plus two Christmas productions—including a dinner theater show at the Hotel del Coronado—and a summer production at the Lyceum Theatre in Horton Plaza. You won't see anything by David Mamet or Martin McDonagh here—Lamb's keeps things on the safe, noncontroversial side. You will see well-acted, well-designed plays, both premieres and classics, such as recent productions of *Amadeus, Metamorphoses,* and *Hamlet.* The theater also operates Encore Café adjacent to its playhouse; it serves lunch, afternoon tea, and light pretheater meals. The box office is open Tuesday through Saturday from noon to 7pm, Sunday from noon to 5pm. 1142 Orange Ave., Coronado. © 619/437-0600. www.lambsplayers.org. Tickets $24–$44. Street parking is usually available nearby. Bus: 901, 902, or 904.

San Diego Repertory Theatre Founded in 1976, the Rep mounts plays and musicals at the Lyceum Theatre in Horton Plaza, which consists of the 545-seat Lyceum Stage and the 260-seat Lyceum Space. The theater acts as a "cultural town hall," hosting nearly daily events, exhibits, and shows, in addition to the Rep's work. The Rep has a strong multicultural bent—it has had a long association with Chicano playwright Luis Valdez, and produces the annual African-American Kuumba Fest and the Jewish Arts Festival. It also stages a yearly production of *A Christmas Carol,* lauded for its clever reinterpretations. Past hits have included the premieres of *Three Mo' Divas* and the Tony-nominated *It Ain't Nothin' But the Blues,* as well as *Who's Afraid of Virginia Woolf?,* and *Culture Clash in Bordertown,* a work based on the San Diego–Tijuana region. Situated at the entrance to Horton Plaza, the modern two-level subterranean theaters are tucked behind a tile obelisk. The box office is open Tuesday through Sunday from noon to 6pm (or curtain time). 79 Broadway Circle, in Horton

Plaza. ⓒ **619/544-1000.** www.sandiegorep.com. Tickets $27–$42. Free validated parking at Horton Plaza Shopping Center. Bus: All Broadway routes.

CLASSICAL MUSIC

La Jolla Music Society ⭐   This well-respected organization has been bringing marquee names to San Diego since 1968. Past performers include Pinchas Zukerman, Emanuel Ax, Chick Corea, Joshua Bell, the American Ballet Theatre, and other world-class artists. About half of the 40-plus annual shows are held October through May in the 500-seat Sherwood Auditorium at the Museum of Contemporary Art; others are presented at the acoustically excellent Neurosciences Institute, downtown's Copley Symphony Hall, and the restored North Park Theatre. The annual highlight is SummerFest, a 3-week series of concerts, forums, open rehearsals, talks, and artist encounters—it's held in August and is broadcast live on NPR. At Sherwood Auditorium, 700 Prospect St., La Jolla. ⓒ **858/459-3728.** www.ljms.org. Tickets $20–$105.

San Diego Symphony ⭐   The organization first took shape when a group of musicians gathered to perform at the US Grant Hotel in 1910. Over time, the symphony grew and prospered with the city, but floundered for a decade starting in the late 1980s in conjunction with several years of local recession, inept management, and the malaise that gripped many fine orchestras around the country. In 2002, enduring financial stability arrived with the announcement of a $120-million bequest by Joan and Irwin Jacobs (founder and CEO of Qualcomm). The bequest has allowed the organization to lure top talent, including resident conductor Jahja Ling. The symphony's home is the former Fox Theatre, a 1929-era French rococo-style downtown landmark, restored and now known as Copley Symphony Hall. The season runs October through May. A Summer Pops series, with programs devoted to big band, Broadway, and Tchaikovsky, is held weekends from July to early September on the Embarcadero—always bring a sweater and possibly a blanket for these pleasantly brisk evenings on the water. The box office is open Monday through Thursday from 10am to 6pm, Friday 10am to 5pm, weekends from noon to 5pm, and on performance days from noon until intermission. 750 B St., at Seventh Ave. ⓒ **619/235-0804.** www.sandiego symphony.com. Tickets $20–$85. Bus: 1, 3, or 25. Trolley: Fifth Ave.

OPERA

San Diego Opera ⭐⭐   One of the community's most successful arts organizations, San Diego Opera celebrated its 40th anniversary in 2005. Under the leadership of Ian Campbell since 1983, the annual season runs from late January to mid-May, with five offerings at downtown's 3,000-seat Civic Theatre, as well as occasional recitals at smaller venues. The productions range from well-trod warhorses like *Carmen* to lesser-known works like Samuel Barber's *Vanessa,* all performed by local singers and name talent from around the world. The annual lineup is announced in May, and nonsubscription tickets go on sale by December. The box office is open Monday through Friday 8:30am to 4:30pm, or you can order tickets online. At the Civic Theatre, 1200 Third Ave. ⓒ **619/533-7000** (box office) or 619/232-7636 (admin). www.sdopera.com. Tickets $27–$172. Bus: 2, 7, 9, 29, 34, or 35. Trolley: Civic Center.

DANCE

The **San Diego Dance Alliance** is the umbrella organization for the local dance community (ⓒ **619/230-8623;** www.sandiegodance.org). The alliance puts on the **Nations of San Diego International Dance Festival** in January, spotlighting the city's ethnic dance groups and emerging artists. The website provides links to more than 50 local dance outfits.

Among San Diego's major dance companies is the **California Ballet** (© **858/560-5676;** www.californiaballet.org), a classical company that produces four shows annually at the Civic Theatre downtown and elsewhere—*The Nutcracker* is a Christmas tradition. **San Diego Ballet** (© **619/294-7378;** www.sandiegoballet.org) and **City Ballet** (© **858/274-6058;** www.cityballet.org) also focus on classical dance pieces. For modern dance, check out **Malashock Dance** (© **619/260-1622;** www.malashock dance.org), **Eveoke Dance Theatre** (© **619/238-1153;** www.eveoke.org), **Jean Isaacs' San Diego Dance Theater** (© **858/484-7791;** www.sandiegodancetheater. org), and **McCaleb Dance** (© **858/488-5559;** www.mccalebdance.org).

2 Live Entertainment

LIVE MUSIC

Maddeningly, many artists still bypass San Diego in favor of another night in LA. On the plus side—especially when it comes to acts that haven't pushed through to the mainstream—if they do play locally, chances are it's in a venue smaller than what you'd find them in up north. *Note:* If you're under 21, much of the city's nightlife will be off-limits to you.

SMALL- & MEDIUM-SIZE VENUES

4th & B   In a former bank building downtown, 4th & B is a no-frills venue made comfortable with haphazardly placed seating (balcony theater seats, occasional cabaret tables on the main floor) and a handful of bar/lounge niches—one actually inside the old vault. The genre is barrier-free; everything from live music and DJs to boxing and comedy shows. Look into advance tickets; the box office is open Monday through Saturday from 10am to 5pm. 345 B St., Downtown. © 619/231-4343. www.4thandB.com.

Acoustic Music San Diego *Finds*   One of San Diego's most unique venues is a nearly 100-year-old church in Normal Heights, which hosts shows presented by Acoustic Music San Diego. Programming ranges from Americana and blues to bluegrass and Celtic, with past performers including roots rockers Dave Alvin and Rosie Flores, neo-troubadors Peter Case and Mary Gauthier, and musical storytellers like David Wilcox and Ramblin' Jack Elliott. Most artists sign autographs and hawk merchandise between sets in the church's adjacent auditorium. 4650 Mansfield St., Normal Heights (south of Adams Ave.). © 619/303-8176. www.acousticmusicsandiego.com.

The Belly Up Tavern *Finds*   This club in Solana Beach, a 30-minute drive from downtown, has played host to critically acclaimed and international artists of all genres. The eclectic mix ranges from Lucinda Williams to Etta James to Frank Black to The Roots. A funky setting in recycled Quonset huts underscores the venue's uniqueness. Look into advance tickets, if possible, though you can avoid excessive Ticketmaster fees by purchasing your tickets at the box office. 143 S. Cedros Ave., Solana Beach (1½ blocks from the Coaster stop). © 858/481-9022 (recorded info) or 858/481-8140 (box office). www.bellyup.com.

The Casbah   It may have a total dive ambience, and passing jets overhead sometimes drown out ballads, but this blaring Little Italy club has a well-earned rep for showcasing bands that either are, were, or will be famous. Past headliners at the 200-capacity club have included Nirvana, Smashing Pumpkins, White Stripes, and local act Rocket From the Crypt. Look into advance tickets if possible; live music can be

No Smoking

In 1998, California enacted legislation that banned smoking in all restaurants and bars. As a rule, don't light up in any public area indoors. If you're looking to light up in clubs, lounges, and other nightspots with outdoor terraces, check with the staff first.

counted on at least 6 nights a week. Every month or two the Casbah turns into Jivewire, with wall-to-wall bodies on the small dance floor and new wave, disco, and hip-hop classics on the sound system. Doors open 8:30pm. 2501 Kettner Blvd., at Laurel St., near the airport. ℭ 619/232-4355. www.casbahmusic.com. Cover charge usually under $12.

Croce's Nightclubs   Croce's is a cornerstone of Gaslamp Quarter nightlife: a loud, crowded, and mainstream gathering place. Two separate clubs operate a couple of doors apart: You'll find a variety of jazz stylings at Croce's Jazz Bar 7 nights a week (8:30pm–12:30am), and usually rhythm and blues at Croce's Top Hat Friday and Saturday (9:30pm–1am). The music blares onto the street, making it easy to decide whether to go in or not. The clubs are named for the late Jim Croce and are owned by his widow, Ingrid, who was a vital component of the Gaslamp's revitalization. The cover charge is waived if you eat at the pricey restaurant. 802 Fifth Ave. (at F St.). ℭ 619/233-4355. www.croces.com. Cover $5–$10.

House of Blues ✦   Whatever your feelings about corporate music entities, there's no denying House of Blues knows how to do things right. A visual feast of amazing outsider art fills this multiroom venue. There's a restaurant serving Southern-inspired cuisine (and the Sunday gospel brunch is a definite hoot—though be prepared to praise Jesus), a swag store, a bar, and an 1,100-person capacity concert space. HOB's booking power brings in an eclectic range of music, from worldbeat to punk (and yes, blues, too). A fair number of these are acts that might not have played in San Diego, if not for HOB. VIP dinner packages are available; and the restaurant is open for lunch. 1055 Fifth Ave., Downtown (between Broadway and C St., steps away from the Fifth Ave. trolley stop). ℭ 619/299-2583. www.hob.com/sandiego.

Humphrey's ✦   This locally beloved 1,300-seat outdoor venue is set on the water next to bobbing yachts. The annual lineup covers the spectrum of entertainment—rock, jazz, blues, folk, and comedy. Chris Isaak, Etta James, Lyle Lovett, India.Arie, and San Diego–bred Jewel are among the many name acts that have played here. Although there's not a bad seat in the house, you can often snag a seat in the first seven rows by buying the dinner/concert package ($52 extra) for the adjoining restaurant of the same name—the food's nothing special, but if sitting up front is of value to you, it's a good deal. Concerts are held from mid-May to October only, and most shows go on sale in early April (seats are also available through Ticketmaster). 2241 Shelter Island Dr., Point Loma. ℭ 619/523-1010 (general info) or 619-224-3577 (reservations). www.humphreysbythebay.com.

LARGE VENUES

There's a worthwhile concert just about any night of the week—you just need to know where to find it. The free *San Diego Weekly Reader,* published on Thursdays (and distributed in tourist areas as *The Weekly*), is the best source of concert information, listing dozens of shows in any given week; check the website at www.sdreader.com for an advance look. Tickets typically go on sale 4 to 10 weeks before the event—dates are usually announced in the *Reader* or the Sunday *San Diego Union-Tribune*. Depending on the popularity of a particular artist or group, last-minute seats are often available through the box office or **Ticketmaster** (© **619/220-8497;** www.ticketmaster.com). You can also go through a broker like **Advance Tickets** (© **800/776-8497;** www.advance tickets.com) if you're willing to pay a higher price for prime tickets at the last minute.

The city has two monster venues. The **ipayOne Center at the Sports Arena** (© **619/225-9813;** www.sandiegoarena.com) is west of Old Town. Built in 1967, the 15,000- to 18,000-seat indoor venue has middling acoustics, but many big-name concerts are held here because of the seating capacity and availability of paid parking. **Qualcomm Stadium** (© **619/641-3131**), in Mission Valley, is a 71,000-seat outdoor stadium and is used only a few times a year for things like motocross or major music tours. The parking lot also gets used as the location for the **Street Scene** music festival in late summer.

The **Open Air Theater** (© **619/594-6947**), on the San Diego State University campus, northeast of downtown along I-8, is a more intimate 4,000-seat outdoor amphitheater. It has great acoustics—if you can't get a ticket, you can sit outside on the grass and hear the entire show. **Cox Arena** (© **619/594-6947**), also at SDSU, has equally superb acoustics in an indoor, 12,000-seat facility that is used for bigger draws—these venues are easily accessed by San Diego Trolley. **Coors Amphitheatre** (© **619/671-3600**) is a slick facility seemingly a stone's throw north of the Mexican border, in Chula Vista. Built in 1999, the 20,000-seat venue has excellent acoustics and good sightlines, and it lures many of the summer tours. The drawbacks: overpriced snacks and drinks, and a location 25 to 45 minutes south of downtown (depending on traffic).

The **Spreckels Theatre,** 121 Broadway (© **619/235-9500**), and **Copley Symphony Hall,** 750 B St. (© **619/235-0804**), are wonderful old vaudeville houses, which also are used by touring acts throughout the year; past shows have included Annie Lennox, Sting, Margaret Cho, and *Forever Tango*. For both venues, tickets are available at the box office or through Ticketmaster.

COMEDY CLUBS

The Comedy Store   Yes, it's a branch of the famous Sunset Strip club in Los Angeles, and yes, plenty of L.A. comics make the trek to headline Friday and Saturday shows here. Less prominent professional comedians perform live Wednesday and Thursday, and Sunday's open-mic night can be hilarious, horrendous—or maybe both. Shows start at 8pm, with later shows on weekends. 916 Pearl St., La Jolla. © **858/454-9176.** www.thecomedystore.com. Cover $5–$20 (plus two-drink minimum). Bus: 30.

3 The Bar & Coffeehouse Scene

BARS, COCKTAIL LOUNGES & DANCE CLUBS
DOWNTOWN

Downtown is the busiest place for nightlife. You'll find something going on just about every night, but the best nights (or worst, depending on your tolerance for crowds) are Thursday through Saturday, when the 20-somethings pour in and dance clubs spring into action. Here are some of the best spots, but keep in mind this is an ever-changing scene.

Airport   This sexy, minimalist gem on the northern edge of Little Italy has one of the best shows in town. From its very cool interior patio, you can almost touch the planes as they come roaring in for a landing at nearby Lindberg Field. Keeping to the theme, bartenders are in pilots' uniforms, waitresses are in classic flight attendant miniskirts. 2400 India St. (just south of Laurel St.), Little Italy. ℂ 619/685-3881. www.airportsd.com.

Altitude Skybar Twenty-two stories up in the Gaslamp Quarter Marriott, this long, narrow open-air space looks down on PETCO Park and the Convention Center. The best view of downtown is curiously walled off by a water sculpture that backs the bar. No worries—there's still lots to look at, as well as fire pits and DJ-spun grooves. 660 K St. (between Sixth and Seventh aves.), Gaslamp Quarter. ℂ 619/446-6088.

The Beach The Beach is the rooftop bar of the W hotel. What makes it truly unique is that most of the floor is sand—you can take your shoes off (drinks are served in plastic) even in winter when the sand is heated. A gas fire pit adds to the ambience, as do the cabanas lining one wall. Don't forget your flip-flops, shovel, and pail. The hotel's two other bars, Living Room and Magnet, are also smart. 421 B St. (at State St.), Downtown. ℂ 619/231-8220.

The Bitter End With three floors, this Gaslamp Quarter hot spot manages to be a sophisticated martini bar, dance club, and relaxing cocktail lounge all in one. On weekends, you're subject to the velvet rope treatment, and there's always a strict dress code in play—no shorts, no tennis shoes. Don't miss the plush upstairs bar. Open daily from 3pm to 2am. 770 Fifth Ave. (at F St.), Gaslamp Quarter. ℂ 619/338-9300. www.thebitter end.com. Cover Thurs $5 after 9:30pm, Fri–Sat $10 after 8:30pm.

Jbar Considerably more earthbound than Altitude (see above), Jbar is on the fourth-floor pool deck of the Hotel Solamar. Let's see: Fire pits, check. Cabanas, check. Comfy lounges, check. A menu of small-plate edibles from the first-floor restaurant, check. Cool music playing overhead, check. Excellent views of the Gaslamp Quarter action, check. Yup, everything you need for a great evening. 616 J St. (at Sixth Ave.), Gaslamp Quarter. ℂ 619/531-8744. www.jsixsandiego.com.

Martini Ranch/Shaker Room This split-level bar boasts more than 50 kinds of martinis (or martini-inspired concoctions). Downstairs resembles an upscale sports bar showing sports TV and music videos. If the sensory overload addles your brain, traipse upstairs to relax in scattered couches, love seats, and conversation pits. The Shaker Room, a dance club next door, operates Wednesday through Sunday from 9pm (Martini Ranch is open nightly). 528 F St. (at Sixth Ave.), Gaslamp Quarter. ℂ 619/235-6100. www.martiniranchsd.com. Cover $10 Fri–Sat after 8:30pm.

Olé Madrid Loud and energetic, this dressy dance club features a changing lineup of celebrated DJs spinning house and hip-hop. The adjoining restaurant has tapas and sangria (lunch and dinner; weekend brunch). Live music and dancing (jazz, pop, salsa) Thursday through Sunday from 7pm; Friday and Saturday: DJs after 10pm, live flamenco dancing 7 to 10pm. 751 Fifth Ave. (between F and G sts.), Gaslamp Quarter. ℂ 619/557-0146. www.olemadrid.com. Cover $5–$15 after 10pm.

On Broadway This retro swanky hangout in a converted 1925 bank building has five rooms covering the musical gamut: house, techno, hip-hop, R&B—using a 90,000-watt sound system—plus a sushi bar with live music (reservations suggested) and a billiards room in the former bank vault. Dress to impress. Open Friday and Saturday, from 6pm. 615 Broadway (at Sixth Ave.), Downtown. ℂ 619/231-0011. www.obec.tv. Cover $15 and up, starting at 8pm.

The Onyx Room/Thin   Hipsters dive into Onyx, a cutting-edge underground (literally) club where the atmosphere is lounge, the drinks are up, and the music is cool. Live jazz is featured on Tuesdays. The Onyx Room opens Tuesday through Saturday from 9pm. At street level is hyper-modern **Thin,** run by the same crew and open Tuesday through Saturday from 7pm (Fri at 5pm). 852 Fifth Ave., Gaslamp Quarter. ℂ **619/235-6699.** www.onyxroom.com. Cover Fri–Sat $10 (covers both bars).

Princess Pub & Grille   A local haunt for Anglophiles and others thirsting for a pint o' Bass, Fuller's, Watney's, or Guinness, this slice of Britain (in Little Italy . . . go figure) also serves up overpriced bangers 'n' mash, steak-and-kidney pie, and other pub grub. The after-work crowd can be festive, and if you drink enough, the food starts to taste good. 1665 India St., Little Italy. ℂ **619/702-3021.** www.princesspub.com.

Sevilla   This Latin-themed club is the spot for salsa lessons Tuesday through Thursday, and samba lessons on Sunday, at 8pm, followed by live bands at 10pm. Friday and Saturday is a Latin/Euro dance club and Monday is Latin hip-hop. Sevilla also has a tapas bar and dining room (Café Sevilla) open from 5pm (till 11pm weeknights, till 1am Fri–Sat). Live flamenco and Gypsy dinner shows are staged each weekend. 555 Fourth Ave., Gaslamp Quarter. ℂ **619/233-5979.** www.cafesevilla.com. Cover $6–$12.

Sidebar   Don't bother looking for signage. This place is too cool for that. Sidebar is found inside a 19th-century building with exposed bricks and beams, contemporized with Noguchi furniture and flat-screen TVs showing video art. There are roomy lounges and a sidewalk patio; plus you can get slices of New York–style pizza. 536 Market St. (corner of Sixth Ave. and Market St.), Gaslamp Quarter. ℂ **619/696-0946.** www.sidebarsd.com.

Stingaree   This $6 million, 3-level club has become *the* hot new destination in the Gaslamp Quarter. It has more than 22,000 square feet of space, a fine dining component, a handful of bars and private nooks, and a rooftop deck with cabanas and a fire pit. The decor is chicly mod and retro; the cover charge ($20) is definitely contemporary. The name is a throwback, too—back in San Diego's Wild West days, this area was known as the Stingaree. 454 Sixth Ave. (between Island Ave. and J St.), Gaslamp Quarter. ℂ **619/544-9500.** www.stingsandiego.com.

Top of the Hyatt *(Moments*   This is San Diego's ultimate bar with a view, the 40th floor of the West Coast's tallest waterfront building. You'll get a wide view of the city, harbor, and Coronado. The bar opens at 3pm daily and is an unparalleled spot from which to watch the sunset. 1 Market Pl. (at Harbor Dr.), Downtown. ℂ **619/232-1234.**

Yard House   Part of a minichain of beer joints spreading across America, this massive outfit doesn't brew its own suds but has a long bar lined with tap after tap, some 130 in all. You'll find everything from little-known Hollywood Blonde to Hemp Ale

---

Party Time

On weekends, lines begin forming outside popular venues by 10pm, so if there's a place you really want to check out, go early to avoid the queue. Some downtown clubs also serve dinner, providing another (albeit pricey) way around the line. All establishments (including liquor and grocery stores) must stop selling alcohol at 2am. Some bars even set their clocks ahead 20 minutes or so to make sure lingering drinkers have turned in their glasses by the magic hour.

---

and other curiosities—just don't you dare order a boring old Coors Light. There's also a full menu, but the entrees are less than successful. Instead, pop in from 3 to 6pm and get half-off appetizers and drink specials. On Friday and Saturday nights, the basement sports a sleek lounge. 1023 Fourth Ave. (at Broadway). ℭ **619/233-9273.** www.yard house.com.

ELSEWHERE IN SAN DIEGO

Lips   Drag review, with or without dinner. There's a different show nightly, like Bitchy Bingo on Wednesday and celebrity impersonations on Thursday. Shows start at 7pm Sunday and Tuesday through Thursday; weekends have two seatings (Fri 6:30 and 9pm; Sat 6 and 8:30pm), and dinner reservations guarantee seating. Sunday brunch 11am to 2pm. 2770 Fifth Ave. (at Nutmeg St.), Hillcrest. ℭ **619/295-7900.** www.lipsshow. biz. Cover $3 Thurs–Sat.

Nunu's Cocktail Lounge   Lots of 1960s Naugahyde style without the attitude, plus a kitchen that whips up burgers, liver-and-onions, and the like for an eclectic crowd. 3537 Fifth Ave. (at Ivy Lane), Hillcrest. ℭ **619/295-2878.**

Ould Sod   Irish through and through, this little gem sits in a working-class neighborhood northeast of Hillcrest, hosting a very local crowd. There's an Irish jam session on Tuesday; more live music on Wednesday and Friday; and karaoke on Thursday and Saturday. 3373 Adams Ave., Normal Heights. ℭ **619/284-6594.** www.theouldsod.com. Cover for bands $3.

Turf Supper Club *(Finds)*   The gimmick at this retro steakhouse is cheap, "grill your own" dinners. Steaks ($7–$15) are delivered raw, but seasoned, on a paper plate with sides—you do the rest. *Tip:* Feel free to ask for grilling suggestions from the staff. The decor and piano bar (on Sun) are pure 1950s, and approved by the cocktail crowd; the volume level other nights is not always conducive to intimate dining. 1116 25th Ave., Golden Hill. ℭ **619/234-6363.**

COFFEEHOUSES WITH PERFORMANCES

Claire de Lune Coffee Lounge *(Finds)*   Together with the revived North Park Theatre across the street, and a few other new businesses, this coffeehouse has created a happening little scene in the neighborhood. There's usually entertainment Thursday through Saturday, ranging from poetry to belly dancing. Every Friday there's a free-form dance in Claire de Lune's adjacent Sunset Ballroom. 2906 University Ave. (at Kansas), North Park. ℭ **619/688-9845.** www.clairedelune.com.

Lestat's Coffee House   Named for literature's second most famous vampire, this local's favorite is open 24/7. There's entertainment nightly, ranging from guitar-strumming troubadours (some of the city's best) and rock bands, to comics and open-mic hopefuls (Monday). 3343 Adams Ave. (at Felton St.), Normal Heights. ℭ **619/282-0437.** www. lestats.com.

Twiggs Tea and Coffee Co. *(Finds)*   Tucked away in a peaceful neighborhood, this popular coffeehouse has an adjoining room for live music Thursday through Sunday, poetry readings every other Monday, and an open-mic night on Wednesday. 4590 Park Blvd. (south of Adams Ave.), University Heights. ℭ **619/296-0616.** www.twiggs.org. Sometimes there's a $6–$12 cover for high-profile acts.

Free Summer Nights

Beach Bonfires Fire pits are free to the public in Pacific Beach, around Mission Bay, and at La Jolla Shores. Head out early to stake your claim, as they tend to get snagged pretty quickly. Glass is never permitted on the sand, and alcohol isn't allowed past 8pm. Be sure to check signs for local laws.

Music Every night of the week, San Diego County is a chorus of free music. On select Sunday nights from June through August, the hills of Alpine come alive with the sound of music at the **Alpine Summer Concert Series** (© 619/445-7330). Head south of downtown and across the Coronado bridge for more free Sunday nighttime music at the **Annual Coronado Promenade Concerts** at Spreckels Park (© 619/437-8788). Fridays in North County really are all that jazz. Parks throughout Carlsbad kick off the weekend with free jazz concerts. Call © 760/434-2904 for information. Spreckels Organ Pavilion presents **Twilight in the Park Summer Concerts** (© 619/239-0512) Tuesday, Wednesday, and Thursday nights in Balboa Park; while on Monday evenings, the Spreckels Organ Society offers its **Summer Organ Festival** (© 619/702-8138).

Festivals Celebrate San Diego's diverse communities at these free festivals, which keep the party alive well past sunset. The annual **Ocean Beach Street Fair & Chili Cook-Off** ((© 619/226-2193) is held from 10am to 8pm in late June. **Independence Day celebrations,** held throughout the county, include Coronado (© 619/437-8788), La Jolla (© 858/454-1444), and Oceanside (© 760/754-4512). The annual **Encanto Street Fair & Cultural Arts Festival** (© 619/266-0936), a multiethnic-themed festival in mid-August, features entertainment, food, vendors, and a custom car show from 10am to 10pm. **Celebrate Chula Vista** (© 619/420-6603) is held at the end of August on this South Bay community's waterfront. It's a family event featuring sports demonstrations, entertainment, food, and fireworks from 11am to 9pm.

4 Gay & Lesbian Nightlife

HILLCREST & UPTOWN

Bourbon Street This bar has several spaces, including an elegant outdoor patio meant to evoke jazzy New Orleans, a game room for darts or pool, a performance area (karaoke, drag shows, live music), and a lounge where DJs spin house music. A good share of gay and straight women show up on Fridays. Open daily from 4pm to 2am; Tuesday is karaoke night, Wednesday is "Fabulous Bingo." 4612 Park Blvd. (near Adams Ave.), University Heights. © 619/291-4043. www.bourbonstreetsd.com.

The Brass Rail San Diego's oldest gay bar (since 1960), this Hillcrest institution is neon-loud, with dancing nightly, and a come-as-you-are attitude. Thursday and Saturday are Latino Night, hip-hop reigns on Friday, Monday is open turntable night. 3796 Fifth Ave. (at Robinson St.), Hillcrest. © 619/298-2233. www.brassrailsd.com. Cover Fri–Sat $7.

The Flame   For 20 years, it was the city's top lesbian hangout; now, The Flame sits mostly idle except for weekends. It's boy's night on Friday, while a revolving schedule of dance clubs are in residence on Saturday and other occasional nights. It's a great space with a large dance floor and a cool neon sign out front. 3780 Park Blvd. at Robinson Ave. ⓒ 619/295-4163. www.flame-sd.com. Call for cover charge information.

Flicks   The first video bar in town, Flick's features VJs drawing from a database of 15,000 music and comedy clips, as well as various weekly special events, including Texas hold 'em tournaments on Thursday and The Dating Game on Monday. Tuesday is Girls Night Out (that is, for lesbians). 1017 University Ave., Hillcrest. ⓒ 619/297-2056. www.sdflicks.com. Cover Mon $2.

Numbers   It's a predominantly male crowd at this busy dance emporium, with three bars, two dance floors, and go-go boy dancers. Friday is Bad Kitties (ladies' night). Open Tuesday through Sunday from 1pm. 3811 Park Blvd. (at University Ave.), Hillcrest. ⓒ 619/294-9005. www.numbers-sd.com. Cover $3–$5.

Top of the Park   The penthouse bar of the Park Manor Hotel, which is adjacent to Balboa Park, is a very popular social scene on Friday evenings from 5 to 10pm. 525 Spruce St. (at Fifth Ave.), Hillcrest. ⓒ 619/291-0999. www.parkmanorsuites.com.

ELSEWHERE IN SAN DIEGO

Moby Dick's   This bar offers bay views and a garden patio in a rambling 1914 structure that also serves as the gay-oriented Harbor House hotel in Little Italy. There's free pool and darts, and it makes a great jumping off point from which to explore Little Italy. 642 W. Hawthorn (at State St.), Little Italy. ⓒ 619/338-9942. www.mobydicksbar.com.

Six Degrees   This casual lesbian gathering place north of Little Italy has an outdoor patio (where Sunday barbecues are held, from 4–7pm), and hosts a variety of entertainment, from DJs and live bands to go-go dancers and karaoke. Closed Thursday. 3175 India St. (at Spruce St.). ⓒ 619/296-6789. www.sixdegrees-sd.com.

5 More Entertainment

EVENING BAY CRUISES

Hornblower Cruises   Aboard the 151-foot antique-style yacht *Lord Hornblower*, you'll be entertained—and encouraged to dance—by a DJ playing a variety of music. The three-course meal is standard-issue banquet style, but the scenery is marvelous. Boarding is at 6:30pm, and the cruise runs from 7 to 10pm. 1066 N. Harbor Dr. (at Broadway Pier). ⓒ 888/467-6256 or 619/686-8715. www.hornblower.com. Tickets Sun–Fri $61, Sat $66 adults, 40% off for children ages 4–12; drinks cost extra. Bus: 2. Trolley: Embarcadero.

San Diego Harbor Excursion   This company offers nightly dinner packages, with choice of four entrees, dessert, and cocktails. For an additional $35 per couple, you can guarantee yourself a private table with window, plus a bottle of champagne, wine, or cider. A DJ plays dance music during the 2½-hour outing. Boarding is at 7pm, and the cruise lasts from 7:30 to 10pm. 1050 N. Harbor Dr. (at Broadway Pier). ⓒ 800/442-7847 or 619/234-4111. www.harborexcursion.com. Tickets $58 adults ($77 with alcoholic beverages), $36 children ages 4–12, free for children under 4; all prices $5 higher on Fri–Sat. Bus: 2. Trolley: Embarcadero.

CINEMA

A variety of multiscreen complexes around the city show first-run films. In the heart of the Gaslamp Quarter, you'll find Pacific's **Gaslamp 15,** Fifth Avenue at G Street, downtown (© **619/232-0400**); the 15 theaters all offer stadium seating with large screens and great sound systems. The AMC chain operates swarming complexes in both the **Mission Valley** and **Fashion Valley** shopping centers (© **858/558-2262**); both have free parking, but popular films sell out early on weekends. Current American independent and foreign films play at Landmark's five-screen **Hillcrest Cinema,** 3965 Fifth Ave., Hillcrest, which offers 3 hours of free parking (© **619/819-0236**); the **Ken Cinema,** 4061 Adams Ave., Kensington (© **619/819-0236**); and the four-screen **La Jolla Village,** 8879 Villa La Jolla Dr., La Jolla, also with free parking (© **619/819-0236**).

The **Museum of Photographic Arts** in Balboa Park (© **619/238-7559;** www.mopa. org) and the **Museum of Contemporary Art San Diego** in La Jolla (© **858/454-6985;** www.mcasd.org) both have ongoing film programs that are worth investigating. The **IMAX Dome Theater** at the Reuben H. Fleet Science Center (© **619/238-1233;** www.rhfleet.org), also in Balboa Park, features movies in the early evening projected onto the 76-foot tilted dome screen (later screenings on weekends). Planetarium shows are held the first Wednesday of the month.

CASINOS

San Diego County has 18 Native American Indian tribes—more than any other county in the nation. Half of them operate casinos in east and north San Diego County, and the **Convention & Visitors Bureau** (© **619/232-3101;** www.sandiego.org) publishes an *Official Casino Guide* with a comprehensive listing and discount coupons. Locations are shown on the "Eastern San Diego County" map on p. 269.

The most easily accessible casino from the downtown area is **Viejas Casino,** 5000 Willows Rd. in Alpine (© **800/847-6537;** www.viejas.com)—it's a straight shot out I-8 (exit Willows Rd.), less than a half-hour's drive away. Besides the usual table games, slots, bingo, and satellite wagering, Viejas presents an outdoor summer concert series that draws major artists; there is also an outlet center with more than 50 brand-name retailers. At press time, the casino was also adding 48,000 square feet of new space, which will encompass a VIP lounge and high-end bar, as well as more room for gaming.

The **Barona Valley Ranch Resort and Casino** is at 1932 Wildcat Canyon Rd., Lakeside (© **888/722-7662** or 619/443-2300; www.barona.com). Take I-8 east to Highway 67 north. At Willows Road, turn right and continue to Wildcat Canyon Road; turn left, and continue 6 miles to the 7,500-acre Barona Reservation (allow 40 min. from downtown). The casino features 2,000 Vegas-style slots, 59 table games, and an offtrack betting area. The resort, which includes 397 guest rooms and an 18-hole championship golf course, restricts alcohol consumption (the hotel, steakhouse, and golf course only), but allows smoking (the Indian reservations are exempt from California's nonsmoking laws).

Sycuan Resort & Casino is outside El Cajon, at 5469 Casino Way (© **800/279-2826** or 619/445-6002; www.sycuancasino.com). Follow I-8 east for 10 miles to the El Cajon Boulevard exit. Take El Cajon 3 blocks to Washington Avenue, turning right and continuing on Washington as it turns into Dehesa Road. Stay on Dehesa for 5 miles, and follow the signs (allow 30 min. from downtown). Sycuan features 2,000 slots, 65 game tables, a 1,200-seat bingo palace, an offtrack betting area, and a 450-seat theater that features name touring acts; Sycuan's 54 holes of golf are also some of San Diego's best.

Finds   Running with the Grunion

The **Grunion Run** is a wacky local tradition. If someone invites you down to the beach for a late-night fishing expedition, armed only with a sack and flashlight, don't be afraid. Grunion are 5- to 6-inch silvery fish that wriggle out of the water to lay their eggs in the sand. They make for decent eating (coated in flour and cornmeal, and then fried), providing you don't mind catching them by hand, but it's fun just to watch the action. April to early June is peak spawning season in Southern California (which, with Baja California, is the only place you'll find grunion). The grunion runs happen twice a month, after the highest tides and during the full or new moon, and anywhere from a few dozen to thousands of grunion can appear during a run. The fish prefer wide, flat, sandy beaches (such as Mission Beach); you'll spot more grunion if you go to a less-populated stretch of beach, with a minimum of light. For more information, go to the little critters' website: **www.grunion.org**.

To bet on the ponies, go to the **Del Mar** racetrack during the local racing season (July to mid-Sept); see p. 186 in chapter 7 for more details. At any time of the year, you can also bet on races being run far and wide at **Surfside Race Place,** at the Del Mar fairgrounds (© **858/755-1167;** www.surfsideraceplace.com).

6 Only in San Diego

San Diego's top three attractions—the **San Diego Zoo, Wild Animal Park,** and **Sea-World**—keep extended summer hours. SeaWorld caps its Summer Nights off at 9:30pm with a **fireworks** display nightly. You can catch them from SeaWorld or anywhere around Mission Bay.

Drive-ins may be all but a thing of the past, but San Diego's most unique movie venue is experienced at **Movies Before the Mast** (© **619/234-9153;** www.sdmaritime. org), aboard the *Star of India* at the waterfront Maritime Museum. During July and August, movies of the nautical genre (such as *The Perfect Storm* or *20,000 Leagues Under the Sea*) are shown on a special "screensail" Fridays and Saturdays at 7pm.

In summer, free concerts are offered at the Spreckels Organ Pavilion in Balboa Park on Monday (organ recitals) and Tuesday through Thursday nights (bands, dance, and vocal groups) as part of **Twilight in the Park** (© **619/239-0512;** www.balboapark.org). Concerts run from mid-June to August and begin at 7:30pm. Also in the park, **Starlight Theatre** presents four Broadway musicals in the Starlight Bowl from mid-June to mid-September (© **619/544-7827;** www.starlighttheatre.org). This venue is in the flight path to Lindbergh Field, and when planes pass overhead, singers stop in midnote, frozen like a statue, and wait for the roar to cease (really—we don't make this stuff up).

11

Side Trips from San Diego

Popular day trips include the beaches and inland towns of **"North County"** (as locals call the part of San Diego County north of the I-5/I-805 junction), as well as our south-of-the-border neighbor, **Tijuana.** All are less than an hour away.

If you have time for a longer trip, you can explore some distinct areas (all within 2 hours of the city) such as the **Disneyland Resort** in Anaheim; the wine country of **Temecula;** the gold-mining town of **Julian,** known for its apple pies; and the vast **Anza-Borrego Desert.** Whichever excursion you choose, you're in for a treat.

1 North County Beach Towns: Spots to Surf & Sun

The string of picturesque beach towns that dot the coast of San Diego County from Del Mar to Oceanside make great day-trip destinations for sun worshipers and surfers. *Be forewarned:* You'll be tempted to spend the night.

ESSENTIALS

GETTING THERE **Del Mar** is only 18 miles north of downtown San Diego, **Carlsbad** about 33 miles, and **Oceanside** approximately 36 miles. If you're driving, follow I-5 north; Del Mar, Solana Beach, Encinitas, Carlsbad, and Oceanside all have freeway exits. The northernmost point, Oceanside, will take about 45 minutes. The other choice by car is to wander up the old coast road, known as Camino del Mar, the "PCH" (Pacific Coast Highway), Old Highway 101, and County Highway S21.

From San Diego, the **Coaster** commuter train provides service to Solana Beach, Encinitas, Carlsbad, and Oceanside, and **Amtrak** stops in Solana Beach—just a few minutes north of Del Mar—and Oceanside. The Coaster makes the trip almost hourly on weekdays, four times on Saturday; Amtrak passes through 11 times daily each way. Call © **619/685-4900** for transit information or check with Amtrak at © **800/872-7245** or www.amtrak.com. United Express and America West Express fly into the **McClellan Palomar Airport,** 3 miles east of I-5 in Carlsbad.

VISITOR INFORMATION The **San Diego North Convention and Visitors Bureau,** based in Escondido (© **800/848-3336** or 760/745-4741; www.sandiego north.com), can answer your questions about North County as well as the Anza-Borrego desert.

DEL MAR ⋒⋒

A small community, Del Mar is home to just over 4,500 inhabitants in a 2-square-mile municipality. The town has adamantly maintained its independence, eschewing incorporation into the city of San Diego. It's one of the most upscale communities in the greater San Diego area, yet Del Mar somehow manages to maintain a casual, small-town ambience that radiates personality and charm. Come summer, the town swells as visitors flock in for the thoroughbred horseracing season and the county's San Diego Fair.

The history and popularity of Del Mar are inextricably linked to the **Del Mar Racetrack & Fairgrounds,** 2260 Jimmy Durante Blvd. (© 858/793-5555; www.del marfair.com). In 1933, actor Bing Crosby developed the Del Mar Turf Club, enlisting the help of Pat O'Brien and other celebrity friends. Soon, Hollywood stars like Lucille Ball, Desi Arnaz, Betty Grable, and Bob Hope were seen around Del Mar, and the town experienced a resurgence. An $80-million grandstand opened in 1993, built in the Spanish mission style of the original structure. Racing season is late July through mid-September.

Two excellent beaches flank Del Mar: **Torrey Pines State Beach** to the south and **Del Mar State Beach.** Both are wide, well-patrolled strands popular for sunbathing, swimming, and surfing (in marked areas). The sand stretches north to the mouth of the San Dieguito Lagoon, where people bring their dogs for a romp in the sea. Beyond the surf and the turf, the hub of activities for most residents and visitors is **Del Mar Plaza,** 1555 Camino del Mar, an open-air shopping center with fountains, sculptures, and palazzo-style terraces. There are good restaurants and shops, and super views to the sea, especially at sunset.

ESSENTIALS

For more information about Del Mar, contact or visit the **Del Mar Regional Chamber of Commerce Visitor Information Center,** 1104 Camino del Mar, Del Mar (© 858/755-4844; www.delmarchamber.org), which also distributes a detailed folding map of the area. The hours of operation vary according to volunteer staffing, but usually approximate weekday business hours. There's also a city-run website at **www.delmar.ca.us**.

FUN ON & OFF THE BEACH

Two excellent beaches flank Del Mar: **Torrey Pines State Beach** to the south and **Del Mar State Beach.** Both are wide, well-patrolled strands popular for sunbathing, swimming, and surfing (in marked areas). Torrey Pines is accessed from I-5 via Carmel Valley Road; take a left on McGonigle Road to a large parking area. For Del Mar Beach, take 15th Street west to Seagrove Park, where college kids can always be found playing volleyball and other lawn games while older folks snooze in the shade. Just past the park is the sand, though parking spaces are in short supply on weekends and any day in summer. There are **free concerts** in the park during July and August; for information, contact the City of Del Mar (© 858/755-9313). The sand stretches north to the mouth of the San Dieguito Lagoon, where people frequently bring their dogs to frolic in the surf. There are restrooms and showers near the park.

Beyond the surf and the turf, the hub of activities for most residents and visitors is **Del Mar Plaza,** a multistory structure at the corner of Camino Del Mar and 15th Street. This is one stylish shopping center and there are good restaurants and shops, and super views to the sea, especially at sunset. Also check out the **Del Mar Library,** built in 1914 as St. James Catholic Church and restored in the 1990s by the city. For many years it was the only place of worship between San Diego and San Clemente. Back then, Jimmy Durante and Desi Arnaz were parishioners; the ushers included Bing Crosby and Pat O'Brien.

Northern San Diego County

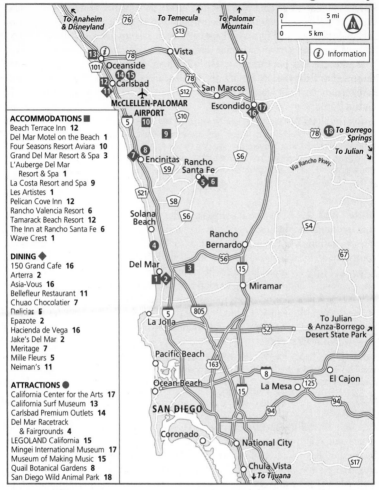

ACCOMMODATIONS ■
Beach Terrace Inn **12**
Del Mar Motel on the Beach **1**
Four Seasons Resort Aviara **10**
Grand Del Mar Resort & Spa **3**
L'Auberge Del Mar
   Resort & Spa **1**
La Costa Resort and Spa **9**
Les Artistes **1**
Pelican Cove Inn **12**
Rancho Valencia Resort **6**
Tamarack Beach Resort **12**
The Inn at Rancho Santa Fe **6**
Wave Crest **1**

DINING ◆
150 Grand Cafe **16**
Arterra **2**
Asia-Vous **16**
Bellefleur Restaurant **11**
Chuao Chocolatier **7**
Delicias **5**
Epazote **2**
Hacienda de Vega **16**
Jake's Del Mar **2**
Meritage **7**
Mille Fleurs **5**
Neiman's **11**

ATTRACTIONS ●
California Center for the Arts **17**
California Surf Museum **13**
Carlsbad Premium Outlets **14**
Del Mar Racetrack
   & Fairgrounds **4**
LEGOLAND California **15**
Mingei International Museum **17**
Museum of Making Music **15**
Quail Botanical Gardens **8**
San Diego Wild Animal Park **18**

Most evenings near dusk, brightly colored **hot-air balloons** punctuate the skies just east of the racetrack; they're easily enjoyed from the racetrack area (and by traffic-jammed drivers on I-5). If you find a balloon ride appealing, this is a great place to do it. See "Outdoor Activities" in chapter 7 for more details.

WHERE TO STAY
Very Expensive
L'Auberge Del Mar Resort & Spa ✸✸✸   On the site of the historic Hotel del Mar (1909–69), the luxurious yet intimate L'Auberge manages to attract casual week-enders as easily as the rich-and-famous horse set, who flock here during summer racing season. In 2002, the resort enhanced the lower-level full-service spa, polished up the poolside ambience, and revamped the dining room. The result is an atmosphere

of relaxation and welcome. Guest rooms exude the elegance of a European country house, complete with marble bathrooms, architectural accents, well-placed casual seating, and the finest bed linens and appointments. Twenty-five rooms boast fireplaces; all have a private balcony or terrace (several with an unadvertised view to the ocean). The hotel is across the street from Del Mar's main shopping and dining scene, and a short jog from the sand. J. Taylor's, the hotel's California/Mediterranean dining room, easily stands as one of Del Mar's finest restaurants; at the very least, don't miss its legendary breakfast of huevos rancheros.

1540 Camino del Mar (at 15th St.), Del Mar, CA 92014. ℂ 800/245-9757 or 858/259-1515. Fax 858/755-4940. www.laubergedelmar.com. 120 units. $325–$410 double; from $600 suite. AE, DC, MC, V. Valet parking $20. Take I-5 to Del Mar Heights Rd. west, and then turn right onto Camino del Mar Rd. **Amenities:** Restaurant; bar; 2 outdoor pools; tennis courts; indoor/outdoor fitness center; full-service spa; Jacuzzi; concierge; courtesy van; limited room service (6:30am–10pm); laundry service; dry cleaning. *In room:* A/C, TV w/pay movies, CD player, dataport, minibar, coffeemaker, hair dryer, iron, safe.

Expensive

Wave Crest 🐟🐟   On a bluff overlooking the Pacific, these gray-shingled bungalow condominiums are beautifully maintained and wonderfully private—from the street it looks nothing like a hotel. The studios and suites surround a lovingly landscaped courtyard; each has a queen-size bed, sofa bed, reproduced artwork, stereo, full bathroom, and fully equipped kitchen with dishwasher. The studios sleep two people; the one-bedroom accommodates up to four; two-bedroom units can sleep six. Some units face the garden or (pretty) street; rooms with ocean views are about $25 extra. In racing season (mid-June to mid-Sept), 90% of the guests are track-bound. It's a 5-minute walk to the beach, and shopping and dining spots are a few blocks away. There is an extra fee for maid service.

1400 Ocean Ave., Del Mar, CA 92014. ℂ 858/755-0100. www.wavecrestresort.com. 31 units. $195–$220 studio; from $265 suite. Weekly rates available. MC, V. Free parking. Take I-5 to Del Mar Heights Rd. west, turn right onto Camino del Mar, and drive to 15th St. Turn left and drive to Ocean Ave., and turn left. **Amenities:** Outdoor pool; Jacuzzi; coin-op laundry. *In room:* TV/DVD, kitchen.

Moderate

Del Mar Motel on the Beach *Finds*   The only property in Del Mar right on the beach, this simply furnished little white-stucco motel has been here since 1946. All rooms are of good size and are well kept (except for a number of worn-out lampshades); upstairs units have one king-size bed, and downstairs rooms have two double beds. Most of them have little in the way of a view, but two oceanfront rooms sit right over the sand (and are dressed up with fake plants and larger bathrooms). This is a good choice for beach lovers because you can walk along the shore for miles, and families can be comfortable knowing a lifeguard station is right next door, as are popular seaside restaurants Poseidon and Jake's. The motel has a barbecue and picnic table for guests' use.

1702 Coast Blvd. (at 17th St.), Del Mar, CA 92014. ℂ 800/223-8449 for reservations, or 858/755-1534. www.del marmotelonthebeach.com. 44 units (upper units w/shower only). $259–$299 double; call for heavily reduced Oct–May rates. AE, DC, DISC, MC, V. Free parking. Take I-5 to Via de la Valle exit. Go west, and then south on Hwy. 101 (Pacific Coast Hwy.); veer west onto Coast Blvd. *In room:* A/C, TV, fridge, coffeemaker, hair dryer, iron.

Les Artistes *Finds*   What do you get when you take a 1940s motel, put it in the hands of Sulana Sae-Onge, a Thai architect with a penchant for prominent painters? The answer is an intriguingly funky, disarmingly informal hotel, just a few blocks from downtown Del Mar, that's an art primer with European and Asian touches.

None of the rooms has an ocean view, and an empty lot sits awkwardly between the hotel and busy Camino del Mar, but charming touches abound—like a lily and koi pond, Asian chimes, and climbing bougainvillea—that you feel only privacy. Ten rooms have been redone as tributes to favored artists, two more were given a Japanese makeover. Artists spotlighted include Diego Rivera, whose room gives you the feeling of stepping into a warm Mexican painting, while the Monet room has an almost distractingly abstract swirl of color. Other subjects include O'Keeffe, Erté, Remington Botero, and Gauguin, while the Japanese Furo room is so authentic that a soaking tub is carved into the bathroom floor—the details are eye-filling. Downstairs rooms in the two-story structure have tiny private garden decks. Guests are also treated to free drinks down the street at Sae-Onge's **Cafe Secret,** 1140 El Camino Real (© **858/481-4239**), a Euro-style bistro serving breakfast and lunch.

944 Camino del Mar, Del Mar, CA 92014. © 858/755-4646. www.lesartistesinn.com. 12 units. $115–$195 double. Rates include continental breakfast. DISC, MC, V. Free parking. From I-5 go west on Del Mar Heights Rd., and then left onto Camino Del Mar Rd. Pets accepted with $50 cash deposit plus $30 cleaning fee. *In room:* TV.

WHERE TO DINE

Head to the upper level of the centrally located Del Mar Plaza, at Camino del Mar and 15th Street. You'll find **Il Fornaio Cucina Italiana** ✿ (© **858/755-8876**), for moderately priced and pleasing Italian cuisine and an *enoteca* (wine bar) with great ocean views; **Pacifica Del Mar** ✿✿ (© **858/792-0476**), which serves outstanding seafood; as well as **Epazote** (see review below). Head west from the plaza on 15th Street and you'll run into neighborhood favorite **Sbicca** ✿, 215 15th St. (© **858/481-1001**), serving modern American cuisine sweetened with great wine deals; and next to Jake's (also below), right on the beach, is **Poseidon,** 1670 Coast Blvd. (© **858/755-9345**), good for modestly priced California cuisine and fabulous sunsets. There are more winning vistas to go along with your wining and dining at lagoon-side **Cuvee** ✿, 2334 Carmel Valley Rd. (© **858/259-5878**), a great place to stop after a visit to Torrey Pines State Reserve.

The racetrack crowd congregates at **Bully's Restaurant,** 1404 Camino del Mar (© **858/755-1660**), for burgers, prime rib, and crab legs; the gold-card crowd heads for special-occasion meals at acclaimed **Pamplemousse Grill** ✿✿✿, 514 Via de la Valle (© **858/792-9090**); while **Blackhorse Grille,** 3702 Via de la Valle (© **858/523-0007**), also takes its inspiration from North County's horsey set and features an interpretive American cuisine. And if you're looking for fresh seafood—and lots of it—make a beeline to the Del Mar branch of San Diego's popular **Fish Market**, 640 Via de la Valle (© **858/755-2277**), near the racetrack (and reviewed on p. 109).

Arterra ✿✿ CALIFORNIAN   The name of this restaurant derives from "art of the earth," and the moniker is no mere marketing gimmick. On-site kitchen master Carl Schroeder crafts his menu based on what's available at Chino or Be Wise, the local farms specializing in heirloom vegetables. Needless to say, the menu is regularly adapted to meet the schedule of Mother Earth. You'll never eat rigid hothouse tomatoes—that's because Arterra doesn't serve them in winter, when tomatoes don't grow naturally in San Diego. But come in summer and you'll feast on a plate of ravishing heirloom tomatoes lightly garnished with pickled corn and warm goat cheese. Patrons can also sample four-, five-, and seven-course chef's tasting meals with wine pairings; there is a sushi bar as well. Housed in a drab, modern Marriott hotel, the broad dining room is impressive, cast in gold and purple tones, with accents of glass and copper, and plush leather banquettes. Arterra is run under the auspices of Bay Area chef Bradley Ogden, but it's basically all Schroeder's show. The breakfast, by the way, is superlative, and worth the trip by itself.

11966 El Camino Real (next to I-5 in the Marriott Del Mar), Carmel Valley. (© 858/369-6032. www.arterrarestaurant. com. Reservations recommended. Main courses $8–$17 breakfast, $16–$23 lunch, $25–$37 dinner. AE, DC, DISC, MC, V. Breakfast Mon–Fri 6:30–10:30am and Sat–Sun 7–11:30am; lunch Mon–Fri 11:30am–2pm; dinner daily 5:30–9:30pm; bar menu 11:30am–midnight. Free parking with validation, or $3 for valet parking.

Epazote ❧ SOUTHWESTERN/ASIAN FUSION   This splendid perch sits a couple stories above Camino del Mar, and although you're set back a few blocks from the beach, the unimpeded sea views are regal. The food is a mostly successful blend of Southwest themes with Asian accents, like fajitas done with mahimahi, chili-seared ahi bathed in a tequila-citrus butter, and shiitake mushroom and leek spring rolls. The bar has 72 different kinds of tequila, and the house margarita—made with fresh lime and lemon juice, Triple Sec, and Grand Chevalier and served in individual shakers over rocks—is one of the best in San Diego. Epazote also serves a Sunday brunch.

1555 Camino del Mar (at 15th St.), Del Mar Plaza. (© 858/259-9966. www.epazotedelmar.com. Reservations recommended on weekends. Main courses $9–$12 brunch, $8–$16 lunch, $13–$28 dinner. AE, DC, DISC, MC, V. Mon–Thurs 11:30am–9:30pm; Fri–Sat 11:30am–10:30pm; Sun 11am–9:30pm. Free parking in garage with validation. Bus: 101.

Jake's Del Mar ❧ SEAFOOD/CALIFORNIAN   The spirit of "aloha" permeates this Hawaiian-owned seafood-and-view outpost. Occupying a building originally constructed in 1910, Jake's has a perfect seat next to the sand so that diners on a series of terraces behind glass get straight-on views of the beach scene—sunbathers, surfers, and the occasional school of dolphins pass by (lunch here is *Endless Summer* no matter the weather). The predictable menu can't live up to the panorama, but it's prepared competently and service is swift (too swift, actually—don't let them rush you). At lunch you'll find cedar plank salmon in white corn–vermouth sauce, or shrimp fettuccini Provençal; sandwiches and salads round out the offerings. Dinner brings in the big boys: Maine lobster tails, giant scampi, and rack of lamb, for example. To enjoy the scene without the wallet wallop, come for happy hour (Mon–Fri 4–6pm and Sat 2:30–4:30pm), when a shorter bar/bistro menu is half-price and the mai tais are just $3.

1660 Coast Blvd. (at 15th St.), Del Mar. (© 858/755-2002. www.jakesdelmar.com. Reservations recommended. Main courses $9–$15 lunch, $18–$42 dinner. AE, DC, DISC, MC, V. Tues–Sat 11:30am–2:30pm; Sun brunch 10am–2pm; daily 5–9pm (Fri–Sat till 9:30pm). Valet parking $2–$3. Bus: 101.

SOLANA BEACH, ENCINITAS & CARLSBAD ❧

North of Del Mar and a 45-minute drive from downtown San Diego, the pretty communities of Solana Beach, Encinitas, and Carlsbad provide many reasons to linger on the California coast: good swimming and surfing beaches, small-town atmosphere, an abundance of antiques and gift shops, and a seasonal display of the region's most beautiful flowers.

Carlsbad was named for Karlsbad, Czechoslovakia, because of the similar mineral (some say curative) waters each produced. Carlsbad's once-famous artesian well was capped in the 1930s, but was redrilled in 1994, and the healthful water is flowing once more. Carlsbad is also a noted commercial flower-growing region, along with its neighbor Encinitas. A colorful display can be seen at **Carlsbad Ranch** (© **760/431-0352**) each spring, when 45 acres of solid ranunculus fields bloom into a breathtaking rainbow visible even from the freeway. In December, the nurseries are alive with holiday poinsettias.

VISITOR INFORMATION

The **Solana Beach Visitor Center** is near the train station at 103 N. Cedros (© **858/350-6006;** www.solanabeachchamber.com). The **Encinitas Visitors Center** is in a nondescript shopping mall immediately west of the I-5, at 138 Encinitas Blvd. (© **800/953-6041** or 760/753-6041; www.encinitaschamber.com). The **Carlsbad Visitor Information Center,** 400 Carlsbad Village Dr. (in the old Santa Fe Depot; © **800/227-5722** or 760/434-6093; www.carlsbadca.org), has information on flower fields and nursery touring.

FAMILY FUN

LEGOLAND California ★ *Kids*   The ultimate monument to the world's most famous plastic building blocks, LEGOLAND is the third such theme park, following branches in Denmark and Britain (and now Germany) that have proven enormously successful. Forty minutes north of downtown San Diego, the Carlsbad park offers a full day of entertainment for families. In addition to 5,000 LEGO models, the park is beautifully landscaped with 1,360 bonsai trees and other plants from around the world, and features more than 50 rides, shows, and attractions.

Attractions include hands-on interactive displays; a life-size menagerie of tigers, giraffes, and other animals; and scale models of international landmarks (the Eiffel Tower, Sydney Opera House, and so on), all constructed of LEGO bricks. "Mini-Land" is a 1:20 scale representation of American achievement, from a New England pilgrim village to Mount Rushmore and a replica of Washington, D.C. There's a DUPLO building area to keep smaller children occupied, and a high-tech ride where older kids can compete in LEGO TECHNIC car races. To give the park a little more appeal for older kids, there are three relatively gentle but fun roller coasters. Dino Island features the Coastersaurus, a roller coaster that climbs and dives through a menagerie of life-size LEGO brick dinos. The most recent attractions are **Knights' Tournament,** a "robo-coaster" that allows you to choose the intensity of your ride experience, and **Wild Woods,** a 25,000-square-foot miniature golf course that plays through more than 40 LEGO forest creatures.

The park is geared toward children ages 2 to 12, and there's just enough of a thrill-ride component that preteens will be amused, while most teenagers will find LEGOLAND a bit of a snooze. *A touring tip:* When the park opens, many visitors

---

Shoppers' Delight

From Adidas to Hilfiger, Bose to Wedgwood, some of the biggest names in fashion and retail are elbow to elbow at **Carlsbad Premium Outlets,** Paseo del Norte via Palomar Airport Road (© **888/790-7467** or 760/804-9000; www.premium outlets.com). This smart, upscale outlet mall features some 90 stores, including Crate & Barrel, Barney's New York, Nine West, and Harry & David—everything from soup (Le Gourmet Chef) to nuts (Sweet Factory). It even has a fine-dining component: Bellefleur Winery & Restaurant (p. 246) anchors one end of the shopping center.

hop in line for the first rides encountered (neither of which are special); it's better to head to the back side of the park where lines are shorter for the first hour or so.

1 Legoland Dr. ⓒ 877/534-6526 or 760/918-5346. www.legoland.com. $53 adults, $43 seniors and children 3–12, free to children under 3. AE, DISC, MC, V. July–Aug daily 10am–8pm; June daily 10am–5 or 6pm; off season Thurs–Mon 10am–5 or 6pm. Closed Tues–Wed Sept–May, but open daily during Christmas and Easter vacation periods. Parking $8. From I-5 take the Cannon Rd. exit east ½ mile, following signs for Legoland Dr.

FLOWER POWER

Carlsbad and its neighbor Encinitas make up a noted commercial flower-growing region. The most colorful display can be seen each spring at the **Flower Fields at Carlsbad Ranch,** 5704 Paseo del Norte, just east of I-5 on Palomar Airport Road; see p. 14 in chapter 2 for additional information on this seasonal event, or contact ⓒ 760/431-0352; www.theflowerfields.com. Also popular is **Weidners' Gardens,** 695 Normandy Rd., Encinitas (ⓒ 760/436-2194; www.weidners.com). Its field of 25,000 tuberous begonias blooms from mid-May to August, fuchsias and impatiens are colorful between March and September, and the holiday season brings an explosion of pansies and poinsettias, as well as the opportunity to dig your own pansies. Touring the grounds is free; Weidners is open November 1 to December 22 and March 1 through Labor Day, 9:30am to 5pm (closed Tues).

Even if you don't visit during the spring bloom—or during December, when area nurseries are alive with holiday poinsettias—there's plenty for the avid gardener to enjoy throughout the year. In fact, North County is such a popular destination for horticultural pursuits there's a **North County Nursery Hoppers Guide** in Encinitas. It's a comprehensive leaflet describing all the area growers and nurseries, including a map that shows where to find flowers; it's available at local visitor centers, or by mail—contact Weidners' Gardens for more information. Also read about the gardens at the Self-Realization Fellowship below.

Quail Botanical Gardens ⓕ   You don't have to possess a green thumb to be satisfied with an afternoon at this wonderful botanical facility. Boasting the country's largest bamboo collection, plus 35 acres of California natives, exotic tropicals, palms, cacti, Mediterranean, Australian, and other unusual collections, this serene compound is crisscrossed with scenic walkways, trails, and benches. Guided tours are given Saturdays at 10am, and there's a gift shop and nursery. The gardens are free to everyone on the first Tuesday of the month.

230 Quail Gardens Rd., Encinitas. ⓒ 760/436-3036. www.qbgardens.com. Admission $8 adults, $5 seniors and military, $3 children 3–12, free for children under 3. AE, MC, V. Daily 9am–5pm. From San Diego take I-5 north to Encinitas Blvd.; go ½ mile east, left on Quail Gardens Dr.

MORE FUN THINGS TO SEE & DO

Going from south to north, the hub of activity for Solana Beach is South Cedros Avenue, 1 block east of and parallel to the Pacific Coast Highway. In a 2-block stretch (from the train station south) are many of San Diego's best furniture and home-design shops, antiques stores, art dealers, and boutiques selling imported goods. You'll also find **The Belly Up Tavern,** one of San Diego's most appealing concert venues (p. 225).

In Encinitas, everyone flocks to **Moonlight Beach,** the city's long-suffering sandy playground. After overcoming a nasty sewage problem caused by a nearby treatment plant (don't ask), and receiving a much-needed replacement of eroded sand, Moonlight is back to its old, laid-back self. It offers plenty of facilities, including free parking, volleyball nets, restrooms, showers, picnic tables, and fire grates, and the company of fellow sunbathers. The beach entrance is at the end of B Street (at Encinitas Blvd.).

Also in Encinitas is the appropriately serene **Swami's Beach.** It's named for the adjacent Self-Realization Fellowship (see below), whose lotus-shaped towers are emulated in the pointed wooden stairway leading to the sand from First Street. This lovely little beach is surfer central in the winter. It adjoins little-known **Boneyard Beach,** directly to the north. Here, low-tide coves provide shelter for romantics and nudists; this isolated stretch can be reached only from Swami's Beach. There's a free parking lot at Swami's, plus restrooms and a picnic area.

The **Self-Realization Fellowship** was founded in 1920 by Paramahansa Yogananda, a guru born and educated in India, and the exotic-looking domes are what remain of the retreat originally built in 1937 (the rest was built too close to the cliff edge and tumbled into the sea). Today the site serves as a spiritual sanctuary for holistic healers and their followers, with meditation gardens and a gift shop that sells Fellowship publications and distinctive arts and crafts from India. The serene, immaculate gardens line a cliff, with often beautiful flower displays and koi ponds—they're a terrific place to cool off on a hot day. The gardens are entered at 215 K St. and are open Tuesday through Saturday 9am to 5pm and Sundays 11am to 5pm; admission is free. The bookstore is at 1105 Second St., between J and K streets (© **760/753-2888;** www.yogananda-srf.org).

While in Encinitas, don't miss a stop at **Chuao Chocolatier,** one of the top artisan chocolate makers in the country. The selection includes bonbons of soft banana and brown sugar caramel, and truffles of orange blossom and honey ganache. Though the prices are rich, one taste and you'll be hooked. All of the sensuous chocolates are handcrafted right on the premises—it's in the Lumberyard mall at 937 S. Coast Hwy. (© **888/635-1444;** www.chuaochocolatier.com).

Carlsbad is a great place for antiquing. Whether you're a serious shopper or seriously window-shopping, park the car, and stroll the 3 blocks of **State Street** between Oak and Beech streets. There are about two dozen shops in this part of town, where diagonal street parking and welcoming merchants lend a village atmosphere. Wares range from estate jewelry to country quilts, from inlaid sideboards to Depression glass. You never know what you'll find, but there's always something.

What about those therapeutic waters that put Carlsbad on the map? They're still bubbling at the **Carlsbad Mineral Water Spa,** 2802 Carlsbad Blvd. (© **760/434-1887;** www.carlsbadmineralspa.com), an ornate European-style building on the site of the original well. Step inside for mineral baths ($65 for 30 min.), massages, or body treatments in the spa's exotic theme rooms—or just pick up a refreshing bottle of this "Most Healthful Water" to drink on the go.

Carlsbad has two beaches, each with pros and cons. **Carlsbad State Beach** parallels downtown and is a fine place to stroll along a wide concrete walkway. It attracts outdoors types for walking, jogging, and inline skating, even at night (thanks to good lighting). Although the sandy strand is narrow, the beach is popular with bodysurfers, boogie boarders, and fishermen—surfers tend to stay away. Enter on Ocean Boulevard at Tamarack Avenue; there's a $4 fee per vehicle. Four miles south of town is **South Carlsbad State Beach,** almost 3 miles of cobblestone-strewn sand. A state-run campground at the north end is immensely popular year-round, and area surfers favor the southern portion. You may on occasion run into some tar blobs along the shoreline, but it's not a major concern here. There's a $4 per vehicle fee at the beach entrance, along Carlsbad Boulevard at Poinsettia Lane.

Just a stone's throw from LEGOLAND is a diversion for music lovers, the **Museum of Making Music,** 5790 Armada Dr. (© **877/551-9976** or 760/438-5996; www. museumofmakingmusic.org). Visitors go on a journey from Tin Pan Alley to MTV, stopping along the way to learn historic anecdotes about the American music industry or to try playing drums, guitars, or a digital keyboard. It's open Tuesday through Sunday from 10am to 5pm; admission is $5 for adults, $3 for children ages 4 to 18, seniors, students, and military.

You can enjoy everything but wing-walking on a vintage biplane from **Biplane, Air Combat & Warbird Adventures** (© **800/759-5667** or 760/438-7680; www. barnstorming.com). Two of the six aircraft even have an open cockpit. Flights leave from McClellan-Palomar Airport in Carlsbad, taking up to two passengers per plane on scenic flights down the coast. Weekday prices start at $274 for two-person, 20-minute biplane rides (weekend rates higher). Or, go for an Air Combat flight for a 2-hour mission that includes a 50-minute "dogfight" with another biplane "opponent" ($498 for one, or $996 if you bring your own adversary). If that's not thrilling enough, opt for a flight in a warbird, which includes loops and rolls with *you* at the helm ($556 and up). Lastly, there's a 30-minute "Great Gatsby" fly/dine package—snuggle up for a sunset flight for two aboard a 1920s biplane followed by dinner at the Four Seasons Aviara—$669 for two including tax, tip, and parking. *Bargain-hunter's tip:* Big discounts are available through the website, or ask when you call.

WHERE TO STAY
Very Expensive
Four Seasons Resort Aviara ★★★   In 1997, the top-drawer Four Seasons chain opened their first ocean-view golf and tennis resort in the continental United States, and Aviara quickly overtook nearby La Costa in the battle for chic movers and shakers—not to mention winning over the local residents, who head here for summer jazz concerts and the exceptional signature restaurant, Vivace. The resort offers every over-the-top comfort with the ease that sets Four Seasons apart; when not wielding club or racquet, guests can lie by the dramatically perched pool, relax in a series of carefully landscaped gardens, or luxuriate in the expanded spa where treatments incorporate regional flowers and herbs. A new recreation center also offers everything from basketball and sand volleyball to croquet and bocce ball. The ambience here is one of both privilege and comfort; rooms are decorated with soothing neutrals and nature prints that evoke the many birds in the surrounding Batiquitos Lagoon. In fact, the name Aviara is a nod to the egrets, herons, and cranes that are among the 130 bird species nesting in the protected coastal wetlands. The hotel's Arnold Palmer–designed golf course was designed to keep the wetlands intact and incorporates native marshlike plants throughout its 18 holes to help blend with the surroundings. The once-barren hills around the Four Seasons have since been built up with multimillion-dollar homes, but you can quickly escape to the wildness of the lagoon on a nature trail with several different access points.

7100 Four Seasons Point, Carlsbad, CA 92009. © **800/332-3442** or 760/603-6800. Fax 760/603-6801. www.four seasons.com/aviara. 329 units. $405–$585 double; from $725 suite. Children 17 and under stay free in parent's room. AE, DISC, MC, V. Valet parking $22. From I-5, take Poinsettia Lane east to Aviara Pkwy. S. **Amenities:** 4 restaurants; 2 bars; 2 outdoor pools; golf course; tennis courts; health club; recreation center; 15,000-sq.-ft. spa; Jacuzzi; bike rental; surf lessons; concierge; business center; José Eber salon; 24-hr. room service; in-room massage; babysitting;

laundry service; dry cleaning. *In room:* A/C, TV w/pay movies, DVD, VCR, CD player, PlayStation, dataport, minibar, coffeemaker, hair dryer, iron, safe.

La Costa Resort and Spa 🕊🕊   La Costa's $100 million renovation redefines the resort's California ranch–style motifs in a campuslike setting, with 45-foot bell towers, white stucco walls, and red tile roofs. Rooms have been refashioned with leather headboards and beds trimmed in Egyptian-cotton linens, dark walnut desks, metal accents, and bathrooms with quaint pedestal sinks; the effect is a nod to the influence of W-style big-city hotels, without being a total immersion in modernist élan. There's a huge new spa with 42 treatment rooms and outdoor sunning areas, a second pool, a sprawling gym, and the (Dr. Deepak) Chopra Center, which offers services and products relating to mind/body healing and transformation; the revamped clubhouse also includes a state-of-the-art fitness center. BlueFire Grill, the stylish bar and signature restaurant, faces out onto a lovely plaza and features three distinctly different, chic spaces, and the new Costa del Sol Ballroom is the largest such facility in the North County (La Costa now has 100,000 sq. ft. of indoor/outdoor meeting and banquet space). The resort has also added 149 privately owned luxury villas, which can also be rented. The 400-acre property boasts two championship 18-hole golf courses (home of the annual WGC-Accenture Match Play Championship), and a 21-court racquet club (home of the WTA Acura Tennis Classic).

Costa del Mar Rd., Carlsbad, CA 92009. 📞 800/854-5000 or 760/438-9111. Fax 760/931-7585. www.lacosta.com. 511 units. $300–$475 double; from $550 suite. Children under 18 stay free in parent's room. $20/day resort fee. Golf, spa, and tennis packages available. AE, DC, DISC, MC, V. Valet parking $25 overnight, self-parking $10. From I-5 take La Costa Ave. east; left on El Camino Real. **Amenities:** 4 restaurants; bar; 4 outdoor pools; 2 golf courses; tennis courts; spa; 6 Jacuzzis; bike rentals; concierge; business center; salon; 24-hr. room service; babysitting; laundry service; dry cleaning. *In room:* A/C, TV w/pay movies, dataport, minibar, coffeemaker, hair dryer, iron.

Expensive

Tamarack Beach Resort 🕊   This resort property's rooms, in the village across the street from the beach, are restfully decorated with beachy wicker furniture. Fully equipped suites—similar to Maui-style vacation condos—have stereos, full kitchens, washers, and dryers. The pretty Tamarack has a pleasant lobby and a sunny pool courtyard with barbecue grills. Dini's by the Sea is a good restaurant that is popular with locals.

3200 Carlsbad Blvd., Carlsbad, CA 92008. 📞 800/334-2199 or 760/729-3500. Fax 760/434-5942. www.tamarack resort.com. 77 units. $205–$235 double; from $300 suite. Children 12 and under stay free in parent's room. Rates include continental breakfast. AE, MC, V. Free underground parking. **Amenities:** Restaurant; outdoor pool; 2 Jacuzzis; exercise room. *In room:* A/C, TV/VCR, DVD, fridge, coffeemaker, hair dryer, iron.

Moderate

Beach Terrace Inn 🕊   At Carlsbad's only beachside hostelry (others are across the road or a little farther away), the rooms and the pool/Jacuzzi all have ocean views. This downtown property is tucked between rows of high-rent beach cottages and touts its scenic location as its best quality. The extra-large rooms suffer from generic "furnished bachelor pad"–style interiors, but some have balconies, fireplaces, and kitchenettes. Suites are affordable and have separate living rooms and bedrooms, making this a good choice for families. VCRs and films are available at the front desk. You can walk everywhere from here—except LEGOLAND, which is a 5-minute drive away.

2775 Ocean St., Carlsbad, CA 92008. 📞 800/433-5415 or 760/729-5951. Fax 760/729-1078. www.beachterrace inn.com. 49 units. $165 double; from $215 suite. Children 12 and under stay free in parent's room. Extra person $20. Rates include continental breakfast. AE, DC, DISC, MC, V. Free parking. **Amenities:** Outdoor pool; Jacuzzi; coin-op laundry; dry cleaning. *In room:* A/C, TV w/pay movies, dataport, fridge, coffeemaker, hair dryer, iron, safe.

Pelican Cove Inn ⓐ   Two blocks from the beach, this Cape Cod–style bed-and-breakfast hideaway combines romance with luxury. Hosts Kris and Nancy Nayudu see to your every need, from furnishing guest rooms with feather beds and down comforters to providing beach chairs and towels or preparing a picnic basket (with 24 hr. notice). Each room features a fireplace and private entrance; some have private spa tubs. The Pacific Room is most spacious, while the airy La Jolla Room has bay windows and a cupola ceiling. Courtesy transportation from the Carlsbad or Oceanside train stations is available.

320 Walnut Ave., Carlsbad, CA 92008. ⓒ 888/735-2683 or 760/434-5995. www.pelican-cove.com. 10 units. $90–$210 double. Rates include full breakfast. Extra person $15. AE, MC, V. Free parking. From downtown Carlsbad, follow Carlsbad Blvd. south to Walnut Ave.; turn left and drive 2½ blocks. *In room:* TV, no phone.

WHERE TO DINE

Always crowded is **Fidel's,** known for reliably tasty Mexican food and kickin' margaritas. The restaurant has a location in Solana Beach at 607 Valley Ave. (ⓒ **858/755-5292**), and there's a **Fidel's Norte** branch in Carlsbad at 3003 Carlsbad Blvd. (ⓒ **760/729-0903**).

One of the county's fine dining destinations is also in Carlsbad—the Aviara resort's **Vivace** ⓐⓐⓐ, 7100 Four Seasons Pt. (ⓒ **760/603-6999**). Bruce Logue, a veteran of the New York restaurant scene and protégé of Mario Batali, became head chef here in 2005. His arrival coincided with the unveiling of Aviara's **Brioso** wine bar, which offers Logue's antipasto menu and 30 California and Italian vintages by the glass, all accompanied by Pacific views through floor-to-ceiling windows. The architectural centerpiece of Carlsbad is **Neiman's,** 2978 Carlsbad Blvd. (ⓒ **760/729-4131**), a restored Victorian mansion complete with turrets, cupolas, and waving flags. Inside, there's a casual cafe and bar where LeRoy Neiman lithographs hang on the walls. The menu includes rack of lamb, macadamia-crusted salmon, filet mignon, and prime rib. There are also burgers, pastas, and salads. Sunday brunch is a tremendous buffet of breakfast and lunch items; happy hour, Monday through Friday, 3 to 6pm, offers draft beers and well drinks for as little as $2, plus food specials.

In Encinitas, look for **Vigilucci's,** 505 S. Hwy. 101 (at D St.; ⓒ **760/942-7332**), where the wafting fragrance of garlic always draws a crowd in for authentic southern Italy trattoria fare served in a lively atmosphere accented with old-world touches like stained glass and a grand mahogany bar; and the nearby **Siamese Basil,** 527 S. Coast Hwy. 101 (ⓒ **760/753-3940**), whose innocuous facade and bland interior belie a well-deserved reputation for fresh, zesty Thai food and a friendly attitude—you can even choose your spice quotient, from toddler-safe 1 to fire-alarm 10.

Bellefleur Restaurant ⓐ CALIFORNIAN/MEDITERRANEAN   This busy restaurant boasts a "California winery" experience, although there's no wine country evident among the surrounding outlet mall and car dealerships. But its cavernous, semi-industrial dining room, coupled with the wood-fired and wine-enhanced aromas emanating from a clanging open kitchen, do somehow evoke the ambience of California wine-producing regions like Santa Barbara and Napa. In addition to the main seating area, there's an open-air dining patio, a tasting bar, and a glassed-in barrel aging room. The place can be noisy and spirited, drawing exhausted shoppers for cuisine that incorporates North County's abundant produce with fresh fish and meats. Lunchtime sandwiches and salads surpass the shopping-mall standard, while dinner choices include charbroiled pork chops finished with apple and cinnamon compote, and jumbo shrimp stuffed with seafood, baked and topped with a lobster-sherry sauce. Sunday brunch is served from 10am to 2pm.

5610 Paseo del Norte, Carlsbad. © 760/603-1919. www.bellefleur.com. Reservations suggested. Lunch $9–$18; dinner $18–$33. AE, DISC, MC, V. Mon–Thurs 11am–9pm; Fri–Sat 11am–10pm; Sun 10am–9pm.

Meritage ★★ CALIFORNIAN   This appealing charmer is in the attractive Lumberyard Mall in the heart of Encinitas, and the cuisine embraces California styles with easygoing flair. Start with delicious, tender panko-cornmeal-crusted calamari, or try the grilled vegetable plate, which reveals the bold flavors of local (often organic) produce. Then move on to the mains, which range from pasta dishes embellished with more bright vegetables to organic chicken breast stuffed with apples, brie, and sweet onions, to rosemary-horseradish crusted filet mignon. The duck breast in orange-spice cognac sauce with chestnut-sage risotto is also a winner. On Monday and Wednesday nights, wine lovers are treated to half off almost all bottles, a great time to take a chance on an exotic vintage (which the restaurant specializes in; great selection by the glass, too); or come on Thursdays and celebrate Martini Night with $4 pours.

897 S. Coast Highway 101, Encinitas. © 760/634-3350. www.meritage1.com. Reservations suggested for Fri–Sat evenings. Lunch $8–$13; dinner $17–$29. AE, DISC, MC, V. Daily 11:30am–3pm (Sat–Sun noon—3pm) and 5–9:30pm (till 10:30pm Fri–Sat).

OCEANSIDE

The northernmost community in San Diego County (actually, it's a city of 170,000), Oceanside is inextricably linked to the military. Camp Pendleton, one of the nation's largest military bases, established in 1942, is immediately north, and the city's fortunes rise and fall with the Marines. For example, the abundant dry cleaners and barbershops downtown continue to cling desperately to life (half of their customers are Marines deployed in Iraq).

Oceanside claims almost 4 miles of beaches and has one of the West Coast's longest over-the-water wooden piers, measuring 1,954 feet (595.5m). The 1950s-style diner at the end of the pier, **Ruby's,** is a great place for a quick and inexpensive lunch over the ocean. The wide, sandy beach, pier, and well-tended recreational area with playground equipment and an outdoor amphitheater are within easy walking distance of the train station.

VISITOR INFORMATION

Oceanside's **California Welcome Center,** 928 North Coast Hwy. (© **800/350-7873** or 760/722-1534; www.oceansidechamber.com), provides information on local attractions, dining, and accommodations.

EXPLORING OCEANSIDE

One of the nicest things to do in Oceanside is to stroll around the city's upscale **harbor.** Bustling with pleasure craft, it's lined with condominiums and boasts a Cape Cod–themed shopping village. A launch ramp, visitor boat slips, and charter fishing are here. The **Harbor Days Festival** in mid-September typically attracts 100,000 visitors for a crafts fair, entertainment, and food booths; call © **760/722-1534** for more details.

Probably the area's most important attraction is **Mission San Luis Rey** ★ (© **760/757-3651;** www.sanluisrey.org), a few miles inland at 4050 Mission Ave. Founded in 1798, it's the 18th and largest of California's 21 missions (you might recognize it as the backdrop for one of the Zorro movies). You can tour the mission, its impressive church, exhibits, grounds, and cemetery; the cost is $5 for adults and $3 for students. Hours are daily from 10am to 4pm.

For a wide selection of rental watercraft, head to **Boat Rentals of America** (© 760/722-0028), on Harbor Drive South. It rents everything from kayaks, WaveRunners, and electric boats for relaxed harbor touring, to 14- and 22-foot sailboats, fishing skiffs, and Runabout cruisers. Even if you have no experience, there's plenty of room for exploration in the harbor. Sample rates: single kayak, $15 per hour; powerboat, from $55 per hour; and WaveRunner, $95 per hour. Substantial winter discounts are available; Boat Rentals keeps seasonal hours, so call for specific information.

Beyond Camp Pendleton, Oceanside's other main identity is with surfers, and there's no better place to learn the lore than the **California Surf Museum,** 223 North Coast Hwy. (© 760/721-6876; www.surfmuseum.org). Founded in 1985, both surf devotees and curious onlookers will delight in the museum's unbelievably extensive collection. Boards and other relics chronicle the development of the sport. Many belonged to surfers whose names are revered by local surfers, including Hawaiian Duke Kahanamoku and local daredevil Bob Simmons. Vintage photographs, beach attire, 1960s beach graffiti, and surf music all lovingly bring the sport to life—there's even a photo display of the real-life Gidget. A gift shop offers unique items, including memorabilia of famous surfers and surf flicks, plus novelty items like a surf-lingo dictionary. The museum is open daily from 10am to 4pm; admission is free, but donations are requested. Oceanside's world-famous surfing spots attract competitions, including the **Longboard Surf Contest** held in August (www.oceansidelongboardsurfingclub.org).

The **Oceanside Beach** starts just outside Oceanside Harbor, where routine harbor dredging makes for a substantial amount of fluffy, clean white sand. It runs almost 4 miles south to the Carlsbad border. Along the way you can enjoy the **Strand,** a grassy park that stretches along the beach between Fifth Street and Wisconsin Avenue. Benches with scenic vistas abound, and the Strand also borders on the Oceanside Pier, which in turn is usually flanked by legions of bobbing surfers. Parking is at metered street spaces or in lots, which can fill up on nice summer days. Harbor Beach, which is separated from the rest by the San Luis River, charges $5 admission per vehicle. Farther south, there is no regulated admission, and after Witherby Street or so, parking is free (but in demand) along residential streets. Around the pier are restrooms, showers, picnic areas, and volleyball nets.

WHERE TO STAY & DINE

The inexpensive-to-moderate **Oceanside Marina Inn,** 2008 Harbor Dr. N. (© 800/252-2033 or 760/722-1561; www.omihotel.com), boasts a scenic perch way at the mouth of the harbor and offers a quiet, nautical setting for those who want to stay overnight. Despite dingy hallways, the rooms are spacious, light, and refurnished in an attractive, vaguely colonial-tropical (think Bombay Company) style. An ocean-view pool and spa, complimentary breakfast, and romantic gas fireplace in every room make the deal even sweeter.

Several surf-and-turf harborside restaurant stalwarts are close by, including **Joe's Crab Shack** (© 760/722-1345), **Jolly Roger** (© 760/722-1831), and **Monterey Bay Canners** (© 760/722-3474).

Elsewhere in Oceanside, you can get a side helping of history with your burger and fries at the original **101 Cafe,** 631 S. Coast Hwy. (© 760/722-5220). This humble diner dates from the earliest days of the old coast highway that was the only route between Los Angeles and San Diego until 1953 brought the interstate.

2 North County Inland: From Rancho Santa Fe to Palomar Mountain

The coastal and inland sections of North County are as different as night and day. Inland you'll find beautiful barren hills, citrus groves, and conservative ranching communities where agriculture plays an important role.

Rancho Santa Fe is about 27 miles north of downtown San Diego; from there the scenic Del Dios Highway (S6) leads to Escondido, 32 miles north of San Diego. Nearly 70 miles from the city is Palomar Mountain in the Cleveland National Forest, which spills over the border into Riverside County.

RANCHO SANTA FE

Exclusive Rancho Santa Fe was once the property of the Santa Fe Railroad, and the eucalyptus trees the railroad grew created a stately atmosphere. The area was "discovered" in the early 1900s by movie director Theodore Reed, who encouraged his friends Douglas Fairbanks and Mary Pickford to purchase property as an investment; they bought 800 acres in 1924. After just a few minutes in town today, it becomes apparent that Rancho Santa Fe is a playground for the über wealthy, though not in the usual pretentious sense. Proving the adage that true breeding makes everyone feel at ease, and that it's gauche to flaunt your money, this upscale slice of North County is a sweet little town that's enjoyed by everyone. Primarily residential Rancho Santa Fe has just two hotels that blend into the eucalyptus groves surrounding the town. Shopping and dining—both quite limited, and refined—revolve around a couple of understated blocks known locally as "the Village." There are more real estate businesses than anything else; The homes advertised all list for well into seven digits. Welcome to perhaps the most affluent community in the United States.

ESSENTIALS

GETTING THERE   From San Diego, take I-5 north to Lomas Santa Fe (County Hwy. S8) east; it turns into Linea del Cielo and leads directly into the Village. If you continue through town on Paseo Delicias, you'll pick up the Del Dios Highway (County Hwy. S6), the scenic route via Lake Hodges to Escondido and the **Wild Animal Park.**

WHERE TO STAY

The Inn at Rancho Santa Fe ✿✿   Spanish Colonial Revival–style tile-roofed cottages are nestled throughout this resort's 23 acres; the decor is English country–flavored and sturdy, and many rooms have fireplaces, kitchenettes, and secluded patios; standard hotel rooms are found in the original lodge building—all are generously sized. A collection of antique, hand-carved model sailing ships is on display in the lobby, and beautifully landscaped grounds contain towering eucalyptus, colorful flowers, and expansive rolling lawns (a favorite among the canine guests welcomed at the inn). A nifty extra is guest membership at Rancho Santa Fe Golf Club, and within a few hundred feet of your room are three of San Diego's finest restaurants: **Delicias** (see review below), **Mille Fleurs** (see review below), and the Inn's own **Dining Room.** A five-year plan to upgrade the rooms and facilities will be completed in 2009, and great care is being taken to preserve the historic property's architecture and charm.

5951 Linea del Cielo (P.O. Box 869), Rancho Santa Fe, CA 92067. ℭ **800/843-4661** or 858/756-1131. Fax 858/759-1604. www.theinnatrsf.com. 87 units. $255–$310 double; from $495 suite. AE, DC, MC, V. Free parking. From I-5, take the Lomas Santa Fe exit, following signs to Rancho Santa Fe. The Inn is in the center of town. Pets accepted. **Amenities:** Restaurant; bar; outdoor pool; tennis courts; fitness room; limited room service (7:30am–9pm); in-room massage; babysitting; coin-op laundry and laundry service; dry cleaning. In room: A/C, TV, hair dryer, dataport, safe.

Rancho Valencia Resort ✦✦✦   Sister property of the La Valencia Hotel (p. 88) in La Jolla, Rancho Valencia is the only Relais & Châteaux property in Southern California. It's a luxurious tennis-resort hideaway set on 40 beautifully landscaped acres, featuring 49 stand-alone, hacienda–style accommodations, all with fireplaces, custom furniture, and colorful tilework. As of press time, the resort was still putting the finishing touches on what is sure to be a highly impressive spa. The $12 million facility encompasses 2.5 acres and has five pools, including a designated Watsu pool, indoor/outdoor treatment rooms, and couples rooms with fireplaces and private outdoor showers and tubs. Rancho Valencia's main dining room, with its oak-beamed ceilings, fireplace, and large picture windows, is at once rustic and sophisticated. Ask for table 42—you'll have unobstructed sunset vistas and be able to watch the hot-air balloons drift by. Outdoor dining is available on the patio overlooking the tennis courts and the valley beyond, or in the old-world courtyard anchored by a small fountain and framed in bougainvillea. Playing privileges are offered at four nearby golf courses.

5921 Valencia Circle (P.O. Box 9126), Rancho Santa Fe, CA 92067. ✆ 800/548-3664 or 858/756-1123. Fax 858/756-0165. www.ranchovalencia.com. 49 units. $390–$645 double; from $520 suite. AE, DC, MC, V. Free parking. From I-5 take the Del Mar Heights exit heading east, go left on El Camino Real, right on San Dieguito Rd., right on Rancho Digueño Rd., and make an immediate left onto Rancho Valencia Dr. Pets $75 per day. **Amenities:** Restaurant; bar; pool; Jacuzzi; tennis courts; spa; 24-hr. room service; dry cleaning; shoe shine. *In room:* A/C, 2 TVs, DVD w/pay movies, CD player w/selection of CDs, dataport, minibar, fridge, coffeemaker, hair dryer, safe, fireplace, private garden patio, daily paper.

WHERE TO DINE

If you're looking for a casual lunch, breakfast, or snack, seek out **Thyme in the Ranch,** 16905 Avenida de Acacias (✆ **858/759-0747**), a bakery/cafe that's open Tuesday through Saturday from 7am to 3pm. Hidden on a small plaza behind chic Mille Fleurs, this tiny treasure is well known (as evidenced by constant lines at the counter). Salads, sandwiches, soup, and quiche are the menu mainstays—all delicious—but the baked treats are extra-special.

Delicias ✦✦✦ CALIFORNIAN   Featuring a mélange of antiques and wicker, accented by woven tapestries and floor-to-ceiling French doors, this cozy restaurant with an outdoor patio is equally appropriate for a casual meal or special occasion. Service is attentive and personable, and the food is delicious. Intriguing—but not overly complex—flavor blends are the hallmark of a menu that ranges from the zesty Pacific Rim to the sunny Mediterranean, interpreted with a subtle French accent. Pan-roasted Alaskan halibut comes with lobster risotto, morel mushrooms, and fava beans; and rack of lamb is served with a goat cheese–herb potato cake and dried fig and apricot compote. Even mac-and-cheese gets a fresh spin, primped with prosciutto, peas, shaved truffles, and *six* cheeses.

6106 Paseo Delicias. ✆ 858/756-8000. Reservations recommended on weekends. Main courses $13–$22 lunch, $20–$39 dinner. AE, DC, MC, V. Mon–Fri 11:30am–2:30pm; Sun–Thurs 5:30–9pm; Fri–Sat 5:30–10pm.

Mille Fleurs ✦✦✦ FRENCH   Chef Martin Woesle has been wowing critics and patrons for years at this landmark restaurant, owned by the same restaurateur who operates **Bertrand at Mister A's** (p. 111). Although Mille Fleurs has that French name and a Gallic country cottage atmosphere, Woesle doesn't like to limit himself to just a French palette—he mixes in elements of American and Californian cuisine, and gives nods to tastes from his native Germany. Every dish, every dessert is a special here— there is a new menu daily, highlighted by whatever Woesle has found during his morning sojourn to nearby Chino Farm. Expect something along the lines of squab breast and foie gras salad with arugula in a black truffle vinaigrette, or venison chop with potato noodles, fresh cherries, and asparagus flan in port wine sauce. The sky's the limit with the dizzying wine list, one of the best in San Diego. There is also a reasonably priced prix-fixe meal Sunday through Tuesday evenings; the bar has live entertainment Wednesday through Saturday evenings. The charming outdoor patio is a great spot for lunch; and if you want to have a really private dinner, ask for the "Booth," a very intimate space that seats up to 8.

6009 Paseo Delicias. ✆ 858/756-3085. www.millefleurs.com. Reservations recommended. Main courses $16–$28 lunch, $29–$36 dinner. AE, DC, MC, V. Mon–Fri 11:30am–2pm; daily 6–9:30pm (from 5:30pm Sat).

ESCONDIDO

Best known as the home of the San Diego Wild Animal Park (p. 140), Escondido is a city of 138,000, founded near the site of the historic battlefield where the bloodiest fight of the Mexican-American war of 1846 was fought. Escondido is surrounded by agriculture, particularly citrus and avocado (neighboring Fallbrook is called the avocado capital of the world). Grand Avenue, old Escondido's downtown main drag, is experiencing a well-conceived renewal, with historic storefronts filled by new restaurants and an antiques district with a mother lode of finds. Two of the biggest are **Escondido Antique Mall,** 135 W. Grand (✆ **760/743-3210**) and **Hidden Valley Antique Emporium,** 333 E. Grand (✆ **760/737-0333**), each holding dozens of individual dealers.

This is also the site of the $81-million **California Center for the Performing Arts,** an attractive 12-acre campus that includes two theaters, an art museum, and a conference center. It's worth the 45-minute drive to Escondido (along I-15 north to the Valley Parkway exit) just to see the appealing postmodern architecture of this facility, which opened in 1994. Performances by the San Diego Symphony, renowned soloists, and national dance companies are a regular event, with ticket prices below what you might expect in a big city. To find out what's playing and to get tickets, call ✆ **800/ 988-4253,** or visit www.artcenter.org.

As the heart of a major agricultural area, it's not surprising that the farmers' market on Tuesday afternoons is one of the county's best. Another attraction is **Orfila Vineyards,** on the way to the Wild Animal Park (see "Special-Interest Sightseeing" in chapter 7). One mile east of the Wild Animal Park is the **San Pasqual Battlefield State Historic Park** (✆ **760/737-2201**); there's a picnic area, a half-mile loop trail, and a small museum that details the bloody clash of 1846 in which *Californios* loyal to Mexico, armed only with lances, repulsed—at least temporarily—invading U.S. troops.

Visitor information is available at the **San Diego North Convention and Visitors Bureau,** 360 N. Escondido Blvd. in Escondido (✆ **800/848-3336** or 760/745-4741; www.sandiegonorth.com), open Monday through Friday, 8:30am to 5pm.

Mingei International Museum ✦ An offshoot of the wonderful Balboa Park museum (p. 148) devoted to "art of the people," this 21,000-square-foot Escondido branch opened in 2003 at the site of an abandoned JCPenney's department store. Rotating exhibitions offer folk art, crafts, and design from countries around the world; displays might encompass textiles, costumes, jewelry, toys, pottery, paintings, or sculpture. Although not as concentrated as the Balboa Park facility, there are often fine shows well worth the trip.

155 W. Grand Ave. ✆ **760/735-3355.** www.mingei.org. Admission $6 adults, $3 seniors, children 6–17 and students with ID, free for children under 6. AE, MC, V. Tues–Sat 1–4pm. From San Diego take I-15 north to Valley Pkwy.; go 1 mile east, it turns into Grand Ave.

Finds **Touring Temecula's Wineries**

Over the line in Riverside County, 60 miles north of San Diego via I-15, Temecula is known for its 20-plus wineries and the increasingly noteworthy vintages they produce. The town's very name (pronounced "ta-*meck*-you-la") provides the first clue to this valley's success in the volatile winemaking business/art. It translates (from a Native American language) as "where the sun shines through the mist," which identifies two of the three climatological factors necessary for viticulture. The third is Rainbow Gap, an opening to the south through the Agua Tibia Mountains, which allows cool afternoon sea breezes to enter the 1,500-foot elevation. Franciscan missionaries planted the first grapevines here in the early 1800s, but the land ended up being used primarily for raising cattle. The 87,000-acre Vail Ranch operated from 1904 until it was sold in 1964. Grapevines began to take root in the receptive soil again in 1968, and the first Temecula wines were produced in 1971.

Most of the wineries are strung along Rancho California Road, and harvest time is generally from mid-August to September. But visitors are welcome year-round to tour, taste, and stock up. Among the more notable are **Callaway Vineyard & Winery** (② 800/472-2377 or 951/676-4001; www.callaway coastal.com), the biggest winery in the region and also the best known. In-depth tours are offered throughout the day between 11am and 3pm (4pm weekends), and they have a casual bistro, Allie's. Across the street from Callaway stands another old-timer, **Thornton Winery** (② 951/699-0099; www. thorntonwine.com), which makes a good choice if you visit only one location, for Thornton provides an all-in-one overview of Temecula's wine country. It has a striking setting, fragrant herb garden, extensive gift shop, and

WHERE TO STAY & DINE

Interesting accommodations in Escondido are limited, though the city may soon be moving forward with a major downtown hotel project. The **Welk Resort Center,** 8860 Lawrence Welk Dr. (② **800/932-9355**), is a moderate-to-expensive resort a few miles north. Lodging is in one- and two-bedroom condo-style "villas," and the property offers golf, tennis, and live theatrical entertainment.

Asia-Vous 🐀🐀🐀 FRENCH/ASIAN With all the cultural growth occurring in Escondido, North County's largest city, it's no wonder big-time cooking has made an appearance as well. The twist, though, is that it wasn't brought to town by some transplanted hired gun looking for a place in the sun—it's being served up by chef/owner Riko Bartolome, who grew up 15 minutes from his restaurant. Bartolome, one of San Diego's finest chefs, transformed a former tax preparer's office into an intimate, stylish space that has been a hit since it opened in 2004. Taking advantage of local, seasonal products, he applies Asian accents to classic French and European cooking, offering items like Sea of Cortez scallops with saffron-potato ragout, housemade gnocchi with lobster, squash blossoms, and Tahitian vanilla bean, and almond-duck Schnitzel with sweet-and-sour cabbage and Chinese black bean-apricot sauce. World-class food.

award-winning restaurant, and tours are offered on weekends, between 11am and 4pm.

At **Mount Palomar Winery** (© 800/854-5177 or 951/676-5047; www.mount palomar.com), you might see unfamiliar names on some labels. Take the informative tour to learn about the process of handcrafting Mediterranean varietals like Sangiovese, Cortese, and Rhône-style blends of French grapes and even cream sherry. Perhaps the most welcoming tasting room is the nouvelle yellow farmhouse of the **Maurice Car'rie Winery** (© 951/676-1711; www. mauricecarriewinery.com), which produces 14 varietals, and has opened an on-site Pacific Rim eatery, The Plantation House. Farther up the road is another venture by this family, **VR La Cereza Vineyard and Winery** (© 951/ 699-6961)—the souvenir-minded will love VR's gift shop, filled with logo items and wine-related gifts. Each of these last two wineries is open daily from 10am to 5pm, and also has gourmet deli items for composing a picnic to enjoy in Maurice Car'rie's rose-filled front garden and patio.

For detailed information on Temecula wine touring, contact the **Temecula Valley Winegrowers Association** (© 800/801-9463 or 951/699-6586; www. temeculawines.org) and request the *Wine Country* pamphlet, a guide with winery locations, hours, and a brief description of each. The **Temecula Valley Chamber of Commerce,** 26790 Ynez Ct. (© 866/676-5090 or 951/676-5090; www.temecula.org), has a *Visitors Guide* and can provide info on accommodations, golf, fishing, and the region's famous **Temecula Valley Balloon & Wine Festival,** held in June (see "San Diego Calendar of Events" in chapter 2).

417 W. Grand Ave. © 760/747-5000. www.asiavousrestaurant.com. Reservations recommended. Main courses $11–$18 lunch, $17–$39 dinner. AE, DC, MC, V. Tues–Fri 11:30am–2:30pm; Tues–Sat 5–9pm. Free parking behind the building. From San Diego take I-15 north to Valley Pkwy.; go 1 mile east, it turns into Grand Ave.

Hacienda de Vega 🎋🎋 *(Finds* MEXICAN   San Diego County has an abundance of Mexican restaurants, but a shortage of places that specialize in *Mexican* Mexican—that is, food as one would encounter in an upscale Mexico City venue. Hacienda de Vega is a 1.6-acre, oasis-like escape just south of downtown Escondido, in a ranchero that opens onto a lovely garden with a large pond—a waterfall eliminates most of the freeway noise. Start with one of several margarita options—the tamarind-flavored variety offers a vibrant twist on this classic—and move on to an appetizer sampler that will prime your taste buds with potato/chorizo quesadillas, *sopes,* and ceviche. The menu features robust dishes like chicken in mole sauce, seared pork loin lathered in a beer-and-potato sauce, and *chipotlacos,* which is zesty pork carnitas wrapped up like an enchilada. Or come on Sunday when a wonderful brunch highlights five different authentic stews. Yes, the menu holds fajitas, burritos, and tacos for those who need them, but take a risk on Mrs. Vega's specialties and you may be pleasantly surprised.

2608 S. Escondido Blvd. © 760/738-9805. www.haciendadevega.com. Reservations recommended for dinner. Main courses $6.50–$12 lunch (till 3:30pm), $12–$19 dinner; Sun all-you-can-eat brunch $19. AE, DC, MC, V. Mon–Thurs

11:30am–9pm; Fri–Sat 11:30am–10pm; Sun brunch 10am–3pm; Sun dinner 5–9pm. Free parking. From San Diego and I-15 north, take the Central City Pkwy. exit; after 1 mile, turn right onto Citracado Pkwy. and take an immediate right onto the frontage road, S. Escondido Blvd.

150 Grand Cafe 👯👯 AMERICAN   The original standard-bearer for fine dining in Escondido, this delightful cafe has a reputation that stretches across the county. Just around the corner from the performing arts center on a charming stretch of historic Grand Avenue that practically screams Norman Rockwell, 150 Grand serves sophisticated, contemporary American cuisine using the best local products. The restaurant embraces an Americana vibe—patrons are greeted by a bold, room-length mural that pays homage to artist Edward Hopper, and the main dining room is as comfy as a living room and, in fact, actually looks like one (fireplace, bookshelves, and all). Chef/owner Carlton Greenawalt takes full advantage of the region's fresh product and proximity to wineries, creating an ever-changing menu of dishes such as raspberry and Zinfandel braised salmon, pecan-crusted pork loin in cranberry-ruby port reduction, and tangerine-honey glazed duck breast. There's also a bar and outdoor seating.

150 W. Grand Ave. 🕐 **760/738-6868.** www.150grandcafe.com. Reservations recommended, especially for weekend nights. Main courses $11–$15 lunch, $20–$33 dinner. AE, DC, MC, V. Mon–Sat 11:30am–2:30pm; Mon–Sat 5–9pm. Free parking on the street. From San Diego take I-15 north to Valley Pkwy.; go 1 mile east—it turns into Grand Ave.

PALOMAR MOUNTAIN

At an elevation of 5,600 feet, **Palomar** is a tiny mountain community 70 miles north of downtown San Diego. The village probably wouldn't be here today but for its famous observatory. From San Diego, take I-15 north to Highway 76 east, and turn left onto County Highway S6—a serpentine road climbs to the summit. Even if you don't want to inch your way to the top, drive the 3 miles to the lookout or just beyond it to the campground, grocery store, restaurant, and post office.

For many years the largest telescope in the world, **Palomar Observatory** 👯 (🕐 **760/742-2119**) has kept a silent vigil over the heavens since 1949. The project was proposed and funded with $1 million from the Rockefeller Foundation in 1928, but it took another 2 decades to find a suitable site, build the 135-foot-high dome, perfect the massive mirror (made from the then-new glass blend Pyrex), and build a road to the summit. Owned by the California Institute of Technology, the telescope's 200-inch mirror weighs 530 tons—it took 2 days to haul the mirror up the Palomar road. Now completely computerized, the telescope is still actively searching the skies—in 2003, Palomar was where the planetoid Sedna, the most distant object in our solar system, was discovered.

Start your visit in the museum, which is open daily from 9am to 4pm and has a continuously running informative video that makes a walk up the hill to the observatory more meaningful. The gift shop is open weekends only, daily during the summer. Palomar is primarily a research facility, and you'll only be able to look at (not through) the mammoth telescope. Behind-the-scenes tours are offered Saturdays, April through October, at 11:30am and 1:30pm. Tickets ($5 adults, $2.50 children) are available at the gift shop and tours are limited to a maximum of 25 people. Try to visit the observatory in the morning; late in the day, you'll have the sun in your eyes as you travel back down the mountain.

3 The Disneyland Resort & Knott's Berry Farm

95 miles N of San Diego

The sleepy Orange County town of Anaheim grew up around Disneyland. Now, even beyond the "Happiest Place on Earth," the city and its neighboring communities are kid-central. Sprawling suburbs have become a playground of family-oriented hotels, restaurants, and unabashedly tourist-oriented attractions. Also nearby is Knott's Berry Farm, another theme park, in Buena Park.

ESSENTIALS

GETTING THERE   From San Diego, take I-5 north. For the Disneyland Resort, exit at Disney Way; dedicated off ramps from both the right-hand lane *and* the left-hand commuter lane lead into the attractions' parking lots and surrounding streets. The drive from downtown San Diego takes approximately 1 hour and 45 minutes in average traffic.

Eleven **Amtrak** (© **800/872-7245;** www.amtrak.com) trains go to Anaheim daily from San Diego. The one-way fare is $19 to $23, and the trip takes about 2 hours; From Anaheim station, take a 10-minute taxi ride (budget around $11) to the Disneyland Resort.

VISITOR INFORMATION   The **Anaheim/Orange County Visitor & Convention Bureau,** 800 W. Katella Ave. (© **888/598-3200** or 714/765-8888; www.anaheim oc.org), can fill you in on area activities and shopping shuttles. It's across the street from the Disneyland Resort, inside the convention center. It's open Monday through Friday from 8am to 5pm. The **Buena Park Convention & Visitors Office,** 6601 Beach Blvd., Suite 200 (© **800/541-3953** or 714/562-3560; www.buenapark.com), provides specialized information on the neighboring area, including Knott's Berry Farm.

THE DISNEYLAND RESORT 🐭🐭🐭

It's not called "The Happiest Place on Earth" for nothing, you know. The theme park that originally opened in 1955 has sprouted siblings in Florida, Tokyo, and even France, but nothing compares with the original. Disneyland has always capitalized on being the archetype—and the world's first family-oriented mega-theme park. Nostalgia is a big part of the appeal (in 2005, the resort celebrated its 50th anniversary) and despite many advancements and evolutions over the years, Disneyland remains true to the vision of founder Walt Disney.

In 2001, Disney unveiled an additional theme park (California Adventure), a shopping/dining/entertainment district (Downtown Disney), and more on-site hotels (Disney's Grand Californian and Disney's Paradise Pier). Though still considerably smaller than Walt Disney World Resort in Orlando, the head Mouseketeers also changed the name of the Anaheim branch to "The Disneyland Resort," reflecting a greatly expanded array of entertainment options; it's no longer a (long) day trip from San Diego. What does this all mean for you? Well, first of all, you'll probably want to think seriously about budgeting more time (and yes, more money) for your Disney visit—you'll need at least 48 hours to see it all. If you have less time, plan carefully so you don't skip what's important to you; in the pages ahead we'll describe what to expect throughout the resort. And, most of all, get ready to have fun—there's lots of great stuff to check out.

ADMISSION, HOURS & INFORMATION   Admission to *either* Disneyland or California Adventure, including unlimited rides and all festivities and entertainment, is $59 for adults and children age 10 and up, $57 for seniors 60 and over, $49 for children 3 to 9, and free for children under 3; parking is $10. Note that a 1-day, one-park ticket allows you into one park *only.* There are several types of multiday tickets available—the 3-day version allows in-and-out privileges between the parks (though 3 full days is probably more time than you need to tour the two parks). The 3-day ticket costs $169, or $139 for children. In addition, some area accommodations offer lodging packages that include admission for 1 or more days. One other option worth investigating is the "Southern California Attractions CityPass," which incorporates a 3-day Disneyland/California Adventure ticket, plus 1-day tickets to Universal Studios Hollywood, SeaWorld, and the San Diego Zoo; the price is $199 for adults, $159 for children 3 to 9. Finally, residents of Southern California are usually offered off-season (nonsummer/holiday) discounts, provided they can show a drivers license with a Southern California zip code.

Disneyland and California Adventure are open every day of the year, but operating hours vary daily, so I strongly recommend that you call for information that applies to the specific day(s) of your visit (© **714/781-4565**), particularly if you're doing Disneyland as a day trip from San Diego (you'll need at least 10–12 hr. to see most of this park). The same information, including ride closures and show schedules, can also be found online at **www.disneyland.com**. Generally speaking, Disneyland opens at 9am and closes around 8pm, with extended hours on weekends, holidays, and during the summer; California Adventure, which requires less time to tour, is open from 10am to 6pm, and longer hours also apply many days.

If you plan to arrive when the ticket booths are most busy—from when the park gates open until about noon—purchase your tickets in advance and get a jump on the crowds. Advance tickets may be purchased through Disneyland's website (www. disneyland.com), at Disney stores in the United States, or by calling the ticket mail-order line (© **714/781-4043**).

DISNEY TIPS   The theme parks are busiest from mid-June to mid-September and on weekends and school holidays year-round. Peak touring hours are from 11am to 5pm; visit the most popular rides before and after these hours, and you'll cut your waiting times substantially. Disneyland still draws the lion's share of the visitors, so by all means try to see it on a weekday (though note that shorter operating hours may negate some of the time saved waiting in lines); California Adventure is still relatively easy to conquer, even on weekends.

Many visitors tackle the parks systematically, beginning at the entrance and working their way clockwise around the park. But a better plan of attack is to arrive early and dash to the most popular rides: the Indiana Jones Adventure, Star Tours, Space Mountain, Big Thunder Mountain Railroad, Splash Mountain, the Haunted Mansion, the Many Adventures of Winnie the Pooh, and Pirates of the Caribbean in Disneyland; and Soarin' Over California, Grizzly River Run, the Tower of Terror, and California Screamin' in California Adventure. Lines for these rides can last an hour or more in the middle of the day.

However, this time-honored plan of attack is increasingly obsolete thanks to the **FASTPASS** system. Here's how it works: Say you want to ride Splash Mountain (probably the parks' top draw), but the line is long—*so* long the wait sign indicates a 90-minute crawl. Now you can head to the automated FASTPASS ticket dispensers, through which you swipe the magnetic strip of your entrance ticket—the machine spits out a FASTPASS that denotes a time to return later that day. When you come

Value   The Art of the (Package) Deal

If you intend to spend 2 or more days in Disney territory, it pays to investigate the bevy of packaged vacation options available. Start by contacting your hotel (even those in Los Angeles or San Diego). Many vacation packages include Disneyland and/or California Adventure (and other attractions) with their inclusive packages; see "Packages for the Independent Traveler" in chapter 2 for contact information. Also, put a call in to the official Disney travel agency, **Walt Disney Travel Co.** (© **800/225-2024** or 714/520-5050). You can request a glossy catalog by mail, or log onto **www.disneyland.com** to peruse package details, take a virtual tour of participating hotel properties, and get online price quotes for customized, date-specific packages. Their packages are value-packed time-savers with abundant flexibility. Hotel choices range from the official Disney hotels to one of 42 "neighbor hotels" in every price range and category; a wide range of available extras includes admission to other Southern California attractions and tours (such as Universal Studios or a Tijuana shopping spree), and behind-the-scenes Disneyland tours, all in limitless combinations. Every time I check, rates are highly competitive, considering each package includes multiday admission, early park entry, free parking (at the Disney hotels), souvenirs, and coupon books.

back you'll use the FASTPASS entrance, which bypasses most of the queue. Essentially, you're reserving a place in line, and the beauty of the system is that it evens out the flow of traffic. However, note that the most popular attractions can "sell out" of FASTPASS slots by early afternoon. Also, craft your itinerary carefully: You cannot obtain a FASTPASS for a second attraction until the window for the first ride has opened. At least 14 rides between the two parks are equipped with FASTPASS; for a complete list for each park, check your official map/guide when you enter.

Since many of the more popular rides have a set number of seats, Disney tries to fill unused single seats with a line bypass for **solo riders.** At the FASTPASS distribution area, ask the attendant for a single rider's pass (a coupon that advances you to the front of the line to await the first single seat available).

Parents should note that a number of rides have minimum height requirements of 40 inches or more. Couples touring with someone under the height requirement can perform the **"baby pass"** at many attractions: Both parents get in line and one is allowed to wait while the other rides; then they trade the child for the other to ride (so that parents don't have to wait in the line separately). The majority of attractions favored by preteens are found in Disneyland but, following some criticism that it wasn't kid-friendly enough, A Bug's Land was added to California Adventure and seems to be keeping the moppets happy.

TOURING DISNEYLAND ✯✯✯
The Disneyland complex is divided into eight theme "lands," each of which has rides and attractions related to that land's theme. You'll find the practical things you might need, such as stroller and wheelchair rentals and storage lockers, just outside the park's main gate.

MAIN STREET U.S.A. At the park's entrance, Main Street U.S.A. is a cinematic version of turn-of-the-20th-century small-town America. The whitewashed Rockwellian fantasy is lined with gift shops, candy stores, a soda fountain, and a silent theater that continuously runs early Mickey Mouse films.

Because there are no big-ticket rides, it's best to tour Main Street during the middle of the afternoon, when lines for popular attractions are longest, or in the evening, when you can rest your feet in the theater that features **"Great Moments with Mr. Lincoln,"** a patriotic (and AudioAnimatronic) look at America's 16th president. There's always something happening on Main Street; stop in at the information booth to the left of the main entrance for a schedule of the day's events. The **Disneyland Railroad** starts its circular journey around the park here, with stops at New Orleans Square, Mickey's Toontown, and Tomorrowland, but you can reach all of these places on foot just about as fast, so don't use it as a shortcut to the other side of the park. The railroad also passes through dioramas of the Grand Canyon and Primeval World between the Tomorrowland and Main Street stations.

ADVENTURELAND Inspired by exotic Asia, Africa, and South America, the central icon of Adventureland is a giant tree, home to **Tarzan's Treehouse,** a stagnant attraction based on the animated film. Its safari-themed neighbor is the **Jungle Cruise,** where passengers board *African Queen*–style river boats and explore the animal "life" along an Amazon-like river—the quip-a-second banter of the captains is filled with groaner jokes. A spear's throw away is the **Enchanted Tiki Room,** one of the most sedate attractions in Adventureland. Inside, you can sit down and watch an 18-minute musical comedy featuring electronically animated tropical birds, flowers, and "Tiki gods."

The **Indiana Jones Adventure** ✸✸ is Adventureland's marquee attraction. Based on the Steven Spielberg films, this ride takes you into the Temple of the Forbidden Eye, aboard joltingly realistic all-terrain vehicles. Riders follow Indy and experience the perils of bubbling lava pits, whizzing poison darts, shrieking serpents, collapsing bridges, and the familiar cinematic tumbling boulder (an effect that's very realistic!). *Parents of children be warned:* The volume on this ride is ear-splitting.

NEW ORLEANS SQUARE Overlooking the "Rivers of America" and Tom Sawyer Island, New Orleans Square is a beautifully detailed re-creation of the Crescent City. There are just two rides here, but both are popular classics. The **Haunted Mansion** ✸ is a high-tech ghost house inhabited by 999 ghouls, goblins, and other spirits; the clever events inside are as funny as they are scary.

Even more fanciful is the epic **Pirates of the Caribbean** ✸✸✸, one of Disneyland's best-loved attractions. Visitors float on boats through underground caves to the Spanish Main, entering a story of swashbuckling, cannon-fire battles, and buried treasure. Even in the middle of the afternoon you can dine by the light of cool moonlight and fireflies and to the sound of crickets in the **Blue Bayou** restaurant, situated in the middle of the ride itself—other than the tasty Monte Cristo sandwich, the food is nothing special, but the ambience is exquisitely serene.

CRITTER COUNTRY An ode to the backwoods, Critter Country is a corner of Frontierland without those pesky settlers. **The Many Adventures of Winnie the Pooh** ✸ is a 2003 addition to Disneyland—a gentle excursion through the Hundred Acre Wood (beware the heffalumps and woozles!). Everyone loves **Splash Mountain** ✸✸✸, an immensely popular log flume ride. Based on the Disney movie *Song of the South,* the ride is lined with about 100 characters that won't stop singing "Zip-A-Dee-Doo-Dah." Be prepared to get wet, especially if someone sizable is in the front seat of your log. During my last visit, on a nonsummer, nonholiday Friday, the line topped 2 hours, 15 minutes at 6pm. There's also **Davy Crockett's Explorer Canoes** ✸, a perfect escape from the lines and crowds as you paddle free-floating, steady canoes around Tom Sawyer Island.

FRONTIERLAND   Inspired by 19th-century America, the centerpiece of Frontierland is the Rivers of America, sailed by the **Mark Twain Riverboat,** a detailed re-creation of a Mississippi-style paddle-wheel steamer, and the **Sailing Ship Columbia,** a three-masted replica of the windjammer that first sailed the American flag around the world (both travel the same route—something that is possible only in Disney's world). The river circles **Tom Sawyer Island,** which is reached by a brief raft ride; kids love to investigate the island, replete with a do-it-yourself play area with balancing rocks, caves, and a rope bridge. The **Big Thunder Mountain Railroad** ✸✸ is a runaway roller coaster that races through a deserted 1870s gold mine—lots of fun here, and it's a relatively moderate coaster for those who might not be up to the more aggressive rides.

On weekends and holidays, and daily during summer, head to the Frontierland after dark to see the **FANTASMIC! show** ✸. It mixes magic, music, live performers, and sensational special effects. Just as he did in *The Sorcerer's Apprentice,* Mickey Mouse appears and uses his magical powers to create giant water fountains, enormous flowers, and fantasy creatures. There are plenty of pyrotechnics, lasers, and fog, as well as a 45-foot-tall dragon that breathes fire and sets the water of the Rivers of America aflame. Best viewing is directly in front of Pirates of the Caribbean, but this is also the most crowded area (get there early).

MICKEY'S TOONTOWN   This is a colorful, whimsical world inspired by the film *Who Framed Roger Rabbit?*—a wacky, gag-filled land populated by 'toons. There are several rides, including **Roger Rabbit's Car Toon Spin,** and a miniature roller coaster with just a 35-inch height requirement, **Gadget's GoCoaster.** But they take a back seat to Toontown itself—a trippy, smile-inducing world without a straight line or right angle in sight.

FANTASYLAND   With its storybook theme, this is the catchall land for stuff that doesn't quite fit anywhere else, much of it based on Walt Disney's animated classics. Most of the rides are geared to the under-six set, including the **King Arthur Carrousel, Dumbo the Flying Elephant,** and the **Casey Jr. Circus Train.** Some, like **Mr. Toad's Wild Ride** and **Peter Pan's Flight** ✸, appeal to grown-ups as well. You'll also find **Alice in Wonderland, Snow White's Scary Adventures, Pinocchio's Daring Journey,** and more.

The most famous lure is **It's a Small World** ✸, an indoor river ride through a Gen-Xer's saccharine nightmare of all the world's children singing the song everybody loves to hate, yet the single-digit set adores this attraction, as does the blue-rinse crowd. Fantasyland's biggest thrill is the **Matterhorn Bobsleds** ✸✸, a zippy roller coaster through chilled caverns and drifting fog banks. It's one of the park's classics (and not found in Disney's sibling parks).

TOMORROWLAND   Conceived as an optimistic look at the future, Tomorrowland employs an angular, metallic look popularized by futurists like Jules Verne.

The jet-propelled, long-time favorite **Space Mountain** ✸✸✸ offers a pitch-black indoor roller coaster that assaults your equilibrium—it's the park's heartiest thrill ride, and was overhauled in 2005 with redesigned rockets, an "on board" soundtrack, and revamped special effects. **Buzz Lightyear Astro Blasters** blasts you through an interactive, moving arcade game aboard your own Star Cruiser. **Star Tours** ⟡⟡ is a Disney–George Lucas joint venture that spins off the Star Wars myth in a flight simulator. The 40-passenger StarSpeeders encounter a space-load of misadventures on the way to the Moon of Endor. The **Astro Orbitor** is a kid-friendly spinning spacecraft ride, while the **Autopia** offers every under-15-year-old's fantasy: driving gas-powered cars along a scenic track. The attraction **"Honey, I Shrunk the Audience"** ⟡ is an eye-popping presentation by the "Imagination Institute" that rides on the characters and plot from the hit film *Honey, I Shrunk the Kids*.

The **Disneyland Monorail** ⟡ stops in Tomorrowland, transporting passengers to and from a stop outside the park, between the Disney resorts and Downtown Disney. You don't have to get off at this stop, and the ride offers a good scenic overview of the entire resort complex.

TOURING CALIFORNIA ADVENTURE ⟡⟡

Despite the localized angle, California Adventure experienced a lukewarm reception when it opened in 2001. Initial visitors complained the park didn't have enough to do (yet admission was priced the same as Disneyland), that there wasn't enough for pre-teens, and that half the rides were dressed-up, carny-style attractions that could be found at your average county fair (rather than one-of-a-kind adventures like Pirates of the Caribbean). Disney responded to the criticisms by adding a number of shows and attractions, including a half-dozen kiddie rides, and in 2004 the elaborate The Twilight Zone Tower of Terror arrived—the park's precarious reputation is starting to turn around. Two things that distinguish California Adventure from Disneyland: it averages less than half the attendance of Disneyland, making it a decidedly less crowded experience; and you can get a cold beer, glass of wine, or cocktail inside this theme park (alcohol is not served inside Disney).

With a grand entrance designed to resemble one of those "Wish you were here" scenic postcards, California Adventure starts out with a bang. Beneath a scale model of the Golden Gate Bridge (watch for the monorail passing overhead), handmade tiles of across-the-state scenes glimmer on either side. Just inside, an enormous gold titanium "sun" shines all day, illuminated by computerized heliostats that follow the real sun's path. From this point, visitors can head into four distinct themed areas, each containing rides, interactive attractions, and live-action shows. Stroller and wheelchair rental and lockers are just inside the main gate, on the right.

THE GOLDEN STATE   This multidimensional area represents California's history, heritage, and physical attributes. Sound boring? Actually, two of the park's biggest crowd-pleasers are here. Inside a weathered corrugated test pilots' hangar is **Soarin' Over California** ⟡⟡, the ride that immediately rose to the top on everyone's run-to-get-in-line-first list (it's equipped with FASTPASS but often sells out by midday anyway). It uses cool technology to combine suspended, hang glider–style seats with a spectacular IMAX movie experience—riders literally "soar" over California's scenic wonders.

Nearby, the park's iconic "Grizzly Peak" towers over the **Grizzly River Run** ⟡⟡, a splashy gold-country ride through caverns and along craggy slopes; it culminates with a wet plunge into a bubbling geyser field. Kids can cavort nearby on the **Redwood Creek Challenge Trail,** a forest playground with smoke-jumper cable slides, net climbing, and swaying bridges.

On the back side of Grizzly Peak is the Robert Mondavi–sponsored **Golden Vine Winery,** which boasts a demonstration vineyard, a Mission-style "aging room" (with a back-to-basics presentation on the art of winemaking), tastings, and the park's most upscale eatery, the **Vineyard Room** (see "Where to Dine in the Anaheim Area," later in this section). **Pacific Wharf** was inspired by Monterey's Cannery Row, and features varied food counters. Also here is **Golden Dreams,** a 22-minute, Whoopi Goldberg-narrated film about California's history and heritage as seen through the eyes of its immigrants.

A BUG'S LAND   The Golden State blends seamlessly into this newer, pint-sized section of the park. At its entrance is **Bountiful Valley Farm,** constructed to pay tribute to California's rich agriculture, demonstrating cultivation techniques. The 3-D attraction **"It's Tough To Be A Bug"** ⊕ uses advanced film technology to expand on *A Bug's Life* characters Flik and Hopper, who lead the audience on a slap-happy underground romp with bees, termites, grasshoppers, stink bugs, spiders, and a few surprises that keep everyone hopping, ducking, and laughing along.

Just beyond is **Flik's Fun Fair,** featuring five smaller amusements that are perfect for younger visitors. The set is an amusingly detailed backyard garden, primed with a leaky spigot and towering clover, allowing visitors to view the world through a bug's perspective.

PARADISE PIER   Journey back to the glory days of California's beachfront amusement attractions on this fantasy boardwalk. Highlights include **California Screamin'** ⊕⊕, a classic roller coaster that replicates the whitewashed wooden white-knucklers of the past—but with state-of-the-art steel construction and a smooth, computerized ride. The 0-to-50 takeoff packs quite a thrill. There's also the **Maliboomer,** a trio of towers (modeled after He-Man sledgehammer tests) that catapults riders to the tip-top bell, and then lets them down bungee-style with dangling feet; the **Orange Stinger,** a whooshing swing ride inside an enormous orange, complete with orange scent piped in; **Mulholland Madness,** a wacky wild trip along L.A.'s precarious hilltop street; and the **Sun Wheel Carousel,** featuring unique zigzagging cars that bring new meaning to the familiar ride.

Most of the rides in Paradise Pier have minimum height requirements, but younger tikes can content themselves with the undersea-themed **King Triton's Carousel.** There are all the familiar boardwalk games (complete with stuffed prizes), and guilty-pleasure fast foods like pizza, corn dogs, and burritos.

HOLLYWOOD PICTURES BACKLOT   If you've visited Disney in Florida, you'll recognize many elements of this ersatz Hollywood movie studio lot. Pass through a classic studio archway flanked by gigantic golden elephants, and you'll find yourself on a surprisingly realistic "Hollywood Boulevard." In the **Disney Animation** building, visitors can participate in six different interactive galleries. For example: Learn how to draw Disney characters at the Animation Academy; listen to a Disney illustrator invent "Crush," the surfin' turtle dude from *Finding Nemo;* and even take a computerized personality test to see which Disney character you resemble most.

At the end of the street, the replica movie palace **Hyperion Theater** presents the live-action musical show *Disney's Aladdin,* a large-scale 40-minute musical production—the show is performed several times daily. The Backlot includes **Jim Henson's MuppetVision 3D** ⊕, an on-screen blast from the past featuring Kermit, Miss Piggy, Gonzo, Fozzie Bear—and even hecklers Waldorf and Statler. Saving the best for last,

California Adventure's big tingle is **The Twilight Zone Tower of Terror** 𝕽𝕽𝕽—another import from Orlando. Guests board a possessed elevator that travels through the bowels of a creepy hotel—you'll witness a parade of spiffy effects before making a sudden plunge down the 13-story shaft. The Tower of Terror is a monstrous classic.

DOWNTOWN DISNEY 𝕽

Borrowing another page from Central Florida's successful Disney compound, **Downtown Disney** is a district filled with restaurants, shops, and entertainment for all ages. For strolling with kids in tow, upscale dining, or just partying into the night, this colorful and sanitized "street scene" fills the bill. It's not a theme park, so you can visit admission-free, but note that this isn't a place for bargain hunting—whether it's a cup of coffee or a choice bit of Disneyana, nothing is cheap.

The promenade begins at the amusement park gates and stretches toward the Disneyland Hotel; there are 26 shops, boutiques, and snack stops, and 12 restaurants, live music venues, and entertainment options.

Highlights include **House of Blues,** the restaurant/club that features Delta-inspired cuisine and big-name music; **Ralph Brennan's Jazz Kitchen,** a spicy mix of New Orleans traditional foods and live jazz; **ESPN Zone,** the ultimate sports dining and entertainment experience, including an interactive game room; **Tortilla Jo's,** for tantalizing Latin cuisine, and **World of Disney,** the largest Disney shopping experience in the West, with a vast and diverse range of toys, souvenirs, and collectibles. There is also a 12-screen stadium-seating movie theater, LEGO Imagination Center, Sephora cosmetics store, and much more.

Even if you're not staying at one of the Disney hotels, Downtown Disney is worth a visit. Locals and day-shoppers take advantage of the no-gate free entry and validated Downtown Disney parking lots (3 hr free, longer with restaurant or theater validation).

KNOTT'S BERRY FARM 𝕽

Cynics say that Knott's Berry Farm is for people who aren't smart enough to find Disneyland. The reality is that Knott's simply can't compete with the Disney allure, but instead focuses on newer and faster thrill rides that target Southern California youths and families instead.

Like Disneyland, Knott's Berry Farm is not without historical background. Rudolph Boysen crossed a loganberry with a raspberry, calling the resulting hybrid the boysenberry. In 1933, Buena Park farmer Walter Knott planted the boysenberry and launched Knott's berry farm on 10 acres of leased land. When things got tough during the Depression, Mrs. Knott set up a roadside stand, selling pies, preserves, and home-cooked chicken dinners. Within a year she was selling 90 meals a day. Lines became so long that Walter decided to create an Old West Ghost Town as a diversion for waiting customers.

Today the amusement park offers a whopping 165 shows, attractions, and high-tech rides that are far more thrilling than most of the rides at the Disneyland Resort. Granted, it doesn't have nearly the magical appeal of Disneyland, but if you're more into fast-paced amusement rides than swirling tea cups, spend your money here.

GETTING THERE   Knott's Berry Farm is at 8039 Beach Blvd. in Buena Park, about 10 minutes north of Disneyland. From I-5 north, exit south onto Beach Boulevard and follow the signs.

ADMISSION, HOURS & INFORMATION   Admission to the park, including unlimited access to all rides, shows, and attractions, is $45 for adults and kids 12 and over, $15 for seniors over 60 and for children 3 to 11; children under 3 are admitted free. After 4pm, admission is $22.50 for adults. Parking is $9. Like Disneyland, Knott's offers discounted admission for Southern California residents during much of the year, so if you're bringing local friends or family members along, be sure to take advantage of the bargain. Knott's Berry Farm's hours vary both during the week and week to week, so call ahead. The park is always open 10am to 6pm weekdays, until 10pm Saturdays, and until 7pm Sundays; during the summer peak season and holidays, hours are extended. Knott's is closed Christmas Day. Special hours and prices are in effect during Knott's Scary Farm in late October (a hugely popular event). Stage shows and special activities are scheduled throughout the day. Pick up a schedule at the ticket booth. For more information, call © **714/220-5200** or log onto **www.knotts.com**.

TOURING THE PARK

Despite all the high-tech multimillion-dollar rides, Knott's Berry Farm still maintains much of its original Old West motif, and is divided into six themed areas spread across 150 acres. **RipTide** is a floorless gondola ride featuring 13 full 360-degree vertical arcs, the **Xcelerator** launches you from 0 to 82mph in 2.3 seconds, and the **Silver Bullet** is a 55mph roller coaster with six inversions. Other attractions include the **California MarketPlace,** the farm's version of Downtown Disney, and **Knott's Soak City U.S.A.,** a 21-ride water-adventure park right next to Knott's Berry Farm (separate admission required).

OLD WEST GHOST TOWN   The park's original attraction is a collection of refurbished 19th-century buildings relocated from deserted Old West towns. You can pan for gold, ride an authentic stagecoach, take rickety train cars through the Calico Mine, get held up aboard the Denver and Rio Grande Calico Railroad, and watch the stunt spectacular at the Wagon Camp Theatre. If you love wooden roller coasters, don't miss the clackity **GhostRider.**

FIESTA VILLAGE   Here you'll find a south-of-the-border theme. That means festive markets, strolling mariachis, and wild rides like **Montezooma's Revenge** and **Jaguar,** a roller coaster that includes two heart-in-the-mouth drops and a loop that turns you upside down.

WILD WATER WILDERNESS   This 3½-acre attraction is styled like a turn-of-the-20th-century California wilderness park. The top ride is a white-water adventure called **Bigfoot Rapids,** with a long stretch of artificial rapids; it's the longest ride of its kind in the world. You can also look **Mystery Lodge** right in the eye—it's a truly amazing high-tech, trick-of-the-eye attraction based on the legends of local Native Americans. Don't miss this wonderful theater piece.

CAMP SNOOPY   This will probably be the youngsters' favorite area. It's meant to re-create a wilderness camp in the picturesque High Sierra. Its 6 rustic acres are the playgrounds of Charles Schulz's beloved beagle and his pals, Charlie Brown and Lucy, who greet guests and pose for pictures. The 30 rides here, including the **Charlie Brown Speedway** and **Lucy's Tugboat,** are tailor-made for the six-and-under set.

INDIAN TRAILS   This Native American interpretive center on the outskirts of Ghost Town is a nod to Native Americans. Exhibits include authentic tepees, hogans, and big houses. There are also daily educational events such as native craft making, storytelling, music, and dance.

THE BOARDWALK   This theme area is a salute to Southern California's beach culture. The main attractions are the **Xcelerator, RipTide,** the 30-story **Supreme Scream,** and a white-water adventure called **Perilous Plunge,** the world's tallest, steepest (think four-story waterfall), and wettest water ride.

WHERE TO STAY IN THE ANAHEIM AREA
EXPENSIVE

The Disneyland Hotel ⭐⭐ *Kids*   The holy grail of Disney-goers has always been this, the "Official Hotel of the Magic Kingdom." A monorail connection via Downtown Disney means you'll be able to return to your room anytime, whether to take a much-needed nap or to change your soaked shorts after your Splash Mountain or Grizzly Peak adventure. The theme hotel is an attraction unto itself, and the best choice for families with small children. The rooms aren't fancy, but they're comfortably furnished and all have balconies. In-room amenities include movie channels (with free Disney Channel, naturally) and cute-as-a-button Disney-themed toiletries and accessories. The hotel has every kind of service desk imaginable; the Neverland Pool Complex themed after Peter Pan and Captain Hook (complete with a white-sand beach); and a video game center.

The complex includes Disney's adjoining 489-room **Paradise Pier Hotel** with a whimsical beach boardwalk theme that ties in with the Paradise Pier section of the California Adventure park across the street. A bonus is the private entrance to that park via your hotel room key. Although the hotel was remodeled and received a new pool in 2004, it is still fairly generic compared to the other two Disney hotels.

1150 Magic Way, Anaheim. (*C*) **714/956-6425.** Fax 714/956-6582. www.disneyland.com. 990 units. $240–$275 double, plus $10 per night resort fee; from $525 suite. AE, DC, DISC, MC, V. Free parking. **Amenities:** 6 restaurants; 3 bars; 3 outdoor pools; health club; Jacuzzi; children's programs; game room; concierge; shopping arcade; room service; babysitting; laundry service; dry cleaning. *In room:* A/C, TV w/pay movies, dataport, minibar, fridge, coffeemaker, hair dryer, iron, safe.

Disney's Grand Californian Hotel ⭐⭐ *Kids*   Disney didn't miss the details when constructing this enormous version of an Arts and Crafts–era lodge (think Yosemite's Awahanee, Pasadena's Gamble House), hiring craftspeople throughout the state to contribute one-of-a-kind tiles, furniture, sculptures, and artwork. Taking inspiration from California's redwood forests, Mission pioneers, and plein-air painters, designers managed to create a nostalgic yet state-of-the-art high-rise hotel. Enter through subtle (where's the door?) stained-glass sliding panels to the hotel's centerpiece, a six-story "living room" with a William Morris–designed marble "carpet," angled skylight seen through exposed support beams, display cases of Craftsman treasures, and a three-story walk-in "hearth" whose fire warms Stickley-style rockers and plush leather armchairs. The hotel opens onto a landscaped area with a pair of swimming pools.

Guest rooms are spacious and smartly designed, carrying through the Arts and Crafts theme surprisingly well considering the hotel's grand scale. The best ones overlook the parks (but you'll pay for that view). Despite the sophisticated air of the Grand Californian, this is a hotel that truly caters to families, with a bevy of room configurations including one with a double bed plus bunk beds with trundle. Since the hotel provides sleeping bags (rather than rollaways) for kids, this standard-size room will sleep a family of six—but you have to share the bathroom.

Guests of the hotel can enter California Adventure through a private entrance, avoiding the crush at the main entrance, and another entrance leads directly into Downtown Disney and its long roster of dining and shopping options.

1600 S. Disneyland Dr., Anaheim. ℂ **714/956-6425** (central reservations) or 714/635-2300. Fax 714/956-6099. www.disneyland.com. 745 units. $280–$455 double, plus $10 per night resort fee; from $695 suite. AE, DC, DISC, MC, V. Free parking. **Amenities:** 3 restaurants; bar; 2 outdoor pools; health club; spa; Jacuzzi; children's center (open evenings only); concierge; business center; 24-hr. room service; laundry service; dry cleaning; concierge-level rooms. *In room:* A/C, TV w/pay movies, dataport, minibar, coffeemaker, hair dryer, iron, safe.

Sheraton Anaheim Hotel 𝔸 This hotel rises to the festive theme-park occasion with its fanciful English Tudor architecture; it's a castle that lures business conventions, Disney-bound families, and local high school proms. The public areas are quiet and elegant—intimate gardens with fountains and koi ponds, plush lobby and lounges—which can be a pleasing touch after a frantic day at the amusement park. The rooms are modern and unusually spacious, but otherwise not distinctive. A large swimming pool sits in the center of the complex, surrounded by attractive landscaping. Don't be put off by the high rack rates; rooms commonly go for $100 to $130, even on busy summer weekends.

900 South Disneyland Dr. (at I-5), Anaheim. ℂ **800/325-3535** or 714/778-1700. Fax 714/535-3889. www.sheraton.com. 489 units. $149–$195 double; from $275 suite. AE, DC, MC, V. Free parking. **Amenities:** 2 restaurants; bar; outdoor pool; health club; Jacuzzi; concierge; 24-hr. room service; coin-op laundry and laundry service; dry cleaning. *In room:* A/C, TV w/pay movies, dataport, fridge, minibar, coffeemaker, hair dryer, iron, safe.

MODERATE

Anaheim Vagabond Hotel 𝔸 *Value* You can easily cross the street to Disneyland's main gate, or take the Anaheim Plaza's free shuttle. Once you return, you'll appreciate the way this hotel's clever design shuts out the noisy world. In fact, the seven two-story garden buildings remind me more of 1960s Waikiki than busy Anaheim. The Olympic-size heated outdoor pool and whirlpool are unfortunately surrounded by Astroturf, and the plain motel-style furnishings are beginning to look a little tired. On the plus side, nothing's changed about the light-filled modern lobby, nor the friendly rates, which often drop as low as $49.

2145 S. Harbor Blvd., Anaheim. ℂ **800/522-1555** or 714/971-5556. Fax 714/971-5580. www.vagabondinn.com. 300 units. $79–$150 double; from $185 suite. Rates include continental breakfast. AE, DC, DISC, MC, V. Free parking. **Amenities:** Restaurant; bar; outdoor pool; Jacuzzi; limited room service (8am–11pm); coin-op laundry and laundry service; dry cleaning. *In room:* A/C, TV, dataport, microwave, coffeemaker, hair dryer, iron.

Candy Cane Inn 𝔸𝔸 *Value* Take your standard U-shaped motel court with outdoor corridors, spruce it up with cobblestone drives and walkways, old-time street lamps, and flowering vines engulfing the balconies of attractively painted rooms, and you have the Candy Cane. The face-lift worked, making this gem near Disneyland's main gate a treat for the stylish bargain hunter. The rooms are decorated in bright floral motifs with comfortable furnishings, including queen beds and a separate dressing and vanity area. Breakfast is served in the courtyard, where you can also splash around in a heated pool.

1747 S. Harbor Blvd., Anaheim. ℂ **800/345-7057** or 714/774-5284. Fax 714/772-5462. www.candycaneinn.net. 173 units. $92–$139 double. Rates include expanded continental breakfast. AE, DC, DISC, MC, V. Free parking. **Amenities:** Outdoor pool; Jacuzzi; health club; coin-op laundry and laundry service; dry cleaning. *In room:* A/C, TV, fridge, coffeemaker, hair dryer, iron.

Knott's Berry Farm Resort Hotel 𝔸 *Kids* Within easy walking distance of Knott's Berry Farm, this spit-shined Radisson (the former Buena Park Hotel) also offers a free shuttle to Disneyland, 7 miles away. The pristine lobby has the look of a business-oriented hotel, and that is it. But vacationers can also benefit from the elevated level of service. Ask about "Super Saver" rates (as low as $99—with breakfast—at press time), plus Knott's or Disneyland package deals. The rooms in the nine-story tower were tastefully redecorated when Radisson took over. Doting parents can even treat their kids to a Peanuts-themed room with Snoopy turndown service.

7675 Crescent Ave. (at Grand), Buena Park. ℂ 800/333-3333 or 714/995-1111. Fax 714/828-8590. www.knottshotel.com. 320 units. $159–$199 double; from $234 suite. AE, DC, DISC, MC, V. Parking $9. **Amenities:** 2 restaurants; bar; outdoor pool; outdoor tennis court (lit for night play); health club; Jacuzzi; video-game room; concierge; courtesy Disneyland shuttle; 24-hr. room service; coin-op laundry and laundry service; dry cleaning. *In room:* A/C, TV w/pay movies, fax, dataport, coffeemaker, hair dryer, iron, safe.

Portofino Inn & Suites 🖈 *Kids*   This complex of low- and high-rise all-suite buildings sports a cheery yellow exterior and family-friendly interior. The location couldn't be better: Directly across the street from California Adventure's back side, they'll shuttle you straight to the front gate. Designed to work as well for business travelers from the nearby Convention Center as for Disney-bound families, the Portofino offers contemporary, stylish furnishings as well as vacation-friendly rates and suites for any family configuration. Families will want one of the many "Kids Suites," which have bunk beds and sofa sleeper, plus TV, fridge, and microwave—and that's just in the kids' room; Mom and Dad have a separate bedroom with grown-up comforts like double vanity, shower massage, and a TV.

1831 S. Harbor Blvd. (at Katella), Anaheim. ℂ **800/398-3963** or 714/782-7600. Fax 714/782-7619. www.portofino innanaheim.com. 190 units. $140–$190 double; from $200 suite. AE, DC, DISC, MC, V. Free parking. **Amenities:** Restaurant; outdoor pool; health club; Jacuzzi; video-game room; tour desk; coin-op laundry and laundry service; dry cleaning. *In room:* A/C, TV w/pay movies, dataport, coffeemaker, hair dryer, iron.

INEXPENSIVE

Howard Johnson Hotel 🖈   This hotel occupies an enviable location, directly opposite Disneyland, and guest rooms were renovated in 2000. They're divided among several low-profile buildings, all with balconies opening onto a central garden with two heated pools for adults and one for children. Garden paths lead under eucalyptus and olive trees to a splashing circular fountain. During the summer you can see the nightly fireworks display at Disneyland from the upper balconies of the park-side rooms. Try to avoid the rooms in the rear buildings, which get some freeway noise. Services and facilities include airport shuttle and family lodging/Disney admission packages. All in all it's pretty classy for a HoJo.

1380 S. Harbor Blvd., Anaheim. ℂ **800/446-4656** or 714/776-6120. Fax 714/533-3578. www.hojoanaheim.com. 320 units. $99–$149 double. AE, DC, DISC, MC, V. Free parking. **Amenities:** Restaurant; 2 outdoor pools; Jacuzzi; concierge; game room; limited room service (7am–11pm); coin-op laundry and laundry service; dry cleaning. *In room:* A/C, TV w/pay movies, dataport, fridge, coffeemaker, hair dryer, iron.

Travelodge Anaheim   On the back side of Disneyland, this modest hotel appeals to the budget-conscious traveler who isn't willing to sacrifice everything. All rooms have a refrigerator and microwave; breakfast is served in a refurbished train dining car; and you can relax by the large outdoor heated pool and Jacuzzi while using the laundry room. The extra-large family rooms accommodate virtually any brood, and shuttles run regularly to the park.

1057 W. Ball Rd., Anaheim. ℂ **800/222-3639** or 714/774-7600. Fax 714/535-6953. www.travelodge.com. 95 units. $62–$72 double; $72 family room. Rates include full breakfast. AE, DC, DISC, MC, V. Free parking. **Amenities:** Outdoor pool; Jacuzzi; coin-op laundry. *In room:* A/C, TV, fridge, microwave, hair dryer, iron.

WHERE TO DINE IN THE ANAHEIM AREA

If you're visiting the Disneyland Resort, chances are good you'll probably eat at one of the many choices inside the theme parks or at Downtown Disney; there are plenty of restaurants to choose from for all tastes. At Disneyland, in the Creole-themed **Blue Bayou,** you can sit under the stars inside the Pirates of the Caribbean ride—no matter what time of day it is. California Adventure features two sit-down options: **Ariel's Grotto,** where Disney characters serve fish and chips, lasagna, hamburgers, and such in a faux-1920s beachfront setting; and the **Vineyard Room,** which offers upscale prix-fixe wine-country cuisine matched to California wines (the more casual Golden Vine Terrace is downstairs). Make reservations early in the day for dinner, as they all fill up pretty quickly.

At Knott's Berry Farm, try the fried-chicken dinners and boysenberry pies at historic **Mrs. Knott's Chicken Dinner Restaurant** (see below for full review). Also listed are some of the best bets in the surrounding area, including nearby **Orange,** whose historic downtown is home to several of the region's best dining options—if you're willing to drive 10 to 15 minutes.

EXPENSIVE

Anaheim White House ✿✿ FRENCH/ITALIAN   Once surrounded by orange groves, this stately 1909 colonial-style mansion now sits on a wide industrial street just 5 minutes from Disneyland. It's set back, though, framed by lawns and gardens, and exudes gentility and nostalgia. The home is nicely restored inside and out; the restaurant opened in 1981, named after its stylistic cousin in Washington, the White House. Owner Bruno Serato maintains this architectural treasure, serving northern Italian cuisine—with a French accent—in elegant white-on-white rooms on the main and second floors. Dinner courses are whimsically named for fashion giants (Dolce & Gabbana whitefish, Prada rack of lamb), and sometimes arrive on oddly shaped platters that work better as artwork than dishware. Prices tend to reflect the expense-account and well-heeled retiree crowd, but lunch prices (including a terrific prix fixe) deliver the same bang for fewer bucks. *Tip:* Use their website to make online reservations.

887 Anaheim Blvd. (north of Ball Rd.), Anaheim. ✆ **714/772-1381.** www.anaheimwhitehouse.com. Reservations recommended at dinner. Main courses $11–$25 lunch, $20–$36 dinner. AE, MC, V. Mon–Fri 11:30am–2:30pm and 5–10pm; Sat–Sun 5–10pm.

MODERATE

Citrus City Grille ✿✿ CALIFORNIAN   Though housed in Orange's second-oldest brick building, this sophisticated crowd-pleaser is furnished without an antique in sight, paying homage to the town's agricultural (citrus) legacy with a bold industrial chic. World-inspired appetizers range from Hawaiian-style ahi *poke* (raw tuna salad) to Southeast Asian coconut-shrimp tempura accented with spiced apricots. Main courses come from the Mediterranean (pasta and risotto), Mexico (*carne asada* with avocado-corn relish), the American South (authentic Louisiana gumbo), and your mom's kitchen (meatloaf smothered in gravy and fried onions). Gleaming bar shelves house myriad bottles for the extensive martini menu, and outdoor foyer tables are nicely protected from the street.

122 N. Glassell St. (½ block north of Chapman), Orange. ✆ **888/668-7474** or 714/639-9600. www.citruscitygrille.com. Reservations recommended. Main courses $9–$14 lunch, $14–$29 dinner. AE, DC, MC, V. Mon–Sat 11am–10pm.

INEXPENSIVE

Felix Continental Cafe 𝒜 CUBAN/SPANISH If you like the recreated Main Street in the Magic Kingdom, you'll love the historic 1886 town square in the city of Orange, on view from the cozy sidewalk tables outside the Felix Continental Cafe. Dining on traditional Cuban specialties (such as citrus-marinated chicken, black beans and rice, and fried plantains) and watching traffic spin around the magnificent fountain and rose bushes of the plaza evokes old Havana or Madrid rather than the cookie-cutter Orange County communities just blocks away. The food is praised by restaurant reviewers and loyal locals alike.

36 Plaza Sq. (at the corner of Chapman and Glassell), Orange. ℂ **714/633-5842.** www.felixcontinentalcafe.com. Reservations recommended for dinner. Main courses $7–$15. AE, DC, MC, V. Mon–Fri 11am–10pm; Sat–Sun 8am–10pm.

Mrs. Knott's Chicken Dinner Restaurant 𝒜 (Kids) AMERICAN Knott's Berry Farm got its start as a down-home diner in 1934, and you can still get a hearty all-American meal without even entering the theme park. The restaurant that started it all, descended from Cordelia Knott's Depression-era farmland tearoom, stands just outside the park's entrance, with plenty of free parking for patrons. Looking just as you'd expect—country cute, with window shutters and paisley aplenty—the restaurant's featured attraction is the original fried chicken dinner, complete with soup, salad, buttermilk biscuits, mashed potatoes and gravy, and a slice of famous pie. Country-fried steak, pot roast, roast turkey, and pork ribs are options, as well as sandwiches, salads, and a terrific chicken potpie. Boysenberries abound (of course), from breakfast jam to traditional double-crust pies, and there's even an adjacent takeout shop that's always crowded.

8039 Beach Blvd. (near La Palma), Buena Park. ℂ **714/220-5080.** Reservations for parties of 12 or more only. Main courses $5–$9; complete dinners $13. DC, DISC, MC, V. Daily 7am–8:30pm (till 9pm Fri, 9:30pm Sat).

4 Julian: Apple Pies & More

60 miles NE of San Diego; 31 miles W of Anza-Borrego Desert State Park

A trip to Julian (pop. 3,000) is a trip back in time. The old gold-mining town, now best known for its apples, has a handful of cute B&Bs, but its popularity is based on the fact that it provides a chance for city-weary folks to get away from it all, an asset best appreciated if you visit weekdays, when things are a little quieter here.

People first ventured into these fertile hills—elevation 4,225 feet—in search of gold in the late 1860s. They discovered it in 1870 near where the Julian Hotel stands today, and 18 mines sprang up like mushrooms. During all the excitement, four cousins—all former Confederate soldiers from Georgia, two with the last name Julian—founded the town of Julian. The mines produced up to an estimated $13 million worth of gold in their day.

In October 2003, Julian was virtually engulfed by the devastating Cedar Fires. Firefighters made a stand to protect the town, against what seemed insurmountable odds. For a few days it was touch-and-go, and hundreds of homes in the surrounding hillsides were lost. But the central historic part of Julian was saved, along with all of the town's famed apple orchards. Today, you can stand on Main Street again without knowing a catastrophe visited just a few hundred yards away. But keep in mind that most of Julian's residents do live on the outskirts, and more than a third lost their homes and livelihoods.

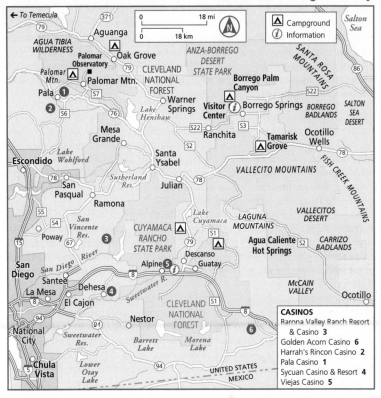

ESSENTIALS

GETTING THERE   You can make the 90-minute trip on Highway 78 or I-8 to Highway 79. I suggest taking one route going and the other on the way back. Highway 79 winds through Rancho Cuyamaca State Park, while Highway 78 traverses open country and farmland. If you come via Cuyamaca, you'll see plenty of residual fire damage, a tragic sight for longtime San Diegans who have spent many happy days amid these old oak trees, but a spectacle containing its own austere beauty at the same time.

VISITOR INFORMATION   The **Julian Chamber of Commerce** is at the corner of Main and Washington streets (© **760/765-1857;** www.julianca.com). Staffers always have enthusiastic suggestions for local activities. The office is open daily from 10am to 4pm.

   Main Street in Julian is only 6 blocks long, and some lodgings, shops, and cafes are on it or a block away. Town maps and accommodations fliers are available from Town Hall, on Main Street at Washington Street. Public restrooms are behind the Town Hall. There's no self-service laundry (so come prepared), but you'll find a post office, a liquor store, and a few grocery stores.

SPECIAL EVENTS   Julian's popular **Arts and Crafts Show** is held every weekend between mid-September and the end of November. Local artisans display their wares;

there's also plenty of cider and apple pie, plus entertainment and brilliant fall foliage. The apple harvest takes place September through October.

The **Wildflower Show** is a weeklong event sponsored by the local Women's Club featuring displays of native plants. Held in Julian's historic Town Hall and initiated in 1926, the show takes place in early May. The **Julian Weed Show** displays and sells artwork and arrangements of wildflowers and indigenous plants gathered from the San Diego area during the second half of August.

TOURING THE TOWN

Radiating the dusty aura of the Old West, Julian offers an abundance of early California history, quaint Victorian streets filled with apple-pie shops and antiques stores, crisp fresh air, and friendly people. While Wal-Mart and McDonald's have invaded formerly unspoiled mountain resorts like Big Bear and Mammoth, this 1880s gold-mining town has managed to retain a rustic, woodsy sense of its historic origins, despite the arrival of a Subway sandwich shop.

Be forewarned, however, that downtown Julian can be exceedingly crowded during the fall harvest season. Consider making your trip during another season (or midweek) to enjoy this unspoiled relic with a little privacy. Rest assured, apple pies are baking around town year-round. But autumn is perfect: The air is crisp and bracing, and Julian sees a dusting (and often more) of snow during the winter; spring prods patches of daffodils into bloom.

The best way to experience Julian is on foot. Two or three blocks of Main Street offer plenty of diversions for an afternoon or longer, depending on how much pie you stop to eat. And don't worry, you'll grow accustomed to constant apple references very quickly here—the fruit has proven to be more of an economic boom than gold ever was.

After stopping in at the chamber of commerce in the old Town Hall—check out the vintage photos of Julian yesteryear—cross the street to the **Julian Drug Store & Miner's Diner,** 2130 Main St. (© **760/765-3753**), an old-style soda fountain serving sparkling sarsaparilla—plus burgers and sandwiches—and conjuring images of boys in buckskin and girls in bonnets. Built in 1886, the brick structure is on the National Historic Register—like many other well-preserved buildings in town—and is jam-packed with local memorabilia.

The **Eagle and High Peak Mines,** built around 1870, at the end of C Street (© **760/765-0036**), although seemingly a tourist trap, offer an interesting and educational look at the town's one-time economic mainstay. Tours take you underground to the 1,000-foot hard-rock tunnel to see the mining and milling process; antique engines and authentic tools are on display. Tours are usually given beginning at 10am, but hours vary so it's best to call ahead; admission is $10 for adults, $5 for children 6 to 16, $1 for children under 6.

You'll probably see one of Suzanne Porter's horse-drawn carriages clip-clopping around town. Some might think it touristy, while others will wax nostalgic for New York's Central Park, but a ride from **Country Carriages** (© **760/765-1471**) is a quintessential Julian experience. Even the locals get into the act, snuggling under a blanket on romantic evening rides to celebrate anniversaries and birthdays. The carriages are always booked solid on Christmas Eve and reservations are highly recommended for any time of year. A 30-minute rambling drive down country roads and through town is $30 per couple. Winter hours are Monday and Thursday (usually no rides Tues–Wed, but it can be arranged) 11am to 4pm, Friday through Sunday 11am to 7pm; hours are extended for summer.

APPLE PIES

Before you leave, you must try Julian's apple pies; you'll need to sample them all to judge whether the best pies come from Mom's Pies or the Julian Pie Company or Apple Alley Bakery or the Julian Café. Stop by the aptly named **Mom's Pies,** 2119 Main St. (© **760/765-2472**). Its special attraction is a sidewalk plate-glass window through which you can observe the mom-on-duty rolling crust, filling pies, and crimping edges. The shop routinely bakes several varieties of apple pie and will, with a day's notice, whip up apple-rhubarb, peach-apple crumb, or any one of a number of specialties. There's a country cafe in the store, in case a cup of coffee and a slice of fresh pie prove irresistible. Another great bakery is the **Julian Pie Company,** 2225 Main St. (© **760/765-2449**). This blue-and-white cottage boasts a small front patio with umbrella tables, a frilly indoor parlor, and a large patio deck in back where overhanging apples are literally up for grabs. The shop serves original, Dutch, apple-mountain berry, and no-sugar-added pies as well as walnut apple muffins and cinnamon cookies made from pie-crust dough. Light lunches of soup and sandwiches are offered weekdays, 11am to 2pm. Both shops are open daily from 9am to 5pm.

SHOPPING

One of the simple pleasures of any weekend getaway is window- or souvenir-shopping in unfamiliar little shops like those lining both sides of Main Street. Keep an eye open for the old barn housing the **Warm Hearth,** 2125 Main St. (© **760/765-1022**). Country crafts, candles, and woven throws sit among the woodstoves, fireplaces, and barbecue grills that make up the shop's main business.

Nearby is the **Julian Cider Mill,** 2103 Main St. (© **760/765-1430**), where you can see cider presses at work October through March. It offers free tastes of the fresh nectar, and jugs to take home. Throughout the year, the mill also carries the area's widest selection of food products, from apple butters and jams to berry preserves, several varieties of local honey, candies, and other goodies.

A terrific browsing store is the **Bell, Book and Candle Shoppe,** 2007 Main St. (© **760/765-1377**), which specializes in only one of the above—candles, candles, and more candles. It sells pillars, tapers, hand-carved representational candles, custom personalized candles, candlesticks, and holders-plus incense, essential oils, and a few other gift items.

You'll have to step uphill 1 block to find the charming **Julian Tea & Cottage Arts,** 2124 Third St. (© **760/765-0832;** www.juliantea.com), where afternoon tea is served amid a treasure-trove of tea-brewing tools and other tea-themed paraphernalia. If that sounds too frilly for you, head upstairs to the **Culinary Cottage,** home to stylish housewares, fine cookbooks, and gourmet foods (often available for tastings).

Book lovers will enjoy stopping into the **Old Julian Book House,** 2230 Main St. (© **760/765-1989**). Run by P. J. Phillips, a dedicated purveyor of new and antiquarian volumes alike, it carries a smattering of maps, sheet music, CDs, and ephemera, too. This small shop also has a comprehensive, computerized book search to help track down out-of-print or scarce material throughout the country. Most of the Main Street merchants are open daily from 10am to 5pm.

Wineries have a presence in the area, too, including rustic **Menghini Winery,** 1150 Julian Orchards Dr. (© **760/765-2072**), and **Witch Creek Winery,** 2100 Main St. (© **760/765-2023;** www.witchcreekwinery.com). Menghini has a small gift shop and rolling picnic grounds that serve to host special events throughout the year, while Witch Creek is a simple tasting room right in town.

There are also a number of **roadside fruit stands and orchards** in the Julian hills; during autumn they're open all day, every day, but in the off-season some might open only on weekends or close entirely. Most stands sell, depending on the season, apples, pears, peaches, cider, jams, jellies, and other homemade foodstuffs. Many are along Highway 78 between Julian and Wynola (3 miles away); there are also stands along Farmers Road, a scenic country lane leading north from downtown Julian. Happy hunting.

Ask any of the San Diegans who regularly make excursions to Julian—no trip would be complete without a stop at **Dudley's Bakery,** Highway 78, Santa Ysabel (© **800/225-3348** or 760/765-0488; www.dudleysbakery.com), for a loaf or three of bread. Loaves are stacked high, and folks are often three deep at the counter clamoring for the nearly 20 varieties of bread baked fresh daily. Choices range from raisin-date-nut to jalapeño, with some garden-variety sourdough and wheat grain in between. Dudley's is a local tradition; built in 1963, it has expanded several times to accommodate its ever-growing business. The bakery is open Wednesday through Sunday from 8am to 5pm (and may close early on Sun).

HISTORIC CEMETERIES

What's a visit to any historic hamlet without a peek at the headstones in the local cemetery? If this activity appeals to you, then Julian's **Pioneer Cemetery** is a must-see. Contemporary graves belie the haphazard, overgrown look of this hilly burial ground, and the eroded older tombstones tell the intriguing story of Julian's rough pioneer history and ardent patriotism. You can drive in from A Street, but I prefer climbing the steep stairway leading up from Main Street around the corner; until 1924 this ascent was the only point of entry, even for processions. As you climb, imagine carrying a coffin up these steps in the snow.

OUTDOOR PURSUITS IN & AROUND JULIAN

Within 10 miles of Julian are numerous hiking trails that traverse rolling meadows, high chaparral, and oak and pine forests; fire damage is visible, but it's not a barren moonscape—oaks have recovered, but pine trees have not, though seedlings are springing up. Hiking here makes for a fascinating look at how Mother Nature works, and the additional good news is that you can actually see more of the vistas than you could before. The most spectacular hike—not affected by the fires—is at **Volcan Mountain Preserve,** north of town along Farmers Road; the trail to the top is a moderately challenging hike of around 3½ miles round-trip, with a 1,400-foot elevation gain. From the top, hikers have a panoramic view of the desert, mountains, and sea. Free docent-led hikes are offered year-round (on weekends, about one per month); for a schedule, call © **760/765-2300** or check www.volcanmt.org.

The 26,000-acre **Cuyamaca Rancho State Park,** along Highway 79 between Julian and I-8, was badly burned during the October 2003 forest fires. As of press time, all but 2 trails had been reopened, but if you're looking for a conifer forest here, you may be disappointed. For a map and further information about park status, stop in at **park headquarters** on Highway 79 (© **760/765-0755;** www.cuyamaca.us). Completely reopened is **William Heise County Park,** outside Pine Hills, which was also severely burned.

Eight miles south of Julian (and not part of the state park), **Lake Cuyamaca** has a tiny community at the 4,600-foot elevation that centers on lake activities, primarily boating and fishing for trout (stocked year-round), plus bass, catfish, bluegill, and sturgeon. There's a general store and restaurant at the lake's edge. The fishing fee is $5 per day, $2.50 per day for kids 8 to 15, free for children under 8. A California State fishing license is required and sold here: $12 for the day, or $35 per year. Rowboats are $15 per day, and motorboat rentals run $38 for the day ($29 after 1pm). In the summer, canoes and paddleboats can be rented by the hour for $10. For boat rental, fishing information, and RV or tent sites, call © **877/581-9904** or 760/765-0515 or see www.lakecuyamaca.org.

For a different way to tour, try **Llama Trek** (© **800/526-2725** or 760/765-1890; www.wikiupbnb.com). You'll lead the llama, which carries packs, for hikes to see rural neighborhoods, a historic gold mine, mountain and lake views, and apple orchards. Rates for the 4-hour trip run $95 per person ($75 for children under 10) and include lunch.

WHERE TO STAY

Julian is B&B country, although five tragically burned during the fires (several are rebuilding). The B&Bs fill up months in advance for the fall apple harvest season. Many (but not all) are affiliated with the **Julian Bed & Breakfast Guild** (© **760/ 765-1555;** www.julianbnbguild.com), a terrific resource for personal assistance in locating accommodations. The 13 members include private cabins and other options as well.

Julian Gold Rush Hotel ⚘   Built in 1897 by freed slave Albert Robinson, this frontier-style hotel is a living monument to the area's gold boom days—it's one of the oldest continually operating hotels in Southern California. Centrally located at the crossroads of downtown, the Julian Gold Rush Hotel isn't as secluded or plush as the many B&Bs in town, but if you seek historically accurate lodgings in Queen Anne style to complete your weekend time warp, this is the place. The 14 rooms and two cottages have been authentically restored (with nicely designed private bathrooms added where necessary) and boast antique furnishings; some rooms are also authentically tiny, so claustrophobics should inquire when reserving. Upstairs rooms are engulfed by a mélange of colorful wallpapers. An inviting private lobby is stocked with books, games, literature on local activities, and a wood-burning stove.

2032 Main St. (at B St.), Julian, CA 92036. © **800/734-5854** or 760/765-0201. Fax 760/765-0327. www.julian hotel.com. 16 units. $120–$165 double; $160–$210 cottages. Rates include full breakfast and afternoon tea. AE, MC, V. Take I-8 east to Highway 79. *In room:* No phone.

Orchard Hill Country Inn ⚘⚘ ⓥalue   Hosts Darrell and Pat Straube offer the most upscale lodging in Julian—a surprisingly posh, two-story Craftsman lodge and 12 cottages on a hill overlooking the town. Ten guest rooms, a lovely dining room (serving a gourmet dinner 4 nights a week, reservations required), and a great room with a massive stone fireplace are in the lodge. The 12 cottages are spread over 3 acres and offer romantic hideaways. All units feature contemporary, nonfrilly country furnishings, and snacks. While rooms in the main lodge feel somewhat hotel-ish, the cottage suites are secluded and luxurious, with private porches, fireplaces, wet bars, whirlpool tubs in most, and robes. Several hiking trails lead from the lodge into adjacent woods. Check for specials and packages on the website.

2502 Washington St., at Second St. (P.O. Box 2410), Julian, CA 92036. © **800/716-7242** or 760/765-1700. Fax 760/765-0290. www.orchardhill.com. 22 units. $225–$240 double; from $305 for cottages. Extra person $25. 2-night minimum stay if including Sat. Rates include breakfast and hors d'oeuvres. AE, MC, V. From Calif. 79, turn left on Main St., and then right on Washington St. **Amenities:** Restaurant; bar; library; mountain bikes; hiking trails. *In room:* A/C, TV/VCR (extensive video library), CD player, hair dryer, iron.

WHERE TO DINE

Julian Grille ✸ AMERICAN   Set in a cozy cottage festooned with lacy draperies, flickering candles, and a warm hearth, the Grille is the nicest eatery in town. Lunch here is an anything-goes affair, ranging from soups, sandwiches, and large salads to charbroiled burgers and hearty omelets. Dinner features grilled and broiled meats, seafood, and prime rib. I'm partial to delectable appetizers like baked brie with apples and mustard sauce and the "Prime Tickler" (chunks of prime rib served cocktail-style *au jus* with horseradish sauce). Dinners include soup or salad, hot rolls, potatoes, and a vegetable.

2224 Main St. (at A St.). ✆ 760/765-0173. Reservations required Fri–Sun. Main courses $8–$13 lunch, $15–$28 dinner (entrees $11–$13 Tues–Thurs). AE, D, MC, V. Daily 11am–4pm (from 10:30ampm Sun); Tues–Sun 5–9pm.

Romano's Dodge House ✸ ITALIAN   Occupying a historic home just off Main Street (vintage photos illustrate the little farmhouse's past), Romano's is proudly the only restaurant in town not serving apple pie. It's a home-style Italian spot, with red-checked tablecloths and straw-clad Chianti bottles. Romano's offers individual lunch pizzas, pastas bathed in rich marinara sauce, veal parmigiana, chicken cacciatore, and the signature dish, pork Juliana (loin chops in a whiskey-apple cider sauce). There's seating on a narrow shaded porch, in the wood-plank dining room, and in a little saloon in back.

2718 B St. (just off Main). ✆ 760/765-1003. www.romanosjulian.com. Reservations required for dinner Fri–Sat, recommended other nights. Main courses $8–$17. No credit cards. Wed–Mon 11:30am–8:30pm.

JULIAN AFTER DARK

No one will mistake Julian for the Gaslamp Quarter. After dark, you are pretty much left to your own devices here, but the **Pine Hills Lodge,** 2960 La Posada Way, about 2 miles from Julian off Pine Hills Road (✆ 760/765-1100; www.pinehillslodge.com), offers occasional Saturday night entertainment. Look for concerts by bands in a country or Americana vein, preceded by a barbecue buffet in this rustic facility that dates to 1912. Dinner features barbecued baby back pork ribs, baked chicken, baked beans, salads, veggies, and thick sheepherder's bread. With advance notice, the kitchen will prepare a vegetarian meal or accommodate other dietary restrictions. Dinner starts at 5:30pm, the show begins at 7pm, and the ticket costs $40.

5 Anza-Borrego Desert State Park ✸

90 miles NE of San Diego; 31 miles E of Julian

The sweeping 600,000-acre Anza-Borrego Desert State Park, the largest state park in the contiguous United States, lies mostly within San Diego County, and for many city-weary residents, a couple days here is just the ticket to rejuvenate overburdened minds.

A sense of timelessness pervades this landscape; travelers tend to slow down and take a long look around. The desert is home to fossils and rocks dating from 540 million years ago; human beings arrived only 10,000 years ago. The terrain ranges in elevation from 15 to 6,100 feet above sea level. It incorporates dry lake beds, sandstone canyons, granite mountains, palm groves fed by year-round springs, and more than 600 kinds of desert plants. After the winter rains, thousands of wildflowers burst into bloom, transforming the desert into a brilliant palette of pink, lavender, red, orange, and yellow. The giant ocotillo bushes flower extravagantly, hummingbirds fill the air, and an occasional migratory bird stops off en route to the Salton Sea. The park got its name from the rare bighorn sheep, or *borrego*, which can sometimes be spotted navigating rocky hillsides. The other half of the name came from the Spanish soldier Anza, who in 1774 led a group of 242 men, women, and children, plus cattle and horses, from the Gulf of Mexico to the California coast (eventually founding a community at the present location of San Francisco).

Many people visit the area with little interest in the flora and fauna. They're here to relax and sun themselves in tiny Borrego Springs, a town surrounded by the state park but exempt from regulations limiting commercial development. It is, however, somewhat remote, and its supporters proudly proclaim that Borrego Springs is and will remain what Palm Springs used to be—a small, charming resort community, with more empty lots than built ones. Yes, there are a couple of country clubs, some chic fairway-view homes, a luxury resort, and a regular influx of vacationers, but it's still plenty funky. One of the valley's unusual sights is scattered patches of tall, lush palm tree groves, perfectly square in shape: Borrego Springs' tree farms are a major source of landscaping trees for San Diego and surrounding counties.

When planning a trip here, keep in mind that temperatures rise to as high as 125°F (52°C) in July and August. Winters days are very comfortable with temperatures averaging around 70°F (21°C) December through January, but note that nighttime temps can drop to freezing—hypothermia is as big a killer out here as the heat.

ESSENTIALS

GETTING THERE   Anza-Borrego Desert State Park is about a 2-hour drive from San Diego. The fastest route is I-15 north to the Poway (S4) exit to its end, left on 67 north to Ramona, which turns into 78 east, to Santa Ysabel. From here, go left on 79, right on S2, and left on S22. Alternatively, follow I-8 east past Alpine to Highway 79. Follow 79 north for 23 miles to Julian; take a right on 78, and then a left on S3 to Borrego Springs. Another (longer) option is to take I-8 to Ocotillo, and then San Diego's loneliest highway, Highway S2, north. Along this 40-mile stretch you'll follow the Southern Overland Stage Route of 1849 (be sure to stop and notice the view at the Carrizo Badlands Overlook) to 78 east into Borrego Springs. The closest airport with scheduled service is Palm Springs, 75 minutes away by car.

GETTING AROUND   You don't need a four-wheel-drive vehicle to tour the desert, but you'll probably want to get off the main highways and onto the Jeep trails. The Anza-Borrego Desert State Park Visitor Center staff (see below) can tell you which Jeep trails are in condition for two-wheel-drive vehicles. The Ocotillo Wells area of the park has been set aside for off-road vehicles such as dune buggies and dirt bikes. To use the Jeep trails, a vehicle has to be licensed for highway use.

ORIENTATION & VISITOR INFORMATION   In Borrego Springs, a town completely surrounded by the state park, Palm Canyon Drive is the main drag. Christmas Circle surrounds a grassy park at the entry to town; the "mall" is just west and contains many of the town's businesses. The architecturally striking **Anza-Borrego Desert State Park Visitor Center** (© 760/767-4205; www.anzaborrego.statepark.org) lies 2 miles west of Borrego Springs; it's cut into the side of a hill and is totally invisible from the road. In addition to a small museum, it supplies information, maps, and two 15-minute audiovisual presentations, one on the bighorn sheep and the other on wildflowers; an interpreted loop trail is also on site. The visitor center is open October through May daily from 9am to 5pm, June through September weekends from 9am to 5pm. You should also stop by the **Desert Natural History Association,** 652 Palm

Wildflowers Bloom in the Desert

The natural beauty of the Anza-Borrego Desert State Park is enhanced by the almost magical appearance of desert wildflowers in the spring. The full bloom is only for 2 to 6 weeks—usually from late February through March, depending on rainfall in winter. The park provides a 24-hour wildflower hot line (© 760/767-4684) as well as a post-card notification program that will alert you about 2 weeks prior to optimum bloom. Visitor Center (© 760/767-4205; www.anzaborrego.statepark.org) hours are 9am to 5pm daily from October to June 1, weekends only in summer.

Canyon Dr. (© 760/767-3098; www.abdnha.org), whose sleek Borrego Desert Nature Center and Bookstore features an impressive selection of guidebooks, historical resources, educational materials for kids, native plants, and regional crafts, and a mini-museum display that includes a pair of frighteningly real taxidermied bobcats. This is also your best source for information on the nearby Salton Sea.

For information on lodging, dining, and activities, contact the **Borrego Springs Chamber of Commerce,** 786 Palm Canyon Dr. (© **800/559-5524** or 760/767-5555; www.borregosprings.org).

EXPLORING THE DESERT

Remember that when you're touring in this area, hydration is of paramount importance. Whether you're walking, cycling, or driving, always have a bottle of water at your side. The temperatures in the desert vary like the winds. So, do yourself a favor and dress in layers to protect yourself from the elements. If you will be out after dusk, or anytime during January and February, warm clothing is also essential.

You can explore the desert's stark terrain on one of its many trails or on a self-guided driving tour; the visitor center can supply maps. For starters, the **Borrego Palm Canyon self-guided hike** ⊛ starts at the campground near the visitor center, and is 1½ miles each way. It's a beautiful, easy-to-moderately difficult hike (depending on what Mother Nature has been up to), winding around boulders and through dry washes to a waterfall and a native grove of massive fan palms. It's grand for photos early in the morning, and keep an eye out for the rare bighorn sheep on the canyon walls above.

You can also take a guided off-road tour of the desert with **California Overland** (© **866/639-7567** or 760/767-1232; www.californiaoverland.com). View spectacular canyons, fossil beds, ancient Native American sites, caves, and more in military-style vehicles. There are 2-, 4-, and 8-hour (as well as overnight) excursions, and most include a visit to the awesome view point at Font's Point, where you can look out on the Badlands—named by the early settlers because it was an impossible area for moving or grazing cattle. Along the way, you'll learn about the history and geology of the area. Tours include drinks, snacks (or gourmet lunch on longer treks), and pickup at any Borrego Springs lodgings; prices start at $45 for the standard 2-hour adventure.

Whether you tour with California Overland or on your own, don't miss the sunset view of the Borrego Badlands from **Font's Point.** Savvy travelers plan ahead and bring champagne and beach chairs for the nightly ritual. *Note:* The road to Font's Point—just past mile marker 29 on Palm Canyon Drive—is often suitable only for four-wheel-drive vehicles; check with the visitor center for current conditions.

If you have only 1 day to spend here, a good day trip from San Diego would include driving over on one route, going to the visitor center, hiking to Palm Canyon, having a picnic, and driving back to San Diego using another route.

GOLF

The **Borrego Springs Resort,** 1112 Tilting T Dr. (© **888/826-7734** or 760/767-3330; www.borregospringsresort.com), has three 9-hole courses—you'll play more than 6,700 yards over any 18 holes. There are four sets of tees to accommodate all levels of play, five lakes, a driving range, clubhouse, and pro shop; **The Arches Restaurant** and **Fireside Lounge and Bar** are in the clubhouse. The greens fee for 18 holes (cart included) is $65 Monday to Thursday, $75 Friday to Sunday in the high season (Oct–May); and $35 Monday to Thursday, $40 Friday to Sunday in the off season (June–Sept). Discounts are available for afternoon play.

WHERE TO STAY

Borrego Springs is small, but there are enough accommodations to suit all travel styles and budgets. Peak season—from November to April—corresponds with the most temperate weather and wildflower viewing. Most hotels also post lower midweek rates. Another decent option is **Palm Canyon Resort,** 221 Palm Canyon Dr. (© **800/242-0044** or 760/767-5341; www.pcresort.com), a large complex that includes a moderately priced hotel, RV park, restaurant, and recreational facilities.

EXPENSIVE

La Casa del Zorro Desert Resort ✿✿   This oasis, 5 miles southeast of Borrego Springs, was built in 1937, and the tamarisk trees that were planted then have grown up around it. So have the many charming tile-roofed casitas, originally neighboring homes bought by the resort's longtime owners, San Diego's Copley newspaper family. Over time the property has grown into a cohesive blend of discretely private cottages and luxurious one- and two-story hotel buildings—each blessed with personalized service and unwavering standards—that make La Casa del Zorro unequaled in Borrego Springs. Courtesy carts ferry you around the lushly planted grounds and to the resort's stunning pool area by the immaculate tennis courts. The cheapest rooms are suites, and the Deluxe category buys a fireplace and plush marble bathrooms for just $5 more. Most of the 19 casitas have a fireplace and pool, up to four bedrooms, and they all have minifridges and microwaves (though a dearth of dishes and utensils will probably force you into the lodge's fine, expensive dining room). The clubby atmosphere is a bit conservative, but the resort's regulars—most from San Diego—book their favorite casita year after year. Outdoor diversions include horseshoes, Ping-Pong, volleyball, jogging trails, basketball, shuffleboard, and a life-size chess set.

3845 Yaqui Pass Rd., Borrego Springs, CA 92004. © **800/824-1884** or 760/767-5323. Fax 760/767-5963. www.lacasa delzorro.com. 79 units. $455–$460 double; from $495 casitas (summer rates considerably less). Extra person $20. AE, DC, DISC, MC, V. **Amenities:** 2 restaurants (men required to wear jacket and a collared shirt at dinner in the Butterfield); bar; 5 pools; 9-hole putting green; 6 tennis courts; health club; spa; 4 Jacuzzis; bike rental; activities desk; courtesy car to golf; business center; salon; limited room service (7am–11pm); in-room massage; babysitting. *In room:* A/C, TV/VCR w/pay movies, dataport, minibar, coffeemaker, hair dryer, iron.

MODERATE

Borrego Valley Inn 🞻   This pueblo-style charmer opened in 1998 and is close to town, which mitigates the lack of a restaurant on the property. There are, however, two pools, one of which is clothing optional. Rooms come in three sizes, but each has a private patio with a separate entrance (so you can wander out and gaze at the sunset or stars), Saltillo tile floors, and a Southwestern decor; larger rooms have a kitchenette. The El Presidente Suite sleeps four and boasts a full kitchen and a 500-square-foot private patio with a propane barbecue grill.

405 Palm Canyon Dr., Borrego Springs, CA 92004. © 800/333-5810 or 760/767-0311. www.borregovalleyinn.com. 15 units. $170–$220 double including continental breakfast; from $245 suite. 2-night minimum seasonal weekends. Extra person or pet $25. DISC, MC, V. No children under age 14. **Amenities:** 2 pools; 2 Jacuzzis; restaurant (breakfast only); activities desk. *In room:* A/C, TV, dataport, CD player, minifridge, hair dryer.

The Palms at Indian Head 🞻🞻 *Finds*   This classic mid-20th-century desert retreat is ideal for nostalgia lovers. Originally opened in 1947, then rebuilt after a fire in 1958, the lodge was a favorite hideaway for San Diego's and Hollywood's elite, playing host to movie stars like Bing Crosby, Clark Gable, and Marilyn Monroe. Rescued from extreme disrepair in 1993, the fervent contemporary owners, David Leibert and Cindy Wood, cleared away the most dilapidated guest bungalows and began renovating the resort. Ten rooms are in the main building, while two newer suites close to the pool have a fireplace and wet bar, and offer a little more privacy. Staying here is comfortable and satisfying, and although the property is a little rough around the edges, the old glamour is tangible, and sweeping views across the undeveloped desert set an easygoing mood. The Palms at Indian Head also boasts a restaurant, the Krazy Coyote (see "Where to Dine," below), and a fabulous, completely restored 42×109–foot Olympic-length pool, which will eventually be joined by the original subterranean grotto bar behind viewing windows at the deep end. The inn occupies the most envied site in the valley—shaded by palms, adjacent to the state park, with a panoramic view across the entire Anza-Borrego region.

2220 Hoberg Rd., Borrego Springs, CA 92004. © 800/519-2624 or 760/767-7788. Fax 760/767-9717. www.the palmsatindianhead.com. 12 units. $189–$229 double including continental breakfast; 2-night minimum seasonal weekends. Extra person $20. DC, DISC, MC, V. **Amenities:** Restaurant; bar; huge pool; Jacuzzi; limited room service (8am–8pm); laundry service. *In room:* A/C, TV, fridge, coffeemaker.

CAMPING

The park has two developed campgrounds. **Borrego Palm Canyon,** with 117 sites, is 2½ miles west of Borrego Springs, near the visitor center. **Tamarisk Grove,** at Highway 78 and county road S3, has 27 sites. The overnight rate at both is $20 without a hookup, or $29 with a hookup at Palm Canyon. Both have restrooms with pay showers (bring quarters) and a campfire program; reservations are required in winter/spring high season. Primitive and backcountry camping are also allowed, making this one of the few parks in the country where you can just pull off the road and find yourself a spot to commune with nature. For more information, check with the visitor center (© 760/767-4205; www.anzaborrego.statepark.org).

WHERE TO DINE

Pickings are slim in Borrego Springs, but your best bet—if you're not willing to break the bank at **La Casa del Zorro**'s classy but pricey dining room—is still the very good **Krazy Coyote.** Offering a daily board of gourmet light meals for around $10, **Badlands Market & Cafe,** 561 Palm Canyon Dr. in the Mall (© 760/767-4058), is also a prepared-foods deli (picnic lunch, anyone?) and store that features imported mustards, marinated sun-dried tomatoes, delicate desserts, and other sophisticated treats; it's open daily from 8am to around 3pm. Or you could also follow legions of locals into the downtown mainstay **Carlee's Place,** 660 Palm Canyon Dr. (© **760/767-3262**), a casual bar and grill with plenty of neon beer signs, a well-worn pool table, and a fuzzy-sounding jukebox. Carlee's is the watering hole of choice for motorcycle brigades that pass through town on recreational rides—the food is tasty, hearty, and priced just right. The first choice for a diner-esque breakfast is **Kendall's Cafe** (© **760/767-3491**), also in the Mall; steaks, teriyaki, and Mexican combo platters are available for lunch and dinner (but our other recommendations are better).

Krazy Coyote Saloon & Grille ⊕ ECLECTIC   The same style and attention to detail that pervades David Leibert and Cindy Wood's retro lodge is evident in this dinner-only restaurant, which overlooks the hotel's swimming pool and the vast desert beyond. An eclectic menu encompasses prime steaks, fresh fish, and individual gourmet pizzas. The evening ambience is welcoming and romantic, as the sparse lights of tiny Borrego Springs twinkle on the desert floor below. The couple also runs **Red Ocotillo** ⊕, 818 Palm Canyon Dr. (© **760/767-7400**). Set in a 1940s-era Quonset hut, this all-day spot serves upscale comfort food, refreshing salads, and creative burgers, daily 7am to 9pm, Friday and Saturday until 10pm. Look for the neon EAT sign here.

In the Palms at Indian Head, 2220 Hoberg Rd. © **760/767-7788.** Reservations highly recommended. Main courses $17–$50. AE, DC MC, V. Wed–Sun 5:30–8:30, Fri–Sat till 9pm; closed in summer.

6 Tijuana: Going South of the Border

17 miles S of San Diego

Like many large cities in developing nations, Tijuana is a mixture of new and old, rich and poor, modern and traditional. With about two million people—many of them transient—it's the second-largest city on the west coast of North America; only Los Angeles is larger. The *maquiladoras*—foreign-owned factories where appliances, furniture, and other goods are assembled by poorly paid, often underage workers and little environmental or labor oversight—thrive here like no other place in Mexico, providing the U.S. and other countries with bargain imports. The Mexico you may be expecting—charming town squares and churches, women in colorful embroidered skirts and blouses, bougainvillea spilling over walls—is found in a different guidebook (if you plan to spend a few days here or in Baja California, pick up a copy of *Frommer's Portable Los Cabos & Baja*).

What you will find in Tijuana is a local populace that seems no more or less happy than their north-of-the-border counterparts. Yes, there is poverty, though less visible than a decade ago, and often nerve-wracking sanitary conditions, but the city is a more vibrant cultural center than many visitors expect. You won't really see this aspect unless you venture away from Avenida Revolución—the prime tourist stripand Mexico's fourth-largest city is undeniably also a thriving business center. Much of the tourism that Tijuana generates is by under-21 types looking for a place to buy cheap liquor, as well as pharmacy traffic. Drugstores offer all manner of pills, either not conventionally or not inexpensively available in the U.S., including Viagra, sold (seemingly) by the bucketful.

Note that, in the post-9/11 era, the border crossing can be an ordeal; read "Getting There," below, before heading across *la frontera*.

Tijuana Safety Alert

Violence has risen dramatically in Tijuana, mostly due to the presence of organized crime. Brazen abductions and killings have plagued the city, but tourists are not the targets—drug cartels wage turf wars, businessmen are extorted, political scores are settled, and wealthy *Tijuaneros* are kidnapped for ransom. There is petty crime, too, so don't flash a lot of cash and expensive jewelry, and stick to populated areas. *Mordida*, "the bite," is also still known to occur. That's when uniformed police officers extort money in exchange for letting you off some infraction, like a traffic ticket. If you do find yourself dealing with an official, never offer a bribe—you may find yourself in much more trouble than you bargained for. And if you do meet up with corruption, you have little recourse but to comply, and then report any incident to the **U.S. Consulate** in Tijuana at ℂ **664/622-7400.**

ESSENTIALS
GETTING THERE

BY TROLLEY   The easiest way to get to Tijuana from downtown San Diego is to hop aboard the bright-red **San Diego Trolley** headed for San Ysidro and get off at the last stop, San Ysidro. From the trolley stop, cross the street and head up the ramp that accesses the border-crossing bridge. Tijuana's shopping and nightlife district, Avenida Revolución, is a $5 taxi ride from the border, or you can walk the mile into the tourist area. The trolley is simple and inexpensive, and takes just 40 minutes from downtown San Diego; the one-way fare is $2.50. The last trolley to San Ysidro departs downtown around midnight (3am on Sat); the last returning trolley from San Ysidro is at 1am (2am on Sat).

Coming home, the border crossing for pedestrians can require as little as a few minutes midweek, or more than 2 hours on weekend and holiday afternoons. This isn't called the busiest border crossing in the world for nothing. At press time, proof of citizenship is required of U.S. citizens; a passport is best, but a birth certificate (original or notarized), with a photo ID, will do. But **as of December 31, 2007,** all land arrivals into Mexico require a valid **U.S. passport,** or for frequent U.S.–Mexico border crossers, a PASS (People Access Security Service) system card. Air and sea arrivals require a passport **as of December 31, 2006.** Check with the **U.S. Department of State** (ℂ **202/647-5225** or see www.travel.state.gov) before your visit. Non–U.S. citizens will need a passport, an I-94, a multiple-entry visa, or a Resident Alien Card to return to the U.S.

BY CAR   I recommend leaving the car behind (unless you want to explore more of Baja California), and not just because the traffic can be challenging. But if you prefer to drive, take I-5 south to the Mexican border at San Ysidro. The drive takes under a half-hour from downtown San Diego. Although the southbound border crossing rarely requires more than a few minutes, allow at least 1 hour to cross the border coming back to the U.S., or a minimum of 2 hours on weekends or holidays. An alternative option if you're going only to Tijuana is to drive to the border and park in one of the long-term parking lots on the U.S. side for about $6 to $10 a day; a shuttle takes you to Avenida Revolución for $2. Once you're in Tijuana, it's easier to get around by taxi than to adopt to the local driving standards.

Tijuana

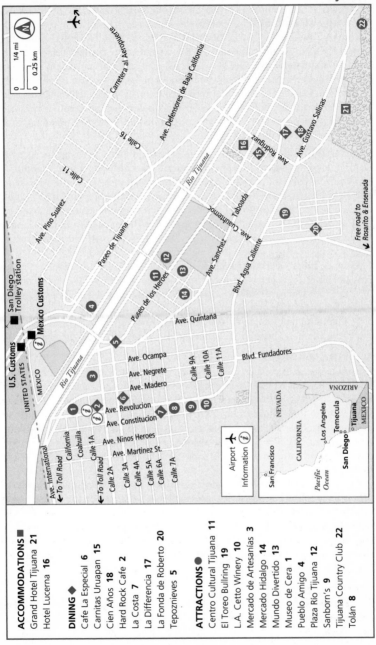

ACCOMMODATIONS ■
Grand Hotel Tijuana **21**
Hotel Lucerna **16**

DINING ◆
Cafe La Especial **6**
Carnitas Uruapan **15**
Cien Años **18**
Hard Rock Cafe **2**
La Costa **7**
La Differencia **17**
La Fonda de Roberto **20**
Tepoznieves **5**

ATTRACTIONS ●
Centro Cultural Tijuana **11**
El Toreo Bullring **19**
L.A. Cetto Winery **10**
Mercado de Artesanías **3**
Mercado Hidalgo **14**
Mundo Divertido **13**
Museo de Cera **1**
Pueblo Amigo **4**
Plaza Río Tijuana **12**
Sanborn's **9**
Tijuana Country Club **22**
Tolán **8**

Many car-rental companies in San Diego, like **Avis** (© **800/230-4898**) and **West Coast Rent a Car** (© **619/544-0606**), allow their cars to be driven into Baja California, at least as far as Ensenada; **Bob Baker Ford** (© **619/297-5001**) allows larger rental vehicles to be driven the entire 1,000-mile stretch of the Baja Peninsula. Mexican auto insurance of around $26 a day is required, and you can obtain it from your car-rental agency in San Diego; at various shops in San Ysidro, just north of the border; or from a stateside AAA office, if you're a member. Don't even think about driving in Mexico unless you have an auto insurance policy that covers you. Mexican auto insurance is not compulsory, but if you are involved in an accident, you must be able to prove you can take financial responsibility

BUS TOURS Bus tours are easy, but they give you only a few hours in Tijuana in the afternoon, so you miss evening activities. **Baja California Tours** (© **800/336-5454** or 858/454-7166; www.bajaspecials.com), based in La Jolla, offers a daily tour that visits Tijuana, Rosarito, and Ensenada, where you'll have lunch, for $65 ($40 for children 3–11). You can also use them as transportation to Tijuana ($31 round-trip) or Rosarito ($40). The buses pick up at many San Diego hotels from La Jolla south, between 7:30 and 9am, returning to San Diego between 6:30 and 7pm. They also offer day trips to Baja's wineries, overnight trips, and other packages.

Contact Tours (© **800/235-5393** or 619/477-8687; www.contactours.com) also offers a tour of Tijuana, for $31 per person ($18 for children 3–11, or up to two children free with two paying adults); departures from downtown San Diego are at 9am, leaving Tijuana at 3pm; and an afternoon tour leaves at 1pm, heading out from Tijuana at 5:30pm. **Five Star Tours** (© **619/232-5049;** www.efivestartours.com) offers a $50 round-trip fare into Tijuana from downtown San Diego (additional passengers are $5).

GETTING AROUND

If you've come to Tijuana on the San Diego Trolley or if you leave a car on the U.S. side of the border, you will walk through the border crossing. The first structure you'll see on your left is a **Visitor Information Center,** open Monday through Saturday from 9am to 5pm, Sunday from 8am to 3pm; they'll have maps, safety tips, and brochures that cover the city's highlights. From here, you can easily walk into the center of town or take a taxi. If you're walking, a good landmark is the tall silver archway—this marks the intersection of First Street and Avenida Revolución, the main tourist strip.

Taxicabs are easy to find; they queue up around most of the visitor hot spots, and drivers often solicit passengers. It's customary to agree upon the rate before stepping into the cab, whether you're going a few blocks or hiring a cab for the afternoon. One-way rides within the city cost $5 to $8, and tipping is optional. Some cabs are "local" taxis, frequently stopping to take on or let off other passengers during your ride; they are less expensive than private cabs. Metered taxis (*taxi libre*)—the cars are white with red stripes—are often a little cheaper than cabs with a negotiated rate.

VISITOR INFORMATION

The **Tijuana Tourism Board** has a website that will get you started: **www.tijuana online.org**. You can request a free visitors' guide by mail via the site. The **Baja Information Guide** is an online "newspaper" that covers Tijuana, Rosarito, and Ensenada; it's available at **www.bajatouristguide.com**. You can also request information and maps from the **Baja California Information Office** in San Diego (© **800/522-1516** in California, Arizona, or Nevada; 800/225-2786 in the rest of the U.S. and Canada; or

619/299-8518). The organization—which is not a government entity and is supported by commissions from hotel bookings—is in Mission Valley at 6855 Friars Rd., Suite 26; it's open Monday through Friday from 9am to 5pm.

Once in Tijuana, you can pick up visitor information at the **Mexican Tourism Office,** Plaza Viva Tijuana (© **664/973-0430**), open Monday through Friday from 8am to 8pm, Saturday and Sunday from 9am to 1pm; and the **National Chamber of Commerce,** at the corner of Avenida Revolución and Calle 1 (© **664/682-8508**), open weekends only. Both are extremely helpful with maps and orientation, local events of interest, and accommodations.

The Mexican Tourism Office provides legal assistance for visitors who encounter problems while in Tijuana. The following countries have consulate offices in Tijuana: the **United States** (© **664/622-7400**), **Canada** (© **664/684-0461**), and the **United Kingdom** (© **664/681-7323**).

SOME HELPFUL TIPS   The city does not take time for an afternoon siesta; you'll always find shops and restaurants open, as well as people in the streets, most of which are safe for walking—observe the same precautions you would in any large city. Most people who deal with the traveling public speak English, often very well. To maneuver around someone on a crowded street or in a shop, say *"con permiso"* ("with permission").

CLIMATE & WEATHER   Tijuana's climate is similar to San Diego's, though somehow the streets always seem a little hotter. Still, don't expect sweltering heat just because you're south of the border, and remember that the Pacific waters won't be much warmer than those off San Diego. The next closest beaches after Playas de Tijuana are about 24km (15 miles) south of the city.

CURRENCY   The Mexican currency is the peso, but you can easily visit Tijuana (or Rosarito, for that matter) without changing money—dollars are accepted just about everywhere. Many prices are posted in American (indicated with the abbreviation "dlls.") and Mexican ("m.n.," *moneda nacional*) currencies—both use the "$" sign. Bring a supply of smaller-denomination ($1, $5, and $10) bills; although change is readily given in American dollars, many merchants are reluctant to break a $20 bill for small purchases. Visa and MasterCard are accepted in many places, but some places will only grudgingly take your card; don't be surprised if the clerk scrutinizes your signature and photo ID. When using credit cards at restaurants, it's a nice gesture to leave the tip in cash. At press time, the dollar was worth about 10 pesos.

TAXES & TIPPING   A sales tax of 10%, called an IVA, is added to most bills, including those in restaurants. This does not represent the tip; the bill will read *IVA incluído,* but you should add about 10% for the tip if the service warrants.

EXPLORING TIJUANA

One of the first major tourist attractions below the border is also one of the strangest— the **Museo de Cera** ("Wax Museum"), Calle 1 between Avenidas Revolución and Madero (© **664/688-2478**). Come to think of it, what wax museum isn't strange? But that doesn't explain the presence of Whoopi Goldberg, Laurel and Hardy, and Bill Clinton in an exhibit otherwise dominated by figures from Mexican history. If you aren't spooked by the not-so-lifelike figures of Aztec warriors, brown-robed friars, Spanish princes, and 20th-century military leaders (all posed in period dioramas), step into the Chamber of Horrors, where wax werewolves and sinister sadists lurk in the shadows. When the museum is mostly empty, which is most of the time, the dramatically lit Chamber of Horrors can be a little creepy. This side-street freak show is open daily from 10am to 6pm; admission is $1.60.

For many visitors, Tijuana's main event is bustling **Avenida Revolución,** the street whose reputation precedes it. Beginning in the 1920s, American college students, servicemen, and hedonistic tourists discovered this street as a bawdy center for illicit fun. Some of the original attraction has fallen by the wayside: Gambling was outlawed in the 1930s, back-alley cockfights are also illegal, and the same civic improvements that repaved Revolución to provide trees, benches, and wider sidewalks vanquished the girlie shows whose barkers once accosted passersby. Drinking and shopping are the main order of business these days. While young people from across the border knock back tequila shooters and dangle precariously at the upstairs railings of glaring neon discos, bargain-hunters peruse the never-ending array of goods (and not-so-goods) for sale. You'll find the action between calles 1 and 9; the information center (see above) is at the north end. To help make sense of the tchotchkes, see "Shopping," below.

Visitors can be easily seduced, then quickly repulsed, by tourist-trap areas like Avenida Revolución, but it's important to remember there's more to Tijuana than American tourism. Tijuana's population, currently around two million, makes it the fourth-largest city in Mexico. While many residents live in poverty-ridden shanty-towns (you can see these *colonias* spread across the low hills surrounding the city), Tijuana has a lower unemployment rate than most of Mexico, thanks to the rise in *maquiladoras*—more than 212,000 are employed in these factories in Baja. High-rise office buildings testify to increased prosperity and the rise of a white-collar middle class, whose members shop at modern shopping centers away from the tourist zone. And there's tourism from elsewhere in northern Mexico; visitors are drawn by the availability of imported goods and the lure of the big city experience.

If you're looking to see a different side of Tijuana, the best place to start is the **Centro Cultural Tijuana** *(★)*, Paseo de los Héroes, at Avenida Independencia (*(C)* **664/ 687-9600**). You'll easily spot the ultramodern Tijuana Cultural Center complex, designed by irrepressible modern architect Pedro Ramírez Vásquez. Its centerpiece is a gigantic sand-colored dome that houses an Omnimax Dome Theater, which screens at least two different 45-minute films daily, in Spanish (subjects range from science to space travel). On Saturdays and Sundays at 3pm there is an English-language film. Tickets are $4.50 for adults and $2.50 for children.

Inside, the center houses the museum's worthwhile collection of Mexican artifacts from pre-Hispanic times through the modern political era, plus a gallery for visiting exhibits. They have included everything from the works of Diego Rivera to a disturbing, well-curated exhibit chronicling torture and human-rights violations through the ages. Music, theater, and dance performances are held in the center's concert hall and courtyard (check out the schedule in advance at **www.cecut.gob.mx**). There's a cafe and an excellent museum bookshop. The center is open Tuesday through Sunday from 10am to 6pm; admission to the museum's permanent exhibit is $2.20. Don't be discouraged if the Cultural Center sounds like a field trip for schoolchildren; it's Tijuana's must-see on my list.

The center also gets you away from the tourist kitsch and into the more sophisticated **Zona Río** (river area), where you can admire the wide, European-style **Paseo de los Héroes.** The boulevard's intersections are marked by gigantic traffic circles *(glorietas),* at the center of which stand statuesque monuments to leaders ranging from Aztec Emperor Cuauhtémoc to Abraham Lincoln. Navigating the congested *glorietas* will require your undivided attention, so it's best to pull over to admire the monuments. In the Zona Río you'll find some classier shopping, a colorful local marketplace, and some of Tijuana's best restaurants.

The Zona Río also possesses the ultimate kid destination, **Mundo Divertido,** Paseo de los Héroes at Calle José Maria Velasco (© **664/634-3213**). Literally translated, it means "world of amusement," and one parent described it as the Mexican equivalent of "a Chuck E. Cheese's restaurant built inside a Malibu Grand Prix." Let kids choose from miniature golf, batting cages, a roller coaster, a kid-size train, a video-game parlor, and go-carts. If you're in luck, the picnic area will be festooned with streamers and piñatas for some happy tike's birthday party. The park is open daily, from around 11am to 10pm. Admission is free, and several booths inside sell tickets for the rides.

The fertile valleys of Baja Norte produce most of Mexico's wine, and many high-quality vintages are exported to Europe; most are unavailable in the United States. For an introduction to Mexican wines, stop into **L.A. Cetto Winery (Cava de Vinos),** Av. Cañón Johnson 2108, at Avenida Constitución Sur (© **664/685-3031;** www.cettowine.com). Shaped like a wine barrel, the building's striking facade is made from old oak aging barrels in an inspired bit of recycling. In the entrance stand a couple of wine presses (dating from 1928) that Don Angel Cetto used in the early days of production. His family still runs the winery, which opened this impressive visitor center in 1993. L.A. Cetto bottles both red and white wines, some of them award winners, including petite sirah, nebbiolo, and cabernet sauvignon. Most bottles are under $10, while the special reserves are worth the investment. The company also produces tequila, brandy, and olive oil, all for sale here. Admission is $2 for tour and tastings (for those 18 and over only; kids under 18 are admitted free with an adult but cannot taste the wines), $5 with souvenir wine glass. It's open Monday through Saturday from 10am to 5pm.

SHOPPING

Tijuana's biggest attraction is shopping—ask any of the millions of people who cross the border each year to do it. They come to take advantage of reasonable prices on a variety of merchandise: terra-cotta and colorfully glazed pottery, woven blankets and serapes, embroidered dresses and sequined sombreros, onyx chess sets, beaded necklaces and bracelets, silver jewelry, leather bags and *huarache* sandals, "rain sticks" (bamboo branches filled with pebbles that simulate the patter of raindrops), hammered tin picture frames, thick drinking glasses, novelty swizzle sticks, Cuban cigars, and Mexican liquors like Kahlúa and tequila. You're permitted to bring $800 worth of purchases back across the border (sorry, no Cuban cigars allowed), including 1 liter of alcohol per person (for adults 21 and older). If your total purchases will come anywhere near the $800 per person limit, it's a good idea to have receipts on hand for the border crossing. Customs officers are familiar with the average cost of handcraft items.

When most people think of Tijuana, they picture **Avenida Revolución,** which appears to exist solely for the extraction of dollars from American visitors. Dedicated shoppers quickly discover most of the curios spilling out onto the sidewalk look alike, despite the determined sellers' assurances that their wares are the best in town. Browse for comparison's sake, but duck into one of the many *pasajes,* or passageway arcades, for the best souvenir shopping. There, you'll find items of a slightly better quality and merchants willing to bargain. Some of the most enjoyable *pasajes* are on the east side of the street between calles 2 and 5; they also provide a pleasant respite from the quickly irritating tumult of Avenida Revolución.

Tips Exploring Beyond Tijuana

If you have a car, venture into Baja California for a long day trip or an overnight getaway. Beyond the border city of Tijuana are the resort towns of **Rosarito Beach** (just 29km [18 miles] south of Tijuana) and **Ensenada** (42 miles farther south). Between Tijuana and Ensenada, you'll find the former lobster hamlet of **Puerto Nuevo** (12 miles south of Rosarito). You'll also find **Foxploration,** a theme park that includes a film set and shows how films are made. *Note:* Most U.S. auto insurance policies don't cover drivers or their vehicles south of Tijuana; Mexican auto insurance is advised. See "Getting Around" on p. 55 in chapter 4.

Two well-maintained roads link Tijuana and Puerto Nuevo: the scenic, coast-hugging toll road (marked *cuota* or 1-D; $3.50 each way), and the free but slower public road (marked *libre* or 1). Start out on the toll road, but cut over to the free road at the first Rosarito Beach exit so that you can stop and enjoy the view at a leisurely pace. You can also visit Rosarito Beach and Ensenada on a tour (see "Bus Tours," p. 282). *Note:* Most restaurants and even hotels along this stretch do *not* accept credit cards.

Once a tiny resort town that remained a secret despite its proximity to Tijuana, Rosarito Beach developed explosively in the 1980s; it's now garish and congested beyond recognition. But it remains popular for a couple of reasons: 1) It's the first beach resort town south of the border, and 2) its reputation continues to lure visitors. For years, the **Rosarito Beach Hotel** (© **866/767-2748** or 661/612-0144; www.rosaritobeachhotel.com) was the preferred hideaway of celebrities and other fashionable Angelinos, most famously movie star Rita Hayworth and her husband, Prince Aly Khan. The hotel remains the most interesting place in town; check out its expert tile and woodwork, as well as the lobby's panoramic murals. Also worth a look are the colorful Aztec images in the main dining room, the magnificently tiled restrooms, and the glassed-in bar overlooking the sparkling pool and beach. Peek into the original owner's mansion, now home to a spa and gourmet restaurant.

When it's not too crowded, you can while away a few hours in Rosarito. Swim or take a horseback ride at the beach, and then munch on fish tacos or tamales from one of the many family-run stands along **Bulevar Benito Juárez,** the town's main (and only) drag. You can wet your whistle at the local branch of Ensenada's enormously popular **Papas & Beer.** On the blocks north of the Rosarito Beach Hotel, you'll find stores typical of Mexican border towns: curio shops, cigar and *licores* (liquor) stores, and *farmacias* (where drugs like Retin-A, Prozac, Viagra, and Zithromax—all available at low cost and without a pre-scription—share shelf space with unguents, liniments, and, yes, even snake oil). Rosarito is also a center for **carved furnishings** (plentiful downtown along Bulevar Benito Juárez), and **pottery** (best purchased at stands along the old highway south of town).

A few miles south of Rosarito Beach, at Km 32.8 on the free road, is **Foxploration,** the state-of-the-art production facility used for *Titanic, Pearl*

Harbor, and *Master and Commander: The Far Side of the World,* and now a seaside theme park. Admission fees are $12 for adults, $9 for children and seniors; Foxploration is open Saturday and Sunday from 10am to 6:30pm, and Wednesday through Friday from 9am to 5:30pm. For more information, call ℂ **866/369-2252** (from the U.S.) or 661/614-9000 (in Mexico), or go to www.foxploration.com.

From Rosarito, drive south and stop at **Puerto Nuevo,** a tiny, portless fishing village with more than 30 restaurants—all serving the same menu! Around 1952, fishermen's wives started serving local lobsters from the kitchens of their simple shacks; many eventually built small dining rooms onto their homes or constructed restaurants. The result is a crustacean lover's paradise, where a feast of lobster, beans, rice, salsa, limes, and fresh tortillas costs $15 to $25. Not all the restaurants have names; **Ortega's** is probably the oldest, and has expanded to five locations in the village, but Puerto Nuevo regulars prefer the smaller, family-run spots, where mismatched dinette sets and chipped plates underscore the earnest service and personally prepared dinners. The above-average picks include **La Casa de la Langosta** (which has a branch in Rosarito Beach), **Malecón de Puerto Nuevo, El Galleón,** and **Tony's.**

About 16km (10 miles) farther south, roughly halfway between Rosarito and Ensenada, is **La Fonda,** a beloved hotel and restaurant (ℂ **646/155-0307**). San Diegans make the drive on Sunday morning for La Fonda's outstanding buffet brunch, an orgy of meats, traditional Mexican stews, *chilaquiles* (a saucy egg-and-tortilla scramble), fresh fruit, and pastries (about $12 per person). The best seating is under thatched umbrellas on La Fonda's tiled terrace overlooking the breaking surf; there's a bar, and strolling mariachis entertain most of the time. It's open daily from 9am to 10pm; Sunday's buffet brunch runs from 10am to 3:30pm.

Continue your journey for several more miles to **Ensenada.** Within this city of 150,000, you'll find good shopping, natural beauty, a friendly atmosphere, and some of the best fishing around—in fact, it bills itself as the "Yellowtail Capital of the World." Deep sea charters take visitors out on cruises for a chance at albacore, barracuda, and bonito.

Silver jewelry is popular in the market stalls and in nearby stores. When shopping, look for the "925" stamp impressed in the jewelry to identify the piece as sterling silver rather than silver plating. Prices are good, ranging from $3 for silver bangles to $10 for large dangle earrings. Textiles are prevalent throughout the market, also. Serapes and blankets sell for $5 to $15, and Mexican dresses for about $20, depending on the detail and amount of embroidery.

When you're ready to take a break from shopping, stop by the **Bodegas de Santo Tomas,** a historic winery open for tours (and tasting) by the public. If your tastes run more toward beer, try Hussong's Cantina, which opened for business in 1892. Cruise passengers and college students alike pack into this busy bar, so popular it now bottles its own beer, Hussong's Cerveza.

An alternative is to visit **Sanborns,** Avenida Revolución between calles 8 and 9 (© **664/688-1462**), a branch of the Mexico City department store long favored by American travelers. It sells an array of regional folk art and souvenirs, books about Mexico in Spanish and English, and candies and bakery treats. You can have breakfast in the sunny cafe. There's another location in Zona Río.

One of the few places in Tijuana to find better-quality crafts from a variety of Mexican states is **Tolán,** Avenida Revolución between calles 7 and 8 (© **664/688-3637**). In addition to the obligatory selection of standard souvenirs, you'll find blue glassware from Guadalajara, glazed pottery from Tlaquepaque, crafts from the Oaxaca countryside, and distinctive tile work from Puebla. Prices at Tolán are fixed, so you shouldn't try to bargain the way you can in some of the smaller shops and stands.

If a marketplace atmosphere and spirited bargaining are what you're looking for, head to **Mercado de Artesanías (Crafts Market),** Calle 2 and Avenida Negrete. Vendors of pottery, clayware, clothing, and other crafts fill an entire city block.

Shopping malls are as common in Tijuana as in any big American city; you shouldn't expect to find typical souvenirs, but shopping alongside residents and other intrepid visitors is often more fun than feeling like a sitting-duck tourist. The biggest, and most convenient, is **Plaza Río Tijuana** (on Paseo de los Héroes at Av. Independencia). It's an outdoor plaza, anchored by several department stores, that features dozens of shops and casual restaurants. This is the place to buy shoes.

For a taste of everyday Mexico, visit **Mercado Hidalgo** (1 block west at Av. Sánchez Taboada and Av. Independencia), a busy indoor-outdoor marketplace where vendors display fresh flowers and produce, sacks of dried beans and chiles by the kilo, and a few souvenir crafts, including some excellent piñatas. Morning is the best time to visit the authentic farmers' market—you'll be more comfortable paying with pesos, because most sellers are accustomed to a local crowd.

SPORTS

BULLFIGHTING While this spectacle employs the same disregard for animal rights as the now-illegal cockfights once popular in Tijuana, bullfighting does occupy a prominent place in Mexican heritage. A matador's skill and bravery is closely linked with cultural ideals regarding machismo, and some of the world's best competitors perform at Tijuana's two stadiums. The season starts in late spring (usually the end of Apr) at **El Toreo** (© **664/686-1510**), 3km (2 miles) east of downtown on Bulevar Agua Caliente at Avenida Diego Rivera. In August, the bullfights move to **Plaza de Toros Monumental,** or Bullring-by-the-Sea (© **664/680-1808**), 9.5km (6 miles) west of downtown on Highway 1-D, before the first toll station. It's perched at the edge of the ocean and the California border. The season runs through October, with events held Sunday at 4pm (check www.bullfights.org). Ticket prices range $16 to $53 (premium seats are on the shady side of the arena). Tickets are for sale at the bullring or in advance in San Diego from **Five Star Tours** (© **619/232-5049;** www.efivestar tours.com). If you want to catch the bullfights but don't want to drive, Five Star Tours offers bus trips to attend. It charges $20 round-trip, plus the cost of your bullfight ticket (prices vary). Or you can easily take a taxi from the border to El Toreo—figure around $7 one way; the fare to Bullring-by-the-Sea is less predictable, but shouldn't be much more than $10.

GOLF Once the favorite of golfing celebrities and socialites (and a very young Arnold Palmer) who stayed at the now-defunct Agua Caliente Resort, the **Tijuana Country Club,** Bulevar Agua Caliente at Avenida Gustavo Salinas (© **888/217-1165**

or 664/104-7545), is near the Caliente Racetrack and behind the Grand Hotel Tijuana. It's about a 10-minute drive from downtown. The well-maintained course attracts mostly business travelers staying at nearby hotels, many of which offer golf packages (see Grand Hotel Tijuana in "Where to Stay," below). Weekend greens fees are $60 per person, $38 during the week. Stop by the pro shop for balls, tees, and a limited number of other accessories; the clubhouse also has two restaurants with cocktail lounges.

WHERE TO STAY

When calculating room rates, remember that hotel rates in Tijuana are subject to a 12% tax. Also note that this guide uses the term "double" when listing rates, referring to the American concept of "double occupancy." However, in Mexico a single room has one bed, a double has two, and you pay accordingly.

Grand Hotel Tijuana ✦ This unusually high (32-story) mirrored twin tower is visible from all over the city. Modern and sleek, it opened in 1982—the height of Tijuana's prosperity—under the name "Fiesta Americana," a name locals (and many cab drivers) still use. Popular for business travelers, visiting celebrities, and society events, the hotel has the best-maintained public and guest rooms in Tijuana, which helps make up for what it lacks in regional warmth. Rooms have spectacular views of the city from the top floors. The lobby has dark carpeting and 1980s mirrors and neon accents that feel like a Vegas hotel/casino. It gives way to several ballrooms and an airy atrium that serves elegant international cuisine at dinner and weekend brunch. Next to it is a casual Mexican restaurant; beyond there, the Vegas resemblance resumes with an indoor shopping arcade and a sports and race book. Golf packages with the adjacent Tijuana Country Club start at $161 for 2 weekdays, $205 on weekends.

Agua Caliente 4500, Tijuana. © **866/472-6385** or 664/681-7000. Fax 664/681-7016. www.grandhoteltijuana.com. 422 units. $135–$190 double; from $270 suite. AE, MC, V. Covered parking. **Amenities:** 3 restaurants; 3 bars; outdoor heated pool; tennis courts; Jacuzzi; sauna; car-rental desk; business center; shopping arcade; sports and race book; 24-hr. room service; in-room massage; babysitting; laundry service; dry cleaning. *In room:* A/C, TV w/pay movies, dataport, minibar, hair dryer, iron.

Hotel Lucerna Once the most chic hotel in Tijuana, the neoclassical Lucerna now offers reliable accommodations with lots of personality. The hotel is in the Zona Río, away from the noise and congestion of downtown, so a quiet night's sleep is easy. It's kept in great shape for the international visitors who enjoy Lucerna's proximity to the financial district, and the staff's friendly and attentive service reflects this clientele. The five-story hotel's rooms all have balconies or patios, but are otherwise unremarkable. Sunday brunch is served outdoors by the swimming pool.

Av. Paseo de los Héroes 10902, Zona Río, Tijuana. www.hotel-lucerna.com.mx. © **800/582-3762** or 664/633-3900. 168 units. $148–$153 double; from $193 suite. AE, DC, MC, V. **Amenities:** 2 restaurants; 2 bars; outdoor pool; exercise room; car-rental desk; tour desk; business center; 24-hr. room service; babysitting. *In room:* A/C, TV, dataport, hair dryer.

WHERE TO DINE

Although the irresistible aroma of street food—*carne asada* (marinated beef grilled over charcoal) tucked into corn tortillas for starters—is everywhere, less well known is that Tijuana has restaurants of real quality, despite the presence of a Hard Rock Cafe that lures many of the visitors. The following places are worth the taxi trip, and *la comida* (lunch) is the main meal of the day; restaurants are busiest around 2:30pm. Do not drink water unless it comes straight from a bottle (this includes ice, or uncooked vegetables like lettuce that have been washed) or you might leave Tijuana with a going-away gift; restaurants listed below generally have sanitary conditions, but it doesn't hurt to be cautious.

For an unusual treat, be sure to stop by **Tepoznieves,** a nostalgic ice cream parlor that carries traditional Mexican flavors like you've never seen: try *nardos,* concocted from the tangy tuberose flower; *nopal,* made from cactus; *beso de angel* (angel's kiss), melding pine nuts, strawberry, and cherry; or *petalo de rosas* (rose petals), which seduces with roasted petals and honey. There are two locations: the shopping center Plaza Minarete, at Blvd. Sanchez Taboada 4002 (off Paseo de los Héroes), and at Playas de Tijuana on Paseo Pedregal (© **664/634-6532**).

Cafe La Especial ✪ MEXICAN   Tucked away in a shopping *pasaje* at the bottom of some stairs (turn in at the taco stand of the same name), this restaurant is a well-known shopper's refuge. It offers home-style Mexican cooking at reasonable (though not dirt-cheap) prices. The gruff, efficient waitstaff carries out platter after platter of carne asada served with fresh tortillas, beans, and rice—it's La Especial's most popular item. Traditional dishes like tacos, enchiladas, and burritos round out the menu, augmented by frosty cold Mexican beers.

Av. Revolución 718 (between calles 3 and 4), Zona Centro. © **664/685-6654**. Menu items $3–$12. No credit cards. Daily 9am–10pm.

Carnitas Uruapan ✪ MEXICAN   *Carnitas,* a beloved dish in Mexico, consists of marinated pork roasted on a spit until it's falling-apart tender, and then served in chunks with tortillas, salsa, cilantro, guacamole, and onions. It's the main attraction at Carnitas Uruapan, where the meat is served by the kilo (or portion thereof) at long, communal wooden tables to a mostly local crowd, accompanied by mariachi music. A half kilo of carnitas is plenty for two people, and costs around $12, including beans and that impressive array of condiments. It's a casual feast without compare, but vegetarians need not apply.

Bulevar Díaz Ordáz 550 (across from Plaza Patra), La Mesa. © **664/681-6181**. Menu items under $8. No credit cards. Daily 7am–3am. Follow Bulevar Agua Caliente south toward Tecate. It turns into Bulevar Díaz Ordáz, also known as Carretera Tecate and Hwy. 2.

Cien Años ✪✪ MEXICAN   Perhaps Tijuana's finest restaurant, this is where *Gourmet* editor Ruth Reichl famously dined on ant roe and mescal worms, though most of the menu is less, er, exotic. The elegant Zona Río eatery offers artfully blended Mexican flavors you expect (tamarind, poblano chiles, and mango), but with a host of offerings that date back to traditional Mayan and Aztec preparations, all stylishly presented. Cien Años also serves breakfast, and the creativity is evident here, too, with dishes like omelets stuffed with cactus, mushrooms, and cheese in a mango sauce. Though modestly priced, Cien Años is dressy by San Diego and Tijuana standards, and reservations are a good idea for dinner.

José María Velazco 1407, Zona Río. © **664/634-3039**. Reservations recommended. Main courses $8–$21. AE, MC, V. Daily 8am–11pm (till midnight Fri–Sat, till 10pm Sun).

La Costa ✪ MEXICAN-STYLE SEAFOOD   Fish gets top billing here, starting with the hearty seafood soup. There are combination platters of half a grilled lobster, stuffed shrimp, and baked shrimp; fish filet stuffed with seafood and cheese; and several abalone dishes. The oldest seafood restaurant in Tijuana, La Costa is very popular with San Diegans, and the food lives up to its reputation.

Calle 7, no. 8131 (just off Av. Revolución), Zona Centro. © **664/685-8494**. Reservations recommended. Main courses $8–$20. AE, MC, V. Daily 10am–11pm (till midnight Fri–Sat).

La Diferencia ✹✹ MEXICAN   This wonderful restaurant is in a nondescript building in the Zona Río, but inside is a delightful courtyard with a fountain, birdcages, and muraled walls. Salsa is handmade at your table, and then the creative appetizers are wheeled out—if you ever wanted to try fried crickets, this is the place, but most of the dishes are made with delicate sauces offering a variety of unusual spices and flavors. Entrees include steaks, seafood, and chicken.

Blvd. Sanchez Taboada 10611-A, Zona Río. ✆ 664/634-3346. Reservations recommended. Main courses $9–$22. AE, MC, V. Daily noon–11pm.

La Fonda de Roberto ✹ MEXICAN   A short drive (or taxi ride) from downtown Tijuana, La Fonda's colorful dining room opens onto the courtyard of a kitschy 1960s motel, complete with retro kidney-shaped swimming pool. The festive atmosphere is perfect for enjoying a variety of regional Mexican dishes, including a decent chicken mole and generous portions of *milanesa* (beef, chicken, or pork pounded paper thin, and then breaded and fried). A house specialty is *queso fundido,* deep-fried cheese with chiles, and mushrooms served with freshly made corn tortillas.

In the La Sierra Motel, Blvd. Cuauthémoc Sur Oriente 2800 (on the old road to Ensenada). ✆ 664/686-4687. Reservations recommended. Most dishes $5–$11. MC, V. Daily 9am–10pm.

TIJUANA AFTER DARK

Perhaps Tijuana's most popular disco is the dance club **Balak** in Pueblo Amigo, Vía Rápida Ote 9211 (✆ 664/682-9222). It's open Fridays and Saturdays, from 9pm to 3am. Also notable is **Baby Rock Discoteca,** Av. Diego Rivera 1482, Zona Río (✆ 664/634-2404). A cousin to Acapulco's lively Baby O, it features everything from DJs to live *rock en español,* Thursday through Saturday, 9pm to 4am.

A recent addition to Tijuana's nightlife are "sports bars," cheerful watering holes that feature satellite wagering from all over the United States, as well as from Tijuana's Caliente Racetrack. The most popular bars cluster in **Pueblo Amigo,** Vía Oriente, and Paseo Tijuana in the Zona Río, a new center designed to resemble a colonial Mexican village. Even if you don't bet on the horses, you can soak up the atmosphere. Two of the town's hottest nightspots, **Rodeo Santa Fe** (✆ 664/682-4967), which features Mexico's versions of country music, *banda* and *norteño,* and **Señor Frogs** (✆ 664/682-4962), are also in Pueblo Amigo. Pueblo Amigo is less than 2 miles from the border, a short taxi ride or—during daylight hours—a pleasant walk.

Appendix: San Diego in Depth

San Diego is best known for beaches and palms, pandas and orcas, sailors and surfers, not to mention some of the world's finest weather. Los Angeles and San Francisco may have bypassed San Diego in size or importance during the 19th century, but our city is the "Plymouth Rock of the Pacific Coast." Here's where the first European settlement took root on the west coast of what would become the United States of America, long before there was a border.

1 The Arrival of Spanish Mission "Style"

San Diego's first residents were probably the San Dieguitos, 8,000 to 11,000 years ago, followed by the La Jollan culture, which populated the coastal mesas until about 1,000 to 3,000 years ago. The Diegueños followed about 1,500 years ago, and existed in two groups: the Ipai, who lived along the San Diego River and northeast toward what is now Escondido, and the Tipai, or Kumeyaay, who lived south of the river into Baja California and east toward Imperial Valley. The men mostly went naked while the women wore a modest cover of woven fibers and animal skins. Meat was not a major part of the diet, but acorns were—the *metates* they used for grinding into flour are sprinkled around the county—and seeds, berries, smaller prey, and shellfish rounded out their menu. Their basket-weaving and pottery talents were such that the vessels they made could hold water. The Kumeyaay were quite peaceful, even though the individual settlements often didn't speak the same dialect as neighboring communities.

After Columbus "discovered" the New World and the Aztecs had been conquered, stories of the fertile Pacific Coast to the north started to percolate. So certain was Spain of the riches that lay ahead, they had already chosen a name for it: California. In 1542, Portuguese explorer **Juan Rodríguez Cabrillo** set out from Navidad, on the west coast of Central America, principally in search of a northwest passage that might provide an easier crossing between the Pacific Ocean and Europe. En route he landed in a place he charted as San Miguel, spending 6 days to wait out a storm and venture ashore, doing a meet-and-greet with three fearful Kumeyaay (who had heard tales of Europeans killing Indians to the east and south) before heading north along the coast. Cabrillo would not live to complete his journey—he died some weeks later, following complications from a broken bone suffered in a skirmish with Chumash Indians on one of the Channel Islands, off the coast of Santa Barbara. Although Cabrillo wrote favorably about what he saw, it would be 60 years before Europeans visited San Miguel again—they were more concerned with the mythical northern passage. Even Sir Francis Drake, as he looted his way from Peru to San Francisco, apparently overlooked San Miguel. When Spanish explorer Sebastián Vizcaíno sailed into the bay with three small ships on the feast day of San Diego de Alcalá, he renamed it in honor of the saint. But despite Vizcaíno calling it "a port which must be the best to be found in all the South Sea," San Diego Bay was all but ignored by invaders for the next century and a half.

In 1768, Spain, fearing that Russian colonies in Northern California might soon threaten Spanish settlements in Central America, decreed the founding of colonies in Southern California. The following year, following an arduous 110-day voyage from the tip of Baja California, the *San Carlos* arrived into San Diego Bay on April 29, 1769, leading "the sacred expedition" of **Father Junípero Serra**, a priest who had been charged with the task of spreading Christianity to the natives. Serra would arrive about 2 months later via an overland route.

The site for the first mission was selected just above the San Diego River, on a prominent hill that offered views onto plains, mesas, marshes, and the sea. The **Presidio de San Diego** was the first of what would be 21 missions in California; a fort was built to surround and protect the settlement. The first years were laborious and fraught with sickness and famine—by late summer the river would become an unreliable trickle and the land immediately surrounding the Presidio was infertile. The Indians were hostile to the Spanish, though eventually they were subdued by firepower. After 4 years, Father Serra requested permission to relocate the mission to Nipaguay, a site 6 miles up the valley, next to an existing Kumeyaay village.

Over the course of 3 years, delayed by a ransacking courtesy of resentful Indians from neighboring tribes, the new **Mission San Diego** was built, and dedicated in 1777. The new location was well chosen, and in 1817 a dam was built—probably the first major irrigation project in the West—which allowed the crew to grow wheat, barley, vineyards, olives, and dates and bring in herds of cattle and sheep. Although the mission provided the Indians with a more sustainable existence, it came at a price: Their culture was mostly lost; communities were shattered by foreign diseases from which they had no natural immunities; and Indians who defied the Spaniards or deserted the new settlements were punished by whipping or confinement. From 1790 to 1800, mission records noted that 1,600 Indians had been baptized—and more than half of them died in the same period.

In 1798, Father Lasuen and the Franciscans founded **Mission San Luis Rey** on a site near what would become Oceanside, in northern San Diego County. The church, erected in 1811–15, is perhaps the finest existing example of mission style, with its composite of Spanish, Moorish, and Mexican architecture.

In 1821, as what is now known as **Old Town** started to take shape, Mexico declared independence from Spain. California's missions were secularized; the Mexican government lost all interest in the natives and instead focused on creating sprawling rancheros. The Mexican flag flew over the Presidio, and in 1825, San Diego became the informal capital of the California territory. Freed of Spanish restrictions, California's ports suddenly opened to trade, and for a period, the town was a hub for the hide trade. Ships brought in silks from the Orient, colognes from France, and gunpowder and clothing from Boston, and left San Diego with leather. But the mission era had come to an ignominious close: The trademark roof tiles used for mission structures were taken away and recycled into new houses built in Old Town, while the adobe walls dissolved into the soil.

2 The Missions Give Way to Gold

The **Mexican-American War** took root in 1846, spreading from Texas west, creating brutal battles between the Californios and the Americans. By 1847 the Californios had surrendered, the treaty of Guadalupe-Hidalgo was signed a year later, and Mexico was paid $15 million for what became the southwestern United

States. In 1848, gold was discovered near Sacramento and the **gold rush** began—in 1 year, San Francisco grew from a town of less than 1,000 residents to 26,000. The road to statehood was paved with gold: In 1850, California was made the 31st state, and San Diego was established as both a city and county, formally confirming its future.

In 1850, William Heath Davis, a San Francisco financier, purchased 160 acres of bayfront property with plans to develop a "new town." Residents of Old Town scoffed, and despite Davis' construction of several prefabricated houses and a wharf, the citizens stayed rooted at the base of the Presidio and labeled the project "Davis' Folly." But in 1867, another developer, Alonzo Horton, also saw the potential of the city and bought 960 acres of bayfront land for $265. Calling it "the prettiest place for a city I ever saw," Horton laid out the grid pattern of streets, completed Davis' wharf, and built a hotel and new homes. Notably, he designated a huge 1,400-acre spread to the northeast as a city park. This time, people started moving in to the new town, and by 1869 San Diego had a population of 3,000; a devastating fire in Old Town in 1872 proved to be the final blow for the original settlement. A crucial catalyst for San Diego's development came in 1870, when gold was discovered in the mountains 60 miles northeast of town. Over the course of 4 swift but lucrative years, $13 million in ore was extracted and the town of Julian blossomed.

San Diego's gold rush was soon replaced by **whaling** as a major industry. Every winter, herds of Pacific gray whales migrated between the feeding territory of Alaska and calving grounds around the tip of Baja California. Peninsular Point Loma jutted into their course, and the easygoing whales, often traveling less than a mile from shore, were simple prey. Whalers from New England moved to the area, and by 1871, whaling was lucrative business. The mammoth carcasses were hauled ashore at Ballast Point, where the animals were butchered and their flesh rendered into oil. But like the gold rush, whaling petered out—the number of whales dwindled and they learned to avoid San Diego Bay (it wasn't until the 1940s that the endangered Pacific gray whale started to make a recovery).

3 Location, Location, Location

The city endured brief bouts of boom and bust but slowly developed, with real-estate speculation providing the fuel for growth. In 1884, entrepreneurs Hampton L. Storey, who had founded a successful Chicago piano-building business, and Elisha S. Babcock, Jr., the director of both a railroad and telephone company, sailed over to Coronado for a day of rabbit hunting. The desolate "island"— really a peninsula of sandy terra firma that protected San Diego Bay—was uninhabited, but Babcock saw its potential as a luxury destination. The two formed a company and purchased Coronado and the land to the northwest (known as North Island, even though it, like Coronado, was connected by way of an isthmus of sand). They subdivided the land in 1886 and sold it for substantial profit, and then went about creating a fantastic storybook hotel, in the style of the epic beach resorts of Florida. Built in just 11 months, the $1.5-million **Hotel del Coronado** was the city's first link to tourism, and the world's largest resort hotel.

Babcock and Storey also helped establish a streetcar system for San Diego; by 1888, 37 miles of trolley track canvassed the city. Around the same time, San Francisco–based sugar baron John D. Spreckels dived into San Diego's real-estate market, soon owning two newspapers, downtown buildings, the streetcar network, and much of Coronado. Suburbs like La Jolla and Chula Vista began to take shape. But much of the 1880s real-estate speculation was based on the prospect of a rail line linking San Diego to the rest of the country—by 1890 it was understood that San Diego would be served only by a spur line from Los Angeles. The real-estate market swooned.

A pivotal moment came in 1910 when the 40,000 citizens approved a $1 million bond measure to host a world's fair, ostensibly to celebrate completion of the Panama Canal, but with another, larger purpose: to promote the city to the world. Despite a competing event in San Francisco, San Diego's 1915 **Panama-California Exposition** was a fabulous success, and saw the development of 1,400-acre **Balboa Park** into fairgrounds of lasting beauty. Nursery owner Kate Sessions brought in and planted trees from around the world (particularly eucalyptus and jacaranda from the southern hemisphere, which remain iconic symbols of the county today); the undulating canyons and mesas were landscaped; an outdoor organ pavilion was created; and an arched bridge was built over Cabrillo Canyon, looking much like a Roman aqueduct. Plaster workers were brought over from Italy to create the delicate flourishes on a village of Spanish colonial structures lining a graceful prado. Theodore Roosevelt, William Taft, Thomas Edison, and a slew of movie stars were among the luminaries who attended the fair; Fatty Arbuckle and Mabel Normand starred in a one-reel film about their visit. The barrage of publicity from the 2-year fair touted San Diego's climate and location, and helped put the city on the map.

As the fair came to a close, a local doctor, Harry Wegeforth, was driving with his brother when he heard the far-off roar from a lion that had been brought in as a sideshow for the expo. "Wouldn't it be wonderful to have a zoo in San Diego?" asked Dr. Harry. A zoological society was created and the **San Diego Zoo** was born. At first the zoo was a motley collection of cages that lined Park Boulevard, but in 1921 the city gave the zoo a permanent home: 100 acres in the heart of Balboa Park. (Actually, in a compromise with the private, nonprofit Zoological Society, the city owns the land and the animals while the society administers its operation.) The park's canyons were ideal for containing diseases that might infect the entire menagerie, and over time proved ideal for creating naturalistic environments for the animals. Exotic species, most of them never before seen in America, came swiftly, such as rare Hawaiian birds, kangaroos, and koalas.

4 The Navy Builds a Home

The Hotel Del and the Exposition proved that tourism could be a successful component of San Diego's economy, but it was the military that proved to be the city's backbone. Toward the end of the 19th century, the **U.S. Navy** began using San Diego as a home port. In 1908, the navy sailed into the harbor with its battleship fleet and 16,000 sailors—the War Department laid plans to dredge the bay to accommodate even larger ships. Aviator Glenn Curtiss convinced the Navy to designate $25,000 to the development of aviation, and soon after he opened a flying school at North Island, the northwestern lobe of the Coronado peninsula. World War I meant construction projects, and North Island was established as a marine base. The Navy built a shipyard at 22nd Street in downtown, and constructed a naval training station and hospital in 1921. America's first aircraft carrier docked in San Diego in 1924.

San Diego's notable aviation history began 2 decades before the Wright Brothers, in 1883, when John Montgomery built and piloted a glider from a hillock near the Mexican border, soaring 600 feet into the air. In 1911, the first successful amphibious takeoff and landing was performed by Glenn Curtiss at North Island. The same year, Curtiss also piloted the first ship-to-shore flight, and received the first radio communication in the air. Aviator T. Claude Ryan started Ryan Aviation to build military and civilian aircraft and equipment. In 1927, Ryan built *The Spirit of St. Louis* for Charles A. Lindbergh, a young airmail pilot; only a few weeks after taking off from North Island, Lindbergh landed in Paris and was toasted as the first to fly solo across the Atlantic. In 1928, San Diego's airport was dedicated as **Lindbergh Field.**

Although the Great Depression stalled growth, the military economy meant San Diego made it through the slump relatively unscathed. In 1931, the *San Diego Union* wrote that the Depression's "effects here are nothing like as severe as those reported from industrial and agricultural centers in other parts of the country." In 1935, Reuben H. Fleet moved his 400 employees at Consolidated Aircraft (later Convair) from Buffalo, New York, to San Diego. A second world's fair, the 1935–36 **California-Pacific International Exposition,** allowed the Spanish colonial architecture in Balboa Park to be expanded, and many tourists became residents.

To alleviate some of the Depression's sting, the federal government created the **Works Progress Administration (WPA)** program in the late 1930s to provide work for artists during lean years. Local artists were supplied with funds to create public art, much of which still exists today; the mural in the La Jolla Post Office by Belle Baranceanu and Donal Hord's water fountain sculpture in front of the County Administration Center are notable examples.

But San Diego had thrown its lot in with the military, which allowed the city to prosper when World War II broke out. The attack on Pearl Harbor on December 7, 1941, mobilized the United States into a massive war machine, and San Diego was dramatically transformed. The headquarters for the Pacific Fleet were moved to the city, and the population swelled to build aircraft and ships as factories operated around the clock, employing thousands of residents. Balboa Park's ornate buildings were converted into hospitals, and the bay was crisscrossed with huge nets to prevent Japanese subs from entering the harbor. In 1942, President Franklin Roosevelt signed orders authorizing the War Department to detain Japanese-Americans; almost 2,000 San Diegans were held in camps like Manzanar at the foot of the Sierra Mountains, near Death Valley.

5 An Identity Beyond the Navy & Beaches

The end of the war didn't signal an end to San Diego's prosperity. New neighborhoods sprouted to house the thousands of military families that had been stationed here, and city leaders again cast an eye toward tourism as an economic rainmaker in times of peace. In 1945, voters approved a $2-million plan to dredge and sculpt Mission Bay from former mud flats, allowing the communities of Mission Beach and Pacific Beach to expand greatly. By the late 1940s, the local fishing fleet comprised hundreds of boats; the catch was processed by local canneries and supplied two-thirds of the nation's tuna, a $50-million-a-year business. The Korean and Vietnam wars didn't impact San Diego like World War II, but the military link kept the city humming in the 1950s and 1960s.

In 1969, the graceful **San Diego-Coronado Bay Bridge** opened and the ferries that linked downtown to the "island" were shut down. Downtown stumbled the way many urban centers did in the 1960s and 1970s, filled after dark with the homeless and inebriated. In 1974, the **Gaslamp Quarter**—the new name for Alonzo Horton's New Town—was designated as a historic district. Little occurred to revitalize downtown at first, but a redevelopment plan was established and the first step was to create **Seaport Village,** a waterside shopping complex, at the south end of the Embarcadero, in the early '80s. In 1985, a $140-million shopping center next to Horton Plaza opened to raves for its charmingly jumbled architecture, and San Diegans responded immediately, coming downtown to shop as they hadn't in a generation. Entrepreneurs financed the revitalization of the Gaslamp Quarter, and condos were built in the area between Horton Plaza and Seaport Village (although most sat empty for some years). A second wave of development was spurred with the opening of the new convention center between the Gaslamp and the bay in 1989, and the Quarter was cemented as a destination for restaurants and nightlife.

In the late '90s, a plan to build a downtown ballpark took shape, albeit with considerable opposition and delays, largely due to the significant city funding required and challenges to what was seen as a sweetheart deal for the team owner. Backed strongly by the mayor and the local newspaper, the San Diego Padres got its ballpark, and downtown's redevelopment area extended a few blocks east—the $474-million **PETCO Park** opened to great fanfare in 2004. The stadium has proven to be a boon to some downtown businesses and a nuisance to others; meanwhile, San Diego still awaits its long-promised downtown library. With less-than-elegant timing, the city's NFL team, the Chargers, began fishing for a new stadium, threatening it would move elsewhere if it didn't get what it wanted. As of January 1, 2007, the Chargers are free to shop around for another hometown—stay tuned.

Traffic congestion and public transportation are increasingly vexing issues—San Diego sprawls over a huge area, hemmed in on two sides by an ocean and a border. Mass transit has been slow to find a way to serve commuters. In 1981, the **San Diego Trolley** opened, providing a link between downtown and the Tijuana border crossing. By using existing rail corridors, costs were kept down and the system quickly found itself operating in the black. The trolley lines were extended, north into Mission Valley and east to Lemon Grove and Santee. A new section, opened in 2005, adds San Diego State University into the mix, and another $750-million extension in a few years will take the trolley north to the University of California, San Diego. But as a housing boom stretches the city's metropolitan area east and north, **gridlock** has emerged as a hot-button topic. Residents look north to Los Angeles as an example of all they don't want San Diego to become, yet slow-growth ballot propositions designed to limit backcountry development haven't proven popular with local voters. The large Camp Pendleton Marine Corps Base, just north of Oceanside, serves as a crucial "natural" barrier that prevents Los Angeles and San Diego from merging.

The postmillennial "dot-bomb" fallout did not ravage the city, largely because a diversified tech economy meant jobs could be cycled from one sector to another. Today's San Diego owes a lot to **medical and high-tech industries**—biotechnology, pharmaceutical, and telecommunications in particular, with companies like Qualcomm and Pfizer based here. One economic think tank declared the city to be the nation's number one "biotech cluster," supported by a steady flow of research from academic institutions like U.C. San Diego, the Scripps Research Institute, and the Salk Institute. The local biotech industry also provides a home base for the greatest concentration of science-based Nobel Prize winners in the world and is directly responsible for more than 36,000 jobs and some $5.8 billion in income. An infusion of talent and fresh perspective has helped the city grow beyond its beach/Navy/zoo profile—money has filtered into the arts, nourished the dining scene, and empowered an unfettered real-estate market, which has run red-hot since 1999 (though many are now seeing signs of an inevitable cool-down).

Buying property in San Diego produces sticker shock for those unfamiliar with California prices—in fact, the National Association of Builders declared the city the second least affordable area in the country. In 2005, the average cost of a new detached home was $861,000 (a 350% increase from 1996); while the median price for an existing family home was $560,000, compared to a national average of $225,000. And while the condo building-boom continues unabated, the vast majority of those are luxury projects, leaving many in the city unable to get a foothold in the housing market. The upshot is that for the first time in a decade, more people left San Diego than moved here from other parts of the country.

And now city leaders face an even larger problem than affordable housing. A tragicomic series of political scandals—including a tainted mayoral election (and an ensuing ascension of three different mayors over an 8-month period), the conviction of two city council members on charges of doing the bidding of a strip-club operator (a third accused councilman dropped dead before he went to trial), and one majorly thieving Congressman (Rep. "Duke" Cunningham)—is topped by a $2 billion deficit in the city pension fund. Creative bookkeeping is suspected, prompting city, U.S. attorney, FBI, IRS, and Securities and Exchange Commission investigations, and leading the *New York Times* to dub San Diego "Enron by the sea." The first federal indictments were handed down early in 2006 and repercussions are expected to be widespread. Possibilities include layoffs of city employees, privatization of some city services, cutbacks in services, higher utility costs, and higher taxes (though current mayor Jerry Sanders has promised no tax hikes).

Tourism remains good news for the city, though. Visitors power San Diego's third-biggest industry (behind manufacturing and the military), spurred on by a convention-friendly downtown. In 2005, 27.2 million visitors came to the city, generating $5.8 billion for the local economy. Besides the obvious—the beach, the zoo, and the weather—San Diego livin' is easy (if you can afford it), and although it's the country's seventh largest city, San Diego retains a small-town feel. It's a clean and safe (by big-city standards), imminently approachable place blessed with a glorious location and climate, and with a nightlife and arts scene that tenaciously battles for equal attention. Historically, San Diego has risen and deflated in spasms of growth and bust, usually tied to real-estate ventures. It's pretty obvious where we are in the cycle right now. Welcome to boomtown.

Index

See also Accommodations and Restaurant indexes, below.

RESTAURANTS

FROMMER'S® COMPLETE TRAVEL GUIDES

FROMMER'S® DOLLAR-A-DAY GUIDES

FROMMER'S® PORTABLE GUIDES

FROMMER'S® CRUISE GUIDES

FROMMER'S® DAY BY DAY GUIDES

Amsterdam
Chicago
Florence & Tuscany

London
New York City
Paris

Rome
San Francisco
Venice

FROMMER'S® NATIONAL PARK GUIDES

Algonquin Provincial Park
Banff & Jasper
Grand Canyon

National Parks of the American West
Rocky Mountain
Yellowstone & Grand Teton

Yosemite and Sequoia & Kings
  Canyon
Zion & Bryce Canyon

FROMMER'S® MEMORABLE WALKS

Chicago
London

New York
Paris

Rome
San Francisco

FROMMER'S® WITH KIDS GUIDES

Chicago
Hawaii
Las Vegas
London

National Parks
New York City
San Francisco

Toronto
Walt Disney World® & Orlando
Washington, D.C.

SUZY GERSHMAN'S BORN TO SHOP GUIDES

Born to Shop: France
Born to Shop: Hong Kong, Shanghai
  & Beijing

Born to Shop: Italy
Born to Shop: London

Born to Shop: New York
Born to Shop: Paris

FROMMER'S® IRREVERENT GUIDES

Amsterdam
Boston
Chicago
Las Vegas
London

Los Angeles
Manhattan
New Orleans
Paris

Rome
San Francisco
Walt Disney World®
Washington, D.C.

FROMMER'S® BEST-LOVED DRIVING TOURS

Austria
Britain
California
France

Germany
Ireland
Italy
New England

Northern Italy
Scotland
Spain
Tuscany & Umbria

THE UNOFFICIAL GUIDES®

Adventure Travel in Alaska
Beyond Disney
California with Kids
Central Italy
Chicago
Cruises
Disneyland®
England
Florida
Florida with Kids

Hawaii
Ireland
Las Vegas
London
Maui
Mexico's Best Beach Resorts
Mini Las Vegas
Mini Mickey
New Orleans
New York City

Paris
San Francisco
South Florida including Miami &
  the Keys
Walt Disney World®
Walt Disney World® for
  Grown-ups
Walt Disney World® with Kids
Washington, D.C.

SPECIAL-INTEREST TITLES

Athens Past & Present
Cities Ranked & Rated
Frommer's Best Day Trips from London
Frommer's Best RV & Tent Campgrounds
  in the U.S.A.

Frommer's Exploring America by RV
Frommer's NYC Free & Dirt Cheap
Frommer's Road Atlas Europe
Frommer's Road Atlas Ireland
Retirement Places Rated

FROMMER'S® PHRASEFINDER DICTIONARY GUIDES

French

Italian

Spanish

IF YOU BOOK IT, IT SHOULD BE THERE.

Only Travelocity guarantees it will be, or we'll work
with our travel partners to make it right, right away.
So if you're missing a balcony or anything else you
booked, just call us 24/7. **1-888-TRAVELOCITY.**

travelocity

You'll never roam alone.